ZAGAT®

Washington, DC
Baltimore
Restaurants
2012

LOCAL EDITORS
Olga Boikess and Marty Katz
STAFF EDITOR
Josh Rogers

Published and distributed by
Zagat Survey, LLC
4 Columbus Circle
New York, NY 10019
T: 212.977.6000
E: washbalt@zagat.com
www.zagat.com

ACKNOWLEDGMENTS

We thank Charlie Adler, Chuck Alexander, American Institute of Wine and Food-DC Chapter, Bernice August, Baltimore Foodies, Greg Bland, Ira Brady, Capital Alumni Network, Jean and Gary Cohen, John Deiner, Kerry Craven DuBard, Lori Edwards, Elaine Eff, Christine Fillat, Bill, Lorraine and Megan Fitzsimmons, Gail Forman, French Wine Society, Dalia Goldgor, Alexandra Greeley, Henry "Hoppy" Hopkins III, Stuart and Nadine Jacobs, Barbara Johnson, Michael Karlan, Danny Katz, Kristen Leary, Les Dames d'Escoffier-DC, Judie Levenson, Mark Longerbeam, Bob Madigan, Ron Matz, Barbara Moore, Ann Morrison, Nycci Nellis, Jo-Ann Neuhaus, Bernard Onken, Rebecca Penovich, Bonita Preston, Professionals in the City-DC, Randi Rom, Dave Sarfaty, Trish Schweers, Donna Shirdon, Will Shore, Emily Shrift, Steven Shukow, Laura Strachan, Katherine Tallmadge, Tastedc.com, Thingstododc.com, Ian Turner, Washington Wine Academy, Ryan Wegman, David Wolff and Michael Zwaig with special thanks to Jodi Lannen Brady and Jennifer Barger, as well as the following members of our staff: Aynsley Karps (editorial assistant), Brian Albert, Sean Beachell, Maryanne Bertollo, Danielle Borovoy, Reni Chin, Larry Cohn, Nicole Diaz, Kelly Dobkin, Alison Flick, Jeff Freier, Matthew Hamm, Justin Hartung, Marc Henson, Natalie Lebert, Mike Liao, James Mulcahy, Polina Paley, Chris Walsh, Jacqueline Wasilczyk, Art Yaghci, Sharon Yates, Anna Zappia and Kyle Zolner.

The reviews in this guide are based on public opinion surveys. The ratings reflect the average scores given by the survey participants who voted on each establishment. The text is based on quotes from, or paraphrasings of, the surveyors' comments. Phone numbers, addresses and other factual data were correct to the best of our knowledge when published in this guide.

Contents

Ratings & Symbols

Zagat Top Spot	Name	Symbols		Cuisine	Zagat Ratings			
					FOOD	DECOR	SERVICE	COST

Area, Address & Contact	**Z Tim & Nina's ◑** *Steak* ▽ 23 │ 19 │ 8 │ $25

Capitol Hill | 1600 J St. NW (Statesmen's Way │ 202-555-6000 | www.zagat.com

Review, surveyor comments in quotes

This "meat-and-greet mecca" boasts the ultimate "see-or-avoid-being-seen" experience, with one-way glass booths ("you can look out but others can't look in") and a "hot line to the family quarters at the White House"; in the absence of waiters, you "pick your own salad" from the hydroponic planters, but the "real attraction" is the low price since "lobbyists pay for most meals."

Ratings   **Food, Decor** & **Service** are rated on a 30-point scale.

0	–	9	poor to fair
10	–	15	fair to good
16	–	19	good to very good
20	–	25	very good to excellent
26	–	30	extraordinary to perfection
▽			low response	less reliable

Cost   The price of dinner with a drink and tip; lunch is usually 25% less. For unrated **newcomers** or **write-ins,** the price range is as follows:

I	$25 and below	E	$41 to $65
M	$26 to $40	VE	$66 or above

Symbols

Z	highest ratings, popularity and importance
◑	serves after 11 PM
Ⓢ Ⓜ	closed on Sunday or Monday
⊄	no credit cards accepted

Maps   Index maps show restaurants with the highest Food ratings in those areas.

About This Survey

This **2012 Washington, DC/Baltimore Restaurants Survey** is an update reflecting significant developments since our last Survey was published. It covers 1,350 restaurants in the Washington, DC/Baltimore area, including 119 important additions. We've also indicated new addresses, phone numbers and other changes. Like all our guides, this one is based on input from avid local consumers. Our editors have synopsized this feedback, highlighting representative comments (in quotation marks within each review). To read full surveyor comments – and share your own opinions – visit **ZAGAT.com,** where you'll also find the latest restaurant news, special events, deals, reservations, menus, photos and lots more, all for free.

ABOUT ZAGAT: In 1979, we started asking friends to rate and review restaurants purely for fun. The term "user-generated content" had not yet been coined. That hobby grew into Zagat Survey; 32 years later, we have over 375,000 surveyors and cover airlines, bars, dining, fast food, entertaining, golf, hotels, movies, music, resorts, shopping, spas, theater and tourist attractions in over 100 countries. Along the way, we evolved from being a print publisher to a digital content provider, e.g. **ZAGAT.com** and Zagat mobile apps (for iPad, iPhone, Android, BlackBerry, Windows Phone 7 and Palm webOS). We also produce marketing tools for a wide range of blue-chip corporate clients. And you can find us on Twitter (twitter.com/zagat), Facebook, Foursquare and just about any other social media network.

THREE SIMPLE PREMISES underlie our ratings and reviews. First, we believe that the collective opinions of large numbers of consumers are more accurate than those of any single person. (Consider that our surveyors bring some 883,000 annual meals' worth of experience to this survey, visiting DC/Baltimore-area restaurants year-round, anonymously – and on their own dime.) Second, food quality is only part of the equation when choosing a restaurant, thus we ask our surveyors to separately rate food, decor and service and report on cost. Third, since people need reliable information in a fast, easy-to-digest format, we strive to be concise, offer extensive indexes and provide our content on every platform – print, online and mobile.

THANKS: We're grateful to our local editors, Olga Boikess, a Washington lawyer and avid diner who has edited this Survey since 1987, and Marty Katz, a Baltimore writer, photographer and barbecue researcher who has worked with us since 1995. Thank you, guys. We also sincerely thank the thousands of surveyors who participated – this guide is really "theirs."

JOIN IN: To improve our guides, we solicit your comments; it's vital that we hear your opinions. Just contact us at **nina-tim@zagat.com.** We also invite you to join our surveys at **ZAGAT.com.** Do so and you'll receive a choice of rewards in exchange.

New York, NY
July 27, 2011

Nina and Tim

Nina and Tim Zagat

What's New

DC ain't no second-tier dining town. For proof, just consider the top-flight chefs and restaurateurs who've been dreaming up new concepts to keep customers coming – and to accommodate their thinner wallets.

EXPANDING EMPIRES: Despite the financial climate, virtually every major DC food personality recently launched an exciting new venture (or is gearing up to do so) – often a more affordable, casual offshoot of their flagship operations. Michel Richard led the way with **Michel** in Tysons Corner, an urbane French that's more like his popular **Central** than his high-end **Citronelle**; and Fabio Trabocchi's **Fiola** in Penn Quarter offers approachable versions of the fare served at his erstwhile fancy Italian **Maestro.** Also delivering top-notch eats in relaxed digs are Robert Wiedmaier's Bethesda Belgian **Mussel Bar**; Cathal Armstrong's Old Town pub **Virtue Feed & Grain**; Todd Gray's seafood-strong **Watershed** in NoMa; and **Estadio,** a Logan Circle Spaniard from **Proof** talents.

NYC IN DC: The Big Apple has sewn more seeds in the capital, notably 'cue champ **Hill Country,** red-sauce juggernaut **Carmine's** and the New Englandy **Luke's Lobster** (all near Verizon Center); famed burger joint **Shake Shack** below Dupont Circle and at Nationals Park; sugary snack specialist **Serendipity 3** in Georgetown; and **P.J. Clarke's** saloon, a patty toss from the White House. In turn, **Casa Nonna,** an Italian comfort-fooder, debuted in Dupont Circle and then headed to NYC.

QUICK AND CASUAL: Cheap eats on the run have been given a boost by the likes of Spike Mendelsohn, whose populist **We, The Pizza** joins his other Capitol Hill fueling station, **Good Stuff Eatery.** Mediterranean and Indian spins on the **Chipotle** quick-serve model are being piloted at **Cava Mezze Grill** in Bethesda and **Merzi** in Penn Quarter, with clones of each planned (and Chipotle's own spin-off, the Asian **ShopHouse,** is in the works). Meanwhile, food trucks flourished, with **Red Hook Lobster Pound** in the vanguard.

MORE FOR BALTIMORE: Baltimore's Hampden is emerging as a serious dining destination with edgy New American fare at **Alchemy** and Belgian-Continental bites at **Corner BYOB.** Elsewhere, Bronx-born actor Chazz Palminteri launched **Chazz,** an upscale Italian/pizzeria in Harbor East; underserved West Baltimore got a much needed Mediterranean (**Waterstone**); Cuba arrived in Towson via **Havana Road**; and Pikesville's **Suburban House** deli rose from the ashes. On the Shore, Easton's **Banning's** (a pub) and **Brasserie Brightwell** (American/French), plus St. Michaels' upcoming **Big Pickle FoodBar** (deli/New American) attest to the region's steady recovery. In late 2011, **Woodberry Kitchen** hopes to open casual siblings nearby and **Oregon Grille** will refurbish Brooklandville's **Valley Inn.** Looking further ahead, **Volt's** Bryan Voltaggio is readying two different new concepts for 2012.

Washington, DC
Baltimore, MD
July 27, 2011

Olga Boikess
Marty Katz

Most Popular in DC

1. Zaytinya | *Med./Mideast.*
2. 2 Amys | *Pizza*
3. Central Michel | *Amer./French*
4. Citronelle | *French*
5. Inn at Little Washington | *Amer.*
6. Rasika | *Indian*
7. Jaleo | *Spanish*
8. Kinkead's | *Seafood*
9. Blue Duck Tavern | *Amer.*
10. 2941 | *Amer.*
11. 1789 | *Amer.*
12. Clyde's | *Amer.*
13. Old Ebbitt Grill | *Amer.*
14. L'Auberge/François | *French*
15. Capital Grille | *Steak*
16. Komi | *Med.*
17. Eve | *Amer.*
18. Brasserie Beck | *Belgian/French*
19. BlackSalt | *Amer./Seafood*
20. CityZen | *Amer.*
21. Five Guys | *Burgers*
22. Ray's The Steaks | *Steak*
23. Ruth's Chris | *Steak*
24. Founding Farmers | *Amer.*
25. Lebanese Taverna | *Lebanese*
26. BLT Steak | *Steak*
27. Acadiana | *Contemp. LA*
28. Vidalia | *Amer.*
29. Palm | *Seafood/Steak*
30. Tosca | *Italian*
31. Morton's | *Steak*
32. Marcel's | *Belgian/French*
33. Nora | *Amer.*
34. Legal Sea Foods | *Seafood*
35. Matchbox | *Amer.*
36. Oyamel | *Mex.*
37. Prime Rib | *Steak*
38. Bistrot du Coin | *French*
39. DC Coast | *Seafood*
40. Ray's Hell | *Burgers*
41. Tabard Inn | *American*
42. Oceanaire | *Seafood*
43. Carlyle | *American*
44. Obelisk | *Italian*
45. Corduroy | *American*
46. Ben's Chili Bowl | *Diner*
47. Palena | *American*
48. Proof* | *American*
49. Bistro Bis | *French*
50. Black Market Bistro | *Amer.*

Many of the above restaurants are among the Washington, DC, area's most expensive, but if popularity were calibrated to price, a number of other restaurants would surely join their ranks. To illustrate this, we have added two pages of Best Buys starting on page 16.

---

* Indicates a tie with restaurant above

Top map (regional):

MARYLAND · VIRGINIA · DISTRICT OF COLUMBIA · WASHINGTON · Arlington · Alexandria · Falls Church · Vienna · Tysons Corner · McLean · Bethesda · Rockville · Potomac · Silver Spring · Wheaton · Colesville · Fairland · Fairland · College Park · Hyattsville · Cheverly · Suitland · Temple Hills · Oxon Hill · Camp Springs · Bellsville · Darnestown · Seneca · Great Falls · Reston · Oakton · Fairfax · Burke · Springfield · Kings Park · Annandale · Franconia · Potomac River

Listings (starred): Freddy's Lobster & Clams · Mussel Bar · Michel · Bayou Bakery · Maìa · Tang · Atlas · Watershed · Medium Rare · Toki Underground · Ba Bay · The Pizza · We · Virtue Feed & Grain · Fiorella Pizzeria · e Caffè

Bottom map (downtown detail):

SHAW · LOGAN CIRCLE · DUPONT CIRCLE · MT VERNON SQUARE · CHINATOWN · DOWNTOWN · MCPHERSON SQUARE · FARRAGUT SQUARE · LAFAYETTE SQUARE · FOGGY BOTTOM · WEST END · GEORGETOWN · THE ELLIPSE · The White House · DUMBARTON OAKS PARK · MONTROSE PARK · ROCK CREEK PARK · Theodore Roosevelt Island · Potomac River · Kennedy Center

Listings (starred): El Centro D.F. · Estadio · Lincoln · P.J. Clarke's · Galileo III · Carmine's · Fiola · Hill Country · Shake Shack · Bayou

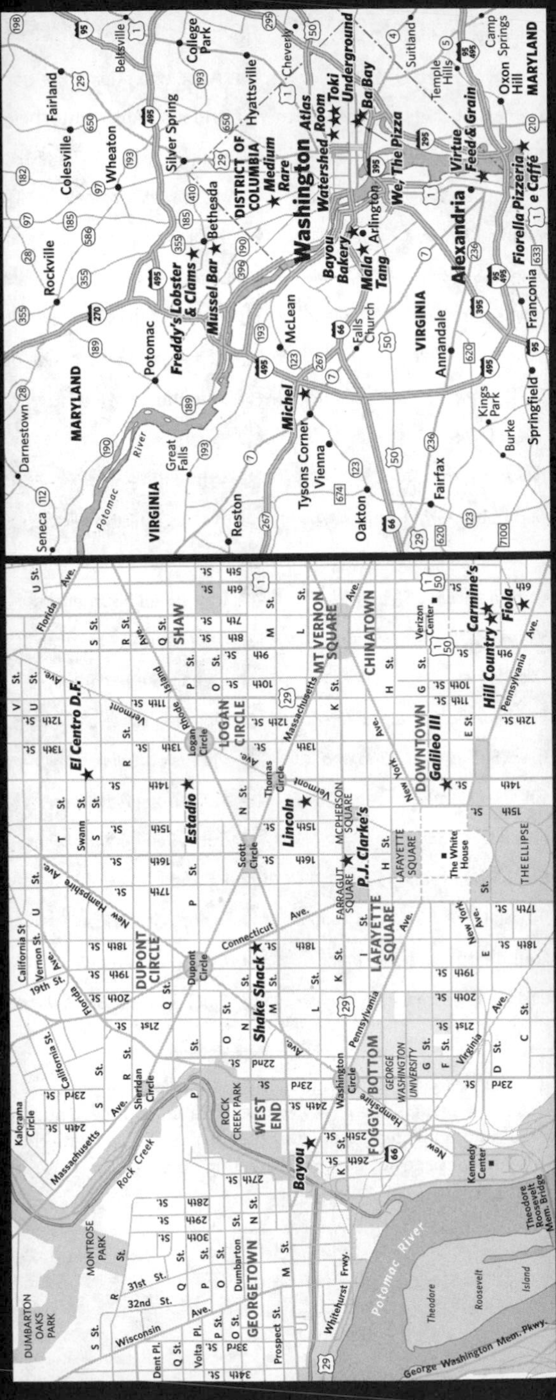

Key Newcomers

Our editors' choices among this year's arrivals. Full list, page 207.

Atlas Room | *Eclectic* | Clever eats elevate namesake neighborhood

Ba Bay | *Vietnamese* | Tour modern Vietnam without leaving the Hill

Bayou | *Cajun/Creole* | Big Easy food, drink and music close to Georgetown

Bayou Bakery | *Southern* | Down-home cooking near Arlington's Courthouse

Carmine's | *Italian* | NYC import brings *abbondanza* to Penn Quarter

El Centro D.F. | *Mexican* | 14 Street NW's high-octane taqueria/tequileria

Estadio | *Spanish* | Tapas and spiked slushies above Logan Circle

Fiola | *Italian* | Fabio Trabocchi's elegant return to the Penn Quarter

Fiorella Pizzeria | *Pizza* | Roman pies and pizzazz in National Harbor

Freddy's Lobster/Clams | *Seafood* | New England–style shack in Bethesda

Galileo III | *Italian* | Roberto Donna's flagship reincarnated Downtown

Hill Country | *BBQ* | Texas 'cue stampedes the Penn Quarter

Lincoln | *American* | Small plates and spirited drinks honor Abe Downtown

Mala Tang | *Chinese* | Tangy hot pots evoke Chengdu in Arlington

Medium Rare | *Steak* | Affordable set-menu dining in Cleveland Park

Michel | *French* | Michel Richard at the Ritz in Tysons Corner

Mussel Bar | *Belgian* | Robert Wiedmaier muscles into Bethesda

P.J. Clarke's | *Pub* | Renowned NYC pub grub near the White House

Red Hook Lobster | *Seafood* | Crustaceans on a roll in DC and beyond

Shake Shack | *Burgers* | NYC legend slides into Nats Park and Dupont

Toki Underground | *Taiwanese* | Low-cost Atlas slurp shop

Virtue Feed & Grain | *Pub* | Auld Sod in Old Town via Cathal Armstrong

Watershed | *American/Seafood* | Todd Gray's all-purpose venue in NoMa

We, The Pizza | *Pizza* | Spike Mendelsohn's idiosyncratic Cap Hill pie place

---

Slated to open soon are *Top Chef* star Mike Isabella's small-plate Italian **Graffiato,** near Verizon Center, and gonzo toque RJ Cooper's New American **Rogue 24,** in Mount Vernon Square. Homegrown restaurant groups are also adding to their portfolios: **Society Fair,** an Old Town market, butcher, bakery, wine bar and eatery expected in fall 2011 (from the **Eve** crew); **Pearl Dive Oyster Palace** on 14th Street (Black Restaurant Group); **Sugo Macaroni & Pizza Bar** in Rockville (a **Cava/Mamma Lucia** joint venture); **Daikay,** a Penn Quarter izakaya/ramen shop (via **Sushiko**); and West End all-Americans **District Commons** and **Burger, Tap & Shake** in late summer 2011 (Passion Food Hospitality). Out-of-towners heading inside the beltway include Bobby Flay (**Bobby's Burger Palace** outlets planned on K Street and in College Park, MD) and *Top Chef* winner Richard Blais whose Atlanta-based **Flip Burger** will land in Penn Quarter.

Top Food

<u>29</u> Marcel's | *Belgian/French*
Inn at Little Washington | *Amer.*
Komi | *Amer./Med.*

<u>28</u> CityZen | *American*
Rasika | *Indian*
Makoto | *Japanese*
Eve | *American*
Citronelle | *French*
Palena | *American*

<u>27</u> L'Aub. Provençale | *French*
Prime Rib | *Steak*
Obelisk | *Italian*
Tosca | *Italian*
Corduroy | *American*
L'Aub. Chez François | *French*

<u>26</u> 2941 | *American*
Blue Duck Tavern | *American*
Pasta Plus | *Italian*
Honey Pig | *Korean*
Minibar | *Nuevo Latino*

Central Michel | *Amer./French*
Ray's The Steaks | *Steak*
Ray's Hell Burger | *Burgers*
Sushi Taro | *Japanese*
Amsterdam Falafel | *Mideast.*
Thai Square | *Thai*
Kinkead's | *Seafood*
Nora | *American*
BlackSalt | *American/Seafood*
Peking Gourmet | *Chinese*
Masala Art | *Indian*
Il Pizzico | *Italian*

<u>25</u> Zaytinya | *Med./Mideast.*
Capital Grille | *Steak*
El Pollo Rico | *Peruvian*
Equinox | *American*
Persimmon | *American*
Ruth's Chris | *Steak*
Sushiko | *Japanese*
Mannequin Pis | *Belgian*

BY CUISINE

AMERICAN (NEW)

<u>29</u> Inn at Little Washington
Komi
<u>28</u> CityZen
Eve
Palena

AMERICAN (TRAD.)

<u>26</u> Blue Duck Tavern
<u>24</u> Ray's/Classics
<u>23</u> Majestic
Matchbox
Tuscarora Mill

BURGERS

<u>28</u> Palena
<u>26</u> Ray's Hell Burger
<u>23</u> Matchbox
<u>22</u> Five Guys
<u>21</u> Good Stuff Eatery

CHINESE

<u>26</u> Peking Gourmet
<u>24</u> Burma Road
A&J
<u>23</u> Mark's Duck Hse.
Joe's Noodle Hse.

FRENCH (BISTRO)

<u>26</u> Central Michel Richard
<u>25</u> Brasserie Beck
<u>24</u> Montmartre
La Côte d'Or
<u>23</u> Bistrot Lepic

FRENCH (CLASSIC)

<u>27</u> L'Auberge Provençale
L'Auberge Chez François
<u>24</u> Et Voila
La Chaumière
Brabo/Tasting Room

FRENCH (NEW)

<u>29</u> Marcel's
<u>28</u> Citronelle
<u>25</u> Bistro Bis
<u>24</u> Adour at the St. Regis
<u>-</u> Bistro Provence

GREEK/MED.

<u>29</u> Komi
<u>25</u> Zaytinya
Mourayo
<u>24</u> Cava
<u>23</u> Evo Bistro

Excludes places with low votes, unless otherwise indicated

Vote at ZAGAT.com

INDIAN

- 28 Rasika
- 26 Masala Art
- 24 Passage to India
- Bombay Club
- Delhi Club

ITALIAN

- 27 Obelisk
- Tosca
- 26 Pasta Plus
- Il Pizzico
- 24 Al Tiramisu

JAPANESE

- 28 Makoto
- 26 Sushi Taro
- 25 Sushiko
- Kaz Sushi Bistro
- Yamazato

MEXICAN

- 24 Oyamel
- 23 Taqueria Nacional
- Taqueria Distrito Federal
- 22 Guajillo
- Azucar

MIDDLE EASTERN

- 26 Amsterdam Falafel
- 25 Zaytinya
- Afghan
- 24 Layalina
- Kabob Palace

NUEVO LATINO

- 25 Maté∇
- 23 Ceiba
- 19 Mio
- 18 Caribbean Breeze
- – Cuba Libre

PAN-ASIAN

- 25 Source
- 22 Spices
- 21 Raku
- Asian Spice
- 20 Asian Bistro/Zen

PIZZA

- 25 2 Amys
- 23 Matchbox
- 22 Pete's Apizza
- Pizzeria Paradiso
- Agrodolce

SEAFOOD

- 26 Kinkead's
- BlackSalt
- 24 PassionFish
- Pesce
- Oceanaire

SOUTH AMERICAN

- 25 El Pollo Rico
- 24 Fogo De Chão
- Crisp & Juicy
- 23 Chima
- La Canela

SOUTHERN

- 24 Vidalia
- 23 Acadiana
- Crème
- 22 Georgia Brown's
- 21 Art & Soul

SOUTHWEST/TEX-MEX

- 21 Sweetwater Tavern
- 19 Uncle Julio's
- 18 Cactus Cantina
- California Tortilla
- Mi Rancho

SPANISH

- 24 Guardado's
- 23 Taberna del Alabardero
- 22 Jaleo
- 19 Bodega-Spanish Tapas
- 17 La Tasca

STEAKHOUSES

- 27 Prime Rib
- 26 Ray's The Steaks
- 25 Capital Grille
- Ruth's Chris
- J&G Steakhouse

THAI

- 26 Thai Square
- 25 Rabieng
- Ruan Thai
- Duangrat's
- 23 Bangkok54

VIETNAMESE

- 25 Four Sisters
- 24 Pho 75
- Minh's
- 23 Present
- 22 Huong Viet

BY SPECIAL FEATURE

BREAKFAST

- 25 J&G Steakhouse
  - Bistro Bis
- 22 Café du Parc
  - Bread Line
- 20 Johnny's Half Shell

BRUNCH

- 26 Blue Duck Tavern
- 25 Rabieng
  - Black Market Bistro
- 24 Bombay Club
  - Tabard Inn

CHEF'S TABLE

- 29 Inn at Little Washington
- 28 Citronelle
- 27 Tosca
- 26 2941
  - Blue Duck Tavern

CHILD-FRIENDLY

- 25 2 Amys
  - Black Market Bistro
- 24 Guardado's
  - Kabob Palace
- 23 Eamonn's

DINING ALONE

- 29 Marcel's
- 28 Palena
- 26 Kinkead's
- 25 Zaytinya
  - 2 Amys

HOTEL DINING

- 29 Inn at Little Washington
- 28 CityZen
  - (Mandarin Oriental)
  - Citronelle
  - (Latham Hotel)
- 27 L'Auberge Provençale
- 26 Blue Duck Tavern
  - (Park Hyatt)

MEET FOR A DRINK

- 26 Central Michel Richard
- 25 Zaytinya
  - Source
- 24 Proof
- 21 Art & Soul

POWER SCENES

- 27 Tosca
- 26 Central Michel Richard
  - Kinkead's
- 25 Bistro Bis
  - Charlie Palmer Steak

PRIVATE ROOMS

- 29 Marcel's
- 28 CityZen
  - Rasika
  - Citronelle
- 27 Tosca

SMALL PLATES/TAPAS

- 25 Zaytinya
- 24 Guardado's
  - Cava
  - Oyamel
- 23 Cork

TRENDY

- 28 CityZen
  - Rasika
- 25 Zaytinya
- 23 Masa 14
- 22 Birch & Barley/Churchkey

WORTH A TRIP

- 29 Inn at Little Washington
  - Washington, VA
- 27 L'Auberge Provençale
  - Boyce, VA
- 25 Trummer's On Main
  - Clifton, VA
- 24 Ashby Inn/Paris, VA
- 23 Iron Bridge Wine Co.
  - Warrenton, VA

BY LOCATION

ADAMS MORGAN

- 26 Amsterdam Falafel
- 24 Cashion's Eat
- 23 Pasta Mia
  - La Fourchette
- 22 Himalayan Heritage

ALEXANDRIA (OLD TOWN)

- 28 Eve
- 24 Brabo/Tasting Room
  - Hank's Oyster
- 23 Eamonn's
  - Grille

BETHESDA

25	Persimmon
24	Guardado's
	Passage to India
24	Haandi
23	Black's Bar

CAPITOL HILL

25	Bistro Bis
	Charlie Palmer Steak
24	Montmartre
	Cava
23	Toscana Café

CLARENDON

26	Ray's The Steaks
24	Pho 75
	Delhi Club
22	Tallula/EatBar
21	Tandoori Nights

CLEVELAND PARK/
WOODLEY PARK

28	Palena
25	2 Amys
23	Indique
	Tono Sushi
22	New Heights

CRYSTAL CITY

25	Ruth's Chris
	Morton's
24	Kabob Palace
22	Jaleo
20	Legal Sea Foods

DOWNTOWN

25	J&G Steakhouse
	Brasserie Beck
24	Adour at the St. Regis
	Oceanaire
	Fogo De Chão

DUPONT CIRCLE

29	Komi
27	Obelisk
26	Sushi Taro
	Nora
25	Mourayo

FALLS CHURCH

26	2941
	Peking Gourmet
25	Rabieng
	Duangrat's
24	Pho 75

GEORGETOWN/
GLOVER PARK

28	Citronelle
25	Sushiko
	1789
24	La Chaumière
23	Hook

GOLDEN TRIANGLE

27	Prime Rib
25	Equinox
	BLT Steak
24	Oval Room
	Bombay Club

PENN QUARTER

28	Rasika
27	Tosca
26	Minibar
	Central Michel Richard
25	Zaytinya

ROCKVILLE

26	Il Pizzico
24	Pho 75
	Bob's Noodle Bistro
	Sushi Damo
	Cava

SILVER SPRING

24	Mandalay
	Ray's The Classics
	Crisp & Juicy
22	Azucar
	Urban BBQ

TYSONS CORNER

25	Capital Grille
	Morton's
24	Fleming's Steak
	Palm
23	Chima

U STREET CORRIDOR

24	Etete
	Dukem
23	Crème
22	Ben's Chili Bowl
21	DC Noodles

WEST END

29	Marcel's
26	Blue Duck Tavern
23	Ris
21	Westend Bistro
	Circle Bistro

Top Decor

28 Inn at Little Washington	Lightfoot
27 Trummer's On Main	L'Auberge Provençale
CityZen	24 Charlie Palmer Steak
2941	Zola
26 Oya	Bombay Club
Marcel's	Morrison-Clark
L'Auberge Chez François	Blue Duck Tavern
Jockey Club	Co Co. Sala
Adour at the St. Regis	Sei
25 Prime Rib	Ping Pong Dim Sum
Citronelle	Corduroy
Eve	Ashby Inn
Source	Marrakesh
1789	Capital Grille
Rasika	Tabard Inn
J&G Steakhouse	701
Eventide	Bourbon Steak
Fahrenheit/Degrees	23 Occidental Grill & Seafood
Mie N Yu	Oval Room
Birch & Barley/Churchkey	Nora

OUTDOORS

Addie's	L'Auberge Chez François
Bistro Provence	Lauriol Plaza
Blue Duck Tavern	Old Angler's
Café du Parc	Poste Moderne
J&G Steakhouse	701
Johnny's Half Shell	2941

PRIVATE ROOMS

Adour at the St. Regis	Fiola
Birch & Barley/Churchkey	Marcel's
Citronelle	Nora
CityZen	Taberna del Alabardero
Clyde's	Tosca

ROMANCE

Birch & Barley/Churchkey	Michel
Co Co. Sala	1905
Cork	Nora
Eventide	Palena
Firefly	Rasika
Marvin	Tabard Inn

VIEWS

Arlington Rooftop	Old Angler's
Bond 45	Perrys
Charlie Palmer Steak	Sequoia
El Centro D. F.	Source
Eventide	Tabaq Bistro
J&G Steakhouse	2941

Top Service

29| Inn at Little Washington

28| Komi
CityZen
Marcel's

27| L'Auberge Chez François
Eve
Prime Rib
Obelisk

26| Citronelle
Tosca
2941

25| Trummer's On Main
L'Auberge Provençale
1789
Capital Grille
Corduroy
Bombay Club
Guardado's
Nora
Layalina

Fogo De Chão
Morton's
Ruth's Chris
Rasika
Blue Duck Tavern
Yamazato
Makoto

24| Kazan
Oval Room
Vidalia
Charlie Palmer Steak
Minibar
Palm
Palena
Siroc
La Côte d'Or
Tavira*
Adour at the St. Regis
Bourbon Steak
Kinkead's

Best Buys

Everyone loves a bargain, and DC offers plenty of them. All-you-can-eat options are mostly for lunch and/or brunch. For prix fixe menus, call ahead for availability.

ALL YOU CAN EAT

- 25 Afghan
- 24 Fogo De Chão
  - Delhi Club
  - Kabob Palace
  - Haandi
- 23 Angeethi
  - Indique Heights
- _ Diya

BAR LUNCH

- 28 Eve ($15)
- 24 Proof ($12)
- 23 Bourbon Steak ($21)
  - Bibiana Osteria ($15)
  - 701 ($15)
  - Ris ($15)
- _ Estadio ($10)

CHICKEN ROASTERS

- 25 El Pollo Rico
- 24 Crisp & Juicy
- 22 Edy's Chicken∇
  - La Limeña*∇
- 20 Chix
  - Nando's Peri Peri
- 18 Pollo Campero
  - Don Pollo

DINERS

- 24 Oohhs & Aahhs∇
  - C.F. Folks
- 22 Ben's Chili Bowl
- 20 Florida Ave. Grill
- 18 Open City
- 17 Diner
  - Luna Grill
- 16 Commissary
- _ Fast Gourmet

EARLY-BIRD/ PRE-THEATER

- 29 Marcel's ($58)
- 28 Rasika ($30)
- 27 Tosca ($38)
  - J&G Steakhouse ($39)
  - Duangrat's ($10)
- 24 La Côte d'Or ($20)
  - Oval Room ($35)
- 23 Zola ($40)

PRIX FIXE LUNCH

- 27 Tosca ($35)
- 26 Central Michel Richard ($20)
  - BlackSalt ($18)
- 25 J&G Steakhouse ($24)
  - Source ($30)
  - Charlie Palmer Steak ($25)
- 24 PassionFish ($17)
- _ Michel ($21)

PRIX FIXE DINNER

- 25 Mannequin Pis ($30)
- 24 Ray's The Classics ($23)
  - Bombay Club ($29)
- 23 La Bergerie ($45)
  - Me Jana ($40)
  - Bastille ($39)
- 22 Dino ($37)
- _ Medium Rare ($20)

PUB FOOD

- 20 Daniel O'Connell's
- 19 Clyde's
  - Againn
- 18 Stoney's Lounge
  - Irish Inn/Glen Echo
  - Franklin's
- 17 Fadó Irish Pub
- _ Virtue Feed & Grain

QUICK BITES

- 26 Amsterdam Falafel
- 24 Horace & Dickey's∇
- 22 Rocklands
  - Surfside
- 21 Tackle Box
- 19 Maoz Vegetarian∇
- _ Cava Mezze Grill
- _ Merzi

SANDWICHES/WRAPS

- 22 Bread Line
- 21 Moby Dick
- 19 Chop't Creative Salad
  - Maoz Vegetarian∇
- 18 Calif. Tortilla
- 17 Pret A Manger
- _ Bayou
- _ Fast Gourmet
- _ Paul

Vote at ZAGAT.com

BEST BUYS: BANG FOR THE BUCK

In order of Bang for the Buck rating.

1. Amsterdam Falafel
2. Buzz
3. Taylor Gourmet
4. Taqueria Distrito Federal
5. Five Guys
6. Taqueria Nacional
7. Ben's Chili Bowl
8. El Pollo Rico
9. California Tortilla
10. Sweetgreen
11. Chop't Creative Salad
12. Elevation Burger
13. Urban Burger
14. Pho 75
15. Crisp & Juicy
16. Chix
17. Pollo Campero
18. Kabob Palace
19. A&J
20. Good Stuff Eatery
21. Ray's Hell Burger
22. BGR Burger Joint
23. Bob & Edith's
24. Eamonn's
25. C.F. Folks
26. Bread Line
27. Nando's Peri-Peri
28. Amma Vegetarian
29. Lighthouse Tofu/Vit Goel Tofu
30. Teaism
31. Moby Dick
32. Chinatown Express
33. Pret A Manger
34. Pete's Apizza
35. Urban BBQ
36. Thai Basil
37. Tryst
38. Vegetable Garden
39. Hard Times Cafe
40. Florida Ave. Grill

BEST BUYS: OTHER GOOD VALUES

American Ice Co.
Angeethi
Bangkok Golden Thai
Breadsoda
Burma Road
Café Assorti
Capital City Diner
Cosmopolitan Grill
Curry Mantra
DC Noodles
Dukem
Eatonville
Edy's Chicken
Etete
Ethiopic
Fast Gourmet
Four Sisters
Freddy's Lobster/Clams
Granville Moore's
Hollywood East
Honey Pig
Horace & Dickey's
Huong Viet
Joe's Noodle Hse.
India Palace
La Caraqueña
La Limeña
Maoz Vegetarian
Maple Ave Restaurant
Masala Art
Matchbox
Medium Rare
Merzi
Nava Thai
Oohhs & Aahhs
Palena
Pho 14
Pizzeria Paradiso
Ravi Kabob House
Ray's the Steaks at East River
Rocklands
Room 11
Ruan Thai
Seventh Hill Pizza
Shake Shack
Spice Xing
Standard
Surfside
Tackle Box
Ted's Bulletin
Thai Square
Toki Underground
Toscana Café
2 Amys
We, The Pizza
Yuan Fu

WASHINGTON, DC
RESTAURANT
DIRECTORY

FOOD | DECOR | SERVICE | COST

A&J ⌷ *Chinese* `24` `10` `18` `$15`

Rockville | Woodmont Station | 1319C Rockville Pike (Wootton Pkwy.), MD | 301-251-7878

Annandale | 4316B Markham St. (Little River Tpke.), VA | 703-813-8181

"Short on style, long on taste", these "dependable" Rockville and Annandale "dim sum joints" serve "amazing Taiwanese snack food" – "small plates that zing with authenticity and originality" – at "stunningly low" prices in "cramped" quarters ("school cafeterias have better decor"); order "from the menu or point at the carts", but "hit the ATM before arriving" because it's "cash only."

Acacia Bistro ⌷ *Italian* `22` `17` `23` `$36`

Upper NW | 4340 Connecticut Ave. NW (Yuma St.) | 202-537-1040 | www.acaciabistro.com

The "interesting, eclectic menu" at this Van Ness Italian bistro showcases the talents of Ligurian chef Liliana Dumas (ex Assaggi Mozzarella Bar and Locanda), known for her "sublime" desserts; add "accommodating" staffers who "smile but don't hover", "terrific" wines paired with "small, well-executed plates", "airy" industrial decor and sidewalk seating, and you have a "gem" in a "neighborhood devoid of good choices."

⌷ Acadiana *Contemp. Louisiana* `23` `22` `23` `$47`

Mt. Vernon Square/Convention Center | 901 New York Ave. NW (9th St.) | 202-408-8848 | www.acadianarestaurant.com

For a "taste of N'Awlins in the capital", "homesick" Southerners head to this Mt. Vernon Square "fixture" for Louisiana "bayou cooking gone upscale", including "tasty" gumbo and "sensational biscuits" that "make your mouth water just thinking about them"; the "sumptuous room" and "sassy" staff extend the "who dat?" feel, plus there's a "perfect" patio for a sunset Sazerac; still, "bring the defibrillator" – it's "delicious, but not what the doctor would recommend."

Acqua al 2 *Italian* `-` `-` `-` `M`

Capitol Hill | 212 Seventh St. SE (North Carolina Ave.) | 202-525-4375 | www.acquaal2dc.com

Elegant rusticity pervades this Tuscan import tucked across from Eastern Market on Capitol Hill, where the extensive, enticing menu – the same one offered at its locations in Florence, Italy – includes authentic pastas and steaks, plus sampler plates for sharing; the dining room boasts flattering lighting, charming antique appointments and intimate nooks, and there's a cozy copper-topped bar with perches by windows overlooking the passing street scene.

Addie's *American* `23` `18` `22` `$42`

White Flint | 11120 Rockville Pike (Edson Ln.) | Rockville, MD | 301-881-0081 | www.addiesrestaurant.com

A "cute little house right on the Pike" (across from White Flint Mall) provides "cozy" quarters for "fresh", "delicious" New American food, enhanced by a "staff that helps you enjoy your meal" and "inviting" patios that provide a "delightful" escape from the oft-"crowded", "funky" interior; "as with all the Black restaurants"

	FOOD	DECOR	SERVICE	COST

(BlackSalt, et al.), dishes are "innovative without being wacky" and one should "save room for dessert."

🅩 Adour at the St. Regis *American/French* | 24 | 26 | 24 | $82 |

Downtown | St. Regis | 923 K St. NW (16th St.) | 202-509-8000 | www.adour-washingtondc.com

"Superb" contemporary French-American fare and "elegant service" define Alain Ducasse's "tucked-away" venue in Downtown's stately St. Regis Hotel, where white-leather appointments, "stunning chandeliers and glass wine displays" overseen by a "genius sommelier" set the stage for an "extravagant" meal; penny-pinchers pale at the "New York prices", but from the "terrific" amuse-bouche and "beautiful" plating ("hot dogs would be presented lavishly" here) to the "divine" macarons, most agree it's "worth it."

Afghan *Afghan* | 25 | 13 | 21 | $26 |

Greater Alexandria | 2700 Jefferson Davis Hwy. (Raymond Ave.) | Alexandria, VA | 703-548-0022 | www.afghanrestaurantva.com

There's "not much to look at", but this Alexandria Afghan's "hearty comfort food" makes it just the place for trenchermen ("cheap, varied lunchtime buffet"), vegetarians ("plenty of choices"), "finicky in-laws" ("menu never changes") and kids (no decor to damage); go for a "tasty" trip to another culture, with "friendly" servers as guides, sometimes enlivened by music from the adjoining banquet hall.

Againn 🅩 *British* | 19 | 23 | 22 | $42 |

Downtown | 1099 New York Ave. NW (11th St.) | 202-639-9830 | www.againndc.com

"English pub food goes upscale" at this "trendy", "somewhat masculine" Downtown eatery outfitted with dark wood, "super-cozy" booths and a "comfortable" zinc-topped bar that hosts a "lively" happy hour with an "impressive whiskey and cocktail menu"; while its "refined focus" on the likes of bangers and mash (featuring housemade charcuterie) strikes some as "average British food at not-so-average prices", the "inviting atmosphere" keeps 'em coming back.

Agora *Turkish* | - | - | - | I |

Dupont Circle | 1527 17th St. NW (bet. P & Q Sts.) | 202-332-6767 | www.agoradc.net

Patterned on similar spots in proprietor Latif Guler's hometown on the Aegean Sea, this brick-walled Turk in Dupont Circle features industrial-feeling chandeliers and a wood-fired oven and charcoal grill; an affordable small-plates-only menu (with Greek influences) includes lots of seafood and vegetables and makes use of olive oil bottled on Guler's family farm, while a patio provides a primo perch for sipping ouzo, wines and Mediterranean beers.

Agrodolce *Italian* | 22 | 16 | 19 | $31 |

Germantown | Milestone Shopping Ctr. | 21030 J Frederick Ave. (Rte. 355), MD | 301-528-6150 | www.agrodolcerestaurant.com

At its "best in fair weather" when the terrace "delights", this Germantown "gem" brings Italian "flair" to the northern Montgomery County dining scene, with "authentic flavors" and "reasonably priced" wines; if the "somewhat spartan" interior is less appealing (i.e. "noise"), the "accommodating" help keeps the vibe *dolce.*

A La Lucia   *Italian* | 22 | 17 | 21 | $37 |

Old Town | 315 Madison St. (bet. Fairfax & Royal Sts.) | Alexandria, VA | 703-836-5123 | www.alalucia.com

"Hidden" in north Old Town, this "friendly neighborhood place" features "uncomplicated" Italian cooking – notably, "outstanding" homemade pasta in "rich but delicious" variations – delivered with a "personal touch" by vets who "know their business"; although seating in the "spartan" dining room is "tight", the "price is right", with deals like a 25% discount on vino (Sunday–Tuesday evenings and lunch daily) and a nightly $31.95 three-course dinner.

Al Crostino   *Italian* | 21 | 16 | 20 | $41 |

U Street Corridor | 1324 U St. NW (bet. 13th & 14th Sts.) | 202-797-0523 | www.alcrostino.com

With its "amazing gnocchi" and other "tasty" Italian fare, this "charming", "informal" U Street bistro saves you a "flight to Rome" – "especially if you go for the (often pricey) specials"; "spot-on" servers give character to the "tiny", rather "drab" space that "can be intimate" but can also feel "crowded."

Al Tiramisu   *Italian* | 24 | 19 | 22 | $54 |

Dupont Circle | 2014 P St. NW (bet. Hopkins & 20th Sts.) | 202-467-4466 | www.altiramisu.com

"Engaging" chef-owner Luigi Diotaiuti adds a spark to this Italian "hot spot" off Dupont Circle, where romantics dig into "wonderful seafood and pasta" next to a "crackling fireplace" in "quaint" (if "tight") quarters; its "authentic cooking", "terrific" wines and "professional waiters" whose "sense of humor keeps fine dining from being a bore" make "seats hard to get"; P.S. "ask for the price of the specials", as they "can be a big surprise."

🆕 **America Eats Tavern**   *American* | – | – | – | M |

Penn Quarter | 405 Eighth St. NW (bet. D & E Sts.) | 202-393-0812

Star chef José Andrés will showcase the nation's culinary history in this six-month pop-up launching July 4 in the former Café Atlántico space; an edible extension of the nearby National Archives' exhibit 'What's Cooking, Uncle Sam?', the midpriced menu spotlights American classics ranging from burgoo to oysters Rockefeller, while the wine list and decor will also reflect the Americana theme; P.S. Minibar remains open through 2011 on the second floor of the tri-level space.

American Flatbread   *Pizza* | 21 | 14 | 20 | $22 |

Ashburn | Broadlands Mktpl. | 43170 Southern Walk Plaza (Wynridge Dr.), VA | 703-723-7003 | www.americanflatbread.com

Sourcing locally is the mantra of this "healthy", "straight-from-Vermont" pizza chain, whose "kid-friendly" Ashburn outlet churns out "amazing" crusty flatbreads (courtesy of a wood-burning oven) with "unique toppings", all paired with "terrific" salads and washed

FOOD | DECOR | SERVICE | COST

down with "top-notch" craft beers or wine; even if the large, "minimalistic" premises is presided over by "chatty" servers who can be "overwhelmed", enthusiasts just "love the place."

NEW American Ice Co. ● *BBQ* | - | - | - | I |

U Street Corridor | 917 V St. NW (bet. 10th St. & Vermont Ave.) | 202-758-3562

Nightlife impresarios Eric and Ian Hilton (Marvin, Patty Boom Boom) lend their cool cred to this affordable V Street NW venture where friends can catch up over counter-service BBQ and PBRs; the former garage's bare-bones, industrial-chic decor is dimly lit, while a courtyard patio is destined to be quite the scene in warm weather.

American Tap Room ● *American* | - | - | - | M |

NEW Bethesda | Bethesda Row | 7278 Woodmont Ave. (Elm St.), MD | 301-656-1366
Reston | Reston Town Ctr. | 1811 Liberty St. (Market St.), VA | 703-834-0400
www.americantaproom.com

Both locations of this sudsy twosome boast big bars pouring craft brews to complement an ample selection of midpriced American fare, with lots of flat-screens and outdoor seating as further draws; twenty- and thirtysomethings crowd the hopping bar scene at the original in Reston Town Center, while perks at the Bethesda outpost include an open kitchen, fireplace and live piano music.

Amici Miei *Italian* | 20 | 18 | 19 | $37 |

Potomac | 1093 Seven Locks Rd. (Wootton Pkwy.), MD | 301-545-0966 | www.amicimieiristorante.com

A "tony" Potomac crowd swears by this "strip-mall gem", basking in its "upscale", "welcoming atmosphere" and the ability to enjoy "homemade pastas" and other "well-prepared" Italian fare in a "convenient" locale; while a few skeptics snap about "squeezed" seating, a "predictable" menu and "coffee-shop" decor, most are pleased to have this "decent" option in a foodie "wasteland."

Amma Vegetarian Kitchen *Indian* | 22 | 11 | 17 | $17 |

Vienna | 344 Maple Ave. E. (bet. Beulah Rd. & Park St.), VA | 703-938-5328 | www.ammavegkitchen.com

Ok, it's "not a place to impress your girlfriend", but partisans praise the "plethora" of South Indian vegetarian "treats" – including "delicious dosas" – at this "authentic" Vienna "hole-in-the-wall" ("almost like home cooking from my mom"); expect "basic" decor and possibly the "tastiest meal for the price."

☑ Amsterdam Falafelshop ● *Mideastern* | 26 | 10 | 17 | $9 |

Adams Morgan | 2425 18th St. NW (Columbia Rd.) | 202-234-1969 | www.falafelshop.com

"Hip, fresh and oh-so-cheap" chirp revelers who hit this Adams Morgan "late-night standby" for its "golden" fries and "awesome" falafel, "little balls of heaven" crushed into pita to make "more room" for the "amazing array of salads and sauces" from the toppings bar; amenities are scant (i.e. "no plates or utensils"), but if

	FOOD	DECOR	SERVICE	COST

"you take quality and divide by cost", you get the DC Survey's No. 1 Bang for the Buck.

Angeethi *Indian* `23` `17` `19` `$22`

Herndon | 645 Elden St. (bet. Jackson & Monroe Sts.), VA | 703-796-1527
Leesburg | 1500 E. Market St. (bet. Battlefield & River Creek Pkwys.), VA | 703-777-6785
www.angeethiva.com

For a "fantastic variety" of Indian "regional specialties" that "eschews the typical blah butter chicken for regional specialties", this Herndon subcontinental (there's a Leesburg branch too) "can't be beat"; sure, it's not big on decor, but the "great-deal" lunch spread is "well attended" ("not tired and dried out"), and servers "don't play the 'you got the buffet so forget getting a second soda' game."

Ardeo + Bardeo *American/Wine Bar* `21` `20` `21` `$43`

Cleveland Park | 3311 Connecticut Ave. NW (bet. Macomb & Ordway Sts.) | 202-244-6750 | www.bardeo.com

Serving "contemporary American cuisine with style and charm" at "surprisingly affordable prices", this "modern-feeling" Cleveland Park eatery provides "minor stargazing" possibilities, and its "helpful but never intrusive" staffers earn it "ardent" fans; a major post-Survey remodeling included knocking down a wall to combine the bistro and wine bar into a single space that oozes rusticity, while new kitchen talent updated the menu with shareable small plates; P.S. there's "lovely" rooftop seating in the summer.

Argia's *Italian* `19` `17` `20` `$33`

Falls Church | 124 N. Washington St. (bet. Broad St. & Park Ave.), VA | 703-534-1033 | www.argias.com

Falls Church denizens "love the small-town feel" of this "bustling neighborhood" Italian near the State Theatre, whose "appealing" specials and "well-selected" wines provide a "welcome break from typical 'boring 'burb bites'"; equally appealing are the "money-saving" family-sized platters, "lively bar" and a staff that "makes you feel at home" – although it's a "noisy" home.

NEW Arlington Rooftop ☻ *American* `-` `-` `-` `M`

Clarendon | 2424 Wilson Blvd. (Barton St.), VA | 703-528-3030 | www.arlingtonrooftopbarandgrill.com

The building's not tall, but the views soar at this rooftop arrival in the Courthouse-Clarendon corridor serving a midpriced American menu of classic surf 'n' turf and updated pub favorites; DC monuments are the backdrop on the outdoor deck that also features a sleek bar, while inside is a high-ceilinged, two-story dining room with huge windows, a massive old-fashioned bar and countless flat-screens tuned for sports-minded locals.

Art & Soul *American* `21` `21` `20` `$46`

Capitol Hill | Liason Capitol Hill | 415 New Jersey Ave. NW (bet. D & E Sts.) | 202-393-7777 | www.artandsouldc.com

Chef Art Smith's "swanky, modern" hotel bar/lounge and dining room on Capitol Hill serves "chic", "Southern-influenced" American fare that "attracts a cool crowd of young power brokers"; "art is there, both on the walls [and] the plates" (in the "beautifully presented" "haute cuisine meets comfort food") and sometimes in person, though some folks' "high expectations" are "not realized" – "sorry, Oprah", it's "ok, but nothing super special."

Artie's *American*   23 | 20 | 23 | $34

Fairfax | 3260 Old Lee Hwy. (Fairfax Blvd.), VA | 703-273-7600 |
www.greatamericanrestaurants.com

"Year in and year out", this Fairfax "mainstay" offers an "easy night out" ("blue jeans *or* business") with its "casual but upscale" American fare, delivered by "perky" servers in a "bustling" dining room awash in "dark wood and boating memorabilia"; the "no-res" policy makes "long waits" common, but a "call-ahead service" and "excellent" bar that's "more than just a holding pen for the hungry masses" keep things at an even keel.

Arucola *Italian*   19 | 15 | 19 | $36

Upper NW | 5534 Connecticut Ave. NW (bet. McKinley & Morrison Sts.) |
202-244-1555 | www.arucola.com

"Before the movies" at the Avalon in Upper NW, this "neighborhood trattoria" lures loyalists with "reliable pastas and pizzas", an "antipasto cart" and "reasonably priced" wine; still, surveyors can't agree on whether the chow's "uninspiring" or "first-rate" (sometimes it's both on "the same occasion"), and service can also be capricious – "inflexible" or "earnest", but with an "easy tolerance" of kids; in any event, it's best in "nice weather", when there's outdoor seating.

Ashby Inn Ⓜ *American*   24 | 24 | 23 | $59

Paris | The Ashby Inn | 692 Federal St. (Rte. 50), VA | 540-592-3900 |
www.ashbyinn.com

This "quaint little inn nestled" in Paris, VA, has long been a "charming spot for a romantic (and delicious) meal", and that tradition continues with the arrival of "accomplished" chef Tarver King (ex South Carolina's Woodlands Resort), whose "imaginative" New American fare is "well worth the drive"; enjoy the "beautiful view from the terrace" during brunch or, after dining in its "cozy", "tavern"-like interior, move outdoors for dessert; P.S. also closed Tuesdays.

Asia Bistro *Asian*   20 | 17 | 19 | $28

Pentagon City | Pentagon Row | 1301 S. Joyce St. (Army Navy Dr.) |
Arlington, VA | 703-413-2002 | www.asia-bistro.com

Zen Bistro & Wine Bar *Asian*

Pentagon City | Pentagon Row | 1301 S. Joyce St. (Army Navy Dr.) |
Arlington, VA | 703-413-8887 | www.zen-bistro.com

A "fun little sushi place", this Pentagon Row eatery entices Arlingtonians with a "nice mix of Asian fusion dishes", along with the "usual rolls", in a "slightly clubby atmosphere" featuring moody lighting; even if a few insist it's "not worth traveling" here for what "feels like chain" fare, most agree it's a "good place for a drink" (ditto Zen, its next-door wine bar offshoot).

Asia Nine *Asian* `18` `17` `18` `$30`

Penn Quarter | 915 E St. NW (bet. 9th & 10th Sts.) | 202-629-4355 |
www.asianine.com

Offering "something for everyone", including a "broad selection of
sake", this "hopping" Pan-Asian in "sleek" Penn Quarter digs is a
"hangout for nearby law people" at lunch and useful "after the E
Street theater"; but even an "excellent happy hour" can't conquer
critics who cite "inconsistent" service and food, deeming it "meh."

Asian Spice *Asian* `21` `20` `19` `$28`

Chinatown | 717 H St. NW (bet. 7th & 8th Sts.) | 202-589-0900 |
www.asianspice.us

Raise the red lantern for this "creative" Chinatown Pan-Asian, a
"quiet respite" that's "not on the beaten path . . . just yet"; but that
may change, since a "diverse" clientele applauds its "friendly" staff,
"great" patio and "reasonable prices" for "delicately" prepared and
"playfully" named offerings that "run the gamut" from Chinese to
Malaysian to Thai and "start out hot and only get hotter."

Assaggi Mozzarella Bar *Italian* `21` `19` `19` `$46`

Bethesda | 4838 Bethesda Ave. (bet. Arlington Rd. & Woodmont Ave.),
MD | 301-951-1988 | www.assaggirestaurant.com

Assaggi Osteria *Italian*

McLean | 6641 Old Dominion Dr. (Holmes Pl.), VA | 703-918-0080 |
www.assaggiosteria.com

"Fill up" on the "generous" mozzarella plates at this "buzzy", open-to-
the-street Bethesda Italian and its "welcoming" McLean offshoot, and
there may not be room for "wonderful pasta dishes" and other "interesting entrees" or the "nice selection" of wine; service gets mixed
marks ("very good" vs. "disinterested"), but overall it's "casual dining
with a slightly upscale feel", reflected in tabs that can be "a bit pricey."

NEW Atlas Room Ⓜ *Eclectic* `–` `–` `–` `M`

Atlas District | 1015 H St. NE (bet. 10th & 11th Sts.) | 202-388-4020 |
www.theatlasroom.com

This Eclectic rookie uplifts its namesake neighborhood's dining
scene with a rotating selection of midpriced creative eats, its quirky
menu focusing on local ingredients served several ways and in three
portion sizes; the narrow, romantically lit dining room is lined with colorful vintage maps and includes a lounge with high-tops in the back.

Austin Grill *Tex-Mex* `15` `15` `17` `$23`

Penn Quarter | 750 E St. NW (bet. 7th & 8th Sts.) | 202-393-3776
Rockville | Rockville Town Sq. | 36 Maryland Ave. (bet. Jefferson St. &
Montgomery Ave.), MD | 301-838-4281
Silver Spring | 919 Ellsworth Dr. (bet. Fenton St. & Georgia Ave.),
MD | 240-247-8969 ☽
Old Town | 801 King St. (Columbus St.) | Alexandria, VA | 703-684-8969
Springfield | 8430 Old Keene Mill Rd. (Rolling Rd.), VA | 703-644-3111
www.austingrill.com

"Longhorns missing home" stampede this Southwestern chainlet for
a "Tex-Mex fix" – bolstered by "monster-sized margaritas" – in a

"flashy", "festive" (i.e. "loud") atmosphere "well suited for families"; the food's "nothing fancy" and for some downright "pedestrian", but the menus are "varied enough to keep everyone happy" and the "price point hits the spot"; P.S. there's "live entertainment" at some branches.

Azucar *Mexican/Pan-Latin*   22 | 16 | 20 | $27

Silver Spring | Layhill Shopping Ctr. | 14418 Layhill Rd. (Bel Pre Rd.), MD | 301-438-3293 | www.azucarrestaurant.net

"Oh, yum", it's "worth the effort" to find this Silver Spring "strip-mall success" whose Mexican and Pan-Latin fare is "much more than just burritos, enchiladas and fajitas", although "delicious" versions are served here; sure, it may have a "nondescript" atmosphere, but "efficient" service and affordable "creative" cooking (like "outstanding" duck with olives) add up to an "enjoyable evening."

NEW Ba Bay Ⓜ *Vietnamese*   - | - | - | M

Capitol Hill | 633 Pennsylvania Ave. SE (bet. 6th & 7th Sts.) | 202-547-1787 | www.babaydc.com

In the Capitol Hill storefront that once housed Locanda, this intimate, modern Vietnamese entry offers a midpriced menu that refines traditional recipes; expect the likes of chile-spiked charcuterie and a sophisticated pho plus playful desserts and a cosmopolitan cocktail program that blends Western techniques with Far Eastern flavors.

Bamian *Afghan*   23 | 18 | 21 | $27

Falls Church | 5634 Leesburg Pike (Carlin Springs Rd.), VA | 703-820-7880 | www.bamianrestaurant.com

"Try anything with eggplant" at this "affordable" Falls Church Afghan with a "kitchen that knows its flavors – indeed, it "makes yogurt seem sexy and lamb chops positively sensual"; the "caring staff" and "cavernous" "banquet hall"–like space make it a real "find", especially when "enhanced by Afghan music" on weekends.

Banana Café & Piano Bar *Cuban/Puerto Rican*   18 | 15 | 15 | $25

Capitol Hill | 500 Eighth St. SE (E St.) | 202-543-5906 | www.bananacafedc.com

Go bananas at this "funky" Capitol Hill "favorite" for Cuban and Puerto Rican fare, with "shareable" plates and a popular Sunday brunch; ok, it's "not the greatest food" and service can be "slow", but the "kitschy Havana" decor and second-floor piano bar make it a "fun spot for a night out with friends", plus there's "fabulous" outdoor seating for enjoying the "hot DC summer."

Bangkok54 *Thai*   23 | 19 | 20 | $27

Arlington | 2919 Columbia Pike (Walter Reed Dr.), VA | 703-521-4070 | www.bangkok54restaurant.com

At this "refreshingly genuine" Thai bistro in Arlington, "even old standbys seem new due to the fresh ingredients and chef's delicate hand", and best of all, the "beautiful presentation" and "efficient" service come at a "reasonable" price; despite decor inspiring "Zen serenity", a meal here is "better than going to the gym – you'll sweat", especially if you don't "adjust the spice factor."

	FOOD	DECOR	SERVICE	COST

Bangkok Golden Thai
Restaurant *Laotian/Thai*

-	-	-	I

Falls Church | Seven Corners Ctr. | 6397 Seven Corners Ctr.
(bet. Arlington Blvd. & Leesburg Pike), VA | 703-533-9480 |
www.bangkokgoldenrestaurant.com

Fiery and fragrant Laotian food, a hard-to-find cuisine inside the
Beltway, is the no-longer-secret specialty of this simple Falls Church
Southeast Asian; long known locally for its inexpensive daily Thai
buffet, it's attracting adventuresome eaters who've discovered that
the chefs are happy to prepare their native dishes – now, several
dozen are listed on the menu; P.S. although expert diners hand roll
sticky rice into scoops for the food, chopsticks and cutlery can be
supplied to novices.

Bangkok Joe's *Thai*

21	21	18	$30

Georgetown | Washington Harbour | 3000 K St. NW
(Thomas Jefferson St.) | 202-333-4422 | www.bangkokjoes.com

"Come for the dumplings" decree devotees of this "chill" Thai at
Georgetown's Washington Harbour whose "fresh, flavorful and affordable" fare is "perfect" before a "movie across the street or for a
prom night dinner for 20" (it "manages all party sizes well"); add in
"generally friendly service", "creative cocktails" and Potomac views,
and you get a "pleasant end to a day."

Bar Pilar *American*

21	18	17	$28

Logan Circle | 1833 14th St. NW (bet. S & T Sts.) | 202-265-1751 |
www.barpilar.com

"Bring friends" and "share everything" at this "hip", "tunnellike"
hideaway above Logan Circle, where the "delicious" New American
small plates, "top-notch" beers and "happening vibe" continue to
"jazz up the 14th Street corridor"; service can be "spotty" and it's
"too noisy" for some, but "food that keeps getting better and better"
ensures that it's "elbow to elbow" on weekends; P.S. a summer 2011
expansion upstairs will enlarge its kitchen and double seating.

Bastille *French*

22	19	19	$45

Old Town | 1201 N. Royal St. (Bashford Ln.) | Alexandria, VA |
703-519-3776 | www.bastillerestaurant.com

Chef-owners Christophe Poteaux and Michelle Garbee-Poteaux's
"wonderful" Gallic bistro, "tucked away" in north Old Town, offers a
"homey", "woody" ambiance and some of the "best (but least
costly) French meals" around; indeed, you'll feel "transported to a
small village in France", complete with service tinged with a bit of
that "French attitude"; P.S. there's a three-course $29 Sunday prix
fixe ("a steal") and "excellent" Sunday brunch.

NEW Bayou M *Cajun/Creole*

-	-	-	M

West End | 2519 Pennsylvania Ave. NW (bet. 25th & 26th Sts.) |
202-223-6941 | www.bayouonpenn.com

This funky Big Easy–inspired arrival in the West End near
Georgetown offers midpriced Cajun-Creole cooking for lunch and
dinner, plus microbrews and cocktails mixed at the downstairs bar;

upstairs, vibrant red walls, recessed nooks and colorful posters set the scene for live music nightly, from blues to zydeco and beyond.

NEW Bayou Bakery *Southern* — | — | — | M

Courthouse | 1515 N. Courthouse Rd. (15th St.) | Arlington, VA | 703-243-2410 | www.bayoubakeryva.com

In a primo corner space in Arlington's Courthouse area, this new Southern bakery, coffee bar and eatery serves casual fare with a New Orleans influence like buttermilk biscuits, beignets, boudin and jambalaya, as well as nightly $12 'Chew Dat' hot-plate specials and plenty of baked sweets from chef David Guas; the down-home digs feature salvaged shutters, reclaimed barn wood and mason jar light fixtures.

Bazin's on Church Ⓜ *American* 23 | 20 | 23 | $44

Vienna | 111 Church St. NW (bet. Center St. & Lawyers Rd.), VA | 703-255-7212 | www.bazinsonchurch.com

"Blazin' with flavor", this "boisterous" bistro with a "nice chef-owned feel" serves up "unfussy (but delicious)" New American fare and "interesting" wines in Vienna, a draw for those hankering for "DC-level [dining] close to home"; a "friendly" staff stays "on top of things" and "huge windows and exposed brick" enhance the "hip" vibe, but caution: the "noise level" makes it "near impossible to have a conversation" at busy times.

Beacon Bar & Grill *American* 17 | 17 | 18 | $34

Scott Circle | Beacon Hotel | 1615 Rhode Island Ave. NW (17th St.) | 202-872-1126 | www.beaconbarandgrill.com

"Amazing happy-hour specials" and one of the "best brunch deals" in town (with "all-you-can-drink cocktails" and an occasional "piano player") are the main attractions of this "trendy"-looking New American in a Scott Circle–area hotel; its "worth-a-visit" rooftop bar gets slammed in fine weather, but unimpressed chowhounds who dis "so-so food" and "slow" service wish they "had more nice things to say."

Belga Café *Belgian* 23 | 17 | 19 | $39

Capitol Hill | 514 Eighth St. SE (bet. E & G Sts.) | 202-544-0100 | www.belgacafe.com

Fans "mussel their way into" this "beyond cramped" Capitol Hill "standby" to enjoy "innovative" Belgian fare, plus "classics" like "excellent" moules frites and an "even better beer selection" (the "real star" here); the brick interior is "on the noisy side" and the "personable" servers "can be brusque", but nab a sidewalk table for the "leisurely brunch" and you'll get a "great European vibe."

Benjarong *Thai* 22 | 19 | 21 | $27

Rockville | Wintergreen Plaza | 885 Rockville Pike (Edmonston Dr.), MD | 301-424-5533 | www.benjarongthairestaurant.com

At "one of Rockville's best Thais", the "prices are so low you can burn yourself out" sampling its myriad "spot-on" dishes, including "dependably excellent" seafood and "unique specials" – just "be careful on the spice levels"; "gracious service" in "spacious", "com-

"fortable" quarters complete the package, so no wonder it's "been around as long as it has."

Ben's Chili Bowl ● ♥ *Diner*

22 | 12 | 18 | $12

U Street Corridor | 1213 U St. NW (bet. 12th & 13th Sts.) | 202-667-0909 | www.benschilibowl.com

"No matter what time of day", this "authentically local" "U Street classic" offers "glorious people-watching" while you "clog your arteries" with "worth-the-wait" half-smokes (spicy hot dogs), the "best" chili-cheese fries and "thick shakes that wash down the grease"; "check the diet at the door" and enjoy the "cheerful", "barking line cooks" who order up the "cheap" eats – heck, "if it's good enough for Obama, it's good enough for you."

Ben's Next Door ● *American*

20 | 20 | 19 | $30

U Street Corridor | 1211 U St. NW (bet. 12th & 13th Sts.) | 202-667-8880 | www.bensnextdoor.com

"Homey" American "comfort food" "with a twist" meets "half-smokes" and other Ben's Chili Bowl standards at the U Street legend's adjacent spin-off, which also pours "strong drinks" into the mix; picky types say it's a "bit of a mishmash" that lacks "wow", but a "sociable" staff and "upscale" digs with "lots of TVs and a long bar" keep most "happy"; P.S. live music/DJs several nights a week.

Bernie's Delicatessen ◪ *Deli*

▽ 25 | 14 | 22 | $17

Fairfax | 4328 Chain Bridge Rd. (bet. Canfield & School Sts.), VA | 703-691-1269 | www.berniesonline.com

This "breath of fresh corned beef" "in the 'burbs" comes from Bernie Socha, who fine-tuned his recipes at Wagshal's in DC before opening a "traditional" "NY-style deli" that satisfies cravings for "overstuffed sandwiches" and "remarkable" 'beer can' chicken; the converted Fairfax convenience store features vintage photos and a few tables, with beer, wine and meat by the pound "aimed at carryout."

Bezu ◪ *American/French*

23 | 22 | 22 | $58

Potomac | Potomac Promenade Shopping Ctr. | 9812 Falls Rd. (River Rd.), MD | 301-299-3000 | www.bezurestaurant.com

This "intimate bistro" in a "nondescript" Potomac strip mall shifted its focus post-Survey, with a new chef – Francis Layrle, who cooked for many years at the French Embassy in DC – steering the menu in a Gallic–New American direction (not reflected in the Food score); devotees no doubt hope that its "attentive" service remains unchanged, and time will tell if the menu revamp wins over faultfinders who felt it was "trying much too hard" given its location.

BGR, The Burger Joint *Burgers*

21 | 13 | 15 | $15

Dupont Circle | 1514 Connecticut Ave. NW (bet. Dupont Circle & Q St.) | 202-299-1071

Bethesda | 4827 Fairmont Ave. (Woodmont Ave.), MD | 301-358-6137

Old Town | 106 N. Washington St. (bet. Cameron & King Sts.) | Alexandria, VA | 703-299-9791

NEW Arlington | 3129 Lee Hwy. (Custis Memorial Pkwy.), VA | 703-812-4705

(continued)

BGR, The Burger Joint

NEW Clarendon | 3024 Wilson Blvd. (Highland St.), VA |
703-566-1446

NEW Springfield | 8420 Old Keene Mill Rd. (Rolling Rd.), VA |
703-451-4651

www.bgrtheburgerjoint.com

Patty down at this "surprisingly good" chainlet, where "humongous" burgers full of secret "mojo sauce" "could feed a family" and the "superb sweet potato fries" set it "apart from the competition"; sure, the music is "blaring", it's "not exactly cheap" and "there's no real service", but "order at the counter" and "tour" the "cool" mosaic tabletops and "music albums on the walls" while waiting for your grub; P.S. "tasty" veggie and tuna burgers are also available.

Bibiana Osteria-Enoteca ☒ *Italian*   23 | 23 | 23 | $53

Downtown | 1100 New York Ave. NW (entrance on H St. bet. 11th & 12th Sts.) | 202-216-9550 | www.bibianadc.com

With its "enticing" takes on regional Italian "classics", "unusual" wines and "professional" service, this "sophisticated" Downtowner has become an "excellent addition to an area in need of better restaurants"; expect an "elegant experience without breaking the bank", and while there may be a "few bumps" (e.g. "loud or brusque at times"), "they're so low they're usually ignored."

Biergarten Haus *German*   - | - | - | M

Atlas District | 1355 H St. NE (bet. 13th & 14th Sts.) | 202-388-4053 | www.biergartenhaus.com

Dust off your lederhosen: this massive re-creation of a Bavarian beer hall brings a touch of the old country to the Atlas District, courtesy of a wide array of bottled and draft brews and a full menu of hearty (and affordable) German fare like bratwurst and potato pancakes; you'll find exposed-beam ceilings and red-chestnut bars inside, with a 4,000-sq.-ft. cobblestone 'garden' out back where guests can revel at long tables while strolling squeezebox players entertain.

NEW Big Cheese Truck ⊄ *Sandwiches*   - | - | - | E

Location varies; see website | no phone | www.bigcheesetruck.com

Grilled cheese sandwiches are given zesty spins by this DC- and NoVa-area four-wheeler, which adds the likes of chipotle or artichoke hearts to the cheap, basic comfort classics built on artisan loafs; what's more, the sweets menu proves that a sandwich for dessert is not an oxymoron – think Nutella and roasted banana on walnut-raisin bread.

Birch & Barley/Churchkey ☒ *American*   22 | 25 | 23 | $36

Logan Circle | 1337 14th St. NW (bet. P St. & Rhode Island Ave.) | 202-567-2576 | www.birchandbarley.com

Something "big" is brewing at this hopshead "paradise" above Logan Circle – just ask the "youthful crowd" packing the "gorgeous" upstairs bar/lounge (Churchkey) that pairs "great" New American small plates with a 500-plus-count "beer list that'll make your head spin, literally and figuratively"; below, Birch & Barley's "beautiful" dining room (flickering oil lamps, brick walls) sets the scene for "seasonal, creative" fare delivered by a "knowledgeable" crew – and best of all, it's "decently priced"; P.S. oenophiles salute a "wonderful" wine list.

Bistro Bis *French*   25 | 22 | 22 | $55

Capitol Hill | Hotel George | 15 E St. NW (bet. Capitol St. & New Jersey Ave.) | 202-661-2700 | www.bistrobis.com

"Power brokers and power eaters" alike converge at this "sophisticated" New French bastion on Capitol Hill for "top-flight" bistro fare "mixed with neat American twists"; an "exceptional bar" and "savvy servers" mean you can take a "client here and look good" or a "date for a special occasion", particularly if you want to "rub shoulders with senators"; whatever the reason, it's "upscale, but worth it."

Bistro Cacao *French*   - | - | - | M

Capitol Hill | 320 Massachusetts Ave. NE (bet. 3rd & 4th Sts.) | 202-546-4737 | www.bistrocacao.com

This "charming" Capitol Hill rookie is bringing French bistro cuisine like escargots and steak frites (at "relatively reasonable prices") to the vintage townhouse that once housed Two Quail; the quaint, romantic hideaway is filled with art and artifacts (plus lawyers and lobbyists) with a wine bar expected in July 2011.

Bistro D'Oc *French*   21 | 17 | 20 | $40

Downtown | 518 10th St. NW (bet. E & F Sts.) | 202-393-5444 | www.bistrodoc.com

Opposite Ford's Theatre, Francophiles find the "coziest cold-weather spot Downtown": chef-owner Bernard Grenier's "unpretentious" bistro, which "transports" diners across the pond with "can't-miss duck confit and cassoulet" and "casual service (just like France!)"; a few *non*-sayers snipe about "underwhelming" decor, but "reasonable" prices for Languedoc wines and a pre-theater "steal" ($25) have most proclaiming it a "real treat."

Bistro Français ◑ *French*   19 | 17 | 18 | $41

Georgetown | 3124 M St. NW (bet. 31st St. & Wisconsin Ave.) | 202-338-3830 | www.bistrofrancaisdc.com

The "food never changes" at this Gallic "old friend" that keeps "late hours" while providing "classic bistro" fare and enough "indifferent service" for Georgetown diners to "feel French"; *oui*, the "old world"–style dining rooms may be a "bit dated", but no matter: it's still the "place to go" for a "post–Kennedy Center nosh", "standout" eggs Benedict and "three-course dinner" deals.

Bistro La Bonne ◑ *French*   - | - | - | I

U Street Corridor | 1340 U St. NW (bet. 13th & 14th Sts.) | 202-758-3413 | www.bistrolabonne.com

French posters line this narrow, brick-walled Gallic bistro on U Street that dishes up moules, steak frites and coq au vin at neighborhood-friendly prices, along with accessible wines and beers on tap; Francophiles can indulge Julia Child–inspired food fantasies with sauce béarnaise on the entrecôte, and classic desserts like floating island and chocolate mousse.

🆕 Bistro LaZeez *Mideastern*

- | - | - | I

Bethesda | 8009 Norfolk Ave. (bet. Auburn & Del Ray Aves.), MD | 301-652-8222 | www.bistrolazeez.com

Sidewalk tables under bright-yellow umbrellas invite passersby to stop at this small Middle Eastern in Bethesda and sample the boldly flavored Syrian and Lebanese homestyle staples; it hasn't taken long for area foodies to take note and sign on for an inexpensive culinary voyage to the Levant.

Bistro L'Hermitage Ⓜ *French*

▽ 24 | 22 | 24 | $55

Woodbridge | 12724 Occoquan Rd. (Rte. 641), VA | 703-499-9552 | www.bistrolhermitage.com

In an "area that thrives on every chain restaurant in the world", it's a "pleasure" to discover this "hidden gem of French cuisine" near the historic Occoquan area of Woodbridge, where "Francophiles" fawn over "excellently prepared" fare and a "château ambiance" (e.g. "exposed brick", candlelight); it's "passionately run" by owner-manager Youssef Essaki (ex Marcel's), who's done everything from making the curtains to supervising the staff.

Bistro Provence Ⓜ *French*

- | - | - | M

Bethesda | 4933 Fairmont Ave. (bet. Norfolk Ave. & Old Georgetown Rd.), MD | 301-656-7373 | www.bistroprovence.org

This Bethesda showcase for chef-owner Yannick Cam's refined New French fare offers affordable small plates plus heartier entrees; flanked by tall Victorian-style street lamps, the handsome, Provençal-accented surroundings feature airy cafe seating, tables in the rear where guests can watch Cam in his open kitchen and a secluded, stone-walled courtyard.

Bistrot du Coin ❶ *French*

21 | 19 | 17 | $35

Dupont Circle | 1738 Connecticut Ave. NW (bet. R & S Sts.) | 202-234-6969 | www.bistrotducoin.com

There "always seems to be a party" at this "energy-filled" French bistro located above Dupont Circle, where there's also "excellent food for the price" (e.g. "mussel buckets") and "cheap house wine"; it's set in a "chaotic" Gallic atmosphere replete with "too-close tables", "deafening" noise and "authentically insouciant" servers, but even solace-seekers who can't nab a "quieter" seat "near the fold-away windows" or at the "expansive bar" agree it's a "fun romp."

Bistrot Lafayette *French*

20 | 18 | 22 | $47

Old Town | 1118 King St. (bet. Fayette & Henry Sts.) | Alexandria, VA | 703-548-2525 | www.bistrotlafayette.com

"Lovely service" and "reliably good" Gallic "comfort food" like steak and frites bring a little bit of "ooh-la-la" to Old Town at chef-owner Keo Koumtakouns' "rustic" bistro; while the "intimate" space can get "noisy and crowded", the prix fixe lunch and Monday half-price wine deals assuage most, as does the weekends-only "piano bar upstairs" (sadly, "nary a single song sung in French").

FOOD | DECOR | SERVICE | COST

Bistrot Lepic & Wine Bar French
23 | 19 | 21 | $49

Georgetown | 1736 Wisconsin Ave. NW (S St.) | 202-333-0111 | www.bistrotlepic.com

Capturing the "heart of Paris between its cramped walls", this Upper Georgetown boîte serves "delicious", "authentically French" cuisine – "artery-cloggers" like "cheeks and feet and organs" – at tables that are a "bit too close for private conversation"; its sunny "small-restaurant charm" and "gracious staff" make it "heavenly for lunch", while the "quietly chic", "affordable" upstairs wine bar offers "well-chosen" small plates and a "romantic" roost for "tweetups."

Blackfinn Restaurant & Saloon American
14 | 15 | 16 | $26

Downtown | 1620 I St. NW (16th St.) | 202-429-4350 | www.blackfinndc.com

Bethesda | 4901 Fairmont Ave. (Norfolk Ave.), MD | 301-951-5681 | www.blackfinnbethesda.com

If you're "looking to watch a football game" in "loud" company while tucking into a "diverse menu" of American grub, this "affordable" pub-themed chain duo in Bethesda and Downtown DC "is for you"; overall, "good drinks" and "great happy-hour deals" score more points than the "mediocre" chow, though fans really "go for the TVs and young, collegiate crowd."

Black Fox Lounge ● Continental
- | - | - | M

Dupont Circle | 1723 Connecticut Ave. (bet. R & S Sts.) | 202-483-1723 | www.blackfoxlounge.com

A large triptych of the English countryside reclaimed from the Watergate Hotel's Circle Bar greets guests at this Dupont revival of the type of clubby lounges that once ruled Washington's nightlife scene; a black marble bar, Persian rugs, leather sofas and live jazz set the scene for quiet, grown-up conversation over classic cocktails and a small, midpriced Continental menu; P.S. a baby grand downstairs offers an intimate piano-bar experience on select evenings.

Black Market Bistro American
25 | 22 | 23 | $41

Garrett Park | 4600 Waverly Ave. (Strathmore Ave.), MD | 301-933-3000 | www.blackmarketrestaurant.com

At this "unpretentious" "little find" in "leafy" Garrett Park "next to railroad tracks" (but "on the right side of the tracks"), the Black restaurant family and its "accommodating" staff dole out "wonderful" American "comfort food" in a "Norman Rockwell"–esque Victorian house; "grab a seat on the porch" to escape the "noise" inside and "make reservations", as it's "popular with the locals" – especially during its "wonderful Sunday brunch."

☑ BlackSalt American/Seafood
26 | 19 | 22 | $53

Palisades | 4883 MacArthur Blvd. NW (U St.) | 202-342-9101 | www.blacksaltrestaurant.com

They "shore" please at this Palisades New American, "another winner" in the Blacks' "empire" whose "wake-up-your-mouth" fin fare is "simply but expertly prepared" and "graciously" served by staffers who "make every person feel special"; choose among the "classy" raw bar, a more "elegant" dining room or the "minimalist" main area where you may be seated next to "some high-powered Washingtonian" – or just "pick up fresh seafood" from the "first-rate" market up front ("a cheaper option") and "grill it at home."

Black's Bar & Kitchen *American*   23 | 23 | 21 | $47

Bethesda | 7750 Woodmont Ave. (bet. Norfolk Ave. & Old Georgetown Rd.), MD | 301-652-5525 | www.blacksbarandkitchen.com

"Everyone is prettier than you are" at this "upscale" Bethesda New American, where an "over-30 crowd" gets its "martini and oyster" fix and downs other "interesting, enjoyable" fare ("especially seafood") in "teak, sleek and way cool" environs, complete with a "Zen patio" with pool; if it's a bit "pricey" for some, regulars suggest sampling its "incredible happy hour" and "real-value" Sunday brunch.

Black Squirrel ● *Pub Food*   – | – | – | E

Adams Morgan | 2427 18th St. NW, 2nd fl. (bet. Belmont St. & Columbia Rd.) | 202-232-1011 | www.blacksquirreldc.com

Bringing "much needed refinement to the frat boy scene" in Adams Morgan, this "beer-lovers' hideaway" boasts an "encyclopedic" range of suds, from "liters of Hofbräu" to "raspberry lambic", plus a smattering of pub grub; the bar on each level of the triplex offers a different list of brews, but an "understated charm" and "comfortable" vibe runs throughout.

⊉ BLT Steak ⊠ *Steak*   25 | 22 | 23 | $67

Golden Triangle | 1625 I St. NW (bet. 16th & 17th Sts.) | 202-689-8999 | www.bltsteak.com

Hard by the White House, this temple to "power politics and red meat" strikes a "perfect balance between a testosterone-filled steak place and fine dining", with "modern", "highbrow" decor and "deferential" help; the beef's "amazing, but so is the seafood", and if some are "shocked at the price", devotees insist it's "worth every penny"; tip: "pre-meal enticements" like "awesome popovers" can lead to prematurely "stuffed tummies", so "save room."

⊉ Blue Duck Tavern *American*   26 | 24 | 25 | $62

West End | Park Hyatt | 1201 24th St. NW (bet. M & N Sts.) | 202-419-6755 | www.blueducktavern.com

"Lucky ducks" are "cosseted" by a "marvelous" staff at this "outstanding" West End New American, a "farm-to-table" "delight" spotlighting chef Brian McBride's "innovative" "comfort cuisine" – including "perfect french fries" and "wickedly scrumptious" apple pie; add in "atmospheric" decor both "inside and out" (e.g. a "fountain on the terrace") and prices that are "reasonable for the quality", and, yes, it's "all it's quacked up to be."

Blue Rock Inn ⊠ *American*   – | – | – | M

Sperryville | Blue Rock Inn | 12567 Lee Hwy. (5 mi. west of Hwy. 522 N.), VA | 540-987-3388 | www.thebluerockinn.com

Cap a drive in the Virginia countryside with a stop at this vintage farmhouse near Sperryville, where midpriced New American fare is imbued with local seasonal ingredients; area vineyards are well represented on its varied wine list, available for sampling in the cozy dining room, on a patio offering spectacular views of the Blue Ridge Mountains or in a snug pub offering light fare; P.S. also closed Tuesdays.

Bob & Edith's Diner ● *Diner*

| 17 | 9 | 17 | $14 |

Arlington | 2310 Columbia Pike (Wayne St.), VA | 703-920-6103
Travel "back in time" at this "old-fashioned diner", a "cramped", "post-hangover" haven open 24/7 where you can "watch the cooks" dish up "old-school" vittles and scope out the Arlington "characters who make the ambiance interesting"; health addicts shudder, but at least it's "cheap" and "quick", prompting poetic types to quip "sit down, eat, get out, repeat."

Bobby Van's Grill ⊠ *Steak*

| 21 | 19 | 21 | $58 |

Downtown | 1201 New York Ave. NW (12th St.) | 202-589-1504
Bobby Van's Steakhouse *Steak*
Downtown | 809 15th St. NW (bet. H & I Sts.) | 202-589-0060
www.bobbyvans.com
"More casual than its competitors", these "high-end" carnivoriums still attract a "who's who of Washington" – as well as the "not-so-powerful" – for "signature steaks" and "dependable" side dishes "served by pros" in "macho" "wood-paneled" digs; skeptics, however, advise sticking to the "decent bar scene" for "happy hour and a bite" as a way to sidestep "pricey dinner menus."

Bob's Noodle Bistro ⊅ *Taiwanese*

| 24 | 9 | 16 | $18 |

Rockville | 305 N. Washington St. (bet. Beall Ave. & Martins Ln.), MD | 301-315-6668
"Opt for great Taiwanese food over decor" at this "super-authentic cheap eat" in Rockville, where "diners who know this cuisine" head for "fine regional" fare, including "yum yum" dim sum (weekends); its "small dining area" can get "crowded" and service can be "slow", but no matter – it's a "food adventure", and "everyone walks out with leftovers"; P.S. cash only.

Bodega-Spanish Tapas & Lounge *Spanish*

| 19 | 21 | 19 | $34 |

Georgetown | 3116 M St. NW (bet. 31st St. & Wisconsin Ave.) | 202-333-4733 | www.bodegadc.com
"Low light and rich colors" enhance the "stylish" vibe at this "lively" tapas-centered Spaniard in Georgetown where nibblers "get a bunch of plates and share them" and romance flourishes at "tables tucked in corners and recesses"; if some suggest it's the "same old, same old", at least it's "handy for a snack" and some "great sangria."

Bombay Bistro *Indian*

| 23 | 13 | 21 | $27 |

Rockville | Bell's Corner | 98 W. Montgomery Ave. (Adams St.), MD | 301-762-8798 | www.bombaybistrova.com
It's "not the fanciest" place around, but this Rockville "benchmark" for "high-quality" "Indian home cooking" has a legion of fans anyway, as much for its "wonderful lunch buffet" (with "vegetarian

dishes that even non-vegetarians love") and sit-down menu as its "friendly" staffers, who "try hard to make sure you're happy"; "reasonable prices" are another reason it's "often crowded."

Bombay Club Indian

24 | 24 | 25 | $49

Golden Triangle | 815 Connecticut Ave. NW (bet. H & I Sts.) | 202-659-3727 | www.bombayclubdc.com

"Dress up, be pampered and savor" Indian cooking that "never disappoints" at this Golden Triangle "retreat", whose "luxurious" "British Colonial" atmosphere lures "White House types" and romantics alike, what with its "widely spaced tables", "gracious" service and "piano playing softly in the background"; if some swear it's "reasonably priced" (for "white-tablecloth" dining, that is), thriftier sorts may consider its "amazing" Sunday brunch buffet for $21 (or $28 with "unlimited champagne") more of a "steal."

Bombay Tandoor Indian

22 | 19 | 23 | $24

Tysons Corner | 8603 Westwood Center Dr. (Leesburg Pike) | Vienna, VA | 703-734-2202 | www.bombaytandoor.com

"They really know how to kick things up with spice" at this "excellent" subcontinental tucked away in Tysons Corner, impressing expats who toast tastes "so close to home"; "accommodating" staffers, "decent prices" (especially for the "delicious" lunch buffet) and a "spacious" setting with "elegant tapestries and romantic lighting" also help "set it above" its compatriots.

Bond 45 Italian

- | - | - | M

National Harbor | National Harbor | 149 Waterfront St. (St. George Blvd.), MD | 301-839-1445 | www.bond45.com

NYC restaurant impresario Shelly Fireman is behind this Italian steak-and-seafood import from the Big Apple, anchored in National Harbor with spectacular Potomac River views, plush dining alcoves and old-world chandeliers, as well as private dining and a seasonal outdoor patio; on the midpriced menu is authentic housemade mozzarella and burrata, organic beef, huge lobsters and more, while famed mixologist Dale DeGroff created the cocktails poured at the long vintage bar.

NEW Bookhill Bistro American

- | - | - | M

Georgetown | 1639 Wisconsin Ave. NW (bet. Q St. & Reservoir Rd.) | 202-338-0001

Situated in a handsome row house, this Upper Georgetown arrival offers moderately priced New American creations from chef-owner (and certified sommelier) Matthew Mohler, formerly of Middleburg's Goodstone Inn and the shuttered Le Paradou; the airy, bi-level space is open from mid-morning through dinner, while an outdoor patio adds extra enticement.

Boulevard Woodgrill American

19 | 16 | 16 | $31

Clarendon | 2901 Wilson Blvd. (Fillmore St.), VA | 703-875-9663 | www.boulevardwoodgrill.com

Clarendon locals feel "right in the mix" at this "hip, hot spot for dining outdoors", where "straightforward" American chow and "fantastic Bloody Marys" at its "good-value" brunch create a "wait" for tables; the less impressed say it's "just ok", citing "pleasantly ordinary" decor and merely "decent" food as reasons why it's "better for happy hour and appetizers."

Bourbon ☉ *Pub Food*   16 | 17 | 18 | M

Adams Morgan | 2321 18th St. NW (Belmont Rd.) | 202-332-0801
Glover Park | 2348 Wisconsin Ave. NW (Observatory Ln.) | 202-625-7770
www.bourbondc.com

They stock "all the bourbon you could ever want under one roof", "from the typical Tennessee choices to limited-batch Kentucky bourbons", at these "great neighborhood bars" in Adams Morgan and Glover Park; aside from whiskey, "young and hip" locals come to "watch games on TV", "catch up with friends" and enjoy "simple" American "pub fare with a twist" at "reasonable prices."

Bourbon Steak *Steak*   23 | 24 | 24 | $76

Georgetown | Four Seasons Hotel | 2800 Pennsylvania Ave. NW (28th St.) | 202-944-2026 | www.michaelmina.net

The "delightful" New American cuisine can be "as thrilling as the frequent celebrity sightings" at this Georgetown "power place" from Michael Mina, who "scores a home run" at the Four Seasons Hotel with "designer steaks", "terrific" seafood and "arguably the best burger" in town; predictably "professional" service, a "buzzy bar" and "eye-catching" decor ("warm" hues, polished wood, dark leather) also entice, and while a few nostalgists "miss the Garden Terrace" and fret over "noise" and "whopping" tabs, most deem it "worth the splurge."

Brabo by Robert Wiedmaier/   24 | 21 | 23 | $51
Tasting Room *Belgian/French*

Old Town | Lorien Hotel & Spa | 1600 King St. (bet. Diagonal Rd. & West St.) | Alexandria, VA | 703-894-3440 | www.braborestaurant.com

Robert Wiedmaier (Marcel's, Brasserie Beck) wins "gustatory bravos" for this "sparkling addition to Old Town", a "sophisticated" Belgian-French hotel restaurant (Brabo) proffering "intriguing" fare and a "deep wine list" in "spacious digs"; naturally, a "swanky clientele" has put it on the "power rotation", while more "relaxed" types who dis its "minimalist" decor and detect a "stuffy" vibe head next door to the "ultracasual" Tasting Room, replete with "mussels with muscle", "excellent" service and "moderate prices."

☒ Brasserie Beck *Belgian/French*   25 | 23 | 22 | $48

Downtown | JBG Bldg. | 1101 K St. NW (11th St.) | 202-408-1717 | www.beckdc.com

"Mussels and beer rule" at this "super-charged" Downtown brasserie, the "more casual, cavernous sister" of Marcel's but no less a "mouthwatering Belgian experience"; with "food that packs a punch", a "ridiculously long" brew list and a "beautiful" space (an "authentic" replica of a European train station bistro), no wonder it's frequently "too crowded and loud"; P.S. "you can do damage to your credit card bill" if you follow all of the "knowledgeable" servers' "great recommendations."

Brasserie Monte Carlo *French/Mediterranean* | 20 | 17 | 21 | $39

Bethesda | 7929 Norfolk Ave. (Cordell Ave.), MD | 301-656-9225 | www.bethesdarestaurant.com

If owner Sonny Abraham has his way, you'll "hit the jackpot" at his "intimate" French-Med Bethesda brasserie, where "romantic interludes" or "quiet evenings with friends" are enhanced by "super meals" full of "interesting flavors" and "reasonably priced" wine; it's "slightly cramped", so "get an outdoor table to watch the passersby while you dine."

Bread & Brew *American/Coffeehouse* | ▽ 22 | 15 | 19 | $16

Dupont Circle | 1247 20th St. NW (N St.) | 202-466-2676 | www.breadandbrew.com

"Deciding where to have lunch in Dupont Circle got easier" after this inexpensive American opened its doors; from its "hearty" breakfast on, there's "something for everybody", thanks to "imaginative sandwiches", "constantly changing soups and quiches", gourmet coffee and "happy-hour specials" in the basement bar, plus homey touches like "quirky" trivia nights that make folks "glad to have this in the neighborhood."

Bread Line 🅖 *Bakery/Sandwiches* | 22 | 9 | 14 | $14

World Bank | 1751 Pennsylvania Ave. NW (bet. 17th & 18th Sts.) | 202-822-8900 | www.breadline.com

At this "one-of-a-kind" weekday bakery/cafe near the White House and World Bank, expect "creative" "world cuisine on paper plates", including "superior sandwiches and soups", "marvelous bread" and "hand-cut" fries; it's a "bit pricey" but "well worth it", and given the "crowds" packing its "sterile" industrial space, there's "surprisingly quick service" and seating (indoor and out) that's "less impossible than it looks."

Breadsoda ☽ *American* | - | - | - | M

Glover Park | 2233 Wisconsin Ave. NW (bet. Hall & W Pls.) | 202-333-7445 | www.breadsoda.com

"It's all about bringing your friends" to this "hidden basement bar" in Glover Park serving "affordable drinks" along with a selection of sandwiches, salads and other American eats; the "friendly" staff sets a "chill, laid-back" vibe as do the extensive entertainment options: board games, darts, Ping-Pong, pool, shuffleboard and Wii.

B. Smith's *Southern* | 20 | 21 | 19 | $44

Capitol Hill | Union Station | 50 Massachusetts Ave. NE (Columbus Circle) | 202-289-6188 | www.bsmith.com

Within this "celebrity-chef outpost" in Union Station, "soaring pillars" and "architectural details galore" greet guests hankering for a "touch of Southern cooking" served with a side of "people-watching" (read: "folks from the Hill"); even if unimpressed surveyors swipe at "hit-or-miss" fare, "Amtrak with an attitude" service and "high prices", the majority maintains it's still the "least worst place for a real meal" in the terminal.

Buca di Beppo *Italian*   16 | 16 | 18 | $28
Dupont Circle | 1825 Connecticut Ave. NW (Florida Ave.) | 202-232-8466
Gaithersburg | 122 Kentlands Blvd. (Great Seneca Hwy.), MD |
301-947-7346
www.bucadibeppo.com

"Loads of red-sauced pastas" fuel the "merry" "gluttony" at these family-style Italian chain spots in Dupont and Gaithersburg that are always "crowded with groups" indulging in "monster portions" amid "kitschy", "over-the-top" decor (including "wacky photos"); despite "average" fare, the "ridiculously perky" crew, relatively "cheap" tabs and "Dean Martin songs" make it a staple for big "get-togethers" in a "Mamma Leone's" vein.

Buck's Fishing & Camping Ⓜ *American*   20 | 16 | 17 | $47
Upper NW | 5031 Connecticut Ave. NW (Nebraska Ave.) |
202-364-0777 | www.bucksfishingandcamping.com

The "backwoods lodge" vibe lives on at this "down-home" Upper NW New American, under the stewardship of newish chef Vickie Reh, whose menu tweaks added a burger and snacks for sharing but retained "one of the best steaks in town"; still, some find the "well-prepared" seasonal menu "too limited" and a "tad expensive given the setting", while others bemoan the "communal" seating ("*please don't seat me at the long table*").

Buddha-Bar ❷ *Asian/French*   - | - | - | E
Mt. Vernon Square/Convention Center | 455 Massachusetts Ave. NW (bet. 4th & 5th Sts.) | 202-377-5555 | www.buddhabardc.com

DC's outpost of this Asian-inspired restaurant/nightlife chain is set in a massive, multimillion-dollar space in the Convention Center/ Capitol Hill corridor, replete with Asian tattoo art, gold-burnished walls, rococo chandeliers and dark-wood dining areas, all presided over by the chain's signature giant Buddha statue; a pricey Pan-Asian and French-inflected menu that includes sushi accompanies wines, sake and cocktails, while a DJ keeps the place humming.

Burma *Burmese*   20 | 10 | 19 | $22
Chinatown | 740 Sixth St. NW (bet. G & H Sts.) | 202-638-1280

Xenophiles climb the stairs to this Burmese near Verizon Center for "subtly seasoned", "East Asia meets South Asia" dishes – including a "fabulous" green tea leaf salad – that offer "complex flavors"; it's got "no ambiance" and an "efficient, if somewhat indifferent, staff" (possibly due to "language barriers"), but it offers the "rare highlight" of "affordable food" in "one of the trendier" parts of town.

Burma Road *Burmese/Chinese*   24 | 14 | 23 | $24
Gaithersburg | 617 Frederick Ave. (bet. Deer Park Rd. & I-370), MD |
301-963-1429 | www.burmaroad.biz

Servers who "make you feel like the guest of honor" will "patiently explain the entrees" at this "bright" Gaithersburg "hole-in-the-wall", though admirers aver "you can't go wrong" with any of its "stellar" Burmese and Chinese dishes (e.g. ginger salad "incredibly alive with flavor"); so it's "not going to be featured in *Architectural Digest*" – with prices this "cheap", who cares?

Busara *Thai* 20 | 18 | 19 | $25

Reston | Reston Town Ctr. | 11964 Market St. (bet. Explore & Library Sts.), VA | 703-435-4188
Tysons Corner | 8142 Watson St. (International Dr.) | McLean, VA | 703-356-2288
www.busara.com

"Monthly specials are indeed special" at these "dependable" Thais favored for "quick, good and reasonably priced meals"; the "brightly colored" Tysons Corner outlet offers a "casual atmosphere" for lunch or dinner, while families "can always get in" to the more "corporate"-looking Reston locale, even when other spots are "full"; P.S. the bars in both are weeknight "hangouts."

Busboys & Poets ◗ *American/Eclectic* 18 | 19 | 16 | $23

Mt. Vernon Square/Convention Center | CityVista | 1025 Fifth St. NW (K St.) | 202-789-2227
U Street Corridor | 2021 14th St. NW (V St.) | 202-387-7638
Shirlington | Village at Shirlington | 4251 S. Campbell Ave. (Arlington Mill Dr.) | Arlington, VA | 703-379-9756
www.busboysandpoets.com

"Part bookstore, part bar, part lounge, part restaurant": "you don't just get a meal" at this "one-of-a-kind" chain that combines "reasonably priced" American-Eclectic fare with "food for thought" (e.g. weekly "poetry readings") in "cozy" environs "buzzing" with the "granola crowd"; service is "painfully slow" and some dismiss the "down-home" dishes as "nothing poetic", but free WiFi means they're "perfect places" to "crank open your laptop and hang out."

Buzz *Coffeehouse* 22 | 20 | 21 | $12

Greater Alexandria | 901 Slaters Ln. (Potomac Greens Dr.) | Alexandria, VA | 703-600-2899 | www.buzzonslaters.com ◗
NEW **Ballston** | 818 N. Quincy St. (entrance on Wilson Blvd.) | Arlington, VA | 703-650-9676 | www.buzzbakery.com

Is this "bustling" "gem" a "coffee bar, lounge or bakery"? ponder partisans who insist it's "worth the trip" to Alexandria's Potomac Yards to sample its "addictive" cupcakes, "tasty sandwiches" and "espresso martinis" (yes, it "keeps buzzing late into the evening"); a "courteous" staff and "family-friendly" vibe are other pluses, but there's a problem: "when people sit down they never seem to leave"; P.S. the Ballston branch opened in spring 2011.

Cactus Cantina *Tex-Mex* 18 | 15 | 17 | $25

Cleveland Park | 3300 Wisconsin Ave. NW (Macomb St.) | 202-686-7222 | www.cactuscantina.com

A "bit of Tex, a bit more Mex" and a "rowdy" vibe powers this Cleveland Park "institution", what with "el machino cranking out fresh tortillas" for "wonderful fajitas" and "young couples" downing "fantastic frozen drinks" on the patio to escape the "toddlers-gone-wild scene" inside; the "price is right" for "huge portions" of "good, simple food", though some hombres want more – "love the margaritas and the guac, everything else? not so much."

Cafe Asia *Asian* 18 | 15 | 16 | $25

Golden Triangle | 1720 I St. (bet. 17th & 18th Sts.) | 202-659-2696
Rosslyn | 1550 Wilson Blvd. (N. Pierce St.), VA | 703-741-0870
www.cafeasia.com

"Young professionals" start the night with "sake bombs" and "cheap sushi" at the "unbeatable happy hours" of these "cavernous" Rosslyn/ DC Pan-Asians, "staples" for "tasty" lunches as well; the "Ikea-tastic" trappings "reflect a lot of conversation", but the "crowds don't seem to mind", and besides, "delivery and to-go" options fuel the "fires of toiling associates" in Golden Triangle law firms.

Café Assorti *Asian/E European* ∇ 22 | 19 | 20 | $21

Arlington | 1800 Wilson Blvd. (bet. Quinn & Rhodes Sts.), VA | 703-465-0036 | www.cafeassorti.com

"Sunny decor", "friendly" staffers and a "wide assortment" of "savory pies, dumplings and salads" derived from Eastern European and Asian cuisines greet noshers at this "mostly unknown" Arlington cafe/bakery; though a "little more explanation" would help neophytes understand its "unique" fare, overall it's a "nice change of pace" in an "uncluttered" space; P.S. "outdoor seating" is a "welcome addition to the neighborhood."

Café Bonaparte *French* 20 | 20 | 19 | $30

Georgetown | 1522 Wisconsin Ave. NW (bet. P & Volta Sts.) | 202-333-8830 | www.cafebonaparte.com

"Even the emperor himself would be happy" at this "petite" boîte, a "bit of Paris in Georgetown" whose "intimate" charm (read: "tight seating") and "simple" French fare, "superior salads" and "terrific" coffee concoctions keep it hopping; it's "authentic right down to the service", so plan accordingly "if time is of any importance."

Cafe Citron ❶ *Pan-Latin* 14 | 14 | 14 | $33

Dupont Circle | 1343 Connecticut Ave. NW (Dupont Circle) | 202-530-8844 | www.cafecitrondc.com

Duponters desiring a "pitcher of sangria" and a "lively night scene" hit this "packed" Pan-Latin "after dinner" when it morphs into a "dance bar" (there's a free salsa class on Monday and Wednesday) for "young people"; while it does dish up inexpensive, "mediocre" takes on "traditional Central American and Caribbean cuisine", even some admirers agree it's more of an "evening spot" ("wait, people still eat here?").

Cafe Deluxe *American* 18 | 16 | 19 | $30

Cleveland Park | 3228 Wisconsin Ave. NW (Macomb St.) | 202-686-2233
Bethesda | 4910 Elm St. (Woodmont Ave.), MD | 301-656-3131
Tysons Corner | 1800 International Dr. (Greensboro Dr.) | McLean, VA | 703-761-0600
www.cafedeluxe.com

"Neighborhood stalwarts" for everything from "informal business meetings" to an "early dinner" with the kids, this "has-it-all" trio of

FOOD | DECOR | SERVICE | COST

"reasonably priced" American bistros delivers "comfort food" (grilled cheese, "big juicy burgers", "fresh salads") with "noisy", "cheerful" accommodation; if critics who complain there's "nothing deluxe" about them "can't understand the crowds", at least "great martinis" "help tide wait times"; P.S. the happy-hour and Monday "half-price wine" specials are "huge bargains."

Cafe Divan *Turkish* | 22 | 18 | 19 | $32 |

Glover Park | Georgetown Hill Inn | 1834 Wisconsin Ave. NW (34th St.) | 202-338-1747 | www.cafedivan.com

Glover Park "diners looking for something a little different" turn to this "Turkish delight", a veritable "mecca for lamb lovers" offering "tasty" kebabs and other "delicious Ottoman cuisine" (including "small bites at great prices" and seafood), plus "yummy" wines; fireplaces add "warmth" to the "attractive" multiwindowed dining room, but if you want your own space, the "loungelike" 'Sea Room' can be rented for "fun" parties.

Café du Parc *French* | 22 | 20 | 21 | $48 |

Downtown | Willard InterContinental Washington | 1401 Pennsylvania Ave. NW (bet. 14th & 15th Sts.) | 202-942-7000 | www.cafeduparc.com

You almost "expect to see Edith Piaf singing in the corner" at the Willard InterContinental's "bustling" French brasserie, where dreamers who think they're "back in Paris" partake of "deliciously rich" fare like "melt-in-your-mouth" pork and enjoy "professional" care; even those few who find meals "not all that special" for the price and deem its "airy" interior "bland" find it hard to resist its "lovely terrace" – a "perfect place" to "people-watch on a gorgeous day."

Café Dupont *American/French* | ∇ | - | 22 | 18 | $34 |

Dupont Circle | Dupont Circle Hotel | 1500 New Hampshire Ave. NW (19th St.) | 202-483-6000 | www.doylecollection.com

Just off Dupont Circle in a recently renovated hotel, this under-the-radar restaurant gets noticed for its "open, inviting" look, a result of the "handsome furniture and wall of windows"; a post-Survey cuisine shift to French-bistro–style offerings, like mussels and steak frites, outdates the Food score; P.S. Bar Dupont next door still offers modern American fare in a contemporary setting.

Cafe Milano ❷ *Italian* | 20 | 20 | 19 | $61 |

Georgetown | 3251 Prospect St. NW (bet. Potomac St. & Wisconsin Ave.) | 202-333-6183 | www.cafemilano.com

It's "see and be seen" at this Georgetown "standard" where "DC's glitterati (both real and wannabe)" sup on "high-end" Northern Italian cuisine and "$18 glasses of wine" while "potential scandals heat up" around them; there's an "excellent" bar scene, primo "people-gazing" (e.g. "Hil and Bill") and chow that's "better than you'd expect", but unless "your name regularly appears on the *Washington Post*'s front page", prepare for "long waits" and "smug" treatment.

	FOOD	DECOR	SERVICE	COST

Café Olé *Mediterranean* | 21 | 12 | 19 | $28 |

Upper NW | 4000 Wisconsin Ave. NW (Upton St.) | 202-244-1330 | www.cafeoledc.com

At this "friendly" Upper NW cafe, Tenleytowners find it's "easy to make a meal" on "real-deal" meze and "marvelous Mediterranean salads" with "modest prices"; outsiders can dine alfresco on its "delightful" patio, tucked away just enough so "you aren't eating car exhaust or being watched by passersby"; P.S. a post-Survey refurb transforming the interior into a bistro-style affair (earth tones, swanky black furnishings) is not reflected in the Decor score.

Café Pizzaiolo *Italian/Pizza* | 18 | 11 | 18 | $21 |

Arlington | 507 S. 23rd St. (Eads St.), VA | 703-894-2250

Pizzaiolo Café on Fern *Italian/Pizza*

Greater Alexandria | 1623 Fern St. (Kenwood Ave.) | Alexandria, VA | 703-717-9324

www.cafepizzaiolo.com

"Go for the pizza" proclaim partisans of this "family-friendly" duo of "little Italian joints" spinning "New York–style" pies adorned with "fresh ingredients" and "chewy" crusts; though "noisy, child-filled" rooms with "minimalist decor" might not make it the best choice for date night, the "neighborhood vibe (complete with board games)" and "down-home" service are "hard to beat."

Café Saint-Ex *Eclectic* | 20 | 18 | 17 | $31 |

Logan Circle | 1847 14th St. NW (T St.) | 202-265-7839 | www.saint-ex.com

Folks sure "get hoppy" about the "beer and brunch" (eggs Benedict, "amazing" fried-green-tomato BLTs) at this 14th Street "hipster hangout", a weekend "crowd" magnet sporting a *Little Prince/*aviation theme and oozing "understated cool"; other times, it offers a "relaxed" atmosphere for "tasty" Eclectic fare, including a "good- value" prix fixe enjoyed in the "cozy" interior or on the "lovely" patio; P.S. there's a DJ downstairs "for late-night debauchery" Monday–Saturday.

Cafe Taj *Indian* | 19 | 14 | 20 | $27 |

McLean | 1379 Beverly Rd. (Old Dominion Dr.), VA | 703-827-0444 | www.mycafetaj.com

"Flavorful" Indian food that's "not too spicy" and "doesn't cost a king's ransom" brings this McLean neighborhood stalwart a "large carry-out trade"; its dining room ("more elegant than many", if a "little run-down") offers a "decent buffet lunch" and is "quiet enough for conversation with dinner."

Cajun Experience *Cajun/Creole* | - | - | - | I |

NEW **Dupont Circle** | 1825 18th St. NW (bet. Swann & T Sts.) | 202-670-4416

Leesburg | 14 Loudoun St. SE (bet. Church & King Sts.), VA | 703-777-6580

www.cajunexperience.biz

These Dupont Circle and Leesburg bistros channel southern Louisiana with gumbo, jambalaya and other Cajun-Creole specialties, prepared using family recipes from owners Bryan and Melissa

	FOOD	DECOR	SERVICE	COST

Crosswhite; cozy settings suit the comfort cuisine, while lunch deals (like Leesburg's po' boy, gumbo and beignet for $12.95) make the 'experience' especially affordable.

California Tortilla *Tex-Mex* | 18 | 11 | 17 | $11 |

Chinatown | Gallery Pl. | 728 Seventh St. NW (bet. G & H Sts.) | 202-638-2233
Cleveland Park | 3501 Connecticut Ave. NW (Ordway St.) | 202-244-2447
Bethesda | 4862 Cordell Ave. (bet. Norfolk & Woodmont Aves.), MD | 301-654-8226
Olney | Olney Village Ctr. | 18101 Village Center Dr. (Olney Sandy Spring Rd.), MD | 301-570-2522
Potomac | Cabin John Shopping Ctr. | 7727 Tuckerman Ln. (Seven Locks Rd.), MD | 301-765-3600
College Park | 7419 Baltimore Ave. (Knox Rd.), MD | 301-927-8500
Rockville | Rockville Town Sq. | 199 E. Montgomery Ave. (Courthouse Sq.), MD | 301-610-6500
Silver Spring | Burnt Mills Shopping Ctr. | 10721A Columbia Pike/ Colesville Rd. (Hillwood Dr.), MD | 301-593-3955
Courthouse | 2057 Wilson Blvd. (bet. Courthouse Rd. & Uhle St.) | Arlington, VA | 703-243-4151
Fairfax | Fair Lakes Promenade Shopping Ctr. | 12239 Fair Lakes Pkwy. (Monument Dr.), VA | 703-278-0007
www.californiatortilla.com
Additional locations throughout the DC area

"Festive", "friendly" and "often crowded", these "zippy" fast-food "favorites" dish up "hefty" burritos that are "actually flavorful (not just hot peppers and rice)" and lots of other "no-frills" Tex-Mex choices, all complemented by a "wall of hot sauces"; snagging a seat can be "harder than crossing the border", so get it "to go" – after all, there's "always some sort of special" that makes meals a "deal."

Capital City Diner Ⓜ *Diner* | - | - | - | I |

Northeast | 1050 Bladensburg Rd. NE (bet. K & L Sts.) | 202-396-3467 | www.capitalcitydiner.com

This vintage 1940s diner car residing in Trinidad – a Northeast neighborhood with few, if any, other places to eat sitting down – looks like it's been there forever, sporting classic industrial design with counter stools and booths plus an old-fashioned Frigidaire filled with sodas; the menu offers traditional fare, including breakfast available all day (and all night on weekends).

☒ Capital Grille *Steak* | 25 | 24 | 25 | $63 |

Penn Quarter | 601 Pennsylvania Ave. NW (6th St.) | 202-737-6200
Chevy Chase | Wisconsin Place | 5310 Western Ave. (Wisconsin Circle), MD | 301-718-7812
Tysons Corner | 1861 International Dr. (Leesburg Pike) | McLean, VA | 703-448-3900
www.thecapitalgrille.com

"Superb" cuts of beef are "served with style" to "lots of suits" at these "top-notch" chain links that seem to be "hiding undercover as a locals' steakhouse and doing a good job of it"; boasting a "fantastic" wine list, "superior" service and a "manly club atmosphere", they're "wonderful" "for a date" or "impressing a client", so "if you're on an expense account, go for it."

Capitol City Brewing Company *Pub Food* | 18 | 17 | 18 | M |

Capitol Hill | 2 Massachusetts Ave. NE (bet. Capitol & 1st Sts.) | 202-842-2337 ●

Downtown | 1100 New York Ave. NW (bet. 11th & 12th Sts.) | 202-628-2222

Shirlington | 4001 Campbell Ave. (I-395) | Arlington, VA | 703-578-3888 ●

www.capcitybrew.com

"Hopping at happy hour" with tourists and locals looking to "watch the game" or "unwind after work", this trio of brewpubs boasts a "nice selection of unique beers on tap" plus a large menu of pubby eats (including "highly recommended" hot pretzels); detractors say they're "big and loud" and about "what you expect from a local chain", but at least the prices are reasonable.

NEW **CapMac** 🖂🖩 *American* | - | - | - | I |

Location varies; see website | 914-489-2897 | www.capmacdc.com

Riffing on the food stands that once lined the streets of NYC's Little Italy, this roving pastaria recently elbowed its way into the DC food-truck scene, serving several varieties of mac 'n' cheese, including its signature: cheddar, pimento and Cheez-It crumble; beef Bolognese, chicken parm meatballs and a few other items, including some desserts, round out the affordable lunchtime menu.

Capri *Italian* | 20 | 15 | 20 | $41 |

McLean | Giant Shopping Ctr. | 6825 Redmond Dr. (Chain Bridge Rd.), VA | 703-288-4601 | www.caprimcleanva.com

Patrons of this Italian "standby" in McLean get the "friendly treatment from the owner on down", which combined with "dependable" pasta and seafood makes this the "kind of place everyone likes to have in their neighborhood"; "unmemorable" "1960s-era" decor (posters, fishing nets) aside, tony locals deem it "good enough to take guests."

NEW **Carbon Peruvian** | - | - | - | I |
Chicken & Grill *Peruvian*

Rockville | Rockville Town Ctr. | 100 Gibbs St. (bet. Beall Ave. & Middle Ln.), MD | 301-251-1944

Charcoal-grilled, marinated birds are just the start of an inexpensive South American culinary flight at this cheery new Rockville roaster, where adventuresome diners down Peruvian specialties like beef hearts, tripe and interesting fruit drinks; its counter-serve staff spells out the possibilities, which can be eaten at colorful tables or at home – if you can withstand the aromatic temptation to gobble in transit.

Caribbean Breeze *Nuevo Latino* | 18 | 18 | 16 | $29 |

Ballston | 4100 N. Fairfax Dr. (Randolph St.) | Arlington, VA | 703-812-7997 | www.caribbeanbreezeva.com

This Nuevo Latino spices up the Ballston corridor with "great happy hours", "dancing on weekends" and fare that earns "decent" ratings from expats and isn't "over-the-top expensive"; while mojitos mixed by "knowledgeable" barkeeps help fusspots "forget about" the interior's lack of decor, vets vow its "outside patio" and 'urban waterfall' make it "worth the trip."

Caribbean Feast ⊠ *Jamaican* — | — | — | I

Temple Hills | 4715 Raleigh Rd. (St. Barnabas Rd.), MD | 301-316-1260 | www.caribbean-feast.com

If you're jonesing for "tasty" Jamaican grub like "goat curry" and fried plantains, this Temple Hills spot that relocated from Rockville delivers the "good stuff"; it's "fun but fatty", and you'll save enough money for next year's Caribbean vacation; P.S. jerk chicken may be the signature dish, but expect Pan-island options.

Carlyle *American* 24 | 21 | 23 | $36

Shirlington | 4000 Campbell Ave. (Quincy St.) | Arlington, VA | 703-931-0777 | www.greatamericanrestaurants.com

Whether it's for a "first date" or "birthday celebration", this "lively" Shirlington New American seems to be on everyone's "go-to" list for "high-quality comfort food" (plus a "twist of modern flavor") with a "modest price tag"; the team service "gets it done" and there's a "hopping bar scene", but for a more "refined" atmosphere – think "soft colors" and dark woods – head upstairs; P.S. success brings "large crowds" and "long waits", so "call ahead" for reservations.

NEW Carmine's *Italian* — | — | — | M

Penn Quarter | 425 Seventh St. NW (bet. D & E Sts.) | 202-737-7770 | www.carminesnyc.com

Blockbuster doesn't even begin to describe this 700-seat Penn Quarter arrival (it's bigger than its NYC parent) serving a classic family-style Southern Italian menu with each dish portioned for two to four; it's done up in retro '30s-era decor with acres of polished cherry wood, a light brigade of vintage chandeliers, a massive lounge equipped with WiFi and phone chargers plus nine private dining rooms.

NEW Casa Nonna *Italian* — | — | — | M

Dupont Circle | 1250 Connecticut Ave. NW (N St.) | 202-629-2505 | www.casanonna.com

This midpriced trattoria below Dupont Circle has enlisted chef Amy Brandwein (ex Fyve) to turn out stylish takes on Italian classics, including pizza, all served in Tuscan-esque environs with a bar/lounge and mosaic-tiled wood-fired ovens; changing monthly, a four-course family dinner celebrates a different region of Italy on Sunday nights.

Casa Oaxaca Ⓜ *Mexican* 18 | 16 | 15 | $31

Adams Morgan | 2106 18th St. NW (bet. California St. & Wyoming Ave.) | 202-387-2272

Inspired by Mexico's "culinary capital", this "quaint" Adams Morgan townhouse awash in "vibrant colors" helps diners "discover" its cuisine with "fantastic" moles and other "truly authentic" regional favorites, along with crowd-pleasers like guacamole and berry-flavored margaritas; while a few fret over "middling to good service" and sigh the fare's "not quite making the cut", they're outvoted by those who say go and "enjoy."

Cashion's Eat Place ⓜ *American* | 24 | 20 | 22 | $50 |

Adams Morgan | 1819 Columbia Rd. NW (bet. Biltmore St. & Mintwood Pl.) | 202-797-1819 | www.cashionseatplace.com

"Inventive" seasonal cooking that's "plate-licking good" draws an urbane clientele to chef/co-owner John Manolatos' "romantic" New American, an Adams Morgan "classic" that's "still at the top of its game"; a "funky but pleasurable" vibe means it's equally suitable for a "date, dinner with friends" or "eating alone at the bar", though "A-types might bristle" at "friendly" service that can be "slow-paced"; P.S. an "affordable" brunch is especially enjoyable on the patio.

Cassatt's Café *New Zealand* | 18 | 13 | 18 | $25 |

Arlington | 4536 Lee Hwy. (Woodstock St.), VA | 703-527-3330 | www.cassattscafe.com

For a "bit of New Zealand flare", Arlingtonians head to this "surprising little find" in a strip mall for "delicious" kiwi specialties, "excellent desserts" and "outstanding breakfasts"; "service has been improving" over time, but expect to wait when it's "packed for Sunday brunch"; P.S. art-filled walls pay homage to the cafe's namesake, painter Mary Cassatt.

Caucus Room ⓩ *American* | 21 | 22 | 22 | $60 |

Penn Quarter | 401 Ninth St. NW (D St.) | 202-393-1300 | www.thecaucusroom.com

The "waiters will even cut your wife's pork chop for her" at this "traditional" New American in the Penn Quarter, where the "high-powered of DC" dive into "great cuts of meat", "huge sides" and "classic cocktails" in "intimate" clubby nooks; it's "vintage Washington", though the unimpressed say "watching the deal-making is more fun" than meals that are "not particularly impressive for the price"; P.S. post-Survey, it added a less formal area up front where a lower-priced menu is in the works.

Cava *Greek* | 24 | 18 | 20 | $35 |

Rockville | 9713 Traville Gateway Dr. (Shady Grove Rd.), MD | 301-309-9090

Cava Mezze *Greek*

Capitol Hill | Cava on Capitol Hill | 527 Eighth St. SE (Pennsylvania Ave.) | 202-543-9090
www.cavamezze.com

"Flaming cheese", "hot waiters" and a "chic, young crowd" converge at these "always packed" gathering spots in Rockville and on Barracks Row dishing up "scrumptious" "homestyle" Greek tapas, plus "recession-friendly" wines and "signature cocktails"; the "delightfully dark" premises exude a "clublike atmosphere", but with tables "inches" apart, it can get "cramped" and "unbearably loud", so arrive "early to enjoy (relative) quiet"; P.S. decor-minded surveyors give the edge to the Cap Hill location and its rooftop patio.

	FOOD	DECOR	SERVICE	COST

NEW Cava Mezze Grill *Greek* | - | - | - | I |

Bethesda | 4832 Bethesda Ave. (bet. Arlington Rd. & Woodmont Ave.),
MD | 301-656-1772 | www.cavagrill.com

Buzzing from day one, this hip counter-serve entry in Bethesda puts
a low-cost, fast-casual spin on the Greek grilled meats, falafel and
tasty spreads popularized at its sit-down siblings Cava and Cava
Mezze; diners assemble customized pitas, bowls and salads at the
rear counter, then sit at long tables in its smart-looking, barn-board-
paneled storefront; P.S. new outlets are in the works.

Ceiba *Nuevo Latino* | 23 | 22 | 21 | $46 |

Downtown | 701 14th St. NW (G St.) | 202-393-3983 |
www.ceibarestaurant.com

While "it's the little extras" – like the meal-ending caramel corn –
"that make this one special", admirers allow it's the "innovative"
menu of "delicious", "beautifully presented" Nuevo Latino fare that
makes it "worth going back to time and again"; it's further enhanced
by "on-the-ball" staffers who work the "subtle, moody" dining space
and the "delightful" lounge, which lures the Downtown happy-hour
brigade with "well-executed tapas" and "nightly drink specials."

☒ Central Michel Richard ☒ *American/French* | 26 | 21 | 23 | $54 |

Penn Quarter | 1001 Pennsylvania Ave. NW (11th St.) | 202-626-0015 |
www.centralmichelrichard.com

"Stylish, great food, fun, exciting, chic" – chef Michel Richard's "genius" makes it all come together at this Penn Quarter "gem", a "bustling" New American–French brasserie where "comfort food gone way
beyond your imagination" comes with "polished" service in an "airy
California atmosphere"; yes, the "hopping bar scene" and "high-
energy" dining room can be "noisy" ("sit in back" by the open kitchen),
but "amazing" meals for "prices you can afford" quiet most skeptics.

Cesco Trattoria *Italian* | 22 | 17 | 21 | $45 |

Bethesda | 4871 Cordell Ave. (Norfolk Ave.), MD | 301-654-8333 |
www.cescomd.com

Chef Francesco Ricchi's "wonderful" Tuscan cooking draws a steady
clientele to his "quiet" Bethesda trattoria, where staffers (including
some "genuine Italian waiters") accommodate "special requests"
and "somebody with taste chooses the wines"; when a few fuss that
the "steady" menu and "old-school" decor "need some oomph",
fans retort "but then prices would shoot up to pay for the redo."

C.F. Folks ☒ *Eclectic* | 24 | 7 | 18 | $15 |

Golden Triangle | 1225 19th St. NW (bet. M & N Sts.) | 202-293-0162 |
www.cffolksrestaurant.com

"Oddball in a good way", this weekday, lunch-only "hole-in-the-
wall" in the Golden Triangle turns out "high-quality" Eclectic fare at
"bargain prices"; along with "extraordinary specials" and some of
"DC's finest" crab cakes, expect "repartee [that's] almost as good
as the sandwiches" and "lots of characters"; P.S. limited seating "in-
vites you to do takeout."

	FOOD	DECOR	SERVICE	COST

Charlie Palmer Steak Ⓩ *Steak* 25 | 24 | 24 | $69

Capitol Hill | 101 Constitution Ave. NW (bet. 1st St. & Louisiana Ave.) | 202-547-8100 | www.charliepalmer.com

"Don't be surprised to find a senator" sitting nearby at this "swank" Capitol Hill "powerhouse", a "carnivore's must" that "breaks from steakhouse convention" with a "beautiful", "modern" setting (no "stodgy mahogany" here), "delicious seafood" and an all-American wine list with selections "from every state"; it's got a noted "lobbying scene", but "you don't have to know someone" to receive "standout service", and while an "expense account" comes in handy here, so do prix fixe lunches ($25) and "no corkage" nights.

Cheesecake Factory *American* 19 | 18 | 18 | $28

Upper NW | Chevy Chase Pavilion | 5345 Wisconsin Ave. NW (Western Ave.) | 202-364-0500 ◑

White Flint | White Flint Mall | 11301 Rockville Pike (Nicholson Ln.) | Rockville, MD | 301-770-0999 ◑

Clarendon | Market Common Clarendon | 2900 N. Wilson Blvd. (Fillmore St.), VA | 703-294-9966

Fairfax | Fair Oaks Shopping Ctr. | 11778 Fair Oaks Mall (Lee Jackson Memorial Hwy.), VA | 703-273-6600

Tysons Corner | Tysons Galleria | 1796 International Dr. (Greensboro Dr.) | McLean, VA | 703-506-9311

Sterling | Dulles Town Ctr. | 21076 Dulles Town Circle (Nokes Blvd.), VA | 703-444-9002

www.thecheesecakefactory.com

"Humongous portions and humongous lines" characterize this American chain where the "textbook"-size menu offers a "broad price spectrum" to keep families "stuffed and happy"; the "herd 'em in, herd 'em out" feel isn't for everyone and critics knock "mass-produced" fare and "overdone" decor, but overall it's a "crowd-pleaser", especially when it comes to the "amazing" namesake dessert.

Chef Geoff's *American* 19 | 17 | 19 | $37

Upper NW | 3201 New Mexico Ave. NW (Lowell St.) | 202-237-7800

Tysons Corner | Fairfax Sq. | 8045 Leesburg Pike (Gallows Rd.) | Vienna, VA | 571-282-6003

Chef Geoff's Downtown *American*

Downtown | 1301 Pennsylvania Ave. NW (E St.) | 202-464-4461

www.chefgeoff.com

"No gimmicks", just "good food for good value": that's the "simple formula" powering these "affordable" Americans in Tysons Corner and DC where there's "something for everyone", from happy-hour "burger bargains" and "wonderful Sunday jazz brunches" to meal specials and "big-as-your-thigh beers"; if critics carp about grub and service that's "just ok", more "walk away happy and full."

Chesapeake Room ◑ *American/Seafood* – | – | – | M

Capitol Hill | 501 Eighth St. SE (E St.) | 202-543-1445 | www.thechesapeakeroom.com

As its name suggests, this midpriced seafood-slanted American on Capitol Hill's Barracks Row celebrates the region's bounty with contemporary takes on classics using locally sourced, seasonal products (think Senate bean soup jazzed up with house-cured bacon) and an interesting menu of local brews and wines; the shipshape setting includes bespoke paintings of water and wildlife, while its covered outdoor terrace, complete with upholstered high-back seats, is likely to become some of the burgeoning neighborhood's most sought after real estate.

Chima Brazilian

23 | 22 | 23 | $58

Tysons Corner | 8010 Towers Crescent Dr. (Leesburg Pike) | Vienna, VA | 703-639-3080 | www.chimasteakhouse.com

They bring "meat on a sword until you say stop" at this "authentic Brazilian" churrascaria hidden in a Tysons high-rise, where the "all-you-can-eat" parade of "top-quality" cuts, plus a "huge" salad buffet ("offered alone" for vegetarians), require a "second stomach" to "justify the cost"; its "circus" vibe, fueled by the "best caipirinhas", is "great for groups", though finicky types say it's "fun to do *once*."

China Bistro Chinese

▽ 23 | 11 | 18 | $22

Rockville | 755 Hungerford Dr. (Martins Ln.), MD | 301-294-0808

At this storefront Asian in Rockville, "top-of-the-line" dumplings in unusual combos (e.g. pork with dill) and tasty "small plates" are the draw; it's best if you can "come during off-peak", as there's "no seating to speak of", and "speak Chinese", but don't worry: "worst case, you can always point"; P.S. small prices make it popular for takeout.

China Garden Chinese

17 | 12 | 13 | $26

Rosslyn | Twin Towers | 1100 Wilson Blvd., 2nd fl. (bet. Kent & Lynn Sts.), VA | 703-525-5317 | www.chinagardenva.com

Cantonese connoisseurs confide it's "worth finding your way to the second floor" of this Rosslyn office tower for some of the area's "best weekend dim sum" – but "get there early" since it can be "tough to get a table"; "decent", affordable Chinese fare is dished up the rest of the week, though detractors decry bland decor and "offhand service."

China Jade Chinese

– | – | – | I

Rockville | 16805 Crabbs Branch Way (Shady Grove Rd.), MD | 301-963-1570 | www.chinajaderockville.com

"Off the beaten path" in a Rockville strip mall, this spot mines the world of "fiery" Sichuan food with a long and varied menu from chef Liu Chaosheng, including "amazing" noodle soups, dumplings and spicy whole fish; P.S. there's also a roster of Cantonese specialties from chef Chun Lee.

China Star Chinese

▽ 24 | 6 | 16 | $19

Fairfax | Fair City Mall | 9600 Main St. (Pickett Rd.), VA | 703-323-8822 | www.chinastarfood.com

The Sichuan offerings at this Fairfax strip-maller are so "fiery hot" they "may be a little too authentic for some", but for heat-seekers it's the "place to go"; expect "dishes available almost nowhere else" ("spicy braised fish" included), served by staffers who "try to be helpful" in decor-deficient digs; P.S. there's also an American-Chinese menu.

Chinatown Express *Chinese*

21 | 6 | 14 | $14

Chinatown | 746 Sixth St. NW (H St.) | 202-638-0424

At few places in "disappearing" Chinatown ("er, "Chinablock") will one find an "old guy making noodles in the window" – and they're some of the "best in town" to boot; the "sublime" dumplings, "fresh-made" soups and other "excellent" "cheap eats" at this "no-frills" Chinese also help make it a "favorite of locals", who generally disregard "robotic" service and decor that "couldn't be much worse."

Ching Ching Cha *Tearoom*

▽ 20 | 23 | 25 | $20

Georgetown | 1063 Wisconsin Ave. NW (M St.) | 202-333-8288 | www.chingchingcha.com

"Experience a traditional Chinese teahouse" at this "one-of-a-kind" Georgetown "oasis" pouring more than 70 types of "expertly brewed" tea – from oolongs to greens – in a "relaxed, lovely" atmosphere; "small bites" like dumplings and cookies "let you reenergize" before beginning an "M Street trade mission", though you can get an early start by bagging some teaware in its on-site shop.

Chix *Eclectic*

20 | 9 | 19 | $14

U Street Corridor | 2019 11th St. NW (U St.) | 202-234-2449 | www.chixdc.com

The "cheap, healthy and full-of-flavor" Eclectic eats at this "green-friendly" U Street "pollo joint" have stayed off "everyone else's radar" exult savvy surveyors who go for "organic chicken at its slow-cooked finest"; vegetarians revel in the "tasty sides", but those who cry fowl cite "blah" decor and "hit-or-miss" cooking.

Chop't Creative Salad *American*

19 | 11 | 17 | $12

Chinatown | 730 Seventh St. NW (bet. G & H Sts.) | 202-347-3225
Downtown | Metro Ctr. | 618 12th St. NW (G St.) | 202-783-0007
Dupont Circle | 1300 Connecticut Ave. NW (N St.) | 202-327-2255
NEW **Farragut** | 1629 K St. NW (17th St.) | 202-688-0333 🗲
Golden Triangle | 1105 19th St. NW (L St.) | 202-955-0665 🗲
NEW **Northeast** | Union Station | 50 Massachusetts Ave. NW (Capitol St.) | 202-688-0330
Rosslyn | 1735 N. Lynn St. (Wilson Blvd.), VA | 703-875-2888
www.choptsalad.com

Get "just about anything your little heart desires" at these "design-your-own-salad" imports offering "tons" of "super-duper-fresh" ingredients that get "tossed" (or occasionally "chopped to smithereens") into "big", "healthy", somewhat "pricey" meals; the "chop dudes" dice quickly, so "lines move fast", but limited seating means they're "more for carryout"; P.S. "excellent" wraps are also available.

Chutzpah *Deli*

18 | 9 | 15 | $18

Fairfax | Fairfax Towne Ctr. | 12214 Fairfax Towne Ctr. (Monument Dr.), VA | 703-385-8883 | www.chutzpahdeli.com

Mavens call this Fairfax deli the "straight-out-of-lower-NYC real deal" for "heaping pastrami sandwiches", matzo brei "just like bubbe used to make" and traditional "counter-case lures" like smoked fish; then again, critics kvetch it's all "attitude with no substance" and "charges way too much for way too little" – even if it's one of the "only places to get your tongue pickled in Virginia."

Circa *American*   17 | 18 | 16 | $30

Dupont Circle | 1601 Connecticut Ave. NW (Q St.) | 202-667-1601 ◐
NEW **Clarendon** | 3010 Clarendon Blvd. (Garfield St.), VA | 703-522-3010
www.circacafes.com

A "perfect Dupont location" coupled with a "delightful, cozy" interior and "scenic" outdoor seating make this "bustling" New American a "hot-ticket meeting place"; too bad naysayers suggest "slow" service and "uninspired" bistro fare make this a better choice for "drinks over dinner"; P.S. a second branch in Clarendon opened post-Survey; a third in Foggy Bottom is expected in summer 2011.

Circle Bistro *American*   21 | 17 | 20 | $46

West End | One Washington Circle Hotel | 1 Washington Circle NW (New Hampshire Ave.) | 202-293-5390 | www.thecirclehotel.com

Despite a "convenient" West End location offering "easy access" to the Kennedy Center, this "low-key" New American falls "somewhat off the radar", notwithstanding "innovative seasonal" cooking that impresses locavores ("who knew root veggies could be this enticing?"); it's all served by "professional" staffers in a "chic", sometimes "noisy" space, though supporters save their highest praise for the "pre-theater prix fixe", perhaps "one of the best deals in town."

NEW Cities ⊠ *Eclectic*   - | - | - | M

Golden Triangle | 919 19th St. NW (bet. I & K Sts.) | 202-331-3232 | www.citieswashington.com

This glamorous new Eclectic resto-lounge near the World Bank allows patrons to wine and dine in four international destinations without leaving its svelte surroundings, thanks to images of the featured locales displayed on flat-screens wrapping around the dining room; the midpriced bar and dinner menus revolve every few months to match a new set of points on the globe, offering iconic items along with representative beers, wines and cocktails.

☑ Citronelle ⊠Ⓜ *French*   28 | 25 | 26 | $106
(aka Michel Richard Citronelle)

Georgetown | Latham Hotel | 3000 M St. NW (30th St.) | 202-625-2150 | www.citronelledc.com

"If heaven had its own dining room", it might look a lot like Michel Richard's "exquisite" Georgetown New French, where the "master chef's" "joie de vivre" still inspires each plate, and a "stunning" wine list and servers who "make you feel special" add to the "unforgettable memories"; naturally, tabs are "up there", but that's the price of "culinary nirvana" (the lounge menu is a bit "more limited" and a bit easier on the wallet); P.S. for a "special splurge, eat at the chef's table."

City Lights of China *Chinese*   19 | 12 | 17 | $25

Dupont Circle | 1731 Connecticut Ave. NW (bet. R & S Sts.) | 202-265-6688 | www.citylightsofchina.com

(continued)

	FOOD	DECOR	SERVICE	COST

(continued)

City Lights of China

Bethesda | 4820 Bethesda Ave. (Woodmont Ave.), MD | 301-913-9501 | www.bethesdacitylightsofchina.com

At this "venerable basement mainstay" above Dupont Circle and its more "modern" Bethesda sib, "basic" Chinese dishes – including "reliable" dumplings – are made "any way you want", and some are "even healthy"; naysayers yawn that it's all "so-so", though "great delivery" means "dinner parties for six can be arranged in 20 minutes."

⦚ CityZen ⦚⦚ *American* | 28 | 27 | 28 | $105 |

SW | Mandarin Oriental | 1330 Maryland Ave. SW (12th St.) | 202-787-6006 | www.mandarinoriental.com

Scoring a "trifecta" of near "perfection on all fronts", this "first-class" New American in the Mandarin Oriental showcases chef Eric Ziebold's "creative brilliance" in a "sleek and sensual" setting with "top-tier" servers and a "fantastic" sommelier; from the "intriguing" six-course tasting menu to the "heavenly mini–Parker House rolls", it's a "transformational experience" that's "worth every penny"; P.S. "smaller" three-course prix fixes in the more casual bar ($50) and dining room ($80) are likewise rife with "delectable delights."

⦚ Clyde's ☾ *American* | 19 | 21 | 20 | $32 |

Chinatown | Gallery Pl. | 707 Seventh St. NW (bet. G & H Sts.) | 202-349-3700

Georgetown | Georgetown Park Mall | 3236 M St. NW (bet. Potomac St. & Wisconsin Ave.) | 202-333-9180

Chevy Chase | 5441 Wisconsin Ave. (bet. Montgomery St. & Wisconsin Circle), MD | 301-951-9600

Rockville | 2 Preserve Pkwy. (bet. Tower Oaks Blvd. & Wootton Pkwy.), MD | 301-294-0200

Greater Alexandria | Mark Ctr. | 1700 N. Beauregard St. (bet. Rayburn Ave. & Seminary Rd.) | Alexandria, VA | 703-820-8300

Reston | Reston Town Ctr. | 11905 Market St. (bet. Reston & Town Ctr. Pkwys.), VA | 703-787-6601

Tysons Corner | 8332 Leesburg Pike (Rte. 123) | Vienna, VA | 703-734-1901

Broadlands | Willow Creek Farm | 42920 Broadlands Blvd. (bet. Belmont Ridge Rd. & Claiborne Pkwy.), VA | 571-209-1200 www.clydes.com

"As reliable as a Timex", these locally bred, family-friendly "saloons" supply "simple, filling" and "affordable" American chow in "inviting" themed settings ("cruise ship", "hunting lodge", etc.); fussy sorts suggest they're a bit "stale", but from "classic" burgers to "creative vegetarian options", there's "something for everyone", and "on-the-ball service", "tasty monthly specials" and "active happy hours" mean there are "crowds" as well.

NEW Coal Fire *Pizza* | 20 | 16 | 17 | $18 |

Gaithersburg | 116 Main St. (Kentlands Blvd.), MD | 301-519-2625 | www.coalfireonline.com

See review in the Baltimore Directory.

FOOD | DECOR | SERVICE | COST

Coastal Flats *Seafood*

21 | 19 | 21 | $32

Fairfax | Fairfax Corner | 11901 Grand Commons Ave. (Monument Dr.), VA | 571-522-6300

Tysons Corner | Tysons Corner Ctr. | 1961 Chain Bridge Rd. (International Dr.) | McLean, VA | 703-356-1440

www.greatamericanrestaurants.com

"You can almost smell the sea breeze" at this "solid" fish house duo that hooks mallgoers seeking a "respite from shopping"; the lure: "tasty" crab cakes, lobster rolls and other fin fare served by a "speedy" staff navigating "noisy, crowded" spaces with a "Florida" feel, courtesy of sculptured "sea life hanging from the ceilings" and plantation shutters; P.S. "call ahead" to "avoid long waits."

Co Co. Sala *Eclectic*

22 | 24 | 19 | $40

Penn Quarter | 929 F St. NW (bet. 9th & 10th Sts.) | 202-347-4265 | www.cocosala.com

"Calling all sweet tooths": part boutique "part restaurant, part lounge and mostly dessert bar", this "posh" Penn Quarter "chocoholic's dream" seemingly "incorporates its namesake bean" into every "inventive" Eclectic dish in a "sexy, un-DC-like" setting (dark walls that flow like molten chocolate, plush velvet banquettes); if "inattentive" service sometimes kills the sugar buzz, you'll still "feel very in the scene – and pay for the privilege."

Coeur de Lion *American*

20 | 20 | 20 | $56

Downtown | Henley Park Hotel | 926 Massachusetts Ave. NW (10th St.) | 202-414-0500 | www.henleypark.com

"Somewhat off the beaten path" near the Convention Center, this "lovely, intimate" Downtown hotel restaurant goes "out of its way" to establish a "relaxed atmosphere" for diners digging into "well-prepared" (if "unremarkable") New American fare; it's best if you "pair it with entertainment", as exposed-brick walls and a Saturday pianist and vocalist encourage a "romantic" vibe.

Columbia Firehouse *American*

20 | 21 | 19 | $35

Old Town | 109 S. St. Asaph St. (King St.) | Alexandria, VA | 703-683-1776 | www.columbiafirehouse.com

Set in a "historic firehouse" in the heart of Old Town, this upscale American "oozes style" with its exposed brick, "abundant stained glass" and "airy, bright atrium"; if the "solid" comfort-food menu "doesn't match the decor" it's still a decent "value" and tipplers toast the "lovely", "social bar."

Comet Ping Pong *Pizza*

20 | 15 | 16 | $23

Upper NW | 5037 Connecticut Ave. NW (Nebraska Ave.) | 202-364-0404 | www.cometpingpong.com

"Lots of neighborhood types" – "oldies, twentysomethings, families with babies" – bop into this "quirky" Van Ness "pizza and Ping-Pong" palace for "tasty" "New Haven–style" pies and "some of DC's best wings"; service is "so-so" and people are on both sides of the net regarding the "industrial setting" ("witty and chic" vs. "tired" and "noisy"), but occasional live music on weekends is a plus.

	FOOD	DECOR	SERVICE	COST

Commissary *American* | 16 | 16 | 17 | $25 |

Logan Circle | 1443 P St. NW (bet. 14th & 15th Sts.) | 202-299-0018 |
www.commissarydc.com

Bring your laptop to this "laid-back" Logan Circle "hangout", where
the "comfortable" setting (think "living room chairs"), "free Internet"
and "simple" American eats served all day make it an "affordable"
spot to "do work"; despite the "promising atmosphere", unsatisfied
sorts "wish it would improve the food" and service, suggesting its
"bar and lounge area" is "where it shines."

Comus Inn ⓜ *American* | 21 | 22 | 20 | $46 |

Dickerson | 23900 Old Hundred Rd. (Comus Rd.), MD | 301-349-5100 |
www.thecomusinn.com

"Breathtaking views" of Sugarloaf Mountain provide a backdrop for
"romantic evenings", live bands, popular Sunday brunches and "one
of the best happy hours around" at this New American nestled in
what's left of the Montgomery County countryside; set in a historic
house, it features tabs that "might not be for the weak-kneed",
though budget-minders should ask about weekend/midweek meal
deals; P.S. also closed Tuesday.

Coppi's Organic *Italian* | 21 | 21 | 19 | $34 |

U Street Corridor | 1414 U St. NW (bet. 14th & 15th Sts.) |
202-319-7773 | www.coppisorganic.com

"Yummy", locally sourced Ligurian specialties, "crispy" pizza and
wine served in tumblers ("just like at home!") attract U Street "regulars" and a pre-theater contingent who want to keep this "family-
owned" eatery a "secret"; it's "nothing mind-blowing", but the
"romance and candlelight" and "attentive" servers who "care about
their customers" have cognoscenti chirping *"ciao bello."*

ⓩ Corduroy ⓢ *American* | 27 | 24 | 25 | $63 |

Mt. Vernon Square/Convention Center | 1122 Ninth St. NW (bet. L &
M Sts.) | 202-589-0699 | www.corduroydc.com

Chef Tom Powers' "remarkably sophisticated" New American
cuisine has finally found its "niche" – and it's virtually "outside the
Convention Center door" in a townhouse that provides an "elegant",
"conversation-conducive" setting for his "creativity"; a "well-priced
wine list" that's "thorough without being overwhelming" and a "professional" staff complement the "powerful" cooking, while an
"underutilized" upstairs bar provides a "perfect retreat", along with
a three-course prix fixe (a $30 "steal").

Cork ⓜ *American* | 23 | 20 | 20 | $41 |

Logan Circle | 1720 14th St. NW (bet. R & S Sts.) | 202-265-2675 |
www.corkdc.com

At this "insanely popular" Logan Circle destination, a "top-
notch" selection of "affordable" European wines, "deceptively simple but flavorful" New American small plates and "superb" pairing
recommendations from "educated" servers "make for a wonderful night out"; snagging a table in its "dark", "exposed-brick" quarters ("are we in Paris?") can be a "challenge", so try its "call-ahead"

system, make an early reservation or "just hang by the bar" – it's "worth a wait."

Cosmopolitan Grill Ⓜ *E European* — | — | — | I

Greater Alexandria | 7770 Richmond Hwy. (Belford Dr.) | Alexandria, VA | 703-360-3660 | www.restaurant-cosmopolitan.com

Discover "interesting" Eastern European fare in this unassuming Alexandria mall stop that's "full of warmth", if not stylish decor; diners "feel the care coming through" in the signature Bosnia burger, the "amazing goulash", the "freshly baked breads" and the fish sandwich "steal", all served with "friendly", "no rush" aplomb.

Counter, The *Burgers* ▽ 21 | 17 | 18 | $18

Reston | 11922 Democracy Dr. (Bluemont Way), VA | 703-796-1008 | www.thecounterburger.com

Build a burger to your specs "from meat type to sauces and other toppings" (including "adventurous" choices like grilled pineapple) at this Reston branch of the West Coast chain, which also serves up "excellent" sweet potato fries and 'adult milkshakes' courtesy of the fully stocked bar; take your "inexpensive" eats home or chow down in the "modern" industrial setting at a long counter or diner-inspired tables tended by "friendly" servers.

Crème *Southern* 23 | 17 | 18 | $34

U Street Corridor | 1322 U St. NW (13th St.) | 202-234-1884

True, there's a "paucity of space" at this "tiny" U Street American, but it still crams in a lot of "delicious Southern cooking", from "perfect short ribs" to some of the "best shrimp and grits in town"; fortunately, the "fun, hip" vibe "makes up for the claustrophobic feel", as do the "solicitous" servers and moderate tabs; P.S. the weekend brunch "rocks" but "get there before the doors open" or prepare to wait.

Crisp & Juicy *Peruvian* 24 | 6 | 15 | $12

Upper NW | 4533 Wisconsin Ave. (River Rd.) | 202-966-1222
Gaithersburg | 18312 Contour Rd. (Lost Knife Rd.), MD | 301-355-7377
Rockville | Sunshine Sq. | 1331G Rockville Pike (Templeton Pl.), MD | 301-251-8833
Silver Spring | 1314 E. West Hwy. (Colesville Rd.), MD | 301-563-6666
Silver Spring | Leisure World Plaza | 3800 International Dr. (Georgia Ave.), MD | 301-598-3333
Wheaton | Westfield Mall | 11160 Veirs Mill Rd. (University Blvd. W.), MD | 301-962-6666
Arlington | 4540 Lee Hwy. (Woodstock St.), VA | 703-243-4222
Falls Church | 913 W. Broad St. (bet. Spring & West Sts.), VA | 703-241-9091
www.crispjuicy.com

It's "true to its name" chirp champions of the "tasty", "moist" rotisserie birds from this "no-frills" Peruvian chicken chain, where "$10 will buy enough for four people" – including "amazing dipping sauces" and "dependable" sides like "addictive fried yuca"; with decor that's "best described as early shabby", it's "more appropriate for take-out", though the "aroma will drive you crazy on the way home."

	FOOD	DECOR	SERVICE	COST

Crystal Thai *Thai*

22 | 15 | 20 | $28

Arlington | Arlington Forest Shopping Ctr. | 4819 Arlington Blvd.
(Park Dr.), VA | 703-522-1311 | www.crystalthai.com

"Year in and year out", this "no-nonsense" Arlington Thai in a "non-descript" strip mall "churns out" "excellent traditional" dishes ("soft shell crab heaven") at "affordable prices"; factor in a "friendly" staff garbed in traditional attire and a "cozy" setting, and you've got "one of the best around."

Cuba de Ayer Ⓜ *Cuban*

23 | 15 | 22 | $26

Burtonsville | 15446 Old Columbia Pike (Spencerville Rd.), MD |
301-476-9622 | www.cubadeayerrestaurant.com

The "mom-and-daughter" team behind this "quaint" strip-mall *cocina* dishes up some of the "best Cuban food north of Miami", as evident by the "expats" and Burtonsville locals enjoying the "simple, homestyle" fare ("ropa vieja, picadillo, vaca frita", etc.) that's "easy on the budget"; the place looks "a bit like a '50s" diner, but no matter: everyone's "there for the food."

NEW Cuba Libre Restaurant & Rum Bar *Nuevo Latino*

- | - | - | M

Penn Quarter | 801 Ninth St. NW (H St.) | 202-408-1600 |
www.cubalibrerestaurant.com

The flashy digs of this huge Penn Quarter Nuevo Latino boast a grand central piazza that looks straight out of Old Havana, complete with wrought-iron balconies, stucco walls and ornate building facades replicated from vintage photographs; its creative fare comes at moderate prices and is bolstered by trendy cocktails and an *Old Man and the Sea*–length rum list; P.S. there are plans to add late-night weekend dancing as at the other locations in Atlantic City, Orlando and Philly.

Cubano's *Cuban*

21 | 17 | 18 | $30

Silver Spring | 1201 Fidler Ln. (Georgia Ave.), MD | 301-563-4020 |
www.cubanosrestaurant.com

"Leave the bongos at home" when heading to this "adventure into Cuban fare" "tucked away" in Downtown Silver Spring, as you'll want to concentrate on the "large portions" of "traditional" fare like "delicious ropa vieja"; a "chatty" staff, "outside seating" and "wonderfully bright, colorful rooms" add to the "Caribbean" vibe, which really kicks in after one or two of its "excellent mojitos."

NEW Curry Mantra *Indian*

- | - | - | I

Fairfax | 9984 Main St. (bet. Fairfax Sq. & Tedrich Blvd.) |
Fairfax City, VA | 703-218-8128 | www.dccurrymantra.com

A wide-ranging menu of northern and southern Indian specialties (including many vegetarian options) broadens the appeal of this affordable subcontinental newcomer in Fairfax; the warm reds and golds of the traditional decor evoke its namesake, which figures in a variety of authentically spiced dishes, though many customers can't resist ordering items cooked in the tandoor glimpsed through a window into the kitchen.

	FOOD	DECOR	SERVICE	COST

Da Domenico ⊠ *Italian* | 21 | 16 | 23 | $44

Tysons Corner | 1992 Chain Bridge Rd. (Leesburg Pike) | McLean, VA |
703-790-9000

"If you can tolerate all the singing", you're likely to "enjoy" this Tysons Corner "hideaway" where "old-school" Italian fare like "excellent" veal chops come with an "opera serenade" on the side; while "friendly" staffers ensure there's always "someone taking care of you", even supporters say a "little updating would be welcome" ("the '80s are calling, and they want their decor back").

Daniel O'Connell's Restaurant ● *Pub Food* | 20 | 23 | 22 | $33

Old Town | 112 King St. (bet. Lee & Union Sts.) | Alexandria, VA |
703-739-1124 | www.danieloconnells.com

"Gorgeous decor" incorporating salvaged church pews and other fixtures from the "homeland" sets the scene for "boisterous fun" and "surprisingly good" pub fare at this bi-level "Irishman's heaven" in Old Town; natch, the "friendliest bartenders" "pull a good pint" to go with the "delicious shepherd's pie", and not even "upscale" pricing can deter those who swear it's like they're "back in Dublin."

Darlington House ● *American* | 20 | 20 | 20 | $38

Dupont Circle | 1610 20th St. NW (bet. Hillyer Pl. & Q St.) |
202-332-3722 | www.darlingtonhousedc.com

It's in a "former residence", so it's no surprise this "charming" Dupont Circle eatery feels like a "friend's well-appointed home" (albeit one with an "intimate date-night atmosphere"); while the service and "light, fresh" Italian-influenced New American fare don't exactly excite surveyors, that's not the case with its downstairs den tendering "tasty cocktails" and "must" mini-pizzas.

DC Boathouse *American* | 15 | 15 | 16 | $33

Palisades | 5441 MacArthur Blvd. (Cathedral Ave.) |
202-362-2628

Don't expect a "fancy feast" at this Greek-owned, family-friendly "neighborhood hangout", just "basic" American "comfort food" served in a "noisy" space decked with college T-shirts and "crewing decor"; Palisides resident or not, you "won't feel out of place here", though some claim the "lofty prices" for merely "decent" food would sink the place if its customers weren't "captive" (few other options are nearby).

DC Coast *American* | 23 | 22 | 22 | $53

Downtown | Tower Bldg. | 1401 K St. NW (14th St.) | 202-216-5988 |
www.dccoast.com

Out-of-towners can see firsthand "what the K Street scene is all about" at this "top-flight" "power-lunch" locus awash in "swanky", "art deco–style" trappings and "imaginative", predictably "pricey" New American fare with a seafood hook; choose between the "high-energy", sometimes "frantic" dining room and the "intimate" balcony (both "professionally" tended by "spot-on" servers), or grab a seat at the "hopping bar" and start "eavesdropping" – "you may learn something important."

	FOOD	DECOR	SERVICE	COST

DC Noodles *Thai*

21 | **15** | **19** | **$21**

U Street Corridor | 1410 U St. NW (bet. 14th & 15th Sts.) |
202-232-8424 | www.dcnoodles.com

When U Streeters are "fixin' for noodles of any Asian variety", this
"basics-only" "gem" answers the call: from its Thai specialties to
Vietnamese pho; the "generous portions" are "fresh, light" and
"tasty"; the "nothing fancy" space gets "noisy" and jurists quarrel
over tabs ("cheap" to a "tad overpriced"), but there's no denying it's
"welcome on a cold day."

DC Slices ☒⇥ *Pizza*

- | **-** | **-** | **I**

Location varies; see website | no phone | www.dcslices.com

Fresh dough and toppings are baked in the back of this food truck, a
peripatetic pizza-maker that travels around the city selling slices
and whole pies – think cheese, veggie, pepperoni, sausage and
Hawaiian; look for it Monday, Wednesday, Friday and Saturday for
lunch, as well as late-night Friday and Saturday.

NEW DC-3 *Hot Dogs*

- | **-** | **-** | **I**

Capitol Hill | 423 Eighth St. SE (bet. E St. & Pennsylvania Ave.) |
202-546-1935 | www.eatdc3.com

The talents behind Matchbox and Ted's Bulletin bring char-grilled
franks to Capitol Hill, dispensing them from a stainless-steel
counter resembling an airplane wing, a nod to its namesake; the
meat-in-a-bun menu reads like a busy pilot's flight log, with service
from DC (half-smoke) to NYC (Nathan's), Seattle (deep-fried cod),
Seoul (beef dog with kimchi) and points beyond; P.S. sweet-tooths
take note: there's cotton candy and soft-serve ice cream.

Dean & DeLuca *Eclectic*

22 | **15** | **16** | **$26**

Georgetown | 3276 M St. NW (33rd St.) | 202-342-2500 |
www.deananddeluca.com

At this Georgetown outpost of NYC's "upscale" purveyor of "drool-
worthy" Eclectic chow, "high-quality ingredients and prep" lure
"spendy types" in search of "gourmet takeout" or an "on-the-run
lunch"; there's "no decor" – "it's a grocery store", after all – but a
"nice outdoor" seating area offers the "best people-watching"
ops; still, many decry the "unreasonable prices" and warn "lines
can get long."

Delhi Club *Indian*

24 | **14** | **22** | **$26**

Clarendon | 1135 N. Highland St. (Clarendon Blvd.), VA | 703-527-5666 |
www.delhiclub.com

If only this "tiny", "no-nonsense" Clarendon subcontinental
"were larger" – there'd be less jostling for the "few tables" hug-
ging the large front windows and more space for the "dedicated
staff" to serve the "tasty, authentic" Indian food ("butter chicken is
worth the trip alone"); a "great" lunch buffet enhances the deal, as
do the "affordable prices."

Delhi Dhaba *Indian*

18 | **9** | **16** | **$20**

Bethesda | 7236 Woodmont Ave. (Elm St.), MD | 301-718-0008

(continued)

Delhi Dhaba

Courthouse | 2424 Wilson Blvd. (Barton St.) | Arlington, VA | 703-524-0008
www.delhidhaba.com

"Easy to miss", these "go-to places for Indian takeout" in Bethesda and Courthouse specialize in curries, tandoori chicken and a "mix-and-match" buffet at "cafeteria prices"; "flavors could be a little perkier", but at least the "Bollywood movies playing" add spice to the otherwise "unremarkable locations" (particularly at Wilson Boulevard).

Dickson Wine Bar *Eclectic*

– | – | – | M

U Street Corridor | 903 U St. NW (bet. 9th & 10th Sts.) | 202-332-1779 |
www.dicksonwinebar.com

This hot wine bar offers U Street NW denizens a polished setting for chilling after work (or before heading out to the nearby clubs), plus an intriguing Eclectic menu with banh mi sandwiches, salads and housemade charcuterie, all paired with organic and biodynamic wines along with ingenious cocktails; the open, three-story space makes use of reclaimed materials, and sight lines from its stylish counter perches and communal tables add people-watching appeal.

Diner, The ● *Diner*

17 | 14 | 17 | $19

Adams Morgan | 2453 18th St. NW (bet. Belmont & Columbia Rds.) |
202-232-8800 | www.dinerdc.com

The "true diner" eats "won't knock your socks off" and "long waits" are common (especially for brunch), but this "friendly" "standby" "serves food 24 hours a day" in a town where few spots do, so "does anything else matter?"; expect an "eclectic crowd" digging into "grilled cheese, chicken fingers" and "all-day breakfast" under the "tin ceiling", many in "clubbing clothes or pajamas" after a "long night in Adams Morgan."

Dino *Italian*

22 | 17 | 20 | $43

Cleveland Park | 3435 Connecticut Ave. NW (bet. Macomb & Ordway Sts.) | 202-686-2966 | www.dino-dc.com

"Linger over pasta" at this "lively", "unpretentious" Cleveland Park Italian from "affable" chef-owner Dean Gold ("you can't miss him in his Hawaiian shirts"), whose "foodie glee" is reflected in the "inventive" menu of midpriced "small plates" and "seasonal specialties"; true, the "faux-*cucina* decor" leaves some cold, but most are too busy sipping through the "fantastic" "opus" of a wine list – "ever had a white from Slovenia?" – to notice.

Dish + Drinks *American*

∇ 19 | 16 | 19 | $41

Foggy Bottom | The River Inn | 924 25th St. NW (bet. I & K Sts.) |
202-338-8707 | www.dishanddrinks.com

For a "pre–Kennedy Center meal", this Foggy Bottom resto-bar in the River Inn dishes out "decent" American "comfort food" augmented by an "excellent wine list"; though "tables are limited, there's great art" by the likes of William Wegman gracing the "cozy" (some say "sterile") space, which might distract those who feel it's "too expensive in relation to the quality."

	FOOD	DECOR	SERVICE	COST

District ChopHouse & Brewery *Steak* | 18 | 18 | 19 | $39 |

Penn Quarter | 509 Seventh St. NW (bet. E & F Sts.) | 202-347-3434 |
www.chophouse.com

"Go ahead, blow the diet – eat the meat and potatoes" at this "reasonably priced" Penn Quarter beef temple where chopaholics settle into leather seats for "great steaks", "monstrous" salads and other "satisfying" fare, washed down with "fresh" suds; true, a few find it "ho-hum", but if you've got tickets for a "game at Verizon Center", "frenetic but good" servers make sure you're there at tip-off.

NEW District of Pi *Pizza* | – | – | – | I |
(aka Pi on Wheels)

Location varies; see website | www.pi-dc.com

Deep-dish, cornmeal-crusted pies that reportedly appease the Eater-in-Chief's Chicago-style pizza cravings are piled with rafts of fresh toppings at this advance mobile unit of a St. Louis–based chain; the truck will continue spinning its wheels after a spiffy Penn Quarter brick-and-mortar location opens at 910 F Street NW (scheduled to open as we go to press).

NEW Diya *Indian* | – | – | – | M |

Tysons Corner | 2070 Chain Bridge Rd. (bet. Gosnell Rd. & Leesburg Pike) | Vienna, VA | 703-970-7500 | www.diyatysons.com

At this swanky new Tysons Corner Indian, the offerings range from curried goat to traditional vegetarian dishes to South Asian takes on burgers (spiced minced lamb, paneer and vegetables) and pizza (naan topped with the likes of chicken tikka) – along with an extensive lunchtime buffet; its setting features a window-wrapped modern bar/lounge, ivory-and-silver-toned dining rooms and party spaces that accommodate up to 400 guests.

Dogfish Head Alehouse *Pub Food* | 18 | 15 | 19 | $25 |

Gaithersburg | 800 W. Diamond Ave. (Quince Orchard Rd.), MD | 301-963-4847

Fairfax | 13041 Lee Jackson Memorial Hwy. (bet. Majestic Ln. & Springfellow Rd.), VA | 703-961-1140

Falls Church | Seven Corners Ctr. | 6363 Leesburg Pike (Rte. 7), VA | 703-534-3342

www.dogfishalehouse.com

Hopsheads hit these "noisy" suburban alehouses for the "legendarily quirky brews" of its eponymous Rehoboth Beach supplier, soaking up the suds with "decent" Delmarva-rooted "pub fare" (Chesapeake pizza, anyone?); the "Cracker Barrel"–like premises are "surprisingly family-friendly", but since beer's the "star here", expect a "young" crowd – just "bring your patience and a table sponge."

Dolce Vita *Italian* | 23 | 16 | 22 | $33 |

Fairfax | 10824 Lee Hwy. (Main St.), VA | 703-385-1530 | www.dolcevitafairfax.com

They "turn back the clock 40 years" at this "little bit of Italy" in Fairfax, thanks to "dishes like mama makes" ("pizza to classics") and a "warm atmosphere" enriched by "owners always on hand to greet patrons"; it's "small and crowded", but *paesani* say "go here" any-way, if only to be "serenaded by strolling [musicians]!" on weekends.

Domku Bar & Café 🅼 *E European/Scandinavian*

| 18 | 15 | 14 | $28 |

Petworth | 821 Upshur St. NW (bet. 8th St. & Georgia Ave.) | 202-722-7475 | www.domkucafe.com

This Petworth "hangout" proffers a "quirky hybrid of Scandinavian and Polish" cuisine, including "pierogi, kielbasa" and Swedish meatballs, plus "sandwiches and burgers for those afraid to ask what goulash is"; locals wash it down with "amazing" aquavits in a "shabby-chic" set-ting, but even fans caution that "well-meaning but overburdened" staffers sometimes deliver service "redolent of the Eastern Bloc."

Don Pollo *S American*

| 18 | 7 | 14 | $14 |

Chevy Chase | 7007 Wisconsin Ave. (bet. Bradley Blvd. & Leland St.), MD | 301-652-0001

Langley Park | 2065 University Blvd. E. (bet. Guilford & Riggs Rds.), MD | 301-434-5001

Rockville | Twinbrooke Shopping Ctr. | 2206 Veirs Mill Rd. (bet. Atlantic Ave. & Meadow Hall Dr.), MD | 301-309-1608 www.donpollorestaurant.com

These South American rotisseries skewer "crispy, succulent" *pollo a la brasa* that prompts partisans to ponder "is there anything else on the menu?" (well, yes: "outstanding" traditional sides like sweet plantains); it all makes for an "easy" take-out meal that's a "serious bargain", good news since the venues are nothing to crow about.

Duangrat's *Thai*

| 25 | 18 | 21 | $31 |

Falls Church | 5878 Leesburg Pike (Glen Forest Dr.), VA | 703-820-5775 | www.duangrats.com

Open since 1987, this "grand old lady of Thai cuisine" still does it all "superbly", "branching out beyond pad Thai" with "innovative" takes on "whole flounder" and other Siamese specialties; its "low-key" Falls Church space (a bit "faded" to some) and "staffers in traditional garb" enhance its rep as the "real deal", with "prices that reflect it."

Dubliner, The ❶ *Irish*

| 16 | 19 | 19 | M |

Capitol Hill | Phoenix Park Hotel | 520 N. Capitol St. NW (F St.) | 202-737-3773 | www.dublinerdc.com

"Arrive early, get a seat and sing along" with "a combination of tour-ists, locals, Eire-o-philes" and "Hill types" at this "cozy" "authentic Irish" pub near Union Station where "bartenders know how to pour a perfect Guinness" to accompany the moderately priced eats; P.S. you'll encounter "excellent crowds on St. Patty's Day."

Dukem ❶ *Ethiopian*

| 24 | 14 | 18 | $22 |

U Street Corridor | 1114-1118 U St. NW (12th St.) | 202-667-8735 | www.dukemrestaurant.com

"Sample multiple dishes" while sipping "honey wine" at these "scrumptious" U Street and Baltimore (Mt. Vernon) Ethiopians, "old-school" affairs where "cabbies get takeout" and a budget-minded "young crowd" uses "spongy" injera bread to scoop up "hearty", sometimes "fiery" fare from "veggie items to meat stews"; "so-so decor and service" bedevil both, but "who cares? we get to eat with our hands!"; P.S. insiders suggest checking out the occasional "live music" (DC only) and Ethiopian coffee ceremony on Sunday afternoon (both locations).

Eamonn's – A Dublin Chipper/PX *Irish*   23 | 15 | 17 | $17

Old Town | 728 King St. (Columbus St.) | Alexandria, VA | 703-299-8384 | www.eamonnsdublinchipper.com

"You have to fight to get a seat" at this "gold standard" for "fresh-from-the-fryer" fish 'n' chips from Irish-born Cathal Armstrong (Eve), especially "when rookies don't share" its few tables; still, that doesn't deter Old Towners from queueing up for "huge portions" of the "absolute best" "heart attack on a plate (um, in a bag)" and a Guinness to "wash it all down"; P.S. seal the deal with a "fried Milky Way" or head upstairs for a "custom cocktail" from PX, its "elegant speakeasy" lounge.

Eat First ● *Chinese*   20 | 7 | 15 | $20

Chinatown | 609 H St. NW (bet. 6th & 7th Sts.) | 202-289-1703

It helps to "know how to read Chinese", but "get something listed on the wall" at this "no-frills" Chinatown "go-to" – "you'll be pleasantly surprised"; otherwise, there's a second "English menu" featuring "delicious, incredibly cheap" standards you "can count on", notably "excellent noodle soups"; if a few fret it's "lost some of its wok chi", more say "don't let the shabby decor fool you."

Eatonville *Southern*   19 | 21 | 20 | $32

U Street Corridor | 2121 14th St. NW (bet. V & W Sts.) | 202-332-9672 | www.eatonvillerestaurant.com

"They've captured the South" at this affordable U Streeter "paying homage" to author Zora Neale Hurston, so expect an "inviting" atmosphere ("beautiful" murals, "porch seating") and "soul food with style"; factor in a "great happy hour", "live jazz" and "killer cocktails", and y'all are in for an "all-around good time", though wary well-wishers fear it's trying to "be too much to too many"; P.S. it's the sib of nearby Busboys & Poets.

NEW Eat Wonky *Eclectic*   - | - | - | I

Location varies; see website | 202-709-6659 | www.eatwonky.com

With its wacky logo and color-splashed paint job, it's hard to miss this truck in trendy DC neighborhoods, serving a hodgepodge of hearty treats on the cheap including specialty poutine (fries smothered in cheese curds and gravy), hot dogs, grilled cheese and whoopie pies; P.S. you can also find it at DC United and Washington Capitals games, DC Rollergirls, ladies arm-wrestling and other sporting events.

Edy's Chicken   *Peruvian*   ▽ 22 | 9 | 17 | $11

Falls Church | Leesburg Plaza | 5240 Leesburg Pike (bet. Jefferson St. & Leesburg Ct.), VA | 703-820-5508

"Insider foodies" cackle about the "crisp rotisserie chicken you won't soon forget" and the "best" yuca fries from this bright, decor-free

Peruvian–Pan-Latin fast-food coop on Leesburg Pike; the "cheap eats" come with "delicious sauces", and there are even "nice" desserts.

Eggspectations *American* | 19 | 16 | 17 | $20 |

Silver Spring | 923 Ellsworth Dr. (bet. Fenton St. & Georgia Ave.), MD | 301-585-1700

Chantilly | Westone Plaza | 5009 Westone Plaza Dr. (Westfields Blvd.), VA | 703-263-7444

NEW **Leesburg** | Wegman Shopping Ctr. | 1609 Vill. Market Blvd. SE (Market St.), VA | 703-777-4127

www.eggspectations.com

No yolk: there's a lot to "love" about this "reliable" chain's "ginormous" American menu of "tasty" "all-day" morning grub (including a "full page of eggs Benedicts"), "surprisingly good" dinner fare and "yummy cocktails"; then again, the "Cirque du Soleil"–style trappings, "long waits on weekends" and "tolerable" service are "eggs-actly" why some say they're just "ok", though even they agree "it sure beats Waffle House."

8407 Kitchen Bar *American* | - | - | - | M |

Silver Spring | 8407 Ramsey Ave. (bet. Bonifant St. & Wayne Ave.), MD | 301-587-8407 | www.8407kb.com

At this Downtown Silver Spring yearling, local purveyors provide the ingredients for the affordable, seasonal New American menu from Pedro Matamoros (ex Nicaro, Tabard Inn); the smart, contemporary setting features bar, cafe and lounge areas downstairs while upstairs is a more spacious dining room done up with exposed brick, rough wood beams and walls of windows.

NEW El Centro D.F. *Mexican* | - | - | - | M |

Logan Circle | 1819 14th St. NW (bet. S & T Sts.) | 202-328-3131 | www.elcentrodf.com

The prolific Richard Sandoval is behind this new midpriced Mexican comfort-food destination off Logan Circle that's just a few doors down from sister Masa 14; the multistoried building includes a ground-floor taqueria (with take-out options), a basement tequileria pouring 200 selections (including mescals) and a rooftop with two outdoor bars.

El Chalan *Peruvian* | 20 | 12 | 19 | $31 |

Foggy Bottom | 1924 I St. NW (20th St.) | 202-293-2765 | www.elchalandc.com

When "World Bank and IMF" suits aren't feasting on "lomo saltado and pisco sours" in Lima, they're eating the same "authentic" Peruvian fare in this "homey" step-down restaurant near their Foggy Bottom offices; everything from the "wholesome dishes" that "won't leave you bankrupt" to the "old-school" service is "true to the spirit of Peru."

Elephant & Castle *Pub Food* | 15 | 15 | 16 | $26 |

Downtown | 1201 Pennsylvania Ave. NW (12th St.) | 202-347-7707

Foggy Bottom | 900 19th St. NW (I St.) | 202-296-2575

www.elephantcastle.com

"Pip, pip, cheerio" – "if pub's your grub, this is your spot" assure aficionados of these Downtown and Foggy Bottom links of the "fun,

FOOD | DECOR | SERVICE | COST

faux-British" chain whose "outdoor seating" generally compensates for "overwhelmed" waiters and "decent" if "uninspiring" "bar food"; still, lots of "beer, beer, beer" (mainly U.K.) make them an ale-safe choice for a "cold pint on a warm day."

Elevation Burger *Burgers*

18 | 11 | 17 | $12

National Harbor | National Harbor | 108 Waterfront St. (National Harbor Blvd.), MD | 301-749-4014
NEW **Potomac** | 12525 Park Potomac Ave. (Montrose Rd.), MD | 301-838-4010
NEW **Hyattsville** | 5501 Baltimore Ave. (Jefferson St.), MD | 301-985-6869
Arlington | Lee Harrison Shopping Ctr. | 2447 N. Harrison St. (bet. Lee Hwy. & 26th St.), VA | 703-300-9467
Falls Church | 442 S. Washington St. (Annandale Rd.), VA | 703-237-4343
www.elevationburger.com

"Big, juicy burgers", "huge orders of fries" and "homemade milkshakes" elevate this expanding chain of "neighborhood hangouts" where the "meat's organic", the frites are "cooked in olive oil" and vegetarians aren't forgotten (hence the "veggie" patties); generally "nice" staffers guide patrons through the menu, but "disappointed" diners decree it's just a "Five Guys wannabe" with "premium prices."

El Floridano ☒ *Sandwiches*

- | - | - | I

Location varies; see website | 202-286-0643 | www.elfloridanodc.com

From his ornately muraled food truck, former Dino chef Stephan Boillon offers up a few eclectic takes on popular sandwiches, including a banh mi made with BBQ turkey meatloaf; soups change weekly, and tempeh can be substituted for certain sandwich's protein free of charge; P.S. it operates weekdays, with its locale tracked on Twitter (@FLmeetsDC) and Facebook.

El Gavilan *Salvadoran/Tex-Mex*

- | - | - | I

Silver Spring | 8805 Flower Ave. (Hartwell Rd.), MD | 301-587-4197

In Silver Spring, this well-priced Salvadoran "surprise" with a "big following" outdoes the "Tex-Mex chains" with its "excellent" Latin offerings; "great" tamales, "flavorful rice and beans" and tacos al carbon are just a few of the specialties served up by a staff that "never falters."

El Golfo *Pan-Latin*

∇ 21 | 14 | 26 | $28

Silver Spring | 8739 Flower Ave. (Piney Branch Rd.), MD | 301-608-2122 | www.elgolforestaurant.com

The "margaritas can throw you for a loop" at this serape-bedecked Silver Spring "favorite", so "don't drink on an empty stomach"; fortunately, an "excellent" staff makes that difficult, since it's constantly plying patrons with "cut-above" Pan-Latin fare (fajitas, masitas de puerco, etc.) in a "family atmosphere"; P.S. frequent "coupons" drive "inexpensive" tabs even lower.

Ella's Wood-Fired Pizza Pizza

20 | 15 | 18 | $23

Penn Quarter | 901 F St. NW (entrance on 9th St.) | 202-638-3434 | www.ellaspizza.com

"Don't blame the throngs of young professionals" (and families, for that matter) who clog this "reasonably priced" Penn Quarter pizza purveyor – they're here for the "paper-thin" pies with "creative toppings", "tasty" salads and "nice menu of craft beers"; "friendly" staffers skillfully navigate the "sparse-looking" space, a challenge during a "happy hour that can feel like a fraternity party", but that just adds to the "lively atmosphere."

El Manantial Italian/Spanish

▽ 23 | 21 | 26 | $40

Reston | Toll Oaks Village Ctr. | 12050A North Shore Dr. (Wiehle Ave.), VA | 703-742-6466 | www.elmanantialrestaurant.com

Service that "couldn't be better" is the hallmark of this "white-tablecloth Mediterranean", a "hidden jewel" set in an "otherwise plain" Reston strip mall; a wine list with some "outstanding values" dulls the pain of relatively "high prices" elsewhere on the menu, a roster of "lovely" Italian, French and Spanish "standards" that "doesn't change" much but is "consistently well prepared."

El Mariachi Mexican

19 | 12 | 19 | $26

Rockville | 765C Rockville Pike (Wootton Pkwy.), MD | 301-738-7177 | www.elmariachirestaurant.com

A Rockville "standby" since 1991, this "reliable" strip-maller is "way more than a Mexican joint", proffering as it does "tasty Tex-Mex" standards along with some South American cuisine (inlcuding "outstanding" lomo saltado and lengua); with "generous portions", "well-made" margaritas and "reasonable" tabs as added enticements, it's "frequently crowded", much to the chagrin of longtime loyalists who sigh "everyone knows about it now."

El Pike S American

‐ | ‐ | ‐ | I

Falls Church | 6138 Arlington Blvd. (Edison St.), VA | 703-237-1682 | www.pike4you.com

Lodged in a Falls Church strip mall, this homey Bolivian "stalwart" is "well known" for its inexpensive weekend *salteñas* ("juicy" empanadas filled with savory stews); still, other "compelling" specialties like its seafood and chicken dishes are "worth trying" too.

El Pollo Rico Peruvian

25 | 6 | 16 | $11

Wheaton | 2517 University Blvd. (bet. Georgia & Grandview Aves.), MD | 301-942-4419

Arlington | 932 N. Kenmore St. (bet. Fairfax Dr. & Wilson Blvd.), VA | 703-522-3220

NEW **Woodbridge** | 13470 Minnieville Rd. (Smoketown Rd.), VA | 703-590-3160

www.welovethischicken.com

"In the world of spit-roasted-over-charcoal chicken", this Peruvian "standard to measure all" represents a "deliciousness for the cost" value that has "everyone from migrant workers to people with luxury purses" waiting on "looong lines" to get their beaks into its "flavorful, juicy" birds and "terrific" sides and sauces; most go for takeout, but if the Wheaton/Arlington duo's "lack of decor" doesn't ruffle your feathers, "get your Inca Kola and get a seat"; the new Woodbridge location opened post-Survey.

Eola ⌧ Ⓜ *American* — | — | — | VE
Dupont Circle | 2020 P St. NW (Hopkins St.) | 202-466-4441 | www.eoladc.com

There's "some mighty upscale cooking" at this young Dupont Circle New American that offers a $65 market-based prix fixe menu that changes weekly (no à la carte options except at the monthly brunch); set in a lovely townhouse, it's been flying under the radar, but early standouts include creative and unusual desserts highlighting local produce and an interesting cocktail menu.

Equinox *American* 25 | — | 23 | $64
Golden Triangle | 818 Connecticut Ave. NW (bet. H & I Sts.) | 202-331-8118 | www.equinoxrestaurant.com

Emerging lighter, brighter and more modern-looking "post kitchen fire", this New American "oasis of grace and charm" – conveniently set in the Obamas' neighborhood and long favored for "special nights out" – is "still special", showcasing as it does chef/co-owner Todd Gray's "classically elegant approach" to the "freshest, finest local ingredients" (hence, there's "always something interesting and different on the menu"); "professional service" adds to the appeal, making it a relatively "good value at the high end."

NEW Estadio *Spanish* — | — | — | M
Logan Circle | 1520 14th St. NW (Church St.) | 202-319-1404 | www.estadio-dc.com

Logan Circle denizens welcome this wine-centric Spaniard (from the Proof team) offering contemporary takes on regional classics in pintxos and tapas formats, along with reasonably priced Iberian vino and frozen alcoholic slushies; the über-stylish setting incorporates wrought iron, reclaimed timber and colorful tiles, with seating at a large bar, a marble counter facing the open kitchen and window-side tables perfect for scoping vibrant 14th Street.

Etete ◑ *Ethiopian* 24 | 15 | 17 | $25
U Street Corridor | 1942 Ninth St. NW (U St.) | 202-232-7600 | www.eteterestaurant.com

Scoop up "authentic Ethiopian food with flatbread" ("look, ma, no forks") at this "cozy" U Street Corridor destination for "stews from mild to spicy" and some of the "best samosas" at "good prices"; service can be "spotty", but at least staffers are "helpful deciphering the menu" in the "modern, bright" space, where some still feel "packed in like sardines" despite an expansion.

Ethiopic Ⓜ *Ethiopian* — | — | — | I
Atlas District | 401 H St. NE (4th St.) | 202-675-2066 | www.ethiopicrestaurant.com

Woven basket tables are tucked into window alcoves of this affordable Atlas District Ethiopian, where native art decorates walls and

FOOD | DECOR | SERVICE | COST

Et Voila *Belgian/French*   24 | 17 | 21 | $47

Palisades | 5120 MacArthur Blvd. (bet. Arizona Ave. & Dana Pl.) | 202-237-2300 | www.etvoiladc.com

At "one of Palisades' newest gems", "ultrarefined" French-Belgian fare is shuttled through a "charming", "narrow" space by servers who "handle the tight quarters with ease"; *oui*, you're a "little close to your neighbor", but with "tantalizing" cooking (including "classic steak and frites") at "affordable prices" and a "great selection" of brews, few seem to care; P.S. "make reservations" or consider "slurping down its juicy, meaty mussels" at the bar.

☑ Eve, Restaurant ☒ *American*   28 | 25 | 27 | $84

Old Town | 110 S. Pitt St. (bet. King & Prince Sts.) | Alexandria, VA | 703-706-0450 | www.restauranteve.com

"Hitting on all cylinders", this "magical" Old Town New American proffers a choice of "unforgettable" experiences: an "ambrosial" nine-course romp in the "serene" tasting room, or a "gastronomic extravaganza on a smaller scale" in the "hip" bistro and lounge; chef/co-owner Cathal Armstrong "coaxes the best" from his "superb ingredients" (including "vegetables from the garden in back") and "impeccable" staff – from the "mesmerizing mixologist" to the "knowledgeable" sommelier – so naturally devotees deem it well "worth the splurge"; P.S. the $14.98 weekday bar lunch "is a steal."

Evening Star Cafe *American*   22 | 18 | 20 | $35

Del Ray | 2000 Mt. Vernon Ave. (Howell Ave.) | Alexandria, VA | 703-549-5051 | www.eveningstarcafe.net

Del Rayites pack this "relaxed" "neighborhood hangout" for an "excellent" "seasonal menu" of "delicious" American appies and shellfish, plus "fabulous brunches"; "servers with personality" help star-grazers parse through the "broad spectrum of reasonably priced wines" (from the shop next door), enjoyed in a "quirky atmosphere with Erector Set lamps and strong colors"; beware: it "gets loud", especially when there's live music in the lounge upstairs.

Eventide ☒ Ⓜ *American*   20 | 25 | 22 | $48

Clarendon | 3165 Wilson Blvd. (Hudson St.), VA | 703-276-3165 | www.eventiderestaurant.com

From the "elegant chandeliers" and "miles of curtains" in the "gorgeous" dining room to the "fantastic views" from the rooftop lounge, the "retro-sophisticated" vibe at this "Clarendon winner" "blows away" diners who duck in for "creative but simple" New American fare (lamb, pastas, fish); while a "more-than-thoughtful" staff caters to "romantic" types, those more interested in the bottom line can head to the "lively" downstairs pub for its lower-priced "bar menu."

	FOOD	DECOR	SERVICE	COST

Evo Bistro *Mediterranean* | 23 | 16 | 18 | $40 |

McLean | Salona Shopping Ctr. | 1313 Old Chain Bridge Rd. (Dolley Madison Blvd.), VA | 703-288-4422 | www.evobistro.com

Sample a "broad range" of vinos from "wine-o-matics" (via "prepaid cards" so "you can pour your own") and "delicious" "tapas and tagines" at this strip-mall McLean Med; service can be "slow", but it's still a "fun" spot for "entertaining out-of-towners" – just note that all that sipping can "tap out your wallet"; P.S. the Decor score may not reflect an expansion.

Extra Virgin *Italian* | 17 | 17 | 19 | $40 |

Shirlington | 4053 Campbell Ave. (Randolph St.) | Arlington, VA | 703-998-8474 | www.extravirginva.com

If "you're catching a movie in Shirlington" or headed to Signature Theatre, the "friendly" servers at this "neighborhood" Northern Italian will "make you feel welcome"; still, while some dig its "classic dishes with matching wine list", a vocal contingent "want to like this place better", citing "outrageous prices" and "mediocre" chow (though a chef change may shake things up); P.S. there's "live music" Saturday.

Ezmè *Turkish* | – | – | – | M |

Dupont Circle | 2016 P St. NW (bet. Hopkins & 21st Sts.) | 202-223-4304 | www.ezmedc.com

An urbane wine bar and Turkish bistro from the Mezè talents (as its anagrammatic name slyly reveals), this affordable Dupont Circle charmer is tucked into a brick-walled space enlivened by wine racks, colorful tiles and an intimate, glowing bar; diners can pair international vino pours with some 40 shareable plates that showcase ingredients from the garden (vegetables), sea (fish), land (meats) and air (fowl), a concept that was popularized by its Adams Morgan sibling.

Facci *Italian/Pizza* | – | – | – | M |

Laurel | Montpelier Shopping Ctr. | 7530 Montpelier Rd. (Johns Hopkins Rd., off Rte. 29), MD | 301-604-5555 | www.faccirestaurant.com

Naples-born Gino Palma-Esposito imported a huge, wood-burning oven for his Italian restaurant in North Laurel (not far from Columbia) so that his midpriced pies would be smoky and authentic tasting, while his extensive pasta, panini and entree menu also replicates the recipes he ate at home; a contemporary burgundy-and-brick setting works equally well for business lunches, happy-hour get-togethers (when appetizers are half off) or as an evening destination.

Faccia Luna Trattoria *Pizza* | 21 | 16 | 19 | $25 |

Old Town | 823 S. Washington St. (bet. Green & Jefferson Sts.) | Alexandria, VA | 703-838-5998

Clarendon | 2909 Wilson Blvd. (Fillmore St.), VA | 703-276-3099 www.faccialuna.com

"Consistent", "convenient" and "crowded", these pizza 'n' pasta "favorites" in Clarendon and Old Town offer a "comfortable atmosphere" to "get together" with family or friends over "tasty" Italian staples and feel "no pinch when the bill comes"; even if there's "nothing particularly luminous" about the decor, the "can't-be-missed" specials shine (e.g. a $25.25 Monday night special features pizza/salad/wine for two).

Fadó Irish Pub *Irish* | 17 | 21 | 17 | $24 |

Chinatown | 808 Seventh St. NW (bet. H & I Sts.) | 202-789-0066 | www.fadoirishpub.com

"Modeled on a typical Irish pub", these Annapolis and DC "places to gather with friends" (especially for "rugby, footie and a pint") boast a "Dublin feel" thanks to wood paneling, "kitschy" memorabilia and "kicking live music"; service is generally "ok" and the "bar food" is pretty "standard" stuff, but the "perfectly poured" brews compensate; P.S. the Chinatown link is "steps from Verizon Center."

Fahrenheit & Degrees *American* | 22 | 25 | 23 | $60 |

Georgetown | Ritz-Carlton Georgetown | 3100 South St. NW (bet. K & M Sts.) | 202-912-4110 | www.ritzcarlton.com

"Imagine eating in a former incinerator" that's "modern, open and not stuffy" – that's the story at the Georgetown Ritz-Carlton's "cool" dining room, where "quality" New American cuisine and "well-trained" servers have fans wondering why it's not "busier"; foes retort it's "too pricey" for fare that's "not uniformly good enough", but even they agree the place has "unlimited potential"; P.S. the posh Degrees lounge features a 'light fare menu.'

Farmers & Fishers *American* | 18 | 21 | 17 | $39 |

Georgetown | Washington Harbour | 3000 K St. NW (30th St.) | 202-298-0003 | www.farmersandfishers.com

Temporarily closed at press time due to flood damage, this spot in Georgetown's Washington Harbour has fans hoping it reopens soon so they can get their fix of "farm-to-table" American fare featuring "fresh" produce and "excellent" beef (from its North Dakota grower/owners); its "inviting" space – "high ceilings", huge windows, "beautiful long bar" – doesn't always compensate for "pricey" tabs and "kinks in service and inconsistent food", but there's "scenic outdoor seating" and "drinks are amazing, which helps."

Faryab Ⓜ *Afghan* | 23 | 13 | 19 | $31 |

Bethesda | 4917 Cordell Ave. (bet. Norfolk Ave. & Old Georgetown Rd.), MD | 301-951-3484

"Named after an Afghan province", this "family-style" standard-bearer emboldens Bethesda diners – even "timid" ones – to "spice" up their dining "routine" with "kebabs cooked to tender perfection", lamb stews and aushak (raviolis that "rock"); even if the "plain decor" and "uneven service" "don't live up" to the chow, "reasonable prices" make it a real "crowd-pleaser."

NEW Fast Gourmet *Pan-Latin* | - | - | - | I |

U Street Corridor | 1400 W St. NW (14th St.) | 202-448-9217 | www.fast-gourmet.com

Hidden in a working gas station in the U Street Corridor, this new counter-serve has quickly developed a cult following for its cheap, hefty sandwiches – the Uruguayan owners' native *chivito* (meats,

FOOD | DECOR | SERVICE | COST

mozzarella, egg, olives and more on a grilled roll) chief among them – and other Pan-Latin favorites like rotisserie chicken, empanadas and fried plantains; amenities are few – just a few tables and WiFi – but takeout is an option and it's open till 5 AM on weekends.

15 Ria *American*   17 | 17 | 16 | $39

Scott Circle | DoubleTree Hotel | 1515 Rhode Island Ave. NW (15th St.) | 202-742-0015 | www.15ria.com

With a "lovely front terrace [that's] perfect for people-watching", this "solid" Scott Circle American wins praise for chef Janis McLean's "creative" cuisine (including "farm-raised meats"), "lovely brunch" and a "cozy" bar with an extensive bourbon list; still, despite the efforts of a "friendly" staff, some find its DoubleTree digs "a bit off-putting" and the food and service only "decent."

Filomena Ristorante *Italian*   23 | 21 | 22 | $44

Georgetown | 1063 Wisconsin Ave. NW (M St.) | 202-338-8800 | www.filomena.com

"Get the doggy bag ready" – even if you arrive "hungry", the "copious mounds" of "delish" "classics" "efficiently" served at this "old-school Georgetown Italian" (complete with nonna "handmaking pasta in the window") mean there's always leftovers; yeah, "it's touristy" and "overdecorates for every holiday", but it's a "DC favorite, and rightly so"; P.S. bypass "pricey" tabs with the "real-deal" $15.95 Sunday brunch buffet.

Finemondo Ⓢ *Italian*   ▽ 22 | 19 | 20 | $42

Downtown | 1319 F St. NW (bet. 13th & 14th Sts.) | 202-737-3100 | www.finemondo.com

"Eat like you're in Rome" at this open-to-the-street Downtowner with a wood-lined dining room serving "basic" Italian staples "done well"; perhaps the "decor is a little clichéd", but the waiters are "attentive" and there's a "great bar for a quiet chat."

Finn & Porter *Seafood/Steak*   17 | 17 | 17 | $43

Downtown | Embassy Suites Washington DC Convention Ctr. | 900 10th St. NW (K St.) | 202-719-1600

Greater Alexandria | Hilton Alexandria | 5000 Seminary Rd. (Beauregard St.) | Alexandria, VA | 703-379-2346 ◐
www.finnandporter.com

"Surf meets turf" at this hotel-restaurant duo whose "simple" dishes include naturally raised beef, "well-cooked" fish and, in Alexandria, "fresh, good" sushi; service darts between "attentive" and "spotty", meaning the whole enterprise is "nothing earth-shattering", though the Downtown DC location is "convenient to the Convention Center" and Virginia is useful for a "business lunch or after-work drinks."

NEW Fiola Ⓢ *Italian*   - | - | - | M

Penn Quarter | 601 Pennsylvania Ave. NW (entrance on Indiana Ave. bet. 6th & 7th Sts.) | 202-628-2888 | www.fioladc.com

At this much-anticipated Penn Quarter Italian trattoria, chef-owner Fabio Trabocchi offers midpriced, approachable versions of the exquisite cuisine served at his erstwhile Tysons Corner stunner,

Maestro; the beautiful redo of Le Paradou's spacious digs, modeled on a posh Italian villa, boasts dramatic spiral chandeliers, an elegant bar lounge and an alfresco courtyard.

NEW Fiorella Pizzeria e Caffé *Pizza*

| - | - | - | M |

National Harbor | 152 National Plaza (off National Harbor Blvd.), MD | 301-839-1811 | www.fiorellapizzeria.com

As usual for his latest venture – an upscale-rustic pizzeria in National Harbor – impresario Shelly Fireman (of nearby Bond 45) didn't stint on the flash factor: witness the nine-ft. marble Bacchus astride a tortoise, spewing water from its mouth into a sculpted bowl where housemade mozzarella balls gently bob; some 30 varieties of Roman-style (thin-crust) pies are baked in a showpiece, copper-clad imported oven, and a handful of Italian entrees boster the midpriced menu.

Firefly *American*

| 20 | 21 | 19 | $42 |

Dupont Circle | 1310 New Hampshire Ave. NW (N St.) | 202-861-1310 | www.firefly-dc.com

That faux "tree growing in the dining room" ("are we inside? outside?") may "seem a little hokey", but Dupont Circlers have come to "love" it and the rest of this "easygoing" New American; service can be "iffy" and a few deem it a "bit pricey", but chef Daniel Bortnick's "creative" "comfort food" and its "focus on fresh, local ingredients" make most concerns flit away.

Fire Works Pizza *Pizza*

| - | - | - | I |

NEW **Clarendon** | 2350 Clarendon Blvd. (Adams St.) | Arlington, VA | 703-527-8700

Leesburg | 201 Harrison St. SE (Royal St.), VA | 703-779-8400
www.fireworkspizza.com

The talents behind the nearby Tuscarora Mill fitted out a vintage train depot in Leesburg with a wood-fired oven, a stylish bar (incorporating train rails as foot rests) and extensive outdoor seating for this contemporary pizzeria; beer geeks tap into the local brews and bottles on offer, while nearby wineries are also well represented; P.S. a spacious industrial Clarendon sibling recently opened, bringing the wood-fired, oven-baked specialties and microbrews inside the beltway.

☑ Five Guys *Burgers*

| 22 | 9 | 16 | $11 |

Chinatown | 808 H St. NW (bet. 8th & 9th Sts.) | 202-393-2900

Georgetown | 1335 Wisconsin Ave. NW (Dumbarton St.) | 202-337-0400

Bethesda | 4829 Bethesda Ave. (bet. Arlington & Clarendon Rds.), MD | 301-657-0007

Greater Alexandria | 4626 King St. (Beauregard St.) | Alexandria, VA | 703-671-1606

Greater Alexandria | 7622 Richmond Hwy. (Boswell Ave.) | Alexandria, VA | 703-717-0090

Old Town | 107 N. Fayette St. (King St.) | Alexandria, VA | 703-549-7991

Herndon | Fox Mill Ctr. | 2521 John Milton Dr. (Fox Mill Rd.), VA | 703-860-9100

(continued)

(continued)

Five Guys

Springfield | 6541 Backlick Rd. (Old Keene Mill Rd.), VA | 703-913-1337
Manassas | Manassas Corner | 9221 Sudley Rd. (Centerville Rd.),
VA | 703-368-8080
Woodbridge | Marumsco Plaza | 14001 Jefferson Davis Hwy.
(Longview Dr.), VA | 703-492-8882
www.fiveguys.com
Additional locations throughout the DC area

"Juicy, greasy, tasty" burgers "with all the trimmings" "blow away"
the competition according to fans of this "presidential favorite"
(rated Baltimore's No. 1 Bang for the Buck) that's also prized for its
"farm-to-fryer" fries and "free peanuts while you wait"; so even if
doubters "don't get the hype", these "bare-bones" but "cheery"
franchises are "taking the world by storm."

Fleming's Prime Steakhouse &
Wine Bar *Steak*

| 24 | 23 | 24 | $61 |

Tysons Corner | 1960A Chain Bridge Rd. (International Dr.) |
McLean, VA | 703-442-8384 | www.flemingssteakhouse.com

Beef eaters savor the "delicious" steaks, "unique" wines by the glass
and "subdued" ambiance at these "chain-chic" chophouses in
Tysons Corner and Baltimore's Harbor East that offer a "high level of
service", showing impressive "attention to detail" all around; while
the tabs are "prime" too, "seasonal prix fixe menus" are a "recession-
budget treat", and the "affordable happy hour" makes it a "perfect
after-office wind-down spot."

Florida Ave. Grill Ⓜ *Diner*

| 20 | 9 | 20 | $18 |

U Street Corridor | 1100 Florida Ave. NW (11th St.) | 202-265-1586 |
www.floridaavenuegrill.com

The "waitresses are sassy, but your coffee cup never goes empty" at
this U Street Corridor "institution", a "Southern-style" diner slinging
"soul comfort food" like the "best chitlins", "fried chicken and sweet
tea" and pancakes "fluffier than clouds in the sky"; from the "celebrity photos covering the wall" to the "low prices", it's a "flashback to
the '50s" that just "can't be beat."

Flying Fish ❶ *Seafood*

| 19 | 15 | 18 | $40 |

Old Town | 815 King St. (Alfred St.) | Alexandria, VA | 703-600-3474 |
www.flyingfishdc.com

A "lively" vibe permeates this Old Town seafooder, where "freshly
prepared" fin fare is delivered by "witty" waiters (inspired perhaps
by the "kitschy" digs) and the rolls in the downstairs sushi bar are
"creative without being huge and ridiculous"; for party-poopers who
say "boring food" plus "slooow service" equals an "unimpressive"
experience, there's ofton karaoke in the Speakeasy Room.

Fogo De Chão *Brazilian/Steak*

| 24 | 21 | 25 | $59 |

Downtown | 1101 Pennsylvania Ave. NW (11th St.) | 202-347-4668 |
www.fogodechao.com

A "blast" if you're in a "red-meat frenzy", this Brazilian steakhouse
chain (with links in Downtown DC and in Baltimore's Inner Harbor)

proffers skewers laden with "glorious" "hand-carved" cuts that "keep on coming", courtesy of a "fantastic" staff in gaucho get-ups; the "extraordinary" salad bar and "terrific" digs are pluses, but just remember it's an "expensive" all-you-can-eat feast, "so you'd better be hungry"; P.S. "you won't want to see a cow for a year" afterward.

Fojol Bros. of Merlindia ⊅ *Indian* — | — | — | I

Location varies; see website | no phone | www.fojol.com

Music and playful costumes add entertainment value to this Indian-food truck, which offers heaping plates for $6 and $9, plus small-bite offerings and vegetarian options; check Twitter or its website for its location, as it can vary day to day.

Fontaine Caffe & Creperie *French* ▽ 24 | 22 | 22 | $26

Old Town | 119 S. Royal St. (King St.) | Alexandria, VA | 703-535-8151 | www.fontainecaffe.com

Tucked away in Old Town Alexandria, this "tiny", blue-walled French cafe with a few outdoor tables specializes in "imaginative and delicious" savory and sweet crêpes, along with beer, wine and "interesting" Euro ciders (a traditional accompaniment); it's a "lovely place" for a "lunch or a light dinner" when shopping or sightseeing, but "expect a wait at peak periods."

NEW Food Wine & Co. *American* — | — | — | M

Bethesda | 7272 Wisconsin Ave. (bet. Bethesda Ave. & Elm St.), MD | 301-652-8008 | www.foodwineandco.com

The recent arrival of chef Michael Harr (ex Gaylord National Resort) at this neighborhood bistro in Bethesda ups the ambitiousness of its midpriced New American comfort food, which ranges from burgers and pizza to steaks and a raw bar, with craft brews and oodles of wine on hand too; the handsome setting features a huge 18th-century clock from a Parisian train station, wrought-iron chandeliers and tall windows illuminating the warm-toned room.

NEW Ford's Fish Shack *Seafood* — | — | — | M

Ashburn | Ice Rink Plaza | 44260 Ice Rink Plaza (Farmwell Rd., west of Smith Switch Rd.), VA | 571-918-4092 | www.fordsfishshack.com

Lobster pots, buoys and murals depicting shoreside vistas lend a breezy allure to this New England–themed seafood shack land-locked in an Ashburn mall; its family-friendly vibe and moderately priced menu featuring crab cakes, lobster rolls, fried clams and fish have hooked the locals, so go early or call ahead to avoid a wait.

Fortune *Chinese* 20 | 10 | 15 | $23

Falls Church | Seven Corners Ctr. | 6249 Arlington Blvd. (Wilson Blvd.), VA | 703-538-3333

This "enormous" Seven Corners banquet hall is "noisy, chaotic" and "tired" looking, but Sinophiles "aren't here for the ambiance" – they're here for the "daily dim sum", featuring "cart after cart of heavenly delights"; there's a seafood-heavy Cantonese menu at night, but regulars stick to those midpriced "bits of Chinese food", "setting aside part of each plate for take-home."

	FOOD	DECOR	SERVICE	COST

Foti's ☒ *American* ▽ 26 | 21 | 24 | $51

Culpeper | 219 E. Davis St. (East St.), VA | 540-829-8400 |
www.fotisrestaurant.com

Locally sourced "quality ingredients" go into the "delicious, creative" New American fare at this "out-of-town gem" from Inn at
Little Washington alum Frank Maragos, an "upscale" Culpeper "surprise" awash in brick walls, statuary and mahogany tables; the Med-
accented cuisine may be "more accessible" than the bistro itself, but
it's "worth the drive" for an experience that's "right up there with the
best at half the price"; P.S. it's also closed Tuesday.

☒ Founding Farmers *American* 21 | 21 | 18 | $37

World Bank | IMF Bldg. | 1924 Pennsylvania Ave. NW (20th St.) |
202-822-8783 | www.wearefoundingfarmers.com

At this "hopping", farmer-owned roost in the IMF building, "eco-
friendly" "modern design" – think "exposed wood beams" and big
glass windows – sets the stage for an "expansive menu" of "affordable" American "comfort food" with a "hipster Southern" twist
(e.g. "must-try" bacon lollipops); "creative cocktails" and a "notori-
ously busy" brunch add appeal, but unimpressed sorts who dis
"snail-slow service" and "hit-or-miss" eats feel it's "suffering from
instant success" and wonder "why is everyone here?"; P.S. look for a
Potomac, MD, offshoot later in 2011.

Four Sisters *Vietnamese* 25 | 20 | 22 | $29

Merrifield | Merrifield Town Ctr. | 8190 Strawberry Ln. (bet. Gallows Rd. &
Lee Hwy.), VA | 703-539-8566 | www.foursistersrestaurant.com

Firmly ensconced in its "bigger" and "more elegant" Merrifield Town
Center digs, this "best-in-class" Vietnamese continues to proffer an
"overwhelming menu" of "outstanding" pan-regional fare, all executed with "precision and flair" using "spices and marinades that lift
flavors to cosmic dimensions"; the "beautiful" flowers and "hospitable" staff remain as well, prompting partisans to proclaim "the girls
still got it!"

Franklin's *Pub Food* 18 | 19 | 20 | $23

Hyattsville | 5123 Baltimore Ave. (Gallatin St.), MD | 301-927-2740 |
www.franklinsbrewery.com

"For a bit of fun or a bite to eat", this "brightly colored" Hyattsville
haven set in a "refurbished hardware store" is hard to beat, what
with its "ever-changing" menu of "basic" pub-grub fare and "interesting" "house-brewed beer"; the "best part": its "hoot" of a "general store", where "you'll spend all the money you saved on dinner"
on toys, gag gifts and other tchotchkes.

☒☒☒ Freddy's Lobster & Clams *Seafood* – | – | – | I

Bethesda | 4867 Cordell Ave. (bet. Old Georgetown Rd. &
Woodmont Ave.), MD | 240-743-4257 | www.freddyslobster.com

Chef Jeff Heineman coaxes lobsters out of the tank and into rolls
and stews (though not the deep fryer – that's reserved for clams,
Maine shrimp and fish) at this inexpensive Bethesda seafooder that
opened next-door to his American place, Grapeseed; New England

	FOOD	DECOR	SERVICE	COST

fish-shack trappings bedeck the large space, which also includes a bar and patio.

🆕 Fruit Bat ⑤Ⓜ *Pan-Latin* | - | - | - | I |

Atlas District | 1236 H St. NE (bet. 12th & 13th Sts.) | 202-399-2323 | www.dcfruitbat.com

This cheerfully colored, *pequeño* H Street bar specializes in BYOC (that's build-your-own cocktails) plus a *pequeñito* menu of tasty Central and South American street bites; its digs have a fresh feel courtesy of hanging fruit baskets, tropical ferns sprouting from the walls and herbs growing in pots behind the bar, which weekly rotates its list of infusions, such as watermelon-thyme tequila and pineapple-cardamom rum.

Full Kee ● *Chinese* | 22 | 7 | 15 | $19 |

Chinatown | 509 H St. NW (bet. 5th & 6th Sts.) | 202-371-2233 | www.fullkeedc.com

"Order the unusual" at this Chinatown "ducks-in-the-window" "humble star" – though it's known for "wonderful" Hong Kong dumpling soup and noodle dishes, there's a "wider menu" of "mouthwatering" meats, including innards, and "delicious" vegetables (ask about the "daily specials" listed on the wall in Chinese); the decor may be "bare-bones", but the "taste and the price are both very right"; P.S. the same-named Falls Church eatery is under separate ownership.

Full Kee ● *Chinese* | 22 | 11 | 17 | $21 |

Falls Church | 5830 Columbia Pike (Leesburg Pike), VA | 703-575-8232

Assuming the decor doesn't "scare you away", you're in for "some of the best Cantonese food around" at this Falls Church standby "packed" with the local "Asian community"; while it helps to "know your way around a Chinese menu" ("the more unusual the dish, the better your experience"), "helpful" staffers and "affordable" prices ensure it's always a "cut above" – and it's even "open late"; P.S. the Chinatown eatery of the same name is under separate ownership.

Full Key ● *Chinese* | 21 | 8 | 15 | $20 |

Wheaton | Wheaton Manor Shopping Ctr. | 2227 University Blvd. W. (bet. Amherst & Georgia Aves.), MD | 301-933-8388

From "homestyle" noodle soups and fresh seafood to "rich roast meats, bright greens" and hot pots, there's "full-filling" fare in an "incredible mix of flavors" to be had at this "Hong Kong–dominant" Chinese in Wheaton, though be sure to check out the "authentic" specialties rather than settle for the menu's "ubiquitous American-Chinese dishes"; if its "drab" quarters and "taciturn" servers "hark back "decades past", so do its prices.

FunXion ⑤ *American* | - | - | - | I |

Downtown | 1309 F St. (bet. 13th & 14th Sts.) | 202-386-9466 | www.funxion.com

At this ultramod Downtown juice bar, health-conscious (salt- and oil-free) renditions of pizza, burgers and tuna melts are ordered at a counter and then enjoyed at perches along a colorful wall, or taken

FOOD · DECOR · SERVICE · COST

upstairs to a loungey, LED-lit balcony; at night the scene morphs into DysFunxion, where the menu is accompanied by cocktails mixed with exotic, housemade juices and a DJ spinning on Thursday, Friday and Saturday nights.

Fu Shing Cafe *Chinese*

| 21 | 12 | 13 | $18 |

Bethesda | 10315 Westlake Dr. (Lakeview Dr.), MD | 301-469-8878
Gaithersburg | 576 N. Frederick Ave. (Lakeforest Blvd.), MD | 301-330-8484
www.fushingcafebethesda.com

"Recommended" by Chinese "friends" for their "authentic", "low-cost" noodle dishes, soups, hot pots and Taiwanese-style dim sum, these unprepossessing eateries "hidden away" in Gaithersburg and Bethesda contrast "white tablecloths" with an "order-at-the-counter" drill; there's "virtually no service" and fewer "friendly" smiles, but that's probably "why they do so much takeout."

Fyve *American*

| ▽ 17 | 15 | 19 | $55 |

Pentagon City | Ritz-Carlton Pentagon City | 1250 S. Hayes St. (bet. Army-Navy Dr. & 15th St.) | Arlington, VA | 703-412-2760 | www.ritzcarlton.com

Something of a "secret", this "small" Ritz-Carlton resto-lounge named for the nearby Pentagon offers an "understated" contemporary setting and "solid service" for all-day, bistro-style American dining, while its lounge (complete with fireplace) hosts a "busy bar scene"; a post-Survey chef change and menu reboot outdates the Food score, although given the brand's reputation, visitors can expect "good" things.

NEW Galileo III 🈺 *Italian*

| - | - | - | E |

Downtown | 600 14th St. NW (bet. F & G Sts.) | 202-783-0083 | www.galileorestaurant.com

This long-awaited third incarnation of Roberto Donna's sophisticated Italian resides in a stunning Downtown space with an intimate, Tuscan-toned downstairs dining room and an elegant curved bar looking out on the street (plus a private-events balcony); bargain trattoria-style dishes are served at the bar, while dinner choices consist of à la carte, prix fixes (two to four courses) or the revived 'laboratorio' – the extreme multicourse (12–15) blowout for a dozen or so guests.

Georgia Brown's *Southern*

| 22 | 20 | 21 | $44 |

Downtown | 950 15th St. NW (bet. I & K Sts.) | 202-393-4499 | www.georgiabrowns.com

"They stuff you" with "overwhelming" portions of "fancy" "Southern fixin's" at this Downtown "power spot" known for its "lively atmosphere" and "off-da-hook" Sunday jazz brunch "deal" – "eat everything on the buffet", then "get an entree to go"; a few fuss the "crowded" dining room would benefit from an "update", but at least with tables so "close together" you might get some "political gossip" (it's a "hop and skip" from the White House).

	FOOD	DECOR	SERVICE	COST

Geranio *Italian*
22 | 20 | 22 | $47

Old Town | 722 King St. (bet. Columbus & Washington Sts.) | Alexandria, VA | 703-548-0088 | www.geranio.net

A "quaint" Old Town "fixture" since 1976, this "teeny jewel" is a "warm" Italian "oasis" (particularly "with the fire going") featuring "unobtrusive" staffers who serve "ample portions" of "consistently good" fare; vets recommend the "specials", while bean-counters who welcome the "chance to get away from impersonal chains" pounce on its dinner deal "before 7 PM and after 9:30."

Good Fortune *Chinese*
18 | 11 | 16 | $20

Wheaton | 2646 University Blvd. W. (bet. Georgia Ave. & Veirs Mill Rd.), MD | 301-929-8818

At this "old-time" Wheaton Chinese, expect "instant gratification" from the "rolling carts full of little dumplings" at its "tasty" weekend dim sum; while a few fortune-finders fret over a "regular" Cantonese menu that's just "ok", "brusque service" and decor that's "showing its age", loyalists insist "good prices" make it "worth the inconvenience."

Good Stuff Eatery ⊠ *Burgers*
21 | 13 | 15 | $15

Capitol Hill | 303 Pennsylvania Ave. SE (bet. 3rd & 4th Sts.) | 202-543-8222 | www.goodstuffeatery.com

"Juicy" patties get dressed up with the condiment bar's "unparalleled" array of "innovative" fixin's at *Top Chef* also-ran Spike Mendelsohn's "trendy" counter-serve "burger joint"; sure, it's a "zoo at mealtimes" with "Cap Hill staffers" lining up "around the block", but partisans promise the "fries done right", "phenomenal" milkshakes (toasted marshmallow is "what dreams are made of") and a chance to see a "celebrity who isn't in elected office" are "worth the wait" and "splurge."

Granville Moore's *American/Belgian*
23 | 17 | 18 | $27

Atlas District | 1238 H St. NE (bet. 12th & 13th Sts.) | 202-399-2546 | www.granvillemoores.com

The burgeoning Atlas District holds bragging rights to one of the "coolest places in town": this former doctor's office turned New American–Belgian gastropub boasting "fantastic mussels and fries" and "phenomenal" beers; it's "snug", so "good luck getting a table on weekend nights", but those in the know simply "sit at the bar" and trade tales with the "knowledgeable" suds-slingers while checking out the "dingy, dark and utterly real" digs.

Grapeseed ⊠ *American*
21 | 17 | 20 | $49

Bethesda | 4865 Cordell Ave. (bet. Norfolk & Woodmont Aves.), MD | 301-986-9592 | www.grapeseedbistro.com

"Go small plate, entree or mix-and-match" at this "chic" Bethesda New American where food and vino "pairings" recommended by "knowledgeable" staffers are a "wine lover's dream come true"; though the "white-tablecloth" "experience" can be "quite pricey", there are "excellent deals" to be had (especially at lunch), and a recently added chef's table offers a "great view" of the "open kitchen."

	FOOD	DECOR	SERVICE	COST

Green Papaya *Vietnamese*   19 | 19 | 18 | $32

Bethesda | 4922 Elm St. (Arlington Rd.), MD | 301-654-8986 |
www.greenpapayamd.com

Pho-natics "look for excuses to go to Bethesda" so they can savor
the "irresistable" (and "reasonably priced") carmelized sea bass,
"soul-warming" noodle dishes and other "skillfully prepared"
Vietnamese offerings at this "gem"; while a few sniff about "spotty"
service, most appreciate having this "suburban alternative" around
and dig its "calming" vibe, abetted by a waterfall behind the bar.

Grille, The *American*   23 | 21 | 24 | $50

Old Town | Morrison House | 116 S. Alfred St. (bet. King & Prince Sts.) |
Alexandria, VA | 703-838-8000 | www.morrisonhouse.com

"Hidden half a block from all the action" in an Old Town hotel, this
"elegant" New American – which presents "exquisitely prepared"
Virginia-accented dishes "in an atmosphere befitting the
Rockefellers" (with service to match) – feels like a "best-kept secret"; a "small, upscale bar" and live music make it a "nice place to
linger", even if some consider it a "touch pricey."

Grillfish *Seafood*   18 | 17 | 19 | $37

West End | 1200 New Hampshire Ave. NW (M St.) | 202-331-7310 |
www.grillfishdc.com

"You can actually taste the fish" at this West End seafooder whose
"simple", "not-smothered-in-sauce" approach to "fresh" entrees
"still works" though faultfinders label the fin fare "inconsistent"; the
"stuck-in-the-'90s" decor got a minor touch-up but remains largely
unchanged, but the sidewalk terrace with "great people-watching"
and happy hour "no one knows about" are bonuses.

Grill from Ipanema *Brazilian*   20 | 18 | 20 | $36

Adams Morgan | 1858 Columbia Rd. NW (Belmont Rd.) | 202-986-0757 |
www.thegrillfromipanema.com

Travel "back to the beaches of Rio" via this "friendly" Adams
Morgan Brazilian whose "fabulous moqueca" ("Bahia-style seafood
stew") "makes the mouth mambo" and "potent" caipirinhas evoke
"Carnivale at night"; amigos dig the "perfectly serviceable" staff and
expanded space, even if party-poopers pout its "name is cuter than
the food"; P.S. wallet-watchers are drawn to the "fabulous" three-
course brunch ($18.95).

Guajillo *Mexican*   22 | 15 | 18 | $25

Courthouse | 1727 Wilson Blvd. (bet. Quinn & Rhodes Sts.) |
Arlington, VA | 703-807-0840 | www.guajillogrill.com

"Quality chips and salsa with a kick" greet guests at this "lively",
brightly hued Arlington Courthouse–area cantina where the
"well-priced" Mexican *comida* "goes far beyond tacos and burritos" (look for "authentic" "Oaxacan-style" dishes topped in
"standout mole" sauce) and the margaritas pack a "punch"; it's
"small", "often crowded" and service can be "haphazard", but the
"delicious" grub "you'll be busy stuffing into your face" is "worth
the weekend wait."

	FOOD	DECOR	SERVICE	COST

Guardado's ⓜ *Pan-Latin/Spanish*   24 | 16 | 25 | $31

Bethesda | 4918 Del Ray Ave. (bet. Norfolk Ave. & Old Georgetown Rd.), MD | 301-986-4920 | www.guardadosnico.com

"Become part of the extended family" at chef Nicolas Jose Guardado's "cozy little place" nestled on a "quiet" Bethesda side street, where "superb", "generously sized" Spanish-Latin tapas "make it easy" to have an "excellent" meal and "not spend a fortune"; indeed, when diners "get personal attention from the owner", "cramped" seating and dull "decor aren't so important", thus many "intend to return."

Haad Thai *Thai*   20 | 14 | 17 | $24

Downtown | 1100 New York Ave. NW (bet. 11th & 12th Sts.) | 202-682-1111 | www.haadthairestaurant.com

Budget-minded lunchers and the "working-late crowd" converge on this "busy" Downtown Thai for "reliable" fare at "low prices"; expect to "weave your way" through a midday "crowd" to get your takeout, though "fast service" means you don't have to stick around in the "plain" digs too long.

Haandi *Indian*   24 | 17 | 21 | $30

Bethesda | 4904 Fairmont Ave. (Norfolk Ave.), MD | 301-718-0121
Falls Church | Falls Plaza Shopping Ctr. | 1222 W. Broad St. (Gordon Rd.), VA | 703-533-3501
www.haandi.com

Having "stood the test of time", these "reasonably priced" Falls Church and Bethesda subcontinentals still get "as crowded as Calcutta", and "with good reason": "you can't order a bad dish here", from "well-seasoned entrees" that are "flavorful without being overpowering" to "delicious breads"; if the decor is "nothing special", grazers at the "excellent" lunch buffet (a "bargain") are usually too busy "holding in their guts" to notice.

Hama Sushi *Japanese*   ∇ 19 | 17 | 18 | $28

Herndon | Village Center at Dulles | 2415 Centreville Rd. (Sunrise Valley Dr.), VA | 703-713-0088 | www.hama-sushi.com

"Surprisingly good sushi" in Herndon (aka "the outer 'burbs") earns this "little" strip-mall Japanese "lots of loyal customers" who praise the "consistently fine quality" of its fin fare and "long list of salads"; the traditional decor features a landscape mural, and there's a tatami room that's useful for small parties.

Hank's Oyster Bar *American/Seafood*   24 | 16 | 20 | $38

Dupont Circle | 1624 Q St. NW (bet. 16th & 17th Sts.) | 202-462-4265
Old Town | 1026 King St. (bet. Henry & Patrick Sts.) | Alexandria, VA | 703-739-4265 ⓜ
www.hanksrestaurants.com

They "take their seafood seriously" at this "peppy" Old Town/Dupont duo serving up everything from "perfect oysters" and "meaty fried clams" to "authentic lobster rolls" that transport Down East transplants "back to Maine"; exuding a "casual", "staff-in-bluejeans" vibe that belies "somewhat high prices", they're a welcome "breath of fresh (salty) air" in these parts; P.S. the Old Town location remains "small" and "crowded", but a major expansion to be completed in July 2011 will double Dupont's size and add a bar, lounge and private-dining space.

Hank's Tavern & Eats *American*   ▽ 22 | 15 | 16 | $28

Hyattsville | University Town Ctr. | 6507 America Blvd. (bet. Adelphi Rd. & E. West Hwy.), MD | 301-209-0573 | www.hankseats.com

"Step up" to this young American pub in Hyattsville's University Town Center, where the "drinks are plentiful" and the "burgers are tall, well-endowed" and come with a side for only $6.99 at the 50-ft. bar during happy hour; add in multiple TVs, "nice" outdoor seating and a staff that "handles groups well", and most proclaim they're "happy it opened in H-ville."

Hard Times Cafe *American*   19 | 13 | 18 | $18

Bethesda | 4920 Del Ray Ave. (bet. Norfolk Ave. & Old Georgetown Rd.), MD | 301-951-3300

Germantown | 13032 Middlebrook Rd. (Century Blvd.), MD | 240-686-0150 ◑

College Park | 4738 Cherry Hill Rd. (Baltimore Ave.), MD | 301-474-8880

Rockville | Woodley Gdns. | 1117 Nelson St. (Montgomery Ave.), MD | 301-294-9720

Old Town | 1404 King St. (West St.) | Alexandria, VA | 703-837-0050

Clarendon | 3028 Wilson Blvd. (Highland St.), VA | 703-528-2233 ◑

Fairfax | 4069 Chain Bridge Rd. (Sager Ave.), VA | 703-267-9590 ◑

Springfield | Springfield Plaza | 6362 Springfield Plaza (Commerce St.), VA | 703-913-5600 ◑

Manassas | 7753 Sudley Rd. (bet. Broken Branch Ln. & Sudley Manor Dr.), VA | 703-365-8400 ◑

Woodbridge | Potomac Festival Plaza | 14389 Potomac Mills Rd. (bet. Opitz Blvd. & Potomac Mills Rd.), VA | 703-492-2950 ◑ www.hardtimes.com

Additional locations throughout the DC area

"Well-flavored chili" and "cheap beer" make "hard times easier" at these "family-friendly" "roadhouses", where the "generous" bowls of red – in four varieties, including "Cincinnati-style" and "spicy vegetarian" – come with "homemade cornbread", à la carte "fixin's" and "low prices"; service is generally "friendly and helpful", but cowpokes can't agree on whether the "pseudo-Texas decor" is "one-horse-town" "tacky" or just plain "fun."

Harry's Tap Room *Seafood/Steak*   19 | 19 | 19 | $34

Clarendon | Marketplace Commons | 2800 Clarendon Blvd. (Fillmore St.), VA | 703-778-7788 | www.harrystaproom.com

Harry's Smokehouse *BBQ/Burgers*

Pentagon City | The Fashion Centre at Pentagon City | 1100 S. Hayes St. (Army Navy Dr.) | Arlington, VA | 703-416-7070 | www.harryssmokehouse.com

At this "go-to" grill in Clarendon, guests "semi-splurge" on "one of the best brunches around" and a "crowd-pleasing" lunch-dinner menu of "solid" surf 'n' turf; "attentive" staffers can get "overwhelmed" in the "inviting", clubby bi-level space, but "mosh pit"–

like happy hours with "great food" make tipplers wild about it; P.S. post-Survey, the Pentagon City branch changed its name, signaling its brand-new, more affordable menu of house-smoked 'cue, burgers and homey all-American sides.

NEW Härth *American*   - | - | - | M

Tysons Corner | Hilton McLean Tysons Corner | 7920 Jones Branch Dr. (Westpark Dr.) | McLean, VA | 703-847-5000 | www.harthrestaurant.com

An aromatic wood-burning oven is the centerpiece of this Tysons Corner New American serving midpriced, updated comfort fare and a drinks list focused on regional beers and wines; ensconced in the newly renovated Hilton, it's a study in casual elegance, done up with polished wood and eggplant hues, and featuring working stone fireplaces and an on-site terrace garden that provides herbs for the kitchen.

Hee Been *Korean*   20 | 14 | 17 | $29

Greater Alexandria | 6231 Little River Tpke. (Beauregard St.) | Alexandria, VA | 703-941-3737 | www.heebeen.com

An "unbelievable variety" of Korean BBQ "cooked at the table", plus sushi and traditional dishes available from an "incredible" buffet or off a menu, makes this Alexandria Asian a "good" choice "if you're new" to the cuisine; though the glass-and-wood setting is "lacking", meals represent a decent "value", especially during the bargain-priced 'cue special starting at 10 PM.

Heights, The *American*   19 | 19 | 18 | $37

Columbia Heights | Kenyon Sq. | 3115 14th St. NW (Kenyon St.) | 202-797-7227 | www.theheightsdc.com

A "see-and-be-seen spot" for the "Columbia Heights 'in' crowd", this "quintessential neighborhood" American aims for "basic fare at fair prices"; while fans who enjoy "casual meals" in "friendly" surroundings (soaring ceilings, huge windows, "pleasant patio") say it's "improved a lot", contrarians counter it still "misses the mark", tapping "boring" chow and "unreliable" service.

NEW Heritage Asia *SE Asian*   - | - | - | M

Glover Park | 2400 Wisconsin Ave. NW, 2nd fl. (Calvert St.) | 202-333-9006 | www.heritageindiausa.com

This new spiffy spin-off of Heritage India, which shares an entrance with its sibling in Glover Park, travels east into Southern Asian cuisine, offering traditional Thai, Vietnamese and Malaysian dishes alongside subcontinental fare; its second-story setting is warmed with saffron and sienna colors, and features inviting perches at the front bar.

Heritage India *Indian*   22 | 19 | 19 | $36

Dupont Circle | 1337 Connecticut Ave. NW (bet. Dupont Circle & N St.) | 202-331-1414

Glover Park | 2400 Wisconsin Ave. NW (Calvert St.) | 202-333-3120 www.heritageindiausa.com

"Rich, fragrant" Indian food and "upscale" surroundings are the hallmarks of this subcontinental duo with their own personalities: the

| | FOOD | DECOR | SERVICE | COST |

"more adventurous" Dupont outpost specializes in "small plates and 'street food'", "great" happy-hour deals and a lunch-buffet "bargain", while "calmer" Glover Park is known for its "outstanding" curries ("ask for specials not on the menu"); less predictable is the service, which ranges from "friendly" to "contentious."

NEW Hill Country *BBQ*

| - | - | - | M |

Penn Quarter | 410 Seventh St. NW (bet. D & E Sts.) | 202-556-2050 | www.hillcountrywdc.com

Just a lasso toss from Verizon Center, this new, midpriced NYC import pays tribute to legendary Lone Star State meat markets – diners get a meal ticket, hit the serving stations where butchers hand-cut (and weigh) their choices and eat at rustic tables in the street-level dining room; the rollicking space is done up with brick, reclaimed wood and photos of iconic 'cue palaces, and there's live music Tuesday–Saturday evenings in the downstairs honky-tonk.

Himalayan Heritage *Indian/Nepalese*

| 22 | 18 | 21 | $25 |

Adams Morgan | 2305 18th St. NW (Kalorama Rd.) | 202-483-9300 | www.himalayanheritagedc.com

"Even the timid" find fare to savor at this "affordable" Adams Morgan trailblazer serving up "intriguing" Indo-Nepalese dishes "bursting with exotic flavor" and prepped with a "wide range of spices", including "tasty" momos (stuffed dumplings); decorated with native artifacts, it's "cramped yet somehow more cozy than annoying", making it ideal for a "special meal with that special someone."

Hinode *Japanese*

| 19 | 14 | 19 | $30 |

Bethesda | 4914 Hampden Ln. (bet. Arlington Rd. & Woodmont Ave.), MD | 301-654-0908
Rockville | 134 Congressional Ln. (bet. Jefferson St. & Rockville Pike), MD | 301-816-2190
www.hinode-restaurant.com

They're "by no means elegant", but this "family-friendly" Maryland trio is lauded by locals who count on its "solid" sushi, "basic Japanese comfort food" and "bargain" lunch buffet (Bethesda and Rockville); "accommodating" servers make up for decor deficiencies, though the newer Frederick branch "on the creek" has a "good ambiance" and outdoor seating.

Hollywood East Cafe ◉ *Chinese*

| - | - | - | I |

(aka Hollywood East on the Boulevard)

Wheaton | Westfield Shoppingtown | 11160 Veirs Mill Rd. (University Blvd. W.), MD | 240-290-9988 | www.hollywoodeastcafe.com

A beacon for budget-minded Chinese food lovers, this longtime Wheaton favorite reopened in 2010 in new digs – think a sea of red, black and silver in an industrial-modern setting with a bar – inside a sprawling mall; the extensive menu still offers Hong Kong–style dishes with plenty of chef specialties, accompanied by the restaurant's well-regarded dim sum served daily starting at 10 AM on weekends and 11 AM weekdays.

	FOOD	DECOR	SERVICE	COST

☑ Honey Pig Gooldaegee Korean Grill ◑ *Korean* (aka Seoul Gool Dae Gee)

| 26 | 12 | 17 | $24 |

Annandale | 7220C Columbia Pike (Maple Pl.), VA | 703-256-5229

"Gastronomic delights" and a "crazy atmosphere collide" in Annandale at this Korean BBQ "joint", a "24/7" "hoot" whose "cheap, tasty" fare – including "fantastic" grilled meats and deep-fried dishes – takes your mind off the "blaringly loud music" and "funky" decor ("advertising posters" and "sparse tables" in a "warehouse" setting); even if "efficient" servers seem "gruff" to sensitive sorts, most everyone's "gotta go back to see the Pig!"; P.S. there's a newer outpost in Ellicott City.

Hook *American/Seafood*

| 23 | 20 | 21 | $52 |

Georgetown | 3241 M St. NW (bet. Potomac St. & Wisconsin Ave.) | 202-625-4488 | www.hookdc.com

Georgetown "fishophiles" take the bait at this "eco-friendly" New American seafooder with a commitment to "sustainable" fin fare, with chef changes charting a more mainstream course for the menu; "knowledgeable" servers patrol the "unpretentious" space with "minimalist decor matching the simplicity of the preparations", if not the "dining-in-a-palace" prices.

Hooked *Seafood*

| 19 | 17 | 13 | $42 |

Sterling | Potomac Run Ctr. | 46240 Potomac Run Plaza (Cascades Pkwy. & Rte. 7), VA | 703-421-0404 | www.hookedonseafood.com

When this Sterling seafooder swam to a larger, fancier pond in fall 2009, it gained a glitzy, modern dining room and bar (not fully reflected in the Decor rating) and a bit of "noise"; indeed, some are still hooked on the "excellent sushi", but finicky fin fans who fear "success [may] have gone to its head" find it "overpriced" for the "quality of service and food."

Horace & Dickie's Seafood Carryout *Seafood*

| ▽ 24 | 4 | 17 | $14 |

Atlas District | 809 12th St. NE (H St.) | 202-397-6040 | www.horaceanddickies.com

"Eat like a king for less than $10" at this carry-out "hole-in-the-wall" near the Atlas District, where the "delicious fried fish" and "down-home" sides (mac 'n' cheese, collards) come in portions "so generous" customers "routinely make two meals from one platter"; true, "long lines" and zero ambiance "could be a turnoff", but "sweet-as-pie" staffers and "one of DC's best deals" make it anything but.

NEW Hot 'N Juicy Crawfish *Cajun/Creole*

| - | - | - | I |

Woodley Park | 2651 Connecticut Ave. (bet. Calvert St. & Woodley Rd.) | 202-299-9448 | www.hotandjuicycrawfish.com

Eatin' is a messy, hands-on business at this cheap new Woodley Park Cajun-Creole saloon, which explains why the tables are covered with plastic and guests are outfitted with bibs and paper towels; its namesake specialty comes with an assortment of spicy, garlicky sauces (you can also opt for head-on shrimp), and accompaniments include french fries and beer.

H Street Country Club *Tex-Mex* | 15 | 20 | 16 | $29 |

Atlas District | 1335 H St. NE (bet. 13th & 14th Sts.) | 202-399-4722 | www.hstreetcountryclub.com

"Even the most staid Capitol Hill staffers feel like hipsters" at this "cool" Tex-Mex bringing "spice to H Street's sexy revival"; the fare is "hit-and-miss" and tabs can be a "little pricey", but "Skee-Ball", shuffleboard and indoor mini-golf with "whimsical holes poking fun at DC" are "kitschy" crowd-pleasers, prompting partisans to proclaim the "good drinks" and "games are the main attraction here."

Hudson ● *American* | 17 | 19 | 18 | $43 |

West End | 2030 M St. NW (21st St.) | 202-872-8700 | www.hudson-dc.com

An "attractive room" and "happening bar" draw West End explorers to this "trendy" New American that's "perfect for a business lunch" or Sunday brunch but gets "more action at night" since it stays up late; a few find it "expensive for what it's serving" – everything from pizza and fried chicken to grilled fish and steak.

Hunan Dynasty *Chinese* | 17 | 13 | 18 | $28 |

Capitol Hill | 215 Pennsylvania Ave. SE, 2nd fl. (bet. C St. & Independence Ave.) | 202-546-6161 | www.hunandynastydc.com

"They get the job done quick" at this second-floor Chinese that's been catering to Capitol Hill types for 30 years; if civilians with more exotic tastes vote down "ordinary" cooking that's a "little timid" and "inconsistent service", there are "fair prices for the location."

Hunan Manor *Chinese* | 21 | 18 | 20 | $25 |

Burtonsville | 15504 Old Columbia Pike (Spencerville Rd.), MD | 301-476-9638
Silver Spring | White Oak Shopping Ctr. | 11237 New Hampshire Ave. (Columbia Pike), MD | 301-681-5360
www.hunanmanorrestaurant.com
See review in the Baltimore Directory.

Hunter's Head Tavern *British* | ▽ 23 | 24 | 20 | $33 |

Upperville | 9048 John Mosby Hwy./Rte. 50 (Parker St.), VA | 540-592-9020 | www.huntersheadtavern.com

Fish 'n' chip chompers head to the country for "pleasurable" British pub eats and a "Guinness to wash it down" at this "delightful, historic" destination outside Upperville; "summer or winter", there's a "terrific atmosphere" in its "cozy", log-cabin–like dining room or on the patio, though it's easier to "enjoy" if you "know the drill" (i.e. "order at the counter" and servers deliver it to you).

Huong Viet ⊅ *Vietnamese* | 22 | 8 | 19 | $20 |

Falls Church | Eden Ctr. | 6785 Wilson Blvd. (bet. Arlington & Roosevelt Blvds.), VA | 703-538-7110 | www.huong-viet.com

Don't forget to "stop by the ATM" en route to this "cash-only" "best-kept secret" in the Eden Center, but "cheap" prices for an "extensive menu" of "wonderful" Vietnamese fare (e.g. "great pho", grilled specialties, "noodle dishes") mean you won't have to drain your account; there's not much atmosphere, but the staff is "cordial" and it's in an Asian shopping complex that's interesting to explore.

iCi Urban Bistro *American*   ▽ 23 | 21 | 21 | $53

Downtown | Sofitel Lafayette Sq. | 806 15th St. NW (bet. H & I Sts.) | 202-730-8700 | www.iciurbanbistro.com

Tucked into the Sofitel Lafayette Square, this "quiet little" American bistro rolls out a "diverse" menu of "well-prepared seafood", salads, sandwiches and haute pastries with a French twist; service gets mixed marks ("great" vs. "snotty"), but a "beautiful space" replete with contemporary artwork and plush leather chairs makes it a "pleasant" choice for a midpriced repast after visiting Le Bar, the adjacent "up-tempo" watering hole.

Il Canale *Italian/Pizza*   - | - | - | M

Georgetown | 1063 31st St. NW (M St.) | 202-337-4444 | www.ilcanaledc.com

In a Georgetown townhouse off the C&O Canal, this midpriced Italian serves authentic pizza baked in an imported wood-burning oven by Neapolitan pizzaioli, plus pastas and fish and meat specialties dispensed from an open kitchen; the setting includes a modern, neon-lit bar, tables upstairs with views of the street scene below and a seasonal rooftop terrace offering romantic dining under the stars.

Il Fornaio *Italian*   21 | 19 | 19 | $40

Reston | Reston Town Ctr. | 11990 Market St. (bet. Reston & St. Francis Pkwys.), VA | 703-437-5544 | www.ilfornaio.com

Loyalists "love the bread" and "creative" pastas at this "simple" but "civilized" Italian chain link in Reston that "tries and often succeeds in serving authentic fare with monthly regional specials"; though some say service is "not consistent" and find the food "unremarkable", the "attractive" environs help support its "almost-gourmet prices."

Il Pizzico 🗷 *Italian*   26 | 16 | 22 | $41

Rockville | Suburban Park | 15209 Frederick Rd. (Gude Dr.), MD | 301-309-0610 | www.ilpizzico.com

What "looks like a pizza joint" in a Rockville strip plaza is actually "one of the best Italian restaurants" around, with "homemade pasta" that's "close to a religious experience" and "deftly done" seasonal dishes; given the "friendly" vibe, it's no surprise "regulars are greeted with two kisses to the cheeks", but it's the "excellent food at an even better price" that keeps it "crowded."

India Palace Bar & Tandoor *Indian*   - | - | - | I

Germantown | Fox Chapel Shopping Ctr. | 19743 Frederick Rd. (Gunners Branch Rd.), MD | 301-540-3000 | www.indiapalacegermantown.com

Despite its un-palatial strip-mall digs in Germantown, subcontinental connoisseurs swear "this is the place to go for fine Indian cuisine"; bonus: its lunch buffet ($10.95 weekdays, $12.95 weekends) offers "great value", plus you can "try a little of everything."

Indique *Indian*
23 | 21 | 21 | $37

Cleveland Park | 3512-14 Connecticut Ave. NW (bet. Ordway & Porter Sts.) | 202-244-6600 | www.indique.com

Indique Heights *Indian*
Chevy Chase | 2 Wisconsin Circle (Western Ave.), MD | 301-656-4822 | www.indiqueheights.com

"Wonderful" flavors "take Indian food to new places" at these "affordable" Cleveland Park and Chevy Chase sibs; "stylish" decor, "rural" dishes like lamb shank bhana and "knockout" tamarind margaritas make the bi-level DC venue a "lovely spot for a date", while the "serene" Maryland outpost offers "standout" Thalis, "street food done with class" and a lunch buffet that works well for "groups."

☑ Inn at Little Washington *American*
29 | 28 | 29 | $145

Washington | Inn at Little Washington | 309 Middle St. (Main St.), VA | 540-675-3800 | www.theinnatlittlewashington.com

From the "truffle popcorn to the last lick of the sorbet sampler", there's "brilliance in every bite" at Patrick O'Connell's "magical" New American in the Virginia countryside; once again, its "drop-dead gorgeous" setting and "irreproachable" staffers who strive for "perfection in every detail" bring it the No. 1 rating for Decor and Service in the DC Survey – no surprise to those who happily dip into their "life's savings" to "savor" this "exquisite experience"; P.S. "stay the night to keep the fairy tale going."

Iota Club & Café *American*
- | - | - | I

Clarendon | 2832 Wilson Blvd. (bet. Edgewood & Fillmore Sts.), VA | 703-522-8340 | www.iotaclubandcafe.com

Clarendon's pioneering live-music venue now caters to early birds as well as songbirds and night owls in remodeled digs that make it a breakfast-through-dinner stop for gourmet java from its new coffee bar, sandwiches and other cheap American fare, plus alcohol; patrons can choose between counter or wait service in the more open-feeling space that's been WiFi equipped; P.S. shows generally start at 8 PM.

Irene's Pupusas *Central American*
∇ 20 | 8 | 14 | $14

Hyattsville | 2218 University Blvd. E. (Riggs Rd.), MD | 301-431-1550
Laurel | 601 Second St. (Talbott Ave.), MD | 301-362-3371
Wheaton | 11300 Georgia Ave. (University Blvd. W.), MD | 301-933-2118 ◐
Wheaton | 2408 University Blvd. W. (Georgia Ave.), MD | 301-933-4800

At these "low-cost" Central Americans in the Maryland 'burbs, the eponymous stuffed-corn tortillas are "served so hot you can barely touch them", and the "special tacos" conjure the "sun-drenched Caribbean beach" depicted on the walls; service can be "slow" and "blaring jukeboxes rule out conversation", but "Irene knows pupusas."

I Ricchi ☒ *Italian*
24 | 22 | 22 | $63

Dupont Circle | 1220 19th St. NW (bet. M & N Sts.) | 202-835-0459 | www.iricchi.net

Bite into a "slice of Tuscany" at Dupont's Northern Italian "standard", which encourages the "culinary sin of overconsumption" with

FOOD | DECOR | SERVICE | COST

"delicate pastas", "giant pork chops" and other "excellent" selections that taste best on an "expense account"; indeed, a "lot of pre-tax dollars are spent here" since its "rustic yet elegant decor" and "formal" service (some say "condescending") make it "great for client entertainment"; P.S. for a "quicker" bite, sit at the "lively" bar.

Irish Inn at Glen Echo *Irish*

18 | 17 | 19 | $37

Glen Echo | 6119 Tulane Ave. (MacArthur Blvd.), MD | 301-229-6600 | www.irishinnglenecho.com

Come to this "convivial" "corner of Ireland" in Glen Echo often enough, and they may "recognize you" and start spinning "stories about life" in the Auld Sod; aye, an "unhurried" tone pervades its "small", "crowded" dining rooms and "cozy" pub, so plan to linger over casual fare like "terrific" fish 'n' chips or "higher-end meals" out to prove "Irish cuisine isn't an oxymoron" (though with mixed success); P.S. there's occasional live music.

Iron Bridge Wine Company *American*

23 | 20 | 21 | $40

Warrenton | 29 Main St. (1st St.), VA | 540-349-9339 | www.ironbridgewines.com

See review in the Baltimore Directory.

Jackie's *American*

21 | 19 | 19 | $40

Silver Spring | 8081 Georgia Ave. (entrance on Sligo Ave.), MD | 301-565-9700 | www.jackiesrestaurant.com

At the "vanguard of Silver Spring's revivial", this "high-end" Jackie of all trades is a "spirited neighborhood favorite" delivering American "comfort food that's always yummy" ("Elvis burgers rule!"); the "stylish" converted auto-parts shop boasts retro "decor that's a hoot" and "hip" staffers who are usually "attentive", hence the "young crowd" returning "again and again" there and at the adjacent Sidebar, its new cocktail-bar sibling; P.S. chef Diana Davila-Boldin took over the kitchen, post-Survey.

Jackson's Mighty Fine Food & Lucky Lounge *American/Seafood*

20 | 18 | 21 | $34

Reston | Reston Town Ctr. | 11927 Democracy Dr. (Library St.), VA | 703-437-0800 | www.greatamericanrestaurants.com

"Chipper service" and a "rip-roaring bar scene" – inside and out – keep this Reston Town Center spot mighty "packed" with a "hot, hip crowd", while the 1940s-inspired decor provides an "interesting" backdrop for "classic American done right" (including seafood and "heavenly" deviled eggs) and "twists" like sushi; the unimpressed proclaim it's "overpriced for what it is" and "unbearably noisy" as well, so "go early" if you can.

Jackson 20 *American*

18 | 18 | 19 | $42

Old Town | Hotel Monaco | 480 King St. (Pitt St.) | Alexandria, VA | 703-842-2790 | www.jackson20.com

"How can you not like a place with 20 $20 wine choices?" wonder those wowed by the "deal" at this "convenient" hotel American in Old Town, whose "friendly" staff welcomes "tourists" and a "regular clientele" alike; exposed brick, warm lighting and an open kitchen set the stage for "Southern-ish comfort food" that gets mixed marks ("not bad, but not great"), but at least it "isn't as expensive as the surroundings suggest."

Jaipur *Indian*   23 | 18 | 21 | $27

Fairfax | 9401 Lee Hwy. (Circle Woods Dr.), VA | 703-766-1111 | www.jaipurcuisine.com

Upon discovering this "out-of-the-way" subcontinental, Fairfax diners are "transported" to India for "beyond-the-ordinary" meals, with "refined" service and "well-spiced" dishes "so aromatic and delicious" no one "leaves a drop on the plate"; moreover, the lunch buffet is "outstanding in its variety, flavor and cost" (from $9.95), and the dining rooms are "inviting" and "comfy" – once "you get over the pink decor."

⚡ Jaleo *Spanish*   22 | 19 | 19 | $37

Penn Quarter | 480 Seventh St. NW (E St.) | 202-628-7949 ◗
Bethesda | 7271 Woodmont Ave. (Elm St.), MD | 301-913-0003
Crystal City | 2250A Crystal Dr. (23rd St.) | Arlington, VA | 703-413-8181 Ⓜ
www.jaleo.com

"Still happening after all these years", these "hustling, bustling" Spaniards owe their "success" to "star chef" José Andrés' "ever-changing" tapas menu, which lets patrons "pick lots of fabulous small plates" – a concept that's "especially good" for "large groups"; "noisy", "packed" rooms and "big checks" for "tiny bites" vex some, but most are "shouting 'olé!'" after a "few glasses" of the "amazing sangria"; P.S. check out the lunch deals and "great happy hour."

J&G Steakhouse *American/Steak*   25 | 25 | 23 | $67

Downtown | W Hotel | 515 15th St. NW (bet. F St. & Pennsylvania Ave.) | 202-661-2440 | www.jgsteakhousewashingtondc.com

Steps from the White House, Jean-Georges Vongerichten's "bright star" in the W Hotel is anything but a "stodgy Washington steakhouse" (despite its name); indeed, its "fantastic" seafood and "creative" New American options are the real "reasons to go" to this "sophisticated" space blending "old architectural elements" with "modern" cool and "attentive" hospitality – and, happily, most feel it's "worthy" of the "pricey" tabs; P.S. "go upstairs" to the POV bar for cocktails and amazing vistas.

Jerry's Seafood Ⓜ *Seafood*   24 | 15 | 20 | $41

Lanham | Seabrook Station | 9364 Lanham Severn Rd. (94th Ave.), MD | 301-577-0333 | www.jerrysseafood.com

The "decor leaves a bit to be desired", but "oh, the crab bomb" – the "amazing" crustacean concoction "makes up" for the deficiences at these "popular" Maryland fish houses that reel in locals with "delicious" seafood and "excellent" down-home sides ("even the coleslaw is high quality"); penny-pincers who complain about "expensive" prices suggest it's best "if someone else is treating"; P.S. the newer Bowie branch is more "yuppified" than the Lanham original.

	FOOD	DECOR	SERVICE	COST

☑ Jockey Club *American* — 22 | 26 | 22 | $66

Dupont Circle | The Fairfax at Embassy Row Hotel | 2100 Massachusetts Ave. NW (21st St.) | 202-835-2100 | www.thejockeyclub-dc.com

After a "face-lift as fabulous as those of its patrons", this "expensive" "old standby" in The Fairfax at Embassy Row reopened in late 2008 "brighter", more "comfortable" and out to "recapture its Reagan-era vibes"; acolytes applaud the "formal sevice", but the jury is still out on how post-Survey chef and management changes have answered critics who wish the American fare were as "wonderful" as the decor.

Joe's Noodle House *Chinese* — 23 | 9 | 17 | $19

Rockville | 1488C Rockville Pike (Congressional Ln.), MD | 301-881-5518 | www.joesnoodlehouse.com

"Be adventurous" at this Rockville mall "treasure" filled with "fabulous Sichuan specialties" that are "not for the faint of heart or palate" ("so hot that you may break into a sweat just looking at them"); there's "painfully plain decor", "plastic dishes" and "minimal service" since you "order at a counter", but "low prices" and "well-prepared dishes make up for the annoyance"; P.S. the "extensive menu" is "daunting", so ask staffers for "recommendations."

Johnny's Half Shell ☒ *American/Seafood* — 20 | 17 | 19 | $44

Capitol Hill | 400 N. Capitol St. NW (Louisiana Ave.) | 202-737-0400 | www.johnnyshalfshell.net

Capitol Hill "politicos" and their acolytes set sail for Ann Cashion's & John Fulchino's "hip", "high-end" New American seafooder, where "delicious" po' boys, bivalves and other "fresh" fin fare vie for attention with a "hopping" wood-and-marble bar and "live music" on the terrace; notwithstanding nostalgia for its former "intimate" Dupont Circle digs, many agree it's "worth a visit"; P.S. its Taqueria Nacional offers cheap takeout from morn through midday.

Juice Joint Cafe ☒ *Health Food* — ▽ 22 | 8 | 17 | $11

Downtown | 1025 Vermont Ave. NW (K St.) | 202-347-6783 | www.juicejointcafe.com

"Lines get long around lunch" at this "reliable" Downtown nook where vegetarians, vegans and carnivores alike grab "cheap" mid-day repasts on weekdays; French-trained chef Adrien Marsoni (ex Bistrot du Coin) is responsible for the wraps, grilled seafood and other "healthy" fare, complemented by "delicious" smoothies churned out by juiced-up staffers; P.S. "McDonald's-like" seating prompts most to do "takeout."

Juniper *American* — ▽ 21 | 23 | 23 | $50

West End | Fairmont Hotel | 2401 M St. NW (24th St.) | 202-457-5020 | www.fairmont.com

"Everything is done just right" at this "delightful" New American in West End's Fairmont Hotel, whose seasonal Mid-Atlantic dishes attract a "steady clientele" of locals and out-of-towners; while entrees are "tasty and inspired" and service "attentive", it's the "peaceful atmosphere" – including a secluded garden courtyard – that wins the highest praise; P.S. the cheese platter is served with honey from rooftop beehives.

Kabab-ji *Lebanese* ▽ 20 | 19 | 23 | $32

Dupont Circle | 1351 Connecticut Ave. NW (Dupont Circle) | 202-822-8999 | www.kabab-ji.com

From the street, this young Dupont Circle Lebanese import looks like a "casual counter eatery", but once inside, meze mavens find a "swank" environment (imported Beirut brick and marble) with a "lively" bar and "nice selection" of "traditional" small dishes, "excellent" kebabs and sandwiches; early reports find the experience "appealing" but costing more than some "want to pay."

Kabob N Karahi ⚫ *Pakistani* - | - | - | I

Silver Spring | 15521 New Hampshire Ave. (Briggs Chaney Rd.), MD | 301-879-0044 | www.kabobnkarahi.com

A "potpourri of nationalities" frequent this "cheerful" Pakistani-Nepalese standout in Silver Spring's Cloverly neighborhood for "authentic"– that means "spicy" – kebabs, "tasty" *karahi* (curries made in a special wok) and "excellent" *haleem* (chicken and lentil stew); accommodations in its "airy" counter-serve quarters are "user-friendly", and it's a "great value" to boot.

Kabob Palace Family Restaurant *Mideastern* 24 | 9 | 19 | $15

Crystal City | 2333 S. Eads St. (bet. 23rd & 24th Sts.) | Arlington, VA | 703-979-3000

Enthusiastic surveyors run out of "words to describe how good" the food is at this "friendly" Crystal City Middle Easterner serving up "fresh, well-seasoned" lamb and chicken kebabs and homestyle vegetarian sides that "pack a powerful punch"; natch, the "taxi drivers and families" chowing down on the Afghan-Pakistani fare in simple "cafeteria"-like premises already know it's an "excellent value."

Kazan ☒ *Turkish* 22 | 19 | 24 | $37

McLean | Chain Bridge Corner Shopping Ctr. | 6813 Redmond Dr. (Chain Bridge Rd.), VA | 703-734-1960 | www.kazanrestaurant.com

Whatever you do, "go when they have the doner kebab" at chef-owner Zeynel Uzun's "welcoming" McLean Ottoman – it's "sweet nostalgia" for those longing for a taste of "Istanbul"; indeed, "rich flavors" permeate all of the "lovingly prepared" fare here, which explains why acolytes have been trekking to this "supermarket plaza" since 1980, though modest prices and a "low-key" atmosphere don't hurt.

Kaz Sushi Bistro ☒ *Japanese* 25 | 15 | 21 | $46

World Bank | 1915 I St. NW (bet. 19th & 20th Sts.) | 202-530-5500 | www.kazsushi.com

Chef-owner Kaz Okochi is "always doing something innovative with raw fish" at this "low-key" Japanese near the World Bank, where the "incredible" rolls and "amazing small plates" make it one of DC's "most inventive and approachable sushi restaurants"; it's "tough to get a seat" and service can be "distracted", but most find Kaz for celebration anyhow: "you get to dine and not just eat" "without totally breaking the bank."

Kellari Taverna *Greek*   22 | 23 | 22 | $56

Golden Triangle | 1700 K St. NW (Connecticut Ave.) | 202-535-5274 | www.kellaridc.com

An outpost of a "high-end" NYC duo, this veritable "East Coast Athens" in the Golden Triangle showcases the "freshest seafood" – along with "classic" Greek meze, entrees and wines – in a "lavish" dining room where fish perched on "crushed ice" "stare at you"; "attentive service" and "expense-account" pricing make it popular for "biz lunches", though wallet-watchers seeking "great deals" can turn to the three-course prix fixes (from $24.95).

☑ Kinkead's *Seafood*   26 | 22 | 24 | $63

Foggy Bottom | 2000 Pennsylvania Ave. NW (I St.) | 202-296-7700 | www.kinkead.com

"Consistency reigns supreme" at chef-owner Bob Kinkead's piscatorial "aristocrat" in Foggy Bottom, offering "sparkling seafood" "served with style" in a "surprisingly large" space designed to "encourage private conversations" among its "movers-and-shakers" clientele; "you pay a lot, but you get a lot" at this "first choice for a VSD (very special dinner)", but value-seekers can head to the "friendly" downstairs bar/cafe for "lighter fare" and lighter tabs.

Kloby's Smokehouse *BBQ*   - | - | - | M

Laurel | Montpelier Shopping Ctr. | 7500 Montpelier Rd.
(Johns Hopkins Rd.), MD | 301-362-1510 | www.klobysbbq.com

'Cue-heads queue up at this big country-themed joint in a busy Laurel strip mall for piles of pork, poultry and beef at moderate prices, including family-style portions; early success has resulted in an expansion to make way for a bourbon bar and a privatizable spillover room; P.S. take-out options include smoked whole pigs, turkeys and ducks.

☑ Komi 🅢🅜 *American/Mediterranean*   29 | 22 | 28 | $123

Dupont Circle | 1509 17th St. NW (P St.) | 202-332-9200 | www.komirestaurant.com

"Way out of the box and over the top" describes the "dazzling" "food adventure" at chef-owner Johnny Monis' "intimate" Dupont Circle "star", where a *degustazione* "marathon" of "intricate" Med-American courses – from "delectable bite-sized morsels" to "gourmet goat" – are matched "beautifully" with "esoteric wines"; "unpretentious" servers provide a "seamless experience from the front end to the kitchen", and if the "price is high and choices minimal", few dispute it "delivers on the 'wow' scale."

Konami *Japanese*   ▽ 20 | 17 | 18 | $33

Tysons Corner | 8221 Leesburg Pike (Chain Bridge Rd.) | Vienna, VA | 703-821-3400 | www.konamirestaurant.com

Once favored as a "soothing" retreat in bustling Tysons Corner, this "basic sushi joint" now fosters a more "barren/minimalist look", though its little garden remains; while it's "nothing to write home about", it still provides "decent" Japanese fare along with "easy access" for get-togethers in a relatively "large" dining room.

Kora *Italian*

15 | 18 | 14 | $41

Crystal City | 2250B Crystal Dr. (23rd St.) | Arlington, VA | 571-431-7090 | www.korarestaurant.com

NEW Farrah Olivia 🖂 Ⓜ *American*

Crystal City | 2250 Crystal Dr. (23rd St.) | Arlington, VA | 703-445-6571 | www.farrahoiliviarestaurant.com

"Given the owners" – chef Amadou Ouattara and his brother, Morou – even "skeptical" surveyors "want to love" Kora, the midpriced Italian ensconced in a "vast", soaring Crystal City venue; alas, for many it "misses the mark", with "decent but not extraordinary" pizza and pastas, "amateurish" help and a "cold, impersonal" space greatly warmed by a "spacious lounge"; P.S. fans of Morou's erstwhile Farrah Olivia are jazzed that its creative New American menu has been resurrected on Wednesday–Saturday nights in Kora's 40-seat private dining room.

Kotobuki *Japanese*

23 | 8 | 17 | $26

Palisades | 4822 MacArthur Blvd. NW (U St.) | 202-625-9080 | www.kotobukiusa.com

"No-frills fresh fish" at "cheap (but not in a bad way)" prices keeps sushi fans "standing on line" at this Palisades Japanese above the exalted Makoto; "friendly" service compensates for a "shoebox-sized" space that's "low on ambiance and tables", but impatient sorts will want to "get there early" or "opt for takeout"; P.S. *kamameshi*, a traditional rice and vegetable pot, adds to the buzz.

Kramerbooks & Afterwords Cafe ◑ *American*

17 | 14 | 15 | $26

Dupont Circle | 1517 Connecticut Ave. NW (bet. Dupont Circle & Q St.) | 202-387-1462 | www.kramers.com

Hipsters "ramp up for a lively night" then "wind down" afterword at this durable (and "affordable") Dupont Circle "staple" where there's "something for everyone", from "terrific brunches" and "above-average desserts" to a "wild array of books" for "browsing"; true, it's "always packed", service can be "spotty" and the "extensive" American menu is "hit-or-miss", but the fact that "it's open 24/7" on weekends makes it a "go-to spot" for partyers and insomniac page-turners alike.

Kushi *Japanese*

- | - | - | M

Mt. Vernon Square/Convention Center | City Vista | 465 K St. NW (bet. 4th & 5th Sts.) | 202-682-3123 | www.eatkushi.com

Up-and-coming Mount Vernon Square is home to this sizzling Japanese izakaya serving simply seasoned, charcoal-grilled skewers of meats and vegetables, accompanied by sushi and fashionable drinks including exclusive small-batch sakes, shochus and Japanese microbrews on tap; its lofty, industrial space boasts polished steel, reclaimed wood and trendy pendant lighting, with huge sake casks adding an intriguing touch.

	FOOD	DECOR	SERVICE	COST

La Bergerie *French*

23 | 22 | 23 | $61

Old Town | Crilley Warehouse | 218 N. Lee St. (bet. Cameron & Queen Sts.) | Alexandria, VA | 703-683-1007 | www.labergerie.com
"Classics never seem to go out of style" at this Old Town French "favorite" where the gentry celebrate "special occasions" by indulging in "expertly prepared" Gallic standards and a "choice of soufflés"; "luxury-level service" and a "comfortable" dining room complete the package, which some find "under-exciting" and "overpriced", even if "prix fixe options" make it "more of a deal than it used to be."

La Canela *Peruvian*

23 | 22 | 22 | $39

Rockville | Rockville Town Sq. | 141 Gibbs St. (bet. Beall Ave. & Middle Ln.), MD | 301-251-1550
At this "enticing" Peruvian in Rockville Town Square, the "accent is just right" on "delicious" regional dishes that "aren't too exotic for local tastes", although its "wonderful" pisco sour packs a punch; wrought-iron accents, mirrors and "seating on several levels" create a "jewel box"-like setting that's enhanced by "warm, homey" service and "moderate prices."

La Caraqueña *Venezuelan*

- | - | - | I

Falls Church | 300 W. Broad St. (Little Falls St.), VA | 703-533-0076 | www.lacaraquena.com
What this affordable Falls Church Venezuelan lacks in curb appeal (it's tucked into a "motel that looks like something out of *CSI*") is made up for with some of the most "authentic" South American food around, including "excellent" arepas and salteñas with "robust" fillings, Chilean sandwiches, lomo (beef dishes) and "ridiculously delicious *cuatro leches*"; check out the photos of its homeland while waiting for your meal to arrive; P.S. it's closed Tuesday.

La Chaumière ☒ *French*

24 | 23 | 23 | $54

Georgetown | 2813 M St. NW (bet. 28th & 29th Sts.) | 202-338-1784 | www.lachaumieredc.com
With its "blazing" fireplace and "cozy" tables, this "charming" *auberge* could as easily be "in rural France as in Georgetown", a feeling enhanced by the "wonderful" Gallic classics ("prepared like Julia [Child] would have made them") delivered with "world-class" panache; local "cave-dwellers" who find it as "comfortable as an old cashmere cardigan" but far more "romantic" swear that its soufflés are "well worth the wait" – and that prices are actually "reasonable."

La Côte d'Or Café *French*

24 | 20 | 24 | $51

Arlington | 6876 Lee Hwy. (Westmoreland St.), VA | 703-538-3033 | www.lacotedorcafe.com
"Close to I-66" but a world apart, this "quaint" Arlingtonian proffers "solidly good French food" (quiche, steak frites, etc.) with service to match in a "quintessential cafe atmosphere"; if some grumble about "Downtown prices in a suburban locale", *prix*-checkers who take advantage of "excellent-value" specials and "early-bird" dinners assure it's "like dining in France, but a lot cheaper"; P.S. Le Marché, an adjacent market serving breakfast and lunch, opened post-Survey.

	FOOD	DECOR	SERVICE	COST

Lafayette Room *American*   ▽ 25 | 29 | 27 | $73

Golden Triangle | The Hay-Adams | 800 16th St. NW (bet. H & I Sts.) | 202-638-2570 | www.hayadams.com

"Who can beat the view?" ask admirers of this "lovely" Hay-Adams hotel dining room with a White House vista, service that's "above reproach" and "Washington's movers and shakers" confabbing over "wonderful" breakfasts and other American fare; it's an altogether "impressive place to take guests", and a "live pianist" only "adds to the overall ambiance"; P.S. there's no dinner Saturday or Sunday, so check out the "fabulous" brunch instead.

La Ferme *French*   22 | 23 | 22 | $54

Chevy Chase | 7101 Brookville Rd. (bet. Taylor & Thornapple Sts.), MD | 301-986-5255 | www.lafermerestaurant.com

Set in a "romantic" Chevy Chase mansion, this "French farm restaurant" provides a "stately paced culinary experience" for a largely "senior" clientele who dote on its "delicious" cuisine, "accommodating" staff and "excellent value"; the *Sesame Street* generation" may find it "stuffy" and "overpriced", but it remains a popular "place for celebrations" nonetheless.

La Fourchette *French*   23 | 19 | 21 | $38

Adams Morgan | 2429 18th St. NW (bet. Columbia & Kalorama Rds.) | 202-332-3077

On the left bank of "ever-changing" Adams Morgan, this family-run "French standout" has persisted for "over 30 years", offering the kind of "good" "simple food" and service you'd expect in a Parisian counterpart; brunch on the patio is a particular "pleasure" ("poached egg dishes are absolutely heaven"), while the arty wall murals are "worth the trip by themselves."

La Limeña *Cuban/Peruvian*   ▽ 22 | 9 | 20 | $21

Rockville | Ritchie Ctr. | 765 Rockville Pike (1st St.), MD | 301-424-8066

"Bargain"-seekers head to this Rockville strip-maller for *pollo a la brasa* that "falls off the bone" and other Peruvian and Cuban classics like "excellent" *anticuchos*, "fabulous" ceviche and "delicious homemade" *chicha morada* (a purple corn drink); one look at the "simple" surroundings and "plastic silverware" explains the "low prices", but there's no lack of "cheerful" service, so locals in this always-developing area urge "go now, before it all changes."

Landini Brothers *Italian*   22 | 19 | 23 | $46

Old Town | 115 King St. (bet. Lee & Union Sts.) | Alexandria, VA | 703-836-8404 | www.landinibrothers.com

"You can't go wrong" if you choose from the "amazing list of daily specials" "recited" by the "professional servers" ("*bravissimo!*") at this "classic Old Town haunt", where "locals go" for "excellent" pastas, soups and other Italian "gastronomical pleasures"; a "cozy" atmosphere makes it the "perfect date place", but add in "wonderful private rooms" and "outdoor dining", and insiders insist "ya gotta love" the place.

	FOOD	DECOR	SERVICE	COST

Las Canteras ⓜ *Peruvian* — — — M

Adams Morgan | 2307 18th St. NW (Kalorama Rd.) | 202-265-1780 |
www.lascanterasdc.com

"Lima would be proud" of this Adams Morgan Peruvian where amigos down the "best pisco sours" in the ground-floor bar before moving upstairs for "killer ceviche", signature loma saltado and other Andean-inspired selections in a dining room prettified with furniture and chandeliers from the home country; P.S. there's half-price wine on Tuesdays.

La Strada *Italian* ▽ 23 14 20 $33

Del Ray | 1905 Mt. Vernon Ave. (bet. Bellefonte & Howell Aves.) |
Alexandria, VA | 703-548-2592 | www.lastrada-ontheave.com

This Del Ray Northern Italian – the kind of place where "mama makes the mozzarella and grows the herbs" – offers a seasonal menu starring "fresh pasta" complemented by an "extensive" wine list; a "friendly" staff and "old-world" setting that includes a wine room and "alfresco dining" add to the "authentic" vibe, while the option to order single or *famiglia* portions adds to its "good value."

La Tasca *Spanish* 17 19 17 $34

Chinatown | 722 Seventh St. NW (bet. G & H Sts.) | 202-347-9190
Rockville | Rockville Town Sq. | 141 Gibbs St. (bet. Beall Ave. &
Middle Ln.), MD | 301-279-7011
Old Town | 607 King St. (St. Asaph St.) | Alexandria, VA | 703-299-9810
Clarendon | 2900 Wilson Blvd. (Fillmore St.), VA | 703-812-9120
www.latascausa.com

"Faux Spanish settings" with "pillows" on the chairs, wrought iron on the walls and "live music" in the air summon a "fun atmosphere" at this "reasonably priced" chainlet dubbed the "Cheesecake Factory of tapas"; "great for groups", they churn out "traditional" small plates that taste "even better when the sangria is flowing", though not enough to prevent the unimpressed from deeming them merely "ok."

La Tomate *Italian* 18 17 20 $39

Dupont Circle | 1701 Connecticut Ave. NW (R St.) | 202-667-5505 |
www.latomatebistro.com

The "unusual shape" (a "glassed-in triangle") of this "homey" Dupont Circle stalwart seems to garner more attention than its "solid" Italian fare, a sea of "reasonably priced" "red-sauce" "standards" served by staffers who "aim to please"; all in all, it's "nothing spectacular", but its "tree-lined" sidewalk cafe is a "plus", ditto the newly added prosciutto bar.

ⓩ L'Auberge Chez François ⓜ *French* 27 26 27 $81

Great Falls | 332 Springvale Rd. (Beach Mill Rd.), VA | 703-759-3800

NEW Jacques' Brasserie ⓜ *French*

Great Falls | 332 Springvale Rd. (Beach Mill Rd.), VA |
703-759-3800
www.laubergechezfrancois.com

A "five-star" drive down "winding country roads" to Great Falls, VA, sets the mood for an "exceptional experience" at this "French classic" nestled in "gorgeous" surroundings; it's "not as glitzy" as some, but after "professional, caring" servers deliver multiple courses of "rich" Alsatian fare and wine from a "list that'll blow you away", most are won over by its "old-timey elegance" that harks back to a "more relaxed era" – and at a price that makes it a "bargain compared with Downtown" restaurants lacking its enduring "charm"; P.S. more affordable fare is now offered à la carte at dinner downstairs in the comparatively casual and cozy Jacques' Brasserie.

⚡ L'Auberge Provençale *French*

27 | 25 | 25 | $78

Boyce | L'Auberge Provençale | 13630 Lord Fairfax Hwy. (Rte. 50), VA | 540-837-1375 | www.laubergeprovencale.com

"An hour or so outside the city but a world away", this "beautiful" Boyce "getaway" is a "romantic" (and "expensive") fireplace-filled retreat for "lovers of fine food" and the "great outdoors"; "delectable" French tasting menus, an "extensive" wine list and "divine" service make it a "treasure" for a "special" meal, but for a truly "amazing" experience, "stay the night" and have breakfast too.

Lauriol Plaza *Mexican*

18 | 17 | 17 | $30

Dupont Circle | 1835 18th St. NW (T St.) | 202-387-0035 | www.lauriolplaza.com

"Quite the scene!" shout supporters of this "wildly popular" Dupont Circle East triple-decker where "everyone under 30 visiting DC ends up" – hence the "absurdly long waits" "made bearable" by "pitcher after pitcher of margaritas" and "great chips and salsa"; *sí*, it's "often knocked by the 'experts'" for "forgettable" Mexican chow and "hit-or-miss service", but amigos point out that there's a "beautiful view" from the "cool" roof deck, the "price is right" and "it's always a good time."

Lavandou *French*

20 | 17 | 20 | $45

Cleveland Park | 3321 Connecticut Ave. NW (bet. Macomb & Ordway Sts.) | 202-966-3002 | www.lavandoudc.com

The food "outshines the simple decor" at this "sunny" "slice of Provence" in Cleveland Park, but few seem to care since "reliable" French standards like steak frites are offered along with "great nightly specials" during the week (e.g. "all-you-can-eat mussels on Tuesday"); service is "friendly", but when it's crowded you may wonder if the "wine you ordered is going to make it to the table before the check."

Layalina *Lebanese/Syrian*

24 | 21 | 25 | $34

Arlington | 5216 Wilson Blvd. (bet. Emerson & Greenbrier Sts.), VA | 703-525-1170 | www.layalinarestaurant.com

"Go twice and you may become one of the family" at this "hospitable" (and "hidden") Arlington Middle Eastern with a "homestyle feel" and "superlative" Lebanese meze and Syrian entrees; guests settle into "cushioned seats in alcoves" in the "art-and-fabric"–bedecked "lair" then dig into "creative" concoctions best enjoyed with "surprisingly good" native wine and a group of friends; if a few gripe about "portion size" for the price, they "can't complain about the quality."

	FOOD	DECOR	SERVICE	COST

☑ Lebanese Taverna *Lebanese* | 21 | 18 | 18 | $30 |

Woodley Park | 2641 Connecticut Ave. NW (bet. Calvert St. & Woodley Rd.) | 202-265-8681
Bethesda | 7141 Arlington Rd. (bet. Bethesda Ave. & Elm St.), MD | 301-951-8681
Rockville | Rockville Town Sq. | 115A Gibbs St. (bet. Beall Ave. & Middle Ln.), MD | 301-309-8681
Rockville | Congressional Plaza | 1605 Rockville Pike
(bet. Congressional Ln. & Halpine Rd.), MD | 301-468-9086
Silver Spring | 933 Ellsworth Dr. (Rte. 29), MD | 301-588-1192
Arlington | 4400 Old Dominion Dr. (bet. Lorcom Ln. & Upton St.),
VA | 703-276-8681
Arlington | 5900 Washington Blvd. (McKinley Rd.), VA | 703-241-8681
Pentagon City | Pentagon Row | 1101 S. Joyce St. (Army Navy Dr.) |
Arlington, VA | 703-415-8681
Tysons Corner | Tysons Galleria | 1840G International Dr.
(Chain Bridge Rd.) | McLean, VA | 703-847-5244
www.lebanesetaverna.com

Eat a "meal in meze" at this "consistently good" local chainlet, where "flavorful renditions" of "traditional" Lebanese dishes provide plenty of "affordable" options for "meat eaters as well as vegetarians"; staffers "mindful of novices" are "generally eager to answer questions" at the "pleasantly modern" full-service and take-away branches, and while some snarl about "inconsistent" food and service, they're outnumbered by those who make these "perennial favorites" a "return destination."

Le Chat Noir *French* | 18 | 15 | 17 | $38 |

Upper NW | 4907 Wisconsin Ave. NW (41st St.) | 202-244-2044 |
www.lechatnoirrestaurant.com

"Even if you come alone", the "tight" tables at this "quaint" Upper NW French bistro ensure you'll "get to know your dining mates" over "traditional" fare like steak frites and a "wide variety of crêpes and galettes"; dishes are "hit-or-miss" and "sometimes they treat you like an American in Paris", but the "upstairs wine bar" is a "cozy" spot for a glass of vino.

Legal Sea Foods *Seafood* | 20 | 17 | 18 | $39 |

Chinatown | 704 Seventh St. NW (bet. G & H Sts.) |
202-347-0007
Bethesda | Montgomery Mall | 7101 Democracy Blvd., 2nd fl. (I-270),
MD | 301-469-5900
Crystal City | 2301 Jefferson Davis Hwy. (23rd St.) | Arlington, VA |
703-415-1200
Tysons Corner | Tysons Galleria | 2001 International Dr.
(Chain Bridge Rd.) | McLean, VA | 703-827-8900
www.legalseafoods.com

Enjoy some of "Boston's best seafood in your backyard" via this "high-quality" chain that's "deservedly popular" for its "always fresh" offerings, including "legendary New England clam chowder"; though it's a bit "basic" for the "upscale" prices and the "modern" decor isn't for everyone, the staff is "accommodating" and the gluten-free menu earns it "huge props."

	FOOD	DECOR	SERVICE	COST

Leopold's Kafe & Konditorei *Austrian*   22 | 20 | 17 | $31

Georgetown | Cady's Alley | 3315 Cady's Alley (bet. 33rd & 34th Sts.) |
202-965-6005 | www.kafeleopolds.com

A "sweet little secret" set in a Georgetown alley, this "pricey"
Austrian coffeehouse/cafe proffers its "stylish clientele" everything
from "light bites to real meals" to "fabulous" desserts (the "star attractions" here); the "modern, Euro-casual" digs feature service
with a "similar feeling" (i.e. "aloof"), but all is forgiven during "not-
to-be-missed" brunches on the "charming patio."

Le Pain Quotidien *Bakery/Belgian*   18 | 15 | 15 | $22

Capitol Hill | 660 Pennsylvania Ave. SE (bet. 6th & 7th Sts.) |
202-459-9148
Dupont Circle | Blaine Mansion | 2001 P St. (bet. Hopkins &
20th Sts. NW) | 202-459-9176
Georgetown | 2815 M St. NW (bet. 28th & 29th Sts.) |
202-315-5420
Upper NW | 4874 Massachusetts Ave. NW (49th St.) |
202-459-9141
Bethesda | Bethesda Row | 7140 Bethesda Ln. (bet. Bethesda Ave. &
Elm St.), MD | 301-913-2902
Old Town | 701 King St. (N. Washington St.) | Alexandria, VA |
703-683-2273
Clarendon | 2900 Clarendon Blvd. (Filmore St.), VA | 703-465-0970
www.lepainquotidien.com

"You could just eat the bread and jam and be happy" at these Belgian
bakery/cafes, home to "fresh, tasty" sandwiches, soups, pastries
and "organic breakfasts" that fill the need for a "quick bite", even if
it's "kinda pricey" ("the 'pain' is in the price tag"); service is "hit-or-
miss" when "crowds of locals" swarm the communal tables – a
"hippie shtick" that's a "little too Birkenstock-and-granola" for
some – but the "outdoor patios" generally compensate.

Le Refuge ⊠ *French*   21 | 20 | 21 | $46

Old Town | 127 N. Washington St. (bet. Cameron & King Sts.) |
Alexandria, VA | 703-548-4661 | www.lerefugealexandria.com

"After all these years", a "warmly familiar" vibe permeates this
"cozy" Old Town Gallic where a "welcome with an accent" and a
space evoking "Paris in 1940" set the stage for "dependably good"
French "standards"; true, the "food is not at a pinnacle" and you'll be
"sharing your space", but few deny it offers "refuge from the hubbub"
of city life; P.S. "prix fixe specials" prevent tabs from "adding up."

Levante's *Mideastern*   18 | 16 | 18 | $28

Dupont Circle | 1320 19th St. NW (Dupont Circle) | 202-293-3244 |
www.levantes.com

"Watch Dupont Circle go by" while getting a "taste of the
Mediterranean" at this indoor/outdoor Middle Easterner featuring
"authentic" Turkish pizzas, soups, salads and a "cold appetizer platter" that "really hits the spot"; one of the "happiest happy hours in
town" plus an "open, modern space" can make things a "bit loud",
but affordable prices make most dismiss the din.

	FOOD	DECOR	SERVICE	COST

Lia's *American/Italian* — 21 | 19 | 21 | $39

Chevy Chase | 4435 Willard Ave. (Wisconsin Ave.), MD |
240-223-5427 | www.liasrestaurant.com

At this airy "neighborhood joint" "tucked away in Chevy Chase", chef-
restaurateur Geoff Tracy's "well-prepared" Italian–New American
fare takes a "creative" tack that leads to "new layers of flavor"; "reasonable prices" and "excellent" specials make it a "mainstay",
though some warn service can be "uneven" and the industrial-chic
interior "noisy"; P.S. it's a "rising brunch spot" too.

Liberty Tavern ◗ *American* — 21 | 18 | 20 | $37

Clarendon | 3195 Wilson Blvd. (Washington Blvd.), VA |
703-465-9360 | www.thelibertytavern.com

"Depending on which level" you pick at this Clarendon American,
you'll either encounter a "raucous" bar scene packed with "young
professionals" digging into burgers and other "affordable" grub
(downstairs) or an "upscale", more "elegant" space offering "delicious" seasonal fare; "friendly" service and a "solid selection of
draft beer" are always on tap, while a "constantly evolving" menu
keeps "locals coming back"; P.S. it's in the Masonic Lodge building.

Liberty Tree *American/Pizza* — - | - | - | M

Atlas District | 1016 H St. NE (bet. 10th & 11th Sts.) | 202-396-8733 |
www.libertytreedc.com

This inviting bistro on the Atlas District's burgeoning Restaurant
Row dishes up affordable, Yankee-accented New American eats –
lobster pot pies, clam-topped pizza, pigs in blankets – in a cozy 'old-
school' setting with dark-wood wainscoting, cream-colored walls
and white tablecloths.

Lightfoot *American* — 22 | 25 | 22 | $44

Leesburg | 11 N. King St. (Market St.), VA | 703-771-2233 |
www.lightfootrestaurant.com

"Polished dark woods and brass", soaring ceilings and two fireplaces
add to the "character" of this "fabulous"-looking New American set
in a "grand old" Leesburg bank, and its "delicious", sometimes "dar-
ing" cooking is also on the money – particularly when paired with
choices from a "great wine list" by "waiters who know it well"; it's
"not inexpensive", but insiders insist it's "worth every penny."

Lighthouse Tofu *Korean* — 20 | 13 | 19 | $17

Rockville | 12710 Twinbrook Pkwy. (bet. Rockville Pike & Veirs Mill Rd.),
MD | 301-881-1178

Vit Goel Tofu *Korean*

Annandale | 4121 Chatelain Rd. (Columbia Pike), VA | 703-333-3436

Vit Guel Tofu *Korean*

Centreville | Centreville Sq. | 6035 Centreville Crest Ln. (St. Germain Dr.),
VA | 703-825-1550

These "fascinating" Koreans offer "lots of different" tofu stews
packed with seafood, meat and veggies that can be "ordered in var-
ious degrees of spiciness", making for a "perfect" meal on a "cold
winter's evening"; other traditional "delicacies" like noodle dishes

and kalbi (grilled beef) are savored in the simple surroundings, but don't come in a rush as "sometimes servers seem to forget about you"; P.S. Rockville is separately owned.

Lima ⚠ Pan-Latin

20 | 22 | 18 | $40

Downtown | 1401 K St. NW (14th St.) | 202-789-2800 | www.limarestaurant.com

"Watch the beautiful people congregate while sipping a mojito" at this tri-level K Street Pan-Latin, a "cool late-night place" where an indoor waterfall and "basement dance floor" compete for attention with chow like crudo, ceviche and lobster that "you'll be pleasantly surprised by"; partyers proclaim they're here "for the clubbing, not the food", but "knowledgeable" waiters make "spot-on" recommendations nonetheless – if you can hear them over the music.

NEW Lincoln American

- | - | - | M

Downtown | 1110 Vermont Ave. NW (bet. L & M Sts.) | 202-386-9200 | www.lincolnrestaurant-dc.com

Pennies (thousands and thousands of them) carpet the floor of this urbane Downtown American entry serving a midpriced menu of seasonal small plates, craft cocktails, wine and beer; beyond the coppery coinage, other visual references to Abe abound, most notably the Emancipation Proclamation projected on a wall.

Little Fountain Cafe Ⓜ Eclectic

▽ 24 | 20 | 25 | $41

Adams Morgan | 2339 18th St. NW (Belmont Rd.) | 202-462-8100 | www.littlefountaincafe.com

A "top-flight charmer in a generally charm-free neighborhood", this "unexpected refuge" a few steps below the Adams Morgan streetscape provides "well-executed" Eclectic fare, a "sensible" wine list and "thoughtful service" in a "romantic setting" (enhanced by a burbling fountain, of course); those seeking a bit more edge can opt for Angles, its late-night watering hole upstairs where "gourmet meets dive bar"; P.S. prix fixe meals and half-price-wine Wednesdays add to the appeal.

Local 16 American/Pizza

13 | 18 | 17 | M

U Street Corridor | 1602 U St. NW (16th St.) | 202-265-2828 | www.localsixteen.com

"Young professionals", "interns" and "acid jazz" lovers seeking "majorly strong drinks" served by "good-looking" bartenders flock to this U Street townhouse that also serves moderately priced American eats, including pizza; with a popular rooftop patio, it "can get crazy" on weekends and be a "meat market" ("if you can't pull here, you can't pull anywhere"), so if you're claustrophobic stick to the more "relaxed" weekdays.

Logan Tavern American

18 | 17 | 18 | $31

Logan Circle | 1423 P St. NW (bet. 14th & 15th Sts.) | 202-332-3710 | www.logantavern.com

While there's "nothing spectacular" about the "affordable" American grub at this "low-key" Logan Circle "joint", groupies gush that it's "homey, plentiful and just right if you have a hangover" (e.g. "meatloaf only your mother could match"); service can be a "little slow" and some say the "menu could use an update", but even reluctant returnees "hoping for more" admit it's "always crowded for a reason"; P.S. "don't miss" the Bloody Marys at its "great brunch."

L St. Vending ⊠🍴 *Korean* — | — | — | I
(aka Bulgogi Cart)
Downtown | 14th & L Sts. NW | 703-209-5415

Lunch-on-the-run meets "great value" at this little yellow cart on a busy Downtown corner; look for the "mother-and-son team" effortlessly handling "office crowds" jostling for spicy or mild options of traditional Korean fare, including "tasty bulgogi and bibimbop."

NEW Luke's Lobster *Seafood* — | — | — | I
Penn Quarter | 624 E St. NW (bet. 6th & 7th Sts.) | 202-347-3355 | www.lukeslobster.com

Lobster roll aficionados welcome this Penn Quarter outpost of the NYC-based counter-serve crustacean specialist, and its trademark $15 sandwich featuring a quarter pound of meat, dressed with mayo, lemon butter and secret seasoning; shrimp, crab claws and chowders round out the maritime menu while de rigueur fish shack digs (i.e. wood shingles, buoys, traps and nets) complete the rustic look.

Luna Grill & Diner *Diner/Vegetarian* 17 | 14 | 17 | $22
Dupont Circle | 1301 Connecticut Ave. NW (N St.) | 202-835-2280
Shirlington | 4024 Campbell Ave. (Quincy St.) | Arlington, VA | 703-379-7173
www.lunagrillanddiner.com

"Even the pickiest" patrons – vegetarians included – "find something to eat" at these Dupont and Shirlington "comfort-food centrals" full of folks mooning over the "stick-to-your-ribs" diner fare and "breakfast all day"; they "get loud" and "seating is a squeeze", but "don't take them too seriously" and you're in for a "decent" meal; P.S. "half-price pasta" specials vary by location.

Lyon Hall ● *French/German* — | — | — | I
Clarendon | 3100 Washington Blvd. (Highland Ave.), VA | 703-741-7636 | www.lyonhallarlington.com

This casual, stylish French brasserie in Clarendon (from the Liberty Tavern/Northside Social team) offers some 20 draft beers and plenty of wine to accompany affordable Alsatian-inspired fare like house-cured charcuterie, mussels, schnitzel, housemade breads and serious desserts; set in a former trophy shop, the two-story space includes a long, narrow dining room, high tables fronted by huge windows and a marble bar downstairs, plus there's a patio and an upstairs room that's used for private parties.

Maddy's ● *American* — | — | — | I
Dupont Circle | 1726 Connecticut Ave. NW (bet. R & S Sts.) | 202-483-2266 | www.maddysbar.com

This Dupont Circle bar and grill in the former Timberlake's digs features "friendly" sorts serving a reasonably priced roster of casual American eats in "huge" portions (don't even think about the "calorie count"), along with plenty of liquid cheer; the spiffy saloon setting sports a pressed tin ceiling, a skylit back room and cushy booths to accommodate the madding crowds.

NEW Mad Fox Brewing Company *Pub Food*

| - | - | - | M |

Falls Church | Shops at Spectrum | 444 W. Broad St. (bet. Pennsylvania & Virginia Aves.), VA | 703-942-6840 | www.madfoxbrewing.com

Buzzing since it opened in a new Falls Church plaza development, this midpriced pub offers house brews along with a serious list of wine, cider and mead to pair with everything from frickles (fried housemade pickles) and Virginia pork belly with spoon bread to pizza and grilled steaks; tall, gleaming beer vats set the stage at the entrance to the spacious, spiffily designed space, where seating options include a 60-ft. bar, communal tables and plush leather-lined booths along the windows.

Madhatter *American/Pub Food*

| - | - | - | M |

Dupont Circle | 1321 Connecticut Ave. NW (bet. Dupont Circle & N St.) | 202-833-1495 | www.madhatterdc.com

When this fixture relocated a few years ago, it underwent an *Alice in Wonderland*–style transformation befitting its name, morphing from basement dive bar to more upscale dining/drinking destination offering moderately priced American fare to ballast its legendary boozing; its current home – a two-story townhouse below Dupont Circle – abounds in dark wood and whimsy, from the grand dining room with a luminous vaulted ceiling and huge, floating metal top hat, to the intimate upstairs bar and 'upside down' party room.

Maggiano's Little Italy *Italian*

| 18 | 17 | 18 | $33 |

Upper NW | 5333 Wisconsin Ave. NW (bet. Jenifer St. & Western Ave.) | 202-966-5500
Tysons Corner | Tysons Galleria | 2001 International Dr. (Chain Bridge Rd.) | McLean, VA | 703-356-9000
www.maggianos.com

"Bring a crowd and eat family-style for the best experience" at these Upper NW and Tysons Corner links of the "steady-Eddie" Italian chain delivering "gargantuan portions" of "comforting" fare for "reasonable" tabs; its "Little Italy" style and "raucous" environs are a hit with fans, who argue that even if the "assembly-line" food is "nothing special, the total experience is great."

Magnolias at the Mill *American*

| 19 | 23 | 19 | $38 |

Purcellville | 198 N. 21st St. (Main St.), VA | 540-338-9800 | www.magnoliasmill.com

A "pleasant surprise" in the Western Loudoun "exurbs", this "cute-as-can-be" Purcellville outpost occupies an "interestingly" restored "old grain mill" where ultrarustic surroundings (wooden walls and rafters, antique granary equipment, etc.) set the scene for "something-for-everyone" New American fare at a "fair price"; snipers say the service "varies", but it's a local "favorite" "for all occasions" that's reputedly "worth the drive."

FOOD | DECOR | SERVICE | COST

Mai Thai *Thai*
20 | 18 | 18 | $26

NEW **Georgetown** | 3251 Prospect St. NW (bet. Potomac St. & Wisconsin Ave.) | 202-337-2424
Golden Triangle | 1200 19th St. NW (M St.) | 202-452-6870
Old Town | 6 King St. (Union St.) | Alexandria, VA | 703-548-0600
www.maithai.us

Admirers cite these "affordable" options as a "reliable" source of "tasty" Siamese "comfort food" matched with "surprisingly quick" (sometimes almost "too fast") service and an "inventive cocktail list" for those out to Thai one on; the Old Town "waterfront" original offers "awesome views of the Potomac" "if you sit upstairs", while the "chill" Golden Triangle locale is a stylishly "airy" rendezvous that's "never too crowded" (the new Georgetown branch opened post-Survey).

Majestic, The *American*
23 | 18 | 22 | $45

Old Town | 911 King St. (bet. Alfred & Patrick Sts.) | Alexandria, VA | 703-837-9117 | www.majesticcafe.com

This "Old Town fave" from Cathal and Meshelle Armstrong (Eve, Eammon's) puts "wonderful new twists" on the "traditional" American dishes "mom used to make" in a "hip, modern diner" setting overseen by a "caring" staff; the "creative" cocktails and "scrumptious" desserts are also "on target", and while "prices can get a little steep", the "family-style" "Nana's dinner on Sunday nights" is a "great buy" at $22 per person.

☑ Makoto Ⓜ *Japanese*
28 | 20 | 25 | $84

Palisades | 4822 MacArthur Blvd. NW (U St.) | 202-298-6866

"As authentically Japanese as you can get", this "intimate" Palisades kaiseki specialist reaches the "pinnacle of quality" with an "adventurous" chef's menu showcasing eight to 10 courses of "exquisite" "works of art" accompanied by "geishalike service"; "delicate" sushi also figures in a "fabulous experience" that's "like leaving the country for the night" (you'll even trade your shoes for "slippers" on entry), so despite "limited room" and seating on hard "wooden boxes" it's "totally worth" the premium price.

NEW Mala Tang *Chinese*
- | - | - | I

Arlington | 3434 Washington Blvd. (Kirkwood Rd.), VA | 703-243-2381 | www.mala-tang.com

Hot pots and street fare that impart the tangy *mala* sensation (i.e. hot and numbing) are the hallmark of this stylish yet inexpensive Sichuan entry in Arlington's Virginia Square neighborhood from chef/co-owner Liu Chaosheng (China Jade); an arresting mural depicting Chengdu's street-eats vendors dominates the main area, and there's also a sleek bar, dining counter and patio.

Malaysia Kopitiam *Malaysian*
19 | 8 | 18 | $25

Golden Triangle | 1827 M St. NW (bet. 18th & 19th Sts.) | 202-833-6232 | www.malaysiakopitiam.com

A "thick picture menu" of "interesting" chow makes this "low-key" Golden Triangle Malaysian "worth discovering" for fans who agree

| | FOOD | DECOR | SERVICE | COST |

the "dirt-cheap prices" and "helpful" staffers offset "basement" digs that "leave much to be desired"; it "satisfies" with "ample servings" and "more choices than you could ever want", so don't be put off by the "lacking" atmosphere – "it's the food that counts."

Mamma Lucia *Italian* | 18 | 12 | 17 | $24 |

Bethesda | 4916 Elm St. (bet. Arlington Rd. & Woodmont Ave.), MD | 301-907-3399
Olney | Olney Village Ctr. | 18224 Village Center Dr.
(Olney Sandy Spring Rd.), MD | 301-570-9500
College Park | College Park Plaza | 4734 Cherry Hill Rd. (bet. Autovill Dr. & 47th Ave.), MD | 301-513-0605
Rockville | Federal Plaza | 12274M Rockville Pike (Twinbrook Pkwy.), MD | 301-770-4894
Rockville | Fallsgrove Village Shopping Ctr. | 14921J Shady Grove Rd. (bet. Blackwell Rd. & Fallsgrove Blvd.), MD | 301-762-8805
Silver Spring | Blair Shops | 1302 E. West Hwy. (Colesville Rd.), MD | 301-562-0693
Reston | 1428 North Point Vill. (Reston Pkwy.), VA | 703-689-4894
www.mammaluciarestaurants.com

"Lots of families" frequent this area mini-chain of "everyday Italian joints" for "quick" fixes featuring "crusty" "New York–style pizza" and "generous portions" of "reliable" "red-sauce" standards; *certo*, the "generic" ambiance and sometimes "spotty service" "do the concept no favors", but "you leave full" and it "won't break the bank" so they're bound to be "busy."

Mandalay *Burmese* | 24 | 12 | 18 | $25 |

Silver Spring | 930 Bonifant St. (bet. Fenton St. & Georgia Ave.), MD | 301-585-0500 | www.mandalayrestaurantcafe.org

"Different but very palatable", this "family-run" Burmese "find" in Downtown Silver Spring is a "surprising" supplier of "tantalizing dishes" with "lots of vegetarian options", all tailored to your "heat tolerance"; though the "uninspired setting" "could use an update", the fair prices, "personable" service and "kid-friendly" feel make it an "insider's choice" for "solid neighborhood dining."

M&S Grill *Seafood/Steak* | 19 | 19 | 19 | $39 |

Downtown | 600 13th St. NW (F St.) | 202-347-1500
Reston | Reston Town Ctr. | 11901 Democracy Dr. (Discovery St.), VA | 703-787-7766
www.mandsgrill.com

McCormick & Schmick's more "casual", "lower-cost" "alternative", these American grills proffer a "big menu" of "decent" seafood and steaks, "great happy-hour deals" and service that veers between "fine" and "inattentive"; Baltimore's "pleasant harborside" site draws "throngs of tourists" while Downtown and Reston are "often pretty crowded" with suits, and while some grumble they're "not particularly creative", realists shrug "it's a chain": "dependable but predictable."

Mandu *Korean* | 21 | 16 | 19 | $25 |

Dupont Circle | 1805 18th St. NW (bet. S & Swann Sts.) | 202-588-1540

(continued)

Mandu

NEW Mt. Vernon Square/Convention Center | City Vista | 453 K St. NW (bet. 4th & 5th Sts.) | 202-289-6899 ◐
www.mandudc.com

This "casual" Dupont Circle Korean "never fails" when it comes to "traditional" "favorites" (including the "delicious dumplings" it's named for) served in a "comfortable" duplex where the "good value" makes it "worth a return"; the "lively" atmo's abetted by a "steady stream" of house-specialty sojutinis, and its affordable fare is replicated at its handsome and happening new Mount Vernon Square branch.

Mannequin Pis *Belgian*   25 | 19 | 21 | $42

Olney | Olney Ctr. | 18064 Georgia Ave. (Olney Laytonsville Rd.), MD | 301-570-4800 | www.mannequinpis.com

An "intimate" "Belgian bistro" is "seemingly unusual" "in suburban Olney", but this "neighborhood gem" surprises with "terrific" moules frites served by "friendly" staffers and washed down with a "mind-blowing" list of imported brews; the "tables are jammed together like the mussels in the pots" and it's "pricey", but the "experience" is still "worth the drive"; P.S. "go on Monday night" for the prix fixe "steal."

Maoz Vegetarian ⓈVegetarian   ▽ 19 | 16 | 17 | $11

Golden Triangle | 1817 M St. NW (bet. 18th & 19th Sts.) | 202-290-3117 | www.maozusa.com

The Golden Triangle outlet of an Amsterdam-based international chain, this vegetarian quick stop specializes in "fine falafel" with "add-your-own toppings" from the fixin's bar plus maozwatering Belgian or sweet potato fries; with "fast" counter service and communal tables, it adds some "welcome" variety "to the lunch scene."

Maple Ave Restaurant *American/Eclectic*   ▽ 20 | 11 | 20 | $31

Vienna | 147 Maple Ave. W. (Center St. & Courthouse Rd.), VA | 703-319-2177

NEW Maple Ave Xpress ⓈⓂⶡ *American/Eclectic*
(aka Max)

Location varies; see website | no phone
www.mapleaverestaurant.com

Those in the know hail this Vienna spot as a "real find" for "inventive" New American fare courtesy of chef-owner Tim Ma, who displays a "unique" "sensibility" with "fresh" seasonal menus featuring small and "full-sized" plates; though the "tiny room" with picture windows and artwork is a "tight" squeeze, the "amazing food" and "friendly" service have the makings of a "major hit"; P.S. a truck carrying affordable bites from the mother ship's menu now travels to nearby Tysons Corner (and occasionally McLean) Thursday–Saturday.

Ⓩ Marcel's *Belgian/French*   29 | 26 | 28 | $88

West End | 2401 Pennsylvania Ave. NW (24th St.) | 202-296-1166 | www.marcelsdc.com

"Master" chef Robert Wiedmaier "orchestrates" culinary "miracles" at this West End Belgian-French "class" act, where the "superlative"

	FOOD	DECOR	SERVICE	COST

cuisine (e.g. the "famous", foie gras–enriched boudin blanc) earns the No. 1 Food rating in the DC Survey; "stellar service" and a "romantic" Provençal setting (that was recently refreshed) enhance an "exceptional" performance that justifies "dropping serious cash" and putting in "extra treadmill time"; P.S. the pre-theater deal includes complimentary car service to the Kennedy Center.

Mark's Duck House *Chinese*

| 23 | 7 | 15 | $28 |

Falls Church | Willston Ctr. | 6184A Arlington Blvd. (Patrick Henry Dr.), VA | 703-532-2125 | www.marksduckhouse.com

Both the "glorious Peking duck" and the "incredible" dim sum are "claims to fame" at this Falls Church Cantonese, a destination where the "authentic" cooking "never wavers"; "service ranges from abrupt to competent" and the "unremarkable" "decor's in desperate need of an upgrade", but the food "more than compensates" as long as you "cultivate patience" for the "crowds and chaos."

Mark's Kitchen *American*

| ▽ 17 | 10 | 19 | $18 |

Takoma Park | 7006 Carroll Ave. (Laurel St.), MD | 301-270-1884 | www.markskitchen.com

Like a throwback to "Smalltown" USA, this thriving Takoma Park "neighborhood joint" is "reliable enough" for "inexpensive" American eats with intriguing Korean accents in a storefront cafe setting where "friendly" '60s vibes make up for limited decor; being one of the area's "better options for vegetarians", it claims a "cult following" among crunchy regulars who "almost live there."

Marrakesh Palace *Moroccan*

| 20 | 24 | 21 | $40 |

Dupont Circle | 2147 P St. NW (bet. 21st & 22nd Sts.) | 202-775-1882 | www.marrakeshpalace.com

Expect a "fun atmosphere" at this Dupont Circle Moroccan, a "great spot for groups" where "courteous", costumed servers deliver "delicious" standards like couscous and tagines in colorful North African-style digs replete with mosaic tiles, fountains and "entertaining" "belly dancing shows"; though purists sniff it's only "quasi-authentic", it's still an "exotic meal" "without having to get on a plane."

Martin's Tavern *American*

| 20 | 20 | 20 | $33 |

Georgetown | 1264 Wisconsin Ave. NW (N St.) | 202-333-7370 | www.martins-tavern.com

Presidents from Truman on have schmoozed at this "Georgetown mainstay", a "blast from the past" dating to 1933 that still "hits the spot" with "solid" burgers and other Traditional American "classics" ("try the 'hot brown'") in a "lively" "saloon" setting with "wood paneling and brass rails"; rumor has it "JFK proposed to Jackie" in one of the booths, and it remains a politicos' "refuge" with "people-watching" aplenty and a popular weekend brunch.

Marvin ❶ *American/Belgian*

| 21 | 20 | 18 | $40 |

U Street Corridor | 2007 14th St. NW (U St.) | 202-797-7171 | www.marvindc.com

Conceived as a "tribute" to Marvin Gaye, this "trendy" U Street "winner" appeals to a "yuppie-hipster" clientele with "ambitious", "soulful" Belgian-American vittles spanning chicken and waffles to "glorious moules frites", well paired with an "incredible" beer list; the "artful" bistro setup is "vibrant" and "quite loud", especially on weekends when the "thumping" rooftop lounge becomes a "happening" "place to see and be seen."

Masa 14 ◐ *Asian/Latin* 23 | 22 | 21 | $43

Logan Circle | 1825 14th St. NW (bet. S & T Sts.) | 202-328-1414 | www.masa14.com

They "got it right from the get-go" at this Logan Circle yearling from chef-owners Richard Sandoval (Zengo) and Kaz Okochi (Kaz Sushi Bistro), which takes a "meze approach" to "Asian-Latin fusion" fare with "outstanding" "small plates galore" conveyed by "attentive" servers in an "industrial" space with a "long bar" where "singles" sip chic cocktails; but since it's a "hot" ticket for "the under-35 crowd", it can be "hard to get a table."

Masala Art *Indian* 26 | 20 | 22 | $33

Upper NW | 4441B Wisconsin Ave. NW (Albemarle St.) | 202-362-4441 | www.masalaartdc.com

"Wake up your mouth" with "full-bodied" culinary artistry at this "fabulous new" Upper NW Indian, where "innovative versions of classic" subcontinental dishes and "fascinating regional" choices (many "not standard" elsewhere) deliver "much more than you'd expect"; the "storefront" space bedecked with native crafts is tended by a "gracious" staff, and given the "quality" you "cannot beat the value", particularly of the lunch buffet.

Matchbox *American* 23 | 20 | 18 | $28

Capitol Hill | 521 Eighth St. SE (bet. E & G Sts.) | 202-548-0369
Chinatown | 713 H St. NW (bet. 7th & 8th Sts.) | 202-289-4441
NEW **Rockville** | Congressional Plaza | 1699 Rockville Pike (Halpine Dr.), MD | 301-816-0369
www.matchboxchinatown.com

"No one matches" the "crisp, perfectly topped" "wood-fired pizza" and "justly famous" sliders ("like crack on a bun") that make these "well-priced" Chinatown, Capitol Hill and striking new Rockville New Americans "impossible to resist" for "ridiculous" "mobs" of "young professionals"; they're appealingly "neat", "upbeat" locales with "cheerful" service, but even if the Eighth Street offshoot is reportedly "less of a zoo" and Maryland is massive, you better "bring a sleeping bag" for the "long waits" at prime time.

Maté ◐ *Asian/Nuevo Latino* ▽ 25 | 25 | 21 | $36

Georgetown | 3101 K St. NW (31st St.) | 202-333-2006 | www.latinconcepts.com

"Hip and sleek", this Georgetown nightspot serves a "fabulous", sushi-centric "mix" of Latin-leaning Asian fusion fare in a "swanky" contemporary space that "sets the mood for party time" (notably during the lively "weekday happy hour"); it's a "great place to meet" with your mates, but make way for the trendsetters who arrive after 11 PM for the "lounge" scene.

	FOOD	DECOR	SERVICE	COST

Matisse *French/Mediterranean*

	23	20	21	$55

Upper NW | 4934 Wisconsin Ave. NW (Fessenden St.) | 202-244-5222 | www.matisserestaurantdc.com

"Grand designs" crop up in an affluent Upper NW neighborhood at this "high-quality" French-Med "gem", serving "memorable" cuisine with occasional "adventuresome" "twists" in an airy white space with "wrought-iron" details recalling the eponymous artist's style; its mature clientele appreciates a milieu where you "can actually hear" yourself, though the "downtown prices" have some suggesting it "punches a bit above its weight."

Matuba *Japanese*

	21	12	18	$32

Bethesda | 4918 Cordell Ave. (bet. Norfolk Ave. & Old Georgetown Rd.), MD | 301-652-7449 | www.matuba-sushi.com

"Highly reliable and occasionally imaginative", this simple Bethesda Japanese is a local fixture known for its "solid" sushi, fun "conveyer belt" setup and "welcoming" staff; sure, the mall-like digs are "modest", but prices are "reasonable" and it's "fine to bring the kids."

McCormick & Schmick's *Seafood*

	20	20	20	$43

Penn Quarter | 901 F St. NW (9th St.) | 202-639-9330
Golden Triangle | 1652 K St. NW (bet. 16th & 17th Sts.) | 202-861-2233
Bethesda | 7401 Woodmont Ave. (Montgomery Ln.), MD | 301-961-2626
Crystal City | 2010 Crystal Dr. (20th St.) | Arlington, VA | 703-413-6400
Reston | Reston Town Ctr. | 11920 Democracy Dr. (bet. Discovery & Library Sts.), VA | 703-481-6600
Tysons Corner | Ernst & Young Bldg. | 8484 Westpark Dr. (Leesburg Pike) | McLean, VA | 703-848-8000
www.mccormickandschmicks.com

An "enjoyable" choice for "business and pleasure", this "upscale" seafood chain offers a "daily changing" menu of "freshly caught" fare in an "upbeat" atmosphere; though it feels too "stamped-out-of-a-mold" for some, its "professional" service is a plus and the "happy-hour bar menu" wins over the after-work crowd.

NEW Medium Rare *Steak*

	–	–	–	M

Cleveland Park | 3500 Connecticut Ave. NW (Ordway St.) | 202-237-1432 | www.mediumrarerestaurant.com

On a prime corner of Cleveland Park, this mod-looking steakhouse with an open kitchen and an inviting patio offers one simple set menu: a dry-aged sirloin cap cut with a distinctive sauce, salad and frites for $19.50 (vegetarians may sub in a grilled portobello); its concise wine list is also affordable and approachable, there are craft beers on tap and feasts can be rounded off with a homestyle dessert for $8 extra.

Meiwah *Chinese*

	19	14	18	$28

West End | 1200 New Hampshire Ave. NW (M St.) | 202-833-2888
Chevy Chase | Chase Tower | 4457 Willard Ave. (Wisconsin Ave.), MD | 301-652-9882
www.meiwahrestaurant.com

Purveying a "large variety" of "full-flavored Chinese" chow "with a nod to American tastes", these "high-volume" stalwarts in the West

End and Chevy Chase "hit the spot" for a "routine" fix that includes some "healthy options"; but surveyors split on the cost ("reasonable" vs. "slightly pricey"), and given atmospherics akin to a "hectic" "food factory" many "prefer the carryout."

Me Jana *Mideastern* | 23 | 20 | 23 | $34 |

Courthouse | Navy League Bldg. | 2300 Wilson Blvd. (Adams St.) | Arlington, VA | 703-465-4440 | www.me-jana.com

The "über-friendly" "staff treats you like family" at this Arlington Courthouse Mideastern "find", where a "tantalizing" menu highlighting "authentic Lebanese" specialties puts the focus on "delicious" "meze to share" and "comes off without a hitch"; maybe the "prices are set for more elegant dining", but the "inviting" vibes and "romantic" surroundings with a "small patio" are "nice for a splurge."

NEW Meridian Pint ● *American* | - | - | - | M |

Columbia Heights | 3400 11th St. NW (Park Row) | 202-588-1075 | www.meridianpint.com

At this craft beer–focused Columbia Heights newcomer, a rotating selection of 24 domestic drafts is backed by a wide-ranging, mid-priced American menu (from strip steak to vegan choices); the handsome, eco-friendly environs include a ground floor with rough-hewn communal tables and old-fashioned booths, plus a downstairs lounge with pool tables, a glass-enclosed beer cellar (displaying cask-conditioned ale and rare bottles) and booths sporting the much-buzzed-about 'pour-your-own' taps.

NEW Merzi *Indian* | - | - | - | I |

Penn Quarter | 415 Seventh St. NW (bet. D & E Sts.) | 202-656-3794 | www.merzi.com

This modern Indian adds new flavor to the Penn Quarter's fast-casual lineup with an affordable menu that lets diners customize meals using rice, naan, chaat or salad as a base, adding proteins and then topping with sauces and chutneys; assembly-line production makes it perfect for a quick bite in the basic but modern storefront setting, or you can get your creation to go.

Meskerem *Ethiopian* | 20 | 16 | 18 | $27 |

Adams Morgan | 2434 18th St. NW (bet. Belmont & Columbia Rds.) | 202-462-4100 | www.meskeremonline.com

An "exotic" "adventure" awaits at this "popular" "Adams Morgan staple", a "warm" if "understated" triplex where diners park on "hassocks on the floor" to enjoy an "addictive" "array" of "traditional" Ethiopian dishes scooped up with spongy injera bread; the "friendly" staff is "helpful to folks who haven't wrestled with" the genre before, and it offers "excellent value" for a "casual meal with a group."

Mezè ● *Mideastern* | 21 | 18 | 17 | $31 |

Adams Morgan | 2437 18th St. NW (bet. Belmont & Columbia Rds.) | 202-797-0017 | www.mezedc.com

Graze on "tasty" Turkish "standouts" from a "large, tapas-style menu" at this "happenin'" Adams Morgan Mideasterner, a sporty split-level with a bustling sidewalk cafe; there's also a "late-night" snack selec-

	FOOD	DECOR	SERVICE	COST

tion, though you may "feel rushed" when it's overrun with weekend barhoppers binging on "the different flavors" of mojitos; P.S. it offers belly-dancing classes on Sundays and tango lessons Mondays.

Mia's Pizzas *Pizza*

| 21 | 15 | 18 | $24 |

Bethesda | 4926 Cordell Ave. (bet. Norfolk Ave. & Old Georgetown Rd.), MD | 301-718-6427 | www.miaspizzasbethesda.com

Pizzaphiles posit the "wood-fired" wares are "worth a detour" at this "pocket-friendly" "neighborhood" fave in Bethesda, which turns out "quality" "Neapolitan" pies with "creative toppings" (and "don't miss the cupcakes for dessert"); chef-owner Melissa Ballinger and her "pleasant" team foster "upbeat" vibes in a "homey" indoor-outdoor setting where "kids are welcome", but "space is limited" so when things get "busy" you'll "have to wait."

Michael's Noodles *Chinese*

| ∇ 23 | 10 | 21 | $21 |

Rockville | 10038 Darnestown Rd. (Travilah Rd.), MD | 301-738-0370 | www.michaelsnoodles.com

The "challenge is eating your way through" the "extensive menu" at this "small" Rockville "storefront Chinese", a "family favorite" boasting some 250 "yummy" and "authentic" choices, including an impressive "variety" of "unusual" dishes and a specialty beef noodle soup that's a "wonderment"; "bring lots of friends" since you'll want to "order more than" you can handle, especially at these prices.

NEW Michel *French*

| - | - | - | E |

Tysons Corner | Ritz-Carlton Tysons Corner | 1700 Tysons Blvd. (International Dr.) | McLean, VA | 703-744-3999 | www.michelrichardva.com

Michel Richard brings modern French cuisine with American accents to the Ritz-Carlton in Tysons Corner, pairing his signature imaginative creations with boutique wines, affordably priced given the upscale location; the elegant, contemporary setting features textured walls and banquettes, sculptured lights that change colors, a showcase kitchen and a chef's table suspended from the ceiling (look, ma - no legs!).

Mie N Yu *American*

| 17 | 25 | 18 | $45 |

Georgetown | 3125 M St. NW (bet. 31st St. & Wisconsin Ave.) | 202-333-6122 | www.mienyu.com

A "super-cool" interior "like you've stepped into another country" marks this Georgetown New American "wonder", whose "enchanting" series of "Silk Road–themed" rooms include a Moroccan bazaar, Turkish tent and chef's table in a suspended "birdcage"; a "pricey" menu with Asian, Mideastern and Med inflections and service that varies from "helpful" to "slow" "don't measure up to the decor", but "phenomenal" cocktails work for "date nights or celebrations."

Mikaku Ⓜ *Japanese*

| - | - | - | M |

Herndon | McLearen Sq. | 3065J Centreville Rd. (McLearen Rd.), VA | 703-467-0220

"Hidden" in a Herndon mini-mall, this traditional Japanese outpost appeals to sushi connoisseurs with "fantastic" rolls backed up by real-deal tempura, teriyaki and noodles as well as inventive small plates; a commodious if casual space with a tatami room, it's a "favorite" among clued-in locals and "business travelers" destined for nearby Dulles Airport.

Mike's "American" *American* 22 | 19 | 22 | $34

Springfield | 6210 Backlick Rd. (Commerce St.), VA | 703-644-7100 | www.greatamericanrestaurants.com

They aim to "please everyone" at this Springfield "standby" from the Great American Restaurants folks, which "consistently" "wins you over" with "excellent service" and "satisfying" American eats starring "on-point" steaks at a "moderate price"; the "big", sports-themed digs are "always mobbed", but "if you can tolerate the din" and "waiting for a table" (phone first "to get on the list") it sets "the gold standard for family dining."

Minerva *Indian* 21 | 11 | 14 | $19

Gaithersburg | 16240 Frederick Rd. (Shady Grove Rd.), MD | 301-948-9898

Fairfax | 10364 Lee Hwy. (University Dr.), VA | 703-383-9200

Herndon | Village Center at Dulles | 2443 Centreville Rd. (Sunrise Valley Dr.), VA | 703-793-3223

Chantilly | Chantilly Park | 14513B Lee Jackson Memorial Hwy. (Airline Pkwy.), VA | 703-378-7778

www.minervacuisine.com

Fire-eaters attest the "chefs don't believe in holding back the spices" at this "modestly priced" Indian chainlet, where the "rich" "variety" of "delicious" specialties and "terrific" lunch buffets attract sizable support from the "South Asian population"; regulars advise "don't expect much" from the service or surroundings ("you call a few wall-mounted TVs decor?"), but you'll probably be "too satiated" to care.

Minh's Restaurant Ⓜ *Vietnamese* 24 | 16 | 20 | $25

Courthouse | 2500 Wilson Blvd. (Cleveland St.) | Arlington, VA | 703-525-2828 | www.minhrestaurant.com

"Genuine" cooking "at pretty reasonable prices" is "more than enough reason" for "city dwellers to cross the Potomac" to this Arlington Courthouse "neighborhood Vietnamese", a "best bet" for "delicious" "classics" in a room furnished with artifacts of bygone Saigon; its minhions trust the "helpful" servers "for advice on what to order", including the occasional "revelation" "that's not on the menu."

☒ Minibar Ⓜ *Eclectic* 26 | 21 | 24 | $195

Penn Quarter | 405 Eighth St. NW, 2nd fl. (bet. D & E Sts.) | 202-393-0812 | www.minibarbyjoseandres.com

You can "expect the unexpected" from "magician" José Andrés, so "do whatever it takes to score" one of the six $150 seats at his tiny Penn Quarter Eclectic "chef's tasting" happening five nights a week in part of the former Café Atlántico space (the rest of which now hosts the pop-up America Eats through December 2011); it's an "incredible" 30-bite "science class" dealing in "molecular gastronomy" that may be "America's closest approximation" to an "el Bulli experience", thus fans are happy about the rumored expansion in 2012; P.S. ratings include votes for its erstwhile parent.

	FOOD	DECOR	SERVICE	COST

Mio ⓈＮuevo Latino
19 | 18 | 20 | $52

Downtown | 1110 Vermont Ave. NW (L St.) | 202-955-0075 |
www.miorestaurant.com

"In transition" after "ups and downs" staffing the kitchen, this "authentically chic" Downtowner has followers "pleasantly surprised" by chef-owner Manuel Iguina's modern Latin leanings, on display in "quality" dishes like ceviche and oxtail mofongo; "friendly" staffers mind the handsome, earth-toned space, and "excellent" specialty drinks fuel the hopping "happy hour."

Mi Rancho *Tex-Mex*
18 | 14 | 19 | $24

Germantown | 19725A Germantown Rd. (Middlebrook Rd.), MD | 301-515-7480
Rockville | Congressional Plaza | 1488 Rockville Pike (Congressional Ln.), MD | 240-221-2636
Silver Spring | 8701 Ramsey Ave. (Cameron St.), MD | 301-588-4872
www.miranchotexmexrestaurant.com

Compadres get "what they expect" from this "serviceable" Tex-Mex trio, namely "decent" "standard fare", "cold margaritas" and "affordable prices" in "family" cantina settings with "outdoor patios" where "no one will notice your crying baby"; overall they're "adequate and nothing more", but "local" posses in need of a "convenient" "default" "let that slide", so "expect to wait" on weekends.

Mitsitam Café *American*
20 | 14 | 12 | $18

SW | National Museum of the American Indian | 950 Independence Ave. SW (4th St.) | 202-633-7039 | www.mitsitamcafe.com

"Escape the food desert" of the Mall at this cafe in the National Museum of the American Indian, where "different stations" offer a "surprising variety" of "interesting" "Native American cuisine" (plank-roasted salmon, fry bread) with some "wonderful" "regional" variants; "yes, it's a cafeteria" that may be "jammed with tourists", but for Smithsonian-goers "in the know" this is "where to lunch."

Mixt Greens *American/Sandwiches*
- | - | - | I

Golden Triangle | 1200 19th St. NW (M St.) | 202-315-5230 Ⓢ
Golden Triangle | 1700 K St. NW (17th St.) | 202-315-5210
ＮＥＷ **Bethesda** | Wildwood Shopping Ctr. | 10217 Old Georgetown Rd. (Grosvenor Ln.), MD | 301-493-4361
www.mixtgreens.com

This affordable, eco-friendly San Francisco salad and sandwich chain offers items made with high-end ingredients like truffle-roasted spuds, spice-rubbed meats and port wine reduction drizzles; the industrial-mod quarters include an edible living wall upon which seasonal rotating herbs and vegetables are grown to add a gourmet kick to meals.

ＮＥＷ Mixx ● *American*
- | - | - | I

Downtown | Renaissance Hotel | 999 Ninth St. NW (bet. I & K Sts.) | 202-898-9000 | www.marriott.com

This Downtown hotel lounge celebrated its 21st birthday by updating its American small plates, cocktails and wines by the glass – and, thankfully, everything remains affordable; completing the reconception, it traded drab conventioneer decor for sleek accoutrements like a polished-stone bar, curvaceous leather chaises, LED wall art and a bright-yellow Murano glass chandelier, with high-tech conveniences such as free WiFi and an MP3 docking station thrown into the mix.

Moby Dick *Persian* 21 | 7 | 15 | $14

Dupont Circle | 1300 Connecticut Ave. NW (N St.) | 202-833-9788 🛇
Georgetown | 1070 31st St. NW (bet. K & M Sts.) | 202-333-4400
Bethesda | 7027 Wisconsin Ave. (Leland St.), MD | 301-654-1838
Gaithersburg | Market Sq. | 105 Market St. (Kentlands Blvd.), MD | 301-987-7770
Germantown | 12844 Pinnacle Dr. (Century Blvd.), MD | 301-916-1555
Rockville | Fallsgrove Village Shopping Ctr. | 14929A Shady Grove Rd. (bet. Blackwell Rd. & Fallsgrove Blvd.), MD | 301-738-0005
Silver Spring | 909 Ellsworth Dr. (Fenton St.), MD | 301-578-8777
Arlington | 3000 Washington Blvd. (Highland St.), VA | 703-465-1600
Fairfax | 12154 Fairfax Towne Ctr. (Ox Rd.), VA | 703-352-6226
McLean | 6854 Old Dominion Dr. (Chain Bridge Rd.), VA | 703-448-8448
www.mobysonline.com
Additional locations throughout the DC area

Experience "fast food, Persian style" at these "go-to" area "kebab joints", "big favorites" for "reliably tasty" skewers accessorized with the "best hummus", "delicious" rice and "yummy" "fresh" "flatbread" at a "value as large as the white whale"; just know that the "counter service" shifts from "swift" to "slow" at peak times, and those who harpoon the "no-frills" setups "prefer to take out."

NEW Mokomandy *Cajun/Korean* - | - | - | M

Sterling | Great Falls Plaza | 20789 Great Falls Plaza (Lowes Island Blvd.), VA | 571-313-0505 | www.mokomandy.com

Cajun and Korean cuisines get separate but equal treatment at this midpriced Sterling newcomer, where diners order from a varied menu of small, medium and large plates from each culinary tradition; while the innovative mix-and-match concept has grabbed headlines, the date-worthy, casual-chic setting (blond wood, inviting bar, open kitchen) and handcrafted cocktails are getting almost as much local buzz.

Mon Ami Gabi *French* 19 | 19 | 20 | $39

Bethesda | 7239 Woodmont Ave. (Elm St.), MD | 301-654-1234
Reston | Reston Town Ctr. | 11950 Democracy Dr. (Library St.), VA | 703-707-0233
www.monamigabi.com

"Straight out of central casting" with their tiled floors, "rolling wine carts" and chalkboard menus, these "high-energy" French bistros in Bethesda and Reston (links in a nationwide chain) supply "appetizing" favorites à la the "trademark steak frites" plus "super service" "at a fair price"; *oui*, they're "nothing revolutionary", but the "formula works" well enough to "relive that trip" to Paree "before the movie or after shopping."

	FOOD	DECOR	SERVICE	COST

Monocle, The ⓢ *American* — 14 | 17 | 19 | $45

Capitol Hill | 107 D St. NE (1st St.) | 202-546-4488 | www.themonocle.com

"Members of Congress" and "heavyweight" "politicos of every stripe" convene at this "aging" Capitol Hill "institution" "within voting distance of the Senate", where the staff "gets you in and out" "in time for the next hearing" and seeing "who's lunching with whom" is the "best part of the decor"; the Traditional American food's "fair at best", but here "it's about who's eating, not what they're eating."

Montmartre ⓜ *French* — 24 | 18 | 20 | $43

Capitol Hill | 327 Seventh St. SE (Pennsylvania Ave.) | 202-544-1244 | www.montmartredc.com

"Ooh-la-la!" gush Francophiles at this "top-notch" Capitol Hill bistro, an "intimate" "delight" with "mouthwatering", "reasonably priced" French cuisine (mainly meats and seafood) and "charming" service in a "lively" setting likened to "a little bit of Paris"; the "tight" quarters can get "a bit claustrophobic", but it's "lovely to eat on the patio" too.

Moroni & Brother's
Restaurant *Latin American/Pizza* — - | - | - | I

Petworth | 4811 Georgia Ave. NW (Decatur St.) | 202-829-2090 | www.moroniandbrothers.com

Besides turning out "well-executed" wood-fired pizza in the style of Pizzeria Paradiso (the owners are alums), this Petworth "jewel in the rough" accommodates its expat fans with homestyle Salvadoran specialties at breakfast and lunch, along with other Latin American faves; the setup is modest, but that's why it remains a "secret."

Morrison-Clark Restaurant *American* — 23 | 24 | 23 | $55

Downtown | Morrison-Clark Inn | 1015 L St. NW (bet. 10th & 11th Sts.) | 202-898-1200 | www.morrisonclark.com

Recalling a "bygone era", the dining room of this "classic" Downtown inn is an "intimate" enclave of "old-fashioned elegance" where seasonal New American fare is "beautifully prepared and presented" in an atmosphere of "lovely" Victoriana; "romantic" vibes that extend to a veranda and courtyard are fail-safe for sweethearts of "all ages."

Morton's The Steakhouse *Steak* — 25 | 22 | 25 | $66

Georgetown | 3251 Prospect St. NW (bet. Potomac St. & Wisconsin Ave.) | 202-342-6258

Golden Triangle | Washington Sq. | 1050 Connecticut Ave. NW (bet. K & L Sts.) | 202-955-5997

Bethesda | Hyatt Regency | 7400 Wisconsin Ave. (Old Georgetown Rd.), MD | 301-657-2650

Crystal City | Crystal City Shops | 1750 Crystal Dr. (bet. 15th & 18th Sts.) | Arlington, VA | 703-418-1444

Reston | Reston Town Ctr. | 11956 Market St. (Freedom Sq.), VA | 703-796-0128

Tysons Corner | Fairfax Sq. | 8075 Leesburg Pike (Gallows Rd.) | Vienna, VA | 703-883-0800

www.mortons.com

A steakhouse "standard-bearer", this "big-ticket" chain offers "excellently prepared" cuts of beef and "grand sides" "served profes-

	FOOD	DECOR	SERVICE	COST

sionally" amid an "ambiance of wealth and class"; some find it a bit "staid" and wish they'd "lose the raw-meat presentation" and "high" wine pricing, but the many who love its "traditional" ways consider it "one of the best."

Mourayo *Greek*
25 | 19 | 23 | $48

Dupont Circle | 1732 Connecticut Ave. NW (bet. R & S Sts.) | 202-667-2100 | www.mourayous.com

Discover "what Greek food can be" at this "cheerful" Dupont Circle Hellenic, where a "consistently excellent" menu ventures well "beyond spanakopita" with a "wide selection" ranging from "classics" like whole grilled fish to more "innovative" picks; the "first-rate staff" is "helpful guiding diners through the unfamiliar options" and "hard-to-find" wines, and the "smart-looking" room is buoyed by a nautical theme.

Mrs. K's Toll House ⓜ *American*
22 | 23 | 23 | $40

Silver Spring | 9201 Colesville Rd. (Dale Dr.), MD | 301-589-3500 | www.mrsks.com

"Completely endearing", this circa-1930 Silver Spring New American is set in a "quaint" Tudor villa surrounded by "beautiful gardens" where "terrific" "old-style" service ushers in a "solid" menu that shows refreshing "signs of modernizing" these days; long a "place to bring out-of-town visitors" or "gather for special occasions", its "renovated basement wine cellar" now adds "romantic" appeal to the "expensive" but "delightful" package.

Murasaki *Japanese*
22 | 15 | 20 | $37

Upper NW | 4620 Wisconsin Ave. NW (bet. Brandywine & Chesapeake Sts.) | 202-966-0023 | www.murasakidc.com

This "oft-overlooked" Upper NW Japanese is a "neighborhood" "go-to" with a rep for "top-notch" sushi crafted from the "highest quality" fish and served with "no attitude"; the "first-class" eating extends to "authentic" cooked fare, and while the "comfortable" quarters may seem plain, there's "always a table" and a "nice" patio awaits "in warm weather."

🆕 Mussel Bar ➊ *Belgian*
- | - | - | M

Bethesda | 7262 Woodmont Ave. (Elm St.), MD | 301-215-7817 | www.musselbar.com

Chef-restaurateur Robert Wiedmaier pays homage to his Belgian roots at this midpriced Downtown Bethesda newcomer where an open kitchen turns out wood-fired flatbreads, sandwiches, grilled seafood and meat, and, yes, mussels prepared in a variety of ways; an oyster cart roves the stylish dark-wood-paneled space that rings a boat-shaped central bar where beer is poured from a sizable, wide-ranging list.

Myanmar ⓜ *Burmese*
∇ 24 | 6 | 15 | $20

Falls Church | Merrifalls Plaza | 7810C Lee Hwy. (Hyson Ln.), VA | 703-289-0013

"Explore" a "swirl of tastes" at this "inexpensive" Burmese "hole-in-the-wall" in a Falls Church strip center, home to "wonderful", "spicy" specialties like "super" salads and curries that make the "eyes water"; it's "not much to look at" (even with newly "added space") and the service is "not in a hurry", but "adventurous" eaters find the food a "welcome change."

Mykonos Grill ☑ *Greek* | 22 | 19 | 20 | $34 |

Rockville | 121 Congressional Ln. (Rockville Pike), MD | 301-770-5999 | www.mykonosgrill.com

"They get it right" at this "highly enjoyable" Greek off Rockville Pike, a "dependable" outfit for "traditional dishes" (e.g. "yummy" leg of lamb) and "warm" service in a "whitewashed", azure-accented space that "transports you to" the Aegean; despite a somewhat steep "price point", it's "popular" and apt to be "crowded on weekends."

Nage *American/Seafood* | 22 | 16 | 21 | $44 |

Scott Circle | Marriott Courtyard Embassy Row | 1600 Rhode Island Ave. NW (bet. 16th & 17th Sts.) | 202-448-8005 | www.nagerestaurant.com

Fin fans surf into this "special surprise" in the Marriott Courtyard Embassy Row, a Delaware Shore import whose "inventive" New American cuisine "brings the beach to DC" with its focus on "wonderfully prepared" seafood like crab cakes; "personal service" and relatively "cost-effective" tabs please, but surveyors aren't hooked on the quarters, which some say "lack atmosphere."

Nam-Viet *Vietnamese* | 21 | 11 | 17 | $24 |

Cleveland Park | 3419 Connecticut Ave. NW (bet. Macomb & Ordway Sts.) | 202-237-1015

Clarendon | 1127 N. Hudson St. (bet. 13th St. & Wilson Blvd.), VA | 703-522-7110

www.namviet1.com

"Incredibly good, incredibly affordable and somehow never crowded", these long-running Vietnamese – one a "holdout against Clarendon modernization", the other in "high-rent" Cleveland Park – dish up "satisfying meals" in a "quick, quiet" fashion; perhaps they're "nothing fancy", but regulars who "go for the pho" and other "mainstays" like "crispy spring rolls" avow it's a "great way" to "expand your palate."

Nando's Peri-Peri *Chicken* | 20 | 16 | 14 | $16 |

Chinatown | 819 Seventh St. NW (bet. H & I Sts.) | 202-898-1225

Dupont Circle | 1210 18th St. NW (Connecticut Ave.) | 202-621-8603

NEW **Silver Spring** | 924 Ellsworth Dr. (bet. Fenton St. & Georgia Ave.), MD | 301-588-7280

www.nandosperiperi.com

"Big flavor and little prices" cause connoisseurs to cluck over the "delicious rotisserie chicken", "incredible sauces" and "stellar" sides at these hatchlings of a Portuguese/South African chain; the "semi-self service" (order at the counter, then food is brought to tables in the "rustic" rooms) can be a "chaotic process" that "takes longer than it should", but patience is "rewarded" with a "satisfying" "budget meal."

	FOOD	DECOR	SERVICE	COST

Napoleon *French* | 16 | 20 | 14 | $31 |

Adams Morgan | 1847 Columbia Rd. NW (bet. Biltmore St. & Mintwood Pl.) | 202-299-9630 | www.napoleondc.com

"Crêpes, cocktails and a well-dressed crowd" converge at this moody French "hot spot" in Adams Morgan, a Café Bonaparte offshoot with a "great personality" of its own; while there's an "extended" bistro menu, "wiser patrons" stick with the house specialty and "affordable wine" and don't expect much in the way of service; P.S. Thursday-Saturday "after 9 PM it turns into an amazing nightclub" with a DJ.

Nava Thai *Thai* | 23 | 15 | 19 | $23 |

Wheaton | 11301 Fern St. (Price Ave.), MD | 240-430-0495 | www.navathai.food.officelive.com

"Ooh, what's that?" is a common refrain from patrons "looking at the interesting dishes at the next table" at this "worth-the-trip" Wheatonite whose "fresh, tasty" Thai street food offers "lots of flavor at low prices"; ask the "friendly" servers who canvass the "large", somewhat "weird" digs (remnants abound from its previous steakhouse incarnation) to "pump up the heat", but beware: it may "knock your socks off."

Negril Ⓩ *Jamaican* | ∇ 23 | 9 | 16 | $15 |

NEW **Anacostia** | 2863 Alabama Ave. SE (30th St.) | 202-575-7555
U Street Corridor | 2301G Georgia Ave. NW (Bryant St.) | 202-332-3737
NEW **Laurel** | Laurel Shopping Ctr. | 331 Montrose Ave. (Washington Blvd.), MD | 301-490-0808
Mitchellville | Mitchellville Plaza | 12116 Central Ave. (Enterprise Rd.), MD | 301-249-9101
Silver Spring | 965 Thayer Ave. (Georgia Ave.), MD | 301-585-3000
www.negrileats.com

Get "solid grub for the buck" at this chainlet of "cheap, fast and tasty" Jamaicans known for their "mouthwatering" jerk chicken sandwiches, "veggie pastries" with "American-friendly" spicing and generous portions of roti ("always enough for lunch *and* dinner"); service is "warm and friendly" but space is "somewhat limited", so many opt for "takeout."

Neisha Thai *Thai* | 19 | 16 | 19 | $27 |

Upper NW | 4445 Wisconsin Ave. NW (Albemarle St.) | 202-966-7088
Tysons Corner | Tysons Corner Ctr. | 7924 Tysons Corner Ctr. (Chain Bridge Rd.) | McLean, VA | 703-883-3588
www.neisha.net

"Eclectic", somewhat "soothing" spaces replete with faux rock walls and neon (think "cave meets Las Vegas") set the stage for "hearty Thai fare" with "complex flavors" at this "convenient" Tysons Corner/Tenleytown duo; "gracious service" and "value" pricing add to the appeal, as does the "quick take-out" and delivery service.

Nellie's Sports Bar ◐ *Pub Food* | 17 | 19 | 20 | M |

U Street Corridor | 900 U St. NW (9th St.) | 202-332-6355 | www.nelliessportsbar.com

"Catch a 'Skins game" at this "straight-friendly" gay sports bar on U Street where there's "always good eye candy", a "huge roof deck", "cute bartenders" and "decent" pub grub on a midpriced menu that includes a few South American specialties like empanadas and arepas; "lots of theme nights" like "super-fun drag bingo" can lift your spirits "if your team goes south."

New Fortune ● *Chinese* — 22 | 11 | 14 | $24

Gaithersburg | 16515 S. Frederick Ave. (Westland Dr.), MD | 301-548-8886 | www.newfortunedimsum.com

At this "cavernous" Gaithersburg Chinese, it's "all about" the lunchtime "dim sum carts" packed with "Hong Kong–style" delicacies that "keep coming until you're so stuffed you want to cry"; the space has all the "appeal of a high school gym" and features "frantic" servers, but the large number of "Asian diners" attest to its rep as "one of the best."

New Heights *American* — 22 | 20 | 22 | $52

Woodley Park | 2317 Calvert St. NW (Connecticut Ave.) | 202-234-4110 | www.newheightsrestaurant.com

While the enduring "charm" of this "wonderful" Woodley Parker owes something to its perch overlooking Rock Creek Park, it's the "ever-changing" menu of "innovative" New American fare that makes it "irresistible"; add in a "true artist" tending bar downstairs and "knowledgeable" waiters working the intimate, "odd"-shaped quarters, and even critics who flag an occasional "uneven" performance vow to "give it another chance."

New Kam Fong ● *Chinese* — ∇ 24 | 10 | 20 | $25

Wheaton | 2400 University Blvd. (Elkin St.), MD | 301-933-6388

It's the "real deal" squeal Sinophiles, so "get there early" for some of the "area's best dim sum" at this bustling, bright Wheaton storefront with an extensive menu of other "innovative" – and affordable – Chinese fare made with "quality ingredients"; folks daunted by the choices can ask the "engaging staff" or take ordering cues from the hanging BBQ meats or marine life in the aquarium.

NEW Newton's Table *American* — - | - | - | M

Bethesda | 4917 Elm St. (bet. Arlington Rd. & Woodmont Ave.), MD | 301-718-0550 | www.newtonstable.com

Fans of chef Dennis Friedman (ex Bezu) will find some favorites reprised at this newcomer in Downtown Bethesda, where the midpriced New American fare also includes creative takes on sandwiches (notably, a surf 'n' burger) on the lunchtime menu; a soothing water wall is the focal point of the svelte dining room, while a trim bar/lounge provides an area for more causal sips and bites.

NEW Next Stage Ⓜ *Eclectic* — - | - | - | I

SW | Arena Stage | 1101 Sixth St. SW (bet. K & M Sts.) | 202-600-4100 | www.arenastage.org

At the spectacular, newly reopened Arena Stage on the Southwest waterfront, this counter-serve cafe by José Andrés offers an eclectic range of soups, salads, sandwiches and hot entrees, some themed to current productions; its balcony location facing the facility's glass-fronted entrance provides dramatic views for customers in line, who then take their trays to a minimalist seating area; P.S. the cafe is open only for 2.5 hours pre-curtain; lighter, pre-packaged fare is available at Andrés' lower-level stand from 30 minutes before curtain until one hour after each show.

Neyla *Lebanese*
22 | 21 | 18 | $44

Georgetown | 3206 N St. NW (Wisconsin Ave.) | 202-333-6353 | www.neyla.com

Take a "wonderful trip without leaving the District" at this "vibrant" Georgetown nightspot dishing up "well-prepared" Lebanese small plates and full-sized dishes with a Med accent; it's a "bit pricey", but the "expansive veranda, attentive service" and "romantic" interior (think tentlike ceiling and purple hues) lead many to say it's "worth it."

Nick's Chophouse *Steak*
20 | 18 | 18 | $46

Rockville | 700 King Farm Blvd. (bet. Gaither & Shady Grove Rds.), MD | 301-926-8869 | www.nickschophouserockville.com

Local carnivores steer their way to this high-end Rockville steakhouse for a "real white-tablecloth, fine-dining experience" in an airy, chandeliered room; critics who cite "uneven" food and "slow" service find it "too expensive for what you get", though the budget-minded "appreciate" its three-course $23.95 menu (Friday–Sunday).

1905 ⓈⓂ *French*
19 | 21 | 18 | $39

Mt. Vernon Square/Convention Center | 1905 Ninth St. NW (bet. T & U Sts.) | 202-332-1905 | www.1905dc.com

The "funky" decor ("red velvet and dimmed lights") summons a "Parisian hole-in-the-wall" vibe at this U Street "date spot" where "people linger" over affordable French bistro specialties, absinthe, "wine and enchanted conversation"; true, the "small bar" and bi-level townhouse space can stretch servers, but "given how crowded" it gets (particularly on weekends and "live jazz" Thursday nights), most shrug it off; P.S. "Sunday brunch is one of DC's best-kept secrets."

Niwano Hana *Japanese*
∇ 26 | 16 | 20 | $35

Rockville | Wintergreen Plaza | 887 Rockville Pike (Edmonston Dr.), MD | 301-294-0553 | www.niwanohana.com

True, there's lots of "love" for "cheerful" chef-owner Takashi Tanda's "outstanding", über-"fresh" sushi at this affordable Rockville stalwart, but there's also a "surprisingly broad spectrum" of other "delicious" Japanese fare to sample (e.g. noodle dishes and teriyakis); "attentive" staffers keep things moving in the "relatively small quarters", but since it's "always crowded", there's always "carryout."

Nooshi *Asian*
19 | 14 | 17 | $23

Golden Triangle | 1120 19th St. NW (bet. L & M Sts.) | 202-293-3138 | www.nooshidc.com

"Big portions", "affordable prices" and "decent" Pan-Asian chow lure Golden Triangle lunchers to this "sushi and noodle house" whose "shoulder-to-shoulder tables and brusque but efficient service" encourage takeout and delivery; "great happy-hour deals"

| | FOOD | DECOR | SERVICE | COST |

keep it "crowded" "after work" as well ("watch out for groups doing sake bombs in the corner").

☑ Nora Ⓢ *American* | 26 | 23 | 25 | $65 |

Dupont Circle | 2132 Florida Ave. NW (R St.) | 202-462-5143 | www.noras.com

Chef/co-owner Nora Pouillon "put DC on the organic map" more than 30 years ago, and she's still "setting the bar" for late arrivals on the "green train" at this "genteel" "grande dame" above Dupont Circle; only the "freshest" "local ingredients" go into her "sophisticated" New American cooking, complemented by eco-conscious wines and "gracious service" in an "elegant" space adorned with vintage quilts (and "celebrities"); no wonder most depart with one "regret" – wishing they could "afford to eat here more often."

Northside Social *American/Coffeehouse* | - | - | - | I |

Clarendon | 3211 Wilson Blvd. (Fairfax Dr.), VA | 703-465-0145 | www.northsidesocialarlington.com

Caffeinistas and oenophiles pour into this Clarendon coffeehouse/ wine bar in a historic, two-story space, which the Liberty Tavern team has fitted out with laptop-friendly communal tables, window-side ledges, sofas and love seats; the downstairs counter proffers java, teas and freshly squeezed juices along with affordable sandwiches, soups, salads and baked goods, while patrons chill upstairs over vino by the glass or bottle paired with charcuterie and cheeses or the eats served below.

Notti Bianche *Italian* | 20 | 16 | 19 | $48 |

Foggy Bottom | George Washington University Inn | 824 New Hampshire Ave. NW (bet. H & I Sts.) | 202-298-8085 | www.nottibianche.com

"Tucked away" near the Kennedy Center, this "snug little" "pre-theater" "find" in Foggy Bottom delivers a "limited menu" of Italian fare prepared "with care" in a "European pub setting"; a few grumps gripe it's all merely "average", but at least it's "affordable" – and a considerable "savings over the KC's outrageous prices."

Oakville Grille & Wine Bar *American* | 19 | 18 | 19 | $39 |

Bethesda | Wildwood Shopping Ctr. | 10257 Old Georgetown Rd. (Democracy Blvd.), MD | 301-897-9100 | www.oakvillewinebar.com

"Even the pickiest wine snob" finds something to "love" at this Bethesda "neighborhood place" that pairs American entrees and "interesting appetizers" with "affordable" by-the-glass options; some sniff the food's a "little expensive" (and "pedestrian" at that), but they're somewhat soothed by "friendly staffers" who pour it on in a "quiet", white-tableclothed space near Strathmore Hall.

☑ Obelisk ⓈⓂ *Italian* | 27 | 20 | 27 | $87 |

Dupont Circle | 2029 P St. NW (bet. 20th & 21st Sts.) | 202-872-1180

"Balanced perfection" is the keystone of this "tiny" Italian prix fixe "treasure" off Dupont Circle, where "well-chosen wines" complement a "never-ending feast" of "inventive" fare that "changes daily" and is "special without being showy"; it comes at a "surprisingly reasonable cost" given the "quality" and the "high level of service", so "bring a special friend for a fine, long evening" – just be sure to "make reservations" and "go hungry."

Occidental Grill & Seafood *American* 22 | 23 | 23 | $55

Downtown | Willard Plaza | 1475 Pennsylvania Ave. NW (bet. 14th & 15th Sts.) | 202-783-1475 | www.occidentaldc.com

You "can't get any more Washington" than this "clubby" Downtown preserve revered for its "walls adorned with DC's power elite", "excellent" New American surf 'n' turf, "old-fashioned" service and strong "martinis that explain how some bills get through Congress"; it's "not for the thin of wallet" and a few fret it's a little "showbiz", but it's always a "lovely spot for lunch on the terrace."

Oceanaire Seafood Room *Seafood* 24 | 22 | 23 | $61

Downtown | 1201 F St. NW (bet. 12th & 13th Sts.) | 202-347-2277 | www.theoceanaire.com

"First-rate seafood" "impresses" fin fans at this "attractive" "high-end chain" (with links in Downtown DC and Baltimore's Harbor East) delivering "creative" preparations of "jet-fresh" fish matched by "excellent" wines; the group-friendly surroundings are "beautiful" and the "knowledgeable" staff ensures you feel "catered to", so most guests are "happy" to make the "splurge."

Olazzo *Italian* 21 | 16 | 21 | $29

Bethesda | 7921 Norfolk Ave. (Cordell Ave.), MD | 301-654-9496

Silver Spring | 8235 Georgia Ave. (Thayer Ave.), MD | 301-588-2540

www.olazzo.com

They stick to "doing the basics the best" at these "modest" Bethesda/ Silver Spring osterias, so expect "huge portions" of "authentic" food (e.g. "fantastic" lasagna) that could come from an "Italian grandmother's kitchen"; but take note: "small quarters" and "reasonable prices" mean they're often "crowded with long waits", and "half-price wine bottles" on Mondays simply feed the fire; P.S. aesthetes give the decor edge to the "hole-in-the-wall-cozy" Georgia Avenue branch.

Old Angler's Inn ⓜ *American* 19 | 22 | 19 | $56

Potomac | 10801 MacArthur Blvd. (Clara Barton Pkwy.), MD | 301-365-2425 | www.oldanglersinn.com

"Ambiance reigns supreme" at this "romantic" "old friend" near the C&O Canal in Potomac with a "beautiful patio" for outdoor dining and summer entertainment and a "cozy" lounge for "generous" drinks "next to the fireplace"; just "beware" of the "steep stairs" leading to its "old-world" dining room, where the waiters and "pricey" New American fare never quite "match the perfect setting."

ⓩ Old Ebbitt Grill ❶ *American* 20 | 23 | 21 | $40

Downtown | 675 15th St. NW (bet. F & G Sts.) | 202-347-4801 | www.ebbitt.com

"There's a special energy" at this "clubby" mega-saloon "almost in the shadow of the White House", where an "appealing menu" of

American fare that "fits everyone's pocketbook" is served with a side of "famous people"–watching; it's "loud, crowded" and "packed with tourists", but "old-school" service, "multiple bars" and "oysters at any hour" ease the pain, and the fact that it "oozes history" makes eating here a "quintessential DC experience."

Old Glory All-American BBQ *BBQ*   17 | 14 | 16 | $26

Georgetown | 3139 M St. NW (Wisconsin Ave.) | 202-337-3406 | www.oldglorybbq.com

Ok, it's "not the best barbecue", but for "perfectly adequate" ribs, pulled-pork sandwiches and Southern-accented sides in a "loud, fun and casual setting", this open-to-the-street Georgetown "institution" is an "easy choice"; while a few party-poopers pout it's all "about as authentic as an exhibit at Disney World" and "expensive" at that, unflagging supporters happily "leave a plate of bones and a good tip"; P.S. don't miss the "year-round roof deck."

Old Hickory Steakhouse *Steak*   ∇ 23 | 23 | 27 | $43

National Harbor | Gaylord National Hotel | 201 Waterfront St. (St. George Blvd.), MD | 301-965-4000 | www.gaylordhotels.com

A "great view of the Potomac" from its perch in the Gaylord National Hotel sets the stage for "steaks done to perfection" and an extensive wine list at this high-end, dinner-only room; the luxurious "ambiance" comes at a price, of course, but that includes details like a tableside presentation of artisan cheeses by a maitre d'fromage; P.S. a nautically themed bar features cozy white-leather settees.

Oohhs & Aahhs Ⓜ ⇎ *Southern*   ∇ 24 | 5 | 19 | $19

U Street Corridor | 1005 U St. NW (10th St.) | 202-667-7142 | www.oohhsnaahhs.com

"You'll leave stuffed, happy" and possibly "hating yourself the next day" after indulging in the "no-frills soul food at its best" served at this affordable U Street "dive"; "fried-to-perfection" chicken wings and other Southern staples can be washed down with "sweet tea and lemonade", but the "drab" counter-serve environs have some suggesting it's best to do that at home; P.S. no credit cards.

Open City ◑ *Diner*   18 | 15 | 16 | $21

Woodley Park | 2331 Calvert St. NW (24th St.) | 202-332-2331 | www.opencitydc.com

This "diner for the Sunday *New York Times* set" lures Woodley Parkers with a "diverse menu" of American "comfort food", from "primo" "all-day breakfasts" and "gigantic coffees" to "spot-on" pizzas and "awesome Bloody Marys"; it's all provided by "funky, downright friendly" waiters and bartenders in a "low-key" setting that gets a "bit noisy" and "crowded" – especially on weekends, when there's a "huge wait" for brunch.

Open Kitchen *Eclectic*   - | - | - | M

Falls Church | West Metro Plaza | 7115 Leesburg Pike (Broad St.), VA | 703-942-8148 | www.openkitchen-dcmetro.com

True, it's an "odd concept and space", but this "cooking school/bistro/coffee shop" and rentable industrial kitchen complex is "worth the effort to find", sitting as it is in a Falls Church shopping-center space fitted with concrete floors and butcher-block surfaces; diners seated at the "handful of tables" laud "artful" Eclectic cuisine using "fresh ingredients", chefs who "chat with guests" and "personable" staffers; P.S. dinner Wednesday–Saturday only; check hours.

Oriental East *Chinese*   22 | 10 | 14 | $21

Silver Spring | 1312 East-West Hwy. (Colesville Rd.), MD | 301-608-0030 | www.orientaleast.com

It's "one of the most popular dim sum spots" around, so get to this affordable Silver Spring Chinese "before it opens" to avoid "long waits" – and "go with a group" since there are so many "incredible" snack-size plates (e.g. "must-try" shrimp dumplings) whizzing by on fast-moving carts; in comparison, some consider the dinner entrees "decidedly mediocre", with "indifferent" service to match.

Oro Pomodoro *Italian*   18 | 17 | 17 | $29

Rockville | Rockville Town Sq. | 33A Maryland Ave. (bet. Beall Ave. & Middle Ln.), MD | 301-251-1111 | www.oropomodoro.com

Locals head to this "pleasant" Italian in Rockville Town Square for "reasonably authentic pizzas", pastas and "excellent fresh mozzarella appetizers" served in an airy, sometimes "noisy" room (the huge flat-screen TV doesn't help); alas, a fair share gripe that the menu's "execution is not as good as it sounds", the result being "low-end taste at moderate costs"; P.S. there's "nice outdoor seating."

Oval Room ☒ *American*   24 | 23 | 24 | $62

Golden Triangle | 800 Connecticut Ave. NW (bet. H & I Sts.) | 202-463-8700 | www.ovalroom.com

Political and media "stars are aligned" at this "elegant" New American offering "unique and unusual dishes" a "world away from the humdrum" yet just "steps from the White House"; "sit at the bar with a drink and a small plate" or duck into the "quiet, comfortable" dining room minded by servers who are "there when you need them", but note it doesn't come cheap – this is "expense-account" dining that "reeks of Washington in all the right ways."

☑ Oya *Asian*   23 | 26 | 21 | $45

Penn Quarter | 777 Ninth St. NW (H St.) | 202-393-1400 | www.oyadc.com

"Sleek, suave, chic": that just begins to describe the "stunning" "fire-and-ice"–themed interior at this Penn Quarter "original", where a "wall of chains", "vast stretches of marble" and a waterfall set the stage for "beautiful, *Iron Chef*–style" Asian-French creations (including "amazing sushi") and "bargain" prix fixe meals; even if some "wish the food were as exciting" as the decor and tap service as "hit-or-miss", most "can't resist coming back here."

Oyamel ◐ *Mexican*   24 | 21 | 20 | $39

Penn Quarter | 401 Seventh St. NW (D St.) | 202-628-1005 | www.oyamel.com

"Ingredients you won't find elsewhere" ("grasshopper tacos", anyone?) power the "unique flavors" at this midpriced Penn Quarter

Mexican, "another gem from chef José Andrés" that features "authentic" small plates for "adventurous" palates and crowd-pleasers like "guacamole made tableside"; it gets "bring-your-earplugs" loud and service can be "harried", but a "vibrant atmosphere" and "strong margaritas" mean there's always a "party in the room – and in your mouth."

NEW Ozzie's Corner Italian *Italian*

| - | - | - | M |

Fairfax | Fairfax Corner | 11880 Grand Commons Ave. (Monument Dr.), VA | 571-321-8000 | www.greatamericanrestaurants.com

The spirit of New York City's Little Italy infuses this latest mega-eatery from the Great American Restaurant Group in Fairfax Corner (a meatball-toss away from one of the group's Coastal Flats locations); colorful murals, dark-wood fittings, tile flooring and old-fashioned lights set a retro scene, while tons of roomy booths and a marble-topped bar provide spots for noshing on the hearty, midpriced fare.

Pacci's Neapolitan Pizzeria Ⓜ *Pizza*

| - | - | - | M |

Silver Spring | 8113 Georgia Ave. (Sligo Ave.), MD | 301-588-1011 | www.paccispizzeria.com

Neapolitan pizza crafted from imported ingredients and baked in an impressive 800-degree wood-fired oven is proffered at this midpriced Silver Spring pie shop, which features a long window bar and cozy tables in a brick-walled space splashed with olive green and dark red; housemade antipasti, salads, pastas and panini round out the menu, available for dining in or to go; P.S. plans are afoot to open a second Silver Spring location out in the former General Store premises in summer 2011.

Ⓩ Palena *American*

| 28 | 21 | 24 | $63 |

Cleveland Park | 3529 Connecticut Ave. NW (bet. Ordway & Porter Sts.) | 202-537-9250 | www.palenarestaurant.com

"Exemplary" chef-owner Frank Ruta conjures "meals that fire on all cylinders" at his Cleveland Park New American, where diners "savor every morsel" of "wonderful and imaginative" French-Italian-inspired prix fixe selections in an "old-world" dining room staffed by "cordial, attentive" servers; post-Survey, the "absolute steal" casual cafe portion has been expanded to the adjacent light-filled space and fitted out with a marble bar and wood-burning grill, further elevating what may be the "city's top burger" and making it easier to "snag a seat" for expanded lunch and dinner menus.

Palio of Leesburg *Italian*

| - | - | - | M |

Leesburg | 2 W. Market St. (King St.), VA | 703-779-0060 | www.paliooofleesburg.com

This midpriced Leesburgian stakes a claim to fine Italian dining in a two-story historic building; a convivial bar/lounge on the ground floor offers drinks and small plates, while authentic specialties like housemade pastas and osso buco are served above in the gold-and-sienna–toned dining room, decorated with paintings evoking its namesake Tuscan horse race; P.S. lunch and Sunday brunch are quieter than bustling weekend dinners.

	FOOD	DECOR	SERVICE	COST

☑ Palm, The *Seafood/Steak* | 24 | 20 | 24 | $66 |

Golden Triangle | 1225 19th St. NW (bet. M & N Sts.) | 202-293-9091
Tysons Corner | 1750 Tysons Blvd. (Rte. 123) | McLean, VA | 703-917-0200
www.thepalm.com

"Perfect" lobster, "superb" steaks and "hefty" cocktails are the signatures of these "bustling", "special-occasion" chophouse chain links in the Golden Triangle and Tysons Corner with a "dark men's-club" look and "wonderful atmosphere" enhanced by "caricatures of celebs" (and "locals") covering the walls; "old-school" service seals the deal, so while it's "not cheap", most conclude it's "worth it."

Panache Restaurant ☒ *Mediterranean* | 16 | 23 | 19 | $46 |

Golden Triangle | 1725 Desales St. NW (bet. Connecticut Ave. & 17th St.) | 202-293-7760
Tysons Corner | Pinnacle Towers S. | 1753 Pinnacle Dr. (Chain Bridge Rd.) | McLean, VA | 703-748-1919
www.panacherestaurant.com

With its luxe leather chairs, deep-red accents and retro-sleek lines, this "hip" Tysons Corner resto-lounge (with a Golden Triangle sibling) oozes "ambiance", while a Med menu of "generous" small and large plates makes it a "good place" for "large parties" to "try many tastes"; "inventive" cocktails, a deep wine list and "pleasant service" add further panache, but it's not enough for those who deem the fare merely "ok."

🆕 Panas *Pan-Latin* | - | - | - | I |

Dupont Circle | 2029 P St. NW (bet. 20th & 21st Sts.) | 202-223-2964 | www.panasgourmet.com

This sprightly step-down counter-serve entry near Dupont Circle enables hand-held snacking via cheap and flaky empanadas, both savory and sweet, based on regional specialties from across Central and South America; whimsical touches, like a patch of pampas grass affixed to a wall, enliven its modish white-and–burnt orange decor.

Panjshir *Afghan* | 22 | 17 | 22 | $25 |

Falls Church | 924 W. Broad St. (West St.), VA | 703-536-4566 | www.panjshirrestaurant.com

"Afghan comfort food" "done exceptionally well" – from "delicious" kebabs to "superb" vegetable dishes and dumplings – "attracts a loyal clientele" to this "well-priced" Falls Church "longtime favorite"; "warm and welcoming" service adds to the Kabul cool, and homeland artifacts decorate the simple dining space.

Paolo's *Californian/Italian* | 18 | 16 | 17 | $35 |

Georgetown | 1303 Wisconsin Ave. NW (N St.) | 202-333-7353 ●
Reston | Reston Town Ctr. | 11898 Market St. (Reston Pkwy.), VA | 703-318-8920
www.paolosristorante.com

While the free breadsticks and tapenade may be the "best thing" about these "moderately priced" Cal-Itals, "decent" wood-fired pizza, "pasta basics" and salads in "kid-friendly" confines make them an "easy dinner" or lunch; at least they have "lively" bars, and "dining on the sidewalk watching Georgetowners stroll by" or "near the big fountain" in Reston Town Center add a touch of "romance."

Park at Fourteenth ⊠Ⓜ *American* ▽ 21 | 20 | 16 | $38

Downtown | 920 14th St. NW (bet. I & K Sts.) | 202-737-7275 | www.theparkat14th.com

Set in an "amazing old house" near Franklin Square, this "lounge/nightclub" also serves "surprisingly good (and affordable)" American comfort food like crab cakes and steaks; patrons dine on the lower levels and party to a DJ above amid a sea of polished wood and fiery chandeliers, a "wild" setting to some, a "tad pretentious" to others; P.S. food is served Thursday and Friday only; the lounge is open Thursday–Saturday.

Parkway Deli *Deli* 19 | 7 | 18 | $21

Silver Spring | Rock Creek Shopping Ctr. | 8317 Grubb Rd. (E. West Hwy.), MD | 301-587-1427 | www.theparkwaydeli.com

"Close but no cigar" say NYC deli snobs, but Silver Spring denizens happily "jam" the "purple-painted" dining room of this "good ol' standby" for "large breakfasts" and "traditional Jewish" fare like "Bubbe's chicken soup", "overstuffed sandwiches" and a "free pickle bar (need I say more?)"; true, it "isn't New York", but it's a "welcome relief from by-the-book chain eateries" nonetheless.

Pasha Cafe *Mediterranean* ▽ 20 | 12 | 18 | $25

Cherrydale | 3911 N. Lee Hwy. (Pollard St.) | Arlington, VA | 703-528-1111 | www.pashacafe.com

"Delicious, affordable and quick", this "reliable" Med is a "surprisingly good" "find" in an "unprepossessing" Cherrydale strip mall; "extremely nice" folks dish up "outstanding" lamb, Greek salads, kebabs and chicken shawarma (plus "seafood specials" and pizza with Middle Eastern toppings like moussaka) in a simple, wood-accented room, while a "nice patio" adds fair-weather appeal.

Passage to India *Indian* 24 | 21 | 22 | $38

Bethesda | 4931 Cordell Ave. (bet. Norfolk Ave. & Old Georgetown Rd.), MD | 301-656-3373 | www.passagetoindia.info

For a "culinary tour of the entire subcontinent", book passage to this midpriced "standard-bearer for Indian restaurants" in Bethesda and explore its "interesting survey of regional cuisines" (each with its own "delicately balanced" spices); "thoughtful service" by "waiters in tuxedos" add to the "elegant, bordering on formal" atmosphere, as do the interesting "pictures on the wall" and wooden carvings.

Passenger, The ❶ *Eclectic* - | - | - | I

Mt. Vernon Square/Convention Center | 1021 Seventh St. NW (bet. Massachusetts & New York Aves.) | 202-393-0220 | www.passengerdc.com

The "handcrafted drinks" steal the "show" at this "upscale neighborhood dive" in Mount Vernon whose "exciting new mixologists" create "delicious" custom cocktails with a "twist"; a "good selection" of beer and offbeat wines and a "minimal" menu of "enticing" Eclectic eats (i.e. panini and kimchi hot dogs) complete the package; P.S. a re-created dining car in the back room hosts cocktail dinners.

PassionFish *American/Seafood* 24 | 23 | 21 | $49

Reston | Reston Town Ctr. | 11960 Democracy Dr. (Explorer St.), VA | 703-230-3474 | www.passionfishreston.com

"If you like fresh seafood prepared well", school yourself at this "hip" Reston American reeling in suburbanites with "killer" fin fare from an "adventurous" kitchen and "fantastic" oysters, crab claws and the like from its raw bar; it's "somewhat pricey" and "noisy", but "professional service" and a "beautiful, airy" space with a "glass-walled" dining room lend a "sophisticated" downtown feel "without the pretension or the commute."

Pasta Mia S M ≠ *Italian* 23 | 12 | 15 | $24

Adams Morgan | 1790 Columbia Rd. NW (18th St.) | 202-328-9114

For "enormous portions" of "cheap, delicious" Italian fare, Adams Morganites happily hop on the "line out the door" of this "no-reservations, cash-only, closed-on-Sundays-and-Mondays, no-substitutes pasta mecca"; it's a "step above your corner sub shop" decorwise and fussy types say the eats are too "mediocre" to contend with "long waits" and "indifferent service", but no matter: young 'uns call it the "best worst-kept secret" in town.

Z **Pasta Plus** M *Italian* 26 | 15 | 22 | $28

Laurel | Center Plaza | 209 Gorman Ave. (bet. Rtes. 1 & 198), MD | 301-498-5100 | www.pastaplusrestaurant.com

Talk about a "paradox": even "after all these years", Laurel locals find it "hard to believe" that such "affordable and delicious" pastas, brick-oven pizza and "fabulous desserts" can be found in a "run-down strip mall" on a "U.S. 1 median"; an "involved" owner and a "welcoming" staff also "make the difference" at this "wonderful" Italian, so supporters counsel "get there early" or prepare for "lines out the door"; P.S. there's carryout available from the attached market, which is open seven days a week.

Patty Boom Boom ◐ S M *Caribbean* - | - | - | I

U Street Corridor | 1359 U St. NW (bet. 13th & 14th Sts.) | 202-629-1714 | www.pattyboomboomdc.com

Everything is *irie* at this U Street island destination boasting an unusual concept: on the ground floor, there's an industrial-looking takeaway shop doling out inventive varieties of cheap Jamaican patties (e.g. goat meat and guava), while upstairs resides a club where rum concoctions and Red Stripe are poured to the strains of bass-heavy reggae, which comes from both live bands and DJs via a top-of-the-line audio system.

NEW **Paul** *Bakery* - | - | - | I

Penn Quarter | 801 Pennsylvania Ave. (bet. 8th & 9th Sts.) | 202-524-4500 | www.paul-usa.com

This renowned global chain brings 120 years of French artisanal-breadmaking tradition to DC with its newly launched Penn Quarter

U.S. flagship bakery/cafe crafting mouthwatering, inexpensive baked goods, omelets, soups, sandwiches and salads; charming Parisian decor frames tucked-away tables, while an outdoor terrace overlooks the Navy Memorial fountains; P.S. a beer/wine license and plans for a Georgetown branch are in the works.

P. Brennan's ☻ *Pub Food*   - | - | - | I

Ballston | 2910 Columbia Pike (Walter Reed Dr.) | Arlington, VA | 703-553-1090 | www.pbrennans.com

This massive, two-story Ballston pub slings drinks and affordable, contemporary versions of Irish-American classics while also serving as a gathering place for the gentrifying neighborhood; olde (polished wood, warm hues) mixes with moderne (slanted columns, chic lighting) to great effect; P.S. balcony diners can people-watch and enjoy live music several nights a week.

Peacock Cafe *American*   19 | 17 | 18 | $34

Georgetown | 3251 Prospect St. NW (bet. Potomac St. & Wisconsin Ave.) | 202-625-2740 | www.peacockcafe.com

A "nicely dressed, hip crowd" struts its stuff at this "solid" Georgetown cafe favored for "American food without frills" ("fresh salads and delicious soups" included) at "reasonable prices"; "accommodating" waiters sally forth in the "bustling, bright" interior, though everyone tries to "grab a table outside" in "warmer months", particularly for the "fantastic" weekend brunch.

Pedro & Vinny's ⬛Ⓜ⌦ *Mexican*   - | - | - | I

Downtown | 15th & K Sts. NW | 571-237-1875 | www.pedroandvinnys.com

Amigos aver "you can't get better than the burritos" assembled by proprietor John Rider at this legendary Mexican food cart, so expect long lines for one of the "best cheap lunches Downtown"; choose between pinto and black bean or ask for a combo ('black and tan'), then douse with one of his many hot sauces, some homemade.

Peking Gourmet Inn *Chinese*   26 | 14 | 20 | $36

Falls Church | Culmore Shopping Ctr. | 6029 Leesburg Pike (Glen Carlyn Rd.), VA | 703-671-8088 | www.pekinggourmet.com

At this "unassuming" Falls Church Chinese, "mallard mavens" marvel at the "absolutely fantasmic Peking duck" that's "carved tableside" in a "performance worthy of the Kennedy Center"; expect "long waits" ("even with reservations") and a "funky space" featuring "lots of Republicans on the walls", but since "just about everything is better than in Beijing", most maintain "if it's good enough for the Bush family, it's good enough for me."

Perrys *American/Eclectic*   19 | 19 | 18 | $35

Adams Morgan | 1811 Columbia Rd. NW (Biltmore St.) | 202-234-6218 | www.perrysadamsmorgan.com

If the "drag queens are a bit too much" for some at the "must-do" brunch of this "one-of-a-kind" Adams Morgan stalwart, "late-night dining" on its "wonderful rooftop terrace" garners nothing but praise; "reasonably" priced Eclectic–New American fare, "accommodating" service and a "fun, lively" vibe are other reasons to "check it out"; P.S. not reflected in the Food score are menu upgrades by consulting chef Mark Furstenberg (Bread Line and Marvelous Market founder) that have put it on foodie radar screens.

Persimmon *American* | 25 | 17 | 22 | $54 |

Bethesda | 7003 Wisconsin Ave. (bet. Leland & Walsh Sts.), MD | 301-654-9860 | www.persimmonrestaurant.com

Devotees of the "grown-up cooking" at this "sweet gem" actually "dream" about the "gigantic portions" of its "mouthwatering" New American fare, backed by a "careful wine list" and "well-paced service"; the "quaint" quarters are a "bit cramped" and "noisy" and a few sticklers complain the "food's become too familiar" for the price, but it remains one of Bethesda's "special-occasion places"; P.S. check out its lunch "bargain" and "great-buy" sunset dinner.

Pesce *Seafood* | 24 | 17 | 22 | $51 |

Dupont Circle | 2002 P St. NW (bet. Hopkins & 20th Sts.) | 202-466-3474 | www.pescedc.com

"Fish the way fish should be" – "cooked with respect" in "imaginative, reasonably priced, sensible-portioned" dishes and paired with "good, basic" vino and service – is the premise behind Regine Palladin's Dupont Circle seafooder, where the ever-changing chalkboard menu showcases the "freshest ingredients"; plus, a recent "move to a bigger space has done it well", resulting in a "brighter", "more comfortable" (if "spare") setting that works for a "night out" as well as for groups.

Pete's New Haven Style Apizza *Pizza* | 22 | 12 | 16 | $18 |

Columbia Heights | 1400 Irving St. NW (bet. 14th & 15th Sts.) | 202-332-7383

NEW **Upper NW** | 4940 Wisconsin Ave. NW (Fessenden St.) | 202-237-7383

NEW **Clarendon** | 3017 Clarendon Blvd. (Garfield St.), VA | 703-527-7383

www.petesapizza.com

"Cravin' New Haven"–style pizza? head to this midpriced pie shop atop the Columbia Heights Metro for "crispy", "thin-crust" options (notably "garlicky clam") along with "delicious antipasti", pastas and desserts; the drill: "order at the counter" then "share the big table" in the "neighborhoody" industrial space that's "fun even when it's overrun by urban moms and dads with giant strollers", though a beer list with "quality microbrews" provides cold comfort; P.S. branches in Clarendon and Upper NW opened post-Survey.

Petits Plats *French* | 22 | 20 | 21 | $50 |

Woodley Park | 2653 Connecticut Ave. NW (bet. Calvert St. & Woodley Rd.) | 202-518-0018 | www.petitsplats.com

For "honest" French fare presented by servers who "anticipate almost every need", Woodley Parkers turn to this "casual neighborhood" bistro and its "cozy" confines ("sit by the fireplace"); the cooking may not be particularly "inventive", but nevertheless diners are "transported

FOOD | DECOR | SERVICE | COST

to Biarritz" while enjoying "great moules frites" and "superb" chocolate fondant at "fair prices"; P.S. there's carryout downstairs.

P.F. Chang's China Bistro *Chinese* | 20 | 20 | 19 | $30 |

NEW Chevy Chase | Shops at Wisconsin Pl. | 5046 Wisconsin Ave. (Williard Ave.), MD | 301-654-4350

White Flint | White Flint Mall | 11301 Rockville Pike (Nicholson Ln.) | Rockville, MD | 301-230-6933

Ballston | Arlington Gateway | 901 N. Glebe Rd. (Fairfax Dr.) | Arlington, VA | 703-527-0955

Fairfax | Fairfax Corner | 4250 Fairfax Corner Ave. (Monument Dr.), VA | 703-266-2414

Tysons Corner | Tysons Galleria | 1716M International Dr. (Chain Bridge Rd.) | McLean, VA | 703-734-8996

NEW Sterling | Dulles Town Ctr. | 21078 Dulles Town Circle (Nokes Blvd.), VA | 703-421-5540

www.pfchangs.com

"Light, delicious", "Americanized" Chinese food keeps fans "coming back" – especially for the "standout" lettuce wraps – to this "trendy", "stylish" chain; though not everyone is convinced ("overpriced", "ordinary", "loud"), the "consistent" service is a plus, as is the "smart" menu "catering to people with allergies" and other needs.

Phillips *Seafood* | 15 | 14 | 16 | $35 |

SW | 900 Water St. SW (7th St.) | 202-488-8515

Rockville | Legacy Hotel | 1775 Rockville Pike (Bouic Ave.), MD | 301-881-4793

www.phillipsseafood.com

"If you don't mind dining with tourists", this hulking Southwest seafooder (with a newer location in Rockville) offers convenient proximity to the Mall and "decent" prices; then again, locals who maintain its "good days are long gone" deride "rushed" service and advise "you're better off trusting the Gorton's Fisherman"; P.S. Baltimore's Harborplace branch will close in early September 2011, but plans to reopen nearby later in the fall.

NEW Pho DC *Vietnamese* | - | - | - | I |

Chinatown | 608 H St. NW (bet. 6th & 7th Sts.) | 202-506-2888 | www.phodc.com

Warm urbanity pervades this new modern enclave bringing a variety of affordable pho and other French-influenced Vietnamese specialties to Chinatown's bustling dining scene; the brick-walled sliver of a space includes an LED-light color-changing wall and a sleek bar mixing specialty cocktails.

Pho 14 *Vietnamese* | ▽ 26 | 15 | 21 | $15 |

Columbia Heights | 1436 Park Rd. NW (bet. 14th & 15th Sts.) | 202-986-2326 | www.dcpho14.com

Finally, "pho-loving vegetarians" and their carnivorous brethren "don't have to venture out" to the 'burbs for the "excellent, cheap" Vietnamese staple, particularly since the homemade stock at this Columbia Heights "real deal" is "one of the very best"; diners can also order "delicious" banh mi and other "tasty" fare, but it's the

	FOOD	DECOR	SERVICE	COST

namesake dish that's "truly food for the soul"; P.S. an expansion into the storefront next door is ongoing at press time.

Pho 75 🚫 *Vietnamese* | 24 | 5 | 14 | $12 |

Langley Park | 1510 University Blvd. E. (New Hampshire Ave.), MD | 301-434-7844
Rockville | 771 Hungerford Dr. (Mannakee St.), MD | 301-309-8873
Clarendon | 1721 Wilson Blvd. (Quinn St.), VA | 703-525-7355
Falls Church | Eden Ctr. | 3103 Graham Rd. (Arlington Blvd.), VA | 703-204-1490
Herndon | 382 Elden St. (Herndon Pkwy.), VA | 703-471-4145

The "perfect cure for cold days, hangovers and cheap dates", these suburban "centers of the uni-pho-verse" have diners "slurping" "satisfying" Vietnamese soup with add-ins from "innards" to "well-seasoned" beef; yes, the "quick" service slips toward "surly" and the "spartan" spaces feature the "utilitarian decor of a government cafeteria", but most "leave feeling full and happy" and there's "not a big hit on the wallet."

Pie-Tanza *Pizza* | 19 | 12 | 18 | $21 |

Arlington | Lee Harrison Shopping Ctr. | 2503B N. Harrison St. (Lee Hwy.), VA | 703-237-0200
Falls Church | Falls Plaza Shopping Ctr. | 1216 Broad St. (bet. Birch St. & Gordon Rd.), VA | 703-237-0977
www.pie-tanza.com

"Busy, loud and family-oriented", these "simple" "local hangouts" in Falls Church and Arlington dish up "generous portions" of "crisp-crusted pizza" and "hearty, healthful salads full of fresh ingredients", all at "bargain prices"; "large open kitchens" mean kids can "watch" the pies being made while "tired adults" sip a "glass of wine", leading sophisticates to sniff they might be "best for the under-seven crowd."

Ping Pong Dim Sum *Asian* | 21 | 24 | 20 | $36 |

Chinatown | 900 Seventh St. NW (I St.) | 202-506-3740 | www.pingpongdimsum.us

Bringing "new blood to Chinatown's dim sum scene", this "Asian-esque" London import encourages customers to "engage in culinary diplomacy" with "fresh, filling" "fusion tapas" presented in an "urban-chic" setting; service ping-pongs between "gracious" and "awkward" and the "pricey" tabs and "backless seats" pain some, but "nontraditional brunch deals" and a "happy hour worth every single penny you won't spend" keep the place "fun, hip and noisy"; P.S. a Dupont Circle outlet is expected in late summer 2011.

Piola *Italian/Pizza* | 21 | 16 | 17 | $25 |

Rosslyn | 1550 Wilson Blvd. (bet. Oak & Pierce Sts.), VA | 703-528-1502 | www.piola.it

"So many pizzas, so little time" pout pie-mavens smitten by this "low-key" Rosslyn chain link that tops its "thin, chewy" crust some 50 ways ("any combination you could dream up"); plus, a plethora of "real deals" save budget-minded patrons "way more than three coins in a fountain", a theme evoked by sidewalk seating that's like a "mini-vacation to Italia" – and much "nicer than the cramped, noisy" interior.

NEW Pizzeria Da Marco *Pizza*

- | - | - | M

Bethesda | 8008 Woodmont Ave. (bet. Cordell & St. Elmo Aves.), MD | 301-654-6083 | www.pizzeriadamarco.net

Pizza mavens can experience the real deal – authentic Italian pies thrown by a Naples-born pizzaiolo, then baked in a handcrafted imported oven at 900 degrees – at this moderately priced Bethesda newcomer; diners lounge comfortably in the airy, big-windowed, brick-walled space or perch at the sleek marble-topped bar dispensing beer and wine.

Pizzeria Orso *Pizza*

- | - | - | I

Falls Church | 400 S. Maple Ave. (Tinners Hill St.), VA | 703-226-3460 | www.pizzeriaorso.com

This affordable Falls Church Italian changed its lead chef in early 2011, retaining its focus of wood-fired-oven baked pizza, but adding more appetizers like pasta and soup, as well as a children's menu; a sophisticated setting incorporates traditional decor (white tiles side the marble-topped bar) into a high-ceiling, industrial space warmed with Tuscan red and saffron hues, plus it offers outdoor seating; P.S. pet the chainsaw-sculpted, life-sized bear (*orso* is Italian for bear).

Pizzeria Paradiso *Pizza*

22 | 16 | 18 | $26

Dupont Circle | 2003 P St. NW (bet. Hopkins & 20th Sts.) | 202-223-1245

Georgetown | 3282 M St. NW (bet. Potomac & 33rd Sts.) | 202-337-1245

NEW Old Town | 124 King St. (bet. Lee & Union Sts.) | Alexandria, VA | 703-837-1245
www.eatyourpizza.com

Find "paradise on a pizza pie crust" at these "friendly" "must-stops" where "fresh dough and fresher ingredients" add up to "some of the best" 'za for "miles around", though the "awesome beer menus" that include "hard-to-find drafts" may be the "real prize"; the Georgetown venue boasts a "cozy cellar complete with fireplace" and Dupont's "homey" digs are "larger and brighter" (there's also a new post-Survey branch on Old Town's main drag) but no matter: "there's still a wait" "during prime dining hours."

NEW P.J. Clarke's *Pub Food*

- | - | - | M

Downtown | 1600 K St. NW (16th St.) | 202-463-6610 | www.pjclarkes.com

The former Olives space near the White House is now an outpost of the famous NYC-based pub chain, serving midpriced burgers and other brew-friendly grub; the big, handsome setting boasts a huge old-school bar, a semi-open kitchen and an eye-popping solarium enclosing a stairway that leads down to Sidecar, a semi-private dining room offering upscale steak and seafood.

	FOOD	DECOR	SERVICE	COST

Plaka Grill *Greek* ▽ 26 | 17 | 24 | $16

Vienna | 110 Lawyers Rd. NW (Maple Ave.), VA | 703-319-3131 |
www.plakagrill.com

"If this is what gyros are like in Greece, then buy me a ticket" opa-
ine Vienna regulars who frequent this "family-friendly" Hellenic for
"fantastic" grilled meats, "perfect baklava" and other "excellent"
specialties savored in a "low-key" setting akin to an "Athens street
scene"; moreover, its "friendly" owners and staffers "aim to please",
as do prices that offer "real value for your money."

Plume ⌧Ⓜ *American* ▽ 26 | 29 | 29 | $98

Downtown | The Jefferson | 1200 16th St. NW (M St.) | 202-448-3227 |
www.jeffersondc.com

"Expect to be pampered" at this "primo" New American in a
Downtown hotel where the "gorgeous dining experience" comes
with a "historical flair" inspired by Thomas Jefferson's creativity and
culinary passions; hand-painted scenes of Monticello and a vaulted
skylight set the stage for "over-the-top food and service", including
a "knowledgeable wine staff" "eager" to pair a "mind-boggling" list
with classic dishes that are given an "occasional brilliant twist", with
"rarefied prices" to match.

Policy ⌧ *American* 19 | 18 | 18 | $36

U Street Corridor | 1904 14th St. NW (T St.) | 202-387-7654 |
www.policydc.com

"Explore each floor" at this nascent New American in the U Street
Corridor, as there's a "totally different feel" between the two –
"roomy booths" in "red patent leather" on the first, graffiti and
chandeliers in the upstairs lounge; "better-than-expected" small
plates are on offer throughout, but surveyors split on service
("excellent" vs. "not bad") and there's impolitic carping about "ok"
cocktail and wine lists and "lack of any good brews"; in any event,
it's "quite a scene."

Pollo Campero *Peruvian* 18 | 10 | 13 | $12

Columbia Heights | 3229 14th St. NW (Park Rd.) | 202-745-0078
Gaithersburg | Lakeforest Mall | 701 Russell Ave. (Lakeforest Blvd.),
MD | 240-403-0135
Takoma Park | 1355 University Blvd. E. (New Hampshire Ave.), MD |
301-408-0555
Wheaton | 11420 Georgia Ave. (Hickerson Dr.), MD |
301-942-6868
Falls Church | 5852 Columbia Pike (Moncure Ave.), VA |
703-820-8400
Herndon | 496 Elden St. (Grant St.), VA | 703-904-7500
www.campero.com

Pollo-istas proclaim it's "worth going on cholesterol medication" to
peck at the "Central American–style fried chicken" and "yummy
Latin sides" at these "friendly" counter-service "joints"; "eager"
staffers speak "limited English" and the interiors are bustling, "blah"
affairs, but once patrons get their claws on the chow "everyone can
afford", there's little squawking.

	FOOD	DECOR	SERVICE	COST

NEW PORC *BBQ*

| | - | - | - | I |

Location varies; see website | no phone | www.porcmobile.com

This 'Purveyor of Rolling Cuisine' serves up low-cost BBQ with special sauces made from pan drippings (plus a few specialties like vegan sloppy joes) that tastes like it came straight from a ramshackle rural smokehouse rather than a DC-based biodiesel-powered mobile truck; it also confounds expectations when it comes to dessert – who would think of polishing off a pastrami sandwich with decadent chocolate truffles?

Poste Moderne Brasserie *American*

| | 21 | 21 | 18 | $48 |

Penn Quarter | Hotel Monaco | 555 Eighth St. NW (bet. E & F Sts.) | 202-783-6060 | www.postebrasserie.com

Chef Robert Weland puts his stamp on this "easy-to-overlook" New American ensconced in a "historic" Penn Quarter post office, a "sublime" setting for "superb" fare enhanced by "fresh ingredients from the garden" out back (which doubles as a "wonderful courtyard"); service can "rub you the wrong way" and the unimpressed question "all the hype", but a "lively" happy hour, "well-chosen" wine list and "special" brunch make shortcomings fade away poste-haste.

Posto *Italian*

| | 21 | 19 | 21 | $42 |

Logan Circle | 1515 14th St. NW (bet. Church & P Sts.) | 202-332-8613 | www.postodc.com

This "midpriced" Italian "gem on 14th Street" – the "casual outpost of Downtown's Tosca" – has fast become a neighborhood "star" thanks to its "scrumptious" pasta, pizza and meat dishes, "well-chosen"' wines and staffers who ensure that "starting times" at nearby Studio Theatre "aren't missed"; the "cavernous", "stark" surroundings can get "loud" ("feels like I'm in a warehouse"), but not to worry: there's "dining outside in warmer weather."

Potenza *Italian/Pizza*

| | 20 | 19 | 19 | $40 |

Downtown | Woodward Bldg. | 1430 H St. NW (15th St.) | 202-638-4444 | www.potenzadc.com

Eat your "way around Italy" at this "bustling" Downtown spot, where "healthy" portions of "gently priced" fare (including "delicious pizzas and pastas") lure crowds to a "well-designed space" with an "open kitchen", TVs for "sports fans" and old-timey tiled floors; even dissidents who deem it "nothing to write home about" can't resist sampling "pastries and sorbet from the attached cafe" or hitting the "lively bar scene."

Praline *Bakery/French*

| | 19 | 13 | 17 | $35 |

Bethesda | Sumner Pl. | 4611 Sangamore Rd. (MacArthur Blvd.), MD | 301-229-8180 | www.praline-bakery.com

"Head straight to the pastries" suggest sugarhounds who salivate over the "wonderful desserts and baked goods" at this "delightful" eatery "hidden" in a "boring" Bethesda shopping center; grab a "takeaway quiche" from the "fantastic" first-floor bakery or head upstairs for "serviceable" French-accented bistro fare in a

| | FOOD | DECOR | SERVICE | COST |

more "formal" atmosphere, which has greater appeal "when the terrace is open."

Present Restaurant *Vietnamese*

23 | 20 | 21 | $30

Falls Church | 6678 Arlington Blvd. (Annandale Rd.), VA | 703-531-1881 | www.presentcuisine.com

Discover a "treasure trove of Vietnamese fare" with the "coolest names" (the "menu is like reading poetry") at this "amazing" Falls Church strip-maller proffering "delicious, inventive" dishes that are "attractively presented" and served by "warm" staffers who "know what they're talking about"; it's "relaxed and relaxing", a tone abetted by a fountain, "well-spaced tables" and soft colors, but the word is out about one of the area's "best-tasting bargain eating places", so call for reservations.

Pret A Manger *Sandwiches*

17 | 11 | 15 | $15

NEW **Chinatown** | 1155 F St. NW (11th St.) | 202-464-2791
NEW **Farragut** | 1828 L St. NW (19th St.) | 202-689-1982
Golden Triangle | 1825 I St. NW (bet. 18th & 19th Sts.) | 202-403-2992 ⊠
www.pret.com

These "grab 'n' go" lunch counters from "across the pond" spark worker-bee appetites with "delicious" sandwiches, salads and snacks that provide a "healthy alternative to the junk food options available" elsewhere; perhaps, but a few eaters miss the "tasty, funky British recipes" found abroad and gripe it's a "tad expensive for what it is."

ⓩ Prime Rib ⊠ *Seafood/Steak*

27 | 25 | 27 | $68

Golden Triangle | 2020 K St. NW (bet. 20th & 21st Sts.) | 202-466-8811 |
www.theprimerib.com

See review in the Baltimore Directory.

Primi Piatti ⊠ *Italian*

22 | 19 | 22 | $45

Foggy Bottom | 2013 I St. NW (bet. 20th & 21st Sts.) | 202-223-3600 |
www.primipiatti.com

The "waiters seem as if they're imported from Italy" at this "mid-priced" Foggy Bottom "staple" known for its "seriously good" pastas and "solid" Italian "standards"; though some find the "tables too close together", "European-style" sidewalk seating and a cozy vibe mean it's a "lovely place to take a date"; P.S. groups can book magic shows by chef-owner Savino Recine.

Proof *American*

24 | 22 | 21 | $51

Penn Quarter | 775 G St. NW (bet. 7th & 8th Sts.) | 202-737-7663 |
www.proofdc.com

Thanks to an "astonishing" vino list and "knowledgeable" sommeliers, this Penn Quarter "hot spot" eases patrons "out of their [wine] comfort zone" with "perfect pairings in any price range" to enhance the "wonderfully imaginative" New American menu; the "chic" interior is "dark as a cave" ("magnifying flashlights" supplied) and a few quibble over "spotty" service, but the majority is proof positive it's "one of the best restaurants" in town; P.S. the $12 lunch specials at the bar (Tuesday–Friday) "are a real bargain."

	FOOD	DECOR	SERVICE	COST

PS 7's ⊠ *American*   22 | 20 | 21 | $51

Penn Quarter | 777 I St. NW (bet. 7th & 8th Sts.) | 202-742-8550 |
www.ps7restaurant.com

Powered by chef-owner Peter Smith's "whimsical" New American
food and "goddess" Gina Chersevani's "amazing" cocktails, this
"easy-to-miss" Penn Quarterite provides a "haven of peace" for "impressive" "adult" meals in its "stylish" dining room; to sample its
"creativity" "without shelling out big bucks", hit the "ruthless"
happy hour – when "getting a seat" in the "noisy" bar thronged with
"twentysomethings" is "like winning the lottery."

Pupatella Pizzeria ⊠ Ⓜ *Pizza*   - | - | - | I

Arlington | 5104 Wilson Blvd. (Edison St.), VA | 571-312-7230 |
www.pupatella.com

An adorable little pizza cart, famed for its "wonderfully fresh"
Neapolitan fare, has spawned a Greater Arlington brick-and-mortar
pizzeria set in a hip Wilson Boulevard storefront; boasting a bright-
red, Italian-imported wood-fired oven and eye-catching graffiti
murals visible from the street, this spot pumps out affordable, authentic pies and fried food along with Italian wine and beer; P.S. the
original Ballston food cart occasionally comes out of retirement for
rare guest appearances.

Puro Café *Coffeehouse/Mediterranean*   - | - | - | I

Georgetown | 1529 Wisconsin Ave. (bet. P & Q Sts.) | 202-787-1937 |
www.purocafe.com

Nestled amid Upper Georgetown's fashionable boutiques, this affordable cafe serves pastries, interesting salads and panini in Euro-chic
digs with seating by the fireplace in the lounge, at a common table near
the big front windows or on a bamboo-lined, secluded outdoor patio;
an exposed-brick wall, a rustic wood floor and fanciful chandeliers
provide a charming contrast to the ultramod white furnishings.

🆕 Queen Vic Ⓜ *British*   - | - | - | M

Atlas District | 1206 H St. NE (bet. 12th & 13th Sts.) | 202-396-2001 |
www.thequeenvicdc.com

This cozy Brit-themed gastropub arrives on the Atlas District's burgeoning Restaurant Row tapping some 20 U.K. brews accompanied
by moderately priced chef-crafted updates of traditional fare like
all-day English breakfast, ploughman's lunch, Cornish pasties and
Sunday roasts; flat-screens in the bar area show sports and British
telly – fitting as the restaurant is named after a pub in *EastEnders*;
P.S. the attached tuck shop, expected soon, will sell staples like
McVitie's and Ribena.

Rabieng *Thai*   25 | 16 | 21 | $28

Falls Church | Glen Forest Shopping Ctr. | 5892 Leesburg Pike
(Glen Forest Dr.), VA | 703-671-4222 | www.rabiengthai.com

"Simpler and smaller" than its "fancy" nearby sib, Duangrat's, this
"homey" Falls Church "hole-in-the-wall" provides a full range of
"wonderful country Thai cooking" with "just the right amount of
spice" and "terrific" small plates (with "lots of choices") served on

weekends; it's "not edgy" by any stretch, but "polite" servers make it an "attractive" place to dine that "dollar for dollar" offers "great value."

Radius *Italian*   17 | 13 | 16 | $22

Mt. Pleasant | 3155 Mt. Pleasant St. NW (bet. Kenyon St. & Kilbourne Pl.) | 202-234-0808 | www.radiusdc.com

"Reborn under new ownership" (i.e. Todd and Nicole Wiss, ex Poste Moderne Brasserie), this Mt. Pleasant "neighborhood spot" for "not-too-heavy" specialty pizza has added "freshly made pasta" and "other nice Italian" dishes into the mix; if the "dark" space and "erratic" fare and service make some "miss the old" joint, an "excellent" happy-hour deal – $5 for a slice and a beer until 7 PM every day – is "hard to beat."

Rail Stop Ⓜ *American*   ▽ 22 | 19 | 22 | $38

The Plains | 6478 Main St. (Fauquier Ave.), VA | 540-253-5644 | www.railstoprestaurant.com

Locals in The Plains make tracks for this rustic American – a horse-country venue that serves as a "convenient" stop for cityfolk "coming back from the mountains" – offering burgers, steaks, fish and pasta, "spot-on" wine pairings and specials listed on a "big board"; as the name suggests, there's often a "toy train choo-chooing" overhead ("festive at Christmastime"), plus exposed wooden beams and a garden patio.

Raku *Asian*   21 | 15 | 17 | $32

Dupont Circle | 1900 Q St. NW (19th St.) | 202-265-7258
Bethesda | 7240 Woodmont Ave. (bet. Bethesda Ave. & Elm St.), MD | 301-718-8681
www.rakuasiandining.com

"Always busy for a reason", these "fairly priced" Pan-Asian "taste treats" in Bethesda and Dupont Circle deliver "delicious" dishes fusing "Thai, Japanese and Chinese" along with "innovative" rolls from "showbiz" sushi counters; "erratic" service and "hectic, noisy" interiors turn some off, though nabbing a "coveted" sidewalk seat on Q Street helps.

Rangoli *Indian*   - | - | - | I

South Riding | Riding Plaza Mall | 24995 Riding Plaza (Riding Center Dr.), VA | 703-957-4900 | www.rangolirestaurant.us

"Fresh, fragrant and flavorful" Indian food that comes with "white-tablecloth service" and reasonable tabs has put this South Riding strip-maller on foodies' radars; a "huge" menu represents "all parts" of the subcontinent, though "custom requests are met without hesitation" by the "attentive" staff; P.S. there's a lunch buffet every day.

Ⓩ Rasika Ⓢ *Indian*   28 | 25 | 25 | $50

Penn Quarter | 633 D St. NW (bet. 6th & 7th Sts.) | 202-637-1222 | www.rasikarestaurant.com

"Does anyone really not rave about the food?" at this Penn Quarter "winner", where "intensely flavorful" Indian dishes take palates on "wondrous culinary journeys" that have dreamers wishing for an "extra stomach" (for the likes of "crispy" fried spinach that "Popeye

| | FOOD | DECOR | SERVICE | COST |

would kill for"); "deft" servers who "appear to enjoy" their jobs and a "glittering" (if "noisy") atmosphere bolster its status as one of DC's "best restaurants – without 'best restaurant' price tags"; P.S. a second location is planned for the West End in early 2012.

Ravi Kabob House ●▽ *Pakistani*   22 | 4 | 14 | $15
Arlington | 305 N. Glebe Rd. (Pershing Dr.), VA | 703-522-6666
Ravi Kabob House II Ⓜ▽ *Pakistani*
Arlington | 250 N. Glebe Rd. (Pershing Dr.), VA | 703-816-0222
www.ravikabobusa.com
Take it from the "cabbies parked outside" these "kid-tolerant" Pakistani takeouts: the "spicy, pungent kebabs", "tasty" curries and "fresh naan" found within are the "real deal"; no one's raving about the "slow service" and interiors that "make McDonald's look luxe", but fans swear they're some of the "best cheap eats" around.

Z Ray's Hell Burger ▽ *Burgers*   26 | 8 | 14 | $15
(aka Ray's Butcher Burgers)
Courthouse | Colonial Vill. | 1725 Wilson Blvd. (bet. Quinn & Rhodes Sts.) | Arlington, VA | 703-841-0001
NEW Ray's Hell Burger Too ▽ *Burgers*
Courthouse | 1713 Wilson Blvd. (bet. Quinn & Rhodes Sts.) | Arlington, VA | 703-841-0001
"Just ask Prez Obama" – even "he stood in line" for one of the "heavenly" headliners at Michael 'Ray' Landrum's "burger nirvana"; it's "absolute mayhem" within the original Courthouse-area "bare-bones" storefront (the nearby 'Too' spin-off, with table service, opened post-Survey), but "none of that matters" since the "juicy", "fresh-made" patties of "unsurpassed quality" and "high-end" toppings like foie gras are what "it's all about"; "draft root beer", "limited sides" ("finally added fries") and "decent prices" round out the cash-only experience: P.S. a third location in the same strip is rumored.

Ray's The Classics *American*   24 | 16 | 20 | $47
Silver Spring | 8606 Colesville Rd. (Georgia Ave.), MD | 301-588-7297 | www.raystheclassics.com
The "meat can't be beat" – and the seafood is "equally excellent" – at this Downtown Silver Spring American, an outpost of Michael 'Ray' Landrum's value-driven empire with prices that "put the national chains to shame" (plus "free sides!"); it has a "cold, dull" atmosphere and service can be "brusque", but locals are "delighted to have [it] in the 'hood" nonetheless; P.S. a three-course, $22.99 bar menu may be the "best deal in town."

Z Ray's The Steaks *Steak*   26 | 15 | 21 | $43
Clarendon | Navy League Bldg. | 2300 Wilson Blvd. (Wayne St.), VA | 703-841-7297
At this "classic" "carnivore's paradise" in Clarendon, meat mavens opt for "consistently rockin' steaks", "educated servers" and "bargain pricing" over posh amenities – and, true to form, its 2009 move to "bigger digs allowed for reservations" but "no decor (but you're not paying for it)"; while some "don't understand the hype" over things

FOOD | DECOR | SERVICE | COST

like "free sides" and "reasonable" wine, they're vastly outnumbered by those who say it's "all about good quality at a good price."

Ray's The Steaks at East River ☒ *Burgers/Steak*

- | - | - | I

Northeast | 3905 Dix St. NE (bet. 40th St. & Minnesota Ave.) | 202-396-7297

Call it a pioneering endeavor: civic-minded restaurateur Michael 'Ray' Landrum has taken his value-oriented concept to a Northeast DC neighborhood with high unemployment and a dearth of sit-down dining establishments; the American eats – seafood and steak platters priced under $20, plus burgers and a cold-smoked fried chicken that's likely to become a citywide cult classic – are presented in a setting with a pressed-tin ceiling and shiny black granite bar.

NEW Red Hook Lobster Pound *Seafood*

- | - | - | I

Location varies; see website | 202-341-6263 | www.redhooklobsterdc.com

DC and nearby Maryland (and soon NoVa) diners can Twitter their way to a real Down East lobstah-shack experience (without tolls or traffic) thanks to this NYC-bred mobile duo whose proprietors make weekly trips to Maine to source coldwater crustaceans; the $15 rolls are made with mayo (traditional) or butter (Connecticut style), and for dessert there are whoopie pies; P.S. waits can exceed an hour.

Red Hot & Blue *BBQ*

20 | 14 | 18 | $22

Gaithersburg | Grove Shopping Ctr. | 16811 Crabbs Branch Way (Shady Grove Rd.), MD | 301-948-7333
Laurel | 677 Main St. (Rte. 216), MD | 301-953-1943
Greater Alexandria | 6482 Lansdowne Ctr. (Beulah St.) | Alexandria, VA | 703-550-6465
Rosslyn | 1600 Wilson Blvd. (N. Pierce St.), VA | 703-276-7427
Fairfax | 4150 Chain Bridge Rd. (Rte. 236), VA | 703-218-6989
Falls Church | Tower Sq. | 169 Hillwood Ave. (Douglass Ave.), VA | 703-538-6466
Herndon | 2403 Centreville Rd. (Sunrise Valley Dr.), VA | 703-870-7345
Manassas | 8366 Sudley Rd. (Irongate Way), VA | 703-367-7100
Leesburg | Bellwood Commons Shopping Ctr. | 541 E. Market St. (Plaza St.), VA | 703-669-4242
www.redhotandblue.com

Calling it the "best damn barbecue north of Memphis" may be a stretch, but these citified "'cue joints" deliver a pulled pork and "rib fix" good enough to "make a pig of yourself", along with "solid" "sides that will bust yours"; they're "family-friendly" and "reasonably priced", but saucy types taunt that "bland" chow and "crowded, noisy" spaces make them the "McDs of BBQ."

NEW Redline ◑ *American*

- | - | - | M

Chinatown | 707 G St. NW, 2nd fl. (bet. 7th & 8th Sts.) | 202-347-8689 | www.dcredline.com

At this newly minted Chinatown resto-lounge across from Verizon Center, moderately priced, upscale American fare pairs with cocktails, wine and brew; the second-story, brick-walled setting features leather-lined booths equipped with a 'pour-your-own' beer system, while plenty of tech (over 30 HDTV screens and electronic display boards) vies with cityscape views for patrons' attention.

RedRocks ◐ *Pizza* | 21 | 18 | 18 | $24 |

Columbia Heights | 1036 Park Rd. NW (11th St.) | 202-506-1402
NEW Old Town | 904 King St. (bet. Alfred & Patrick Sts.) | Alexandria, VA | 703-717-9873
www.redrocksdc.com

Bringing "delicious brick-oven pizza", "yummy salads" and "interesting beers" to "increasingly popular" (read: gentrifying) Columbia Heights has made the tables in this "rustic" townhouse-turned–pie parlor "more cramped than a football team crammed into an airplane bathroom"; happily, there's a "wonderful" roomy patio where "four-legged pals" are welcome; P.S. Old Town opened post-Survey.

Redwood *American* | 17 | 23 | 16 | $45 |

Bethesda | Bethesda Row | 7121 Bethesda Ln. (bet. Bethesda Ave. & Elm St.), MD | 301-656-5515 | www.redwoodbethesda.com

Sit by the "giant open windows" in the "swank" interior of this wood-and-stone–accented Bethesdan and you'll "feel like you're outside", or just opt for "outdoor dining" on the "lovely" patio; alas, its "seasonal" menu of "flatbreads, pastas, sandwiches" and New American entrees sometimes "falls short" of the "ambiance" ("particularly for the price"), and service "can use some sprucing up" too.

Regent, The *Thai* | ▽ 23 | 20 | 21 | $32 |

Dupont Circle | 1910 18th St. NW (bet. Florida Ave. & T St.) | 202-232-1781 | www.regentthai.com

"Flavorful, well-prepared" Thai dishes in "serene" surroundings (low light, dark wood) offer "good value" and a "quiet" respite in bustling Dupont Circle East; while the menu has the basic "favorites", "interesting specials" given a "bit of a twist" and "warmhearted" hospitality make it more "memorable."

Renato at River Falls *Italian* | 19 | 14 | 18 | $39 |

Potomac | 10120 River Rd. (Falls Rd.), MD | 301-365-1900 | www.riverfallsseafood.com

"Genial" manager Enzo Iachetti "could be voted the mayor of Potomac" by the way he welcomes "regular customers" – including famous faces – to this "upscale" Italian with "consistent" "fresh pasta and seafood" (thanks to its family ties to the fish market next door); most have a "good time here", despite some snickering about "noise" and "ho-hum" fare.

Restaurant at Goodstone Inn & | - | - | - | VE |
Estate *American*

Middleburg | Goodstone Inn & Estate | 36205 Snake Hill Rd. (Foxcroft Rd.), VA | 540-687-4645 | www.goodstone.com

Floor-to-ceiling palladian windows frame the airy yet intimate dining room (30 seats) at this posh country inn near Middleburg, where the bucolic hunt-country vistas serve as a fitting backdrop for a pricey New American menu that features produce grown on the

200-acre preserve; its wine cellar, lined with international vintages, offers a romantic setting of a different sort for small private dinners.

Restaurant 3 *American* (aka 3 Bar & Grill)

| 18 | 18 | 19 | $34 |

Clarendon | 2950 Clarendon Blvd. (Garfield St.), VA | 703-524-4440 | www.restaurantthree.com

Just the spot to "hang with friends" in Clarendon, this "midpriced", "family-friendly" American bistro offers "sophisticated", Southern-accented American cuisine in a "warm, comfortable" space (vintage bar, multiple dining rooms) manned by an "efficient" team; if few deny that "it aims high", the less-impressed lament the "execution leaves something to be desired."

Rice *Thai*

| 22 | 18 | 20 | $32 |

Logan Circle | 1608 14th St. NW (bet. Q & R Sts.) | 202-234-2400 | www.ricerestaurant.com

Expect "specialties not found anywhere else" at this "grown-up" Logan Circle Thai, which pairs a "refined and imaginative" menu ("hotness ordered to taste") with "great mixed drinks" and beer; conversationalists may prefer a "table outside to people-watch", as the exposed-brick interior can get "loud"; P.S. its name evokes the "amazing jasmine sweet rice that comes with every dish."

NEW Ripple ● *American*

| - | - | - | E |

Cleveland Park | 3417 Connecticut Ave. NW (Ordway St.) | 202-244-7995 | www.rippledc.com

Making waves since it opened, this Cleveland Park late-nighter attracts a young, hip crowd with locally sourced, contemporary American fare, artisanal cheeses and charcuterie and trendy snacks (bacon-roasted pecans, anyone?); there's a cozy, hidden-away dining room in the back, while up front there are tables by windows, high-tops and a long bar dispensing sustainable, organic and bio-dynamic wines plus fancy cocktails; P.S. recently expanded next door.

Rí Rá Irish Restaurant Pub *Pub Food*

| 14 | 17 | 17 | $26 |

Bethesda | 4931 Elm St. (bet. Arlington Rd. & Woodmont Ave.), MD | 301-657-1122
Clarendon | 2915 Wilson Blvd. (Fillmore St.), VA | 703-248-9888
www.rira.com

"Stout"-hearted fans of these Bethesda/Clarendon "fantasies of what an Irish restaurant should look like" dig their "traditional" "bar food" that's "fine" for a "comfort meal", "fun" vibe and "amazing selection of beers"; "don't go if you're in a hurry", have a hankering for gourmet chow or "expect to make much conversation" (thanks to the "live bands") – "it's a pub", plain and simple.

Ris *American*

| 23 | 23 | 23 | $49 |

West End | 2275 L St. NW (23rd St.) | 202-730-2500 | www.risdc.com

Chef Ris Lacoste's "welcome return" to the DC dining scene brings the newly "hip West End" a "comfortable" yet "sophisticated" bistro serving "upscale" New American "comfort food", including "not-to-be-missed" lamb shank; "multiple room designs" ("tablecoth" and informal), a sweeping patio and "one of the best bars in town" ensure there's a space for every taste, and while some say a few "kinks" remain, it's generally "excellent from the moment you walk in"; P.S. the specials are a "super value."

NEW Rivers at the Watergate ● Ⓢ *American*   `- | - | - | M`

Foggy Bottom | Watergate | 600 New Hampshire Ave. NW (Virginia Ave.) | 202-333-1600 | www.riversdc.com

It's 100 steps (count 'em) to the Kennedy Center from this sophisticated newcomer offering a midpriced steak-and-seafood-centric American menu plus a popular pre-theater deal designed to suit the needs of ticket-holders and cash-strapped locals alike; the sweeping space features sun-dappled, amber-toned dining rooms and a classy, lively piano bar overlooking a terrace with the Potomac River below.

Rocklands *BBQ*   `22 | 11 | 16 | $18`

Glover Park | 2418 Wisconsin Ave. NW (Calvert St.) | 202-333-2558
Rockville | Wintergreen Plaza | 891A Rockville Pike (W. Edmonston Dr.), MD | 240-268-1120
Greater Alexandria | 25 S. Quaker Ln. (Duke St.) | Alexandria, VA | 703-778-9663
Arlington | 3471 Washington Blvd. (Lincoln St.), VA | 703-528-9663
www.rocklands.com

"Smokey" like "good" BBQ should be, with "mesmerizing" aromas that "draw passersby like moths to a flame", these "oases" in the "BBQ-challenged metro area" get 'cue addicts "dreaming about collards and brisket", pulled pork and "messy, marvelous" ribs; while they generally "ain't much to look at" (i.e. better for "carry-out"), the newer Washington Boulevarder is a "take-out, dine-in and bar super-joint."

Roof Terrace at the Kennedy Center *American*   `15 | 20 | 17 | $59`

Foggy Bottom | Kennedy Ctr. | 2700 F St. NW (bet. New Hampshire & Virginia Aves.) | 202-416-8555 | www.roofterracerestaurant.com

"If you're worried about making the curtain" or craving a Sunday brunch with a "magnificent" skyline view, this upscale New American atop the Kennedy Center fits the bill; alas, critics complain it's an under-performer, with "tired" decor, "spotty" service and "passable" food at "high prices", while forgiving sorts allow "you're paying for the experience" – and the "convenience."

Room 11 *Eclectic*   `- | - | - | I`

Columbia Heights | 3234 11th St. NW (Lamont St.) | 202-332-3234 | www.room11dc.com

Though tipplers trill it's all about the "specialty cocktails" and vino at this "closet-sized" wine bar, the "new cool" in Columbia Heights also delivers "delicious" Eclectic small plates and "tasty snacks" at "reasonable prices"; servers are "friendly" even when the place is "bursting at the seams", and a patio eases congestion in "warmer months."

	FOOD	DECOR	SERVICE	COST

Rosa Mexicano *Mexican*   20 | 20 | 19 | $39

Penn Quarter | Terrell Pl. | 575 Seventh St. NW (bet. E & F Sts.) |
202-783-5522
National Harbor | 153 Waterfront St. (St. George Blvd.), MD |
301-567-1005
www.rosamexicano.com

"Lethal" margaritas that "go down like fruit punch" and "amazing
fresh guac" made tableside pave the way for "solid", often "creative" Mexican fare at these "always busy" NYC imports ("be prepared to wait"); they're "lively and fun", but those who take a less
rosy view complain of "slow service" and "pricey" tabs for "underwhelming" chow; P.S. Penn Quarter is "convenient to Verizon Center", while National Harbor features "beautiful water views."

Roti Mediterranean Grill 🖎 *Mediterranean*   - | - | - | I

World Bank | 1747 Pennsylvania Ave. NW (bet. 17th & 18th Sts.) |
202-466-7684
NEW **NoMa** | 1275 First St. NE (N St.) | 202-618-6969
www.roti.com

Served cafeteria-style, the grilled meats, falafel and Middle Eastern
salads at this World Banker can be folded into pitas, assembled on
platters or added to rice bowls (AM options include breakfast pitas,
yogurt and bagels); a high-ceilinged, big-windowed space evokes
the Mediterranean with glimmering blue and orange hues, terra-
cotta flooring, tiled columns and rustic wood tables that also belie
its chain affiliation and affordable prices; P.S. a NoMa branch
opened post-Survey and several more DC links are in the works.

RT's *Cajun/Creole*   24 | 12 | 22 | $36

Greater Alexandria | 3804 Mt. Vernon Ave. (Glebe Rd.) | Alexandria, VA |
703-684-6010 | www.rtsrestaurant.net

"Check your cholesterol at the door" of this Alexandria "dive" and
dig in to "some of the best" "old-style" Cajun-Creole "cooking this
side of N'Awlins", including "incredible" crawfish beignets and "orgas-
mic" Jack Daniel's shrimp; eat at the vintage bar or let the "veteran
waiters guide you", and ignore the "dated decor" like everyone else.

Ruan Thai *Thai*   25 | 9 | 17 | $19

Wheaton | 11407 Amherst Ave. (University Blvd.), MD | 301-942-0075 |
www.ruanthaiwheaton.com

It's in a "small strip-mall storefront" (two, actually, after its recent
expansion next door) with decor that's "bad at best", but this "superb"
Wheaton Siamese sources "some of the best pad Thai" around and
other "wonderful, authentic" dishes offering budget-minded diners a
chance to "explore"; for those turned off by "slow" service but crave
the "fantastic flavors", "takeout" is always an option.

Russia House ☾ *Russian*   15 | 20 | 18 | E

Dupont Circle | 1800 Connecticut Ave. NW (Florida Ave.) |
202-234-9433 | www.russiahouselounge.com

"Step back in time" at this "huge house" outfitted with "dark wood"
and "velvet curtains" that recalls "St. Petersburg" (or maybe

	FOOD	DECOR	SERVICE	COST

"Minsk") and features expensive Russian small and large plates plus a selection of caviar; "vodka is the drink here" but there's also a "good Baltic beer selection" and you may "spot some hockey players" among the "interesting people" who call this a "home away from home."

Rustico *American* | 21 | 20 | 20 | $32 |

Greater Alexandria | 827 Slaters Ln. (Potomac Greens Dr.) | Alexandria, VA | 703-224-5051
NEW **Ballston** | Liberty Ctr. | 4075 Wilson Blvd. (Randolph St.) | Arlington, VA | 571-384-1820
www.rusticorestaurant.com

Suds-seekers say this "vibrant" Alexandria American achieves a "trifecta of awesomeness" with its "huge book of beers" for "any taste" ("30 on tap" alone), "surprisingly good" hearth-cooked fare ("especially pizza") and "knowledgeable" servers who "always have a smile"; the "chill atmosphere" is enhanced by "fireplaces", exposed brick and an ample bar that gets "pretty packed", plus it's "relatively affordable"; P.S. the Ballston locale, with a massive bar serving an impresive craft-brew selection, opened post-Survey.

NEW **Rustik Tavern** *American/Eclectic* | - | - | - | I |

Bloomingdale | 84 T St. NW (bet. 1st St. & Rhode Island Ave.) | 202-290-2936 | www.rustikdc.com

This American-Eclectic arrival in underserved Bloomingdale offers artisanal pizzas fired in a wood-burning oven plus inexpensive designer sandwiches, small plates and plenty of craft brews and wines; the spiffed-up digs feature a fanciful mural depicting an Albanian village, windowside tables overlooking the street scene and a patio – a scarce amenity in this up-and-coming neighborhood.

Z Ruth's Chris Steak House *Steak* | 25 | 23 | 25 | $62 |

Penn Quarter | 724 Ninth St. NW (bet. G & H Sts.) | 202-393-4488
Dupont Circle | 1801 Connecticut Ave. NW (S St.) | 202-797-0033
Bethesda | 7315 Wisconsin Ave. (Elm St.), MD | 301-652-7877
Crystal City | Crystal Park | 2231 Crystal Dr., 11th fl. (23rd St.) | Arlington, VA | 703-979-7275
Fairfax | 4100 Monument Corner Dr. (Monument Dr.), VA | 703-266-1004
Vienna | 8521 Leesburg Pike (Spring Hill Rd.), VA | 703-848-4290
www.ruthschris.com

Loyalists "love the sizzling platters" of "oh-so-good buttery steaks" at this "top-quality" chophouse chain that comes through with "winning" sides too; delivering "old-style service" in a "traditional" setting, it's "expensive" (and "not for the dieter"), but "utterly reliable", especially when you're "entertaining friends and clients."

Sabai Sabai Simply Thai *Thai* | - | - | - | I |

Germantown | 19847 Century Blvd. (Crystal Lake Blvd.), MD | 301-528-1400 | www.sabaisimplythai.com

Thai food fans travel 'round the Beltway to this stop in Germantown where Srisuda and Fred Hart, the former owners of Rockville's Benjarong, focus on fresh ingredients, bold flavors and appealing presentations; the affordable menu offers a mix of classics and un-

FOOD | DECOR | SERVICE | COST

common street fare (with lots of vegetarian options), while earthy notes in the wood, water and stone lend the space a Zen-like feel – that is, when it's not buzzing with foodie crowds.

Sakana 🗷 *Japanese* ▽ 22 | 13 | 18 | $28

Dupont Circle | 2026 P St. NW (bet. 20th & 21st Sts.) | 202-887-0900
Dupont Circle-ites "craving" "fantastic, fresh" sashimi, sushi and other "reliable favorites" "always return" to this "sweet Japanese oasis" and its "cozy" if lackluster interior; it can "get busy at night", but "friendly" staffers who are "happy to serve you" and "reasonable prices" mean it's "always a treat."

Sakoontra *Thai* ▽ 19 | 16 | 19 | $24

Fairfax | Costco Plaza | 12300C Costco Plaza (Ox Rd.), VA | 703-818-8886 | www.sakoontra.com
From "mildly spiced to set-your-taste-buds-afire, there's something for everyone" at this Fairfax Thai, which features affordable prices and "imaginative" decorative touches like a colorful tuk-tuk; sure, some deem the chow "good but not great", but at least the place offers a "restful" respite from the sea of chain stores surrounding it.

Samantha's *Pan-Latin* ▽ 23 | 11 | 23 | $28

Silver Spring | 631 E. University Blvd. (Piney Branch Rd.), MD | 301-445-7300 | www.samanthasrestaurant.net
Thanks to "excellent", "well-flavored" fare like ropas viejos and ceviche and a "family-friendly" vibe pervading its "comfortable" space, this "serene" Silver Spring Pan-Latin feels "like home – if home is somewhere south of Mexico"; just don't let its "location near a Laundromat and carwash" "deter" you, because there's "much more than fajitas" to "love" here.

Sauca *Eclectic* - | - | - | I

NEW Arlington | 4707 Columbia Pike (Buchanan St.), VA | 703-979-0020
Location varies; see website | no phone 🗷
www.eatsauca.com
Globally inspired meals-on-wheels come courtesy of this member of the DC-area food-truck brigade, which features specially grilled flatbread with a half-dozen toppings and a choice of 22 sauces drawn from cuisines around the world; adding some high-tech pizzazz to the fleet are WiFi, LCD flat-screens and international pay phones (tokens are earned by purchasing food); P.S. a brick-and-mortar counter-serve location recently debuted in Arlington.

NEW Sax ◑ *French* - | - | - | VE

Downtown | 730 11th St. NW (bet. G & H Sts.) | 202-737-0101 | www.saxwdc.com
Virtually every square inch of this sexy new resto/cabaret in a high-ceilinged, balconied space Downtown has been ornately gilded, marbleized, tufted or draped in red velvet by the Oya crew; decadent cocktails and modern French finger food and fondues accompany burlesque and other near-continuous stage entertainment, while waitresses' provacative costumes make prime conversation

starters; P.S. reservations are required, and both diners and drinkers must meet a fairly high minimum per person.

Screwtop Wine Bar Ⓜ *American* | - | - | - | M |

Arlington | Zoso Bldg. | 1025 N. Fillmore St. (bet. 10th & 11th Sts.), VA | 703-888-0845 | www.screwtopwinebar.com

It didn't take long for Arlington enthusiasts to discover this boutique wine bar and specialty food shop that pairs its small-production selections and craft beers with cheese, charcuterie, appetizers and interesting sandwiches; the spiffy-looking, big-windowed space features seating at a long, butcher-block-topped bar (or at tables), while wines, displayed along the walls, can be purchased to enjoy at home.

Sea Catch Ⓩ *Seafood* | 21 | 21 | 19 | $48 |

Georgetown | Canal Sq. | 1054 31st St. NW (bet. K & M Sts.) | 202-337-8855 | www.seacatchrestaurant.com

"Eat outside by the canal" or at the "discreet bar" at this "quiet, relaxing" "Georgetown fishery" where fin fans fall hook, line and sinker for "freshly shucked oysters" and other "solid" seafood "delivered with passion" by waiters who "know their clientele"; "beautiful setting" aside, a few fret over "high prices" and suggest the kitchen could use some "new ideas."

Sea Pearl *American/Californian* | 20 | 21 | 22 | $37 |

Merrifield | Merrifield Town Ctr. | 8191 Strawberry Ln. (bet. Gallows Rd. & Lee Hwy.), VA | 703-372-5161 | www.seapearlrestaurant.com

A "beautiful interior" and "inventive" Cal-American cuisine "with an emphasis on fresh seafood" make this glam sib of nearby Four Sisters seem like a pearl in "restaurant-starved" Merrifield; the deep-blue digs (with a wall carved to resemble ocean waves) can feel a "bit cavernous", but "personalized" care and "pretty" plates packed with "good flavor" make for an "enjoyable" meal; P.S. save some clams at the weekday happy hour.

Sei ☻ *Asian* | 23 | 24 | 20 | $48 |

Penn Quarter | 444 Seventh St. NW (bet. D & E Sts.) | 202-783-7007 | www.seirestaurant.com

From "icy-white decor as cool as the Arctic" to "imaginative sushi" and "clever" Asian-esque small plates (e.g. "wasabi guacamole"), this "excellent addition to Penn Quarter" from the Oya team creates an "experience for all senses"; "informative" staffers "make choosing the right dishes and drinks easy", even if some sei "prices aren't cheap" and it's "loud, loud, loud"; P.S. its "proximity to theaters" makes it popular among Lansburgh and Woolly Mammoth showgoers.

NEW Senart's Oyster & Chop House *American/Seafood* | - | - | - | M |

Capitol Hill | 520 8th St. SE (bet. E & G Sts.) | 202-544-1168 | www.senartsdc.com

Expect a moderately priced raw bar along with seafood and chops, plus old-fashioned cocktails, at this Barracks Row fresh face with an old name (check out the faded lettering outside); the townhouse's

| | FOOD | DECOR | SERVICE | COST |

parlor floor sports a 50-ft. marble bar and photos and murals of vintage oyster-house revelry – some of which may be re-created during the daily happy hour featuring half-price raw-bar items.

Sequoia *American* | 15 | 23 | 15 | $43 |

Georgetown | Washington Harbour | 3000 K St. NW (30th St.) | 202-944-4200 | www.arkrestaurants.com

"Watch the boats on the Potomac" from this "beautiful riverfront setting" in Washington Harbour, with floor-to-ceiling windows and a multilevel deck that becomes a "real scene at happy hour" (hence the "excellent people-watching"); Georgetowners who swear the American "food doesn't live up to the atmosphere" and is "priced for tourists looking to overpay for a memory" advise "just have cocktails on the terrace" or go for the "showy Sunday brunch."

NEW Serendipity 3 ☻ *Dessert* | - | - | - | M |

Georgetown | 3150 M St. NW (Wisconsin Ave.) | 202-333-5193 | www.serendipity3dc.com

The arrival of this iconic NYC dessert cafe in Georgetown has set sweet tooths tingling with signature mugs of 'frrrozen hot chocolate' in many decadent variations, as well as sundaes, cakes and pies, while savory types favor sandwiches, pastas and other moderately priced eats; gussied up with wit and whimsy, the former Nathans location now sports a black, white and pink color scheme and ice cream tables, though the vintage bar that once hosted the neighborhood's who's who still dispenses adult beverages.

Sergio Ristorante Italiano ⊠ *Italian* | ∇ 24 | 16 | 24 | $34 |

Silver Spring | Hilton Silver Springs | 8727 Colesville Rd. (bet. Fenton & Spring Sts.), MD | 301-585-1040 | www.hilton.com

"Yes it's in a hotel, yes it's stuck in the '60s, and, no, it's not a redsauce joint" – rather this Silver Spring redevelopment survivor "hidden" in a Hilton is an "authentic" Italian restaurant that's been dishing up "wonderful" fare at "modest prices" seemingly "forever"; bonus: "gracious" owner Sergio Toni "makes his own pasta everyday" and "knows all the regulars" in his "intimate" dining room.

Sette Osteria *Italian* | 20 | 17 | 19 | $37 |

Dupont Circle | 1666 Connecticut Ave. NW (R St.) | 202-483-3070 | www.setteosteria.com

Perched above Dupont Circle, Cafe Milano's "younger, more casual sibling" delivers "relatively down-to-earth" Italian eats (pasta, pizza, "well-prepared" entrees) that draw "tourists and local traffic" alike to a rather "stark", large-windowed space; waiters "hustle" customers out quickly so it's fine for a "quick bite", and if things start to get "too noisy", there's a "nice outdoor patio"; P.S. pennepinchers can opt for "bargain" half-size portions.

701 *American* | 23 | 24 | 23 | $53 |

Penn Quarter | 701 Pennsylvania Ave. NW (7th St.) | 202-393-0701 | www.701restaurant.com

Close to the Penn Quarter "action", this "swanky" New American is "better looking" than ever since a "sumptuous" makeover, while the "excellent" buzz generated by now-departed toque Adam Longworth seems to have grown louder with the post-Survey arrival of locavore Ed Witt; "gracious" staffers and a "pianist who takes requests" add to the "pleasant atmosphere", plus there's "great people-watching" from the terrace overlooking the Navy Memorial; P.S. the pre-theater prix fixe and $15 bar lunch offer "excellent value."

Seven Seas *Chinese/Japanese*
18 | 12 | 17 | $24

College Park | 8503 Baltimore Ave. (Quebec St.), MD | 301-345-5808 | www.sevenseascp.com
Rockville | Federal Plaza | 1776 E. Jefferson St. (bet. Montrose Rd. & Rollins Ave.), MD | 301-770-5020 | www.sevenseasrestaurant.com

"Excellent fresh fish" hooks habitués of this Rockville Chinese and its College Park offspring, which offer "reliably good", "reasonably priced" Sino specialties and "terrific" sushi and other Japanese fare; they've "been around forever", so "face-lifts" are in order, but supporters insist they're the kind of places "everybody wishes they had in their neighborhood."

☒ 1789 *American*
25 | 25 | 25 | $65

Georgetown | 1226 36th St. NW (Prospect St.) | 202-965-1789 | www.1789restaurant.com

Hark back to a "time when elegance mattered" at this "gorgeous" Georgetown townhouse, where the seasonal New American fare "always delivers", "welcoming" staffers "attend to you as if they've known you for decades" and romance blossoms amid "intimate tables", fireplaces and "classic" decor ("sit downstairs"); expect to find the neighborhood "hoi polloi", "witty pols" and "visiting parents" taking advantage of that rarity: a "pricey place that isn't overpriced", thanks in part to a $35 three-course prix fixe.

Seventh Hill Pizza Ⓜ *Pizza*
▽ 23 | 14 | 18 | $21

Capitol Hill | 327 Seventh St. SE (Pennsylvania Ave.) | 202-544-1911 | www.montmartredc.com/seventhhill

"Chewy" crusts, "fresh ingredients" and "inventive toppings" round out the "top-notch" wood-fired pizzas at this "welcome addition" on Capitol Hill (from the folks at Montmartre next door); now if only its "space were a little bigger", the better to eat the pies right "out of the oven" rather than take them home.

NEW Shake Shack *Burgers*
- | - | - | I

Dupont Circle | 1216 18th St. NW (Connecticut Ave.) | 202-683-9922
SW | Nationals Park | 1500 S. Capitol St. SE | no phone
www.shakeshack.com

Lines out its Dupont Circle door herald DC's first outpost of NYC's iconic 'roadside' burger stand, serving its signature special-sauced burgers, veggie-topped hot dogs and concretes (ultrathick shakes), plus beer and wine; for the uninitiated, the drill goes like this: customers order at the counter, wait for their buzzer to ring, pick up their food and head to the high-ceilinged dining room outfitted in recycled barn-wood and park bench–inspired seating; P.S. the Nationals Park location is only open during games.

	FOOD	DECOR	SERVICE	COST

Shamshiry *Persian* — 22 | 10 | 15 | $25

Tysons Corner | 8607 Westwood Center Dr. (Leesburg Pike) | Vienna, VA | 703-448-8883 | www.shamshiry.com

"Rice is elevated to an art" at this "bit of Tehran" whose "fragrant" Persian preps and "super kebabs" draw a "crowd" of Middle Easterners who "know what to ask for" ("helpful" staffers "walk" novices through the menu); it's set in a "plain" space and "hidden in a Tysons office park", but "real value" can be found here; P.S. "no alchohol" served.

Shula's Steak House *Steak* — 21 | 20 | 21 | $60

Tysons Corner | Marriott Tysons Corner | 8028 Leesburg Pike (Towers Crescent Dr.) | Vienna, VA | 703-506-3256 | www.donshula.com

"Coach does this one right" affirm fans of Don Shula's steakhouse chain link in Tysons Corner serving "good-quality" cuts in a "publike atmosphere"; the "cost vs. value" and "dated", football-themed touches are out-of-bounds for some, though others appreciate that it "impresses" without being too "stuffy."

Sichuan Pavilion *Chinese* — ▽ 23 | 9 | 14 | $21

Rockville | 410 Hungerford Dr. (Beall Ave.), MD | 240-403-7351 | www.scpavilion.com

"You want authentic?" then this "friendly" Rockville "gem" is the "place to go" for "exotic", "outstanding" Sichuan Chinese fare, including "amazing" ma po tofu; it's served in a "pleasant" setting adorned with watery landscapes, but even heat-seekers should beware: the "inexpensive" chow ranges from "peppy" to "too hot to enjoy."

Siroc *Italian* — 24 | 19 | 24 | $50

Downtown | 915 15th St. NW (bet. I & K Sts.) | 202-628-2220 | www.sirocrestaurant.com

"Taste buds jump" at chef/co-owner Martin Lackovic's Downtown "find", a "powerhouse of Italian food" that "deserves more attention than it gets" thanks to its "fantastic" homemade pastas, "interesting" entrees and "shockingly reasonable" lunch tabs; the staff goes "out of its way to please" in the "warm, handsome" quarters, while "outside tables" opposite McPherson Square are ripe for a "romantic dinner."

Slaviya Cafe *E European* — - | - | - | M

Adams Morgan | 2424 18th St. NW (bet. Belmont & Columbia Rds.) | 202-464-2100 | www.slaviya-dc.com

This sleek, relatively large venue brings Eastern Europe to Adams Morgan with a moderately priced menu of spicy, grilled Slavic sausages and meats, plus Balkan fare and American brunch stuff; the modern big-windowed setting features high-tops and banquettes, plus a large centerpiece bar pouring, natch, plenty of vodka; P.S. it pays props to the Eastern European music scene with DJs and live shows.

Smith & Wollensky *Steak* — 22 | 19 | 21 | $62

Golden Triangle | 1112 19th St. NW (bet. L & M Sts.) | 202-466-1100 | www.smithandwollensky.com

Beef eaters hit this "big-time" chophouse chain for "succulent" steaks matched by a "breathtaking" wine list in a "classic" setting; the "old-boy service" strikes some as "arrogant", but others admire its "NYC edge" and say it's worth going "even without an expense account."

NEW Smith Commons Ⓜ American — | — | — | M

Atlas District | 1245 H St. NE (bet. 12th & 13th Sts.) | 202-396-0038 | www.smithcommonsdc.com

This new tri-level spot on the Atlas District's main drag courts twenty- and thirtysomethings with upscale, internationally accented American fare, plus craft beer, wine and fancy drinks; the ground-floor dining room is dressed with burlap curtains, vintage photos and a big bar while the more homey second-story lounge has comfy mismatched chairs and sofas indoors and a patio area oustide; P.S. the third-floor bar/patio rental space is open to the public on weekends.

NEW Socci Italian — | — | — | M

Crystal City | Renaissance Arlington Capital View Hotel | 2800 S. Potomac Ave. (28th St.) | Arlington, VA | 703-413-1300 | www.marriott.com

At this ambitious yet affordable Crystal City hotel arrival, expect contemporary Italian favorites including hearth-fired pizzas in an urbane setting with an open kitchen, a terrazzo bar and a sleek, green-and-white lounge area; on Fridays in nice weather, patrons can play bocce ball on the lawn in front of the patio while sipping signature Bellinis.

NEW Solar Crêpes Ⓩ Crêpes — | — | — | I

Arlington | Location varies; see website, VA | 202-276-6083 | www.solarcrepes.com

Francophiles and locavores collide at this pretty, pink solar-powered food cart now parking in Clarendon and Ballston that rolls up savory and sweet crêpes on the cheap; seasonal, market-based fillings run the gamut from ham and cheese to white-bean hummus to a housemade chocolate-hazelnut spread playfully called 'Knewtella' – and for dessert there's a mean chocolate chip cookie.

Sonoma Restaurant & Wine Bar American 20 | 19 | 17 | $40

Capitol Hill | 223 Pennsylvania Ave. SE (bet. 2nd & 3rd Sts.) | 202-544-8088 | www.sonomadc.com

"Wine country meets Washington" at this "trendy" New American "mere steps from the Capitol", which entices Hill people with a "tasty" selection of "small plates, pizzas and dinners" in a "Napa Valley atmosphere (and wine list to match)"; if sour grapes gripe about "middling" food, "expensive" tabs and "snobby" treatment, even they concede it's one of the "better" options in an area that "should have more quality choices."

Sorak Garden Korean ∇ 23 | 14 | 20 | $32

Annandale | 4308 Backlick Rd. (Little River Tpke.), VA | 703-916-7600

A "step above most Korean BBQs", this "solid" Annandale eatery garners plaudits for its "mix-and-match" menu of "grilled meats" that come with kimchee, "homemade pickles" and other gratis accompaniments (thus, it's a real "value"); there's also a vast menu of "typical" fare like bibimbop and noodle dishes on offer in the "nice digs", which include a sushi bar.

Sorriso *Italian* | 22 | 17 | 20 | $33 |

Cleveland Park | 3518 Connecticut Ave. NW (bet. Ordway & Porter Sts.) | 202-537-4800 | www.sorrisoristorante.net

"All the family members" get in on the action at Pietro Polles' "mom-and-pop" Cleveland Park Italian, proffering "uncommonly well-made" Treviso-style pizza, "excellent specials" ("no two meals are the same") and grapes from the clan's "vineyard in Italy"; it's set in a simple storefront, but the "warm ambiance" and "personal feeling make it special", as does the breezy outdoor seating.

Source, The 🗵 *American* | 25 | 25 | 23 | $67 |

Penn Quarter | Newseum | 575 Pennsylvania Ave. NW (6th St.) | 202-637-6100 | www.wolfgangpuck.com

"Newsworthy" "Modern American–meets-Asian" fare headlines Wolfgang Puck's "dazzling" outpost next to the Penn Quarter's Newseum, where a "stunning" yet "stark" second-story dining room provides a "serene" milieu for "high-end" meals melding "wonderful flavors"; other pluses include a "cordial, responsive" staff and "lively" happy hour, when its downstairs lounge fills with "hip DCers" digging into Far Eastern small plates in an atmosphere akin to "Vegas, LA or New York."

Sou'Wester *American* | 18 | 19 | 18 | $45 |

SW | Mandarin Oriental | 1330 Maryland Ave. SW (12th St.) | 202-787-6990 | www.mandarinoriental.com

Sweeping waterfront views backdrop "refined versions of grandma's cooking" at this Regional American, the "more affordable alternative to CityZen", its sister restaurant in the posh Mandarin Oriental; while the Southern-accented staples – including "hushpuppies, fried chicken, crab imperial" – are generally "palate-pleasing", "spotty" service and a homey, "somewhat undistinctive" space lead a few doubters to deem it merely "so sou."

Spices *Asian* | 22 | 16 | 18 | $30 |

Cleveland Park | 3333A Connecticut Ave. NW (bet. Macomb & Ordway Sts.) | 202-686-3833 | www.spicesdc.com

"Inventive" sushi stars on a "large menu" of "fresh-tasting" Pan-Asian fare ("is there any cuisine it doesn't serve?") at this Cleveland Park neighborhood "staple" whose "unbelievable" ginger salad is worth a "special trip" alone; a "convenient" location across from the Uptown movie theater, "generally quick" service and modest prices keep it "hopping", even if the space is a "bit cafeterialike."

Spice Xing *Indian* | 20 | 19 | 20 | $31 |

Rockville | Rockville Town Sq. | 100B Gibbs St. (Middle Ln.), MD | 301-610-0303 | www.spicexing.com

"Tasty" Indian fare "with a twist" spices up this "classy" Rockville eatery, a "surprise" whose dishes "stray far from traditional tandoori" and include "complex" "layers of flavor" (bonus: it gives "fire to the food" when asked); un-X-cited sorts say it "misses the mark", but the fabric-ceilinged dining room, "helpful" staffers and "reasonable" prices sway most; P.S. the "outstanding" lunch buffet (from $8.95) is a "good deal."

NEW Standard ● Ⓜ *BBQ*   – | – | – | I

Logan Circle | 1801 14th St. NW (S St.) | no phone | www.standarddc.com
Beer, BBQ and brats on the cheap fuel this buzzing biergarten on the trendy stretch of 14th Street NW between Logan Circle and U Street NW, where most of the noshing and guzzling takes place at colorful, communal picnic tables on the streetside patio; the interior, done up in buttery yellow, white tile and gleaming wood, is barely large enough for a small bar and a narrow dining counter.

Star & Shamrock ● *Deli*   – | – | – | I

Atlas District | 1341 H St. NE (bet. 13th & 14th Sts.) | 202-388-3833 | www.starandshamrock.com
Merge an Irish saloon with a Jewish-style deli, and you get this Atlas District original featuring tons of polished wood, a huge three-sided bar and irreverent touches like a liquor display evoking a Hebrew tabernacle; likewise, affordable standards like pastrami and corned beef combos share menu space with a few Old Sod classics, the better to go with the Guinness and whiskeys on hand; P.S. the late-night kitchen attracts crowds from the nearby clubs.

Sticky Rice *Asian/Eclectic*   22 | 19 | 17 | $24

Atlas District | 1224 H St. NE (bet. 12th & 13th Sts.) | 202-397-7655 | www.stickyricedc.com
"Sticky balls", "cheap sushi", "crazy" food combos and "bottomless buckets" of tater tots draw "hipsters" to this "funky" Eclectic-Asian "hot spot" in the trendy Atlas District; "spacy" servers are often "more interested in their tattoos" than waiting tables, but that "just doesn't matter" to party types seeking ballast before they "go drinking"; P.S. karaoke and DJs add to the "boisterous" vibe.

Stoney's Lounge ● *Pub Food*   18 | 10 | 16 | $22

Logan Circle | 1433 P St. NW (bet. 14th & 15th Sts.) | 202-234-1818 | www.stoneysdc.com
Grab a "warm meal and a cold beer" ("better yet, make that a few beers . . .") at this "perfect neighborhood joint" in Logan Circle with some of the DC bar scene's "most reliable comfort food" – including what may be the "best grilled cheese around"; it's got "hole-in-the-wall" appeal to spare, while "reasonable prices", "efficient" service and the "many drafts on tap" make it easy to "enjoy yourself."

Surfside *Californian/Mexican*   22 | 14 | 15 | $19

Glover Park | 2444 Wisconsin Ave. NW (Calvert St.) | 202-337-0004 | www.surfsidedc.com
"Sway to the rhythm of the tropics", sip on "tangy margaritas" and catch up on "Glover Park gossip" at this joint revered for its "exceptional" Cal-Mex fast food ("grilled-fish tacos", burritos, etc.) and "wonderful roof deck"; a "DIY" ordering/pickup system "keeps the prices down", but lines are "whittled" fast and the

	FOOD	DECOR	SERVICE	COST

chow comes out "quickly", making it a "great family-friendly addition" to the area.

Sushi Damo _Japanese_   24 | 23 | 22 | $42

Rockville | Rockville Town Sq. | 36G Maryland Ave. (bet. Jefferson St. & Montgomery Ave.), MD | 301-340-8010 | www.sushidamo.com

Sushi fans, beware: "you can go nuts" choosing among the "creative" and "beautifully presented" raw-fin fare and "interesting seasonal" specials at this "cool" NYC-bred Japanese in Rockville Town Square; the "standout" Zen decor and "gracious" service add to the "pizzazz", cushioning the fact that some bean-counters find it "pricey."

Sushiko _Japanese_   25 | 18 | 21 | $44

Glover Park | 2309 Wisconsin Ave. NW (Calvert St.) | 202-333-4187
Chevy Chase | 5455 Wisconsin Ave. (Western Ave.), MD | 301-961-1644
www.sushikorestaurant.com

"Year after year", this Glover Park "institution" and its Chevy Chase offspring deliver some of the "best sushi around", but what makes them "true standouts" are their "superb" East-West small plates and the "sheer genius" of pairing Japanese food with red and white Burgundies; DC is "low-key" and cramped" and the Marylander "stylish" and a bit more "spacious", but wherever you go, expect "friendly" faces and "decent prices" for what you get.

Sushi Rock _Japanese_   - | - | - | M

Arlington | 1900 Clarendon Blvd. (Scott St.), VA | 571-312-8027 | www.sushirockdc.com

Maki and music meld at this industrial lounge in Arlington's Courthouse neighborhood equipped with iron rebar and chains, wall-sized rock culture images, cymbals as chandeliers and, of course, a guitar-heavy soundtrack (there's also an outdoor patio); the midpriced menu offers creative sushi named after singers and their songs, as well as Asian-influenced steak and salmon dishes and rock-inspired cocktails.

☑ Sushi Taro ☒ _Japanese_   26 | 20 | 22 | $59

Dupont Circle | 1503 17th St. NW (P St.) | 202-462-8999 | www.sushitaro.com

Following a "stunning redesign" and the installation of a "more authentic" Japanese menu, this Dupont Circle East destination offers kaiseki dinners that will "bowl you over" in a "sleek" (not "cozy") setting, plus "exotic" sushi prepared at an intimate "chef's table"; while vocal vets are "sad" to see "no California rolls in sight" and "expensive" tabs at what used to be a "Tokyo-style" haunt, at least the $12.95 "bento box lunch" is a "steal."

Sweet Basil _Thai_   ▽ 21 | 17 | 22 | $29

Bethesda | 4910 Fairmont Ave. (bet. Norfolk Ave. & Old Georgetown Rd.), MD | 301-657-7997 | www.sweetbasilland.com

Patrons are "always greeted with a friendly smile" at this Bethesda Thai where "inventive" curries, exotic salads, noodle dishes and the like draw an admiring clientele; perhaps some of its "innovations" are geared toward "USA tastes", but much here remains "good" say its sweethearts, who happily accept a storefront "ambiance [that's] a bit lacking."

Sweet Ginger *Asian*   19 | 17 | 20 | $26

Vienna | Danor Plaza | 120B Branch Rd. SE (Maple Ave.), VA | 703-319-3922

Loyalists "light the lanterns" and head to this "charming" Vienna standby for "artful" sushi and other "tasty delights" from a "broad sampling of Asian cuisines", including Chinese, Japanese, Malaysian and Thai; despite its "strip-mall" setting, "reasonable prices" and "excellent" service make it just the place "to take guests", plus it's convenient "before a show at nearby Jammin Java."

Sweetgreen *Health Food*   21 | 12 | 15 | $12

NEW **Capitol Hill** | 221 Pennsylvania Ave. SE (bet. 2nd & 3rd Sts.) | 202-547-9338

Dupont Circle | 1512 Connecticut Ave. NW (bet. Dupont Circle & Q St.) | 202-387-9338

Georgetown | 3333 M St. NW (bet. 33rd & 34th Sts.) | 202-337-9338

Logan Circle | 1471 P St. NW (bet. 14th & 15th Sts.) | 202-234-7336

Bethesda | 4831 Bethesda Ave. (bet. Arlington Rd. & Woodmont Ave.), MD | 301-654-7336

NEW **Ballston** | 4075 Wilson Blvd. (Randolph St.) | Arlington, VA | 703-522-2016

NEW **Reston** | 11935 Democracy Dr. (Library St.), VA | 571-203-0082
www.sweetgreen.com

"Healthy and green never tasted so good" swear supporters of these "inexpensive", eco-friendly "takeaways" doling out "fresh, fresh, fresh" salads (and soups) so "unique and tasty" they're sure to satisfy "flavor"-seekers turned off by "wimpy rabbit food"; lunch lines are "crazy long" within the recycled-wood-adorned spaces, but there's "tart, tangy" frozen yogurt that "can't be missed" waiting on the end.

Sweetwater Tavern *Southwestern*   21 | 18 | 21 | $30

Merrifield | 3066 Gatehouse Plaza (Rte. 50), VA | 703-645-8100

Centreville | 14250 Sweetwater Ln. (Multiplex Dr.), VA | 703-449-1100

Sterling | 45980 Waterview Plaza (Loudon Tech Dr.), VA | 571-434-6500
www.greatamericanrestaurants.com

A "popular" choice for "kids/families/dates/everyone", these Southwestern-themed NoVa "crowd" magnets offer "consistently good" American chow and "some of the best brews around"; they're "loud" and there'll be a "long wait unless you call ahead", but the "varied" fare ferried by "enthusiastic" servers means that "everyone will find something they like" – and at "affordable" prices.

Tabaq Bistro ◐ *Mediterranean*   20 | 21 | 17 | $37

U Street Corridor | 1336 U St. NW (bet. 13th & 14th Sts.) | 202-265-0965 | www.tabaqdc.com

A "fabulous" vista greets guests who venture onto the "cool" rooftop terrace at this U Street Med, which proffers "reliable" small plates, kebabs and salads from an extensive menu (also available in dimly lit, lower-level rooms); true, detractors deem it "pretentious and overpriced" with service that's "so-so", but skyline-seekers say that "view makes it worth it"; P.S. bands or DJs entertain Thursdays and Fridays.

Tabard Inn *American* | 24 | 24 | 22 | $44 |

Dupont Circle | Hotel Tabard Inn | 1739 N St. NW (bet. 17th & 18th Sts.) | 202-331-8528 | www.tabardinn.com

With its cozy "nooks and crannies", fires "crackling in the hearth" and "walled garden courtyard", this "quirky" Dupont New American lodged in an "old English"-style inn provides a "delightfully un-Washington" setting for "imaginative" cooking, "interesting wines" and "perennially friendly" service; too bad it's a bit "loud and crowded" at times, particularly when it's presenting "one of the best brunches in DC" ("reserve early").

Taberna del Alabardero *Spanish* | 23 | 23 | 23 | $65 |

World Bank | 1776 I St. NW (18th St.) | 202-429-2200 | www.alabardero.com

Expect a "sophisticated" dining experience "every bit as authentic" as those in Madrid at this "elegant" World Bank Iberian, where an "impeccable" staff works in tandem with an "outstanding" kitchen equally adept at "classic" dishes and more "innovative" fare; it's too "pricey" and "stuffy" for some, but "superb" wines and a happy hour replete with some of the "best tapas" make it *"perfecto"* for many.

Tachibana *Japanese* | 24 | 14 | 19 | $39 |

McLean | 6715 Lowell Ave. (Emerson Ave.), VA | 703-847-1771 | www.tachibana.us

The sushi chefs at this "high-end" McLean Japanese "know exactly what they're doing" with the "impeccably fresh" fin fare on hand, so "sit at the bar" and watch them create "generous" portions of its "fantastic" signature ("no skimpy wafers of fish on rice here"); "interesting traditional" fare that's "often hard to find" and "good-value" lunch specials round out the menu, but beware: even fans fret that the "tired old interior" "has to be spruced up."

Tackle Box *Seafood* | 21 | 14 | 15 | $19 |

NEW Cleveland Park | 3407 Connecticut Ave. NW (bet. Macomb & Ordway Sts.)

Georgetown | 3245 M St. NW (bet. 33rd St. & Wisconsin Ave.) | 202-337-8526
www.tackleboxrestaurant.com

At this "seat-yourself", "fish-shack" spin-off of nearby Hook, Georgetowners dig into "solid, affordable" seafood (including one of DC's "best lobster rolls" and $13.50 meal deals) accompanied by "lots" of "sauces and sides"; expect the "bare minimum" when it comes to decor and service: order at the counter, then "sup with fellow diners" at "communal" picnic tables or head upstairs to Crackle Bar for $2 happy hour 'ritas 5–7 PM; P.S. a second location opened post-Survey in Cleveland Park.

	FOOD	DECOR	SERVICE	COST

Taipei Tokyo *Chinese/Japanese*

16 | 8 | 13 | $18

Rockville | Fallsgrove Village Shopping Ctr. | 14921D Shady Grove Rd. (bet. Blackwell Rd. & Fallsgrove Blvd.), MD | 301-738-8813
White Flint | 11510A Rockville Pike (Nicholson Ln.) | Rockville, MD | 301-881-8388
www.taipei-tokyo.net

These suburbanites' "strange mixture of Chinese on one side and Japanese on the other" (with Thai and "decent sushi" available) may work for a "low-cost" lunch or dinner, although purists pan their "sanitized version of Asian food"; budget-minders counter that "on a good night [they're] surprisingly good", but given the basic settings, "takeout is the way to go"; P.S. White Flint is cafeteria-style, while Rockville is full service.

Tako Grill *Japanese*

23 | 15 | 20 | $37

Bethesda | 7756 Wisconsin Ave. (Cheltenham Dr.), MD | 301-652-7030 | www.takogrill.com

"Top-quality" sushi and sashimi swim to the top of the "pricey" menu at this long-running Bethesda Japanese, which also features robatayaki ("small plates of grilled fish and vegetables"), "unique treats" and a "sake bar"; if "consistency" is where it "shines", the nondescript decor tarnishes the glow a tad; P.S. "try the baby octopus – if you pretend it sticks to your tongue the kids will freak."

NEW TaKorean 🛇 *Korean*

- | - | - | I

Location varies; see website | no phone | www.takorean.com

Borrowing a page from Mr. Softee, this new DC-based truck plays music – but instead of soft-serve it slings spicy Korean tacos with a Mexican twist; the easy-on-the-wallet choices include beef bulgogi, chicken or caramelized tofu, topped with the likes of slaw, Sriracha and lime crème, plus there's Mexican soda to wash it all down.

Tallula/EatBar *American*

22 | 20 | 20 | $42

Clarendon | 2761 Washington Blvd. (Pershing Dr.), VA | 703-778-5051 | www.tallularestaurant.com

"Creative cooking" and "innovative combinations" keep these "hip" Clarendon "hangouts" hopping: go upscale for "super-tasty" New American meals and "fabulous brunches" in Tallula's "intimate" dining room, or venture next door to EatBar, a "noisy" "nosh heaven" for "drinks and a light meal" ("tapas-style" plates rule); both share a "wine list that won't quit" and "efficient" service, making them a "favorite" destination for a "night out on the town."

Tandoori Nights *Indian*

21 | 20 | 20 | $29

Gaithersburg | 106 Market St. (Kentlands Blvd.), MD | 301-947-4007
Clarendon | 2800 Clarendon Blvd. (Edgewood St.), VA | 703-248-8333
www.tandoorinights.com

At these Gaithersburg and Clarendon Indians, "beautiful, artistic" touches like jeweled patio umbrellas and dramatic wall murals create "chic settings" for "consistently good" fare spiced to "satisfy the Americanized palate" (still, the kitchens make a "vindaloo that will

| | FOOD | DECOR | SERVICE | COST |

make you think el Diablo invaded"); they may not be the "most inventive" eateries, but "reasonable prices" and "helpful" service make them "keepers."

Taqueria Distrito Federal *Mexican* | 23 | 10 | 19 | $12 |

Columbia Heights | 3463 14th St. NW (Oak St.) | 202-276-7331
Petworth | 805 Kennedy St. NW (8th St.) | 202-276-7331
www.taqueriadf.com

"Practice your Spanish" on a "mini-vacation to Mexico" at these "real-deal" outposts in Columbia Heights and Petworth proffering "awesome tacos" ("especially the goat"), "great carne asada" and other "authentic" eats; there's "no decor" to speak of, but with prices this "reasonable", you're not paying for it either; P.S. weekend specials include tripe soup and pork tamales.

Taqueria El Charrito | - | - | - | I |
Caminante ⊅ *Mexican/Salvadoran*

Arlington | 2710A Washington Blvd. (Pershing Dr.), VA | 703-351-1177

"Two people can eat for less than $10" at this Mexican-Salvadoran carryout in Arlington, filling up on its "authentic" pupusas, tacos and burritos; the decor's "lacking", so aesthetes may want to "order and eat outside in [their] car", but what matters here is the food – and it's "less than dirt-cheap and very good."

Taqueria La Placita ⊅ *Mexican* | - | - | - | I |

Hyattsville | 5020 Edmonston Rd. (Farragut St.), MD | 301-277-4477

Few aficionados have managed to try all 14 taco versions at this inexpensive Mexican transplant in Hyattsville, where the corn-tortilla-wrapped meats and innards it serves could as easily be found south of the border as in suburban Maryland; expats fill the bright room decorated with a massive mural and interesting artifacts from home, but non-natives do fine, especially if they attempt a bit of Spanish.

Taqueria Nacional ⊠ *Mexican* | 23 | 13 | 18 | $13 |

Capitol Hill | 400 N. Capitol St. NW (Louisiana Ave.) | 202-737-7070 | www.taquerianacional.com

"Senate staffers" (and their bosses) "struggle with hunger pains" while waiting on line for "cheap, delicious" tacos, guacamole, yuca fries and agua fresca at this "walk-up" Cap Hill Mexican positioned behind its *padre*, Johnny's Half Shell; it's only open weekdays for breakfast and lunch and "there's no place to sit", but everyone from poor interns to power players laud it as a "nacional treasure."

Taqueria Poblano *Mexican* | 22 | 14 | 20 | $22 |

Del Ray | 2400B Mt. Vernon Ave. (Oxford Ave.) | Alexandria, VA | 703-548-8226
Arlington | 2503A N. Harrison St. (Lee Hwy.), VA | 703-237-8250
www.taqueriapoblano.com

The fish and duck "tacos are great, and the rest of the menu ain't far behind" at these "cheery" Cal-Mex "hangouts" in Del Rey and Arlington that "sparkle" with "fresh flavors", "reasonable prices and hearty portions"; "accommodating" staffers help make the "cozy" (some say "cramped") digs "family-friendly", even as mom and dad sip "custom margaritas" that "someone knows a bit about mixing"; P.S. both offer breakfast on Sundays.

Tara Thai *Thai*
19 | 17 | 18 | $26

Upper NW | Spring Valley Shopping Ctr. | 4849 Massachusetts Ave. NW (49th St.) | 202-363-4141
Bethesda | 4828 Bethesda Ave. (bet. Arlington Rd. & Woodmont Ave.), MD | 301-657-0488
Gaithersburg | 9811 Washingtonian Blvd. (Sam Eig Hwy.), MD | 301-947-8330
Rockville | Montrose Crossing | 12071 Rockville Pike (Montrose Rd.), MD | 301-231-9899
Falls Church | 7501E Leesburg Pike (Pimmit Dr.), VA | 703-506-9788
NEW Herndon | 13021 Worldgate Dr. (Centreville Rd.), VA | 703-481-8999
Vienna | 226 Maple Ave. W. (bet. Lawyers Rd. & Nutley St.), VA | 703-255-2467
www.tarathai.com

As long as the "soothing" "underwater"-themed decor doesn't "put you in a trance", there's much to "enjoy" about this "middle-of-the-road" Thai chainlet where you "always know what you're getting" (read: "decent" fare, "polite" service, "reasonable prices"); sure, adventurous sorts dis "bland" chow that's "thoroughly Americanized", but the seafood-slanted menu works as an "old standby."

Taste of Burma *Burmese*
∇ 22 | 15 | 18 | $26

Sterling | Countryside Shopping Ctr. | 126 Edds Ln. (bet. Rtes. 7 & 28), VA | 703-444-8510 | www.tasteofburma.com

Discover "authentic tastes from another world" at this "affordable" Sterling Burmese offering more than 100 menu items fusing French, Chinese, Indian, Vietnamese and native flavors in "freshly prepared" dishes (so "be prepared to wait"); regulars suggest "coming with other couples" to sample as many things as possible in the intimate strip-mall space prettified with pillows on the banquettes and fresh flowers.

Taste of Morocco *Moroccan*
20 | 20 | 20 | $33

Clarendon | 3211 N. Washington Blvd. (Wilson Blvd.), VA | 703-527-7468 | www.atasteofmorocco.com

"Mercifully hidden from the usual Clarendon yuppies", this "diamond in the rough" offers midpriced Moroccan fare that's "different from the ordinary", balancing "tartness and sweetness" in dishes like chicken with olives and lemon; diners feel they've entered a "dream world" as they "lounge on cushions and watch the belly dancer" while basking in the "attentive" service.

Taste of Saigon *Vietnamese*
21 | 17 | 19 | $31

Rockville | Rockville Town Sq. | 20 Maryland Ave. (Beall Ave.), MD | 301-424-7222
Tysons Corner | 8201 Greensboro Dr. (International Dr.) | McLean, VA | 703-790-0700
www.tasteofsaigon.com

"Grandma Tu's recipes are tastefully prepared" at these Tysons Corner/Rockville outlets for "Vietnamese home cooking", which forge beyond pho with a "wide range" of French-influenced cuisine, notably dishes with the "signature black pepper sauce"; for most, their "pleasing ambiance", modest prices and "ready-to-please" staff add up to a "quality dining experience", even if a few nostalgists kvetch that Maryland's relatively "new location lacks the charm of the old."

Tavira *Portuguese*   24 | 19 | 24 | $49

Chevy Chase | Chevy Chase Bank Bldg. | 8401 Connecticut Ave. (Chevy Chase Lake Dr.), MD | 301-652-8684 | www.tavirarestaurant.com

It's "hidden in the basement" of a bank building in Chevy Chase, but "walking down a flight of stairs" reveals an "oasis of old-world elegance" that's home to some of the area's "best Portuguese"; smitten surveyors salute fare that's "creative and classically inspired" ("especially fish"), "wonderful" wine and "entertaining" waiters, all of which adds up to a "lovely" "night out without breaking the budget."

Taylor Gourmet *Deli/Italian*   23 | 17 | 19 | $13

Atlas District | 1116 H St. NE (bet. 11th & 12th Sts.) | 202-684-7001
Mt. Vernon Square/Convention Center | 485 K St. NW (bet. 4th & 5th Sts.) | 202-289-8001
NEW **Bethesda** | Bethesda Row | 7280 Woodmont Ave. (Elm St.), MD | 301-951-9001
www.taylorgourmet.com

"Native Philadelphians" may quibble, but DC deli mavens swear these City of Brotherly Love–inspired sandwich-makers "take the Italian hoagie to a new level" of "overstuffed", "salty/cheesy goodness"; you'll "spend more than you would at a Subway", but the "high-quality ingredients" used at the "urban-chic" trio ensure a "great nosh" – one guaranteed to make you "sleep away the afternoon at work."

Teaism *Tearoom*   20 | 16 | 15 | $17

Penn Quarter | 400 Eighth St. NW (D St.) | 202-638-6010
Dupont Circle | 2009 R St. NW (Connecticut Ave.) | 202-667-3827
Golden Triangle | 800 Connecticut Ave. NW (H St.) | 202-835-2233 🎨
www.teaism.com

"Meet the girls" for a "chai latte" or take an Asian-themed detour from sightseeing at this "quaint" trio of counter-service tearooms "hidden" around town; it's a "challenge" finding a table at lunch and they're a "tad pricey", but the brew crew feels "healthy, happy and whole" noshing on the "fresh light fare" and "dangerously delicious" salted oat cookies – reason enough most applaud the "anti-Starbucks."

NEW Teak Wood *Thai*   - | - | - | I

Logan Circle | 1323 14th St. NW (bet. N St. & Rhode Island Ave.) | 202-290-1856 | www.teakwooddc.com

This date-worthy Thai newcomer on trendy 14th Street NW above Logan Circle offers inexpensive traditional dishes plus an extensive sushi selection and drinks served from a teak-sided bar; imported wood carvings, splashing waterfalls, lush plants and statuary create a Thai Buddhist retreat feel, and big front windows make it brighter than its older sibling, The Regent.

	FOOD	DECOR	SERVICE	COST

Teatro Goldoni ⊠ *Italian*

	-	21	21	$59

Golden Triangle | 1909 K St. NW (bet. 19th & 20th Sts.) |
202-955-9494 | www.teatrogoldoni.com

Bargain-hunters still find one of DC's "best bar lunches" here, but a
post-Survey downscaling of this Golden Triangle Italian into a
trattoria, and the departure of chef Enzo Fargione, has resulted in
the addition of small plates and half-portions of hearty traditional cuisine; the setting – a "clubby" Venetian Carnevale–inspired
room – remains unchanged, though "great bartenders" now add
to the buzz with bargain $20 all-the-wine-you-can-drink deals
offered 5–8 PM on weekdays.

Ted's Bulletin *American*

	-	-	-	I

Capitol Hill | 505 Eighth St. SE (bet. E & G Sts.) | 202-544-8337 |
www.tedsbulletin.com

A spiffy setting – ornate art deco accent pieces, a vintage bar,
leather-lined booths, old-school lunch counter – that harks back to
a time when everyday eats were served in classic comfort sets the
stage for homestyle American chow at this Capitol Hill eatery from
the Matchbox team; affordable fare like grilled cheese, T-bones and
old-fashioned supper dishes (plus all-day breakfast) is enlivened by
classic cocktails, malts and fresh-baked goodies.

Tempo *French/Italian*

	▽ 22	18	23	$42

Greater Alexandria | 4231 Duke St. (Gordon St.) | Alexandria, VA |
703-370-7900 | www.temporestaurant.com

"Eating in a garage was never so good" declare devotees of this
"well-priced" French-Italian set in a "former gas station" in Alexandria;
patrons fill their tanks with "outstanding" fish and meat entrees and
"super specials" in a "white-tablecloth" milieu ("lacking" to some,
"light and airy" to others), making for a "pleasant" pit stop prized by
neighbors on nights when they "don't want to cook."

T.H.A.I. *Thai*

	23	18	22	$31

Shirlington | Village at Shirlington | 4029 Campbell Ave. (Randolph St.) |
Arlington, VA | 703-931-3203 | www.thaiinshirlington.com

It's "g.r.e.a.t" spell out supporters of this Shirlington Thai offering
"well-seasoned" dishes that may be "as authentic as they come"; the
the "warmth of the staff", mod interior and "fun" outdoor seating
make it "perfect before or after" nearby Signature Theatre, but beware: you may become "addicted to its 'Big Bowl' lunch specials"
(11:30 AM–4 PM daily), a "good value" for under $10.

Thai at Silver Spring *Thai*

	20	14	17	$22

Silver Spring | 921 Ellsworth Dr. (bet. Fenton St. & Georgia Ave.),
MD | 301-650-0666 | www.thaiatsilverspring.com

A "relative gem in a sea of mediocre chains", this affordable
Silver Spring Thai comes "recommended" for its "highly reliable"
traditional dishes, plus Chinese-American classics; the decor is
"nothing to write home about", but an "ample" dining room and
"decent" service make it a "comfortable" option for a "pre- or
post-movie dinner."

	FOOD	DECOR	SERVICE	COST

Thai Basil *Thai* | 22 | 15 | 21 | $20 |

Chantilly | 14511P Lee Jackson Memorial Hwy. (Airline Pkwy.), VA | 703-631-8277 | www.thaibasilchantilly.com

"There's good reason" that owner-chef Nongkran Daks won the pad Thai *Throwdown! With Bobby Flay* on the Food Network, but the other fare at this "busy, tight" Chantilly Siamese is equally "tasty" (just "pay attention to the heat level"); a few cite "disappointing" meals, but more maintain it's "worth the drive", and an "incredible value" to boot.

Thaiphoon *Thai* | 20 | 16 | 18 | $24 |

Dupont Circle | 2011 S St. NW (bet. Connecticute Ave. & 20th St.) | 202-667-3505
Pentagon City | Pentagon Row | 1301 S. Joyce St. (Army Navy Dr.) | Arlington, VA | 703-413-8200
www.thaiphoon.com

"Cheap and cheerful", these "better-than-you'd-expect" Dupont and Pentagon Row Thais satisfy young crowds with "fruity cocktails" and "quick, tasty" curries, noodle dishes and more; "take a shoehorn to find a seat" at the S Street location or head to Arlington for the patio.

⊠ Thai Square *Thai* | 26 | 8 | 18 | $26 |

Arlington | 3217 Columbia Pike (Highland St.), VA | 703-685-7040 | www.thaisquarerestaurant.com

At this "top-notch" "garden of eatin'" in Arlington, the "nondescript" setting has as much "charm as a 1970s Southeast Asian airport", but its "spicy-as-all-hell" cooking is the "real deal"; as such, expats come here for "outstanding" "dishes found nowhere else", while "limited seating" makes diners feel as if they're "getting a private chef for the evening" for "half the price of fancier places."

Thai Tanic *Thai* | 23 | 15 | 20 | $24 |

Logan Circle | 1326A 14th St. NW (bet. N St. & Rhode Island Ave.) | 202-588-1795 | www.thaitanic.us

Thai Tanic II *Thai*

Columbia Heights | 3462 14th St. NW (Newton St.) | 202-387-0882 | www.thaitanic.us

NEW Tsunami Sushi et Lounge ● *Japanese*

Logan Circle | 1326 14th St. NW, 2nd fl. (Rhode Island Ave.) | 202-588-5599

At this "affordable" Logan Circle "go-to" and its Columbia Heights clone, an urban clientele digs into an "expansive menu" of "Thai-riffic" fare and "inventive drinks"; a few would sink the "disco" decor and "retro sparkly tables", but for many the "plasticky ambiance and silly name add to the charm" and help explain why they're always "crowded and noisy"; P.S. its sleek sushi bar recently debuted upstairs.

NEW Toki | – | – | – | I |
Underground *Taiwanese/Noodle Shop*

Atlas District | 1234 H St. NE, 2nd fl. (bet. 12th & 13th Sts.) | 202-388-3086 | www.tokiunderground.com

Taiwanese-style ramen is the specialty of this inexpensive counterserve newcomer in the Atlas District, which also offers sake, beer and up-to-the-minute Asian-accented cocktails; noodle-heads climb stairs to reach the tiny grunge-mod digs done up with a skateboard ramp on the ceiling, graffiti peeping through rough planks and rope-wrapped wires twisted like trees.

Tonic *American* | 16 | 16 | 15 | $23 |

Foggy Bottom | Quigley's Pharmacy | 2036 G St. NW (bet. 20th & 21st Sts.) | 202-296-0211
Mt. Pleasant | 3155 Mt. Pleasant St. NW (bet. Kenyon St. & Kilbourne Pl.) | 202-986-7661
www.tonicrestaurant.com
"Great draft beers", somewhat "reliable" American chow (burgers, tater tots, etc.), affordable tabs and a "lively" scene make for "one-stop shopping" at these "popular" pubs; Mt. Pleasant features a dining room upstairs and a newly added speakeasy-style cocktail lounge called Last Exit below, while the Foggy Bottom outpost on the GW campus is "filled at happy hour with students and State Department" types – they're "fun" perhaps, but critics complain that overall "nothing stands out."

Tono Sushi *Japanese* | 23 | 16 | 20 | $27 |

Woodley Park | 2605 Connecticut Ave. NW (Calvert St.) | 202-332-7300 | www.tonosushi.com
The "$1-happy-hour" deals may get you "hooked on sushi" at this Japanese "gem" in Woodley Park "tourist land", where "creative" raw fish and "interesting vegetarian" options share the spotlight with "high-quality" dishes from Thai, Chinese, Japanese and other cuisines; it'll "make the whole family happy", but if the undistinguished digs achieve the opposite, there's always "fast" delivery.

Tony & Joe's Seafood Place *Seafood* | 15 | 18 | 16 | $42 |

Georgetown | Washington Harbour | 3000 K St. NW (30th St.) | 202-944-4545 | www.tonyandjoes.com
Scenery-seekers say the "food is secondary" to the "waterfront location" of this "tourist"-friendly American seafooder in Georgetown; true, some "have yet to be disappointed" by the "pricey" raw-bar selections and Sunday brunch, but the unimpressed say "ok" chow and service make it better for "drinks and a light dinner"; P.S. at press time only its boisterous outdoor bar area is open – the main dining area is still closed and undergoing repairs due to extensive flood damage.

Tony Cheng's *Chinese* | 19 | 13 | 17 | $29 |

Chinatown | 619 H St. NW (bet. 6th & 7th Sts.) | 202-371-8669 | www.tonychengsrestaurant.com
"Enjoy both floors" of this Chinatown "favorite": "go upstairs" for "consistently good" seafood and "cheap, authentic" dim sum (the "carts of tasty dumplings don't stop until you do"), or stay at ground level for "all-you-can-eat" Mongolian BBQ that's a "real bargain for bottomless pits"; the setting isn't tony, but generally "efficient" service and a location near Verizon Center still make it a "step above."

	FOOD	DECOR	SERVICE	COST

⟨Z⟩ Tosca ⊠ *Italian* | 27 | 23 | 26 | $66 |

Penn Quarter | 1112 F St. NW (bet. 11th & 12th Sts.) | 202-367-1990 | www.toscadc.com

Celebrated for its "quiet elegance" and "divine" Italian cuisine paired with wines to "match every dish and taste", this Penn Quarter "standout" is lined with "power players" at lunch and "romantic" sorts at night – because "no matter whom you bring here", its "seasoned" pros make the "experience special"; "understated" decor (some say "boring") completes the package, one with "pricey" tabs tempered by a "bargain" $38 pre-theater prix fixe deal; P.S. "try the chef's table in the kitchen."

Toscana Café *Deli/Italian* | 23 | 16 | 18 | $33 |

Capitol Hill | 601 Second St. NE (Talbott Ave.) | 202-525-2693 | www.toscanacafedc.com

Patrons peer at the "backside of Union Station" at this "hard-to-find" Capitol Hill Italian that "churns out" "*delizioso*" pasta dishes", entrees and sandwiches in its eat-in/carry-out street-level "kitchen" and upstairs dining room ("cramped" but cheery); it's still a "little unpolished around the edges", but "skilled cooking", modest prices and "friendly service" add up to a "welcome addition" in an area where "good dining options are scarce."

Tragara *Italian* | 21 | 19 | 22 | $49 |

Bethesda | 4935 Cordell Ave. (bet. Norfolk Ave. & Old Georgetown Rd.), MD | 301-951-4935 | www.tragara.com

"Professional" waiters whisk plates of classic Northern Italian fare to tables at this Bethesda standby, a "special-occasion" "favorite" that fans deem a "thoroughly enjoyable place" to "linger over dinner" or do business at lunch; still, some are less than *dolce* on the place, citing "good but tired" chow and decor that's on the "blah" side.

⟨Z⟩ Trummer's On Main Ⓜ *American* | 25 | 27 | 25 | $60 |

Clifton | 7134 Main St. (bet. Chapel St. & Clifton Creek Dr.), VA | 703-266-1623 | www.trummersonmain.com

This "gorgeous" newcomer in "quaint" Clifton, VA, is "more casual" and less expensive than some other country standouts and offers its own "delightful" brand of "gracious atmosphere and adventurous food"; its "creative, visually stunning" New American fare (including "melt-in-your-mouth" suckling pig) has made it an instant "hot spot", one enhanced by a "homey yet chic" setting with a "modern feel", distinctive service and cocktails that go a long way toward showcasing "wizardry behind the bar."

Tryst ◑ *Coffeehouse* | 19 | 18 | 16 | $19 |

Adams Morgan | 2459 18th St. NW (bet. Belmont & Columbia Rds.) | 202-232-5500 | www.trystdc.com

"Do it all or do nothing" "any time of day" at this "hipster coffeehouse" in Adams Morgan, a "quiet haven" strewn with "comfy couches from multiple decades" and "faces buried in laptops" ("*too much cyberism*" for some); regulars "talk about their problems over great coffee", cocktails and "nothing-to-write-home-about" soups and salads, all accompanied by "decor so bad it's good" and "sketchy service"; P.S. there's occasional live music.

Tuscarora Mill *American*   23 | 21 | 22 | $45

Leesburg | Market Station | 203 Harrison St. SE (Loudoun St.), VA | 703-771-9300 | www.tuskies.com

Over and above its "rustic, historical feel", this "attractively refurbished" mill-turned–New American gathering place in Leesburg grinds out "creative, beautifully executed" cuisine for enthusiasts undeterred by high "DC prices"; an "exceptional" wine list and service to match enhance the experience, while a cafe and bar rich in "character and characters" boasts its own "interesting menu" (e.g. "fabulous corn chowder") and ensures that there's "something for everyone."

Tutto Bene *Italian/S American*   17 | 15 | 18 | $31

Ballston | 501 N. Randolph St. (Glebe Rd.) | Arlington, VA | 703-522-1005 | www.tuttobeneitalian.com

Wedged into "busy" Ballston, this "split personality" "next to a couple of auto shops" serves up "hearty Italian fare like momma used to make" – plus, oddly enough, some of the "best Bolivian food in town" (i.e. "exceptional" *salteñas*); still, service that can be "indifferent" and "out-of-date" decor incorporating "Roman statues" leave some saying they just "don't get the hype."

Z 2941 Restaurant Ⓩ *American*   26 | 27 | 26 | $73

Falls Church | 2941 Fairview Park Dr. (I-495), VA | 703-270-1500 | www.2941.com

Enter past a "shimmering" koi pond and you'll discover "lush views" of a "tranquil" garden and lake from this "top-flight" New American's "impressive" dining rooms, whose "floor-to-ceiling windows", "artisan lighting and huge mirrors" belie its Falls Church office park locale ("who knew?"); the "exquisite" French-accented fare from chef Bertrand Chemel is presented with "polished" professionalism, making it a "special-occasion favorite", and while "being treated this well" is "not inexpensive", there are "good deals" at the bar.

Twisted Vines Bottleshop &   - | - | - | I
Bistro *Eclectic*

Arlington | 2803 Columbia Pike (Walter Reed Dr.), VA | 571-482-8581 | www.twisted-vines.com

Located in Arlington's rapidly developing Columbia Pike neighborhood, this combo wine shop/wine bar/bistro showcases small producer bottlings from around the world, which can be enjoyed at a handsome, wood-backed bar or at tables set under the tin ceiling in the slick, modern space; charcuterie, cheese samplers, salads and a few Eclectic small plates should keep hunger pangs at bay while leaving room for one of the tempting desserts.

Z 2 Amys *Pizza*   25 | 16 | 19 | $25

Cleveland Park | 3715 Macomb St. NW (Wisconsin Ave.) | 202-885-5700 | www.2amyspizza.com

Making "pizza like God intended" (or at least with the Naples pizza association's "blessing"), this "always crowded" Cleveland Parker proffers "sublime" "wood-fired, heat-blistered" pies that vie with its "fantastic charcuterie" as reasons to "battle hungry stroller-wielding" families for space in its "hectic" white-tiled premises; since grown-ups can seek refuge on the "lovely patio" or in the "well-stocked" wine bar and "quieter" upstairs dining room, the vast majority agree that "although wait times are 2 often 2 long", the place is "not 2 be missed."

Ulah Bistro   *American*   18 | 17 | 16 | $29

U Street Corridor | 1214 U St. NW (bet. 12th & 13th Sts.) | 202-234-0123 | www.ulahbistro.com

"People go here for the scene" more than the "decent" if "standard" American menu: that's the word on this "classy yet affordable" U Street bistro; service bounces from "accommodating" to "spotty", but that doesn't deter locals from "hanging out at the bar" or queueing up for brunch on an "outdoor terrace to watch the neighborhood" go by.

Uncle Julio's   *Tex-Mex*   19 | 15 | 18 | $26

Bethesda | 4870 Bethesda Ave. (Arlington Rd.), MD | 301-656-2981
Gaithersburg | 231 Rio Blvd. (Washingtonian Blvd.), MD | 240-632-2150
Ballston | 4301 N. Fairfax Dr. (Taylor St.) | Arlington, VA | 703-528-3131
Fairfax | 4251 Fairfax Corner Ave. (Monument Dr.), VA | 703-266-7760
Reston | Reston Town Ctr. | 1827 Library St. (New Dominion Pkwy.), VA | 703-904-0703
NEW Woodbridge | Stonebridge at Potomac Town Ctr. | 14900 Potomac Town Pl. (Neabsco Mills Rd.), VA | 703-763-7322
www.unclejulios.com

"Homesick Texans" hold up these "always-hopping" Dallas-bred haciendas as "legit" Tex-Mex on account of their "paper-thin" chips, "fire-roasted" salsa and "freshly made" fajitas; some snip they're a "little pricey", and the "über-casual" indoor/outdoor settings can get so "loud" "no one can hear your kid scream", but most "don't care after the first sip of margarita."

NEW Uniontown Bar & Grill ⑤ *American*   - | - | - | I

Anacostia | 2200 Martin Luther King Ave. SE (W St.) | 202-678-8824 | www.utowndc.com

This urbane, affordable newcomer in a historic building on Martin Luther King Avenue brings much needed sit-down dining amenities to underserved, east-of-the-river Anacostia with its small menu of Cajun-influenced Americana; colorful cocktails are poured at the inviting bar, while the sun-washed, high-ceilinged dining room is done up in burnished gold; P.S. a second-floor dining room and kitchen/menu expansion is planned.

NEW Upper Crust   *Pizza*   - | - | - | I

World Bank | 1747 Pennsylvania Ave. NW (bet. 17th & 18th Sts.) | 202-463-0002 | www.theuppercrustpizzeria.com

Boston's famed pizza joint has established a small beachhead on Pennsylvania Avenue near the White House and World Bank; the slick counter-serve spot offers on-the-cheap slice-and-salad com-

FOOD | DECOR | SERVICE | COST

bos and whole pies, as well as calzones and the like to go or to enjoy at perches along the wall.

Urbana *French/Italian*
22 | 21 | 21 | $42

Dupont Circle | Hotel Palomar | 2121 P St. NW (bet. 21st & 22nd Sts.) | 202-956-6650 | www.urbanadc.com

DC insiders descend to this below-street-level "find" in Dupont Circle's Hotel Palomar for an "inventive cocktail" or to wander through the "thoughtful wine list" in its "buzzing" "modern" lounge – but often end up staying for an "imaginative" meal in its "intimate" and "relaxing" dining room; the modestly priced chow ranges from wood-fired pizzas and a raw bar to "imaginative" French-Italian entrees, and service is "attentive."

Urban Bar-B-Que Company *BBQ*
22 | 10 | 17 | $17

Rockville | 2007 Chapman Ave. (Twinbrook Pkwy.), MD | 240-290-4827
Silver Spring | Hillandale | 10163 New Hampshire Ave. (Powder Mill Rd.), MD | 301-434-7427
www.iloveubq.com

For a "10-paper-towel meal" of "tasty" 'cue, urban cowboys dismount at these "no-frills" Maryland counter-servers for "kick-ass" pork ribs, chicken and brisket; yes, it's "not Memphis or Kansas" or "North Carolina BBQ", but with an "impressive range of sauces" and "better-than-usual slaw" and cornbread, few seem to care; P.S. "small" interiors make them prime "carry-out" options.

Urban Burger Company *Burgers*
21 | 11 | 19 | $14

Rockville | Rock Creek Village Ctr. | 5566 Norbeck Rd. (Bauer Dr.), MD | 301-460-0050 | www.eataturban.com

Rockville's "great neighborhood burger place" – a family-friendly offshoot of nearby Urban Bar-B-Que – boasts "juicy" patties served by a "friendly" crew; there's also a "wide variety" of sandwiches, salads and apps, notably the signature 'soul roll', a cheeseburger stuffed in a crispy egg-roll wrapper; P.S. cops, teachers, seniors and others get 10% off already "reasonable" tabs.

Vapiano *Italian*
18 | 16 | 15 | $21

Chinatown | 623 H St. NW (bet. 6th & 7th Sts.) | 202-621-7636
Golden Triangle | 1800 M St. NW (18th St.) | 202-640-1868
NEW **Bethesda** | 4900 Hampden Ln. (Woodmont Ave.), MD | 301-215-7013
Ballston | 4401 Wilson Blvd. (Glebe Rd.) | Arlington, VA | 703-528-3113
Sterling | Dulles Town Ctr. | 21100 Dulles Town Circle (Nokes Blvd.), VA | 703-574-4740
www.vapiano.com

"Like an upscale Sbarro with a lounge", these "German-created" "cafeteria-style" Italians feature "made-to-order" pastas, pizzas and salads consumed at "family-style tables"; they're "packed at lunch" and a "big hit" with young 'uns "carbing up before hitting the clubs" (a "quirky" charge-card system "means there are no hassles dividing the bill"), but those irked by the "crowds" and inconvenience of "getting your own food and drinks" deem them a "tad overpriced."

	FOOD	DECOR	SERVICE	COST

Vaso's Kitchen ⊠ *Greek* | 20 | 13 | 21 | $29 |

Old Town | 1225 Powhatan St. (Bashford Ln.) | Alexandria, VA | 703-548-2747

This "cozy" Old Town "*Cheers*" with a "Cypriot accent" dishes up "straightforward" Greek specialties along with a "warm welcome" that makes diners feel at "home without having to do the dishes"; better yet, the "generous portions" come with "reasonable prices"; P.S. look for the "historic Dixie Pig sign" on the roof.

Vegetable Garden *Chinese/Vegetarian* | 22 | 12 | 19 | $19 |

White Flint | 11618 Rockville Pike (bet. Nicholson Ln. & Old Georgetown Rd.) | Rockville, MD | 301-468-9301 | www.thevegetablegarden.com

"Even die-hard carnivores love" the "tasty, inventive" vegan fare at this White Flint Chinese, where a chef who "produces miracles" has beef eaters enthusing "I can't believe it's not meat"; a "huge selection" (including macrobiotic choices), "low prices and quick service" are other reasons supporters shrug off its "annoying strip-mall location."

NEW Vento *Italian* | - | - | - | M |

Dupont Circle | 2120 P St. NW (bet. 21st & 22nd Sts.) | 202-833-1750 | www.ventorestaurant.com

The Siroc talents have breezed into Dupont Circle to open this chic, more moderately priced sibling offering interesting takes on contemporary Italian fare accompanied by well-priced wines and cocktails; hanging lights in the dining room emit a flattering candlelike glow, and there's also a sexy, spacious lounge and seasonal sidewalk seating.

Veritas Wine Bar *Cheese* | 18 | 19 | 21 | $34 |

Dupont Circle | 2031 Florida Ave. NW (Connecticut Ave.) | 202-265-6270 | www.veritasdc.com

"Low-lit and perfect for canoodling", this Dupont Circle "hole-in-the-wall" lures oenophiles and novices alike who down "witty, original wine flights", plus "yummy cheese and charcuterie"; a "knowledgeable staff" adds to the "mellow atmosphere", while "half-price-bottle Mondays" and "happy-hour deals" accommodate wallet-watchers.

Vermilion *American* | 23 | 21 | 22 | $47 |

Old Town | 1120 King St. (bet. Fayette & Henry Sts.) | Alexandria, VA | 703-684-9669 | www.vermilionrestaurant.com

"Exposed brick, rich reds" and a wine wall make an "inviting" Old Town backdrop for "creative" New American fare from chef Tony Chittum, a "fish god" whose "deft touch" in the kitchen ensures diners "leave with a smile"; plus, "attentive" servers in the "attractive" downstairs lounge and "comfy" upstairs dining room keep the vibe "classy but not pretentious"; P.S. a four-course tasting menu ($59) is a "bargain."

Z Vidalia *American* | 24 | 22 | 24 | $63 |

Dupont Circle | 1990 M St. NW (bet. 19th & 20th Sts.) | 202-659-1990 | www.vidaliadc.com

"Highbrow Low Country cooking" coupled with an "impressive wine list", servers who "remember you and your needs" and a "bright, airy" space make diners "instantly forget" they've "stepped underground" at this "stellar" Dupont New American; true, a few naysayers suggest it's "living on its reputation", but they're vastly outnumbered by those who say it's "worth the splurge" (tip: a "three-course lunch special" trims tabs); P.S. "leave room for dessert."

Village Bistro *Continental*
▽ 23 | 11 | 21 | $39

Courthouse | Colonial Vill. | 1723 Wilson Blvd. (bet. Quinn & Rhodes Sts.) | Arlington, VA | 703-522-0284 | www.villagebistro.com

"Bare-bones bistro decor" doesn't detract from the "real bistro" fare at this Arlington French-Continental, a "comfortable neighborhood place" that's "more than satisfying" for the price (if not downright "delightful"); expect "good food and an easy dining experience", which is why it's "often crowded" with longtime loyalists and "overflow" from nearby Ray's Hell Burger.

Villa Mozart Ⓢ *Italian*
24 | 21 | 23 | $53

Fairfax | 4009 Chain Bridge Rd. (Main St.), VA | 703-691-4747 | www.villamozartrestaurant.com

Chef Andrea Pace's "inventive" Northern Italian menu has Fairfax City *bec fins* "anticipating" "unexpected twists" – "don't miss the beef [carpaccio] with chunks of foie gras" – and "delectable" tastes at this "unpretentious" boîte; a "romantic" if "simple" setting and "experienced" servers "add to the charm", but the "food is the shining star" here; P.S. a "bargain lunch" makes it more accessible to bean-counters.

Vinifera Wine Bar & Bistro *American*
▽ 21 | 19 | 23 | $46

Reston | Westin Reston Heights | 11750 Sunrise Valley Dr. (Reston Pkwy.), VA | 703-234-3550 | www.viniferabistro.com

"Toto, I don't think we're in the suburbs anymore!" gloat vinophiles who've discovered the "excellent wine selection" – including flights that encourage sampling – and "high-quality" New American small plates and entrees at this Westin Reston Heights eatery; what's more, "knowledgeable" servers give "helpful" advice in the dark-wood interior, which some liken to a "hotel lobby" (so "sit out on the deck").

Vinoteca ❶ *Eclectic*
21 | 19 | 20 | $36

U Street Corridor | 1940 11th St. NW (U St.) | 202-332-9463 | www.vinotecadc.com

At the "people's wine bar" off U Street NW, "prices aren't too high", "choices are abundant" and the Eclectic chow is "designed to pair perfectly" with the vino; sippers who perch at the bar for "unbeatable happy hours" or in the "compact", red-tiled dining room generally shrug off "patchy" service and a high "noise level", though a "front patio" helps with the latter in "warmer months."

🆕 Virtue Feed & Grain *Pub Food*
- | - | - | M

Old Town | 106 S. Union St. (bet. King & Prince Sts.) | Alexandria, VA | 571-970-3669 | www.virtuefeedandgrain.com

Courtesy of the Armstrongs (Eve et al.), a massive two-story 19th-century granary in Old Town is now a chicly rough-hewn mega-tavern offering midpriced Irish and American pub favorites; the setup offers something for everyone, including a massive downstairs bar pouring craft beers and 'hoptails' (beer-based cocktails), a walk-up window for to-go items and a game room with pool, darts, video games and big screens for sports fans; P.S. an outdoor deck is also on tap.

NEW **Watershed** *American/Seafood*   – | – | – | M
(aka Todd Gray's Watershed)

NoMa | Hilton Garden Inn | 1225 First St. NE (bet. M & N Sts.) | 202-534-1350 | www.toddgrayswatershed.com

Todd Gray's seafood-focused modern American serving the fast-growing NoMa neighborhood and Hilton guests has something for everyone: a casual cocktail, a nibble or an affordable dinner; the layout is equally versatile and includes a contemporary lounge, stylish dining room (with a marble-topped raw bar) and a secluded outdoor patio.

Westend Bistro by Eric Ripert *American*   21 | 19 | 21 | $58

West End | Ritz-Carlton, Washington DC | 1190 22nd St. NW (M St.) | 202-974-4900 | www.westendbistrodc.com

Partisans proclaim "they've pulled it off" – i.e. the "trend where big-name chefs with formal restaurants go downscale" – at this West End New American, citing "refined" bistro fare with a "unique Eric Ripert twist" (e.g. "ethereal" fish burgers), "professional" but "friendly" service and a "who's-who" bar scene; still, contrarians who expect "exponentially more given all the hype" and its Ritz-Carlton branding gripe about a "hotel-restaurant feel", "unmanageable noise" and "hit-or-miss" fare at "high prices."

NEW **We, The Pizza** Ⓢ *Pizza*   – | – | – | I

Capitol Hill | 305 Pennsylania Ave. SE (bet. 3rd & 4th Sts.) | 202-544-4008 | www.wethepizza.com

Top Chef contestant Spike Mendelsohn's foray into NY-style pies on Capitol Hill (next to his burger joint Good Stuff Eatery) offers affordable slices as well as whole rounds, topped classically or inventively, along with subs, wings and housemade gelato; the smart-looking counter-serve operation, with seating on the second floor, features a huge photo taken at Woodstock and an old-fashioned soda fountain for jerking authentic chocolate egg creams and Italian-inspired drinks.

Wildfire *Seafood/Steak*   19 | 20 | 20 | $42

Tysons Corner | Tysons Galleria | 1714U International Dr. (Chain Bridge Rd.) | McLean, VA | 703-442-9110 | www.wildfirerestaurant.com

"Retro-chic" decor (think "Chicago speakeasy") coupled with a "vast" American surf 'n' turf menu bring a "swanky" feel to this expansive Tysons Corner eatery geared to satisfy "large appetites" at a "reasonable price"; however, a few get fired up about this Windy City export, chiding "mass-produced" meals that are served "fast-food quick" in a "chainlike atmosphere."

NEW **Wild Tomato** Ⓜ *American*   – | – | – | M

Potomac | 7945 MacArthur Blvd. (Seven Locks Rd.), MD | 301-229-0680

The seeds from one fruit sprout another for Persimmon chef-owner Damian Salvatore, whose new nightshade-named American serves

	FOOD	DECOR	SERVICE	COST

pizza, salads and moderately priced entrees to the Potomac gentry; big front windows, food-focused artwork, butcher-block tables and a stone bar create an attractive ambiance for casual dining and informal get-togethers.

Willow ☒ *American* — 24 | 21 | 23 | $50

Ballston | 4301 N. Fairfax Dr. (Utah St.) | Arlington, VA | 703-465-8800 | www.willowva.com

"Celebrate something special" at this "impressive" Ballston New American where "welcoming" staffers "really care about what they serve", namely "consistently excellent" seafood, flatbreads "fit for foodies" and numerous "farm-fresh" finds off a "creative menu" (plus "less expensive" options at the bar); outdoor seating offers relief from a "spacious, modern" dining room that can get too "loud", but all in all, expect an "experience that leaves you feeling good."

Wine Kitchen ☒ *American* — ▽ 21 | 23 | 21 | $39

Leesburg | 7 S. King St. (Market St.), VA | 703-777-9463 | www.thewinekitchen.com

"Free WiFi, $8 lunch specials and good wine" lure Leesburg telecommuters who throng these "lovely", urbane quarters for "affordable" vino flights "smartly" paired with New American small plates; its 'chicken and waffles' has become a cult favorite, inasmuch as the "ingredients support local farms" and reflect the kitchen's creative "aspirations"; P.S. go early, since it doesn't take reservations.

Woo Lae Oak *Korean* — 21 | 18 | 18 | $38

Tysons Corner | 8240 Leesburg Pike (Chain Bridge Rd.) | Vienna, VA | 703-827-7300 | www.woolaeoak.com

"Expats" find the "soul of Seoul" at this Tysons Corner Korean ensconced in a "cavernous", "glammed-up" setting where "solid" barbecue is prepared "at your table", and "standout" soups, dumplings and sushi in the lounge area are "perfect for a casual lunch or large event"; fans insist it's "worth the drive", but critics aren't so sure, citing "inconsistent" service, "ok" chow and "NYC prices."

Woomi Garden *Korean* — ▽ 23 | 16 | 19 | $28

Wheaton | 2423 Hickerson Dr. (bet. Elkin St. & Rte. 97), MD | 301-933-0100 | www.woomigarden.com

"Check out the lunch buffet" at this Wheaton Korean, dubbed "one of the better BBQ and hot-pots spots" by eaters who "overstuff" themselves with "great kalbi and stews", "plentiful" banchan plus "excellent sushi" from a small Japanese menu; it can be "pricey", but "oh, boy" . . . the chow's "addicting", plus it comes with "nice" servers and a "family-friendly" vibe.

X.O. Taste ◑ *Chinese* — ▽ 22 | 13 | 14 | $24

Falls Church | 6124 Arlington Blvd. (Patrick Henry Dr.), VA | 703-536-1630

Take ordering cues from the roast pig "hanging from a hook in the window", the fish tank in the rear or even the name of this "bustling" Falls Church Cantonese – then give the "crispy" pork, "excellent lobster dishes" and "unique" Hong Kong sauce preparations a try; it's "one of the most authentic Chinese restaurants" around, so don't be surprised to find its "cavernous" space filled on weekends (go early since it "doesn't take reservations").

Yama *Japanese*   23 | 16 | 21 | $34

Vienna | Vienna Plaza | 328 Maple Ave. W. (Nutley St.), VA | 703-242-7703

It's "stuck in a strip mall", but this Vienna neighborhood Japanese is a "quiet center of excellence" for "delicious" raw-fish preparations, as well as numerous options for "non-sushi eaters" (including "excellent-value" bento boxes); it's "so good and so consistent" and so "busy", regulars wish they could "keep it to themselves."

Yamazato *Japanese*   25 | 16 | 25 | $31

Greater Alexandria | Beauregard Sq. | 6303 Little River Tpke. (Beauregard St.) | Alexandria, VA | 703-914-8877 | www.yamazato.net

Fans of this "cozy" "mom-and-pop" Alexandria Asian say it "should be called 'Yummy-zato'", inasmuch as it serves "super-fresh fish" that pleases sushi "purists", "interesting" specialty rolls and "delicious" Thai and Japanese cooked entrees that "don't taste like Chung King by way of Bangkok"; "attentive" servers and "fair prices" are other lures, providing you can find it in its "hidden location."

Yosaku *Japanese*   21 | 14 | 20 | $38

Upper NW | 4712 Wisconsin Ave. NW (Chesapeake St.) | 202-363-4453 | www.yosakusushi.com

Some big-name birds roost at this "sushi nest" in Tenleytown, where the patio scene can include famous faces digging into "well-priced" chow; expect "fresh fish" served in a "comfortable" space, along with "authentic" Japanese entrees and a "delicious" "daily bento box."

Yuan Fu *Chinese/Vegetarian*   ∇ 18 | 8 | 18 | $19

Rockville | 798 Rockville Pike (Wootton Pkwy.), MD | 301-762-5937 | www.yuanfuvegetarian.com

The "faux meat is so good" you won't "miss the saturated fat and hormones in the real stuff" declare devotees of this vegan Rockville Chinese; the "lack of decor" is trumped by "eager-to-please" servers ("extra good if you speak Chinese") and modest prices.

ⓩ Zaytinya ◉ *Mediterranean/Mideastern*   25 | 23 | 21 | $42

Penn Quarter | Pepco Bldg. | 701 Ninth St. NW (G St.) | 202-638-0800 | www.zaytinya.com

Foodies "worship" at José Andrés' "cathedral of Eastern Mediterranean" flavors in the Penn Quarter, a "sleek", "airy" space "oozing hipness" and offering a "dazzling array" of "fascinating small plates" covering "Greece to Lebanon with all stops in between"; it's "loud, brash" and "always crowded", but staffers who "keep it real", a "user-friendly wine list" and tabs that "won't suck the money out of your wallet" help make it the Most Popular restaurant in the DC Survey – and render reservations "indispensable."

	FOOD	DECOR	SERVICE	COST

Zeffirelli Ristorante *Italian*   22 | 20 | 21 | $46

Herndon | 728 Pine St. (Station St.), VA | 703-318-7000 |
www.zeffirelliristorante.com

"Classic Italian dishes and service" bring the spirit of NYC's "Little
Italy" to a traditional Herndon setting where "lovely candlelit tables
make special-occasion dining" all the more so; "solid, consistent" fare
and treating customers "like family" have kept it crowded for years.

Zengo *Asian/Pan-Latin*   22 | 23 | 19 | $41

Chinatown | Gallery Pl. | 781 Seventh St. NW (bet. F & H Sts.) |
202-393-2929 | www.modernmexican.com

"Big-city buzz" and the "perfect Zen-tango" of Asian fusion and Latin
cuisine meld with "knockout" design at this bi-level Chinatowner,
where trendies sip "phenomenal" drinks while exclaiming "you have
to try this!" over "innovative" small plates; the less-impressed mut-
ter it's "too noisy" with service that's "pretty casual for the price",
while those in the know warn "wear hip clothing", as there's a "head-
to-toe visual inspection" as you walk upstairs to the dining room.

Zentan ☒ *Asian*   21 | 23 | 17 | $50

Downtown | Donovan House | 1155 14th St. NW (Massachusetts Ave.) |
202-379-4366 | www.zentanrestaurant.com

"Who knew coleslaw could be so interesting?" coo customers after
sampling the 19-ingredient Singapore slaw at celeb chef Susur Lee's
"exotic" Asian in Downtown's Donovan House Hotel, but "bring
friends" because there's "plenty" more to discover (e.g. "creative"
sushi"); service can be "disorganized" and "not everything" on the
menu is a success, but the moodily lit, "contemporary" space is
"jam-packed with beautiful people" nonetheless; P.S. there's a chill
drinks-and-snacks scene at the related rooftop lounge ADC.

Zest, An American Bistro *American*   ∇ 18 | 21 | 18 | $29

Capitol Hill | 735 Eighth St. SE (bet. G & I Sts.) | 202-544-7171 |
www.zestbistro.com

This New American bistro on Capitol Hill's burgeoning Restaurant
Row makes a "strong" first impression with approachable fare – including interesting sandwiches, salads, entrees and wine
choices – and an "eager-to-accommodate" staff; what's more, the
exposed-brick walls and mellow yellow-and-gold palette make for a
"surprisingly pleasant" space that "fits in well with the neighborhood."

Zola *American*   23 | 24 | 21 | $46

Penn Quarter | International Spy Museum | 800 F St. NW (8th St.) |
202-654-0999 | www.zoladc.com

DC's "beautiful people" stake out James Bond "cool" at this "sleek"
Penn Quarter New American attached to the International Spy
Museum, which explains the "clever" decor (concealed doors, secret kitchen views); if the less-intrigued insist the food "takes more
twists and turns" than a good thriller, "creative" cooking and "attentive" service generally result in an "all-around enjoyable" meal,
topped only by the "fantastic" drinks in the "decidedly unquiet" bar;
P.S. the pre-event prix fixe is an "affordable fix."

WASHINGTON, DC INDEXES

LOCATION MAPS

Cuisines

Includes names, locations and Food ratings.

AFGHAN

Afghan	**Alexandria**	25
Bamian	**Falls Ch**	23
Faryab	**Bethesda**	23
Kabob Palace	**Arlington**	24
Panjshir	**Falls Ch**	22

AMERICAN

15 Ria	**Scott Cir**	17
Addie's	**White Flint**	23
☑ Adour/St. Regis	**D'town**	24
Againn	**D'town**	19
NEW America Eats	**Penn Qtr**	–
American Tap	**multi.**	–
Ardeo/Bardeo	**Cleve Pk**	21
NEW Arlington Rooftop	**Clarendon**	–
Artie's	**Fairfax**	23
Ashby Inn	**Paris**	24
Bar Pilar	**Logan Cir**	21
Bazin's/Church	**Vienna**	23
Beacon B&G	**Scott Cir**	17
Ben's Chili	**U St**	22
Ben's Next Door	**U St**	20
Bezu	**Potomac**	23
BGR	**Dupont Cir**	21
NEW Big Cheese	**Location Varies**	–
Birch/Barley	**Logan Cir**	22
Blackfinn	**multi.**	14
Black Mkt.	**Garrett Pk**	25
☑ BlackSalt	**Palisades**	26
Black's Bar	**Bethesda**	23
Black Squirrel	**Adams Mor**	–
☑ Blue Duck	**West End**	26
Blue Rock Inn	**Sperryville**	–
NEW Bookhill Bistro	**Georgetown**	–
Blvd. Woodgrill	**Clarendon**	19
Bread/Brew	**Dupont Cir**	22
Breadsoda	**Glover Pk**	–
Buck's Fishing	**Upper NW**	20
Busboys/Poets	**multi.**	18
Cafe Deluxe	**multi.**	18
Café Dupont	**Dupont Cir**	–
Capital City	**NE**	–
NEW CapMac	**Location Varies**	–
Carlyle	**Arlington**	24
Cashion's Eat	**Adams Mor**	24

Caucus Rm.	**Penn Qtr**	21
☑ Central Michel	**Penn Qtr**	26
Cheesecake	**multi.**	19
Chef Geoff	**multi.**	19
Chesapeake Rm.	**Cap Hill**	–
Chop't	**multi.**	19
Circa	**multi.**	17
Circle Bistro	**West End**	21
☑ CityZen	**SW**	28
☑ Clyde's	**multi.**	19
Co Co. Sala	**Penn Qtr**	22
Coeur de Lion	**D'town**	20
Columbia Firehse.	**Alexandria**	20
Commissary	**Logan Cir**	16
Comus Inn	**Dickerson**	21
☑ Corduroy	**Mt. Vernon Sq**	27
Cork	**Logan Cir**	23
Darlington Hse.	**Dupont Cir**	20
NEW DC-3	**Cap Hill**	–
DC Boathouse	**Palisades**	15
DC Coast	**D'town**	23
Dish/Drinks	**Foggy Bottom**	19
Eggspectations	**multi.**	19
8407 Kit.	**Silver Spring**	–
Eola	**Dupont Cir**	–
Equinox	**Gldn Triangle**	25
☑ Eve	**Alexandria**	28
Evening Star	**Alexandria**	22
Eventide	**Clarendon**	20
Fahrenheit	**Georgetown**	22
Firefly	**Dupont Cir**	20
Fire Works Pizza	**Clarendon**	–
NEW Food Wine	**Bethesda**	–
Foti's	**Culpeper**	26
☑ Founding Farmers	**World Bank**	21
FunXion	**D'town**	–
Fyve	**Arlington**	17
Granville Moore's	**Atlas Dist**	23
Grapeseed	**Bethesda**	21
Grille	**Alexandria**	23
Hank's Tav.	**Hyattsville**	22
Hard Times	**multi.**	19
Harry's	**Clarendon**	19
NEW Härth	**McLean**	–
Heights	**Columbia Hts**	19
Hook	**Georgetown**	23
Hooked	**Sterling**	19

Horace/Dickie	**Atlas Dist**	24	Occidental	**D'town**	22
Hudson	**West End**	17	Old Angler's	**Potomac**	19
iCi	**D'town**	23	⧫ Old Ebbitt	**D'town**	20
⧫ Inn/Little Washington	**Washington**	29	Open City	**Woodley Pk**	18
			Oval Rm.	**Gldn Triangle**	24
Iota Club/Café	**Clarendon**	-	⧫ Palena	**Cleve Pk**	28
Iron Bridge	**Warrenton**	23	⧫ Palm	**multi.**	24
Jackie's	**Silver Spring**	21	Paolo's	**multi.**	18
Jackson's	**Reston**	20	Park/14th	**D'town**	21
Jackson 20	**Alexandria**	18	PassionFish	**Reston**	24
J&G Steak	**D'town**	25	P. Brennan's	**Arlington**	-
⧫ Jockey Club	**Dupont Cir**	22	Peacock Cafe	**Georgetown**	19
Johnny's	**Cap Hill**	20	Perrys	**Adams Mor**	19
Juniper	**West End**	21	Persimmon	**Bethesda**	25
⧫ Komi	**Dupont Cir**	29	NEW P.J. Clarke's	**D'town**	-
Kora/Farrah	**Arlington**	15	Plume	**D'town**	26
Kramerbooks	**Dupont Cir**	17	Policy	**U St**	19
Lafayette Rm.	**Gldn Triangle**	25	Poste Moderne	**Penn Qtr**	21
Lia's	**Chevy Chase**	21	Praline	**Bethesda**	19
Liberty Tav.	**Clarendon**	21	Proof	**Penn Qtr**	24
Liberty Tree	**Atlas Dist**	-	PS 7's	**Penn Qtr**	22
Lightfoot	**Leesburg**	22	Rail Stop	**Plains**	22
NEW Lincoln	**D'town**	-	⧫ Ray's Hell Burger	**Arlington**	26
Local 16	**U St**	13			
Logan Tav.	**Logan Cir**	18	Ray's/Classics	**Silver Spring**	24
Maddy's	**Dupont Cir**	-	⧫ Ray's/Steaks	**Clarendon**	26
NEW Mad Fox Brew	**Falls Ch**	-	Ray's/East River	**NE**	-
Madhatter	**Dupont Cir**	-	NEW Redline	**Chinatown**	-
Magnolias/Mill	**Purcellville**	19	Redwood	**Bethesda**	17
Majestic	**Alexandria**	23	Restaurant 3	**Clarendon**	18
M&S Grill	**multi.**	19	Rest./Goodstone	**Mid'burg**	-
Maple Ave	**Vienna**	20	NEW Ripple	**Cleve Pk**	-
Mark's Kit.	**Takoma Pk**	17	Ris	**West End**	23
Martin's Tav.	**Georgetown**	20	NEW Rivers/Watergate	**Foggy Bottom**	-
Marvin	**U St**	21			
Matchbox	**multi.**	23	Roof Terr.	**Foggy Bottom**	15
NEW Meridian	**Columbia Hts**	-	Rustico	**multi.**	21
NEW Michel	**McLean**	-	NEW Rustik	**Bloomingdale**	-
Mie N Yu	**Georgetown**	17	Screwtop Wine	**Arlington**	-
Mike's	**Springfield**	22	Sea Pearl	**Merrifield**	20
Mitsitam	**SW**	20	NEW Senart's Oyster	**Cap Hill**	-
Mixt Greens	**multi.**	-	Sequoia	**Georgetown**	15
NEW Mixx	**D'town**	-	701	**Penn Qtr**	23
Monocle	**Cap Hill**	14	⧫ 1789	**Georgetown**	25
Morrison-Clark	**D'town**	23	NEW Smith Commons	**Atlas Dist**	-
Mrs. K's	**Silver Spring**	22			
Nage	**Scott Cir**	22	Sonoma	**Cap Hill**	20
New Heights	**Woodley Pk**	22	Sou'Wester	**SW**	18
NEW Newton's	**Bethesda**	-	Sweetwater Tav.	**multi.**	21
⧫ Nora	**Dupont Cir**	26	Tabard Inn	**Dupont Cir**	24
Northside	**Clarendon**	-	Tallula/EatBar	**Clarendon**	22
Oakville Grille	**Bethesda**	19	Ted's Bulletin	**Cap Hill**	-

Tonic	**multi.**	16
Ⓩ Trummer's	**Clifton**	25
Tuscarora Mill	**Leesburg**	23
Ⓩ 2941	**Falls Ch**	26
Ulah Bistro	**U St**	18
NEW Uniontown B&G	**Anacostia**	-
Urbana	**Dupont Cir**	22
Urban Burger	**Rockville**	21
Vermilion	**Alexandria**	23
Ⓩ Vidalia	**Dupont Cir**	24
Vinifera	**Reston**	21
NEW Watershed	**NoMa**	-
Westend Bistro	**West End**	21
NEW Wild Tomato	**Potomac**	-
Willow	**Arlington**	24
Wine Kit.	**Leesburg**	21
Zest	**Cap Hill**	18
Zola	**Penn Qtr**	23

ASIAN

Asia Bistro/Zen	**Arlington**	20
Asia Nine	**Penn Qtr**	18
Asian Spice	**Chinatown**	21
Buddha-Bar	**Mt. Vernon Sq**	-
Cafe Asia	**multi.**	18
Café Assorti	**Arlington**	22
Ching Ching	**Georgetown**	20
Mark's Kit.	**Takoma Pk**	17
Masa 14	**Logan Cir**	23
Maté	**Georgetown**	25
Ⓩ Oya	**Penn Qtr**	23
Raku	**multi.**	21
Source	**Penn Qtr**	25
Sticky Rice	**Atlas Dist**	22
Sweet Ginger	**Vienna**	19
Teaism	**multi.**	20
Zengo	**Chinatown**	22
Zentan	**D'town**	21

AUSTRIAN

Leopold's Kafe	**Georgetown**	22

BAKERIES

Bread Line	**World Bank**	22
Buzz	**multi.**	22
Il Fornaio	**Reston**	21
Leopold's Kafe	**Georgetown**	22
Le Pain Quotidien	**multi.**	18
NEW Paul	**Penn Qtr**	-
Praline	**Bethesda**	19

BARBECUE

NEW American Ice	**U St**	-
Harry's	**Arlington**	19
NEW Hill Country	**Penn Qtr**	-
Kloby's Smokehse.	**Laurel**	-
Old Glory	**Georgetown**	17
NEW PORC	**Location Varies**	-
Red Hot/Blue	**multi.**	20
Rocklands	**multi.**	22
NEW Standard	**Logan Cir**	-
Urban BBQ	**multi.**	22

BELGIAN

Belga Café	**Cap Hill**	23
Brabo	**Alexandria**	24
Ⓩ Brass. Beck	**D'town**	25
Et Voila	**Palisades**	24
Granville Moore's	**Atlas Dist**	23
Le Pain Quotidien	**multi.**	18
Mannequin Pis	**Olney**	25
Ⓩ Marcel's	**West End**	29
Marvin	**U St**	21
NEW Mussel Bar	**Bethesda**	-

BRAZILIAN

Chima	**Vienna**	23
Fogo De Chão	**D'town**	24
Grill/Ipanema	**Adams Mor**	20

BRITISH

Againn	**D'town**	19
Hunter's Head	**Upperville**	23
NEW Queen Vic	**Atlas Dist**	-

BURGERS

BGR	**multi.**	21
Ⓩ Clyde's	**multi.**	19
Counter	**Reston**	21
Elevation Burger	**multi.**	18
Ⓩ Five Guys	**multi.**	22
Good Stuff	**Cap Hill**	21
Harry's	**Arlington**	19
Matchbox	**multi.**	23
Ⓩ Old Ebbitt	**D'town**	20
Ⓩ Palena	**Cleve Pk**	28
Ⓩ Ray's Hell Burger	**Arlington**	26
Ray's/East River	**NE**	-
NEW Shake Shack	**multi.**	-
Urban Burger	**Rockville**	21

BURMESE

Burma	**Chinatown**	20
Burma Rd.	**Gaith'burg**	24

Mandalay | **Silver Spring** 24
Myanmar | **Falls Ch** 24
Taste/Burma | **Sterling** 22

CAJUN

Z Acadiana | **Mt. Vernon Sq** 23
NEW Bayou | **West End** -
Cajun Experience | **multi.** -
NEW Hot 'N Juicy | **Woodley Pk** -
NEW Mokomandy | **Sterling** -
RT's | **Alexandria** 24

CAVIAR

Russia Hse. | **Dupont Cir** 15

CHEESE SPECIALISTS

Veritas | **Dupont Cir** 18

CHICKEN

NEW Carbon Peruvian | **Rockville** -
Chix | **U St** 20
Crisp/Juicy | **multi.** 24
Don Pollo | **multi.** 18
Edy's Chicken | **Falls Ch** 22
El Pollo Rico | **multi.** 25
La Limeña | **Rockville** 22
Nando's | **multi.** 20
Pollo Campero | **multi.** 18

CHINESE

(* dim sum specialist)
A&J* | **multi.** 24
Burma Rd. | **Gaith'burg** 24
China Bistro | **Rockville** 23
China Gdn.* | **Rosslyn** 17
China Jade | **Rockville** -
China Star | **Fairfax** 24
Chinatown Express | **Chinatown** 21
City Lights | **multi.** 19
Eat First | **Chinatown** 20
Fortune* | **Falls Ch** 20
Full Kee (VA) | **Falls Ch** 22
Full Kee (DC) | **Chinatown** 22
Full Key | **Wheaton** 21
Fu Shing | **multi.** 21
Good Fortune* | **Wheaton** 18
Hollywood E.* | **Wheaton** -
Hunan Dynasty | **Cap Hill** 17
Hunan Manor | **multi.** 21
Joe's Noodle Hse. | **Rockville** 23
NEW Mala Tang | **Arlington** -
Mark's Duck Hse.* | **Falls Ch** 23
Meiwah | **multi.** 19

Michael's Noodles | **Rockville** 23
New Fortune* | **Gaith'burg** 22
New Kam | **Wheaton** 24
Oriental E.* | **Silver Spring** 22
Peking Gourmet | **Falls Ch** 26
P.F. Chang's | **multi.** 20
Ping Pong* | **Chinatown** 21
Seven Seas | **multi.** 18
Sichuan Pavilion | **Rockville** 23
Taipei Tokyo | **multi.** 16
Tony Cheng's* | **Chinatown** 19
Vegetable Gdn. | **White Flint** 22
X.O. Taste | **Falls Ch** 22
Yuan Fu | **Rockville** 18

COFFEEHOUSES

Bread/Brew | **Dupont Cir** 22
Buzz | **multi.** 22
Café Bonaparte | **Georgetown** 20
Leopold's Kafe | **Georgetown** 22
Northside | **Clarendon** -
Puro Café | **Georgetown** -
Tryst | **Adams Mor** 19

COFFEE SHOPS/ DINERS

Ben's Chili | **U St** 22
Bob & Edith's | **Arlington** 17
Capital City | **NE** -
Diner | **Adams Mor** 17
Florida Ave. Grill | **U St** 20
Luna Grill | **multi.** 17
Oohhs & Aahhs | **U St** 24
Open City | **Woodley Pk** 18

CONTINENTAL

Black Fox | **Dupont Cir** -

CREOLE

Z Acadiana | **Mt. Vernon Sq** 23
NEW Bayou | **West End** -
Cajun Experience | **multi.** -
NEW Hot 'N Juicy | **Woodley Pk** -
RT's | **Alexandria** 24

CRÊPES

NEW Solar Crêpes | **Arlington** -

CUBAN

Banana Café | **Cap Hill** 18
Cuba de Ayer | **Burtonsville** 23
Cubano's | **Silver Spring** 21
La Limeña | **Rockville** 22

DELIS

Bernie's Deli | **Fairfax**	25
Chutzpah | **Fairfax**	18
Parkway Deli | **Silver Spring**	19
Star/Shamrock | **Atlas Dist**	-
Taylor Gourmet | **multi.**	23
Toscana Café | **Cap Hill**	23

DESSERT

Cheesecake | **multi.**	19
NEW Serendipity 3 | **Georgetown**	-

EASTERN EUROPEAN

Café Assorti | **Arlington**	22
Cosmopolitan Grill | **Alexandria**	-
Domku | **Petworth**	18
Slaviya Cafe | **Adams Mor**	-

ECLECTIC

NEW Arlington Rooftop | **Clarendon**	-
NEW Atlas Rm. | **Atlas Dist**	-
Busboys/Poets | **multi.**	18
Café Saint-Ex | **Logan Cir**	20
C.F. Folks | **Gldn Triangle**	24
Chix | **U St**	20
NEW Cities | **Gldn Triangle**	-
Co Co. Sala | **Penn Qtr**	22
Dean & DeLuca | **Georgetown**	22
Dickson Wine | **U St**	-
NEW Eat Wonky | **Location Varies**	-
El Floridano | **Location Varies**	-
Little Fountain | **Adams Mor**	24
Maple Ave | **Vienna**	20
Mie N Yu | **Georgetown**	17
Z Minibar | **Penn Qtr**	26
NEW Next Stage | **SW**	-
Open Kit. | **Falls Ch**	-
Passenger | **Mt. Vernon Sq**	-
Perrys | **Adams Mor**	19
NEW Redline | **Chinatown**	-
Room 11 | **Columbia Hts**	-
NEW Rustik | **Bloomingdale**	-
Sauca | **multi.**	-
Sticky Rice | **Atlas Dist**	22
Twisted Vines | **Arlington**	-
Vinoteca | **U St**	21

ETHIOPIAN

Dukem | **U St**	24
Etete | **U St**	24
Ethiopic | **Atlas Dist**	-
Meskerem | **Adams Mor**	20

FRENCH

Z Adour/St. Regis | **D'town**	24
Bezu | **Potomac**	23
Bistro Bis | **Cap Hill**	25
Bistro Provence | **Bethesda**	-
Brabo | **Alexandria**	24
Brass. Monte Carlo | **Bethesda**	20
Buddha-Bar | **Mt. Vernon Sq**	-
Z Citronelle | **Georgetown**	28
Et Voila | **Palisades**	24
La Bergerie | **Alexandria**	23
La Chaumière | **Georgetown**	24
La Ferme | **Chevy Chase**	22
La Fourchette | **Adams Mor**	23
Z L'Aub./François | **Grt Falls**	27
Z L'Aub. Provençale | **Boyce**	27
Lavandou | **Cleve Pk**	20
Z Marcel's | **West End**	29
Matisse | **Upper NW**	23
NEW Sax | **D'town**	-
Tempo | **Alexandria**	22
Urbana | **Dupont Cir**	22
Village Bistro | **Arlington**	23

FRENCH (BISTRO)

Bastille | **Alexandria**	22
Bistro Cacao | **Cap Hill**	-
Bistro D'Oc | **D'town**	21
Bistro Français | **Georgetown**	19
Bistro La Bonne | **U St**	-
Bistro L'Hermitage | **Woodbridge**	24
Bistro Provence | **Bethesda**	-
Bistrot du Coin | **Dupont Cir**	21
Bistrot Lafayette | **Alexandria**	20
Bistrot Lepic | **Georgetown**	23
Z Brass. Beck | **D'town**	25
Café Bonaparte | **Georgetown**	20
Café du Parc | **D'town**	22
Café Dupont | **Dupont Cir**	-
Z Central Michel | **Penn Qtr**	26
Fontaine Caffe | **Alexandria**	24
La Côte d'Or | **Arlington**	24
Le Chat Noir | **Upper NW**	18
Le Refuge | **Alexandria**	21
Lyon Hall | **Clarendon**	-
NEW Michel | **McLean**	-
Mon Ami Gabi | **multi.**	19
Montmartre | **Cap Hill**	24
Napoleon | **Adams Mor**	16

1905 | **Mt. Vernon Sq**	19
Petits Plats | **Woodley Pk**	22
Praline | **Bethesda**	19

FRENCH (BRASSERIE)

☑ L'Aub./François | **Grt Falls**	27

GASTROPUB

Againn | British | **D'town**	19
Granville Moore's | Amer./Belgian | **Atlas Dist**	23
NEW Queen Vic | British | **Atlas Dist**	-

GERMAN

Biergarten Haus | **Atlas Dist**	-
Lyon Hall | **Clarendon**	-

GREEK

Cava | **multi.**	24
NEW Cava Mezze Grill | **Bethesda**	-
Kellari Taverna | **Gldn Triangle**	22
Mourayo | **Dupont Cir**	25
Mykonos Grill | **Rockville**	22
Plaka Grill | **Vienna**	26
Vaso's Kit. | **Alexandria**	20

HEALTH FOOD

(See also Vegetarian)

Juice Joint Cafe | **D'town**	22
Sweetgreen | **multi.**	21

HOT DOGS

Ben's Chili | **U St**	22
NEW DC-3 | **Cap Hill**	-
NEW Eat Wonky | **Location Varies**	-
NEW Shake Shack | **multi.**	-

ICE CREAM PARLORS

NEW Serendipity 3 | **Georgetown**	-

INDIAN

Amma Veg. | **Vienna**	22
Angeethi | **multi.**	23
Bombay Bistro | **Rockville**	23
Bombay Club | **Gldn Triangle**	24
Bombay Tandoor | **Vienna**	22
Cafe Taj | **McLean**	19
NEW Curry Mantra | **Fairfax**	-
Delhi Club | **Clarendon**	24
Delhi Dhaba | **multi.**	18
NEW Diya | **Vienna**	-
Fojol Bros. | **Location Varies**	-

Haandi | **multi.**	24
Heritage India | **multi.**	22
Himalayan Heritage | **Adams Mor**	22
India Palace | **Germantown**	-
Indique | **multi.**	23
Jaipur | **Fairfax**	23
Kabob N Karahi | **Silver Spring**	-
Masala Art | **Upper NW**	26
NEW Merzi | **Penn Qtr**	-
Minerva | **multi.**	21
Passage to India | **Bethesda**	24
Rangoli | **S Riding**	-
☑ Rasika | **Penn Qtr**	28
Spice Xing | **Rockville**	20
Tandoori Nights | **multi.**	21

IRISH

Daniel O'Connell | **Alexandria**	20
Dubliner | **Cap Hill**	16
Eamonn's | **Alexandria**	23
Fadó | **Chinatown**	17
Irish Inn/Glen Echo | **Glen Echo**	18
P. Brennan's | **Arlington**	-
Rí Rá | **multi.**	14
Star/Shamrock | **Atlas Dist**	-

ITALIAN

(N=Northern; S=Southern)

Acacia Bistro | **Upper NW**	22
Acqua al 2 | **Cap Hill**	-
Agrodolce | **Germantown**	22
A La Lucia | **Alexandria**	22
Al Crostino | **U St**	21
Al Tiramisu | **Dupont Cir**	24
Amici Miei | **Potomac**	20
Argia's | **Falls Ch**	19
Arucola | **Upper NW**	19
Assaggi | **multi.**	21
Bibiana | **D'town**	23
Bond 45 | **Nat'l Harbor**	-
Buca di Beppo | **multi.**	16
Cafe Milano | **Georgetown**	20
Café Pizzaiolo | **multi.**	18
Capri | **McLean**	20
NEW Carmine's | S | **Penn Qtr**	-
NEW Casa Nonna | **Dupont Cir**	-
Cesco Trattoria | N | **Bethesda**	22
Coppi's Organic | N | **U St**	21
Da Domenico | **McLean**	21
Dino | N | **Cleve Pk**	22
Dolce Vita | **Fairfax**	23
El Manantial | **Reston**	23

Extra Virgin | **Arlington**	17
Facci | **Laurel**	–
Faccia Luna | **multi.**	21
Filomena | **Georgetown**	23
Finemondo | **D'town**	22
NEW Fiola | **Penn Qtr**	–
NEW Galileo III | **D'town**	–
Geranio | N | **Alexandria**	22
Il Canale | **Georgetown**	–
Il Fornaio | **Reston**	21
Il Pizzico | **Rockville**	26
I Ricchi | N | **Dupont Cir**	24
Kora | **Arlington**	15
Landini Bros. | N | **Alexandria**	22
La Strada | **Alexandria**	23
La Tomate | **Dupont Cir**	18
Lia's | **Chevy Chase**	21
Maggiano's | **multi.**	18
Mamma Lucia | **multi.**	18
Notti Bianche | **Foggy Bottom**	20
Z Obelisk | **Dupont Cir**	27
Olazzo | **multi.**	21
Oro Pomodoro | **Rockville**	18
NEW Ozzie's Corner | **Fairfax**	–
Palio of Leesburg | **Leesburg**	–
Paolo's | **multi.**	18
Pasta Mia | **Adams Mor**	23
Z Pasta Plus | **Laurel**	26
Pie-Tanza | **Arlington**	19
Piola | **Rosslyn**	21
Posto | **Logan Cir**	21
Potenza | **D'town**	20
Primi Piatti | **Foggy Bottom**	22
Radius | **Mt. Pleasant**	17
RedRocks | **multi.**	21
Renato/River Falls | **Potomac**	19
Sergio Rist. | **Silver Spring**	24
Sette Osteria | **Dupont Cir**	20
Siroc | **D'town**	24
NEW Socci | **Arlington**	–
Sorriso | **Cleve Pk**	22
Taylor Gourmet | **multi.**	23
Teatro Goldoni | **Gldn Triangle**	–
Tempo | N | **Alexandria**	22
Z Tosca | N | **Penn Qtr**	27
Toscana Café | **Cap Hill**	23
Tragara | N | **Bethesda**	21
Tutto Bene | N | **Arlington**	17
Urbana | **Dupont Cir**	22
Vapiano | **multi.**	18
NEW Vento | N | **Dupont Cir**	–

Villa Mozart | N | **Fairfax**	24
Zeffirelli Rist. | N | **Herndon**	22

JAMAICAN

Caribbean Feast | **Temple Hills**	–
Negril | **multi.**	23
Patty Boom Boom | **U St**	–

JAPANESE
(* sushi specialist)

Flying Fish* | **Alexandria**	19
Hama Sushi* | **Herndon**	19
Hinode* | **multi.**	19
Hooked* | **Sterling**	19
Kaz Sushi* | **World Bank**	25
Konami* | **Vienna**	20
Kotobuki* | **Palisades**	23
Kushi* | **Mt. Vernon Sq**	–
Z Makoto* | **Palisades**	28
Matuba* | **Bethesda**	21
Mikaku* | **Herndon**	–
Murasaki* | **Upper NW**	22
Niwano Hana* | **Rockville**	26
Perrys* | **Adams Mor**	19
Sakana* | **Dupont Cir**	22
Sei | **Penn Qtr**	23
Seven Seas | **multi.**	18
Spices* | **Cleve Pk**	22
Sushi Damo* | **Rockville**	24
Sushiko* | **multi.**	25
Sushi Rock* | **Arlington**	–
Z Sushi Taro* | **Dupont Cir**	26
Tachibana* | **McLean**	24
Taipei Tokyo | **multi.**	16
Tako Grill* | **Bethesda**	23
NEW Teak Wood* | **Logan Cir**	–
Tono Sushi* | **Woodley Pk**	23
Thai Tanic* | **Logan Cir**	23
Woomi Gdn.* | **Wheaton**	23
Yama* | **Vienna**	23
Yamazato* | **Alexandria**	25
Yosaku* | **Upper NW**	21

KOREAN
(* barbecue specialist)

Hee Been* | **Alexandria**	20
Z Honey Pig* | **Annandale**	26
Lighthouse/Vit Goel | **multi.**	20
L St. Vending | **D'town**	–
Mandu | **multi.**	21
NEW Mokomandy | **Sterling**	–
Sorak Gdn.* | **Annandale**	23

NEW TaKorean* | **Location Varies** | - |

Woo Lae Oak* | **Vienna** | 21 |

Woomi Gdn.* | **Wheaton** | 23 |

LAOTIAN

Bangkok Golden | **Falls Ch** | - |

LEBANESE

Kabab-ji | **Dupont Cir** | 20 |

Layalina | **Arlington** | 24 |

Z Lebanese Tav. | **multi.** | 21 |

Me Jana | **Arlington** | 23 |

Neyla | **Georgetown** | 22 |

MALAYSIAN

Malaysia Kopitiam | **Gldn Triangle** | 19 |

MEDITERRANEAN

Agora | **Dupont Cir** | - |

NEW Bistro LaZeez | **Bethesda** | - |

Brass. Monte Carlo | **Bethesda** | 20 |

Café Olé | **Upper NW** | 21 |

Evo Bistro | **McLean** | 23 |

Z Komi | **Dupont Cir** | 29 |

Matisse | **Upper NW** | 23 |

Panache | **multi.** | 16 |

Pasha Cafe | **Arlington** | 20 |

Puro Café | **Georgetown** | - |

Roti Med. | **multi.** | - |

Tabaq Bistro | **U St** | 20 |

Tavira | **Chevy Chase** | 24 |

Z Zaytinya | **Penn Qtr** | 25 |

MEXICAN

Azucar | **Silver Spring** | 22 |

Casa Oaxaca | **Adams Mor** | 18 |

NEW El Centro | **Logan Cir** | - |

El Mariachi | **Rockville** | 19 |

Guajillo | **Arlington** | 22 |

H St. Country | **Atlas Dist** | 15 |

Lauriol Plaza | **Dupont Cir** | 18 |

Oyamel | **Penn Qtr** | 24 |

Pedro & Vinny | **D'town** | - |

Rosa Mexicano | **multi.** | 20 |

Surfside | **Glover Pk** | 22 |

NEW TaKorean | **Location Varies** | - |

Taqueria Distrito | **multi.** | 23 |

Taqueria/Charrito | **Arlington** | - |

Taqueria La Placita | **Hyattsville** | - |

Taqueria Nacional | **Cap Hill** | 23 |

Taqueria Poblano | **multi.** | 22 |

MIDDLE EASTERN

Z Amsterdam Falafel | **Adams Mor** | 26 |

NEW Bistro LaZeez | **Bethesda** | - |

Levante's | **Dupont Cir** | 18 |

Maoz | **Gldn Triangle** | 19 |

Mezè | **Adams Mor** | 21 |

Z Zaytinya | **Penn Qtr** | 25 |

MOROCCAN

Marrakesh | **Dupont Cir** | 20 |

Taste/Morocco | **Clarendon** | 20 |

NEPALESE

Himalayan Heritage | **Adams Mor** | 22 |

NEW ENGLAND

NEW Red Hook | **Location Varies** | - |

NEW ZEALAND

Cassatt's Café | **Arlington** | 18 |

NOODLE SHOPS

Bob's Noodle | **Rockville** | 24 |

Chinatown Express | **Chinatown** | 21 |

DC Noodles | **U St** | 21 |

Full Key | **Wheaton** | 21 |

Nooshi | **Gldn Triangle** | 19 |

Pho 75 | **multi.** | 24 |

NEW Toki | **Atlas Dist** | - |

NUEVO LATINO

Caribbean Breeze | **Arlington** | 18 |

Ceiba | **D'town** | 23 |

NEW Cuba Libre | **Penn Qtr** | - |

La Caraqueña | **Falls Ch** | - |

Maté | **Georgetown** | 25 |

Mio | **D'town** | 19 |

PAKISTANI

NEW Diya | **Vienna** | - |

Kabob N Karahi | **Silver Spring** | - |

Kabob Palace | **Arlington** | 24 |

Ravi Kabob | **Arlington** | 22 |

PAN-LATIN

Azucar | **Silver Spring** | 22 |

Cafe Citron | **Dupont Cir** | 14 |

El Golfo | **Silver Spring** | 21 |

NEW Fast Gourmet | **U St** | - |

NEW Fruit Bat | **Atlas Dist** | - |

Guardado's | **Bethesda** | 24 |

Lima | **D'town** | 20 |

Masa 14 | **Logan Cir** | 23
NEW Panas | **Dupont Cir** | -
Samantha's | **Silver Spring** | 23
Zengo | **Chinatown** | 22

PERSIAN

Moby Dick | **multi.** | 21
Shamshiry | **Vienna** | 22

PERUVIAN

NEW Carbon Peruvian | **Rockville** | -
Crisp/Juicy | **multi.** | 24
Don Pollo | **multi.** | 18
Edy's Chicken | **Falls Ch** | 22
El Chalan | **Foggy Bottom** | 20
El Pollo Rico | **multi.** | 25
La Canela | **Rockville** | 23
La Limeña | **Rockville** | 22
Las Canteras | **Adams Mor** | -
Pollo Campero | **multi.** | 18

PIZZA

Agrodolce | **Germantown** | 22
American Flatbread | **Ashburn** | 21
Café Pizzaiolo | **multi.** | 18
NEW Casa Nonna | **Dupont Cir** | -
Coal Fire | **Gaith'burg** | 20
Comet Ping Pong | **Upper NW** | 20
Coppi's Organic | **U St** | 21
DC Slices | **Location Varies** | -
NEW District/Pi | **Location Varies** | -
Dolce Vita | **Fairfax** | 23
Ella's Pizza | **Penn Qtr** | 20
Facci | **Laurel** | -
Faccia Luna | **multi.** | 21
NEW Fiorella | **Nat'l Harbor** | -
Fire Works Pizza | **multi.** | -
Il Canale | **Georgetown** | -
Kora | **Arlington** | 15
Liberty Tree | **Atlas Dist** | -
Local 16 | **U St** | 13
Mamma Lucia | **multi.** | 18
Matchbox | **multi.** | 23
Mia's Pizzas | **Bethesda** | 21
Moroni/Bro. | **Petworth** | -
Oro Pomodoro | **Rockville** | 18
Pacci's | **Silver Spring** | -
Z Pasta Plus | **Laurel** | 26
Pete's Apizza | **multi.** | 22
Pie-Tanza | **multi.** | 19
Piola | **Rosslyn** | 21

NEW Pizzeria Da Marco | **Bethesda** | -
Pizzeria Orso | **Falls Ch** | -
Pizzeria Paradiso | **multi.** | 22
Posto | **Logan Cir** | 21
Potenza | **D'town** | 20
Pupatella Pizzeria | **Arlington** | -
Radius | **Mt. Pleasant** | 17
RedRocks | **multi.** | 21
Rustico | **Alexandria** | 21
NEW Rustik | **Bloomingdale** | -
Sette Osteria | **Dupont Cir** | 20
Seventh Hill | **Cap Hill** | 23
Sorriso | **Cleve Pk** | 22
Z 2 Amys | **Cleve Pk** | 25
NEW Upper Crust | **World Bank** | -
Vapiano | **multi.** | 18
NEW We, The Pizza | **Cap Hill** | -

PORTUGUESE

Tavira | **Chevy Chase** | 24

PUB FOOD

NEW Arlington Rooftop | **Clarendon** | -
Biergarten Haus | **Atlas Dist** | -
Black Squirrel | **Adams Mor** | -
Bourbon | **multi.** | 16
Capitol City Brew | **multi.** | 18
Z Clyde's | **multi.** | 19
Daniel O'Connell | **Alexandria** | 20
Dogfish Head | **multi.** | 18
Elephant/Castle | **multi.** | 15
Fadó | **Chinatown** | 17
Franklin's | **Hyattsville** | 18
Granville Moore's | **Atlas Dist** | 23
Hunter's Head | **Upperville** | 23
Irish Inn/Glen Echo | **Glen Echo** | 18
Liberty Tav. | **Clarendon** | 21
Liberty Tree | **Atlas Dist** | -
NEW Mad Fox Brew | **Falls Ch** | -
Madhatter | **Dupont Cir** | 17
Nellie's | **U St** | -
P. Brennan's | **Arlington** | -
NEW P.J. Clarke's | **D'town** | -
Restaurant 3 | **Clarendon** | 18
Rí Rá | **multi.** | 14
Stoney's Lounge | **Logan Cir** | 18
NEW Virtue | **Alexandria** | -

RUSSIAN

Russia Hse. | **Dupont Cir** | 15

SALVADORAN

El Gavilan | **Silver Spring**	–
Irene's Pupusas | **multi.**	20
Moroni/Bro. | **Petworth**	–
Taqueria/Charrito | **Arlington**	–

SANDWICHES

Bernie's Deli | **Fairfax**	25
NEW Big Cheese | **Location Varies**	–
Bread/Brew | **Dupont Cir**	22
Bread Line | **World Bank**	22
Buzz | **multi.**	22
C.F. Folks | **Gldn Triangle**	24
Chutzpah | **Fairfax**	18
El Floridano | **Location Varies**	–
NEW Fast Gourmet | **U St**	–
Le Pain Quotidien | **multi.**	18
Mixt Greens | **multi.**	–
Northside | **Clarendon**	–
NEW Paul | **Penn Qtr**	–
Pret A Manger | **multi.**	17
Taylor Gourmet | **multi.**	23
Toscana Café | **Cap Hill**	23

SEAFOOD

NEW Arlington Rooftop | **Clarendon**	–
☒ BlackSalt | **Palisades**	26
Black's Bar | **Bethesda**	23
Chesapeake Rm. | **Cap Hill**	–
Coastal Flats | **multi.**	21
DC Coast | **D'town**	23
Finn/Porter | **multi.**	17
Flying Fish | **Alexandria**	19
NEW Ford's Fish | **Ashburn**	–
NEW Freddy's Lobster | **Bethesda**	–
Grillfish | **West End**	18
Hank's Oyster | **multi.**	24
Harry's | **Clarendon**	19
Hook | **Georgetown**	23
Hooked | **Sterling**	19
Horace/Dickie | **Atlas Dist**	24
NEW Hot 'N Juicy | **Woodley Pk**	–
Jackson's | **Reston**	20
J&G Steak | **D'town**	25
Jerry's Seafood | **Lanham**	24
Johnny's | **Cap Hill**	20
Kellari Taverna | **Gldn Triangle**	22
☒ Kinkead's | **Foggy Bottom**	26
Legal Sea Foods | **multi.**	20
NEW Luke's Lobster | **Penn Qtr**	–

M&S Grill | **multi.**	19
McCormick/Schmick | **multi.**	20
NEW Mussel Bar | **Bethesda**	–
Nage | **Scott Cir**	22
Oceanaire | **D'town**	24
☒ Palm | **McLean**	24
PassionFish | **Reston**	24
Pesce | **Dupont Cir**	24
Phillips | **multi.**	15
Ray's/Classics | **Silver Spring**	24
NEW Red Hook | **Location Varies**	–
Sea Catch | **Georgetown**	21
NEW Senart's Oyster | **Cap Hill**	–
Seven Seas | **multi.**	18
Surfside | **Glover Pk**	22
Tackle Box | **multi.**	21
Tony & Joe's | **Georgetown**	15
NEW Watershed | **NoMa**	–
Wildfire | **McLean**	19

SMALL PLATES

(See also Spanish tapas specialist)

Acacia Bistro | Italian | **Upper NW**	22
Asia Bistro/Zen | Asian | **Arlington**	20
Bar Pilar | Amer. | **Logan Cir**	21
Café du Parc | French | **D'town**	22
Café Olé | Med. | **Upper NW**	21
Cava | Greek | **multi.**	24
Cork | Amer. | **Logan Cir**	23
Dino | Italian | **Cleve Pk**	22
Evo Bistro | Med. | **McLean**	23
Indique | Indian | **multi.**	23
Iron Bridge | Amer. | **Warrenton**	23
NEW Lincoln | Amer. | **D'town**	–
Mezè | Turkish | **Adams Mor**	21
Mikaku | Japanese | **Herndon**	–
NEW Mixx | Amer. | **D'town**	–
Oyamel | Mex. | **Penn Qtr**	24
Policy | Amer. | **U St**	19
Raku | Asian | **Dupont Cir**	21
☒ Rasika | Indian | **Penn Qtr**	28
Source | Amer. | **Penn Qtr**	25
Tabaq Bistro | Med. | **U St**	20
Tallula/EatBar | Amer. | **Clarendon**	22
Tandoori Nights | Indian | **multi.**	21
☒ Zaytinya | Mideast. | **Penn Qtr**	25

SOUTHERN

☒ Acadiana | **Mt. Vernon Sq**	23
Art & Soul | **Cap Hill**	21

NEW Bayou Bakery	**Arlington**	–
B. Smith	**Cap Hill**	20
Crème	**U St**	23
Eatonville	**U St**	19
Florida Ave. Grill	**U St**	20
Georgia Brown	**D'town**	22
Oohhs & Aahhs	**U St**	24
Sou'Wester	**SW**	18
Z Vidalia	**Dupont Cir**	24

SPANISH

(* tapas specialist)

Bodega*	**Georgetown**	19
El Manantial	**Reston**	23
NEW Estadio*	**Logan Cir**	–
Guardado's*	**Bethesda**	24
Z Jaleo*	**multi.**	22
La Tasca*	**multi.**	17
Taberna/Alabardero*	**World Bank**	23

STEAKHOUSES

Z BLT Steak	**Gldn Triangle**	25
Bobby Van's	**D'town**	21
Bond 45	**Nat'l Harbor**	–
Bourbon Steak	**Georgetown**	23
Z Capital Grille	**multi.**	25
Caucus Rm.	**Penn Qtr**	21
Charlie Palmer	**Cap Hill**	25
District ChopHse.	**Penn Qtr**	18
Finn/Porter	**multi.**	17
Fleming's Steak	**McLean**	24
Fogo De Chão	**D'town**	24
Harry's	**Clarendon**	19
J&G Steak	**D'town**	25
M&S Grill	**multi.**	19
NEW Medium Rare	**Cleve Pk**	–
Morton's	**multi.**	25
Nick's Chophse.	**Rockville**	20
Old Hickory	**Nat'l Harbor**	23
Z Palm	**multi.**	24
Z Prime Rib	**Gldn Triangle**	27
Ray's/Classics	**Silver Spring**	24
Z Ray's/Steaks	**Clarendon**	26
Ray's/East River	**NE**	–
Z Ruth's Chris	**multi.**	25
Shula's	**Vienna**	21
Smith/Wollensky	**Gldn Triangle**	22
Wildfire	**McLean**	19

TAIWANESE

NEW Toki	**Atlas Dist**	–

TEAROOMS

Ching Ching	**Georgetown**	20
Teaism	**multi.**	20

TEX-MEX

Austin Grill	**multi.**	15
Cactus Cantina	**Cleve Pk**	18
Calif. Tortilla	**multi.**	18
El Gavilan	**Silver Spring**	–
H St. Country	**Atlas Dist**	15
Mi Rancho	**multi.**	18
Uncle Julio's	**multi.**	19

THAI

Bangkok54	**Arlington**	23
Bangkok Golden	**Falls Ch**	–
Bangkok Joe's	**Georgetown**	21
Benjarong	**Rockville**	22
Busara	**multi.**	20
Crystal Thai	**Arlington**	22
DC Noodles	**U St**	21
Duangrat's	**Falls Ch**	25
Haad Thai	**D'town**	20
NEW Heritage Asia	**Glover Pk**	–
Mai Thai	**multi.**	20
Nava Thai	**Wheaton**	23
Neisha Thai	**multi.**	19
Rabieng	**Falls Ch**	25
Regent	**Dupont Cir**	23
Rice	**Logan Cir**	22
Ruan Thai	**Wheaton**	25
Sabai	**Germantown**	–
Sakoontra	**Fairfax**	19
Sweet Basil	**Bethesda**	21
Tara Thai	**multi.**	19
NEW Teak Wood	**Logan Cir**	–
T.H.A.I.	**Arlington**	23
Thai/Silver Spring	**Silver Spring**	20
Thai Basil	**Chantilly**	22
Thaiphoon	**multi.**	20
Z Thai Sq.	**Arlington**	26
Thai Tanic	**multi.**	23

TURKISH

Agora	**Dupont Cir**	–
Cafe Divan	**Glover Pk**	22
Ezmè	**Dupont Cir**	–
Kazan	**McLean**	22

VEGETARIAN

(* vegan)

Amma Veg.	**Vienna**	22
Z Amsterdam Falafel	**Adams Mor**	26

Luna Grill* | **multi.** 17
Mandalay | **Silver Spring** 24
Maoz | **Gldn Triangle** 19
Mark's Kit. | **Takoma Pk** 17
Vegetable Gdn.* | **White Flint** 22
Yuan Fu* | **Rockville** 18

VENEZUELAN

La Caraqueña | **Falls Ch** -

VIETNAMESE

NEW Ba Bay | **Cap Hill** -
Four Sisters | **Merrifield** 25

Green Papaya | **Bethesda** 19
Huong Viet | **Falls Ch** 22
Minh's | **Arlington** 24
Nam-Viet | **multi.** 21
NEW Pho DC | **Chinatown** -
Pho 14 | **Columbia Hts** 26
Pho 75 | **multi.** 24
Present | **Falls Ch** 23
Taste/Saigon | **multi.** 21

Locations

Includes names, cuisines, Food ratings and, for locations that are mapped, top list with map coordinates.

Washington, DC

ADAMS MORGAN

(See map on page 205)

TOP FOOD

Amsterdam Falafel | *Mideast.* | **B3**	26
Cashion's Eat | *Amer.* | **B3**	24
Pasta Mia | *Italian* | **B3**	23
La Fourchette | *French* | **B3**	23
Himalayan Heritage | *Indian/Nepalese* | **C3**	22
Mezè | *Mideast.* | **B3**	21
Grill/Ipanema | *Brazilian* | **B2**	20

LISTING

☑ Amsterdam Falafel | *Mideast.*	26
Black Squirrel | *Pub*	–
Bourbon | *Pub*	16
Casa Oaxaca | *Mex.*	18
Cashion's Eat | *Amer.*	24
Diner | *Diner*	17
Grill/Ipanema | *Brazilian*	20
Himalayan Heritage | *Indian/Nepalese*	22
La Fourchette | *French*	23
Las Canteras | *Peruvian*	–
Little Fountain | *Eclectic*	24
Meskerem | *Ethiopian*	20
Mezè | *Mideast.*	21
Napoleon | *French*	16
Pasta Mia | *Italian*	23
Perrys | *Amer./Eclectic*	19
Slaviya Cafe | *E Euro.*	–
Tryst | *Coffee*	19

ANACOSTIA

Negril | *Jamaican*	23
NEW Uniontown B&G | *Amer.*	–

ATLAS DISTRICT

NEW Atlas Rm. | *Eclectic*	–
Biergarten Haus | *German*	–
Ethiopic | *Ethiopian*	–
NEW Fruit Bat | *Pan-Latin*	–
Granville Moore's | *Amer./Belgian*	23
Horace/Dickie | *Seafood*	24
H St. Country | *Tex-Mex*	15
Liberty Tree | *Amer./Pizza*	–
NEW Queen Vic | *British*	–
NEW Smith Commons | *Amer.*	–

Star/Shamrock | *Deli*	–
Sticky Rice | *Asian/Eclectic*	22
Taylor Gourmet | *Deli/Italian*	23
NEW Toki | *Taiwanese/Noodle Shop*	–

BLOOMINGDALE

NEW Rustik | *Amer./Eclectic*	–

CAPITOL HILL

Acqua al 2 | *Italian*	–
Art & Soul | *Amer.*	21
NEW Ba Bay | *Viet.*	–
Banana Café | *Cuban/Puerto Rican*	18
Belga Café | *Belgian*	23
Bistro Bis | *French*	25
Bistro Cacao | *French*	–
B. Smith | *Southern*	20
Capitol City Brew | *Pub*	18
Cava | *Greek*	24
Charlie Palmer | *Steak*	25
Chesapeake Rm. | *Amer./Seafood*	–
NEW DC-3 | *Hot Dogs*	–
Dubliner | *Irish*	16
Good Stuff | *Burgers*	21
Hunan Dynasty | *Chinese*	17
Johnny's | *Amer./Seafood*	20
Le Pain Quotidien | *Bakery/Belgian*	18
Matchbox | *Amer.*	23
Monocle | *Amer.*	14
Montmartre | *French*	24
NEW Senart's Oyster | *Amer./Seafood*	–
Seventh Hill | *Pizza*	23
Sonoma | *Amer.*	20
Sweetgreen | *Health*	21
Taqueria Nacional | *Mex.*	23
Ted's Bulletin | *Amer.*	–
Toscana Café | *Deli/Italian*	23
NEW We, The Pizza | *Pizza*	–
Zest | *Amer.*	18

CHINATOWN/ PENN QUARTER

(Including Gallery Place; see map on page 200)

TOP FOOD

Rasika | *Indian* | **H10**	28
Tosca | *Italian* | **G6**	27

Minibar	*Eclectic*	**H9**	26
Central Michel	*Amer./French*	**I7**	26
Zaytinya	*Med./Mideast.*	**F8**	25
Capital Grille	*Steak*	**J10**	25
Ruth's Chris	*Steak*	**F8**	25
Source	*Amer.*	**J10**	25
Proof	*Amer.*	**F9**	24
Oyamel	*Mex.*	**H9**	24
Sei	*Asian*	**H9**	23
701	*Amer.*	**I9**	23
Matchbox	*Amer.*	**E9**	23
Zola	*Amer.*	**G8**	23
Oya	*Asian*	**E8**	23

LISTING

NEW America Eats	*Amer.*	-
Asia Nine	*Asian*	18
Asian Spice	*Asian*	21
Austin Grill	*Tex-Mex*	15
Burma	*Burmese*	20
Calif. Tortilla	*Tex-Mex*	18
Z Capital Grille	*Steak*	25
NEW Carmine's	*Italian*	-
Caucus Rm.	*Amer.*	21
Z Central Michel	*Amer./French*	26
Chinatown Express	*Chinese*	21
Chop't	*Amer.*	19
Z Clyde's	*Amer.*	19
Co Co. Sala	*Eclectic*	22
NEW Cuba Libre	*Nuevo Latino*	-
District ChopHse.	*Steak*	18
Eat First	*Chinese*	20
Ella's Pizza	*Pizza*	20
Fadó	*Irish*	17
NEW Fiola	*Italian*	-
Z Five Guys	*Burgers*	22
Full Kee (DC)	*Chinese*	22
NEW Hill Country	*BBQ*	-
Z Jaleo	*Spanish*	22
La Tasca	*Spanish*	17
Legal Sea Foods	*Seafood*	20
NEW Luke's Lobster	*Seafood*	-
Matchbox	*Amer.*	23
McCormick/Schmick	*Seafood*	20
NEW Merzi	*Indian*	-
Z Minibar	*Eclectic*	26
Nando's	*Chicken*	20
Z Oya	*Asian*	23
Oyamel	*Mex.*	24
NEW Paul	*Bakery*	-
NEW Pho DC	*Viet.*	-
Ping Pong	*Asian*	21
Poste Moderne	*Amer.*	21

Pret A Manger	*Sandwiches*	17
Proof	*Amer.*	24
PS 7's	*Amer.*	22
Z Rasika	*Indian*	28
NEW Redline	*Amer.*	-
Rosa Mexicano	*Mex.*	20
Z Ruth's Chris	*Steak*	25
Sei	*Asian*	23
701	*Amer.*	23
Source	*Amer.*	25
Teaism	*Tea*	20
Tony Cheng's	*Chinese*	19
Z Tosca	*Italian*	27
Vapiano	*Italian*	18
Z Zaytinya	*Med./Mideast.*	25
Zengo	*Asian/Pan-Latin*	22
Zola	*Amer.*	23

CLEVELAND PARK/ WOODLEY PARK

Ardeo/Bardeo	*Amer./Wine*	21
Cactus Cantina	*Tex-Mex*	18
Cafe Deluxe	*Amer.*	18
Calif. Tortilla	*Tex-Mex*	18
Dino	*Italian*	22
NEW Hot 'N Juicy	*Cajun/Creole*	-
Indique	*Indian*	23
Lavandou	*French*	20
Z Lebanese Tav.	*Lebanese*	21
NEW Medium Rare	*Steak*	-
Nam-Viet	*Viet.*	21
New Heights	*Amer.*	22
Open City	*Diner*	18
Z Palena	*Amer.*	28
Petits Plats	*French*	22
NEW Ripple	*Amer.*	-
Sorriso	*Italian*	22
Spices	*Asian*	22
Tackle Box	*Seafood*	21
Tono Sushi	*Japanese*	23
Z 2 Amys	*Pizza*	25

DOWNTOWN

(See map on page 200)

TOP FOOD

J&G Steak	*Amer./Steak*	**G3**	25
Brass. Beck	*Belgian/French*	**C6**	25
Adour/St. Regis	*Amer./French*	**D2**	24
Oceanaire	*Seafood*	**G6**	24
Fogo De Chão	*Brazilian/Steak*	**H6**	24
Siroc	*Italian*	**D3**	24
Bibiana	*Italian*	**D6**	23

Ceiba	*Nuevo Latino*	**F4**	23
DC Coast	*Amer.*	**C4**	23
Morrison-Clark	*Amer.*	**B7**	23

LISTING

Ⓩ Adour/St. Regis	*Amer./French*	24
Againn	*British*	19
Bibiana	*Italian*	23
Bistro D'Oc	*French*	21
Blackfinn	*Amer.*	14
Bobby Van's	*Steak*	21
Ⓩ Brass. Beck	*Belgian/French*	25
Café du Parc	*French*	22
Capitol City Brew	*Pub*	18
Ceiba	*Nuevo Latino*	23
Chef Geoff	*Amer.*	19
Chop't	*Amer.*	19
Coeur de Lion	*Amer.*	20
DC Coast	*Amer.*	23
Elephant/Castle	*Pub*	15
Finemondo	*Italian*	22
Finn/Porter	*Seafood/Steak*	17
Fogo De Chão	*Brazilian/Steak*	24
FunXion	*Amer.*	-
ᴺᴱᵂ Galileo III	*Italian*	-
Georgia Brown	*Southern*	22
Haad Thai	*Thai*	20
iCi	*Amer.*	23
J&G Steak	*Amer./Steak*	25
Juice Joint Cafe	*Health*	22
Lima	*Pan-Latin*	20
ᴺᴱᵂ Lincoln	*Amer.*	-
L St. Vending	*Korean*	-
M&S Grill	*Seafood/Steak*	19
Mio	*Nuevo Latino*	19
ᴺᴱᵂ Mixx	*Amer.*	-
Morrison-Clark	*Amer.*	23
Occidental	*Amer.*	22
Oceanaire	*Seafood*	24
Ⓩ Old Ebbitt	*Amer.*	20
Park/14th	*Amer.*	21
Pedro & Vinny	*Mex.*	-
ᴺᴱᵂ P.J. Clarke's	*Pub*	-
Plume	*Amer.*	26
Potenza	*Italian/Pizza*	20
ᴺᴱᵂ Sax	*French*	-
Siroc	*Italian*	24
Zentan	*Asian*	21

DUPONT CIRCLE

(See map on page 205)

TOP FOOD

Komi	*Amer./Med.*	**G5**	29
Obelisk	*Italian*	**H2**	27

Sushi Taro	*Japanese*	**H5**	26
Nora	*Amer.*	**F1**	26
Ruth's Chris	*Steak*	**F2**	25
Mourayo	*Greek*	**F2**	25
Pesce	*Seafood*	**H2**	24

LISTING

Agora	*Turkish*	-
Al Tiramisu	*Italian*	24
BGR	*Burgers*	21
Bistrot du Coin	*French*	21
Black Fox	*Continental*	-
Bread/Brew	*Amer./Coffee*	22
Buca di Beppo	*Italian*	16
Cafe Citron	*Pan-Latin*	14
Café Dupont	*Amer./French*	-
Cajun Experience	*Cajun/Creole*	-
ᴺᴱᵂ Casa Nonna	*Italian*	-
Chop't	*Amer.*	19
Circa	*Amer.*	17
City Lights	*Chinese*	19
Darlington Hse.	*Amer.*	20
Eola	*Amer.*	-
Ezmè	*Turkish*	-
Firefly	*Amer.*	20
Hank's Oyster	*Amer./Seafood*	24
Heritage India	*Indian*	22
I Ricchi	*Italian*	24
Ⓩ Jockey Club	*Amer.*	22
Kabab-ji	*Lebanese*	20
Ⓩ Komi	*Amer./Med.*	29
Kramerbooks	*Amer.*	17
La Tomate	*Italian*	18
Lauriol Plaza	*Mex.*	18
Le Pain Quotidien	*Bakery/Belgian*	18
Levante's	*Mideast.*	18
Luna Grill	*Diner/Veg.*	17
Maddy's	*Amer.*	-
Madhatter	*Amer./Pub*	-
Mandu	*Korean*	21
Marrakesh	*Moroccan*	20
Moby Dick	*Persian*	21
Mourayo	*Greek*	25
Nando's	*Chicken*	20
Ⓩ Nora	*Amer.*	26
Ⓩ Obelisk	*Italian*	27
ᴺᴱᵂ Panas	*Pan-Latin*	-
Pesce	*Seafood*	24
Pizzeria Paradiso	*Pizza*	22
Raku	*Asian*	21
Regent	*Thai*	23
Russia Hse.	*Russian*	15

Ruth's Chris	*Steak*	25
Sakana	*Japanese*	22
Sette Osteria	*Italian*	20
NEW Shake Shack	*Burgers*	-
Sushi Taro	*Japanese*	26
Sweetgreen	*Health*	21
Tabard Inn	*Amer.*	24
Teaism	*Tea*	20
Thaiphoon	*Thai*	20
Urbana	*French/Italian*	22
NEW Vento	*Italian*	-
Veritas	*Cheese*	18
Vidalia	*Amer.*	24

FARRAGUT

Chop't	*Amer.*	19
Pret A Manger	*Sandwiches*	17

FOGGY BOTTOM/ WORLD BANK

(See map on page 202)

TOP FOOD

Kinkead's	*Seafood*	**G6**	26
Kaz Sushi	*Japanese*	**F7**	25
Taberna/Alabardero	*Spanish*	**F8**	23
Primi Piatti	*Italian*	**G6**	22
Bread Line	*Bakery/Sandwiches*	**H9**	22
Founding Farmers	*Amer.*	**G7**	21

LISTING

Bread Line	*Bakery/Sandwiches*	22
Dish/Drinks	*Amer.*	19
El Chalan	*Peruvian*	20
Elephant/Castle	*Pub*	15
Founding Farmers	*Amer.*	21
Kaz Sushi	*Japanese*	25
Kinkead's	*Seafood*	26
Notti Bianche	*Italian*	20
Primi Piatti	*Italian*	22
NEW Rivers/Watergate	*Amer.*	-
Roof Terr.	*Amer.*	15
Roti Med.	*Med.*	-
Taberna/Alabardero	*Spanish*	23
Tonic	*Amer.*	16
NEW Upper Crust	*Pizza*	-

GEORGETOWN

(See map on page 204)

TOP FOOD

Citronelle	*French*	**C6**	28
1789	*Amer.*	**C2**	25
Morton's	*Steak*	**C4**	25

La Chaumière	*French*	**C7**	24
Hook	*Amer./Seafood*	**C4**	23

LISTING

Bangkok Joe's	*Thai*	21
Bistro Français	*French*	19
Bistrot Lepic	*French*	23
Bodega	*Spanish*	19
NEW Bookhill Bistro	*Amer.*	-
Bourbon Steak	*Steak*	23
Café Bonaparte	*French*	20
Cafe Milano	*Italian*	20
Ching Ching	*Tea*	20
Citronelle	*French*	28
Clyde's	*Amer.*	19
Dean & DeLuca	*Eclectic*	22
Fahrenheit	*Amer.*	22
Filomena	*Italian*	23
Five Guys	*Burgers*	22
Hook	*Amer./Seafood*	23
Il Canale	*Italian/Pizza*	-
La Chaumière	*French*	24
Leopold's Kafe	*Austrian*	22
Le Pain Quotidien	*Bakery/Belgian*	18
Mai Thai	*Thai*	20
Martin's Tav.	*Amer.*	20
Maté	*Asian/Nuevo Latino*	25
Mie N Yu	*Amer.*	17
Moby Dick	*Persian*	21
Morton's	*Steak*	25
Neyla	*Lebanese*	22
Old Glory	*BBQ*	17
Paolo's	*Cal./Italian*	18
Peacock Cafe	*Amer.*	19
Pizzeria Paradiso	*Pizza*	22
Puro Café	*Coffee/Med.*	-
Sea Catch	*Seafood*	21
Sequoia	*Amer.*	15
NEW Serendipity 3	*Dessert*	-
1789	*Amer.*	25
Sweetgreen	*Health*	21
Tackle Box	*Seafood*	21
Tony & Joe's	*Seafood*	15

GLOVER PARK

Bourbon	*Pub*	16
Breadsoda	*Amer.*	-
Cafe Divan	*Turkish*	22
NEW Heritage Asia	*SE Asian*	-
Heritage India	*Indian*	22
Rocklands	*BBQ*	22
Surfside	*Cal./Mex.*	22
Sushiko	*Japanese*	25

GOLDEN TRIANGLE

(See map on page 202)

TOP FOOD

Prime Rib	*Seafood/Steak*	**F5**	27
Equinox	*Amer.*	**G10**	25
BLT Steak	*Steak*	**F11**	25
Morton's	*Steak*	**E9**	25
Oval Rm.	*Amer.*	**G10**	24
Bombay Club	*Indian*	**G10**	24
Palm	*Seafood/Steak*	**B7**	24
C.F. Folks	*Eclectic*	**B7**	24
Kellari Taverna	*Greek*	**F9**	22
Smith/Wollensky	*Steak*	**D7**	22
Teaism	*Tea*	**G10**	20
Mai Thai	*Thai*	**C7**	20
McCormick/Schmick	*Seafood*	**F10**	20

LISTING

Z BLT Steak	*Steak*	25
Bombay Club	*Indian*	24
Cafe Asia	*Asian*	18
C.F. Folks	*Eclectic*	24
Chop't	*Amer.*	19
NEW Cities	*Eclectic*	-
Equinox	*Amer.*	25
Kellari Taverna	*Greek*	22
Lafayette Rm.	*Amer.*	25
Mai Thai	*Thai*	20
Malaysia Kopitiam	*Malaysian*	19
Maoz	*Veg.*	19
McCormick/Schmick	*Seafood*	20
Mixt Greens	*Amer./Sandwiches*	-
Morton's	*Steak*	25
Nooshi	*Asian*	19
Oval Rm.	*Amer.*	24
Z Palm	*Seafood/Steak*	24
Panache	*Med.*	16
Pret A Manger	*Sandwiches*	17
Z Prime Rib	*Seafood/Steak*	27
Smith/Wollensky	*Steak*	22
Teaism	*Tea*	20
Teatro Goldoni	*Italian*	-
Vapiano	*Italian*	18

LOCATION VARIES

(Food Trucks)

NEW Big Cheese	*Sandwiches*	-
NEW CapMac	*Amer.*	-
DC Slices	*Pizza*	-
NEW District/Pi	*Pizza*	-
NEW Eat Wonky	*Eclectic*	-
El Floridano	*Sandwiches*	-

Fojol Bros.	*Indian*	-
NEW PORC	*BBQ*	-
NEW Red Hook	*Seafood*	-
Sauca	*Eclectic*	-
NEW TaKorean	*Korean*	-

MT. PLEASANT

Radius	*Italian*	17
Tonic	*Amer.*	16

MT. VERNON SQUARE/ CONVENTION CENTER

Z Acadiana	*Contemp. LA*	23
Buddha-Bar	*Asian/French*	-
Busboys/Poets	*Amer./Eclectic*	18
Z Corduroy	*Amer.*	27
Kushi	*Japanese*	-
Mandu	*Korean*	21
1905	*French*	19
Passenger	*Eclectic*	-
Taylor Gourmet	*Deli/Italian*	23

NOMA

Roti Med.	*Med.*	-
NEW Watershed	*Amer./Seafood*	-

NORTHEAST

Capital City	*Diner*	-
Chop't	*Amer.*	19
Ray's/East River	*Burgers/Steak*	-

PALISADES

Z BlackSalt	*Amer./Seafood*	26
DC Boathouse	*Amer.*	15
Et Voila	*Belgian/French*	24
Kotobuki	*Japanese*	23
Z Makoto	*Japanese*	28

PETWORTH/ BRIGHTWOOD/ COLUMBIA HEIGHTS

Domku	*E Euro./Scan.*	18
Heights	*Amer.*	19
NEW Meridian	*Amer.*	-
Moroni/Bro.	*Latin Amer./Pizza*	-
Pete's Apizza	*Pizza*	22
Pho 14	*Viet.*	26
Pollo Campero	*Peruvian*	18
RedRocks	*Pizza*	21
Room 11	*Eclectic*	-
Taqueria Distrito	*Mex.*	23
Thai Tanic	*Thai*	23

SCOTT CIRCLE/
LOGAN CIRCLE

15 Ria	*Amer.*	17
Bar Pilar	*Amer.*	21
Beacon B&G	*Amer.*	17
Birch/Barley	*Amer.*	22
Café Saint-Ex	*Eclectic*	20
Commissary	*Amer.*	16
Cork	*Amer.*	23
NEW El Centro	*Mex.*	-
NEW Estadio	*Spanish*	-
Logan Tav.	*Amer.*	18
Masa 14	*Asian/Latin*	23
Nage	*Amer./Seafood*	22
Posto	*Italian*	21
Rice	*Thai*	22
NEW Standard	*BBQ*	-
Stoney's Lounge	*Pub*	18
Sweetgreen	*Health*	21
NEW Teak Wood	*Thai*	-
Thai Tanic	*Japanese/Thai*	23

SW

Z CityZen	*Amer.*	28
Mitsitam	*Amer.*	20
NEW Next Stage	*Eclectic*	-
Phillips	*Seafood*	15
NEW Shake Shack	*Burgers*	-
Sou'Wester	*Amer.*	18

UPPER NW

Acacia Bistro	*Italian*	22
Arucola	*Italian*	19
Buck's Fishing	*Amer.*	20
Café Olé	*Med.*	21
Cheesecake	*Amer.*	19
Chef Geoff	*Amer.*	19
Comet Ping Pong	*Pizza*	20
Crisp/Juicy	*Peruvian*	24
Le Chat Noir	*French*	18
Le Pain Quotidien	*Bakery/Belgian*	18
Maggiano's	*Italian*	18
Masala Art	*Indian*	26
Matisse	*French/Med.*	23
Murasaki	*Japanese*	22
Neisha Thai	*Thai*	19
Pete's Apizza	*Pizza*	22
Tara Thai	*Thai*	19
Yosaku	*Japanese*	21

U STREET CORRIDOR

Al Crostino	*Italian*	21
NEW American Ice	*BBQ*	-
Ben's Chili	*Diner*	22
Ben's Next Door	*Amer.*	20
Bistro La Bonne	*French*	-
Busboys/Poets	*Amer./Eclectic*	18
Chix	*Eclectic*	20
Coppi's Organic	*Italian*	21
Crème	*Southern*	23
DC Noodles	*Thai*	21
Dickson Wine	*Eclectic*	-
Dukem	*Ethiopian*	24
Eatonville	*Southern*	19
Etete	*Ethiopian*	24
NEW Fast Gourmet	*Pan-Latin*	-
Florida Ave. Grill	*Diner*	20
Local 16	*Amer./Pizza*	13
Marvin	*Amer./Belgian*	21
Negril	*Jamaican*	23
Nellie's	*Pub*	17
Oohhs & Aahhs	*Southern*	24
Patty Boom Boom	*Jamaican*	-
Policy	*Amer.*	19
Tabaq Bistro	*Med.*	20
Ulah Bistro	*Amer.*	18
Vinoteca	*Eclectic*	21

WEST END

(See map on page 204)

TOP FOOD

Marcel's	*Belgian/French*	**E9**	29
Blue Duck	*Amer.*	**C9**	26
Ris	*Amer.*	**D9**	23
Westend Bistro	*Amer.*	**D10**	21
Circle Bistro	*Amer.*	**E9**	21

LISTING

NEW Bayou	*Cajun/Creole*	-
Z Blue Duck	*Amer.*	26
Circle Bistro	*Amer.*	21
Grillfish	*Seafood*	18
Hudson	*Amer.*	17
Juniper	*Amer.*	21
Z Marcel's	*Belgian/French*	29
Meiwah	*Chinese*	19
Ris	*Amer.*	23
Westend Bistro	*Amer.*	21

Nearby Maryland

BETHESDA/
CHEVY CHASE

American Tap	*Amer.*	-
Assaggi	*Italian*	21
BGR	*Burgers*	21

NEW Bistro LaZeez	*Mideast.*	-
Bistro Provence	*French*	-
Blackfinn	*Amer.*	14
Black's Bar	*Amer.*	23
Brass. Monte Carlo	*French/Med.*	20
Cafe Deluxe	*Amer.*	18
Calif. Tortilla	*Tex-Mex*	18
Z Capital Grille	*Steak*	25
NEW Cava Mezze Grill	*Greek*	-
Cesco Trattoria	*Italian*	22
City Lights	*Chinese*	19
Z Clyde's	*Amer.*	19
Delhi Dhaba	*Indian*	18
Don Pollo	*S Amer.*	18
Faryab	*Afghan*	23
Z Five Guys	*Burgers*	22
NEW Food Wine	*Amer.*	-
NEW Freddy's Lobster	*Seafood*	-
Fu Shing	*Chinese*	21
Grapeseed	*Amer.*	21
Green Papaya	*Viet.*	19
Guardado's	*Pan-Latin/Spanish*	24
Haandi	*Indian*	24
Hard Times	*Amer.*	19
Hinode	*Japanese*	19
Indique	*Indian*	23
Z Jaleo	*Spanish*	22
La Ferme	*French*	22
Z Lebanese Tav.	*Lebanese*	21
Legal Sea Foods	*Seafood*	20
Le Pain Quotidien	*Bakery/Belgian*	18
Lia's	*Amer./Italian*	21
Mamma Lucia	*Italian*	18
Matuba	*Japanese*	21
McCormick/Schmick	*Seafood*	20
Meiwah	*Chinese*	19
Mia's Pizzas	*Pizza*	21
Mixt Greens	*Amer./Sandwiches*	-
Moby Dick	*Persian*	21
Mon Ami Gabi	*French*	19
Morton's	*Steak*	25
NEW Mussel Bar	*Belgian*	-
NEW Newton's	*Amer.*	-
Oakville Grille	*Amer.*	19
Olazzo	*Italian*	21
Passage to India	*Indian*	24
Persimmon	*Amer.*	25
P.F. Chang's	*Chinese*	20
NEW Pizzeria Da Marco	*Pizza*	-
Praline	*Bakery/French*	19
Raku	*Asian*	21

Redwood	*Amer.*	17
Rí Rá	*Pub*	14
Z Ruth's Chris	*Steak*	25
Sushiko	*Japanese*	25
Sweet Basil	*Thai*	21
Sweetgreen	*Health*	21
Tako Grill	*Japanese*	23
Tara Thai	*Thai*	19
Tavira	*Portug.*	24
Taylor Gourmet	*Deli/Italian*	23
Tragara	*Italian*	21
Uncle Julio's	*Tex-Mex*	19
Vapiano	*Italian*	18

GAITHERSBURG/ DICKERSON/ GERMANTOWN/ OLNEY/ SHADY GROVE

Agrodolce	*Italian*	22
Buca di Beppo	*Italian*	16
Burma Rd.	*Burmese/Chinese*	24
Calif. Tortilla	*Tex-Mex*	18
Coal Fire	*Pizza*	20
Comus Inn	*Amer.*	21
Crisp/Juicy	*Peruvian*	24
Dogfish Head	*Pub*	18
Fu Shing	*Chinese*	21
Hard Times	*Amer.*	19
India Palace	*Indian*	-
Mamma Lucia	*Italian*	18
Mannequin Pis	*Belgian*	25
Minerva	*Indian*	21
Mi Rancho	*Tex-Mex*	18
Moby Dick	*Persian*	21
New Fortune	*Chinese*	22
Pollo Campero	*Peruvian*	18
Red Hot/Blue	*BBQ*	20
Sabai	*Thai*	-
Tandoori Nights	*Indian*	21
Tara Thai	*Thai*	19
Uncle Julio's	*Tex-Mex*	19

NATIONAL HARBOR

Bond 45	*Italian*	-
Elevation Burger	*Burgers*	18
NEW Fiorella	*Pizza*	-
Old Hickory	*Steak*	23
Rosa Mexicano	*Mex.*	20

POTOMAC/ GLEN ECHO

Amici Miei	*Italian*	20
Bezu	*Amer./French*	23

Calif. Tortilla | Tex-Mex	18
Elevation Burger | Burgers	18
Irish Inn/Glen Echo | Irish	18
Old Angler's | Amer.	19
Renato/River Falls | Italian	19
NEW Wild Tomato | Amer.	-

PRINCE GEORGE'S COUNTY

Calif. Tortilla | Tex-Mex	18
Cuba de Ayer | Cuban	23
Don Pollo | S Amer.	18
Elevation Burger | Burgers	18
Facci | Italian/Pizza	-
Franklin's | Pub	18
Hank's Tav. | Amer.	22
Hard Times | Amer.	19
Hunan Manor | Chinese	21
Irene's Pupusas | Central Amer.	20
Jerry's Seafood | Seafood	24
Kloby's Smokehse. | BBQ	-
Mamma Lucia | Italian	18
Negril | Jamaican	23
Ⓩ Pasta Plus | Italian	26
Pho 75 | Viet.	24
Red Hot/Blue | BBQ	20
Seven Seas | Chinese/Japanese	18
Taqueria La Placita | Mex.	-

ROCKVILLE/ GARRETT PARK/ WHITE FLINT

A&J | Chinese	24
Addie's | Amer.	23
Austin Grill | Tex-Mex	15
Benjarong | Thai	22
Black Mkt. | Amer.	25
Bob's Noodle | Taiwanese	24
Bombay Bistro | Indian	23
Calif. Tortilla | Tex-Mex	18
NEW Carbon Peruvian | Peruvian	-
Cava | Greek	24
Cheesecake | Amer.	19
China Bistro | Chinese	23
China Jade | Chinese	-
Ⓩ Clyde's | Amer.	19
Crisp/Juicy | Peruvian	24
Don Pollo | S Amer.	18
El Mariachi | Mex.	19
Hard Times | Amer.	19
Hinode | Japanese	19
Il Pizzico | Italian	26
Joe's Noodle Hse. | Chinese	23

La Canela | Peruvian	23
La Limeña | Cuban/Peruvian	22
La Tasca | Spanish	17
Ⓩ Lebanese Tav. | Lebanese	21
Lighthouse/Vit Goel | Korean	20
Mamma Lucia | Italian	18
Matchbox | Amer.	23
Michael's Noodles | Chinese	23
Mi Rancho | Tex-Mex	18
Moby Dick | Persian	21
Mykonos Grill | Greek	22
Nick's Chophse. | Steak	20
Niwano Hana | Japanese	26
Oro Pomodoro | Italian	18
P.F. Chang's | Chinese	20
Phillips | Seafood	15
Pho 75 | Viet.	24
Rocklands | BBQ	22
Seven Seas | Chinese/Japanese	18
Sichuan Pavilion | Chinese	23
Spice Xing | Indian	20
Sushi Damo | Japanese	24
Taipei Tokyo | Chinese/Japanese	16
Tara Thai | Thai	19
Taste/Saigon | Viet.	21
Urban BBQ | BBQ	22
Urban Burger | Burgers	21
Vegetable Gdn. | Chinese/Veg.	22
Yuan Fu | Chinese/Veg.	18

SILVER SPRING/ TAKOMA PARK/ WHEATON

Austin Grill | Tex-Mex	15
Azucar | Mex./Pan-Latin	22
Calif. Tortilla | Tex-Mex	18
Crisp/Juicy | Peruvian	24
Cubano's | Cuban	21
Eggspectations | Amer.	19
8407 Kit. | Amer.	-
El Gavilan | Salvadoran/Tex-Mex	-
El Golfo | Pan-Latin	21
El Pollo Rico | Peruvian	25
Full Key | Chinese	21
Good Fortune | Chinese	18
Hollywood E. | Chinese	-
Hunan Manor | Chinese	21
Irene's Pupusas | Central Amer.	20
Jackie's | Amer.	21
Kabob N Karahi | Pakistani	-
Ⓩ Lebanese Tav. | Lebanese	21
Mamma Lucia | Italian	18

Mandalay	*Burmese*	24
Mark's Kit.	*Amer.*	17
Mi Rancho	*Tex-Mex*	18
Moby Dick	*Persian*	21
Mrs. K's	*Amer.*	22
Nando's	*Chicken*	20
Nava Thai	*Thai*	23
Negril	*Jamaican*	23
New Kam	*Chinese*	24
Olazzo	*Italian*	21
Oriental E.	*Chinese*	22
Pacci's	*Pizza*	-
Parkway Deli	*Deli*	19
Pollo Campero	*Peruvian*	18
Ray's/Classics	*Amer.*	24
Ruan Thai	*Thai*	25
Samantha's	*Pan-Latin*	23
Sergio Rist.	*Italian*	24
Thai/Silver Spring	*Thai*	20
Urban BBQ	*BBQ*	22
Woomi Gdn.	*Korean*	23

TEMPLE HILLS

Caribbean Feast	*Jamaican*	-

Nearby Virginia

ALEXANDRIA

Afghan	*Afghan*	25
Buzz	*Coffee*	22
☑ Clyde's	*Amer.*	19
Cosmopolitan Grill	*E Euro.*	-
Evening Star	*Amer.*	22
Finn/Porter	*Seafood/Steak*	17
☑ Five Guys	*Burgers*	22
Hee Been	*Korean*	20
La Strada	*Italian*	23
Café Pizzaiolo	*Italian/Pizza*	18
Red Hot/Blue	*BBQ*	20
Rocklands	*BBQ*	22
RT's	*Cajun/Creole*	24
Rustico	*Amer.*	21
Taqueria Poblano	*Mex.*	22
Tempo	*French/Italian*	22
Yamazato	*Japanese*	25

ALEXANDRIA (OLD TOWN)

(See map on page 206)

TOP FOOD

Eve	*Amer.*	**C8**	28
Brabo	*Belgian/French*	**C3**	24

Hank's Oyster	*Amer./Seafood*	**C5**	24
Eamonn's	*Irish*	**C7**	23
Grille	*Amer.*	**C6**	23
Vermilion	*Amer.*	**C5**	23
Majestic	*Amer.*	**C6**	23
La Bergerie	*French*	**B9**	23
Bastille	*French*	**A9**	22
Five Guys	*Burgers*	**C5**	22

LISTING

A La Lucia	*Italian*	22
Austin Grill	*Tex-Mex*	15
Bastille	*French*	22
BGR	*Burgers*	21
Bistrot Lafayette	*French*	20
Brabo	*Belgian/French*	24
Columbia Firehse.	*Amer.*	20
Daniel O'Connell	*Pub*	20
Eamonn's	*Irish*	23
☑ Eve	*Amer.*	28
Faccia Luna	*Pizza*	21
☑ Five Guys	*Burgers*	22
Flying Fish	*Seafood*	19
Fontaine Caffe	*French*	24
Geranio	*Italian*	22
Grille	*Amer.*	23
Hank's Oyster	*Amer./Seafood*	24
Hard Times	*Amer.*	19
Jackson 20	*Amer.*	18
La Bergerie	*French*	23
Landini Bros.	*Italian*	22
La Tasca	*Spanish*	17
Le Pain Quotidien	*Bakery/Belgian*	18
Le Refuge	*French*	21
Mai Thai	*Thai*	20
Majestic	*Amer.*	23
Pizzeria Paradiso	*Pizza*	22
RedRocks	*Pizza*	21
Vaso's Kit.	*Greek*	20
Vermilion	*Amer.*	23
NEW Virtue	*Pub*	-

ARLINGTON

Asia Bistro/Zen	*Asian*	20
Bangkok54	*Thai*	23
NEW Bayou Bakery	*Southern*	-
BGR	*Burgers*	21
Bob & Edith's	*Diner*	17
Busboys/Poets	*Amer./Eclectic*	18
Buzz	*Coffee*	22
Cafe Asia	*Asian*	18
Café Assorti	*Asian/E Euro.*	22

Vote at ZAGAT.com

Café Pizzaiolo	*Italian/Pizza*	18
Calif. Tortilla	*Tex-Mex*	18
Capitol City Brew	*Pub*	18
Caribbean Breeze	*Nuevo Latino*	18
Carlyle	*Amer.*	24
Cassatt's Café	*New Zealand*	18
China Gdn.	*Chinese*	17
Chop't	*Amer.*	19
Crisp/Juicy	*Peruvian*	24
Crystal Thai	*Thai*	22
Delhi Dhaba	*Indian*	18
Elevation Burger	*Burgers*	18
El Pollo Rico	*Peruvian*	25
Extra Virgin	*Italian*	17
Fyve	*Amer.*	17
Guajillo	*Mex.*	22
Harry's	*BBQ/Burgers*	19
◪ Jaleo	*Spanish*	22
Kabob Palace	*Mideast.*	24
Kora/Farrah	*Amer./Italian*	15
La Côte d'Or	*French*	24
Layalina	*Lebanese/Syrian*	24
◪ Lebanese Tav.	*Lebanese*	21
Legal Sea Foods	*Seafood*	20
Luna Grill	*Diner/Veg.*	17
NEW Mala Tang	*Chinese*	–
McCormick/Schmick	*Seafood*	20
Me Jana	*Mideast.*	23
Minh's	*Viet.*	24
Moby Dick	*Persian*	21
Morton's	*Steak*	25
Pasha Cafe	*Med.*	20
P. Brennan's	*Pub*	–
P.F. Chang's	*Chinese*	20
Pie-Tanza	*Pizza*	19
Piola	*Italian/Pizza*	21
Pupatella Pizzeria	*Pizza*	–
Ravi Kabob	*Pakistani*	22
◪ Ray's Hell Burger	*Burgers*	26
Red Hot/Blue	*BBQ*	20
Rocklands	*BBQ*	22
Rustico	*Amer.*	21
◪ Ruth's Chris	*Steak*	25
Sauca	*Eclectic*	–
Screwtop Wine	*Amer.*	–
NEW Socci	*Italian*	–
NEW Solar Crêpes	*Crêpes*	–
Sushi Rock	*Japanese*	–
Sweetgreen	*Health*	21
Taqueria/Charrito	*Mex./Salvadoran*	–
Taqueria Poblano	*Mex.*	22

T.H.A.I.	*Thai*	23
Thaiphoon	*Thai*	20
◪ Thai Sq.	*Thai*	26
Tutto Bene	*Italian/S Amer.*	17
Twisted Vines	*Eclectic*	–
Uncle Julio's	*Tex-Mex*	19
Vapiano	*Italian*	18
Village Bistro	*Continental*	23
Willow	*Amer.*	24

CLARENDON

NEW Arlington Rooftop	*Amer.*	–
BGR	*Burgers*	21
Blvd. Woodgrill	*Amer.*	19
Cheesecake	*Amer.*	19
Circa	*Amer.*	17
Delhi Club	*Indian*	24
Eventide	*Amer.*	20
Faccia Luna	*Pizza*	21
Fire Works Pizza	*Pizza*	–
Hard Times	*Amer.*	19
Harry's	*Seafood/Steak*	19
Iota Club/Café	*Amer.*	–
La Tasca	*Spanish*	17
Le Pain Quotidien	*Bakery/Belgian*	18
Liberty Tav.	*Amer.*	21
Lyon Hall	*French/German*	–
Nam-Viet	*Viet.*	21
Northside	*Amer./Coffee*	–
Pete's Apizza	*Pizza*	22
Pho 75	*Viet.*	24
◪ Ray's/Steaks	*Steak*	26
Restaurant 3	*Amer.*	18
Rí Rá	*Pub*	14
Tallula/EatBar	*Amer.*	22
Tandoori Nights	*Indian*	21
Taste/Morocco	*Moroccan*	20

FAIRFAX

Artie's	*Amer.*	23
Bernie's Deli	*Deli*	25
Calif. Tortilla	*Tex-Mex*	18
Cheesecake	*Amer.*	19
China Star	*Chinese*	24
Chutzpah	*Deli*	18
Coastal Flats	*Seafood*	21
NEW Curry Mantra	*Indian*	–
Dogfish Head	*Pub*	18
Dolce Vita	*Italian*	23
Hard Times	*Amer.*	19
Jaipur	*Indian*	23
Minerva	*Indian*	21

Moby Dick | *Persian* 21

NEW Ozzie's Corner | *Italian* -

P.F. Chang's | *Chinese* 20

Red Hot/Blue | *BBQ* 20

Z Ruth's Chris | *Steak* 25

Sakoontra | *Thai* 19

Uncle Julio's | *Tex-Mex* 19

Villa Mozart | *Italian* 24

FALLS CHURCH

Argia's | *Italian* 19

Bamian | *Afghan* 23

Bangkok Golden | *Laotian/Thai* -

Crisp/Juicy | *Peruvian* 24

Dogfish Head | *Pub* 18

Duangrat's | *Thai* 25

Edy's Chicken | *Peruvian* 22

Elevation Burger | *Burgers* 18

El Pike | *S Amer.* -

Fortune | *Chinese* 20

Full Kee (VA) | *Chinese* 22

Haandi | *Indian* 24

Huong Viet | *Viet.* 22

La Caraqueña | *Venezuelan* -

NEW Mad Fox Brew | *Pub* -

Mark's Duck Hse. | *Chinese* 23

Myanmar | *Burmese* 24

Open Kit. | *Eclectic* -

Panjshir | *Afghan* 22

Peking Gourmet | *Chinese* 26

Pho 75 | *Viet.* 24

Pie-Tanza | *Pizza* 19

Pizzeria Orso | *Pizza* -

Pollo Campero | *Peruvian* 18

Present | *Viet.* 23

Rabieng | *Thai* 25

Red Hot/Blue | *BBQ* 20

Tara Thai | *Thai* 19

Z 2941 | *Amer.* 26

X.O. Taste | *Chinese* 22

GREAT FALLS

Z L'Aub./François | *French* 27

MCLEAN

Assaggi | *Italian* 21

Cafe Taj | *Indian* 19

Capri | *Italian* 20

Evo Bistro | *Med.* 23

Kazan | *Turkish* 22

Moby Dick | *Persian* 21

Tachibana | *Japanese* 24

RESTON/HERNDON

American Tap | *Amer.* -

Angeethi | *Indian* 23

Busara | *Thai* 20

Z Clyde's | *Amer.* 19

Counter | *Burgers* 21

El Manantial | *Italian/Spanish* 23

Z Five Guys | *Burgers* 22

Hama Sushi | *Japanese* 19

Il Fornaio | *Italian* 21

Jackson's | *Amer./Seafood* 20

Mamma Lucia | *Italian* 18

M&S Grill | *Seafood/Steak* 19

McCormick/Schmick | *Seafood* 20

Mikaku | *Japanese* -

Minerva | *Indian* 21

Mon Ami Gabi | *French* 19

Morton's | *Steak* 25

Paolo's | *Cal./Italian* 18

PassionFish | *Amer./Seafood* 24

Pho 75 | *Viet.* 24

Pollo Campero | *Peruvian* 18

Red Hot/Blue | *BBQ* 20

Sweetgreen | *Health* 21

Tara Thai | *Thai* 19

Uncle Julio's | *Tex-Mex* 19

Vinifera | *Amer.* 21

Zeffirelli Rist. | *Italian* 22

SPRINGFIELD/
ANNANDALE

A&J | *Chinese* 24

Austin Grill | *Tex-Mex* 15

BGR | *Burgers* 21

Z Five Guys | *Burgers* 22

Hard Times | *Amer.* 19

Z Honey Pig | *Korean* 26

Mike's | *Amer.* 22

Sorak Gdn. | *Korean* 23

Lighthouse/Vit Goel | *Korean* 20

TYSONS CORNER

Bombay Tandoor | *Indian* 22

Busara | *Thai* 20

Cafe Deluxe | *Amer.* 18

Z Capital Grille | *Steak* 25

Cheesecake | *Amer.* 19

Chef Geoff | *Amer.* 19

Chima | *Brazilian* 23

Z Clyde's | *Amer.* 19

Coastal Flats | *Seafood* 21

Da Domenico | *Italian* 21

NEW Diya | *Indian* — |
Fleming's Steak | *Steak* 24 |
NEW Härth | *Amer.* — |
Konami | *Japanese* 20 |
Z Lebanese Tav. | *Lebanese* 21 |
Legal Sea Foods | *Seafood* 20 |
Maggiano's | *Italian* 18 |
Maple Ave | *Amer./Eclectic* 20 |
McCormick/Schmick | *Seafood* 20 |
NEW Michel | *French* — |
Morton's | *Steak* 25 |
Neisha Thai | *Thai* 19 |
Z Palm | *Seafood/Steak* 24 |
Panache | *Med.* 16 |
P.F. Chang's | *Chinese* 20 |
Shamshiry | *Persian* 22 |
Shula's | *Steak* 21 |
Taste/Saigon | *Viet.* 21 |
Wildfire | *Seafood/Steak* 19 |
Woo Lae Oak | *Korean* 21 |

VIENNA/OAKTON/MERRIFIELD

Amma Veg. | *Indian* 22 |
Bazin's/Church | *Amer.* 23 |
Four Sisters | *Viet.* 25 |
Maple Ave | *Amer./Eclectic* 20 |
Plaka Grill | *Greek* 26 |
Z Ruth's Chris | *Steak* 25 |
Sea Pearl | *Amer./Cal.* 20 |
Sweet Ginger | *Asian* 19 |
Sweetwater Tav. | *SW* 21 |
Tara Thai | *Thai* 19 |
Yama | *Japanese* 23 |

Exurban Virginia

BROADLANDS

Z Clyde's | *Amer.* 19 |

CENTREVILLE/MANASSAS/PRINCE WILLIAM COUNTY

Bistro L'Hermitage | *French* 24 |
El Pollo Rico | *Peruvian* 25 |
Z Five Guys | *Burgers* 22 |
Hard Times | *Amer.* 19 |
Red Hot/Blue | *BBQ* 20 |
Sweetwater Tav. | *SW* 21 |

Uncle Julio's | *Tex-Mex* 19 |
Lighthouse/Vit Goel | *Korean* 20 |

CHANTILLY

Eggspectations | *Amer.* 19 |
Minerva | *Indian* 21 |
Thai Basil | *Thai* 22 |

CLIFTON

Z Trummer's | *Amer.* 25 |

LEESBURG/LANSDOWNE

Angeethi | *Indian* 23 |
Cajun Experience | *Cajun/Creole* — |
Eggspectations | *Amer.* 19 |
Fire Works Pizza | *Pizza* — |
Lightfoot | *Amer.* 22 |
Palio of Leesburg | *Italian* — |
Red Hot/Blue | *BBQ* 20 |
Tuscarora Mill | *Amer.* 23 |
Wine Kit. | *Amer.* 21 |

PURCELLVILLE

Magnolias/Mill | *Amer.* 19 |

STERLING/ASHBURN/SOUTH RIDING

American Flatbread | *Pizza* 21 |
Cheesecake | *Amer.* 19 |
NEW Ford's Fish | *Seafood* — |
Hooked | *Seafood* 19 |
NEW Mokomandy | *Cajun/Korean* — |
P.F. Chang's | *Chinese* 20 |
Rangoli | *Indian* — |
Sweetwater Tav. | *SW* 21 |
Taste/Burma | *Burmese* 22 |
Vapiano | *Italian* 18 |

Virginia Countryside

Ashby Inn | *Amer.* 24 |
Blue Rock Inn | *Amer.* — |
Foti's | *Amer.* 26 |
Hunter's Head | *British* 23 |
Z Inn/Little Washington | *Amer.* 29 |
Iron Bridge | *Amer.* 23 |
Z L'Aub. Provençale | *French* 27 |
Rail Stop | *Amer.* 22 |
Rest./Goodstone | *Amer.* — |

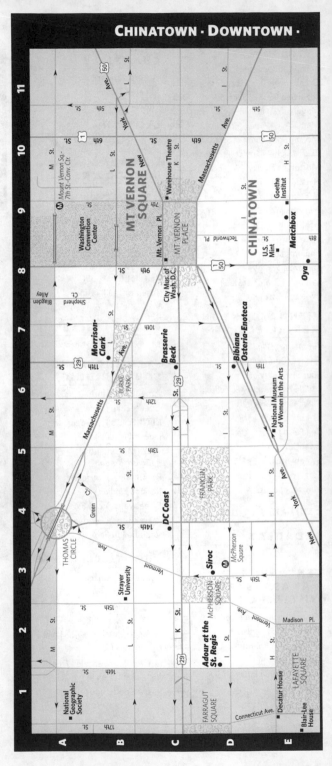

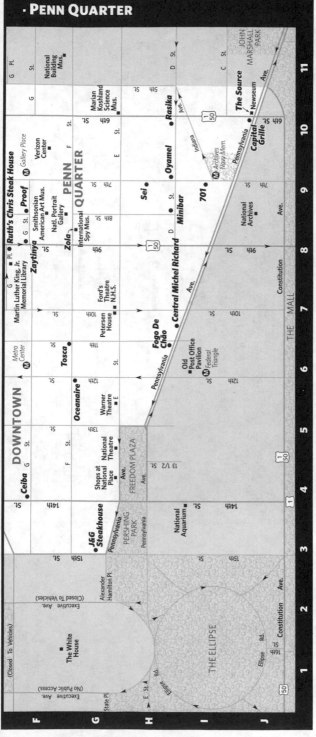

· PENN QUARTER

DOWNTOWN

- Ceiba •
- J&G Steakhouse •
- Tosca •
- Oceanaire •
- Ruth's Chris Steak House •
- Proof •
- Zaytinya •
- Zola •
- Fogo De Chão •
- Central Michel Richard •
- Sei •
- Minibar •
- 701 •
- Oyamel •
- Rasika •
- The Source •
- Capital Grille •

PENN QUARTER

National Building Mus.

Marian Koshland Science Mus.

Newseum

Verizon Center
Gallery Place

Smithsonian American Art Mus.
Natl. Portrait Gallery

International Spy Mus.

Martin Luther King, Jr. Memorial Library

Metro Center

Ford's Theatre N.H.S.

Petersen House

Warner Theatre

National Theatre

Shops at National Place

FREEDOM PLAZA

National Aquarium

Old Post Office Pavilion
Federal Triangle

National Archives

Archives Navy Mem.

JOHN MARSHALL PARK

THE MALL

Constitution Ave.

PERSHING PARK

THE ELLIPSE

The White House
(No Public Access)

Executive Ave. (Closed To Vehicles)

Alexander Hamilton Pl.

Ellipse Rd.

State Pl.

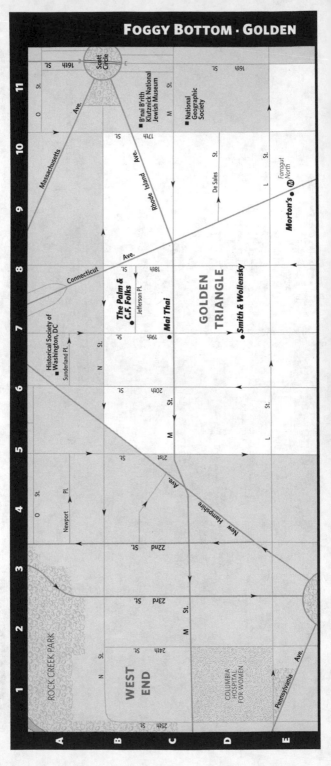

FOGGY BOTTOM · GOLDEN

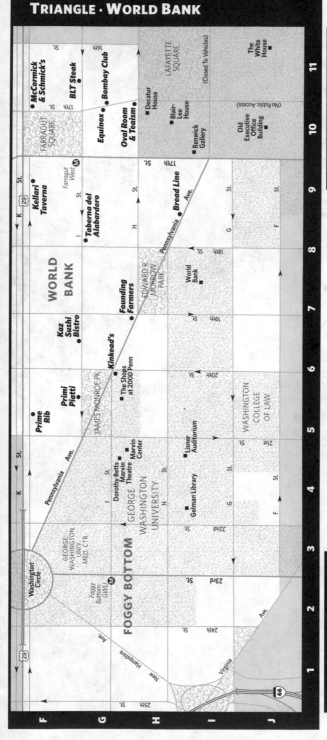

McCormick & Schmick's
BLT Steak
Bombay Club
Equinox
Oval Room & Tealism
Kellari Taverna
Taberna del Alabardero
Bread Line
Founding Farmers
Kaz Sushi Bistro
Kinkead's
Primi Piatti
Prime Rib

LAFAYETTE SQUARE
(Closed To Vehicles)
The White House
Decatur House
Blair-Lee House
Renwick Gallery
(No Public Access)
Old Executive Office Building

FARRAGUT SQUARE
Farragut West

WORLD BANK
EDWARD R. MURROW PARK
World Bank

JAMES MONROE PK.
The Shops at 2000 Penn

WASHINGTON COLLEGE OF LAW

Lisner Auditorium
Marvin Center
Dorothy Betts Marvin Theatre
GEORGE WASHINGTON UNIVERSITY
Gelman Library

GEORGE WASHINGTON UNIV. MED. CTR.

Washington Circle

Foggy Bottom-GWU

FOGGY BOTTOM

Pennsylvania Ave.
New Hampshire Ave.
Virginia Ave.

K St.
16th St.
17th St.
17th St.
Pennsylvania Ave.
18th St.
19th St.
20th St.
21st St.
H St.
G St.
F St.
22nd St.
23rd St.
24th St.
25th St.

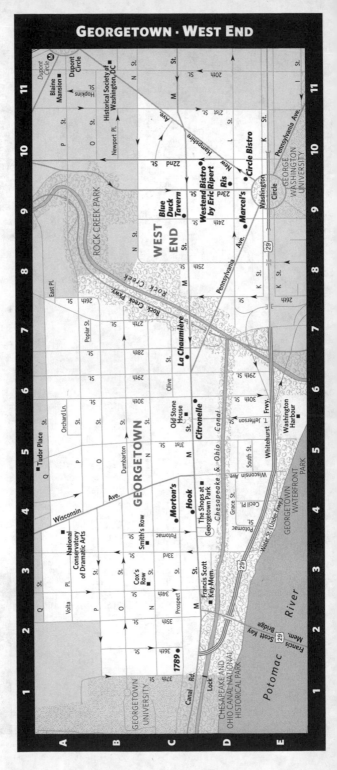

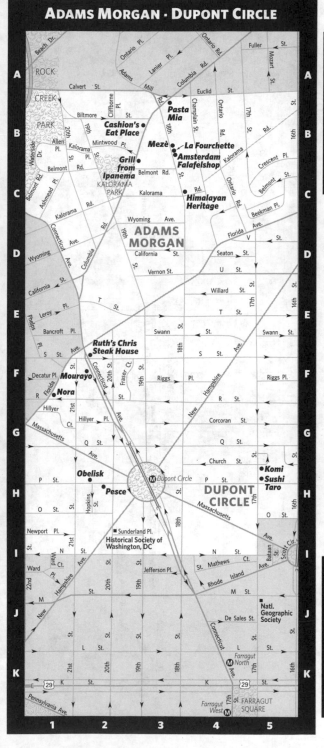

ADAMS MORGAN · DUPONT CIRCLE

Beach Dr.
ROCK
CREEK
PARK
Ontario Pl.
Lanier Pl.
Adams Mill
Calvert St.
Biltmore St.
Cliffborne Pl.
20th
19th
Allen Pl.
Kalorama
Belmont Rd.
Waterside Dr.
Ashmead Pl.
Belmont Rd.
KALORAMA PARK
Kalorama Rd.
Wyoming Ave.
Connecticut Ave.
Columbia Rd.
Wyoming St.
California St.
Leroy Pl.
Bancroft Pl.
Phillips Pl.
S St.
Ave.
21st St.
Hillyer Ct.
Hillyer Pl.
Massachusetts Ave.
Decatur Pl.
Florida
R St.
Fuller St.
Mozart St.
Ontario Rd.
Columbia Rd.
Euclid St.
Champlain St.
18th
17th St.
16th St.
Ontario Rd.
Kalorama Rd.
Crescent Pl.
Belmont St.
Beekman Pl.
Florida Ave.
Seaton St.
U St.
Vernon St.
Willard St.
T St.
Swann St.
S St.
Riggs Pl.
New Hampshire Ave.
Corcoran St.
Q St.
Church St.
P St.
Massachusetts Ave.
O St.
Ward Ct.
N St.
Jefferson Pl.
St. Mathews Ct.
Rhode Island Ave.
M St.
De Sales St.
L St.
Farragut North
K St.
Pennsylvania Ave.
Farragut West
FARRAGUT SQUARE

ADAMS MORGAN

DUPONT CIRCLE

- Pasta Mia
- Cashion's Eat Place
- Mezè
- La Fourchette
- Amsterdam Falafelshop
- Grill from Ipanema
- Himalayan Heritage
- Ruth's Chris Steak House
- Mourayo
- Nora
- Obelisk
- Pesce
- Komi
- Sushi Taro
- M Dupont Circle
- Sunderland Pl.
- Historical Society of Washington, DC
- Natl. Geographic Society

Dupont Circle

29 · Pennsylvania Ave.
29

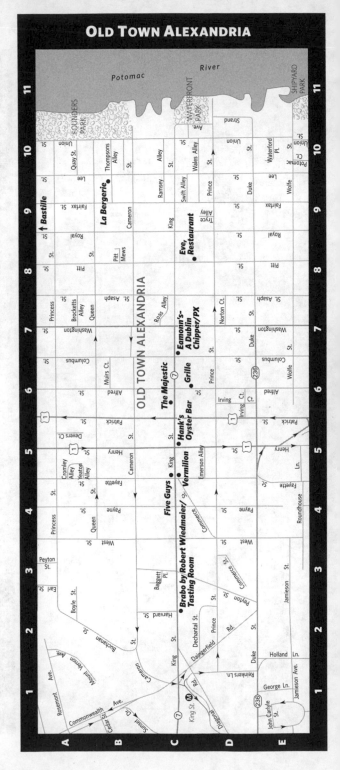

OLD TOWN ALEXANDRIA

Special Features

Listings cover the best in each category and include names, locations and Food ratings. Multi-location restaurants' features may vary by branch.

ADDITIONS

(Properties added since the last edition of the book)

America Eats | **Penn Qtr**
American Ice | **U St**
American Tap | **multi.**
Arlington Rooftop | **Clarendon**
Atlas Rm. | **Atlas Dist**
Ba Bay | **Cap Hill**
Bangkok Golden | **Falls Ch**
Bayou | **West End**
Bayou Bakery | **Arlington**
Big Cheese | **Location Varies**
Bistro LaZeez | **Bethesda**
Black Fox | **Dupont Cir**
Black Squirrel | **Adams Mor**
Bookhill Bistro | **Georgetown**
Bourbon | **multi.**   16
Breadsoda | **Glover Pk**
Capitol City Brew | **multi.**   18
CapMac | **Location Varies**
Carbon Peruvian | **Rockville**
Carmine's | **Penn Qtr**
Casa Nonna | **Dupont Cir**
Cava Mezze Grill | **Bethesda**
Cities | **Gldn Triangle**
Cuba Libre | **Penn Qtr**
Curry Mantra | **Fairfax**
DC-3 | **Cap Hill**
District/Pi | **Location Varies**
Diya | **Vienna**
Dubliner | **Cap Hill**   16
Eat Wonky | **Location Varies**
El Centro | **Logan Cir**
Estadio | **Logan Cir**
Fast Gourmet | **U St**
Fiola | **Penn Qtr**
Fiorella | **Nat'l Harbor**
Food Wine | **Bethesda**
Ford's Fish | **Ashburn**
Freddy's Lobster | **Bethesda**
Fruit Bat | **Atlas Dist**
Galileo III | **D'town**
Härth | **McLean**
Heritage Asia | **Glover Pk**
Hill Country | **Penn Qtr**
Hot 'N Juicy | **Woodley Pk**

Iota Club/Café | **Clarendon**
Kloby's Smokehse. | **Laurel**
Lincoln | **D'town**
Local 16 | **U St**   13
Luke's Lobster | **Penn Qtr**
Mad Fox Brew | **Falls Ch**
Mala Tang | **Arlington**
Medium Rare | **Cleve Pk**
Meridian | **Columbia Hts**
Merzi | **Penn Qtr**
Michel | **McLean**
Mixx | **D'town**
Mokomandy | **Sterling**
Mussel Bar | **Bethesda**
Nellie's | **U St**   17
Newton's | **Bethesda**
Next Stage | **SW**
Ozzie's Corner | **Fairfax**
Panas | **Dupont Cir**
Patty Boom Boom | **U St**
Paul | **Penn Qtr**
Pho DC | **Chinatown**
Pizzeria Da Marco | **Bethesda**
P.J. Clarke's | **D'town**
PORC | **Location Varies**
Queen Vic | **Atlas Dist**
Red Hook | **Location Varies**
Redline | **Chinatown**
Ripple | **Cleve Pk**
Rivers/Watergate | **Foggy Bottom**
Russia Hse. | **Dupont Cir**   15
Rustik | **Bloomingdale**
Sax | **D'town**
Senart's Oyster | **Cap Hill**
Serendipity 3 | **Georgetown**
Shake Shack | **multi.**
Smith Commons | **Atlas Dist**
Socci | **Arlington**
Solar Crêpes | **Arlington**
Standard | **Logan Cir**
TaKorean | **Location Varies**
Teak Wood | **Logan Cir**
Toki | **Atlas Dist**
Uniontown B&G | **Anacostia**
Upper Crust | **World Bank**
Vento | **Dupont Cir**

Virtue | **Alexandria**	-⌐
Watershed | **NoMa**	-⌐
We, The Pizza | **Cap Hill**	-⌐
Wild Tomato | **Potomac**	-⌐

BREAKFAST

(See also Hotel Dining)

Ben's Chili | **U St**	22
Bob & Edith's | **Arlington**	17
Bread Line | **World Bank**	22
Diner | **Adams Mor**	17
Florida Ave. Grill | **U St**	20
Johnny's | **Cap Hill**	20
Le Pain Quotidien | **multi.**	18
McCormick/Schmick | **multi.**	20
🅩 Old Ebbitt | **D'town**	20
Parkway Deli | **Silver Spring**	19
🆕 Paul | **Penn Qtr**	-⌐
Pho 75 | **multi.**	24
Teaism | **multi.**	20

BRUNCH

Ardeo/Bardeo | **Cleve Pk**	21
Birch/Barley | **Logan Cir**	22
Bistro Bis | **Cap Hill**	25
Black Mkt. | **Garrett Pk**	25
🅩 Blue Duck | **West End**	26
Bombay Club | **Gldn Triangle**	24
Café Bonaparte | **Georgetown**	20
Cafe Deluxe | **multi.**	18
Café Saint-Ex | **Logan Cir**	20
Carlyle | **Arlington**	24
Cashion's Eat | **Adams Mor**	24
Chef Geoff | **multi.**	19
🅩 Clyde's | **multi.**	19
Crème | **U St**	23
Et Voila | **Palisades**	24
Evening Star | **Alexandria**	22
Georgia Brown | **D'town**	22
Hank's Oyster | **Dupont Cir**	24
Old Angler's | **Potomac**	19
🅩 Old Ebbitt | **D'town**	20
Perrys | **Adams Mor**	19
Poste Moderne | **Penn Qtr**	21
Rabieng | **Falls Ch**	25
Ris | **West End**	23
Roof Terr. | **Foggy Bottom**	15
Sequoia | **Georgetown**	15
Tabard Inn | **Dupont Cir**	24

BUSINESS DINING

🅩 Acadiana | **Mt. Vernon Sq**	23
Acqua al 2 | **Cap Hill**	-⌐

🅩 Adour/St. Regis | **D'town**	24
Againn | **D'town**	19
🆕 America Eats | **Penn Qtr**	-⌐
Art & Soul | **Cap Hill**	21
Artie's | **Fairfax**	23
Assaggi | **McLean**	21
Bamian | **Falls Ch**	23
Bazin's/Church | **Vienna**	23
Bibiana | **D'town**	23
Bistro Bis | **Cap Hill**	25
Bistro Cacao | **Cap Hill**	-⌐
Bistro Provence | **Bethesda**	-⌐
🅩 BlackSalt | **Palisades**	26
🅩 BLT Steak | **Gldn Triangle**	25
🅩 Blue Duck | **West End**	26
Bobby Van's | **D'town**	21
Bombay Club | **Gldn Triangle**	24
Bombay Tandoor | **Vienna**	22
Bond 45 | **Nat'l Harbor**	-⌐
🆕 Bookhill Bistro | **Georgetown**	-⌐
Bourbon Steak | **Georgetown**	23
Brabo | **Alexandria**	24
🅩 Brass. Beck | **D'town**	25
Buddha-Bar | **Mt. Vernon Sq**	-⌐
Café du Parc | **D'town**	22
Café Dupont | **Dupont Cir**	-⌐
🅩 Capital Grille | **multi.**	25
Carlyle | **Arlington**	24
🆕 Carmine's | **Penn Qtr**	-⌐
🆕 Casa Nonna | **Dupont Cir**	-⌐
Caucus Rm. | **Penn Qtr**	21
Ceiba | **D'town**	23
🅩 Central Michel | **Penn Qtr**	26
Charlie Palmer | **Cap Hill**	25
Chef Geoff | **Vienna**	19
Chesapeake Rm. | **Cap Hill**	-⌐
Chima | **Vienna**	23
🅩 Citronelle | **Georgetown**	28
🅩 CityZen | **SW**	28
🅩 Clyde's | **multi.**	19
🅩 Corduroy | **Mt. Vernon Sq**	27
🆕 Cuba Libre | **Penn Qtr**	-⌐
DC Coast | **D'town**	23
🆕 Diya | **Vienna**	-⌐
Eatonville | **U St**	19
8407 Kit. | **Silver Spring**	-⌐
Equinox | **Gldn Triangle**	25
🆕 Estadio | **Logan Cir**	-⌐
🅩 Eve | **Alexandria**	28
Eventide | **Clarendon**	20
Evo Bistro | **McLean**	23

Extra Virgin | **Arlington**	17
Finn/Porter | **multi.**	17
NEW Fiola | **Penn Qtr**	–
NEW Fiorella | **Nat'l Harbor**	–
Fire Works Pizza | **Clarendon**	–
Fogo De Chão | **D'town**	24
NEW Ford's Fish | **Ashburn**	–
Z Founding Farmers | **World Bank**	21
Four Sisters | **Merrifield**	25
NEW Galileo III | **D'town**	–
Georgia Brown | **D'town**	22
Grille | **Alexandria**	23
Hank's Oyster | **Dupont Cir**	24
Hank's Tav. | **Hyattsville**	22
Harry's | **multi.**	19
NEW Härth | **McLean**	–
NEW Heritage Asia | **Glover Pk**	–
NEW Hill Country | **Penn Qtr**	–
Hook | **Georgetown**	23
Hudson | **West End**	17
Hunan Dynasty | **Cap Hill**	17
iCi | **D'town**	23
Il Fornaio | **Reston**	21
I Ricchi | **Dupont Cir**	24
Jackson's | **Reston**	20
Jackson 20 | **Alexandria**	18
J&G Steak | **D'town**	25
Johnny's | **Cap Hill**	20
Kaz Sushi | **World Bank**	25
Kellari Taverna | **Gldn Triangle**	22
Z Kinkead's | **Foggy Bottom**	26
Konami | **Vienna**	20
Kushi | **Mt. Vernon Sq**	–
Lafayette Rm. | **Gldn Triangle**	25
Z Lebanese Tav. | **Bethesda**	21
Lia's | **Chevy Chase**	21
Lima | **D'town**	20
NEW Lincoln | **D'town**	–
Maddy's | **Dupont Cir**	–
NEW Mad Fox Brew | **Falls Ch**	–
Magnolias/Mill | **Purcellville**	19
Mai Thai | **Gldn Triangle**	20
NEW Mala Tang | **Arlington**	–
M&S Grill | **D'town**	19
Mandu | **Mt. Vernon Sq**	21
Maple Ave | **Vienna**	20
Z Marcel's | **West End**	29
Martin's Tav. | **Georgetown**	20
Masala Art | **Upper NW**	26
Matchbox | **Rockville**	23
McCormick/Schmick | **multi.**	20
NEW Medium Rare | **Cleve Pk**	–
NEW Michel | **McLean**	–
Mon Ami Gabi | **Reston**	19
Monocle | **Cap Hill**	14
Morton's | **multi.**	25
NEW Mussel Bar | **Bethesda**	–
Nage | **Scott Cir**	22
NEW Newton's | **Bethesda**	–
Occidental | **D'town**	22
Oceanaire | **D'town**	24
Z Old Ebbitt | **D'town**	20
Oval Rm. | **Gldn Triangle**	24
Oyamel | **Penn Qtr**	24
NEW Ozzie's Corner | **Fairfax**	–
Palio of Leesburg | **Leesburg**	–
Z Palm | **multi.**	24
PassionFish | **Reston**	24
NEW P.J. Clarke's | **D'town**	–
Plume | **D'town**	26
Poste Moderne | **Penn Qtr**	21
Posto | **Logan Cir**	21
Potenza | **D'town**	20
Present | **Falls Ch**	23
Z Prime Rib | **Gldn Triangle**	27
PS 7's | **Penn Qtr**	22
Rangoli | **S Riding**	–
Z Ray's/Steaks | **Clarendon**	26
Ray's/East River | **NE**	–
Redwood | **Bethesda**	17
Restaurant 3 | **Clarendon**	18
Ris | **West End**	23
NEW Rivers/Watergate | **Foggy Bottom**	–
Rosa Mexicano | **Nat'l Harbor**	20
Rustico | **Arlington**	21
Z Ruth's Chris | **multi.**	25
Sabai | **Germantown**	–
Sea Pearl | **Merrifield**	20
Sei | **Penn Qtr**	23
NEW Senart's Oyster | **Cap Hill**	–
NEW Serendipity 3 | **Georgetown**	–
701 | **Penn Qtr**	23
Sichuan Pavilion | **Rockville**	23
Siroc | **D'town**	24
Smith/Wollensky | **Gldn Triangle**	22
NEW Socci | **Arlington**	–
Source | **Penn Qtr**	25
Sou'Wester | **SW**	18
Spice Xing | **Rockville**	20
Sushi Damo | **Rockville**	24

Vote at ZAGAT.com

NEW Newton's | **Bethesda**	⌐
Plume | **D'town**	26
Poste Moderne | **Penn Qtr**	21
ⓩ Tosca | **Penn Qtr**	27
ⓩ 2941 | **Falls Ch**	26
ⓩ Vidalia | **Dupont Cir**	24
Westend Bistro | **West End**	21

CHILD-FRIENDLY

(Alternatives to the usual fast-food places; * children's menu available)

15 Ria* | **Scott Cir**	17
Artie's* | **Fairfax**	23
Arucola | **Upper NW**	19
Austin Grill* | **multi.**	15
Black Mkt.* | **Garrett Pk**	25
Buzz | **Alexandria**	22
Cactus Cantina* | **Cleve Pk**	18
Cafe Deluxe* | **multi.**	18
Calif. Tortilla* | **multi.**	18
Carlyle | **Arlington**	24
Chef Geoff* | **multi.**	19
ⓩ Clyde's* | **multi.**	19
Coastal Flats* | **Fairfax**	21
Comet Ping Pong | **Upper NW**	20
Eamonn's* | **Alexandria**	23
Elevation Burger | **Falls Ch**	18
El Gavilan | **Silver Spring**	⌐
El Golfo* | **Silver Spring**	21
Ella's Pizza | **Penn Qtr**	20
Guardado's* | **Bethesda**	24
Kabob Palace | **Arlington**	24
ⓩ L'Aub./François* | **Grt Falls**	27
ⓩ Lebanese Tav.* | **multi.**	21
Legal Sea Foods* | **multi.**	20
Maggiano's* | **multi.**	18
Mark's Kit.* | **Takoma Pk**	17
Matuba | **Bethesda**	21
Minerva | **multi.**	21
Mi Rancho | **multi.**	18
Old Glory | **Georgetown**	17
Pete's Apizza* | **Columbia Hts**	22
P.F. Chang's | **multi.**	20
Pizzeria Paradiso | **Dupont Cir**	22
Rabieng | **Falls Ch**	25
Red Hot/Blue* | **multi.**	20
Samantha's | **Silver Spring**	23
Sweetwater Tav.* | **multi.**	21
Taqueria Poblano* | **multi.**	22
Tara Thai* | **multi.**	19
ⓩ 2 Amys | **Cleve Pk**	25
Uncle Julio's* | **multi.**	19

NEW Virtue | **Alexandria**	⌐
NEW Wild Tomato | **Potomac**	⌐

DESSERT SPECIALISTS

ⓩ Acadiana | **Mt. Vernon Sq**	23
ⓩ Adour/St. Regis | **D'town**	24
Black Mkt. | **Garrett Pk**	25
ⓩ BlackSalt | **Palisades**	26
Black's Bar | **Bethesda**	23
ⓩ Blue Duck | **West End**	26
Bread Line | **World Bank**	22
Buzz | **multi.**	22
Carlyle | **Arlington**	24
ⓩ Central Michel | **Penn Qtr**	26
Cheesecake | **multi.**	19
ⓩ Citronelle | **Georgetown**	28
ⓩ CityZen | **SW**	28
DC Coast | **D'town**	23
Equinox | **Gldn Triangle**	25
ⓩ Eve | **Alexandria**	28
NEW Fiola | **Penn Qtr**	⌐
Hook | **Georgetown**	23
iCi | **D'town**	23
ⓩ Inn/Little Washington | **Washington**	29
ⓩ Jaleo | **multi.**	22
Johnny's | **Cap Hill**	20
ⓩ Kinkead's | **Foggy Bottom**	26
Leopold's Kafe | **Georgetown**	22
Le Pain Quotidien | **multi.**	18
Majestic | **Alexandria**	23
NEW Michel | **McLean**	⌐
Northside | **Clarendon**	⌐
ⓩ Palena | **Cleve Pk**	28
NEW Paul | **Penn Qtr**	⌐
Praline | **Bethesda**	19
Ris | **West End**	23
NEW Serendipity 3 | **Georgetown**	⌐
ⓩ 1789 | **Georgetown**	25
ⓩ 2941 | **Falls Ch**	26
Willow | **Arlington**	24
ⓩ Zaytinya | **Penn Qtr**	25

ENTERTAINMENT

(Call for days and times of performances)

American Tap | piano | **Bethesda**	⌐
Banana Café | piano | **Cap Hill**	18
NEW Bayou | live music | **West End**	⌐
Black Fox | varies | **Dupont Cir**	⌐

Bombay Club | piano | **Gldn Triangle**	24
Cafe Asia | DJ | **Rosslyn**	18
Café Saint-Ex | DJ | **Logan Cir**	20
Coeur de Lion | piano/vocal | **D'town**	20
Dukem | Ethiopian music | **U St**	24
Evening Star | live music | **Alexandria**	22
Georgia Brown | jazz | **D'town**	22
🆕 Hill Country | live music | **Penn Qtr**	-
🄯 Kinkead's | piano | **Foggy Bottom**	26
Neyla | belly dancing | **Georgetown**	22
Perrys | drag performers | **Adams Mor**	19
🆕 Sax | varies | **D'town**	-
701 | jazz/piano | **Penn Qtr**	23
Slaviya Cafe | varies | **Adams Mor**	-
Taste/Morocco | belly dancing | **Clarendon**	20
Tutto Bene | varies | **Arlington**	17

FIREPLACES

15 Ria | **Scott Cir**	17
Al Tiramisu | **Dupont Cir**	24
American Tap | **Bethesda**	-
Bastille | **Alexandria**	22
Bistro Bis | **Cap Hill**	25
Bistro D'Oc | **D'town**	21
Bourbon Steak | **Georgetown**	23
Chef Geoff | **Vienna**	19
Circle Bistro | **West End**	21
🄯 Clyde's | **multi.**	19
Columbia Firehse. | **Alexandria**	20
Comus Inn | **Dickerson**	21
Daniel O'Connell | **Alexandria**	20
Eamonn's | **Alexandria**	23
Equinox | **Gldn Triangle**	25
🄯 Eve | **Alexandria**	28
Fadó | **Chinatown**	17
Finn/Porter | **D'town**	17
Fogo De Chão | **D'town**	24
Foti's | **Culpeper**	26
Fyve | **Arlington**	17
Geranio | **Alexandria**	22
Harry's | **Clarendon**	19
Hunter's Head | **Upperville**	23
Il Fornaio | **Reston**	21
🄯 Inn/Little Washington | **Washington**	29

I Ricchi | **Dupont Cir**	24
Irish Inn/Glen Echo | **Glen Echo**	18
La Chaumière | **Georgetown**	24
La Ferme | **Chevy Chase**	22
🄯 L'Aub./François | **Grt Falls**	27
🄯 L'Aub. Provençale | **Boyce**	27
Lia's | **Chevy Chase**	21
Lightfoot | **Leesburg**	22
Little Fountain | **Adams Mor**	24
Magnolias/Mill | **Purcellville**	19
Matisse | **Upper NW**	23
Monocle | **Cap Hill**	14
Morrison-Clark | **D'town**	23
Mrs. K's | **Silver Spring**	22
Old Angler's | **Potomac**	19
🄯 Oya | **Penn Qtr**	23
Petits Plats | **Woodley Pk**	22
Plume | **D'town**	26
Redwood | **Bethesda**	17
Restaurant 3 | **Clarendon**	18
Rustico | **Alexandria**	21
Sea Catch | **Georgetown**	21
🄯 1789 | **Georgetown**	25
Sonoma | **Cap Hill**	20
Tabard Inn | **Dupont Cir**	24
Tavira | **Chevy Chase**	24
🄯 Trummer's | **Clifton**	25
Tuscarora Mill | **Leesburg**	23
🄯 2941 | **Falls Ch**	26
Vapiano | **multi.**	18
Woo Lae Oak | **Vienna**	21
🄯 Zaytinya | **Penn Qtr**	25

FOOD TRUCKS

🆕 Big Cheese | **Location Varies**	-
🆕 CapMac | **Location Varies**	-
DC Slices | **Location Varies**	-
🆕 District/Pi | **Location Varies**	-
🆕 Eat Wonky | **Location Varies**	-
El Floridano | **Location Varies**	-
Fojol Bros. | **Location Varies**	-
L St. Vending | **D'town**	-
Maple Ave | **Vienna**	20
Pedro & Vinny | **D'town**	-
🆕 PORC | **Location Varies**	-
🆕 Red Hook | **Location Varies**	-
Sauca | **Location Varies**	-
🆕 Solar Crêpes | **Arlington**	-

Sweetgreen | multi.   21
NEW TaKorean | -
   Location Varies

HISTORIC PLACES

(Year opened; * building)

1750 | Hunter's Head* | 23
   Upperville
1753 | L'Aub. Provençale* | 27
   Boyce
1786 | Virtue* | **Alexandria**   -
1790 | Eve* | **Alexandria**   28
1800 | Corduroy* | 27
   Mt. Vernon Sq
1829 | Ashby Inn* | **Paris**   24
1841 | Poste Moderne* | 21
   Penn Qtr
1860 | Old Angler's* | **Potomac**   19
1862 | Comus Inn* | **Dickerson**   21
1864 | Morrison-Clark* | **D'town**   23
1869 | Trummer's* | **Clifton**   25
1876 | District ChopHse.* | 18
   Penn Qtr
1883 | Columbia Firehse.* | 20
   Alexandria
1885 | Monocle* | **Cap Hill**   14
1887 | Tabard Inn* | **Dupont Cir**   24
1888 | Lightfoot* | **Leesburg**   22
1890 | Inn/Little Washington* | 29
   Washington
1890 | La Bergerie* | **Alexandria** 23
1890 | Nora* | **Dupont Cir**   26
1897 | Irish Inn/Glen Echo* | 18
   Glen Echo
1900 | Standard* | **Logan Cir**   -
1901 | Bookhill Bistro* | -
   Georgetown
1904 | Occidental* | **D'town**   22
1905 | Magnolias/Mill* | 19
   Purcellville
1907 | Liberty Tav.* | **Clarendon** 21
1908 | B. Smith* | **Cap Hill**   20
1909 | Ben's Chili* | **U St**   22
1920 | Matchbox* | **Cap Hill**   23
1925 | Eventide* | **Clarendon**   20
1930 | Mrs. K's | **Silver Spring**   22
1932 | Fahrenheit* | 22
   Georgetown
1932 | Majestic* | **Alexandria**   23
1933 | Martin's Tav. | 20
   Georgetown
1944 | Florida Ave. Grill | **U St** 20
1946 | Lyon Hall* | **Clarendon**   -
1954 | L'Aub./François | 27
   Grt Falls

HOTEL DINING

Ashby Inn
   Ashby Inn | **Paris**   24
Beacon Hotel
   Beacon B&G | **Scott Cir**   17
Blue Rock Inn
   Blue Rock Inn | **Sperryville**   -
Donovan House
   Zentan | **D'town**   21
DoubleTree Hotel
   15 Ria | **Scott Cir**   17
Dupont Circle Hotel
   Café Dupont | **Dupont Cir**   -
Embassy Suites
   Finn/Porter | **D'town**   17
Fairfax at Embassy Row
   Z Jockey Club | **Dupont Cir** 22
Fairmont Hotel
   Juniper | **West End**   21
Four Seasons Hotel
   Bourbon Steak | **Georgetown**   23
Gaylord National Hotel
   Old Hickory | **Nat'l Harbor**   23
George, Hotel
   Bistro Bis | **Cap Hill**   25
Georgetown Hill Inn
   Cafe Divan | **Glover Pk**   22
George Washington Univ. Inn
   Notti Bianche | 20
   Foggy Bottom
Goodstone Inn & Estate
   Rest./Goodstone | **Mid'burg**   -
Hay-Adams, The
   Lafayette Rm. | **Gldn Triangle** 25
Henley Park Hotel
   Coeur de Lion | **D'town**   20
Hilton Alexandria
   Finn/Porter | **Alexandria**   17
Hilton Garden Inn
   NEW Watershed | **NoMa**   -
Hilton McLean Tysons Corner
   NEW Härth | **McLean**   -
Hilton Silver Springs
   Sergio Rist. | **Silver Spring** 24
Hyatt Regency
   Morton's | **Bethesda**   25
Inn at Little Washington
   Z Inn/Little Washington | 29
   Washington
Latham Hotel
   Z Citronelle | **Georgetown** 28

L'Auberge Provençale
  🅩 L'Aub. Provençale | **Boyce**   27

Legacy Hotel
  Phillips | **Rockville**   15

Liason Capitol Hill
  Art & Soul | **Cap Hill**   21

Lorien Hotel & Spa
  Brabo | **Alexandria**   24

Mandarin Oriental
  🅩 CityZen | **SW**   28
  Sou'Wester | **SW**   18

Marriott Court. Embassy Row
  Nage | **Scott Cir**   22

Marriott Tysons Corner
  Shula's | **Vienna**   21

Monaco, Hotel
  Jackson 20 | **Alexandria**   18
  Poste Moderne | **Penn Qtr**   21

Morrison-Clark Inn
  Morrison-Clark | **D'town**   23

Morrison House
  Grille | **Alexandria**   23

One Washington Circle Hotel
  Circle Bistro | **West End**   21

Palomar, Hotel
  Urbana | **Dupont Cir**   22

Park Hyatt
  🅩 Blue Duck | **West End**   26

Phoenix Park Hotel
  Dubliner | **Cap Hill**   16

Renaissance Arlington Capital
  View
  NEW Socci | **Arlington**   ─

Renaissance Hotel
  NEW Mixx | **D'town**   ─

Ritz-Carlton Georgetown
  Fahrenheit | **Georgetown**   22

Ritz-Carlton Pentagon City
  Fyve | **Arlington**   17

Ritz-Carlton Tysons Corner
  NEW Michel | **McLean**   ─

Ritz-Carlton, Washington DC
  Westend Bistro | **West End**   21

River Inn
  Dish/Drinks | **Foggy Bottom**   19

Sofitel Lafayette Sq.
  iCi | **D'town**   23

St. Regis
  🅩 Adour/St. Regis | **D'town**   24

Tabard Inn
  Tabard Inn | **Dupont Cir**   24

Westin Reston Heights
  Vinifera | **Reston**   21

W Hotel
  J&G Steak | **D'town**   25

Willard InterContinental
  Café du Parc | **D'town**   22

LATE DINING

(Weekday closing hour)

NEW American Ice | 2 AM | **U St**   ─

American Tap | varies | **multi.**   ─

🅩 Amsterdam Falafel | varies | **Adams Mor**   26

Austin Grill | varies | **Silver Spring**   15

Ben's Chili | 2 AM | **U St**   22

Ben's Next Door | 1:30 AM | **U St**   20

Bistro Français | 3 AM | **Georgetown**   19

Bistro La Bonne | 12 AM | **U St**   ─

Bistrot du Coin | 12 AM | **Dupont Cir**   21

Black Fox | varies | **Dupont Cir**   ─

Black Squirrel | 2 AM | **Adams Mor**   ─

Bob & Edith's | 24 hrs. | **Arlington**   17

Bourbon | 2 AM | **multi.**   16

Breadsoda | 12 AM | **Glover Pk**   ─

Buddha-Bar | 12 AM | **Mt. Vernon Sq**   ─

Busboys/Poets | 12 AM | **multi.**   18

Buzz | 12 AM | **Alexandria**   22

Cafe Citron | 2 AM | **Dupont Cir**   14

Capitol City Brew | 12 AM | **multi.**   18

Chesapeake Rm. | 1 AM | **Cap Hill**   ─

Circa | varies | **Dupont Cir**   17

🅩 Clyde's | varies | **multi.**   19

Daniel O'Connell | 1 AM | **Alexandria**   20

Darlington Hse. | 12 AM | **Dupont Cir**   20

Diner | 24 hrs. | **Adams Mor**   17

Dubliner | 1:30 AM | **Cap Hill**   16

Dukem | 1 AM | **U St**   24

Eat First | 2 AM | **Chinatown**   20

Finn/Porter | 12 AM | **Alexandria**   17

Flying Fish | 12 AM | **Alexandria**   19

Full Kee (VA) | varies | **Falls Ch**   22

Full Kee (DC)	varies	**Chinatown**	22
Hard Times	varies	**multi.**	19
Hollywood E.	12 AM	**Wheaton**	-
Z Honey Pig	24 hrs.	**Annandale**	26
Hudson	12 AM	**West End**	17
Irene's Pupusas	12 AM	**Wheaton**	20
Kabob N Karahi	12 AM	**Silver Spring**	-
Kramerbooks	1:30 AM	**Dupont Cir**	17
Lyon Hall	2 AM	**Clarendon**	-
Maddy's	1 AM	**Dupont Cir**	-
Mandu	1:30 AM	**Mt. Vernon Sq**	21
Marvin	12 AM	**U St**	21
Masa 14	1 AM	**Logan Cir**	23
Maté	12:30 AM	**Georgetown**	25
NEW Meridian	12 AM	**Columbia Hts**	-
Mezè	1:30 AM	**Adams Mor**	21
NEW Mixx	12:30 AM	**D'town**	-
Nellie's	12 AM	**U St**	17
New Fortune	1 AM	**Gaith'burg**	22
New Kam	12 AM	**Wheaton**	24
Z Old Ebbitt	1 AM	**D'town**	20
Open City	1:30 AM	**Woodley Pk**	18
Passenger	1:30 AM	**Mt. Vernon Sq**	-
Patty Boom Boom	varies	**U St**	-
P. Brennan's	12 AM	**Arlington**	-
NEW P.J. Clarke's	1 AM	**D'town**	-
Ravi Kabob	1 AM	**Arlington**	22
NEW Redline	1 AM	**Chinatown**	-
RedRocks	12 AM	**multi.**	21
Russia Hse.	varies	**Dupont Cir**	15
NEW Sax	varies	**D'town**	-
Sei	12 AM	**Penn Qtr**	23
NEW Serendipity 3	varies	**Georgetown**	-
NEW Standard	1 AM	**Logan Cir**	-
Star/Shamrock	12 AM	**Atlas Dist**	-
Stoney's Lounge	12:45 AM	**Logan Cir**	18
Tabaq Bistro	12 AM	**U St**	20
Tryst	1:30 AM	**Adams Mor**	19

Thai Tanic	varies	**Logan Cir**	23
Vinoteca	12 AM	**U St**	21
X.O. Taste	2 AM	**Falls Ch**	22

MEET FOR A DRINK

Z Acadiana	**Mt. Vernon Sq**	23
Z Adour/St. Regis	**D'town**	24
Againn	**D'town**	19
Agora	**Dupont Cir**	-
NEW America Eats	**Penn Qtr**	-
NEW American Ice	**U St**	-
American Tap	**multi.**	-
Art & Soul	**Cap Hill**	21
Asia Nine	**Penn Qtr**	18
NEW Atlas Rm.	**Atlas Dist**	-
Banana Café	**Cap Hill**	18
Bar Pilar	**Logan Cir**	21
Bastille	**Alexandria**	22
NEW Bayou	**West End**	-
Bazin's/Church	**Vienna**	23
Beacon B&G	**Scott Cir**	17
Ben's Next Door	**U St**	20
Bezu	**Potomac**	23
Bibiana	**D'town**	23
Biergarten Haus	**Atlas Dist**	-
Birch/Barley	**Logan Cir**	22
Bistro Bis	**Cap Hill**	25
Blackfinn	**Bethesda**	14
Black Fox	**Dupont Cir**	-
Black's Bar	**Bethesda**	23
Z BLT Steak	**Gldn Triangle**	25
Z Blue Duck	**West End**	26
Bodega	**Georgetown**	19
Bond 45	**Nat'l Harbor**	-
Bourbon	**multi.**	16
Bourbon Steak	**Georgetown**	23
Brabo	**Alexandria**	24
Z Brass. Beck	**D'town**	25
Bread/Brew	**Dupont Cir**	22
Buck's Fishing	**Upper NW**	20
Buddha-Bar	**Mt. Vernon Sq**	-
Busboys/Poets	**multi.**	18
Buzz	**Arlington**	22
Cafe Citron	**Dupont Cir**	14
Café du Parc	**D'town**	22
Café Dupont	**Dupont Cir**	-
Cafe Milano	**Georgetown**	20
Café Saint-Ex	**Logan Cir**	20
Cajun Experience	**Dupont Cir**	-
Capitol City Brew	**multi.**	18
Caribbean Breeze	**Arlington**	18
NEW Carmine's	**Penn Qtr**	-

NEW Casa Nonna | **Dupont Cir**	—
Casa Oaxaca | **Adams Mor**	18
Caucus Rm. | **Penn Qtr**	21
Cava | **Cap Hill**	24
Ceiba | **D'town**	23
Z Central Michel | **Penn Qtr**	26
Chef Geoff | **multi.**	19
Circa | **Dupont Cir**	17
NEW Cities | **Gldn Triangle**	—
Z Citronelle | **Georgetown**	28
Z CityZen | **SW**	28
Z Clyde's | **multi.**	19
Co Co. Sala | **Penn Qtr**	22
Columbia Firehse. | **Alexandria**	20
Comet Ping Pong | **Upper NW**	20
Commissary | **Logan Cir**	16
Cork | **Logan Cir**	23
Crème | **U St**	23
NEW Cuba Libre | **Penn Qtr**	—
Darlington Hse. | **Dupont Cir**	20
Dickson Wine | **U St**	—
Dino | **Cleve Pk**	22
Dogfish Head | **Falls Ch**	18
Domku | **Petworth**	18
Eatonville | **U St**	19
8407 Kit. | **Silver Spring**	—
NEW El Centro | **Logan Cir**	—
Eola | **Dupont Cir**	—
NEW Estadio | **Logan Cir**	—
Eventide | **Clarendon**	20
Evo Bistro | **McLean**	23
Ezmè | **Dupont Cir**	—
Fahrenheit | **Georgetown**	22
Finn/Porter | **D'town**	17
NEW Fiola | **Penn Qtr**	—
NEW Fiorella | **Nat'l Harbor**	—
Fire Works Pizza | **Clarendon**	—
Fontaine Caffe | **Alexandria**	24
NEW Food Wine | **Bethesda**	—
Z Founding Farmers | **World Bank**	21
NEW Freddy's Lobster | **Bethesda**	—
NEW Fruit Bat | **Atlas Dist**	—
FunXion | **D'town**	—
NEW Galileo III | **D'town**	—
Granville Moore's | **Atlas Dist**	23
Hank's Tav. | **Hyattsville**	22
Harry's | **multi.**	19
NEW Härth | **McLean**	—
Heights | **Columbia Hts**	19
NEW Hill Country | **Penn Qtr**	—
Hook | **Georgetown**	23
Hooked | **Sterling**	19
H St. Country | **Atlas Dist**	15
Hudson | **West End**	17
iCi | **D'town**	23
Il Canale | **Georgetown**	—
Indique | **Chevy Chase**	23
Iota Club/Café | **Clarendon**	—
Jackie's | **Silver Spring**	21
Jackson's | **Reston**	20
Jackson 20 | **Alexandria**	18
Z Jaleo | **multi.**	22
J&G Steak | **D'town**	25
Z Jockey Club | **Dupont Cir**	22
Johnny's | **Cap Hill**	20
Kellari Taverna | **Gldn Triangle**	22
Kora/Farrah | **Arlington**	15
Kushi | **Mt. Vernon Sq**	—
Z Lebanese Tav. | **Bethesda**	21
Lia's | **Chevy Chase**	21
Liberty Tav. | **Clarendon**	21
Liberty Tree | **Atlas Dist**	—
Lima | **D'town**	20
NEW Lincoln | **D'town**	—
Local 16 | **U St**	13
Lyon Hall | **Clarendon**	—
NEW Mad Fox Brew | **Falls Ch**	—
Madhatter | **Dupont Cir**	—
Mai Thai | **Gldn Triangle**	20
Majestic | **Alexandria**	23
NEW Mala Tang | **Arlington**	—
Mandu | **Mt. Vernon Sq**	21
Z Marcel's | **West End**	29
Marvin | **U St**	21
Masa 14 | **Logan Cir**	23
Matchbox | **multi.**	23
Maté | **Georgetown**	25
NEW Meridian | **Columbia Hts**	—
NEW Michel | **McLean**	—
NEW Mokomandy | **Sterling**	—
Mon Ami Gabi | **Reston**	19
Mrs. K's | **Silver Spring**	22
NEW Mussel Bar | **Bethesda**	—
Napoleon | **Adams Mor**	16
Nellie's | **U St**	17
NEW Newton's | **Bethesda**	—
1905 | **Mt. Vernon Sq**	19
Z Old Ebbitt | **D'town**	20
Oro Pomodoro | **Rockville**	18
Z Oya | **Penn Qtr**	23
Oyamel | **Penn Qtr**	24

NEW Ozzie's Corner	**Fairfax**	–
Panache	**Gldn Triangle**	16
Passenger	**Mt. Vernon Sq**	–
PassionFish	**Reston**	24
Patty Boom Boom	**U St**	–
P. Brennan's	**Arlington**	–
Perrys	**Adams Mor**	19
Ping Pong	**Chinatown**	21
NEW Pizzeria Da Marco	**Bethesda**	–
Pizzeria Paradiso	**Alexandria**	22
NEW P.J. Clarke's	**D'town**	–
Plume	**D'town**	26
Policy	**U St**	19
Poste Moderne	**Penn Qtr**	21
Posto	**Logan Cir**	21
Potenza	**D'town**	20
Proof	**Penn Qtr**	24
PS 7's	**Penn Qtr**	22
NEW Queen Vic	**Atlas Dist**	–
Z Rasika	**Penn Qtr**	28
NEW Redline	**Chinatown**	–
RedRocks	**Alexandria**	21
Redwood	**Bethesda**	17
Restaurant 3	**Clarendon**	18
Ris	**West End**	23
NEW Rivers/Watergate	**Foggy Bottom**	–
Room 11	**Columbia Hts**	–
Rosa Mexicano	**Nat'l Harbor**	20
Russia Hse.	**Dupont Cir**	15
Rustico	**multi.**	21
NEW Rustik	**Bloomingdale**	–
Screwtop Wine	**Arlington**	–
Sea Pearl	**Merrifield**	20
Sei	**Penn Qtr**	23
NEW Senart's Oyster	**Cap Hill**	–
701	**Penn Qtr**	23
Slaviya Cafe	**Adams Mor**	–
NEW Smith Commons	**Atlas Dist**	–
NEW Socci	**Arlington**	–
Sonoma	**Cap Hill**	20
Source	**Penn Qtr**	25
Sou'Wester	**SW**	18
NEW Standard	**Logan Cir**	–
Star/Shamrock	**Atlas Dist**	–
Sticky Rice	**Atlas Dist**	22
Stoney's Lounge	**Logan Cir**	18
Sushi Damo	**Rockville**	24
Sushi Rock	**Arlington**	–
Tabaq Bistro	**U St**	20
Tackle Box	**Cleve Pk**	21
Tallula/EatBar	**Clarendon**	22
Tandoori Nights	**multi.**	21
NEW Toki	**Atlas Dist**	–
Tonic	**Foggy Bottom**	16
Z Trummer's	**Clifton**	25
Tryst	**Adams Mor**	19
Thai Tanic	**Logan Cir**	23
Twisted Vines	**Arlington**	–
Z 2 Amys	**Cleve Pk**	25
Ulah Bistro	**U St**	18
NEW Uniontown B&G	**Anacostia**	–
NEW Vento	**Dupont Cir**	–
Veritas	**Dupont Cir**	18
Z Vidalia	**Dupont Cir**	24
Vinifera	**Reston**	21
NEW Virtue	**Alexandria**	–
NEW Watershed	**NoMa**	–
Wildfire	**McLean**	19
Willow	**Arlington**	24
Woo Lae Oak	**Vienna**	21
Z Zaytinya	**Penn Qtr**	25
Zentan	**D'town**	21
Zest	**Cap Hill**	18

OFFBEAT

NEW America Eats	**Penn Qtr**	–
Z Amsterdam Falafel	**Adams Mor**	26
Ben's Chili	**U St**	22
Biergarten Haus	**Atlas Dist**	–
Bob & Edith's	**Arlington**	17
Buca di Beppo	**multi.**	16
Buddha-Bar	**Mt. Vernon Sq**	–
Cafe Citron	**Dupont Cir**	14
Cassatt's Café	**Arlington**	18
Ching Ching	**Georgetown**	20
Comet Ping Pong	**Upper NW**	20
Dukem	**U St**	24
NEW Fast Gourmet	**U St**	–
Florida Ave. Grill	**U St**	20
Franklin's	**Hyattsville**	18
NEW Fruit Bat	**Atlas Dist**	–
NEW Hill Country	**Penn Qtr**	–
H St. Country	**Atlas Dist**	15
Hunter's Head	**Upperville**	23
Kora/Farrah	**Arlington**	15
Kushi	**Mt. Vernon Sq**	–
Lima	**D'town**	20
Malaysia Kopitiam	**Gldn Triangle**	19

Mark's Kit. | **Takoma Pk**	17
Marvin | **U St**	21
Mie N Yu | **Georgetown**	17
Oohhs & Aahhs | **U St**	24
Passenger | **Mt. Vernon Sq**	-
Perrys | **Adams Mor**	19
NEW Sax | **D'town**	-
Sticky Rice | **Atlas Dist**	22
Tabard Inn | **Dupont Cir**	24
Zola | **Penn Qtr**	23

OUTDOOR DINING

(G=garden; P=patio; S=sidewalk; T=terrace)

15 Ria | T | **Scott Cir**	17
Addie's | G, P | **White Flint**	23
NEW American Ice | P | **U St**	-
American Tap | P | **multi.**	-
Arucola | S | **Upper NW**	19
Ashby Inn | T | **Paris**	24
Austin Grill | S | **multi.**	15
Bastille | P | **Alexandria**	22
Biergarten Haus | P | **Atlas Dist**	-
Bistro Bis | P | **Cap Hill**	25
Bistro Provence | P, S | **Bethesda**	-
☑ Blue Duck | P | **West End**	26
Bombay Club | P | **Gldn Triangle**	24
Bread Line | S | **World Bank**	22
Cafe Deluxe | P, S | **multi.**	18
Café du Parc | S | **D'town**	22
Cafe Milano | P | **Georgetown**	20
Café Olé | P | **Upper NW**	21
Café Saint-Ex | P | **Logan Cir**	20
Cashion's Eat | S | **Adams Mor**	24
Chesapeake Rm. | P | **Cap Hill**	-
Circle Bistro | P | **West End**	21
☑ Citronelle | S, T | **Georgetown**	28
Comus Inn | T | **Dickerson**	21
Dean & DeLuca | P | **Georgetown**	22
NEW El Centro | R | **Logan Cir**	-
Equinox | S | **Gldn Triangle**	25
Evening Star | P | **Alexandria**	22
Hank's Oyster | S | **Dupont Cir**	24
iCi | T | **D'town**	23
Indique | P | **Chevy Chase**	23
Irish Inn/Glen Echo | P | **Glen Echo**	18
☑ Jaleo | P | **Bethesda**	22
J&G Steak | P | **D'town**	25
Johnny's | T | **Cap Hill**	20
Juniper | G | **West End**	21
Konami | P | **Vienna**	20

La Fourchette | T | **Adams Mor**	23
☑ L'Aub./François | G | **Grt Falls**	27
☑ L'Aub. Provençale | T | **Boyce**	27
Lauriol Plaza | P, T | **Dupont Cir**	18
Leopold's Kafe | P | **Georgetown**	22
Levante's | S | **Dupont Cir**	18
☑ Marcel's | S | **West End**	29
Marvin | R | **U St**	21
NEW Medium Rare | P, S | **Cleve Pk**	-
Mezè | P | **Adams Mor**	21
Mon Ami Gabi | P | **Bethesda**	19
Mrs. K's | P | **Silver Spring**	22
Neyla | P | **Georgetown**	22
Occidental | P | **D'town**	22
Old Angler's | G, T | **Potomac**	19
Open City | P | **Woodley Pk**	18
Oval Rm. | S | **Gldn Triangle**	24
☑ Palena | S | **Cleve Pk**	28
Paolo's | P | **multi.**	18
Perrys | T | **Adams Mor**	19
Poste Moderne | P | **Penn Qtr**	21
Rail Stop | P, T | **Plains**	22
Raku | P, S | **multi.**	21
Renato/River Falls | S | **Potomac**	19
Ris | P | **West End**	23
Sea Catch | P, T | **Georgetown**	21
Sequoia | T | **Georgetown**	15
Sette Osteria | P | **Dupont Cir**	20
701 | P | **Penn Qtr**	23
Source | P | **Penn Qtr**	25
NEW Standard | G, P, S | **Logan Cir**	-
Tabard Inn | G | **Dupont Cir**	24
Taberna/Alabardero | S | **World Bank**	23
Tony & Joe's | P | **Georgetown**	15
☑ 2941 | G, P | **Falls Ch**	26
☑ 2 Amys | P | **Cleve Pk**	25
Uncle Julio's | P | **multi.**	19
Westend Bistro | S | **West End**	21
☑ Zaytinya | P | **Penn Qtr**	25

PEOPLE-WATCHING

☑ Adour/St. Regis | **D'town**	24
Againn | **D'town**	19
Agora | **Dupont Cir**	-
NEW America Eats | **Penn Qtr**	-
☑ Amsterdam Falafel | **Adams Mor**	26
Art & Soul | **Cap Hill**	21
Asia Nine | **Penn Qtr**	18

Assaggi | **Bethesda**	21
NEW Atlas Rm. | **Atlas Dist**	-
NEW Bayou Bakery | **Arlington**	-
Bibiana | **D'town**	23
Biergarten Haus | **Atlas Dist**	-
Birch/Barley | **Logan Cir**	22
Bistro Bis | **Cap Hill**	25
Bistro Provence | **Bethesda**	-
Bodega | **Georgetown**	19
Bourbon | **Glover Pk**	16
Bourbon Steak | **Georgetown**	23
Brabo | **Alexandria**	24
Z Brass. Beck | **D'town**	25
Bread Line | **World Bank**	22
Buddha-Bar | **Mt. Vernon Sq**	-
Busboys/Poets | **multi.**	18
Cafe Deluxe | **multi.**	18
Café du Parc | **D'town**	22
Café Dupont | **Dupont Cir**	-
Cafe Milano | **Georgetown**	20
Café Saint-Ex | **Logan Cir**	20
NEW Carmine's | **Penn Qtr**	-
Cashion's Eat | **Adams Mor**	24
Caucus Rm. | **Penn Qtr**	21
Z Central Michel | **Penn Qtr**	26
Charlie Palmer | **Cap Hill**	25
Chef Geoff | **Vienna**	19
Circa | **Dupont Cir**	17
Z Citronelle | **Georgetown**	28
Co Co. Sala | **Penn Qtr**	22
Columbia Firehse. | **Alexandria**	20
Comet Ping Pong | **Upper NW**	20
Commissary | **Logan Cir**	16
Cork | **Logan Cir**	23
NEW Cuba Libre | **Penn Qtr**	-
Darlington Hse. | **Dupont Cir**	20
DC Coast | **D'town**	23
DC Noodles | **U St**	21
Dean & DeLuca | **Georgetown**	22
Dickson Wine | **U St**	-
Eatonville | **U St**	19
NEW El Centro | **Logan Cir**	-
Equinox | **Gldn Triangle**	25
NEW Estadio | **Logan Cir**	-
Eventide | **Clarendon**	20
Evo Bistro | **McLean**	23
Ezmè | **Dupont Cir**	-
Fahrenheit | **Georgetown**	22
NEW Fiola | **Penn Qtr**	-
Firefly | **Dupont Cir**	20
Fire Works Pizza | **Clarendon**	-
Z Founding Farmers | **World Bank**	21
NEW Fruit Bat | **Atlas Dist**	-
NEW Galileo III | **D'town**	-
Georgia Brown | **D'town**	22
Hank's Oyster | **Dupont Cir**	24
Heights | **Columbia Hts**	19
NEW Hill Country | **Penn Qtr**	-
Hook | **Georgetown**	23
H St. Country | **Atlas Dist**	15
Hudson | **West End**	17
Indique | **Chevy Chase**	23
Z Inn/Little Washington | **Washington**	29
Jackie's | **Silver Spring**	21
Jackson's | **Reston**	20
Z Jaleo | **multi.**	22
J&G Steak | **D'town**	25
Johnny's | **Cap Hill**	20
Z Kinkead's | **Foggy Bottom**	26
Kramerbooks | **Dupont Cir**	17
Kushi | **Mt. Vernon Sq**	-
Lauriol Plaza | **Dupont Cir**	18
Lia's | **Chevy Chase**	21
Liberty Tav. | **Clarendon**	21
Lima | **D'town**	20
NEW Lincoln | **D'town**	-
Local 16 | **U St**	13
Lyon Hall | **Clarendon**	-
Madhatter | **Dupont Cir**	-
Mai Thai | **Gldn Triangle**	20
Mandu | **Mt. Vernon Sq**	21
Z Marcel's | **West End**	29
Martin's Tav. | **Georgetown**	20
Marvin | **U St**	21
Masa 14 | **Logan Cir**	23
Matchbox | **multi.**	23
NEW Medium Rare | **Cleve Pk**	-
NEW Michel | **McLean**	-
Monocle | **Cap Hill**	14
NEW Mussel Bar | **Bethesda**	-
Z Nora | **Dupont Cir**	26
Northside | **Clarendon**	-
Z Old Ebbitt | **D'town**	20
Oval Rm. | **Gldn Triangle**	24
Z Oya | **Penn Qtr**	23
Oyamel | **Penn Qtr**	24
Z Palm | **Gldn Triangle**	24
Passenger | **Mt. Vernon Sq**	-
PassionFish | **Reston**	24
Ping Pong | **Chinatown**	21
Pizzeria Paradiso | **Alexandria**	22

NEW P.J. Clarke's | **D'town**	-
Poste Moderne | **Penn Qtr**	21
Posto | **Logan Cir**	21
Potenza | **D'town**	20
NEW Queen Vic | **Atlas Dist**	-
Z Ray's Hell Burger | **Arlington**	26
Redwood | **Bethesda**	17
Restaurant 3 | **Clarendon**	18
NEW Ripple | **Cleve Pk**	-
Ris | **West End**	23
Room 11 | **Columbia Hts**	-
Rosa Mexicano | **multi.**	20
Roti Med. | **World Bank**	-
Rustico | **Arlington**	21
Sea Pearl | **Merrifield**	20
NEW Senart's Oyster | **Cap Hill**	-
Sequoia | **Georgetown**	15
701 | **Penn Qtr**	23
NEW Shake Shack | **Dupont Cir**	-
Sonoma | **Cap Hill**	20
Source | **Penn Qtr**	25
Sou'Wester | **SW**	18
NEW Standard | **Logan Cir**	-
Star/Shamrock | **Atlas Dist**	-
Sticky Rice | **Atlas Dist**	22
Sushi Rock | **Arlington**	-
Tabaq Bistro | **U St**	20
Tallula/EatBar | **Clarendon**	22
Tandoori Nights | **Clarendon**	21
NEW Toki | **Atlas Dist**	-
Tryst | **Adams Mor**	19
Z 2941 | **Falls Ch**	26
Twisted Vines | **Arlington**	-
NEW Vento | **Dupont Cir**	-
Veritas | **Dupont Cir**	18
Z Vidalia | **Dupont Cir**	24
Vinifera | **Reston**	21
Vinoteca | **U St**	21
NEW Virtue | **Alexandria**	-
NEW Watershed | **NoMa**	-
Westend Bistro | **West End**	21
Z Zaytinya | **Penn Qtr**	25
Zentan | **D'town**	21
Zola | **Penn Qtr**	23

POWER SCENES

Z Acadiana | **Mt. Vernon Sq**	23
Acqua al 2 | **Cap Hill**	-
Z Adour/St. Regis | **D'town**	24
NEW America Eats | **Penn Qtr**	-
Ardeo/Bardeo | **Cleve Pk**	21
Bamian | **Falls Ch**	23

Bibiana | **D'town**	23
Bistro Bis | **Cap Hill**	25
Bobby Van's | **D'town**	21
Bombay Club | **Gldn Triangle**	24
Bourbon Steak | **Georgetown**	23
Z Brass. Beck | **D'town**	25
Z Capital Grille | **multi.**	25
Caucus Rm. | **Penn Qtr**	21
Z Central Michel | **Penn Qtr**	26
Charlie Palmer | **Cap Hill**	25
Chef Geoff | **Vienna**	19
Z Citronelle | **Georgetown**	28
Z CityZen | **SW**	28
Z Clyde's | **multi.**	19
Z Corduroy | **Mt. Vernon Sq**	27
DC Coast | **D'town**	23
Equinox | **Gldn Triangle**	25
Z Eve | **Alexandria**	28
Evo Bistro | **McLean**	23
NEW Fiola | **Penn Qtr**	-
Fyve | **Arlington**	17
NEW Galileo III | **D'town**	-
NEW Hill Country | **Penn Qtr**	-
Hunan Dynasty | **Cap Hill**	17
iCi | **D'town**	23
Z Inn/Little Washington | **Washington**	29
J&G Steak | **D'town**	25
Johnny's | **Cap Hill**	20
Z Kinkead's | **Foggy Bottom**	26
Landini Bros. | **Alexandria**	22
Z Marcel's | **West End**	29
NEW Michel | **McLean**	-
Monocle | **Cap Hill**	14
Morton's | **multi.**	25
Z Nora | **Dupont Cir**	26
Occidental | **D'town**	22
Z Old Ebbitt | **D'town**	20
Oval Rm. | **Gldn Triangle**	24
Z Palena | **Cleve Pk**	28
Z Palm | **multi.**	24
Potenza | **D'town**	20
Z Prime Rib | **Gldn Triangle**	27
Proof | **Penn Qtr**	24
701 | **Penn Qtr**	23
Sonoma | **Cap Hill**	20
Taberna/Alabardero | **World Bank**	23
Z Tosca | **Penn Qtr**	27
Tuscarora Mill | **Leesburg**	23
Z 2941 | **Falls Ch**	26
Z Vidalia | **Dupont Cir**	24

Vote at ZAGAT.com

Westend Bistro | **West End**	21
Willow | **Arlington**	24
Ⓩ Zaytinya | **Penn Qtr**	25
Zola | **Penn Qtr**	23

PRE-THEATER DINING

(Call for prices and times)

Bistro D'Oc | **D'town**	21
Bistro Français | **Georgetown**	19
Chef Geoff | **Upper NW**	19
Circle Bistro | **West End**	21
J&G Steak | **D'town**	25
Ⓩ Marcel's | **West End**	29
Notti Bianche | **Foggy Bottom**	20
Oval Rm. | **Gldn Triangle**	24
Ⓩ Rasika | **Penn Qtr**	28
Roof Terr. | **Foggy Bottom**	15
701 | **Penn Qtr**	23
Ⓩ Tosca | **Penn Qtr**	27

PRIVATE ROOMS

(Restaurants charge less at off times; call for capacity)

Ⓩ Adour/St. Regis | **D'town**	24
Afghan | **Alexandria**	25
Birch/Barley | **Logan Cir**	22
Bistro Bis | **Cap Hill**	25
Bistro D'Oc | **D'town**	21
Bistrot Lepic | **Georgetown**	23
Ⓩ Brass. Beck | **D'town**	25
B. Smith | **Cap Hill**	20
Cafe Milano | **Georgetown**	20
NEW Carmine's | **Penn Qtr**	-
Caucus Rm. | **Penn Qtr**	21
Ceiba | **D'town**	23
Ⓩ Central Michel | **Penn Qtr**	26
Charlie Palmer | **Cap Hill**	25
Chef Geoff | **multi.**	19
Chima | **Vienna**	23
Ⓩ Citronelle | **Georgetown**	28
Ⓩ CityZen | **SW**	28
Ⓩ Clyde's | **multi.**	19
Ⓩ Corduroy | **Mt. Vernon Sq**	27
DC Coast | **D'town**	23
Duangrat's | **Falls Ch**	25
Equinox | **Gldn Triangle**	25
NEW Fiola | **Penn Qtr**	-
Fleming's Steak | **McLean**	24
NEW Galileo III | **D'town**	-
Geranio | **Alexandria**	22
Heritage India | **Dupont Cir**	22
Irish Inn/Glen Echo | **Glen Echo**	18

Johnny's | **Cap Hill**	20
La Chaumière | **Georgetown**	24
La Ferme | **Chevy Chase**	22
Ⓩ Lebanese Tav. | **Woodley Pk**	21
Lightfoot | **Leesburg**	22
Ⓩ Marcel's | **West End**	29
Matisse | **Upper NW**	23
Monocle | **Cap Hill**	14
Morton's | **multi.**	25
Ⓩ Nora | **Dupont Cir**	26
Occidental | **D'town**	22
Old Angler's | **Potomac**	19
Oval Rm. | **Gldn Triangle**	24
Ⓩ Oya | **Penn Qtr**	23
Ⓩ Palm | **multi.**	24
NEW Pizzeria Da Marco | **Bethesda**	-
Ⓩ Rasika | **Penn Qtr**	28
Sequoia | **Georgetown**	15
701 | **Penn Qtr**	23
Ⓩ 1789 | **Georgetown**	25
Smith/Wollensky | **Gldn Triangle**	22
Taberna/Alabardero | **World Bank**	23
Teatro Goldoni | **Gldn Triangle**	-
Ⓩ Tosca | **Penn Qtr**	27
Tragara | **Bethesda**	21
Ⓩ 2941 | **Falls Ch**	26
Ⓩ Vidalia | **Dupont Cir**	24
Wildfire | **McLean**	19
Woo Lae Oak | **Vienna**	21
Zengo | **Chinatown**	22
Zola | **Penn Qtr**	23

PRIX FIXE MENUS

(Call for prices and times)

Bastille | **Alexandria**	22
Bistro Français | **Georgetown**	19
Bistrot Lafayette | **Alexandria**	20
Ⓩ BlackSalt | **Palisades**	26
Bombay Club | **Gldn Triangle**	24
Ⓩ Central Michel | **Penn Qtr**	26
Charlie Palmer | **Cap Hill**	25
Ⓩ Citronelle | **Georgetown**	28
Dino | **Cleve Pk**	22
Equinox | **Gldn Triangle**	25
Ⓩ Eve | **Alexandria**	28
Ⓩ Inn/Little Washington | **Washington**	29
J&G Steak | **D'town**	25
La Bergerie | **Alexandria**	23
Ⓩ L'Aub./François | **Grt Falls**	27

Makoto | **Palisades**	28
Mannequin Pis | **Olney**	25
Matisse | **Upper NW**	23
NEW Medium Rare | **Cleve Pk**	-
Me Jana | **Arlington**	23
NEW Michel | **McLean**	-
Nora | **Dupont Cir**	26
Obelisk | **Dupont Cir**	27
Palena | **Cleve Pk**	28
PassionFish | **Reston**	24
Ray's/Classics | **Silver Spring**	24
Source | **Penn Qtr**	25
Taberna/Alabardero | **World Bank**	23
Tosca | **Penn Qtr**	27

QUIET CONVERSATION

15 Ria | **Scott Cir**	17
Adour/St. Regis | **D'town**	24
Art & Soul | **Cap Hill**	21
Ashby Inn | **Paris**	24
Bastille | **Alexandria**	22
Bibiana | **D'town**	23
Bistro Cacao | **Cap Hill**	-
Bistro L'Hermitage | **Woodbridge**	24
Bistro Provence | **Bethesda**	-
Blue Rock Inn | **Sperryville**	-
Bombay Club | **Gldn Triangle**	24
NEW Bookhill Bistro | **Georgetown**	-
Bourbon Steak | **Georgetown**	23
Brabo | **Alexandria**	24
Busboys/Poets | **Mt. Vernon Sq**	18
Buzz | **Arlington**	22
Café du Parc | **D'town**	22
Caucus Rm. | **Penn Qtr**	21
Ching Ching | **Georgetown**	20
Circle Bistro | **West End**	21
Citronelle | **Georgetown**	28
Coeur de Lion | **D'town**	20
Commissary | **Logan Cir**	16
Corduroy | **Mt. Vernon Sq**	27
Dickson Wine | **U St**	-
NEW Diya | **Vienna**	-
Eola | **Dupont Cir**	-
Et Voila | **Palisades**	24
Eve | **Alexandria**	28
Eventide | **Clarendon**	20
Fahrenheit | **Georgetown**	22
NEW Fiola | **Penn Qtr**	-
Heritage India | **Glover Pk**	22

Il Canale | **Georgetown**	-
Indique | **multi.**	23
Inn/Little Washington | **Washington**	29
J&G Steak | **D'town**	25
Jockey Club | **Dupont Cir**	22
Kellari Taverna | **Gldn Triangle**	22
La Chaumière | **Georgetown**	24
Las Canteras | **Adams Mor**	-
Leopold's Kafe | **Georgetown**	22
Liberty Tav. | **Clarendon**	21
Little Fountain | **Adams Mor**	24
Makoto | **Palisades**	28
Mandu | **Mt. Vernon Sq**	21
Masala Art | **Upper NW**	26
NEW Michel | **McLean**	-
Morrison-Clark | **D'town**	23
Mrs. K's | **Silver Spring**	22
New Heights | **Woodley Pk**	22
NEW Newton's | **Bethesda**	-
1905 | **Mt. Vernon Sq**	19
Nora | **Dupont Cir**	26
Obelisk | **Dupont Cir**	27
Oceanaire | **D'town**	24
Palena | **Cleve Pk**	28
Plume | **D'town**	26
Puro Café | **Georgetown**	-
Rasika | **Penn Qtr**	28
Ris | **West End**	23
Sea Catch | **Georgetown**	21
1789 | **Georgetown**	25
Siroc | **D'town**	24
Sonoma | **Cap Hill**	20
Source | **Penn Qtr**	25
Sou'Wester | **SW**	18
Taberna/Alabardero | **World Bank**	23
Taste/Saigon | **Rockville**	21
Tosca | **Penn Qtr**	27
Toscana Café | **Cap Hill**	23
Trummer's | **Clifton**	25
Veritas | **Dupont Cir**	18
NEW Watershed | **NoMa**	-
Woo Lae Oak | **Vienna**	21
Zentan | **D'town**	21

ROMANTIC PLACES

Acqua al 2 | **Cap Hill**	-
Agora | **Dupont Cir**	-
Al Tiramisu | **Dupont Cir**	24
Ashby Inn | **Paris**	24
NEW Atlas Rm. | **Atlas Dist**	-

Vote at ZAGAT.com

Bezu | **Potomac**	23
Birch/Barley | **Logan Cir**	22
Bistro Cacao | **Cap Hill**	-
Bistro L'Hermitage | **Woodbridge**	24
Bistro Provence | **Bethesda**	-
Blue Rock Inn | **Sperryville**	-
Bombay Club | **Gldn Triangle**	24
Brabo | **Alexandria**	24
Buddha-Bar | **Mt. Vernon Sq**	-
Busboys/Poets | **Arlington**	18
Casa Oaxaca | **Adams Mor**	18
Cava | **Rockville**	24
Circle Bistro | **West End**	21
Z Citronelle | **Georgetown**	28
Co Co. Sala | **Penn Qtr**	22
Coeur de Lion | **D'town**	20
Z Corduroy | **Mt. Vernon Sq**	27
Cork | **Logan Cir**	23
NEW Cuba Libre | **Penn Qtr**	-
Dickson Wine | **U St**	-
NEW El Centro | **Logan Cir**	-
NEW Estadio | **Logan Cir**	-
Z Eve | **Alexandria**	28
Eventide | **Clarendon**	20
Ezmè | **Dupont Cir**	-
NEW Fiola | **Penn Qtr**	-
Firefly | **Dupont Cir**	20
Green Papaya | **Bethesda**	19
Himalayan Heritage | **Adams Mor**	22
Hook | **Georgetown**	23
Il Canale | **Georgetown**	-
Indique | **Chevy Chase**	23
Z Inn/Little Washington | **Washington**	29
J&G Steak | **D'town**	25
La Bergerie | **Alexandria**	23
La Canela | **Rockville**	23
La Chaumière | **Georgetown**	24
La Ferme | **Chevy Chase**	22
Z L'Aub./François | **Grt Falls**	27
Z L'Aub. Provençale | **Boyce**	27
Le Refuge | **Alexandria**	21
Little Fountain | **Adams Mor**	24
Marrakesh | **Dupont Cir**	20
Marvin | **U St**	21
NEW Michel | **McLean**	-
Montmartre | **Cap Hill**	24
New Heights | **Woodley Pk**	22
NEW Newton's | **Bethesda**	-
Neyla | **Georgetown**	22
1905 | **Mt. Vernon Sq**	19
Z Nora | **Dupont Cir**	26
Z Obelisk | **Dupont Cir**	27
Old Angler's | **Potomac**	19
Z Oya | **Penn Qtr**	23
Z Palena | **Cleve Pk**	28
Present | **Falls Ch**	23
Z Rasika | **Penn Qtr**	28
Redwood | **Bethesda**	17
Rustico | **Arlington**	21
NEW Sax | **D'town**	-
Sea Pearl | **Merrifield**	20
Sei | **Penn Qtr**	23
701 | **Penn Qtr**	23
Z 1789 | **Georgetown**	25
Source | **Penn Qtr**	25
Tabard Inn | **Dupont Cir**	24
Taberna/Alabardero | **World Bank**	23
NEW Teak Wood | **Logan Cir**	-
Z Trummer's | **Clifton**	25
NEW Vento | **Dupont Cir**	-
Zentan | **D'town**	21

SINGLES SCENES

American Tap | **Reston**	-
NEW Arlington Rooftop | **Clarendon**	-
Austin Grill | **multi.**	15
Bar Pilar | **Logan Cir**	21
Beacon B&G | **Scott Cir**	17
Birch/Barley | **Logan Cir**	22
Blackfinn | **Bethesda**	14
Z BLT Steak | **Gldn Triangle**	25
Z Brass. Beck | **D'town**	25
Buddha-Bar | **Mt. Vernon Sq**	-
Cafe Citron | **Dupont Cir**	14
Cafe Deluxe | **multi.**	18
Cafe Milano | **Georgetown**	20
Café Saint-Ex | **Logan Cir**	20
Z Central Michel | **Penn Qtr**	26
Chef Geoff | **Vienna**	19
Circa | **Dupont Cir**	17
Z Clyde's | **multi.**	19
Columbia Firehse. | **Alexandria**	20
Dogfish Head | **Falls Ch**	18
NEW Fruit Bat | **Atlas Dist**	-
Heights | **Columbia Hts**	19
Hook | **Georgetown**	23
H St. Country | **Atlas Dist**	15
Indique | **Chevy Chase**	23
Jackson's | **Reston**	20

Kramerbooks | **Dupont Cir**	17
Liberty Tav. | **Clarendon**	21
Lima | **D'town**	20
Local 16 | **U St**	13
Marvin | **U St**	21
Masa 14 | **Logan Cir**	23
Maté | **Georgetown**	25
Mie N Yu | **Georgetown**	17
Mio | **D'town**	19
Neyla | **Georgetown**	22
☑ Old Ebbitt | **D'town**	20
☑ Oya | **Penn Qtr**	23
Oyamel | **Penn Qtr**	24
Passenger | **Mt. Vernon Sq**	-
Perrys | **Adams Mor**	19
PS 7's | **Penn Qtr**	22
Room 11 | **Columbia Hts**	-
Rustico | **Alexandria**	21
NEW Sax | **D'town**	-
Sequoia | **Georgetown**	15
NEW Standard | **Logan Cir**	-
Star/Shamrock | **Atlas Dist**	-
Tabaq Bistro | **U St**	20
Tony & Joe's | **Georgetown**	15
☑ Zaytinya | **Penn Qtr**	25
Zengo | **Chinatown**	22
Zola | **Penn Qtr**	23

SLEEPERS

(Good to excellent food,
but little known)

Afghan | **Alexandria**	25
Bernie's Deli | **Fairfax**	25
Bistro L'Hermitage | **Woodbridge**	24
Burma Rd. | **Gaith'burg**	24
China Star | **Fairfax**	24
Cuba de Ayer | **Burtonsville**	23
Delhi Club | **Clarendon**	24
Fontaine Caffe | **Alexandria**	24
Grille | **Alexandria**	23
Guardado's | **Bethesda**	24
Horace/Dickie | **Atlas Dist**	24
Jaipur | **Fairfax**	23
Kabob Palace | **Arlington**	24
Layalina | **Arlington**	24
Little Fountain | **Adams Mor**	24
Mandalay | **Silver Spring**	24
Mannequin Pis | **Olney**	25
Masala Art | **Upper NW**	26
Maté | **Georgetown**	25
Minh's | **Arlington**	24

Myanmar | **Falls Ch**	24
Pho 14 | **Columbia Hts**	26
Plaka Grill | **Vienna**	26
Plume | **D'town**	26
Regent | **Dupont Cir**	23
RT's | **Alexandria**	24
Ruan Thai | **Wheaton**	25
Sergio Rist. | **Silver Spring**	24
Sichuan Pavilion | **Rockville**	23
Tavira | **Chevy Chase**	24
Toscana Café | **Cap Hill**	23
Villa Mozart | **Fairfax**	24
Yama | **Vienna**	23
Yamazato | **Alexandria**	25

TEA SERVICE

☑ Blue Duck | **West End**	26
Ching Ching | **Georgetown**	20
Coeur de Lion | **D'town**	20
Fyve | **Arlington**	17
Irish Inn/Glen Echo | **Glen Echo**	18
Seven Seas | **Rockville**	18
Teaism | **multi.**	20

TRANSPORTING EXPERIENCES

NEW America Eats | **Penn Qtr**	-
Biergarten Haus | **Atlas Dist**	-
Bodega | **Georgetown**	19
Bombay Club | **Gldn Triangle**	24
☑ Brass. Beck | **D'town**	25
Buddha-Bar | **Mt. Vernon Sq**	-
Ching Ching | **Georgetown**	20
☑ Clyde's | **multi.**	19
NEW El Centro | **Logan Cir**	-
NEW Freddy's Lobster | **Bethesda**	-
Green Papaya | **Bethesda**	19
Heritage India | **Glover Pk**	22
NEW Hill Country | **Penn Qtr**	-
H St. Country | **Atlas Dist**	15
Hunter's Head | **Upperville**	23
Indique | **Chevy Chase**	23
☑ Inn/Little Washington | **Washington**	29
Kushi | **Mt. Vernon Sq**	-
☑ L'Aub./François | **Grt Falls**	27
☑ Makoto | **Palisades**	28
Marrakesh | **Dupont Cir**	20
Mie N Yu | **Georgetown**	17
Mon Ami Gabi | **Bethesda**	19
Neyla | **Georgetown**	22
☑ Oya | **Penn Qtr**	23

Passenger	**Mt. Vernon Sq**	–
Rosa Mexicano	**Penn Qtr**	20
Wildfire	**McLean**	19
Z Zaytinya	**Penn Qtr**	25
Zengo	**Chinatown**	22
Zola	**Penn Qtr**	23

TRENDY

Z Acadiana	**Mt. Vernon Sq**	23
Againn	**D'town**	19
NEW America Eats	**Penn Qtr**	–
NEW American Ice	**U St**	–
Art & Soul	**Cap Hill**	21
Asia Nine	**Penn Qtr**	18
NEW Atlas Rm.	**Atlas Dist**	–
NEW Ba Bay	**Cap Hill**	–
Banana Café	**Cap Hill**	18
Bangkok Golden	**Falls Ch**	–
Bastille	**Alexandria**	22
NEW Bayou	**West End**	–
NEW Bayou Bakery	**Arlington**	–
Belga Café	**Cap Hill**	23
BGR	**multi.**	21
Bibiana	**D'town**	23
Biergarten Haus	**Atlas Dist**	–
Birch/Barley	**Logan Cir**	22
Bistro Bis	**Cap Hill**	25
Bodega	**Georgetown**	19
Bourbon	**multi.**	16
Brabo	**Alexandria**	24
Z Brass. Beck	**D'town**	25
Buddha-Bar	**Mt. Vernon Sq**	–
Busboys/Poets	**multi.**	18
Cafe Asia	**multi.**	18
Cafe Citron	**Dupont Cir**	14
Café du Parc	**D'town**	22
Cafe Milano	**Georgetown**	20
Café Saint-Ex	**Logan Cir**	20
Cava	**Cap Hill**	24
NEW Cava Mezze Grill	**Bethesda**	–
Ceiba	**D'town**	23
Z Central Michel	**Penn Qtr**	26
Chef Geoff	**Vienna**	19
Circa	**multi.**	17
NEW Cities	**Gldn Triangle**	–
Z CityZen	**SW**	28
Z Clyde's	**multi.**	19
Co Co. Sala	**Penn Qtr**	22
Comet Ping Pong	**Upper NW**	20
Commissary	**Logan Cir**	16
Z Corduroy	**Mt. Vernon Sq**	27

Cork	**Logan Cir**	23
DC Coast	**D'town**	23
Dickson Wine	**U St**	–
Eatonville	**U St**	19
NEW El Centro	**Logan Cir**	–
NEW Estadio	**Logan Cir**	–
Etete	**U St**	24
Z Eve	**Alexandria**	28
Eventide	**Clarendon**	20
Evo Bistro	**McLean**	23
Fahrenheit	**Georgetown**	22
NEW Fiola	**Penn Qtr**	–
NEW Fiorella	**Nat'l Harbor**	–
Fire Works Pizza	**multi.**	–
Z Founding Farmers	**World Bank**	21
Four Sisters	**Merrifield**	25
NEW Freddy's Lobster	**Bethesda**	–
NEW Fruit Bat	**Atlas Dist**	–
FunXion	**D'town**	–
NEW Galileo III	**D'town**	–
Good Stuff	**Cap Hill**	21
Granville Moore's	**Atlas Dist**	23
Hank's Oyster	**Dupont Cir**	24
Heritage India	**multi.**	22
NEW Hill Country	**Penn Qtr**	–
Hook	**Georgetown**	23
H St. Country	**Atlas Dist**	15
Hudson	**West End**	17
Hunan Dynasty	**Cap Hill**	17
iCi	**D'town**	23
Il Canale	**Georgetown**	–
Iota Club/Café	**Clarendon**	–
Jackie's	**Silver Spring**	21
Z Jaleo	**multi.**	22
J&G Steak	**D'town**	25
Johnny's	**Cap Hill**	20
Juice Joint Cafe	**D'town**	22
Z Komi	**Dupont Cir**	29
Kushi	**Mt. Vernon Sq**	–
Leopold's Kafe	**Georgetown**	22
Liberty Tav.	**Clarendon**	21
Lima	**D'town**	20
NEW Lincoln	**D'town**	–
Local 16	**U St**	13
Lyon Hall	**Clarendon**	–
NEW Mala Tang	**Arlington**	–
Mandu	**multi.**	21
Marvin	**U St**	21
Masa 14	**Logan Cir**	23
Matchbox	**multi.**	23

NEW Medium Rare | Cleve Pk	–
NEW Michel | McLean	–
Mie N Yu | Georgetown	17
Ⓩ Minibar | Penn Qtr	26
NEW Mussel Bar | Bethesda	–
Nellie's | U St	17
1905 | Mt. Vernon Sq	19
Ⓩ Oya | Penn Qtr	23
Oyamel | Penn Qtr	24
Ⓩ Palena | Cleve Pk	28
Passenger | Mt. Vernon Sq	–
Patty Boom Boom | U St	–
Peacock Cafe | Georgetown	19
Pete's Apizza | multi.	22
Pho 14 | Columbia Hts	26
Ping Pong | Chinatown	21
NEW Pizzeria Da Marco | Bethesda	–
Pizzeria Paradiso | Alexandria	22
Policy | U St	19
Posto | Logan Cir	21
Potenza | D'town	20
Pret A Manger | Gldn Triangle	17
Proof | Penn Qtr	24
NEW Queen Vic | Atlas Dist	–
Radius | Mt. Pleasant	17
Ⓩ Rasika | Penn Qtr	28
Ⓩ Ray's Hell Burger | Arlington	26
Ⓩ Ray's/Steaks | Clarendon	26
NEW Red Hook | Location Varies	–
RedRocks | multi.	21
Restaurant 3 | Clarendon	18
Rice | Logan Cir	22
Ris | West End	23
Room 11 | Columbia Hts	–
Rosa Mexicano | Nat'l Harbor	20
Rustico | multi.	21
NEW Rustik | Bloomingdale	–
Sea Pearl | Merrifield	20
Sei | Penn Qtr	23
Seventh Hill | Cap Hill	23
NEW Shake Shack | multi.	–
Siroc | D'town	24
NEW Smith Commons | Atlas Dist	–
Source | Penn Qtr	25
NEW Standard | Logan Cir	–
Sticky Rice | Atlas Dist	22
Stoney's Lounge | Logan Cir	18
Surfside | Glover Pk	22
Sushi Damo | Rockville	24

Tackle Box | Cleve Pk	21
Tallula/EatBar | Clarendon	22
NEW Teak Wood | Logan Cir	–
NEW Toki | Atlas Dist	–
Ⓩ Trummer's | Clifton	25
NEW Uniontown B&G | Anacostia	–
NEW Vento | Dupont Cir	–
Veritas | Dupont Cir	18
Vermilion | Alexandria	23
Vinoteca | U St	21
NEW Virtue | Alexandria	–
NEW Watershed | NoMa	–
Westend Bistro | West End	21
NEW We, The Pizza | Cap Hill	–
Wildfire | McLean	19
Woo Lae Oak | Vienna	21
Ⓩ Zaytinya | Penn Qtr	25
Zengo | Chinatown	22
Zentan | D'town	21
Zest | Cap Hill	18

VALET PARKING

15 Ria | Scott Cir	17
Ⓩ Acadiana | Mt. Vernon Sq	23
Ⓩ Adour/St. Regis | D'town	24
Al Tiramisu | Dupont Cir	24
Ardeo/Bardeo | Cleve Pk	21
Art & Soul | Cap Hill	21
Asia Nine | Penn Qtr	18
Asian Spice | Chinatown	21
Assaggi | Bethesda	21
Beacon B&G | Scott Cir	17
Bibiana | D'town	23
Biergarten Haus | Atlas Dist	–
Ⓩ BLT Steak | Gldn Triangle	25
Ⓩ Blue Duck | West End	26
Bobby Van's | D'town	21
Bombay Club | Gldn Triangle	24
Brabo | Alexandria	24
Brass. Monte Carlo | Bethesda	20
Buddha-Bar | Mt. Vernon Sq	–
Café du Parc | D'town	22
Café Dupont | Dupont Cir	–
Ⓩ Capital Grille | multi.	25
Caribbean Breeze | Arlington	18
NEW Carmine's | Penn Qtr	–
NEW Casa Nonna | Dupont Cir	–
Cashion's Eat | Adams Mor	24
Caucus Rm. | Penn Qtr	21
Cava | Cap Hill	24
Ceiba | D'town	23

Central Michel | **Penn Qtr**	26	
Cesco Trattoria | **Bethesda**	22	
Charlie Palmer | **Cap Hill**	25	
Cheesecake | **White Flint**	19	
Chef Geoff | **multi.**	19	
Chima | **Vienna**	23	
Circle Bistro | **West End**	21	
NEW Cities | **Gldn Triangle**	-	
Citronelle | **Georgetown**	28	
CityZen | **SW**	28	
Clyde's | **Vienna**	19	
Co Co. Sala | **Penn Qtr**	22	
Coeur de Lion | **D'town**	20	
NEW Cuba Libre | **Penn Qtr**	-	
DC Coast | **D'town**	23	
Dish/Drinks | **Foggy Bottom**	19	
District ChopHse. | **Penn Qtr**	18	
NEW Diya | **Vienna**	-	
NEW Estadio | **Logan Cir**	-	
Facci | **Laurel**	-	
Fahrenheit | **Georgetown**	22	
Finemondo | **D'town**	22	
Finn/Porter | **D'town**	17	
NEW Fiola | **Penn Qtr**	-	
Fleming's Steak | **McLean**	24	
Fogo De Chão | **D'town**	24	
Georgia Brown | **D'town**	22	
Grapeseed | **Bethesda**	21	
Grille | **Alexandria**	23	
Grill/Ipanema | **Adams Mor**	20	
NEW Härth | **McLean**	-	
Hee Been | **Alexandria**	20	
Heritage India | **multi.**	22	
iCi | **D'town**	23	
Inn/Little Washington | **Washington**	29	
I Ricchi | **Dupont Cir**	24	
Irish Inn/Glen Echo | **Glen Echo**	18	
J&G Steak | **D'town**	25	
Jockey Club | **Dupont Cir**	22	
Juniper | **West End**	21	
Kabab-ji | **Dupont Cir**	20	
Kellari Taverna | **Gldn Triangle**	22	
Lafayette Rm. | **Gldn Triangle**	25	
Lia's | **Chevy Chase**	21	
Lima | **D'town**	20	
Maggiano's | **McLean**	18	
M&S Grill | **D'town**	19	
Marcel's | **West End**	29	
Marrakesh | **Dupont Cir**	20	
Masa 14 | **Logan Cir**	23	
Matchbox | **multi.**	23	

McCormick/Schmick | **multi.**	20	
NEW Medium Rare | **Cleve Pk**	-	
Minibar | **Penn Qtr**	26	
Mio | **D'town**	19	
Mon Ami Gabi | **Bethesda**	19	
Morrison-Clark | **D'town**	23	
Morton's | **multi.**	25	
Nage | **Scott Cir**	22	
New Heights | **Woodley Pk**	22	
NEW Newton's | **Bethesda**	-	
Neyla | **Georgetown**	22	
Nora | **Dupont Cir**	26	
Notti Bianche | **Foggy Bottom**	20	
Occidental | **D'town**	22	
Oceanaire | **D'town**	24	
Old Ebbitt | **D'town**	20	
Oval Rm. | **Gldn Triangle**	24	
Oya | **Penn Qtr**	23	
Palm | **multi.**	24	
Panache | **McLean**	16	
Park/14th | **D'town**	21	
Passage to India | **Bethesda**	24	
Pesce | **Dupont Cir**	24	
Petits Plats | **Woodley Pk**	22	
P.F. Chang's | **Sterling**	20	
Phillips | **Rockville**	15	
NEW P.J. Clarke's | **D'town**	-	
Plume | **D'town**	26	
Policy | **U St**	19	
Poste Moderne | **Penn Qtr**	21	
Potenza | **D'town**	20	
Prime Rib | **Gldn Triangle**	27	
Primi Piatti | **Foggy Bottom**	22	
Proof | **Penn Qtr**	24	
PS 7's | **Penn Qtr**	22	
Rasika | **Penn Qtr**	28	
NEW Rivers/Watergate | **Foggy Bottom**	-	
Rosa Mexicano | **Penn Qtr**	20	
Ruth's Chris | **multi.**	25	
NEW Sax | **D'town**	-	
Sette Osteria | **Dupont Cir**	20	
701 | **Penn Qtr**	23	
1789 | **Georgetown**	25	
Shula's | **Vienna**	21	
Siroc | **D'town**	24	
Slaviya Cafe | **Adams Mor**	-	
Smith/Wollensky | **Gldn Triangle**	22	
NEW Smith Commons | **Atlas Dist**	-	
NEW Socci | **Arlington**	-	

Source | **Penn Qtr** 25

Sou'Wester | **SW** 18

Sushiko | **Glover Pk** 25

Tabaq Bistro | **U St** 20

Tabard Inn | **Dupont Cir** 24

Teatro Goldoni | **Gldn Triangle** –

Z Tosca | **Penn Qtr** 27

Tragara | **Bethesda** 21

Tutto Bene | **Arlington** 17

Z 2941 | **Falls Ch** 26

Ulah Bistro | **U St** 18

Urbana | **Dupont Cir** 22

Vapiano | **Gldn Triangle** 18

NEW Vento | **Dupont Cir** –

Z Vidalia | **Dupont Cir** 24

Vinifera | **Reston** 21

NEW Watershed | **NoMa** –

Westend Bistro | **West End** 21

Wildfire | **McLean** 19

Woo Lae Oak | **Vienna** 21

Z Zaytinya | **Penn Qtr** 25

Zengo | **Chinatown** 22

Zola | **Penn Qtr** 23

VIEWS

NEW Arlington Rooftop | **Clarendon** –

Ashby Inn | **Paris** 24

Blue Rock Inn | **Sperryville** –

Bond 45 | **Nat'l Harbor** –

Café du Parc | **D'town** 22

Charlie Palmer | **Cap Hill** 25

Z Clyde's | **Rockville** 19

NEW El Centro | **Logan Cir** –

Eventide | **Clarendon** 20

NEW Fiorella | **Nat'l Harbor** –

Z Inn/Little Washington | **Washington** 29

J&G Steak | **D'town** 25

Lafayette Rm. | **Gldn Triangle** 25

Z L'Aub./François | **Grt Falls** 27

Mai Thai | **Alexandria** 20

New Heights | **Woodley Pk** 22

Old Angler's | **Potomac** 19

Perrys | **Adams Mor** 19

Phillips | **SW** 15

NEW Rivers/Watergate | **Foggy Bottom** –

Roof Terr. | **Foggy Bottom** 15

Rosa Mexicano | **Nat'l Harbor** 20

Z Ruth's Chris | **Arlington** 25

Sea Catch | **Georgetown** 21

Sequoia | **Georgetown** 15

701 | **Penn Qtr** 23

Source | **Penn Qtr** 25

Sou'Wester | **SW** 18

Tabaq Bistro | **U St** 20

Tony & Joe's | **Georgetown** 15

Z 2941 | **Falls Ch** 26

NEW Virtue | **Alexandria** –

VISITORS ON EXPENSE ACCOUNT

Z Acadiana | **Mt. Vernon Sq** 23

Z Adour/St. Regis | **D'town** 24

Bazin's/Church | **Vienna** 23

Bistro Provence | **Bethesda** –

Z BLT Steak | **Gldn Triangle** 25

Z Blue Duck | **West End** 26

Blue Rock Inn | **Sperryville** –

Bond 45 | **Nat'l Harbor** –

Bourbon Steak | **Georgetown** 23

Z Brass. Beck | **D'town** 25

Z Capital Grille | **multi.** 25

Caucus Rm. | **Penn Qtr** 21

Z Central Michel | **Penn Qtr** 26

Charlie Palmer | **Cap Hill** 25

Z Citronelle | **Georgetown** 28

Z CityZen | **SW** 28

Z Eve | **Alexandria** 28

Eventide | **Clarendon** 20

Fahrenheit | **Georgetown** 22

NEW Fiola | **Penn Qtr** –

Fyve | **Arlington** 17

NEW Galileo III | **D'town** –

Grille | **Alexandria** 23

Z Inn/Little Washington | **Washington** 29

I Ricchi | **Dupont Cir** 24

J&G Steak | **D'town** 25

Z Jockey Club | **Dupont Cir** 22

Z Kinkead's | **Foggy Bottom** 26

Lafayette Rm. | **Gldn Triangle** 25

Z Marcel's | **West End** 29

NEW Michel | **McLean** –

Morton's | **multi.** 25

Oceanaire | **D'town** 24

Z Palena | **Cleve Pk** 28

Z Palm | **multi.** 24

PassionFish | **Reston** 24

NEW P.J. Clarke's | **D'town** –

Plume | **D'town** 26

Z Prime Rib | **Gldn Triangle** 27

Z Ruth's Chris | **multi.** 25

Vote at ZAGAT.com

NEW Sax | **D'town**	–
🄴 1789 | **Georgetown**	25
Shula's | **Vienna**	21
Smith/Wollensky | **Gldn Triangle**	22
Source | **Penn Qtr**	25
🄴 Tosca | **Penn Qtr**	27
🄴 Trummer's | **Clifton**	25
🄴 2941 | **Falls Ch**	26
🄴 Vidalia | **Dupont Cir**	24
Westend Bistro | **West End**	21
Willow | **Arlington**	24
Woo Lae Oak | **Vienna**	21
Zentan | **D'town**	21

WATERSIDE

Phillips | **SW**	15
Sea Catch | **Georgetown**	21
Sequoia | **Georgetown**	15
Sou'Wester | **SW**	18
Tony & Joe's | **Georgetown**	15

WINE BARS

Acacia Bistro | **Upper NW**	22
A La Lucia | **Alexandria**	22
Al Crostino | **U St**	21
Ardeo/Bardeo | **Cleve Pk**	21
Asia Bistro/Zen Wine Bar | **Arlington**	20
Bastille | **Alexandria**	22
Bazin's/Church | **Vienna**	23
Bistrot Lepic | **Georgetown**	23
Cava | **Rockville**	24
Circa | **Dupont Cir**	17
Cork | **Logan Cir**	23
Dickson Wine | **U St**	–
NEW Estadio | **Logan Cir**	–
Evo Bistro | **McLean**	23
Ezmè | **Dupont Cir**	–
Fleming's Steak | **McLean**	24
Grapeseed | **Bethesda**	21
Iron Bridge | **Warrenton**	23
Mrs. K's | **Silver Spring**	22
Oakville Grille | **Bethesda**	19
Posto | **Logan Cir**	21
Proof | **Penn Qtr**	24
Redwood | **Bethesda**	17
NEW Ripple | **Cleve Pk**	–
Room 11 | **Columbia Hts**	–
Screwtop Wine | **Arlington**	–
701 | **Penn Qtr**	23
Sonoma | **Cap Hill**	20
Twisted Vines | **Arlington**	–

Urbana | **Dupont Cir**	22
Veritas | **Dupont Cir**	18
🄴 Vidalia | **Dupont Cir**	24
Vinifera | **Reston**	21
Vinoteca | **U St**	21
Wine Kit. | **Leesburg**	21

WINNING WINE LISTS

Acqua al 2 | **Cap Hill**	–
🄴 Adour/St. Regis | **D'town**	24
Ashby Inn | **Paris**	24
Bastille | **Alexandria**	22
Bibiana | **D'town**	23
Bistro Bis | **Cap Hill**	25
Bistro L'Hermitage | **Woodbridge**	24
🄴 BLT Steak | **Gldn Triangle**	25
🄴 Blue Duck | **West End**	26
Bond 45 | **Nat'l Harbor**	–
Blvd. Woodgrill | **Clarendon**	19
Bourbon Steak | **Georgetown**	23
Brabo | **Alexandria**	24
🄴 Brass. Beck | **D'town**	25
Buck's Fishing | **Upper NW**	20
Café du Parc | **D'town**	22
🄴 Capital Grille | **multi.**	25
Carlyle | **Arlington**	24
Cashion's Eat | **Adams Mor**	24
Caucus Rm. | **Penn Qtr**	21
🄴 Central Michel | **Penn Qtr**	26
Charlie Palmer | **Cap Hill**	25
Chef Geoff | **Vienna**	19
Circa | **Dupont Cir**	17
🄴 Citronelle | **Georgetown**	28
🄴 CityZen | **SW**	28
🄴 Corduroy | **Mt. Vernon Sq**	27
Cork | **Logan Cir**	23
Dino | **Cleve Pk**	22
Equinox | **Gldn Triangle**	25
NEW Estadio | **Logan Cir**	–
🄴 Eve | **Alexandria**	28
Evening Star | **Alexandria**	22
Eventide | **Clarendon**	20
Evo Bistro | **McLean**	23
Fahrenheit | **Georgetown**	22
NEW Fiola | **Penn Qtr**	–
NEW Fiorella | **Nat'l Harbor**	–
Fleming's Steak | **McLean**	24
NEW Food Wine | **Bethesda**	–
NEW Galileo III | **D'town**	–
Grapeseed | **Bethesda**	21
Harry's | **Arlington**	19

Hook | **Georgetown**	23
iCi | **D'town**	23
Il Canale | **Georgetown**	-
Z Inn/Little Washington | **Washington**	29
Jackson 20 | **Alexandria**	18
Z Jaleo | **multi.**	22
J&G Steak | **D'town**	25
Z Jockey Club | **Dupont Cir**	22
Johnny's | **Cap Hill**	20
Kellari Taverna | **Gldn Triangle**	22
Z Kinkead's | **Foggy Bottom**	26
Z Marcel's | **West End**	29
NEW Medium Rare | **Cleve Pk**	-
NEW Michel | **McLean**	-
Z Minibar | **Penn Qtr**	26
Mon Ami Gabi | **multi.**	19
Mrs. K's | **Silver Spring**	22
New Heights | **Woodley Pk**	22
Z Nora | **Dupont Cir**	26
Northside | **Clarendon**	-
Oakville Grille | **Bethesda**	19
Z Obelisk | **Dupont Cir**	27
Occidental | **D'town**	22
Z Old Ebbitt | **D'town**	20
Oval Rm. | **Gldn Triangle**	24
Z Palena | **Cleve Pk**	28
Z Palm | **multi.**	24
Passenger | **Mt. Vernon Sq**	-
PassionFish | **Reston**	24
Plume | **D'town**	26
Posto | **Logan Cir**	21
Z Prime Rib | **Gldn Triangle**	27
Proof | **Penn Qtr**	24
Z Rasika | **Penn Qtr**	28
Ray's/Classics | **Silver Spring**	24
Z Ray's/Steaks | **Clarendon**	26
Redwood | **Bethesda**	17
Ris | **West End**	23
Room 11 | **Columbia Hts**	-
Rustico | **Arlington**	21

NEW Sax | **D'town**	-
Smith/Wollensky | **Gldn Triangle**	22
Sonoma | **Cap Hill**	20
Source | **Penn Qtr**	25
Sushiko | **Glover Pk**	25
Taberna/Alabardero | **World Bank**	23
Tallula/EatBar | **Clarendon**	22
Z Tosca | **Penn Qtr**	27
Z Trummer's | **Clifton**	25
Z 2941 | **Falls Ch**	26
Twisted Vines | **Arlington**	-
Z 2 Amys | **Cleve Pk**	25
Veritas | **Dupont Cir**	18
Z Vidalia | **Dupont Cir**	24
Vinifera | **Reston**	21
Vinoteca | **U St**	21
Westend Bistro | **West End**	21
Willow | **Arlington**	24
Z Zaytinya | **Penn Qtr**	25
Zola | **Penn Qtr**	23

WORTH A TRIP

Boyce, VA	
Z L'Aub. Provençale	27
Clifton, VA	
Z Trummer's	25
Culpeper, VA	
Foti's	26
Dickerson, MD	
Comus Inn	21
Middleberg, VA	
Rest./Goodstone	-
Paris, VA	
Ashby Inn	24
The Plains, VA	
Rail Stop	22
Warrenton, VA	
Iron Bridge	23
Washington, VA	
Z Inn/Little Washington	29

BALTIMORE, ANNAPOLIS AND THE EASTERN SHORE

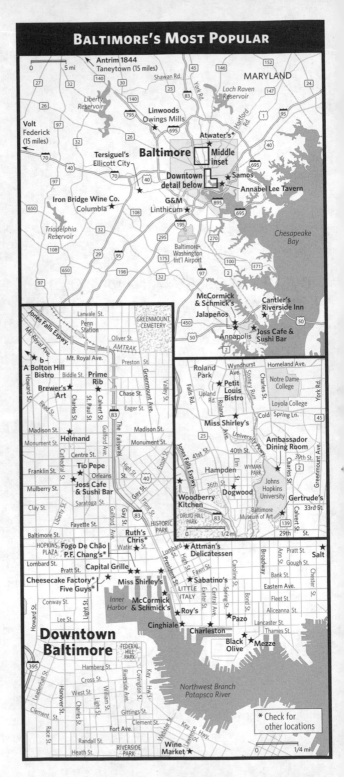

BALTIMORE'S MOST POPULAR

Antrim 1844
Taneytown (15 miles)

MARYLAND

Volt
Frederick
(15 miles)

Linwoods
Owings Mills

Atwater's★

Baltimore

Middle
inset

Tersiguel's
Ellicott City★

Downtown
detail below

Samos★

Annabel Lee Tavern

Iron Bridge Wine Co.
Columbia★

G&M
Linthicum★

Baltimore-
Washington
Int'l Airport

Chesapeake
Bay

McCormick
& Schmick's
Jalapeños

Cantler's
Riverside Inn

Annapolis

Joss Cafe &
Sushi Bar

Jones Falls Expwy.

GREENMOUNT
CEMETERY

Penn
Station

AMTRAK

b
A Bolton Hill
Bistro

Prime
Rib

Brewer's
Art

Helmand★

Tio Pepe★

Joss Cafe
& Sushi Bar★

Roland
Park

Petit
Louis
Bistro★

Notre Dame
College

Loyola College

Miss Shirley's★

Ambassador
Dining Room

Hampden

Woodberry
Kitchen★

Dogwood★

Johns
Hopkins
University

Gertrude's★

DRUID HILL
PARK

Baltimore
Museum of Art

Ruth's
Chris*★

Attman's
Delicatessen★

Salt

Fogo De Chão★
P.F. Chang's*★

Capital Grille★

Sabatino's★

Cheesecake Factory*★
Five Guys*★

Miss Shirley's★

McCormick
& Schmick's★

Roy's★

Inner
Harbor

Pazo★

**Downtown
Baltimore**

FEDERAL
HILL
PARK

Cinghiale★

Charleston★

Black
Olive★

Mezze★

Northwest Branch
Patapsco River

* Check for
other locations

Wine
Market★

232

Vote at ZAGAT.com

Baltimore's Most Popular

All restaurants are in the Baltimore area unless otherwise noted (A=Annapolis and E=Eastern Shore). When a restaurant has locations both inside and out of the city limits, we include the notation BA as well.

1. Woodberry Kitchen | *American*
2. Charleston | *American*
3. Volt | *American*
4. Cinghiale | *Italian*
5. Prime Rib | *Steak*
6. Helmand | *Afghan*
7. Black Olive | *Greek/Seafood*
8. Petit Louis | *French*
9. Pazo | *Mediterranean*
10. Capital Grille | *Steak*
11. Ruth's Chris/A/BA | *Steak*
12. Five Guys/A/BA | *Burgers*
13. Cheesecake/A/BA | *Amer.*
14. Tio Pepe | *Continental/Spanish*
15. Miss Shirley's | *American*
16. Samos | *Greek*
17. Wine Market | *American*
18. Roy's | *Hawaiian*
19. Linwoods | *American*
20. Ambassador Dining Rm. | *Indian*

21. Brewer's Art | *American*
22. Iron Bridge Wine Co. | *American*
23. Fogo De Chão | *Brazilian/Steak*
24. b | *Eclectic*
25. Salt* | *American*
26. Atwater's | *Bakery*
27. G&M | *Seafood*
28. Annabel Lee Tavern | *American*
29. McCormick*/A/BA | *Seafood*
30. Sabatino's | *Italian*
31. Antrim 1844 | *American/French*
32. P.F. Chang's | *Chinese*
33. Attman's Deli | *Deli*
34. Joss Cafe*/A/BA | *Japanese*
35. Dogwood | *American*
36. Jalapeños/A | *Mexican/Spanish*
37. Mezze* | *Mediterranean*
38. Gertrude's | *Chesapeake*
39. Cantler's Riverside/A | *Seafood*
40. Tersiguel's* | *French*

Many of the above restaurants are among the Baltimore area's most expensive, but if popularity were calibrated to price, a number of other restaurants would surely join their ranks. To illustrate this, we have added two lists comprising 58 Best Buys on page 238.

KEY NEWCOMERS

Our editors' choices among this year's arrivals. Full list, page 309.

Alchemy | *American*

Banning's/E | *American*

Big Pickle FoodBar/E | *American*

Bistro Rx | *American*

Brass. Brightwell/E | *Amer./Fr.*

Chazz | *Italian/Pizza*

Corner BYOB | *Continental*

CR Lounge | *American*

Havana Road | *Cuban*

Meet 27 | *American*

---

* Indicates a tie with restaurant above

Top Food

28 Charleston | *American*
Volt | *American*

27 Prime Rib | *Steak*
Samos | *Greek*
Di Pasquale's | *Italian*
Tasting Room | *American*
Thai Arroy | *Thai*
Peter's Inn | *American*
Linwoods | *American*
Salt | *American*

Thai Landing | *Thai*
Jalapeños/A | *Mex./Spanish*
Chameleon Cafe | *Amer.*
Scossa*/E | *Italian*
Faidley's | *Seafood*

26 Helmand | *Afghan*
Woodberry Kitchen | *Amer.*
Honey Pig | *Korean*
Les Folies/A | *French*
O'Learys/A | *Seafood*

BY CUISINE

AMERICAN (NEW)

28 Charleston
Volt
27 Tasting Room
Peter's Inn
Linwoods

AMERICAN (TRAD.)

24 Blue Moon Cafe
Miss Shirley's
22 Friendly Farm
22 Patrick's
21 Dutch's Daughter

CHINESE

28 Grace Garden▽
23 Szechuan House
21 Hunan Manor
20 Cafe Zen
P.F. Chang's

CRAB HOUSES

27 Faidley's
26 Mr. Bill's Terrace Inn▽
23 Costas Inn
Obrycki's
Cantler's Riverside/A

FRENCH

26 Les Folies/A
Tersiguel's
25 Antrim 1844
Petit Louis
23 Café Normandie/A

GREEK

27 Samos
26 Black Olive

24 Ikaros
21 Paul's Homewood/A
Zorba's B&G

INDIAN

24 Flavors/House of India
Akbar
Ambassador Dining Rm.
22 Carlyle Club

ITALIAN

27 Di Pasquale's
Scossa/E
26 La Scala
25 Osteria 177/A
Aldo's

MEXICAN/SPANISH

27 Jalapeños/A
26 Mari Luna
25 Isabella's
24 Tio Pepe
21 Cacique

SEAFOOD

27 Faidley's
26 O'Learys/A
Black Olive
24 Oceanaire
Catonsville Gourmet

STEAKHOUSES

27 Prime Rib
25 Lewnes' Steakhouse/A
Capital Grille
Ruth's Chris/A/BA
Morton's

Excludes places with low votes, unless otherwise indicated

Vote at ZAGAT.com

SUSHI

26	Sushi Sono
25	Joss Cafe/Sushi/A/BA
24	Sushi King
	Edo Sushi
23	Sushi Hana

THAI

27	Thai Arroy
	Thai Landing
23	Lemongrass/A
20	Pad Thai/A
19	Bân Thai

BY SPECIAL FEATURE

BREAKFAST

24	Main Ingredient/A
	Blue Moon Cafe
	Miss Shirley's
22	Stone Mill Bakery
21	City Cafe

BRUNCH

25	Orchard Market
	b
24	Main Ingredient/A
	Ambassador Dining Rm.
23	Jesse Wong's Asean

BUSINESS DINING

28	Charleston
27	Linwoods
25	Lewnes' Steakhouse/A
	Capital Grille
	Ruth's Chris

HOTEL DINING

25	Ruth's Chris (Pier 5)
	Antrim 1844
	Morton's (Sheraton Inner Harbor)
22	B&O American Brasserie (Monaco Baltimore)
20	McCormick & Schmick's (Pier 5)

LOCAL FAVORITES

27	Samos
	Faidley's
26	Mari Luna
22	Jennings∇
21	Zorba's B&G

MEET FOR A DRINK

24	Wine Market
	Pazo
23	Brewer's Art

19	One World Cafe
	13.5% Wine Bar

POWER SCENES

28	Charleston
	Volt
27	Linwoods
26	Woodberry Kitchen
25	Lewnes' Steakhouse/A

QUICK BITES

27	Faidley's
25	Big Bad Wolf BBQ
23	Szechuan House
22	Goldberg's Bagels
18	Jimmy's

TRENDY

25	Hamilton Tavern
23	Clementine
19	13.5% Wine Bar
-	Alchemy
-	Corner BYOB

WATERSIDE

24	Kentmorr/E∇
23	Cantler's Riverside/A
	Narrows/E
22	Carrol's Creek Cafe/A
21	Tabrizi's

WORTH A TRIP

28	Volt
	Frederick
26	Mr. Bill's Terrace Inn∇
	Essex
25	Antrim 1844
	Taneytown
23	Cantler's Riverside/A
	Annapolis
	Narrows/E
	Grasonville

BY LOCATION

ANNAPOLIS
27 Jalapeños
26 Les Folies
25 Osteria 177
Joss Cafe/Sushi
Galway Bay

COLUMBIA
26 Sushi Sono
25 Pho Dat Thanh
24 Sushi King
Flavors/House of India
Akbar

DOWNTOWN NORTH/ MT. VERNON
27 Prime Rib
Thai Landing
26 Helmand
25 Iggies
Joss Cafe/Sushi

EASTERN SHORE
27 Scossa
25 208 Talbot
Out of the Fire
23 Bistro St. Michaels
Narrows

EASTPORT
26 O'Learys
25 Lewnes' Steak
Ruth's Chris
Carrol's Creek
18 Rockfish

FELLS POINT
27 Peter's Inn
26 Black Olive
25 Mezze
24 Blue Moon Cafe
Kali's Court

FREDERICK
28 Volt
27 Tasting Room

25 Isabella's
24 Monocacy Crossing
21 Firestone's

HARBOR EAST
28 Charleston
25 Roy's
24 Oceanaire
Cinghiale
Fleming's Steak

INNER HARBOR
25 Capital Grille
Ruth's Chris
24 Fogo De Chão
Miss Shirley's
Edo Sushi

LITTLE ITALY
26 La Scala
25 Aldo's
24 La Tavola
23 Germano's
Rocco's Capriccio

LUTHERVILLE/ TIMONIUM
24 Sabor
Edo Sushi
23 Szechuan House
Christopher Daniel
22 BlueStone

SOUTH BALTIMORE
27 Thai Arroy
22 Matsuri
Regi's
21 Tabrizi's
Corks

TOWSON
25 Atwater's
Orchard Market
Pho Dat Thanh
23 Sushi Hana
San Sushi/Thai

Vote at ZAGAT.com

Top Decor

<u>27</u> Charleston	Linwoods
Pazo	<u>25</u> Prime Rib
Scossa*/E	Elkridge Furnace
Milton Inn	Oregon Grille
Antrim 1844	<u>24</u> Kali's Court
<u>26</u> Ambassador Dining Rm.	Sotto Sopra
Woodberry Kitchen	B&O American Brasserie
Blue Hill Tavern	Severn Inn/A
Cinghiale	Gertrude's
Volt	Capital Grille

OUTDOORS

Ambassador Dining Rm.	Milton Inn
b	Oregon Grille
Cantler's Riverside	Stone Mill Bakery
Gertrude's	Tabrizi's
Kentmorr/E	Tark's Grill
L.P. Steamers	Wine Market

PRIVATE ROOMS

Broom's Bloom	Mezze
Cafe Hon	Pazo
Capital Grille	Portalli's
Charleston	Sabatino's
Cinghiale	Sushi Hana (Timonium)
Ikaros	Tersiguel's
La Famiglia	Vinny's Cafe

ROMANCE

Ambassador Dining Rm.	Narrows
Antrim 1844	Orchard Market
Chameleon Café	Pairings Bistro
Charleston	Paul's Homewood
Helmand	Samos
Islander Inn	Sotto Sopra
Milton Inn	Zorba's B&G

VIEWS

Blue Hill Tavern	L.P. Steamers
Broom's Bloom	Narrows
Cantler's Riverside	Pope's Tavern/E
Carrol's Creek Café	Robert Morris Inn/E
Charleston	Stone Mill Bakery
Gertrude's	Sushi Sono
Harris Crab	Tabrizi's
Kentmorr/E	Tidewater Grille

Top Service

Best Buys

In order of Bang for the Buck rating.

OTHER GOOD VALUES

BALTIMORE, ANNAPOLIS AND THE EASTERN SHORE RESTAURANT DIRECTORY

Baltimore

Acacia Bistro ▩ *American* | 20 | 18 | 18 | $42
Frederick | 129 N. Market St. (bet. Church & 2nd Sts.) | 301-694-3015 |
www.acacia129.com
"Ask about the daily specials" at this "consistently good" New
American in the heart of Frederick featuring an "inventive" menu
"foodies will enjoy"; sit up front in one of the "traditional" bar's high-
tops or in the narrow space's "inviting" dining rooms, including one
within eyeshot of a "lovely garden"; all in all, it's a "soothing" way to
chow down, that is "unless the shoppers show up with strollers."

Aida Bistro & Wine Bar ▨ *Italian* | 23 | 18 | 22 | $40
Columbia | 6741 Columbia Gateway Dr. (Rte. 175) | 410-953-0500 |
www.aidabistro.com
Newly resettled in warmer, more spacious digs across the street
(outdating its Decor score), this "family-owned" Italian is still "tough
to find" (blame its Columbia "industrial park" locale), but it's "well
worth" the effort, particularly for the "delicious" "home-cooked"
pastas, "small plates" and "ample, reasonable" wine list; tabs that
can run a "bit pricey" chill some, but "warm", generally "attentive"
service from the "friendly" staff thaws most hearts.

Akbar *Indian* | 24 | 17 | 22 | $25
Mt. Vernon | 823 N. Charles St. (bet. Madison & Read Sts.) |
410-539-0944
Columbia | Columbia Mktpl. | 9400 Snowden River Pkwy.
(bet. Berger & Oakland Mills Rds.) | 410-381-3600
www.akbar-restaurant.com
"When you need that Indian food fix", these "reliable" – and
"popular" – subcontinentals dish up an "excellent sampling" of "delicious" fare that's "reasonably priced"; choose between the "cozy,
subterranean" Mt. Vernon space or the Columbia "strip-mall" digs,
both of which provide a "plentiful" lunch buffet that's "good enough
to put you in a food coma (close the office door, it's nap time)."

NEW Alchemy *American* | - | - | - | E
Hampden | 1011 W. 36th St. (bet. Hickory & Roland Aves.) |
410-366-1163 | www.alchemyon36.com
This newcomer on Hampden's 'Avenue' is literally packing them into
its tight, though nicely rehabbed, bi-level space for edgy, expensive
New American tastes; the staff is upping its game as it learns to handle the crowds, and there's craft beer and wine to help smooth over
any early bumps in service.

Aldo's *Italian* | 25 | 24 | 24 | $57
Little Italy | 306 S. High St. (Fawn St.) | 410-727-0700 |
www.aldositaly.com
One bite and you're "back in Rome" at chef-owner Aldo Vitale's "go-
to place for special occasions", where "exquisite" Southern Italian
fare is delivered by "gracious" tux-clad servers in a "romantic setting", courtesy of decor that's "more sophisticated and lighter" than

its Little Italy brethren; it all comes with "expensive" tabs, of course, and detractors detect a "stuffy formality", but those who deem it a "pleasure" "can't wait" to return.

Ambassador Dining Room *Indian*   24 | 26 | 24 | $38

Homewood | Ambassador Apts. | 3811 Canterbury Rd. (bet. 39th St. & University Pkwy.) | 410-366-1484 | www.ambassadordining.com
Connoisseurs "can't say enough" about this "incredibly romantic" Indian "treat" "hidden" in a "nondescript" Homewood apartment building, home to "fantastic" fare that "never disappoints" and tuxedoed servers who "make you feel like a maharajah"; the "elegant" ambiance is abetted by a "sumptuous" space that's "equally wonderful" in any season, thanks to a "lovely garden patio with fountain" and "bookend fireplaces" that "set the mood perfectly" in colder months.

Amicci's *Italian*   21 | 17 | 20 | $27

Little Italy | 231 S. High St. (bet. Fawn & Stiles Sts.) | 410-528-1096 | www.amiccis.com
"Heavy on the garlic, light on the wallet", this "Little Italy standard" lures locals and "out-of-towners" alike with its "generous portions" of "solid" red-sauce classics dished up in a "cozy" space adorned with "wall posters"; vets say "don't miss" the "famous" *pane' rotundo* (shrimp scampi in a breadbowl) – it may be a "heart attack on a plate", but "every table has at least one."

Andy Nelson's BBQ ⊠ *BBQ*   25 | 12 | 19 | $14

Cockeysville | 11007 York Rd. (Wight Ave.) | 410-527-1226 | www.andynelsonsbbq.com
For some of the "best BBQ pig and sweet tea north of Tara", Cockeysville denizens make tracks to this "standout" "smoke shack" owned by the former Baltimore Colt (don't be surprised if "good ol' Andy himself" takes your order at the counter); there's a "picnic-style atmosphere" within and it "looks like a dive from outside", but that "doesn't take away from the taste" – and besides, the "price is right."

An Loi *Vietnamese*   24 | 10 | 19 | $13

Columbia | 7104 Minstrel Way (Snowden River Pkwy.) | 410-381-3188
It's "tucked into a nondescript [Columbia] strip mall", there's "not a lot of ambiance" and "tables are close together", but "who cares" when the "authentic" Vietnamese fare (plus a few Korean options) is this "good"; add in "reasonable prices", and small wonder it's "always crowded."

Annabel Lee Tavern ⊠ *American*   23 | 22 | 22 | $26

Canton | 601 S. Clinton St. (Fleet St.) | 410-522-2929 | www.annabelleetavern.com
Edgar Allan Poe "would be proud" of this "quirky" Canton "hole-in-the-wall" themed for his final poem, with "creative, delicious" and "reasonably priced" New American grub and a "moody", "memorabilia"-packed interior that "gets crowded quickly"; regulars "stopping in after work" and "strangers" are both "treated well here", further boosting its growing rep as a "place to raven about."

☑ Antrim 1844 *American/French*   25 | 27 | 25 | $72

Taneytown | Antrim 1844 | 30 Trevanion Rd. (Rte. 140) | 410-756-6812 |
www.antrim1844.com

"It's a bit of a drive", but this "Maryland must" in a "beautiful old"
Taneytown inn is "worth it" to sample chef Michael Gettier's "wonderful" French-influenced New American meals, "delightful culinary
adventures" accompanied by service to match; be sure to "allow
time for the experience" and "roam the beautiful gardens" or, better
yet, just "get a room" and sleep in.

Asian Court *Chinese*   ▽ 22 | 13 | 17 | $24

Ellicott City | Chatham Station | 9180 Baltimore National Pike
(bet. N. Chatham Rd. & St. Johns Ln.) | 410-461-8388

The aptly named 'Feel Good Noodles' pretty much sum up surveyors' opinions on this "small" Ellicott City strip-maller proffering
what's "easily the area's best dim sum"; there's little ambiance but
most are "glad to have it around" anyway, especially since new
ownership has reportedly improved things like "spotty" service.

Attman's Delicatessen *Deli*   25 | 9 | 17 | $14

East Baltimore | 1019 E. Lombard St. (Exeter St.) | 410-563-2666 |
www.attmansdeli.com

Even "displaced Noo Yawkas" agree that this 96-year-old East
Baltimore "institution" is "what delis are supposed to be": bastions
of "killer kosher dogs", "great pickles" and "amazing corned beef"
packed into "ginormous sandwiches" best consumed after putting
"your cardiologist on speed dial"; while "long lines" move "fast"
thanks to "witty", "brutally efficient" countermen, the "dinky" dining room means there's often "nowhere to sit", though a planned expansion aims to change that.

Atwater's *Bakery*   25 | 15 | 19 | $14

North Baltimore | Belvedere Square Mkt. | 529 E. Belvedere Ave.
(York Rd.) | 410-323-2396

NEW **Catonsville** | 815 Frederick Rd. (bet. Mellor & Newburg Aves.) |
410-747-4120

Towson | 798 Kenilworth Dr. (West Rd.) | 410-938-8775
www.atwaters.biz

"It's all about the soup" at Ned Atwater's "great little lunch spot"
(breakfast too) in "busy" Belvedere Square, which ladles out a "wonderful variety" of "hearty, healthy" creations complemented by
"delicious rustic breads" and "tasty sandwiches"; if its younger
Towson sib is "more cramped" (a drive-thru helps) and "not as fun",
you can expect the same "delicious" if relatively "pricey" fare and,
alas, service that can run "maddeningly slow"; P.S. the newest
branch is a counter-serve in Catonsville.

b – A Bolton Hill Bistro Ⓜ *American*   25 | 21 | 23 | $36

Downtown North | 1501 Bolton St. (Mosher St.) | 410-383-8600 |
www.b-bistro.com

"To b or not to b?": yes, "go there" assert admirers of this "cozy
neighborhood place" whose "inventive" New American fare, "in-

expensive wine list" and "competent, sincere" staff will have you "fantasizing about living in Bolton Hill"; expect a "wonderful atmosphere", albeit one with "sardine-can seating", a bit of "noise" from the crowds and a paucity of "empty tables" – so "sit outside" and enjoy the air.

B&O American Brasserie *American* 22 | 24 | 22 | $43
Downtown | Monaco Baltimore | 2 N. Charles St. (Baltimore St.) | 443-692-6172 | www.bandorestaurant.com

"Step off Charles Street and feel like you're in Manhattan" at this "upscale and chic" New American in a beaux arts building Downtown; while the "inventive" fare (e.g. "perfect pork belly"), "creative" cocktails and "attentive" staff generally please, it's the "beautiful" split-level space and a "cool bar complete with faux leather walls" and velvet stools that leave surveyors swooning.

Bân Thai ⊠ *Thai* 19 | 12 | 19 | $22
Downtown | 340 N. Charles St. (Mulberry St.) | 410-727-7971 | www.banthai.us

The "decor may be a bit faded", but that doesn't faze regulars of this "well-established" North Charles Street Thai proffering "ample, flavorful meals" for a modest price (making it a "decent" option for pre-theater repasts and lunches); "fast service" sweetens the deal for those who insist "even if nothing excels, nothing ever disappoints either."

Baugher's *American* 18 | 10 | 20 | $15
Westminster | 289 W. Main St. (Rtes. 31 & 32) | 410-848-7413 | www.baughers.com

"Go for the fried chicken, stay for the pies" at this "down-home" "throwback" in Westminster where the "dependable" "country cooking" (much of it derived from the Baugher family orchard) is no friend to those "preoccupied with their waistlines"; while it may be short on decor, "good service" and "cheap prices" keep the place "crowded"; P.S. "shop for produce after you eat" at the adjacent farm stand.

Bertha's *Seafood* 18 | 15 | 17 | $26
Fells Point | 734 S. Broadway (Lancaster St.) | 410-327-5795 | www.berthas.com

It may be "Baltimore in the rough", but that doesn't stop the masses from descending on this "divey" Fells Point seafooder for its "claim to fame": "mussels in all their glorious variations" and the "lip-smacking" sauces that accompany them; if "sloppy service" and an otherwise "blah menu" leave some landlubbers "unimpressed", they're outnumbered by those who return "time and time again"; P.S. there's "live music" Tuesday–Saturday and a popular Sunday brunch.

NEW BGR, The Burger Joint *Burgers* 21 | 13 | 15 | $15
Columbia | Columbia Crossing | 6250 Columbia Crossing Circle (Dobbin Rd.) | 443-319-5542 | www.bgrtheburgerjoint.com
See review in the Washington, DC, Directory.

	FOOD	DECOR	SERVICE	COST

Big Bad Wolf's House of Barbeque *BBQ*

| 25 | 8 | 18 | $14 |

Northeast Baltimore | 5713 Harford Rd. (White Ave.) | 410-444-6422 | www.bigbadwolfbarbeque.com

"Little, yellow, different": that's how committed "carnivores" describe Rick and Scott Smith's "eating hot spot", a butter-hued brick house that's become the "center of the barbecue universe in Baltimore" (Hamilton, to be exact); from "amazing pulled pork" and "falling-off-the-bone ribs" to "down-home sides" and "awesome" sauces, you "can't go wrong", though with "little seating", some howl it's best for "carryout."

Birches ☒ *American*

| 24 | 17 | 18 | $30 |

Canton | 641 S. Montford Ave. (Foster Ave.) | 410-732-3000 | www.birchesrestaurant.com

Once they "find parking" (it's not easy), visitors to this "best-kept secret" in Canton "find delight" in its "extensive menu" of "terrific" New American "gourmet comfort food" with a "twist" ("popcorn in your salad?"); sure, the "food takes forever" – blame that wood-fired grill – and the "cozy" tavern setting is a bit "shabby", but most just "can't resist" the place; P.S. there are "tasty weekday specials at the bar."

Bistro Blanc Ⓜ *American*

| - | - | - | E |

Glenelg | 3800 Ten Oaks Rd. (bet. Ivory & Triadelphia Rds.) | 410-489-7907 | www.bistroblancmd.com

Wayfarers in the Howard County hinterlands (i.e. Glenelg) are happy to discover this slick wine bar/restaurant/retail outfit complete with a "cool" self-serve vino-dispensing machine and a pricey New American menu, ranging from braised pork with figs to burgers and rack of lamb; just grab the GPS or call for directions, as it's "tough to find"; P.S. 50% wine bottles on Tuesdays and occasional live music sweeten the deal.

NEW Bistro Rx *American*

| - | - | - | M |

Highlandtown | 2901 E. Baltimore St. (Linwood Ave.) | 410-276-0820 | www.bistrorx.net

This newcomer set in a former corner pharmacy lures northern Highlandtown's pioneering real-estate rehabbers with an addictive prescription: midpriced, arty turns on American pub fare (e.g. bison steak, chorizo-crab mac 'n' cheese, bread puddings) dispensed by a pair of ex–Wine Market chefs; weekday specials, a strong beer list and outdoor seating by Patterson Park are further draws.

☒ Black Olive *Greek/Seafood*

| 26 | 22 | 24 | $52 |

Fells Point | 814 S. Bond St. (Shakespeare St.) | 410-276-7141 | www.theblackolive.com

"Get up close and personal with your food" at this "Greek paradise" set in a "rustic" Fells Point row house, where patrons choose from the "fresh fish on ice" then chill as it's "beautifully cooked" and "deboned and served tableside"; it may be the "closest you can get to the Mediterranean in Baltimore", though "expense-account" pricing leaves budgeteers suggesting it's "best for a special occasion."

Blue Agave
Restaurante y Tequileria ⓜ *Mexican*

20 | 20 | 18 | $32

South Baltimore | 1032 Light St. (Cross St.) | 410-576-3938 |
www.blueagaverestaurant.com

With more than 130 different tequilas on hand, "it's all about the
drinks" (e.g. "dangerous margaritas") at this "casual" South Baltimore
haunt; "exposed brick and plaster walls in earthy tones" provide a
"fun" backdrop to "basic" Mexican eats and "marginal" service.

Bluegrass ⓜ *American*

- | - | - | M

South Baltimore | 1500 S. Hanover St. (Fort Ave.) | 410-244-5101 |
www.bluegrasstavern.com

Set in residential South Baltimore west of the nightlife area, this
modernized corner tavern is crowded with urban dwellers and suburbanites digging into midpriced, locally sourced New American
comfort fare with a Southern twist – think cornbread in iron skillets
and cheddar grits; big windows open the narrow space to covered
sidewalk seating that's suited to sipping the two dozen bourbons on
offer, while valet service eases parking woes.

Blue Hill Tavern *American*

23 | 26 | 21 | $41

Canton | 938 S. Conkling St. (Dillon St.) | 443-388-9363 |
www.bluehilltavern.com

"This trendy joint has it all": "simply stunning" decor that brings
"NYC/Miami/LA (you choose)" to Canton, "terrific" service and
"creative, tasty" New American fare – including "scrumptious"
desserts – in a "wide variety of prices"; add in "lively" bars that become a "hot, hot, hot" scene on weekends, and most concur "you
won't be blue" after a visit; P.S. free valet parking available.

Blue Moon Cafe *American*

24 | 15 | 17 | $17

Fells Point | 1621 Aliceanna St. (bet. Bethel St. & B'way) |
410-522-3940

It slings some of the "best breakfasts around", so "arrive early" on
weekends at this "tiny, cramped" Fells Point "gem" "if you want to
eat in a timely manner"; choose from "biscuits like mama's",
"yummy omelets" or the "world-famous" Cap'n Crunch French
toast, a "religious experience" that's "worth the wait" – and worth
putting up with servers' "take it or leave it" attitude; P.S. open from
7 AM to 3 PM Monday–Wednesday, then open continuously from
7 AM on Thursday until 3 PM on Sunday.

BlueStone *Seafood*

22 | 21 | 21 | $34

Timonium | 11 W. Aylesbury Rd. (Business Park Dr.) | 410-561-1100 |
www.bluestoneonline.net

Providing "reliable" "fresh seafood" in the "desert of suburbia", this
Timonium "hangout" draws a wide-ranging "crowd" (from singles to
sports fans) to its "upscale", "contemporary" quarters, complete
with a "hopping bar" and "half-price bottles of wine on Tuesdays";
it's "often noisy" and service can be "inconsistent", but for the most
part, "everyone's having a good time"; P.S. a post-Survey expansion
and fancy new terrace may outdate the Decor score.

	FOOD	DECOR	SERVICE	COST

Bon Fresco ☒ *Sandwiches* | - | - | - | I |

Columbia | 6945 Oakland Mills Rd. (Snowden River Pkwy.) | 410-290-3434

Chef-owner Gerald Koh (ex DC's Bread Line) bakes crusty ciabatta all day and uses housemade London broil, roast chicken, pork loin and grilled veggies to create some of the "best-tasting sandwiches" around; salads, arty pizzas, desserts and take-home breads complete the menu at this relatively inexpensive counter-service spot buried in a Columbia commercial strip (so grab your GPS).

NEW Breakfast Shoppe *American* | - | - | - | I |

Severna Park | Park Plaza Shopping Ctr. | 552 Ritchie Hwy. (McKinsey Rd.) | 410-544-8599 | www.thebreakfastshoppe.com

Locals who used to line up for the egg specials (e.g. crab-asparagus Benedict, portobello-rosemary omelets) and other breakfast and lunch eats at this daytime American were plenty pleased to follow it down Ritchie Highway to its new Severna Park strip-mall berth; it remains as cheap as ever, but now there's more room to spread out and pack in the calories.

Brewer's Art *American* | 23 | 23 | 20 | $35 |

Mt. Vernon | 1106 N. Charles St. (bet. Biddle & Chase Sts.) | 410-547-6925 | www.thebrewersart.com

Hopsheads "come for the beer and stay for the food" at this "classic" Mt. Vernon townhouse with two "equally delightful" spaces: a "gorgeous bar" and "swanky" dining room where "creative" New American meals "will knock your socks off" and, below that, a "dark, underground" retreat where "hipsters go to not be seen"; it's always a "rare experience", but regulars order a "home-brewed Resurrection Ale" and the "must-try" garlic-rosemary fries to send it "over the top."

Broom's Bloom Dairy ☒ *Ice Cream* | ▽ 27 | 18 | 25 | $10 |

Bel Air | 1700 S. Fountain Green Rd./Rte. 543 (Rte. 136) | 410-399-2697 | www.bbdairy.com

Just "minutes from I-95" but a world apart, this "fabulous" (and "inexpensive") Bel Air cafe "tucked away on a dairy farm" offers a "delicious break from the city"; while it's "known" for "outstanding" ice cream in "many inventive flavors", there's also "tasty, substantial" soups and sandwiches, "live music on weekends" and open space for kids to run around; P.S. a private party room was recently added.

Cacique *Mexican/Spanish* | 21 | 16 | 18 | $28 |

Frederick | 26 N. Market St. (Patrick St.) | 301-695-2756 | www.caciquefrederick.com

Well-sited on Downtown Frederick's Market Street strip, this "friendly" entry plies a "flavorful", "reasonably priced" lineup of "traditional" Spanish dishes and "Mexican favorites" (e.g. "standout" paella and fajitas) chased with sangria and margaritas; a homey hacienda with a handful of sidewalk tables, it's often "filled" but still "romantic" enough "to take a date."

Caesar's Den *Italian*

21 | 19 | 23 | $39

Little Italy | 223 S. High St. (Stiles St.) | 410-547-0820 |
www.caesarsden.com

"One of Little Italy's unsung heroes", this longtime Italian "standby"
supplies comforting "classics" served by staffers who "treat you as
friends"; while the smallish setting and "basic" "old-school" style
strike some as "nothing special", loyalists laud it as "one of the better" picks for a "traditional" fix; P.S. call ahead for reservations.

Cafe Bretton Ⓜ *French*

▽ 24 | 24 | 23 | $48

Severna Park | 849 Baltimore-Annapolis Blvd. (Smith Rd.) |
410-647-8222 | www.cafe-bretton.com

"Like a visit to France without the attitude", this Severna Park French-
Continental pairs a "delightful" menu garnished with "ultrafresh
greens and veggies" "from its own garden" with "attentive service" in
a fireplace-equipped setting that could be a patch of "Provence";
some plead it's "expensive", but well-heeled admirers "love it."

Café de Paris *French*

21 | 19 | 20 | $39

Columbia | 8808 Centre Park Dr. (Rte. 108) | 410-997-3560 |
www.cafedepariscolumbia.com

"You feel like a regular on your first visit" to this "casual" bistro
tucked in a Columbia "office building", where "involved owner" Erik
Rochard oversees a "hospitable" milieu for "well-executed" "country French" fare; a finicky few shrug *comme ci comme ça*, but the
prix fixe menu, "small crêperie" annex and "live jazz" on Tuesdays
and weekends add incentive "for a date."

Café Gia *Italian*

20 | 21 | 19 | $28

Little Italy | 410 S. High St. (Eastern Ave.) | 410-685-6727 |
www.cafegias.com

Known by its "whimsically painted exterior", this "bistro-like" Little
Italy spot serves "solid" "homestyle Italian" cooking in "cute-as-a-
button" art nouveau quarters "under the watchful eye of a mother-
and-daughter" ownership team; while on the "casual" side, it's
considered "a cut above the touristy spots in the area."

Cafe Hon *American*

15 | 18 | 17 | $21

Hampden | 1002 W. 36th St. (Roland Ave.) | 410-243-1230 |
www.cafehon.com

"Watch *Hairspray*" to appreciate the "hometown Bawlmer appeal"
at this way "popular" Hampden "icon", a "nifty '50s" "throwback"
for "simple American eats" served up in "quirky" "diner" digs by a
"spirited" if "slooooow" staff; foes fume it's "living on shtick" with
"unspectacular" food priced "higher than you'd expect", but the
"sass" "makes up for" that so "everybody should go once."

Cafe Nola *American*

▽ 21 | 21 | 20 | $27

Frederick | 4 E. Patrick St. (Market St.) | 301-694-6652 |
www.cafe-nola.com

"If you're not in a rush", this "low-key" Frederick "neighborhood"
hang serves coffeehouse fare by day and an "interesting" New

American dinner menu with some "eclectic choices" that appeal to "vegans, locavores and the like"; works by "local artists" line the walls, and nights occasionally "turn into a hipster scene" as the cool crowd gathers to "listen to indie bands" and poets.

Café Troia *Italian*

21 | 20 | 21 | $48

Towson | 31 W. Allegheny Ave. (Washington Ave.) | 410-337-0133 | www.cafetroia.com

"High quality" is the hallmark of this "upscale" Towson Italian, now settled in "larger digs" across from its original site with an "imaginative Italian" menu showcasing "scrumptious" braised meats; even if critics carp it's "overpriced", "first-rate service" and tasteful, ochre-shaded surroundings "make you feel like you're a bigger big shot" than you are.

Café Tuscany 🗷 Ⓜ *Italian* (fka Bit of Tuscany)

▽ 22 | 17 | 19 | $55

Westminster | 84 E. Main St. (Longwell Ave.) | 410-857-4422 | www.cafetuscanywestminster.com

This "small, charming" family-run storefront in Westminster's old retail center is upping the dining stakes in these parts with a "great wine selection" and "very good" Italian cooking, including Tuscan tastes like exotic pastas (truffle agnolotti), antipasti, panini, pizzas and lamb/vealburgers; an appreciative crowd of professionals, families and dates descends upon the bright front room, quiet back room, patio and newly added sit-down bar.

Cafe Zen *Chinese*

20 | 11 | 18 | $21

North Baltimore | 438 E. Belvedere Ave. (York Rd.) | 410-532-0022 | www.cafezen.us

This "well-established" North Baltimore Chinese "meets a neighborhood need", serving "inventive" house specialties ("healthy" vegetarian plates included) "along with popular favorites" at a "moderate" cost; the staff is "pleasant" and "prompt", and if the "minimalist" setup strikes some as "too sterile", it's a "handy" hangout "before a movie or event at the Senator."

🟏 Capital Grille *Steak*

25 | 24 | 25 | $63

Inner Harbor | 500 E. Pratt St. (Gay St.) | 443-703-4064 | www.thecapitalgrille.com

See review in the Washington, DC, Directory.

Carlyle Club *Indian*

22 | 24 | 23 | $39

Homewood | The Carlyle | 500 W. University Pkwy. (bet. 39th & 40th Sts.) | 410-243-5454

Experience "a different kind" of subcontinental "character" at this Homewood Indian from the "same owner as the Ambassador Dining Room", where "charming waiters" serve "creative" Southern Coastal specialties ("try the dosas") in a "lovely" space with "relaxing" vibes that extend to a patio; while "quiet" and somewhat "underappreciated", supporters say it's a "hidden gem" that "more need to discover."

	FOOD	DECOR	SERVICE	COST

Catonsville Gourmet *Seafood*

| 24 | 18 | 22 | $32 |

Catonsville | 829 Frederick Rd. (bet. Mellor & Newburg Aves.) | 410-788-0005 | www.catonsvillegourmet.com

"Finally", the "name is no longer an oxymoron" thanks to this Catonsville "haven" for "exceptional" seafood from chef/co-owner Rob Rehmert, whose "gill-breathing fresh" roster of raw bar and Eastern Shore classics with occasional Asian inflections "will satisfy even the most discriminating"; "top-shelf" service and a BYO policy that's a "value winner" help explain why the "casually elegant" quarters are typically "packed"; P.S. a "market under the same roof" vends the catch to take home.

Cazbar *Turkish*

| 22 | 21 | 18 | $27 |

Downtown | 316 N. Charles St. (Saratoga St.) | 410-528-1222 | www.cazbar.pro

A "tasty" "introduction to Turkish" fare awaits at this Downtown nook, where "many different meze" and "excellent" specialties like kebabs and manti (beef dumplings) are "served without pretense" "at a reasonable price"; the stylishly "small space" is handy for a "leisurely lunch" or lets you get closer to a date, though it's more "lively" on weekends when "lovely belly dancers" "rock the Cazbar."

Centro 🗵 Ⓜ *Spanish*

| - | - | - | M |

South Baltimore | 1444 Light St. (Fort Ave.) | 443-869-6871 | www.centrotapasbar.com

The former Bicycle space in South Baltimore is humming with a focus on cuisines from Spain and South America, so expect moderately priced fare like Mallorcan chorizo, snacky small plates (e.g. Catalonian almonds) and more-familiar empanadas and paella; cozy dining rooms spread over two row houses provide a pleasant environment for sangria-sipping, plus there's a shaded patio for extra seating in fair weather.

Chameleon Cafe 🗵 Ⓜ *American*

| 27 | 17 | 25 | $42 |

Northeast Baltimore | 4341 Harford Rd. (Montebello Terr.) | 410-254-2376 | www.thechameleoncafe.com

"Hurray!" cheer champions of this "unexpected treasure" in a converted Northeast Baltimore row house, a "top-flight" showcase for chef/co-owner Jeffrey Smith's "dedication" to "seasonal, local" gustation via an "elegantly prepared" New American menu that's like "a symphony for the taste buds" accompanied by "excellent wines"; a "knowledgeable and attentive" team monitors the "simple" but "cozy" setting, and despite "all the buzz" over the "sublime dining", the "price is right."

🗷 Charleston 🗵 *American*

| 28 | 27 | 27 | $85 |

Harbor East | 1000 Lancaster St. (Exeter St.) | 410-332-7373 | www.charlestonrestaurant.com

"The hype is all true" at this "top-of-the-line" Harbor East "jewel" – rated No. 1 for Food, Decor and Service in the Baltimore Survey – which "raises the bar" with the "incomparable" Cindy Wolf's "stellar" New American cuisine, presented on a diner's-choice tasting menu paired with "outstanding wines"; the "impeccable" service and "sheer elegance" of the setting will "sweep you off your feet", so even if you "need to take out a second mortgage", "you won't care."

NEW Chazz: A Bronx Original *Italian/Pizza* − | − | − | M

Harbor East | 1415 Aliceanna St. (Central Ave.) | 410-522-5511 | www.chazzbronxoriginal.com

Actor Chazz Palminteri has enlisted the team behind local high-flier Aldo's for this nostalgaic love letter to the pizza and pasta emporiums of his Arthur Avenue childhood, set in a Harbor East high-rise (the first link in a planned national chain); a huge coal-fired oven elevates pizzamaking to entertainment, while housemade pastas, Italian entrees, an antipasti station and an elegant bar serving craft drinks round out the menu.

Cheesecake Factory *American* 19 | 18 | 18 | $28

Inner Harbor | Harborplace Pratt Street Pavilion | 201 E. Pratt St. (South St.) | 410-234-3990
Columbia | 10300 Little Patuxent Pkwy. (Columbia Pike) | 410-997-9311
NEW Towson | Towson Town Ctr. | 825 Dulaney Valley Rd. (Fairmont Ave.) | 410-337-7411
www.thecheesecakefactory.com
See review in the Washington, DC, Directory.

Chiapparelli's *Italian* 20 | 17 | 21 | $33

Little Italy | 237 S. High St. (Fawn St.) | 410-837-0309
NEW Havre de Grace | 400 N. Union Ave. (Franklin St.) | 410-939-5440
www.chiapparellis.com

"The house salad alone" is "worth the trip" to this '40s-era "standby" in Little Italy (there's also a new Havre de Grace location), famed for "big portions" of "reliable" "old-school Italian" ("wear pants with an elastic waistband") from "'hon'-style" servers who treat you like "long-lost family"; yes, it's "a total time warp" with "dated decor", but the "unpretentious" atmo and fair prices help ensure you "leave happy."

Chicken Rico *Chicken* 26 | 6 | 16 | $11

Highlandtown | 3728 Eastern Ave. (bet. Dean & Eaton Sts.) | 410-522-2950

"So addictive the DEA might have to investigate", this Highlandtown joint's "mouthwatering Peruvian chicken" is seasoned "with many spices", "slow-roasted" on the rotisserie and served with "tasty" sides by a "friendly" counter staff; "bargain" prices and portions "enough for two" boost the appeal, though the "stark" setup with "blaring" "Latin American TV" encourages "carryout."

Chiu's Sushi *Japanese* 23 | 16 | 19 | $28

Harbor East | 608 S. Exeter St. (Fleet St.) | 410-752-9666 | www.chiussushi.com

Chiusy sushi lovers deem this Harbor East Japanese a "solid contender" for "fantastic" "specialty rolls", "assembled masterfully" and presented by an "attentive", kimono-clad staff; maybe the "quaint" "decor is not that attractive", but "your tongue is delighted" and it's in a "convenient location" near Whole Foods, so most maintain it "does just fine."

Christopher Daniel *American*
23 | 19 | 21 | $41

Timonium | Padonia Park Shopping Ctr. | 106 W. Padonia Rd. (Broad Ave.) | 410-308-1800 | www.christopher-daniel.com

"High-end" cooking in a "suburban strip mall" may seem like a "weird combo", but this Timonium New American "continues to amaze" with its "imaginative menu", "first-class" service and "bountiful" Sunday brunch; given the "pricey" outlay, critics are a "little underwhelmed" by the "inelegant decor", but its "sophisticated" ways are still "surprising" in a culinary "desert."

Ciao Bella *Italian*
22 | 20 | 22 | $35

Little Italy | 236 S. High St. (bet. Fawn & Stiles Sts.) | 410-685-7733 | www.cbella.com

"You feel like one of the family" at this Little Italy stalwart, home to "simple, delicious" Italian fare served with a "personal touch" by the "wonderful" owner and staff; some sniff it's "uninventive", but when you're ready to *mangia* the "reasonably priced" menu is "worth a try."

◪ Cinghiale *Italian*
24 | 26 | 25 | $57

Harbor East | 822 Lancaster St. (Exeter St.) | 410-547-8282 | www.cgeno.com

Charleston owners Cindy Wolf and Tony Foreman "work their magic" at this Harbor East Italian, where the "inspired" cooking, "highly attentive" service and "cosmopolitan" atmosphere go "so well together"; the "dressed-down" enoteca serves "quality meats and cheeses" from the in-house salumeria while the "more formal" osteria matches its "memorable" dishes with an "exceptional" wine list, and if it all comes at a "steep price", "you get what you pay for."

City Cafe *American*
21 | 18 | 20 | $24

Mt. Vernon | 1001 Cathedral St. (Eager St.) | 410-539-4252 | www.citycafebaltimore.com

Although "not as casual as before", this Mt. Vernon oasis of "urban chic" "continues to do what it does best", catering to "laid-back" coffee klatches in the "cheerful" front cafe while a more "upscale" rear restaurant serves "tasty", seasonal New American fare; the "high-ceilinged" space with "outside tables" is "accommodating" to both "neighborhood" and theater crowds, and it's there "when you need it."

Clementine Ⓜ *American*
23 | 19 | 21 | $30

Northeast Baltimore | 5402 Harford Rd. (Gibbons Ave.) | 410-444-1497 | www.bmoreclementine.com

This Northeast Baltimore New American "hot spot" is the darling of "boomers" and "hipsters gone to parenting" thanks to chef/co-owner Winston Blick's "super" seasonal "fusion of comfort and trendy foods" including "homemade charcuterie" and desserts from his pastry-chef mom's recipes (Tuesday's $10-per-platter "taco nights" are a "bargain"); the "bohemian setting" and "pleasant" staff lend an "inviting" "local" feel that's further enhanced by "a full bar"; P.S. a related greengrocer/charcuterie market is in the works nearby.

Clyde's ● *American*
19 | 21 | 20 | $32

Columbia | 10221 Wincopin Circle (Little Patuxent Pkwy.) |
410-730-2829 | www.clydes.com
See review in the Washington, DC, Directory.

Coal Fire *Pizza*
20 | 16 | 17 | $18

Ellicott City | 5725 Richards Valley Rd. (Waterloo Rd.) | 410-480-2625 |
www.coalfireonline.com
"If you like thin and crispy", this pie parlor in Ellicott City (with a new
Gaithersburg sibling and another planned for Frederick) has a coal-
burning oven that produces a charred "cracker" crust topped with
"fresh ingredients and your choice of three sauces" delivering different levels of "zesty" "kick"; the "strip-mall" digs suit a "not-bad"
"family choice", though "pizza cognoscenti" firing away at "uneven"
eating opine "it ain't all that."

Corks *American*
21 | 19 | 21 | $42

South Baltimore | 1026 S. Charles St. (bet. Cross & Hamburg Sts.) |
410-752-3810 | www.corksrestaurant.com
Patrons "squeezing past the kitchen" into two "cozy" dining rooms
will find this "renovated" South Baltimore New American has a
"more affordable" but still "well-prepared" bistro menu featuring
fondue, sandwiches and "deals" like half-price steaks Sunday–
Thursday; the "eager" staff also uncorks an "outstanding wine list",
though a few big spenders "prefer the old concept."

NEW Corner BYOB Ⓜ *Continental*
– | – | – | E

Hampden | 850 W. 36th St. (Elm Ave.) | 443-869-5075 |
www.cornerbyob.com
Hampden, increasingly a serious dining destination, may have never
seen the likes of frogs' legs and the other Belgian and Continental
bites that Bernard Dehaene (ex Mannequin Pis in Olney) brings to
this cozy new bistro; do as its name suggests and stop into one of the
two nearby wine sellers first – and bring cash if you can (the restaurant
charges varying fees for credit cards, corkage and carryout).

Costas Inn Crab House ● *Crab House*
23 | 11 | 22 | $38

Dundalk | 4100 N. Point Blvd. (New Battle Grove Rd.) | 410-477-1975 |
www.costasinn.com
"Claws down" "one of the best" for a dose of "real Baltimore", this
"old-fashioned" Dundalk roadhouse is a long-standing "year-round"
source of "yummy steamed" blue crabs delivered fresh daily from
Texas; the menu's otherwise "pedestrian" and the spartan setup
(with "paper tablecloths" if crabs are ordered) "looks like the Elks
Club", but the "reputation" "packs them in"; P.S. call ahead to reserve crabs by size and quantity.

Crêpe du Jour *French*
21 | 16 | 18 | $26

Mt. Washington | 1609 Sulgrave Ave. (bet. Kelly Ave. & Newbury St.) |
410-542-9000 | www.crepedujour.com
"Grab a slightly different" bite at this Mt. Washington bistro, where
a "quirky" expat chef-owner concocts "delightful" "savory and

sweet crêpes" in "cozy" "little" quarters with "back deck seating"; *amis* applaud the "authentic French feel" and "reasonable" prices, though even with a full menu some allege it's "a one-act place."

NEW CR Lounge ⓂAmerican | - | - | - | M |
(aka Crème Restaurant)
Mt. Vernon | 518 N. Charles St. (Centre St.) | 443-869-3381 | www.crloungebalt.com

This pretty, elegant debutante in Mt. Vernon, a sibling of DC's Crème, puts Southern touches on American comfort fare that comes in portions big enough for refueling after a day of culture at the Walters Art Museum, steps away; further pluses include a casual lounge behind the grand dining room, a Sunday brunch and reasonable tabs.

Crush *American* | 22 | 22 | 21 | $40 |
North Baltimore | Belvedere Sq. | 510 E. Belvedere Ave. (York Rd.) | 443-278-9001 | www.crush-restaurant.com

This North Baltimore "neighborhood" "find" is "catching on" owing to a menu of "innovative" New American "winners" from chef/co-owner Daniel Chaustit (ex Christopher Daniel), paired with a "well-conceived wine list"; with "amiable service", an "attractive" interior and a "pleasant" patio, it "fits all occasions" and provides a "trendy and fun" option when you're stepping out to Belvedere Square; P.S. mini-restaurant Demi opened in the basement post-Survey, dishing up globally influenced New American small plates from an open kitchen.

Da Mimmo *Italian* | 22 | 18 | 20 | $52 |
Little Italy | 217 S. High St. (Stiles St.) | 410-727-6876 | www.damimmo.com

Like "a trip back in time", this "Little Italy standby" and onetime "celeb" haunt maintains an old-fashioned "fancy atmosphere" to complement "rich and tasty" Italian dishes (notably "the signature veal chop") that'll make you "forget your diet"; just beware of "snooty" service, and "hold onto your wallet" when the bill arrives, especially when ordering "unpriced specials, which cost plenty."

David Chu's China Bistro *Chinese/Kosher*   ∇ 22 | 14 | 19 | $24 |
Pikesville | 7105 Reisterstown Rd. (bet. Glengyle Ave. & Seven Mile Ln.) | 410-602-5008

"Yes, kosher Chinese food can be delectable" declare devotees of this plain-and-simple Pikesville joint, which supplies observant Sinophiles with generous servings from a beef-leaning menu; being virtually the "only option" of its kind hereabouts, it's often "busy", so some choose to take out; P.S. closed Friday evenings and Saturdays.

Della Notte *Italian* | 22 | 23 | 22 | $42 |
Little Italy | 801 Eastern Ave. (President St.) | 410-837-5500 | www.dellanotte.com

Paying tribute to "schmaltzy, old-school" Italian, this Little Italy "mainstay" "puts a lot of effort into" a "lavish" neoclassical look – complete with marble columns, statuary and a "crazy tree" in the center of the "circular dining room" – that's the backdrop for "well-prepared" standards and a 1,400-label wine lineup served by an "efficient" staff; foes find it "overpriced" and "a little cheesy", but many agree the "free parking lot" is a windfall.

☒ Di Pasquale's Marketplace ☒ *Italian* | 27 | 14 | 19 | $16 |

East Baltimore | 3700 Gough St. (Dean St.) | 410-276-6787 | www.dipasquales.com

"One hundred percent authentic", this "family-run" Italian grocery in East Baltimore dispenses "awesome", "well-priced" deli faves (subs, "brick-oven pizza", "housemade lasagna", etc.) over the counter with "no fuss, no muss"; there's bare-bones seating for a "homey" lunch "in the neighborhood", but you "go for the great food not the atmosphere", so feel free to "take it home"; P.S. closes at 6 PM.

Dogwood ☒Ⓜ *American* | 25 | 18 | 22 | $39 |

Hampden | 911 W. 36th St. (Roland Ave.) | 410-889-0952 | www.dogwoodbaltimore.com

Fans cheer this Hampden New American, where chef Galen Sampson and wife Bridget merge their "farm-to-table philosophy" with a "social mission" "of providing reentry employment" for "ex-offenders" into an "unexpected" culinary "treat" showcasing "inspired dishes" devised from "organic and local ingredients"; with a "funky" basement space, "excellent service" and "reasonable prices" to "add to the enjoyment", it's "a keeper" "with a conscience."

Dukem *Ethiopian* | 24 | 14 | 18 | $22 |

Mt. Vernon | 1100 Maryland Ave. (W. Chase St.) | 410-385-0318 | www.dukemrestaurant.com

See review in the Washington, DC, Directory.

Dutch's Daughter *American* | 21 | 19 | 22 | $40 |

Frederick | 581 Himes Ave. (Rte. 40) | 301-668-9500 | www.dutchs.info

"Really popular" "with the locals", this Frederick faux "mansion" serves "solid", seafood-centric American fare in four "upstairs banquet rooms" as well as a basement bar/lounge that has "a slightly younger feel"; well known for "catering and events" (it's a "hit during prom season") and "Sunday brunch with the family", it's occasionally in dutch with detractors who cite "high" prices for "average food."

Edo Sushi *Japanese* | 24 | 19 | 23 | $30 |

Inner Harbor | Harborplace Pratt Street Pavilion | 201 E. Pratt St. (South St.) | 410-843-9804

Timonium | Padonia Village Shopping Ctr. | 53 E. Padonia Rd. (York Rd.) | 410-667-9200

Owings Mills | Garrison Forest Plaza | 10347 Reisterstown Rd. (Rosewood Ln.) | 410-363-7720

Edo Mae Sushi *Japanese*

Owings Mills | Boulevard Corporate Ctr. | 10995 Owings Mills Blvd. (bet. Gwynnbrook Ave. & Reisterstown Rd.) | 410-356-6818 www.edosushimd.com

While the Harborplace branch of this "quality" quartet boasts "great views", the others' "strip-mall settings belie" the fact that there's "excellent sushi and sashimi" on hand, plus "creative" specialty rolls and "delicious soups"; expect "average to expensive prices" (though BYO helps at the Owings Mills and Timonium outposts), "prompt service" and "good luck" if you "bang on the drum" – or gong – when you "walk in the door."

Eggspectations *American* 19 | 16 | 17 | $20
Ellicott City | Columbia Corporate Park 100 | 6010 University Blvd. (Waterloo Rd.) | 410-750-3115 | www.eggspectations.com
See review in the Washington, DC, Directory.

Elkridge Furnace Inn Ⓜ *American* 24 | 25 | 23 | $49
Elkridge | 5745 Furnace Ave. (bet. Main St. & Race Rd.) | 410-379-9336 | www.elkridgefurnaceinn.com
In an "area with few special-occasion restaurants", this "elegant" Elkridge New American set in a "historic mansion" on the Patapsco River rises to the challenge with "excellent" French-accented cuisine (including "phenomenal desserts") and "service to match"; it's a "lovely place" to simply "walk around the grounds" or to sample numerous activities like cooking classes and wine-tastings.

El Trovador *Mexican/Salvadoran* ▽ 23 | 17 | 18 | $21
Fells Point | 318 S. Broadway (bet. Bank & Gough Sts.) | 410-276-6200
"Reasonable prices", "fast service" and "large servings" of "great" Mexican and Salvadoran fare are the hallmarks of this "no-frills" find just above Fells Point; it's "not exactly cutting edge", but for "good margaritas" in an "attractive" setting (glass portico, wood bar, native artwork), "this is the place."

Ethel & Ramone's Ⓜ *Cajun/Creole* 21 | 15 | 20 | $32
Mt. Washington | 1615 Sulgrave Ave. (Kelly Ave.) | 410-664-2971 | www.ethelandramones.com
"Don't expect real fancy, but do expect real flavors" at this "casual-night-out" "alternative" in Mt. Washington, where "reasonably priced" Cajun-Creole cuisine is "kicked up a notch" thanks to "interesting" Maryland influences ("try the crab cake" for proof); "dated" decor turns off a few who don't dig the old-house setting, but "hard-working" staffers and a "relaxed atmosphere" win over most; P.S. their stand at the Downtown Baltimore farmer's market is unrated.

Faidley's Seafood Ⓩ *Seafood* 27 | 10 | 17 | $20
Downtown West | Lexington Mkt. | 203 N. Paca St. (Lexington St.) | 410-727-4898 | www.faidleyscrabcakes.com
"Go lump or go home" at this "legendary" Lexington Market "mecca for seafood devotees" that opened in 1886 and remains stuck in some sort of "miraculous time warp"; "you eat standing up" at high-top tables amid seafood counters, but since its "fantastic" "crab cakes (broiled please)" are the "standard by which all other Baltimore crab cakes are judged", few seem to care; P.S. "freshly shucked oysters" from its "excellent raw bar" make a "cheap lunch."

FOOD | DECOR | SERVICE | COST

Falls, The *American*

− | − | − | M

Mt. Washington | 1604 Kelly Ave. (Newbury St.) | 410-367-7840 |
www.thefallsmtwashington.com

Mt. Washington professors and professionals find that this all-day
American cafe in a former corner grocery fits many needs: it works
for coffee on couches, drinks at self-serve beer-dispenser tables or
moderately priced full meals in book-lined booths (yes, you can
borrow the books).

Firestone's 🎶 *American*

21 | 19 | 20 | $42

Frederick | 105 N. Market St. (Church St.) | 301-663-0330 |
www.firestonesrestaurant.com

Hit the "cozy" mezzanine if you want some "quiet" time at this
"solid" tin-ceilinged New American in Downtown Frederick with a
"local feel" and a "lively" pub scene at street level; "reliably delicious" eats like its signature cowboy steak are complemented by
an "impressive wine list", though some warn the "usually good" staff
can get overwhelmed when it's "crowded"; P.S. its adjacent shop
proffers gourmet goodies and kitchen accessories.

ⓩ Five Guys *Burgers*

22 | 9 | 16 | $11

Inner Harbor | Harborplace Pratt Street Pavilion | 201 E. Pratt St.
(South St.) | 410-244-7175
Canton | Shoppes at Brewers Hill | 3600 Boston St. (S. Conkling St.) |
410-522-1580
White Marsh | Shops at Nottingham Sq. | 5272 Campbell Blvd.
(Philadelphia Rd.) | 410-933-1017
Bowie | Bowie Town Ctr. | 3851 Town Center Blvd. (Emerald Way) |
301-464-9633
Hanover | Shops at Arundel Preserve | 7690 Dorchester Blvd.
(bet. Arundel Mills Blvd. & Wright Rd.) | 410-799-3933
Glen Burnie | Centre Mall of Glen Burnie | 6711 Ritchie Hwy.
(Ordnance Rd.) | 410-590-3933
Cockeysville | York Market Pl. | 10015 York Rd. (bet. Cranbrook &
Warren Sts.) | 410-667-0818
Towson | 936 York Rd. (Fairmount Ave.) | 410-321-4963
Westminster | 140 Village Shopping Ctr. | 596 Jermor Ln.
(Old Baltimore Rd.) | 410-751-9969
Frederick | Shops at Monocacy | 1700 Kingfisher Dr. (bet. Monocacy Blvd. &
Rte. 26) | 301-668-1500
www.fiveguys.com
Additional locations throughout the Baltimore area
See review in the Washington, DC, Directory.

Fleming's Prime Steakhouse & Wine Bar *Steak*

24 | 23 | 24 | $61

Harbor East | 720 Aliceanna St. (President St.) | 410-332-1666 |
www.flemingssteakhouse.com
See review in the Washington, DC, Directory.

Fogo De Chão *Brazilian/Steak*

24 | 21 | 25 | $59

Inner Harbor | 600 E. Pratt St. (bet. Market Pl. & S. Gay St.) |
410-528-9292 | www.fogodechao.com
See review in the Washington, DC, Directory.

Friendly Farm *American* 22 | 14 | 22 | $28

Upperco | 17434 Foreston Rd. (Mount Carmel Rd.) | 410-239-7400 | www.friendlyfarm.net

"Chicks and ducks and geese scurry about" while you "wait for your table" at this somewhat "pricey" Upperco charmer dishing out "unbelievable portions" of "down-home" American grub (including "fabulous" crab cakes) served "family-style" with "all-you-can-eat" coleslaw, potatoes, green beans and other "flavorful" sides; the "interior's a little old", but the uncowed insist it's "exactly how a farm-fresh, family-run restaurant in the country should look."

G&M *Seafood* 24 | 14 | 19 | $28

Linthicum | 804 N. Hammonds Ferry Rd. (Nursery Rd.) | 410-636-1777 | www.gandmcrabcakes.com

The "sagging floors and funky rooms" at this "wildly popular" Linthicum seafooder are long "gone", but the "outstanding", "softball-sized crab cakes" with "little or no filler" remain, as do their "bargain" prices; still, even "pleasant" service can't sway naysayers who snap that the "famous" specialty "lacks flavor" and the "rest of the menu is subpar" – and some folks even "miss the old dumpier" digs.

Garry's Grill *American* 20 | 16 | 21 | $24

Severna Park | 553 Baltimore Annapolis Blvd. (bet. McKinsey Rd. & Ritchie Hwy.) | 410-544-0499 | www.garrysgrill.com

"One of a vanishing breed", this family-friendly Severna Parker may be "hidden away" in a "nondescript strip mall" and throw off a "luncheonette" vibe, but its young chef-owner cooks up "reliable, innovative" American fare with "flair", including "eclectic specialties", breakfast, salads and burgers; add in "personal" service and "reasonable" prices, and no wonder "they keep on coming."

Germano's Trattoria *Italian* 23 | 15 | 23 | $36

Little Italy | 300 S. High St. (Fawn St.) | 410-752-4515 | www.germanostrattoria.com

"Be sure to ask for the specials" at this "friendly" High Street "mainstay", whose *paesani* rank it among the "best in Little Italy" thanks to its "delicious", "authentic" Tuscan fare and a "well-informed staff"; if the decor doesn't wow surveyors, the "reasonable prices" do, making it a "must" choice for "big and small occasions" alike; P.S. there's cabaret-style entertainment Thursday–Sunday, so "go for the show" as well.

Gertrude's ⓜ *Chesapeake* 23 | 24 | 22 | $37

Charles Village | Baltimore Museum of Art | 10 Art Museum Dr. (N. Charles St.) | 410-889-3399 | www.gertrudesbaltimore.com

"Art and good food make an excellent combination" at chef-owner John Shields' "locavore's heaven", a "sophisticated but unstuffy" eatery at the BMA spotlighting "creative" Chesapeake Regional cuisine; it's a "little pricey", but "$12 entrees on Tuesday nights" soften the blow, as does "prompt and friendly service"; P.S. "eat outside in the sculpture garden" during the "lovely" Sunday jazz brunch.

FOOD | DECOR | SERVICE | COST

Goldberg's New York Bagels *Bagels/Kosher* 22 | 8 | 13 | $11

Pikesville | 1500 Reisterstown Rd. (Old Court Rd.) | 410-415-7001 |
www.goldbergsbagels.com

"Big, fresh and often right out of the oven", the "gobble"-worthy
treasures produced by this "kosher establishment" in Pikesville just
might be the "best bagels" you'll encounter "without going to NYC",
plus there's more robust, sit-down fare; it "isn't a place you visit for
decor or service", but "fight the crowds" anyway – you won't be "disappointed"; P.S. closes early on Fridays, opens late on Saturdays.

Golden West Cafe *New Mexican* 20 | 18 | 13 | $20

Hampden | 1105 W. 36th St. (Hickory Ave.) | 410-889-8891 |
www.goldenwestcafe.com

"Green chilies and sour hipsters abound" at this "noisy" Hampden
"funkateria" where service issues ("will the server be surly or
cheery?") sometimes "overshadow" the affordable chow – "fresh,
tasty" lunch and dinner and "all-day breakfast" with a New Mexican
"flair"; it's a "no-substitutions" "adventure" set in a "Western-
themed" space, but vets who "love" its tofu Buffalo wings and tater
tots" just "keep going back."

Grace Garden 🌃 *Chinese* ▽ 28 | 6 | 21 | $20

Odenton | 1690A Annapolis Rd. (Reece Rd.) | 410-672-3581 |
www.gracegardenchinese.com

Yes, this "ultimate hole-in-the-wall find" in an Odenton retail strip
near Ft. Meade "ain't much to look at", but "suck it up" or you'll miss
the "best Chinese meal you'll have in the area"; from the "fabulous"
tea-smoked duck to the "must-try fish noodles" on the recently updated menu, each of chef Li's "top-notch" offerings ("Sichuan by
way of Hong Kong") is "well prepared and different" – just "bring
some friends", since you'll want to "try lots of dishes"; P.S. call to
ask which items need advance ordering.

Grano Pasta Bar 🌃 *Italian* ▽ 25 | 17 | 23 | $18
(aka Little Grano)

Hampden | 1031 W. 36th St. (Hickory Ave.) | 443-869-3429

Emporio Grano *Italian*
(aka Big Grano)

Hampden | 3547 Chestnut Ave. (36th St.) | 443-438-7521 |
www.granopastabar.com

Boasting "good, simple" pastas and salads without the "high prices
and formality of Little Italy", this "lovely" Hampden duo "only does
a few things and does them well"; locals' loyalties are torn between
the "cozy" original, set in a former tavern, and its newer, larger
Chestnut Avenue sib (aka Big Grano), with a wine bar and deck,
though most agree Baltimore "needs more restaurants like these."

Great Sage Ⓜ *Vegan* 22 | 19 | 21 | $27

Clarksville | Clarksville Square Dr. | 5809 Clarksville Square Dr.
(Clarksville Pike) | 443-535-9400 | www.greatsage.com

For vegan "cuisine that everybody can love" ("even pure carnivores"), head to this "little bit of California in Clarksville" dishing up

"hearty" "old classics and new creations", "great desserts" and "organic beers and cocktails"; it's in an "unlikely" strip-mall location and service "ranges from friendly and helpful to adequate", but supporters sagely shrug it off, concentrating instead on the affordable prices and "lovely" dining room and patio.

Greystone Grill *American*

19 | 18 | 18 | $44

Ellicott City | MDG Corporate Ctr. | 8850 Columbia 100 Pkwy. (Centre Park Rd.) | 410-715-4739 | www.greystonegrill.com

The location – an Ellicott City office building set back from the street – may be "a bit odd" but those who frequent this steakhouse cite "solid" chops, "plenty of parking" and a "nice little bar" as reasons for repeat visits; still, dissenters find it "overpriced" with food and service that's sometimes "not up to par."

Grilled Cheese & Co. *Sandwiches*

- | - | - | I

Catonsville | 500 Edmondson Ave. (I-695) | 410-747-2610
NEW **Eldersburg** | 577 Johnsville Rd. (Sykesville Rd.) | 443-920-3238
www.ilovegrilledcheese.com

Fromage lovers get the grill of their dreams at this old Catonsville house fitted with light wood and a few tables just off of I-695, where numerous cheeses can be combined with chicken, bacon, roasted pepper, crab and veggies to create memorable (and gooey) combos; soup is also ladled out at the affordable counter-service affair, but beware: crowds have already found their whey to it; P.S. the second link in the planned chain opened in early 2011 in Eldersburg.

Gunning's Seafood *Seafood*

- | - | - | M

Hanover | 7304 Parkway Dr. (Coca-Cola Dr.) | 410-712-9404 | www.gunningsonline.com

A "loyal local following" packs this "friendly" Hanover strip-mall seafooder near BWI, so don't be surprised to find "flight crews" noshing alongside business types, after-work revelers and families in the "homey" dining room; the midpriced menu includes fried green pepper rings, pub fare and, natch, crab cakes and piles of steamed crustaceans.

Hamilton Tavern *Pub Food*

25 | 23 | 21 | $23

Northeast Baltimore | 5517 Harford Rd. (Hamilton Ave.) | 410-426-1930 | www.hamiltontavern.com

"Locally famous", this "comfy" nook on Northeast Baltimore's increasingly hot Harford Road is a "small" rehabbed tavern decked out with "old farm tools" where "inventive takes on pub food" (the "fantastic" local natural-beef burger "will make you see God") are chased with a "great beer selection"; a "friendly staff" abets the "convivial atmosphere", but being a "hit" with the hipoisie, it's often "crowded" and "a little loud"; P.S. closed Tuesdays.

Hard Times Cafe *American*

19 | 13 | 18 | $18

Frederick | 1003 W. Patrick St. (Hoke Pl.) | 301-695-0099 | www.hardtimes.com

See review in the Washington, DC, Directory.

	FOOD	DECOR	SERVICE	COST

Harryman House Grill *American* | 22 | 21 | 21 | $38 |

Reisterstown | 340 Main St. (bet. Bond Ave. & Glyndon Dr.) |
410-833-8850 | www.harrymanhouse.com

With its "quaint" setting "in a historic house" built around a circa-1791 "log cabin" room, this Reisterstown New American puts on the "old-fashioned charm" to enhance a "solid" menu that now features both upmarket dishes and "less expensive" grill grub like sandwiches and pizza; expect a "tavernlike atmosphere" that's "convivial" but "noisy" when busy.

NEW Havana Road ⑤ *Cuban* | - | - | - | M |

Towson | 8 W. Pennsylvania Ave. (bet. Washington Ave. & York Rd.) |
410-494-8222 | www.havanaroad.com

Soft salsa music, warm hues and engaging servers transcend this newcomer's tiny Towson commerical-strip setting, allowing diners to concentrate on the important stuff: quiet conversation and chef-owner Marta Inés Quintana's classic Cuban cuisine; moderate tabs and fee-free BYO appeal to the budget-minded; P.S. Quintana's retail line of sauces can be found at area Whole Foods and other gourmet markets.

⏁ Helmand *Afghan* | 26 | 20 | 23 | $31 |

Mt. Vernon | 806 N. Charles St. (bet. Madison & Read Sts.) |
410-752-0311 | www.helmand.com

By "now a Baltimore landmark", this "unique" Mt. Vernon "treasure" is a "consistent" source of "out-of-this-world" Afghan "comfort food" ("don't miss" the pumpkin appetizer) that'll "please any palate" with its "nuanced spicing" of both "traditional meat" and "great vegetarian offerings", which incorporate fresh produce from its organic farm; with "personable" service and "fair prices", it's "naturally" "a popular spot", but "crowded" conditions don't deter legions of fans from "coming back for more."

Henninger's Tavern ⑤ⓜ *American* | 24 | 22 | 23 | $33 |

Fells Point | 1812 Bank St. (bet. Ann & Wolfe Sts.) | 410-342-2172 |
www.henningerstavern.com

A steady "level of quality" "over the years" marks this "cute little" "local joint" in upper Fells Point, a "relaxed" "standby" for "amazing" New American plates prepared in "homemade gourmet" mode and served in snug quarters where the clutter of "eccentric" "artwork" and vintage "memorabilia" provides "lots to look at"; with a "convivial" staff to "add to the charm", it has a well-earned rep as a "real sleeper."

Hinode *Japanese* | 19 | 14 | 19 | $30 |

Frederick | 50 Carroll Creek Way (Patrick St.) | 301-620-2943 |
www.hinodefrederick.com

See review in the Washington, DC, Directory.

Honey Pig Gooldaegee Korean Grill ● *Korean* | 26 | 12 | 17 | $24 |

Ellicott City | Princess Shopping Center | 10045 Baltimore National Pike (Centennial Ln.) | 410-696-2426

See review in the Washington, DC, Directory.

	FOOD	DECOR	SERVICE	COST

House of India *Indian*   `24` `15` `20` `$25`

Columbia | 9350 Snowden River Pkwy. (Oakland Mills Rd.) |
410-381-3844 | www.houseofindiainc.com

NEW Flavors of India ⑤ *Indian*

Columbia | 7185 Columbia Gateway Dr. (Waterloo Rd.) | 410-290-1118 |
www.flavorsofindiainc.com

Patrons get the "king" treatment from the "highly attentive" team at
this affordable subcontinental, a "winner" that "stands out among
the mediocre chains filling Columbia"; the "intimate" interior
"needs some updating", but a "loyal following" has come to expect
"real Indian" here – including "perfect tandoori chicken" – in portions so "large" there's a "take-out cart" to ensure no one "wastes
anything"; Flavors of India opened post-Survey.

Hunan Manor *Chinese*   `21` `18` `20` `$25`

Columbia | 7091 Deepage Dr. (Snowden River Pkwy.) | 410-381-1134 |
www.hunanmanorrestaurant.com

"Order off the native Chinese menu" for a truly "authentic" experience at this "rare delight" in Columbia, though the "huge
plates" of well-priced "Americanized" fare are equally "delicious";
"punctuated by an impressive fish tank", it "tries to look upscale in
decor" and generally succeeds, another reason devotees deem it a
"worthy destination"; P.S. the Burtonsville and Silver Spring
branches are unrated.

Hunan Taste ● *Chinese*   `-` `-` `-` `M`

Catonsville | H-Mart Plaza | 718 N. Rolling Rd. (Rte. 40) | 410-788-8988 |
www.hunantastemd.com

"Darn good" cooking created an initial buzz about this Catonsville
Chinese in the H-Mart strip mall, a modernistic magnet for enter-
prising foodies and émigrés hungry for authentic tastes of the old
country, including spicy ox lung, frog, turtle and organ meats; for the
less adventurous, there's a menu of Americanized fare that's
equally voluminous and reasonably priced.

Iggies Ⓜ *Pizza*   `25` `16` `18` `$16`

Mt. Vernon | 818 N. Calvert St. (Read St.) | 410-528-0818 |
www.iggiespizza.com

This "laid-back" "pizza joint" is an "oddball but endearing" eatery
near Center Stage churning out "crisp, thin-crust" pies with "unique
toppings" "you're not going to get everywhere" (read: duck, pista-
chios); "fantastic salads" and gelato are further options you "order
at a counter" and eat at "crowded" "communal tables", but whatev:
the no-corkage BYO policy "makes this a great deal."

Ikaros *Greek*   `24` `17` `24` `$29`

Greektown | 4805 Eastern Ave. (Oldham St.) | 410-633-3750 |
www.ikarosrestaurant.com

"Plates heaped high" with "superb" Hellenic cooking are the hallmarks of this "old-school" Greektown standard; while the "reasonably priced" chow may be a "gift of the gods, the decor is not", but
partisans proudly declare "we don't care" – they "come for the food"

and to be "pampered" by the "wonderful, attentive" owners and their "pleasant" team; P.S. closed Tuesdays.

Iron Bridge Wine Company *American*　23 | 20 | 21 | $40

Columbia | 10435 State Rte. 108 (Centennial Ln.) | 410-997-3456 | www.ironbridgewines.com

They may be "in the middle of nowhere", but this "cute" if "cramped" "little place" in the Columbia farmland and its newer Virginia sib are "wonderful" spots to "meet and mingle"; while "excellent" New American "small plates" draw "food lovers", it's the "extensive selection of local, U.S. and international" vinos that's the "main draw" here, including monthly "bargains" "worth the ride" alone.

Isabella's Ⓜ *Spanish*　25 | 16 | 20 | $30

Frederick | 44 N. Market St. (Rte. 144) | 301-698-8922 | www.isabellas-tavern.com

"Small tastes of delicious food" deliver big payoffs at this "nifty" Spaniard set in a "spacious" storefront on Frederick's Restaurant Row; sí, the "decor could be more festive", but "don't let that put you off" – the "good selection" of "creative, tasty" tapas and "affordable" wines make for a "fun night out", and there's "quick" service and a "great happy hour" to boot.

Islander Inn *Crab House*　– | – | – | M

Dundalk | 9008 Cuckold Point Rd. (6th St.) | 410-388-0713 | www.islanderinnandcatering.com

Hidden on a remote spit of land past where the road turns rural in Dundalk is this real-deal roadhouse for those who work on the water, serving up truly local crabs plus other midpriced comfort eats from the deep and beyond; out-of-towners who make the trek become instant (and well-fed) friends – as long as they're Ravens fans; P.S. call for the times and details of their many specials, like $1 steamed crabs.

Jack's Bistro Ⓜ *Eclectic*　26 | 17 | 23 | $34

Canton | 3123 Elliott St. (S. Robinson St.) | 410-878-6542 | www.jacksbistro.net

"Adventure" lovers who like to boast "you know what I ate last night?" mob this "guaranteed fun time" in Canton featuring "surprising" Eclectic dishes with "ingredient combos that totally work" (chocolate mac 'n' cheese, "lots of sous vide"); "personable" service and a "charming" tavern setting are other pluses, though even devotees "wish the place were bigger"; P.S. closed Mondays and Tuesdays; food served until 1 AM.

Jennings Cafe ◗ *Pub Food*　▽ 22 | 11 | 24 | $24

Catonsville | 808 Frederick Rd. (Mellor Ave.) | 410-744-3824 | www.jenningscafe.com

Devotees dub this 1958 Catonsville classic "Old Faithful", and for good reason: it "hasn't changed in decades", from the knotty-pine walls and "reasonable prices" down to the "reliable" pub grub like burgers, "excellent crab cakes" and "fresh desserts"; still, it's the "original waitresses from yesterday" who deliver much of its charm – and, yep, server Peggy Bailey "still rocks"; P.S. open Sundays during football season.

Jerry's Seafood *Seafood*

24 | 15 | 20 | $41

Bowie | 15211 Major Lansdale Blvd. (off Northview Dr.) | 301-805-2284 | www.jerrysseafood.com

See review in the Washington, DC, Directory.

Jesse Wong's Asean Bistro *Asian*

23 | 19 | 22 | $27

Columbia | 8775 Centre Park Dr. (Rte. 108) | 410-772-5300 | www.aseanbistro.com

"Go when the piano player" is tickling the ivories at this "creative" Columbia eatery whose "beautifully plated" Pan-Asian fare (e.g. "yum" Pinot Grigio shrimp) exhibits its own flair for "showmanship"; the "refined" decor and "excellent bar" give off an "upscale" vibe despite the "strip-mall setting", while "attentive" servers add to the feeling that this is "not your ordinary" dining experience; P.S. music Friday–Saturday.

Jesse Wong's Kitchen *Asian*

19 | 21 | 19 | $33

Hunt Valley | Hunt Valley Town Ctr. | 118 Shawan Rd. (bet. McCormick & York Rds.) | 410-329-1088 | www.jessewongskitchen.com

This "classy" space in a Hunt Valley shopping center is a "divergence from the norm", exhibiting "creativity" with the "freshest ingredients" in an "unusual selection" of Asian fusion fare and "very good sushi"; service gets mixed grades, but many are quick to praise the "beautiful", "contemporary" space, "abundant Sunday brunch" and tabs that make it a "good value."

Jimmy's *Diner*

18 | 11 | 18 | $14

Fells Point | 801 S. Broadway (Lancaster St.) | 410-327-3273

For "budget breakfasts" in a "friendly atmosphere", everyone from "watermen" and "politicos" to night owls nursing "hangovers" converge at this "colorful" Fells Point "institution"; "quick service" keeps "ridiculous" lines moving, and while it's "not the place for fancy", it *is* the place for "huge portions" of "good ol'-fashioned diner food" and a shot at "being called 'hon'"; P.S. hours are 5 AM to 7 PM.

John Steven, Ltd. *Seafood*

18 | 15 | 17 | $28

Fells Point | 1800 Thames St. (Ann St.) | 410-327-5561 | www.johnstevenltd.com

There's "atmosphere galore" at this "old-fashioned joint" offering a Charm City trifecta: "steamed shrimp, drinking in Fells Point and harbor views" from sidewalk tables; if former champions chide it for "resting on its reputation" with "hit-or-miss" seafood and service, at least suds-seekers can enjoy the "great beer selection" on the "cool little patio."

Josef's Country Inn *Continental*

∇ 28 | 25 | 26 | $40

Fallston | 2410 Pleasantville Rd. (Fallston Rd.) | 410-877-7800

It may feel like a "trip back to old Germany", but *nein,* it's actually a "cozy", decidedly "non-trendy" Continental "find" near Fallston; an "extensive wine list and excellent entrees" (e.g. veal Oscar) are

	FOOD	DECOR	SERVICE	COST

paired with a predictably professional staff, the result being an "attractive" choice for a "special occasion."

Joss Cafe & Sushi Bar *Japanese* | 25 | 16 | 21 | $34 |

Mt. Vernon | 413 N. Charles St. (bet. W. Franklin & Mulberry Sts.) | 410-244-6988 | www.josssushi.com
See review in the Annapolis Directory.

Kali's Court *Mediterranean/Seafood* | 24 | 24 | 22 | $52 |

Fells Point | 1606 Thames St. (Bond St.) | 410-276-4700 | www.kaliscourt.com
"For a special night out", this "romantic" Fells Pointer provides "elegant food in an elegant setting" – that is, "tasty" Med-accented seafood savored in a "lovely" bi-level space replete with "red velvet" and rich woods; if the less-impressed contend it's "noise-ville" with a "snooty" staff and "hefty prices", more vow "we shall return"; P.S. dinner only.

Kings Contrivance, The *American* | 23 | 23 | 22 | $51 |

Columbia | 10150 Shaker Dr. (bet. Rtes. 29 & 32) | 410-995-0500 | www.thekingscontrivance.com
If you're looking for someplace to "take the in-laws when you want to impress", regulars rave that this "special-occasion" "standby" set in a "lovely" "old mansion" in Columbia fits the bill; if the "lovely" setting tends to trump the New American fare ("not overly creative but quite good") and service, you're still in for a "special night out"; P.S. budget-watchers can "save a lot" with early-bird options.

Koco's 🖼️Ⓜ️ *Pub Food* | 26 | 11 | 22 | $30 |

Northeast Baltimore | 4301 Harford Rd. (bet. Overland & Weaver Aves.) | 410-426-3519 | www.kocospub.com
"It's huge, it's gigantic" . . . it's the "amazing crab cake" with "asteroid-sized lumps of meat" (though admittedly imported meat) at this "good ol'" Northeast Baltimore tavern; it's the wrong place if "you're looking for fancy" and the other pub grub is just "so-so", but prices that "won't break the bank", "attentive" service and a "down-to-earth" vibe have fans saying "bring a friend and chow down."

La Famiglia *Italian* | 21 | 23 | 23 | $44 |

Homewood | 105 W. 39th St. (University Pkwy.) | 443-449-5555 | www.lafamigliabaltimore.com
"Who needs Little Italy?" sniff supporters of this "upscale Italian retreat" in Homewood where "charismatic" owner Dino Zeytinoglu "treats you like family" and oversees an "amiable" staff; it's "not cheap", but "delicious" pastas and seafood enjoyed in an "intimate, inviting" space please most, and "free parking" and patio seating are a "plus."

Langermann's *Southern* | – | – | – | M |

Canton | 2400 Boston St. (Hudson St.) | 410-534-3287 | www.langermanns.com
Lodged in a former Canton can company "transformed into a gorgeous space", this "tasteful" Southern-inspired spot from chef/co-owner

Neal Langermann (ex DC's Georgia Brown's) offers "high-end Low Country" favorites from breakfast to late night, including shrimp and grits and fried green tomatoes; a "Bloody Mary"-enriched weekend brunch and outdoor seating sweeten the deal, as do prices that are "not too expensive."

La Scala *Italian* 26 | 23 | 25 | $46

Little Italy | 1012 Eastern Ave. (bet. Central Ave. & Exeter St.) | 410-783-9209 | www.lascaladining.com

"Humongous portions" of "superb" Italian food *and* an "indoor bocce court"? "I'm so there" exclaim enthusiasts of this Little Italy "delight" where "everything's on the money", from chef-owner Nino Germano's "creative" cooking ("love the grilled Caesar salad") to the "old-school service" and "romantic" atmosphere; those who say it's "sure to impress" also "wish they could afford to go weekly."

La Tavola *Italian* 24 | 18 | 22 | $43

Little Italy | 248 Albemarle St. (Fawn St.) | 410-685-1859 | www.la-tavola.com

"Charming and anxious to please", this "slightly offbeat" eatery in Little Italy offers "fabulous" pasta and seafood in a "large", generally placid setting manned by "helpful" waiters; tabs are relatively affordable, but "half-price wine on Wednesdays" and prix fixe specials sweeten the deal.

Laurrapin, The Ⓜ *American* - | - | - | M

Havre de Grace | 209 N. Washington St. (Pennington Ave.) | 410-939-4956 | www.laurrapin.com

Travelers searching for a "meeting point" between "Philly and Washington" discover "pleasant meals in a tavernlike" setting at this Havre de Grace "gem" on the main drag; "inventive" New American entrees and daily specials are delivered by "relaxed" servers, while barhounds poring over the extensive wine and beer list dig into pub grub like sliders and enjoy live entertainment on weekends.

Lebanese Taverna *Lebanese* 21 | 18 | 18 | $30

Harbor East | 719 S. President St. (Lancaster St.) | 410-244-5533 | www.lebanesetaverna.com

See review in the Washington, DC, Directory.

Liberatore's *Italian* 21 | 19 | 22 | $36

Bel Air | 562 Baltimore Pike (Rte. 24) | 410-838-9100
Timonium | Timonium Corporate Ctr. | 9515 Deereco Rd. (Padonia Rd.) | 410-561-3300
Perry Hall | Honeygo Village Ctr. | 5005 Honeygo Center Dr. (Honeygo Blvd.) | 410-529-4567
Eldersburg | Freedom Village Shopping Ctr. | 6300 Georgetown Blvd. (Liberty Rd.) | 410-781-4114
Westminster | 140 Village Shopping Ctr. | 521 Jermor Ln. (Rte. 97) | 410-876-2121 Ⓜ
www.liberatores.com

"Don't let the exteriors fool you" – these separately managed eateries scattered in "office buildings" and strip malls in the Baltimore 'burbs proffer "solid" Italian "favorites" in a "friendly atmosphere"; the less-impressed say tabs are a "little pricey" for "standard-issue" cooking, but they're outnumbered by those who insist it's like visiting "Little Italy without the parking hassles"; P.S. Bel Air and Perry Hall have "live music."

Z Linwoods *American*   27 | 26 | 26 | $56
Owings Mills | 25 Crossroads Dr. (McDonogh & Reisterstown Rds.) | 410-356-3030 | www.linwoods.com

With its "well-heeled clientele" and "stylish" setting, there's a "New York feeling" in the air at this "long-term" Owings Mills "treat" that remains one of the region's "best and most consistent places"; chef/co-owner Linwood Dame's "luscious" New American fare puts "innovative twists on old favorites" ("this guy can cook!"), and while you may wish someone else were "paying the bill", a "charming staff" ensures the experience is "always superb."

Little Spice **S** *Thai*   ▽ 25 | 15 | 20 | $21
Hanover | 1350 Dorsey Rd. (Ridge Rd.) | 410-859-0100 | www.littlespicethairestaurant.com

It's in a "strip mall by BWI airport", but "try the food" at this sister-run "jewel" and "out-of-the-way" Hanover suddenly becomes "Thailand"; dishes with "tremendous depth and complexity" that are "just spicy enough" (and not "just-hot-for-the-sake-of-being-hot") please palates, while the "friendly atmosphere" and fair prices add to an overall "great experience" that's "worth the extra drive."

Louisiana **M** *American/Creole*   22 | 22 | 20 | $54
Fells Point | 1708 Aliceanna St. (S. B'way) | 410-327-2610 | www.louisianasrestaurant.com

"Come with an open mind and a tolerance for spice" when visiting this "delightful" Fells Pointer whose "delicious" New American cuisine incorporates "neat takes on Creole"; if the "gorgeous" space in an old brick townhouse is a bit "lonely" at times (some say it's "underappreciated", others "too expensive"), insiders insist it's still a "special place" for "that special dinner"; P.S. call ahead for opening hours.

L.P. Steamers *Seafood*   23 | 11 | 18 | $27
Locust Point | 1100 E. Fort Ave. (Woodall St.) | 410-576-9294 | www.lpsteamers.com

"It ain't pretty", but this "homey" Locust Point "hole-in-the-wall" provides a "truly authentic setting" for "pickin' crabs" and divin' into "huge piles of french fries", "fried clams" and "excellent shrimp"; "reasonable prices" compensate for service that can be a "little slow", while regulars recommend "heading all the way upstairs to the deck" to enjoy "views of Baltimore" with your "fresh-cooked" crustaceans and "pitchers of beer" (just call servers by cell).

Mama's on the Half Shell *Seafood*   23 | 20 | 20 | $30
Canton | 2901 O'Donnell St. (S. Linwood Ave.) | 410-276-3160 | www.mamasmd.com

Whatever you do, "try the orange crushes" that "crush the competition" at this "classic" corner Cantonite, which also serves up a "great fresh oyster selection" and other "well-prepared" seafood at "moderate prices"; guests can head "upstairs by the fireplace" ("beware of the climb"), laze in the "lively" first-floor bar or "sit outdoors and people-watch", but no matter where they end up, it's likely to be "loud" and "crowded."

Mamie's Cafe *American*   - | - | - | I

Aberdeen | Beards Hill Plaza | 939 Beards Hill Rd. (Rte. 22) | 410-273-8999 | www.mamiescafewithlove.com

Fans feel as if they're "sitting around the table at grandma's house" at this "family-run" charmer wedged into an Aberdeen strip mall just off of I-95; the "high-quality, down-home" American chow (e.g. "open-faced turkey sandwiches", fried chicken, meatloaf) is "remarkably inexpensive", and it's enhanced by "friendly" faces, free desserts and a "fun" space adorned with the owners' 1940s-era photos and collectibles.

Mamma Lucia *Italian*   18 | 12 | 17 | $24

Elkridge | Gateway Overlook | 6630 Marie Curie Dr. (Waterloo Rd.) | 410-872-4894

Frederick | Shops of Monocacy | 1700 Kingfisher Dr. (Rte. 26) | 301-694-2600

www.mammaluciarestaurants.com

See review in the Washington, DC, Directory.

M&S Grill *Seafood/Steak*   19 | 19 | 19 | $39

Inner Harbor | Harborplace Pratt Street Pavilion | 201 E. Pratt St. (South St.) | 410-547-9333 | www.mandsgrill.com

See review in the Washington, DC, Directory.

Marie Louise Bistro *French/Mediterranean*   20 | 20 | 20 | $29

Mt. Vernon | 904 N. Charles St. (Read St.) | 410-385-9946 | www.marielouisebistrocatering.com

"Save room" for the "fresh homemade pastries and gelato" at this "cutesy" Mt. Vernon "find" that can serve as a "launching point for a visit" to the Walters Art Gallery, but it may be difficult after indulging in its "unpretentious" and "affordable" French and Mediterranean fare; an "attentive" team adds to the "comfortable atmosphere", enhanced by a high-ceilinged, brick-walled space.

Mari Luna Mexican Grill M *Mexican/Pan-Latin*   26 | 17 | 22 | $29

Pikesville | 102 Reisterstown Rd. (Seven Mile Ln.) | 410-486-9910

Mari Luna Latin Grill *Mexican/Pan-Latin*

Pikesville | 1010 Reisterstown Rd. (Sherwood Ave.) | 410-653-5151

NEW Mari Luna Bistro M *Mexican/Pan-Latin*

Mt. Vernon | 1225 Cathedral St. (Biddle St.) | 410-637-8013

www.mariluna.com

For "real-deal" fare with a "real-world kick (not too bland, not too spicy)", locals make tracks to this "popular" Reisterstown Road duo – the "hole-in-the-wall" original for "homestyle Mexican goodies" and its "bigger", dressier sibling for Pan-Latin favorites like "excellent" ropo vieja; both offer "welcoming" waiters and "reasonable-to-cheap prices", and if they get a little "loud", that's only "happy diners" exclaiming "*más, más por favor*"; P.S. the new Mt. Vernon branch has an express menu for the pre-symphony crowd.

Matsuri *Japanese* | 22 | 14 | 20 | $29

South Baltimore | 1105 S. Charles St. (Cross St.) | 410-752-8561 | www.matsuri.us

"Even if you're a sushi purist", fans of this midpriced Japanese near the Cross Street Market maintain you should "try the signature rolls" – "you won't be disappointed"; the less-impressed deem the fare (teriyaki and noodle dishes included) "good, but not crazy good", but at least the outdoor tables and "small downstairs" are supplemented by a larger upstairs dining area to handle the crowds.

Matthew's Pizza *Pizza* | 25 | 11 | 18 | $15

Highlandtown | 3131 Eastern Ave. (S. East Ave.) | 410-276-8755 | www.matthewspizza.com

"Old school" right down to the "real Baltimore girls doing the waitressing", this casual Highlandtown "pizza heaven" – which has been "around for over 60 years" – still spins out "awesome" "thick-crust" (and thin-crust) pies packed with "over-the-top taste"; just don't let the casual digs and "long waits" dissuade you, because "when you're this good, you don't have to impress anyone."

McCabe's Ⓜ *Pub Food* | - | - | - | M

Hampden | 3845 Falls Rd. (bet. 37th & 38th Sts.) | 410-467-1000

Burger and crab cake connoisseurs can sate their pub-grub pangs at this brick cave of a tavern in Hampden; beyond those classics, a modernized, midpriced menu pays attention to vegetarian items, local sourcing and comfort fare (roast chicken, bread pudding) – just plan around peak times, as it's tiny.

McCormick & Schmick's *Seafood* | 20 | 20 | 20 | $43

Inner Harbor | Pier 5 Hotel | 711 Eastern Ave. (S. President St.) | 410-234-1300 | www.mccormickandschmicks.com

See review in the Washington, DC, Directory.

NEW **Meet 27** *American* | - | - | - | M

Charles Village | 127 W. 27th St. (Maryland Ave.) | 410-585-8121 | www.meet27americanbistro.yolasite.com

Celiacs celebrate the Charles Village arrival of this long-delayed full-service American spin-off from adjacent gluten-free bakery Sweet Sin that sets out to prove that gluten-free can be tasty for all – from a smattering of Indian and Asian specialties right down to the scratch-made mango-peach ketchup on the fresh-cut fries; the low-lit space is brightened by a mural depicting famous Baltimoreans – and should light up more when the bar side gets its license.

Mekong Delta Cafe Ⓜ🗩 *Vietnamese* | 25 | 8 | 16 | $15

Downtown West | 105 W. Saratoga St. (Cathedral St.) | 410-244-8677

Plunked on the "outskirts of a transitional" Downtown West neighborhood, this "tiny", "family-run" storefront offers a "fabulous array" of "delicious, cheap" Vietnamese fare (including some of the "best pho in Baltimore"); there's "sparse" decor, "inconsistent" service and "long waits" for the "cooked-to-order" chow, but no matter: the "word has gotten out", so go now while you "can fit in the door."

Meli *Eclectic*
22 | 22 | 20 | $40

Fells Point | 1636 Thames St. (S. B'way) | 410-534-6354 | www.kalismeli.com

"Everything has a hint of honey" (that's what *meli* means in Greek, after all) at this "sweet" Fells Point cousin of Kali's Court, which "spoons" out "well-prepared" Eclectic dishes to "lots of attractive people" on "dates"; service can "use a little help" and some are stymied by the "unusual", multilevel layout, but a "great bar" and moderate prices have many buzzing it's "the place to bee"; P.S. there's live jazz Friday and Saturday.

Metropolitan Coffeehouse & Wine Bar *American*
18 | 15 | 14 | $26

South Baltimore | 902 S. Charles St. (Henrietta St.) | 410-234-0235 | www.metrobalto.com

At this South Baltimore "down-home" "hangout", young professionals "catch up with friends" over beers in the upstairs bar while an older crowd digs into "fair to good" New American meals in the coffee shop or at sidewalk tables; service can be "friendly" or "surly" depending on whom you talk to, and even regulars say the place is "old, damp and dark", but those concerns disappear "after a few beers."

Mezze ● *Mediterranean*
25 | 22 | 20 | $35

Fells Point | 1606 Thames St. (Bond St.) | 410-563-7600 | www.kalismezze.com

Avoid the ground floor's "constant traffic" and "sit upstairs" at this "urbane" yet "casual" Fells Point Med that "never gets old", possibly because there's such a "wide selection" of "excellent" small plates and the "wonderful" "homemade sangria" is "always cold" ("better order two pitchers!"); true, service can be "hit-or-miss", but most are too busy having a "good time" to notice; P.S. bean-counters concur it's a "better deal" than next-door sib Kali's Court.

Mick's New American Bistro Ⓜ *American*
- | - | - | M

Frederick | 207 W. Patrick St. (Center St.) | 301-662-0373 | www.micksnewamericanbistro.com

A few blocks west of Frederick's main drag lies this saloon offering novel New American interpretations of pub classics (the house-made pickles are a must-try) at moderate prices; great effort goes into locally sourcing both ingredients and clientele – who don't seem to mind the dark, mostly windowless railroad-style layout for romantic dates or nights out with the kids.

Miguel's Cocina & Cantina *Mexican*
- | - | - | M

Locust Point | Silo Point | 1200 Steuart St. (Clement St.) | 443-438-3139 | www.miguelsbaltimore.com

A towering grain silo converted to luxury condos in Locust Point hosts Michael Marx's tribute to Mexican cooking, where the fare

FOOD | DECOR | SERVICE | COST

warms tongues without burning holes in wallets; dangling Día de los Muertos artwork brightens the soaring concrete ceilings, giant windows offer railyard views and there's always soccer on TV; P.S. GPS is a big help in navigating the area.

☑ Milton Inn *American*

26 | 27 | 25 | $57

Sparks | 14833 York Rd. (Quaker Bottom Rd.) | 410-771-4366 | www.miltoninn.com

"Still a winner after all these years", this "special occasion"–worthy "treat" tucked into a "romantic" Sparks inn (1740) lures locals and out-of-towners alike with "outstanding" New American fare and "superb wines" that are "nicely presented by attentive servers"; it's "rather pricey", but with an "elegant" ambiance enhanced by fireplaces, red brick and a flagstone patio for pre-dinner cocktails or dining, "there's a good reason why it's always crowded."

Minato *Japanese*

22 | 20 | 20 | $27

Downtown North | 1013 N. Charles St. (Eager St.) | 410-332-0332 | www.minatosushibar.com

At this Downtown North row house, a "chichi" interior sets the scene for "generous portions" of "delicious" sushi and Japanese and Vietnamese dishes, delivered via "service with a smile"; if a few deem it all "hit-or-miss", the "great weekly specials", happy hours and "big bowls of noodle soups really hit the spot."

Miss Shirley's *American*

24 | 18 | 20 | $23

Inner Harbor | 750 E. Pratt St. (President St.) | 410-528-5373
Roland Park | 513 W. Cold Spring Ln. (Kittery Ln.) | 410-889-5272
www.missshirleys.com

"Be ready to loosen your belt" after digging into the "huge portions" of "decadent" breakfast and lunch at these "wildly popular" Americans, where everything from omelets to Southern specialties like "delish fried green tomatoes" is "bursting with flavor"; "efficient" servers try to keep up with the "big crowds", but expect "long lines" for the "pricey" grub nonetheless; P.S. regulars report the newer Inner Harbor office-lobby venue is not as "homey" as the Roland Park original; an Annapolis branch is due in fall 2011.

Monocacy Crossing Ⓜ *American*

24 | 17 | 21 | $43

Frederick | 4424A Urbana Pike (bet. Araby Church & Ball Rds.) | 301-846-4204 | www.monocacycrossing.com

"Drive too fast on Urbana Pike" and you "might miss" Rich and Kelly Regan's New American "nestled away" near Frederick, a "romantic" "gem" featuring an "eclectic wine list" and "inventive" cuisine (e.g. "hedonistic duck nachos") that's "prepared with care and served with flair"; it "doesn't look like much from the outside (or inside)", but one bite of the "wonderful" fare and the "surroundings quickly fade into a blur."

Morton's The Steakhouse *Steak*

25 | 22 | 25 | $66

Inner Harbor | Sheraton Inner Harbor Hotel | 300 S. Charles St. (Conway St.) | 410-547-8255 | www.mortons.com
See review in the Washington, DC, Directory.

	FOOD	DECOR	SERVICE	COST

Mr. Bill's Terrace Inn ⊠ *Crab House*   ▽ 26 | 11 | 19 | $38

Essex | 200 Eastern Blvd. (Helena Ave.) | 410-687-5996

"There's no Bill, no terrace and no inn", but "you know you're in Bawlmer, hon", when you step through the doors of this "noisy" Essex seafooder and start hammerin' piles of some of the "best crabs in town" alongside "old Colts and Orioles"; "go early or wait a long time", though whenever you arrive you'll "always feel welcome."

Mr. Rain's Fun House ⊠ *American*   - | - | - | M

Federal Hill | American Visionary Art Museum | 800 Key Hwy. (Covington St.) | 443-524-7379 | www.mrrainsfunhouse.com

Set atop the American Visionary Art Museum, this "artfully funky" concept from the team behind the defunct Sputnik Cafe presents "delightful" if "unusual" New American fare in a "cool" space sprinkled with fanciful flourishes (e.g. "brightly colored animal heads hanging from concrete walls"); "excellent cocktails" delivered by "servers who want you to have a good time" and 'Starving Artists Happy Hours' add to the "funhouse feel."

Obrycki's *Seafood*   23 | 14 | 19 | $38

East Baltimore | 1727 E. Pratt St. (bet. B'way & S. Regester St.) | 410-732-6399 | www.obryckis.com

Act fast to experience this 67-year-old East Baltimore "icon" that plans to close permanently in November after the 2011 crab season; for now, there's still "paper on the tables" along with "wooden mallets" for crushing crustaceans (plus other "solid seafood"); it has "all the atmosphere of a basement" and it's "rather expensive", but most maintain "smash, crash, it's fun"; P.S. Obrycki's has begun its second life as a chain, with outposts at BWI and Cleveland Hopkins airports.

Oceanaire Seafood Room *Seafood*   24 | 22 | 23 | $61

Harbor East | 801 Aliceanna St. (President St.) | 443-872-0000 | www.theoceanaire.com

See review in the Washington, DC, Directory.

One-Eyed Mike's *American*   - | - | - | M

Fells Point | 708 S. Bond St. (Aliceanna St.) | 410-327-0445 | www.oneeyedmikes.com

Away from the Fells Point waterfront bar district, this classic workingman's tavern sitting amid old row houses looks the part (narrow space, hand-carved back bar, tin ceilings) but surprises with ambitious, moderately priced New American plates; patrons have eyes for such palate-pleasers as the Caprese salad and broiled crab cake (sorry, no burger), but the dining room is tiny, so consider noshing with the popular bartenders or on the year-round patio with retractable roof.

One World Cafe *Vegetarian*   19 | 14 | 17 | $19

Homewood | 100 W. University Pkwy. (Canterbury Rd.) | 410-235-5777 | www.one-world-cafe.com

At this "laptop-filled academic den" near Hopkins, "hipsters" and their "parents" dig into "reliable" vegetarian staples, "fish options"

	FOOD	DECOR	SERVICE	COST

and "hard-to-find dishes involving faux meat" in "funky" surroundings (*you* try cramming a "coffee shop, smoothie joint, bar and restaurant" into one space); "cheap" prices keep it busy morning to late night, while an "inviting" vibe empowers patrons to "take their time and enjoy"; P.S. the Homewood locale means parking can be "difficult."

Orchard, The ☒Ⓜ *Eclectic* ▽ 19 | 12 | 17 | $29

Frederick | 45 N. Market St. (Church St.) | 301-663-4912 |
www.theorchardrestaurant.com

For "creative" Eclectic dishes prepared in "wholesome ways" – including a multinational array of "delicious" stir-fries – Frederick locals turn to this "casual-but-classy" eatery set in an unpretentious Market Street storefront; simple decor and service that's "sometimes disorganized" can't dissuade devotees lured by "good prices" and "freshly prepared desserts."

Orchard Market & Café Ⓜ *Persian* 25 | 20 | 24 | $27

Towson | 8815 Orchard Tree Ln. (Joppa Rd.) | 410-339-7700 |
www.orchardmarketandcafe.com

"Don't be afraid of the surroundings" of this Towson "industrial park" Persian: simply "enter and be enchanted" by the "huge portions" of "wonderfully prepared" cuisine – including a "great" Sunday brunch buffet – served by what may be the "nicest staff in town"; the "otherworldly atmosphere" is enhanced by the "lovely" decor (tiles, samovars), while a BYO policy makes it "even less expensive."

Oregon Grille *Seafood/Steak* 25 | 25 | 25 | $63

Hunt Valley | 1201 Shawan Rd. (Beaver Dam Rd.) | 410-771-0505 |
www.theoregongrille.com

Well-heeled nostalgists feel "transported back to the good ol' days" (read: "gentlemen must wear a jacket" at dinner in the main dining room) at this "horsey" Hunt Valley "favorite", a "comfy, clubby" affair where patrons trot in for expensive but "delicious steaks" and seafood; "fireplaces" inside and out, a "garden complete with waterfall" and "live piano" music add to the overall "romantic" mood, though neigh-sayers snipe about a "snooty" vibe and "overpriced" tabs.

Pairings Bistro Ⓜ *American* - | - | - | M

Bel Air | 2105 Laurel Bush Rd. (Emmorton Rd.) | 410-569-5006 |
www.pairingsbistro.com

"Tucked quietly into a small business center" in Bel Air, this "cool" New American is "small but packed" with "imaginative food" and "varied", "affordable" wines (a planned expansion should provide more breathing room); the decor is "unremarkable", but the warm hues and curvy floorplan still make it a standout in these parts, so no wonder acolytes "plan to return."

Pappas *American/Seafood* ▽ 26 | 14 | 25 | $23

Glen Burnie | 6713 Ritchie Hwy. (Americana Circle) |
410-766-3713

(continued)

Pappas

Northeast Baltimore | 1725 Taylor Ave. (Oakleigh Rd.) | 410-661-4357
www.pappascrabcakes.com

Caution: you may "be embarrassed by the moaning sounds emitting from your mouth" while savoring the "perfectly seasoned" crab cakes with "little filler" at this "comfy" Northeast Baltimore "favorite"; the "old-school" decor comes complete with a pianist struggling to be heard in the "crowded, noisy" dining room, filled with everyone from "out-of-town guests" to "grandmas" poring over the menu of "well-priced", seafood-slanted American chow; P.S. the Glen Burnie branch, complete with sports bar, opened post-Survey.

Patrick's *American*

22 | 21 | 21 | $34

Cockeysville | 550 Cranbrook Rd. (Ridgland Rd.) | 410-683-0604 | www.patricksrestaurant.com

Boosters of this Cockeysville "throwback" like its "cozy" "pleasant" setting and "reliable" American eats that please its "older clientele" and newer followers; it's "nothing fancy", but choose among "bar/casual dining/fine dining" to "suit your mood", then dig into "reasonably priced" fare like its signature crab cakes.

✓ Pazo *Mediterranean*

24 | 27 | 23 | $44

Harbor East | 1425 Aliceanna St. (bet. S. Caroline St. & S. Central Ave.) | 410-534-7296 | www.pazorestaurant.com

From the "scrumptious" Mediterranean tapas and entrees to the "wannabe movers-and-shakers" clientele, "everything about this place" from Charleston's Tony Foreman "exudes chic" – including one of the town's "snazziest" venues, a "cavernous" converted machine-tool shop in Harbor East with "high ceilings"; tabs can "add up quickly", but "considerate" servers help ease the pain, as do "great martinis and wine"; P.S. chef and menu tweaks post-Survey outdate the Food score; DJs and dancing have returned on some nights.

Peerce's *American*
(aka The Grille at Peerce's)

- | - | - | E

Phoenix | 12460 Dulaney Valley Rd. (Loch Raven Dr.) | 410-252-7111 | www.thegrilleatpeerces.com

Returning from a multiyear hiatus with a more casual concept under new ownership, this sprawling special-occasion house in Phoenix welcomes back old friends with a pricey menu of American classics (e.g. filet mignon, chicken pot pie, crab cakes); horse and hound prints dot the large dining room, but largely absent are the jackets and ties, which are no longer required; P.S. two vast event rooms host catered parties.

Peppermill *American*

18 | 13 | 20 | $30

Lutherville | Heaver Bldg. | 1301 York Rd. (bet. I-695 & Seminary Ave.) | 410-583-1107 | www.pepmill.com

It's "nothing too fancy", but no matter: the "senior set loves this place" and its "old-fashioned but consistently good" American chow; sure, the "plain setting" could use some "sprucing", but with "fast service", "huge portions", a "convenient location" in a Lutherville office building and "value" pricing, most "don't seem to notice."

Z Peter's Inn Ⓢ Ⓜ *American*   27 | 18 | 22 | $33

Fells Point | 504 S. Ann St. (Eastern Ave.) | 410-675-7313 | www.petersinn.com

Perhaps "Baltimore's worst-kept secret", this "former biker bar" draws Fells Point foodies who vow it's "worth the wait" to sample its "short" "weekly menu" of "spectacular" New American cuisine and "great wines by the glass"; "friendly" servers navigate the "tight", "quirky" quarters featuring decor "right out of [your] father's base-ment", which somehow all seems so "hip" it begs the question "are you cool enough to eat here?"

Z Petit Louis Bistro *French*   25 | 22 | 23 | $46

Roland Park | 4800 Roland Ave. (Upland Rd.) | 410-366-9393 | www.petitlouis.com

For a "fabulous little taste of France" "without the jet lag", Francophiles pack into this "bustling" Roland Parker featuring "perfectly executed bistro classics", an "excellent French wine list" and "first-class" service ("I tip my beret to the staff"); *oui,* "extremely close" tables lead to rampant "eavesdropping" and "deafening" noise levels, but regulars retort "bring an appetite . . . and earplugs"; P.S. euro-pinchers side-step "pricey" tabs with a $20 lunch prix fixe option.

P.F. Chang's China Bistro *Chinese*   20 | 20 | 19 | $30

Inner Harbor | Market Pl. | 600 E. Pratt St. (bet. Market Pl. & S. Gay St.) | 410-649-2750

White Marsh | White Marsh Mall | 8342 Honeygo Blvd. (White Marsh Blvd.) | 401-931-2433

Columbia | Mall in Columbia | 10300 Little Patuxent Pkwy. (Wincopin Circle) | 410-730-5344

Towson | Towson Town Ctr. | 825 Dulaney Valley Rd. (Fairmont Ave.) | 410-372-5250
www.pfchangs.com

See review in the Washington, DC, Directory.

Pho Dat Thanh *Vietnamese*   25 | 11 | 18 | $18

Columbia | 9400 Snowden River Pkwy. (Broken Land Pkwy.) | 410-381-3839

Towson | 510 York Rd. (Pennsylvania Ave.) | 410-296-9118
www.phodatthanh.com

Sure, the atmosphere at this "friendly" Columbia strip-maller and its Towson offspring is "nothing special", but the same can't be said of the "authentic" Vietnamese offerings on tap, which include "phan-tastic pho" ("as close to a health plan as many of us have"), "terrific" noodle dishes and "crowd-pleasing" apps; service can be "wildly in-consistent", but "guilt-inducingly cheap prices" mean you can "hardly go wrong" here.

Pho Nam ⌒ *Vietnamese*   ▽ 23 | 6 | 16 | $13

Catonsville | 6477 Baltimore National Pike (Rolling Rd.) | 410-455-6000

Out Route 40 west of Catonsville, this "pho specialist" ladles out some of the "best broth around", a "rich, meaty" stock savored by the many

Asian emigres who dine here ("so it must be good"); the "plain" strip-mall setting takes nothing away from the "amazing" "family fare", and the "affordable prices" and "fast" service only make it better.

Pierpoint Ⓜ American ▽ 24 | 13 | 25 | $39

Fells Point | 1822 Aliceanna St. (bet. Ann & Wolfe Sts.) | 410-675-2080 | www.pierpointrestaurant.com

The "food speaks for itself" at this "small but efficient" Fells Pointer that continues to turn out "creative, delicious" Chesapeake-inflected New American fare, especially when chef-owner Nancy Longo is "behind the stoves" ("her smoked crab cake is a franchise in itself"); some may "question entering" the narrow, "cramped" space, but few regret it; P.S. a "kid-friendly" vibe extends to the proprietor's popular cooking classes.

Portalli's Italian - | - | - | M

Ellicott City | 8085 Main St. (Maryland Ave.) | 410-720-2330 | www.portallisec.com

Presenting a "classic Italian menu in pleasant surroundings", this bustling boîte set in a former steakhouse attracts families and date-nighters out for an evening on the town in Ellicott City; guests enjoy a full range of midpriced pastas, meat, seafood and specialty cocktails in the high-ceilinged upstairs space (enlivened by a piano player on Fridays and Saturdays) or the more intimate, clubby downstairs room.

Porter's American - | - | - | M

Federal Hill | 1032 Riverside Ave. (Cross St.) | 410-332-7345 | www.portersfederalhill.com

Gentrified Federal Hill is delighted by this homey and intimate dark-wood corner bar and its seasonally adjusted American fare made from local farmer's-market finds; tabs are wallet-friendly, and if you come often enough, you'll be welcomed in the proverbial *Cheers* manner.

☑ Prime Rib Seafood/Steak 27 | 25 | 27 | $68

Downtown North | 1101 N. Calvert St. (Chase St.) | 410-539-1804 | www.theprimerib.com

In Downtown Baltimore and DC's Golden Triangle, the "godfathers of steakhouses" mix "old-world elegance" with "just the right touch of film-noir decadence", live music and "dynamite food" – the "best slab-o-meat in town", "first-rate" crab and "huge" sides – to make each "expensive" meal an "event"; the "retro-classy" digs are attended by "tuxedoed waiters" (there's a business casual "dress code" for customers too), while the bar scenes "will hurt your eyes if you're married."

Regions Ⓜ Eclectic - | - | - | M

Catonsville | 803 Frederick Rd. (Mellor Ave.) | 410-788-0075 | www.regionsrestaurant.com

An upmarket date annex of Catonsville Gourmet, this sleek yearling on a burgeoning Restaurant Row is done up in dark burgundy with black accents and exposed rafters; an oft-changing Eclectic menu offers a mix of big and small plates with a tilt toward different 'regions' (Maryland, France, Asia, etc.), while moderate prices are made even more accessible by a BYO policy with modest corkage fees.

Regi's *American*   22 | 17 | 22 | $32

South Baltimore | 1002 Light St. (E. Hamburg St.) | 410-539-7344 | www.regisamericanbistro.com

Whether you strike up "conversation with locals" at the bar or opt for a "romantic date night" in the "comfortable" dining room, "don't miss" the "grown-up tater tots" at this South Baltimore "comfort place"; an owner who's "always on hand" to greet guests sets a "warm" tone, all the better to enjoy "excellent" New American fare (sourced partially from a rooftop garden/apiary) worth the "waist-line splurge"; P.S. "one of the best brunches in town" can be enjoyed on covered sidewalk tables.

Rocco's Capriccio *Italian*   23 | 17 | 24 | $38

Little Italy | 846 Fawn St. (bet. Albemarle & High Sts.) | 410-685-2710 | www.roccosinlittleitaly.com

If you're lucky, "Rocco himself will come by" your table at his "Little Italy stalwart", which churns out "generous portions" of traditional "Northern Italian specialties" that "compete well" with some of the neighborhood's "big names"; "smallish" rooms and "quaint" decor inspire little passion among surveyors, but "reasonable prices", "nightly specials" and "excellent service" more than compensate.

Rocket to Venus *Eclectic*   19 | 18 | 16 | $23

Hampden | 3360 Chestnut Ave. (W. 34th St.) | 410-235-7887 | www.rockettovenus.com

A "too-cool-for-school crowd" converges on this "funky" "little neighborhood" Eclectic with a "warm feeling on the inside, chill decor on the outside" and a "limited menu" of "way-out food combos" that somehow "work"; it may be where "tragically hip servers go to die" (so expect "'tude" with your "fried pickles"), but it's "cheap", "cool" and "comfortable" – in other words, "Hampden with a capital H."

Roy's *Hawaiian*   25 | 23 | 24 | $47

Harbor East | 720B Aliceanna St. (President St.) | 410-659-0099 | www.roysrestaurant.com

"Every meal is a delight" effuse fans of this "high-end chain" outpost in Harbor East showcasing celeb chef Roy Yamaguchi's "modern mastery" of Hawaiian fusion cuisine, focusing on "beautifully prepared" fish (and "unique" local specialties) among other "innovative creations" with "bold flavors"; the "upbeat" atmosphere and "excellent" service help support the "steep" price, plus the prix fixe menu is a real "deal."

Ruth's Chris Steak House *Steak*   25 | 23 | 25 | $62

Business District | 600 Water St. (bet. Gay St. & Market Pl.) | 410-783-0033
Inner Harbor | Pier 5 Hotel | 711 Eastern Ave. (S. President St.) | 410-230-0033
Pikesville | 1777 Reisterstown Rd. (Hooks Ln.) | 410-837-0033
www.ruthschris.com

See review in the Washington, DC, Directory.

	FOOD	DECOR	SERVICE	COST

Sabatino's ◐ *Italian*   20 | 16 | 21 | $32
Little Italy | 901 Fawn St. (High St.) | 410-727-9414 |
www.sabatinos.com

At this "epitome of Little Italy", "generous" servings of "plain ol' Italian comfort food" and "amazing 'Bookmaker' salads" come courtesy of service that's "very old-school, hon"; sure, the "menu and staff haven't changed in this century or last" and the "nondescript" decor "goes back to the '50s", but its legion of loyalists "like it that way" – plus "it's open late" (3 AM on weekends).

Sabor *Eclectic*   24 | 19 | 23 | $42
Lutherville | Roundwood Shopping Ctr. | 12240 Tullamore Rd. (Padonia Rd.) | 410-628-7227 | www.restaurantsabor.com

"Talented chef" and owner Roddy Domacassé brings a "little ethnic flair" to this "elegant and inventive" Lutherville Eclectic that's "not your average strip-mall spot"; high ceilings and a "glassed-in kitchen" set the stage for "delicious" fare delivered by "knowledgeable" waiters who will "dote on you"; P.S. BYO eases the pain of "downtown prices."

Salsa Grill *Pan-Latin/Peruvian*   - | - | - | M
Woodlawn | 6644 Security Blvd. (bet. I-695 & Woodlawn Dr.) | 410-265-5552 | www.eatsalsagrill.com

Like a "bolt from the blue", this BYO "treasure" in a Woodlawn strip mall "surprises" with an "incredibly tasty" mix of Peruvian, Salvadoran and American chow; it's "not fancy", but the bold blue-and-green space studded with booths and tables becomes packed at lunchtime with hungry "value"-seekers.

☑ Salt Ⓜ *American*   27 | 22 | 25 | $43
East Baltimore | 2127 E. Pratt St. (Collington St.) | 410-276-5480 | www.salttavern.com

Smitten surveyors "kinda love" this "top-notch" "neighborhood secret" crammed into a "tiny" East Baltimore row house, where a "reliable kitchen" turns out an "ever-changing menu" of "beyond-the-norm" New American fare; it's all washed down with "imaginative" cocktails and served by a "comfortably attentive" staff, and if "difficult parking" is a deterrent for some, most say "by all means, go."

Sammy's Trattoria *Italian*   21 | 20 | 19 | $37
Mt. Vernon | 1200 N. Charles St. (Biddle St.) | 410-837-9999 | www.sammystrattoria.com

Convenient for a meal "before or after the Meyerhoff or Lyric", this midpriced Mt. Vernonite proffers "hefty portions" of "tasty" "Italian with flair" in high-ceilinged digs boasting a long bar; parking can be "tough" and service "slow" on "busy nights", but "ever-present" owners who make patrons "feel at home" help matters.

☑ Samos Ⓩ⇄ *Greek*   27 | 12 | 20 | $22
Greektown | 600 S. Oldham St. (Fleet St.) | 410-675-5292 | www.samosrestaurant.com

They "come from miles away and wait for hours" to sample the "real-deal" Hellenic eats at this "well-priced" Greektown "institution", where chef-owners Nick and Mike Georgalas greet you with a "warm smile and open arms" and ensure no one "leaves unsatisfied"; it's "small, cramped" and "nothing fancy", but "quick" service and a BYO policy that "makes it even better" mean most "would go back in a flash"; P.S. "bring cash" and, on weekends, "your patience."

Sam's Kid *Asian* ▽ 24 | 22 | 19 | $23

Fells Point | 811 S. Broadway (bet. Lancaster & Thames Sts.) | 410-522-3663

"From Korea to Japan to China", this Fells Pointer from Indonesian owner-chef Andrea Rani touches all the bases with "creative" Pan-Asian dishes enhanced by "fresh" ingredients and "surprisingly delicious and complex sauces"; add in a "comfortable" if "tony" storefront setting (think bright walls, "funky" purple and red couches), an "accommodating" staff and "modest prices", and it's clear acolytes aren't kidding when they say "welcome to Baltimore!"

San Sushi *Japanese* 23 | 15 | 18 | $25

Cockeysville | 9832 York Rd. (bet. Galloway Ave. & Padonia Rd.) | 410-453-0140

San Sushi Too/Thai One On *Japanese/Thai*

Towson | 10 W. Pennsylvania Ave. (York Rd.) | 410-825-0908

"Go hungry, leave full" at this "delicious" split personality: the original Cockeysville strip-mall BYO "makes you feel like family" while dishing up "delicious, creative" raw-fin fare, while its "casual" Towson sib – a "sea of sushi and college students" – is praised for its "great use of spices", "excellent" Thai food and moody bar; expect "reasonable prices" at both, though York Road costs a bit more.

Sascha's 527 ⚡ *American* 22 | 21 | 20 | $31

Mt. Vernon | 527 N. Charles St. (bet. Centre & Hamilton Sts.) | 410-539-8880 | www.saschas.com

"Dressed up for champagne at beer prices", this Mt. Vernon "find" features a "beautiful", "spacious" dining room (i.e. dramatic draping, high ceilings, rotating artwork) that provides a worthy backdrop for a "fairly edgy" menu of New American fare; despite the "sophisticated" trappings, it's a "comfortable" spot for a "reliable" meal, so "leave your pretension at the door" and enjoy.

Schultz's Crab House *Crab House* - | - | - | M

Essex | 1732 Old Eastern Ave. (Back River Neck Rd.) | 410-687-1020

Crustacean mavens "don't want anyone else" discovering this knotty-pined "throwback to the '60s", an "old-time bar and crab house" offering some of the "best seafood" in Essex; expect "average prices", plenty of "on-street parking" and "good service" – just get there "early on weekends", because you won't be alone.

Shin Chon *Korean* - | - | - | M

Ellicott City | 8801 Baltimore National Pike (Ridge Rd.) | 410-461-3280

"Korean BBQ lovers" converge under the spiffy shiny ductwork above tables at this energetic Ellicott City strip-maller, an unassuming palate-pleaser that's "best with a group" (read: everyone can take turns manning the DIY grills); modest prices and an "attentive" staff are other reasons it's become increasingly "crowded", but those in the know say it's "worth a wait" during the "popular" "weekend dinner hours."

Sotto Sopra *Italian*   24 | 24 | 23 | $49

Mt. Vernon | 405 N. Charles St. (bet. Franklin & Mulberry Sts.) | 410-625-0534 | www.sottosopra.us

"Go here rather than Little Italy" decree devotees of this "warm and receptive" "standout" in a "cozy" Mt. Vernon townhouse, where "creative" – if "expensive" – Italian fare crafted from the "highest-quality ingredients" is presented by "charming servers with an international flair"; "specialty" prix fixes (e.g. "opera performances with dinner" one Sunday a month) add to the "lively atmosphere."

Soup'r Natural 🖼️🅼 *American*   - | - | - | I

Parkton | 17114 York Rd. (Mt. Carmel Rd.) | 443-491-3464 | www.souprnatural.com

At this American yearling in Parkton near hunt country, homeowners, contractors and farmers gather at their own farm-to-table 'community center'; the homey one-room eatery focuses on local production, so naturally, only the freshest ingredients support its soups, salads, sandwiches, entrees and made-from-scratch fountain sodas.

Stanford Grill *American*   - | - | - | M

Columbia | 8900 Stanford Blvd. (Dobbin Rd.) | 410-312-0445 | www.thestanfordgrill.com

A vast horseshoe bar and sea of wooden booths, all within eyeshot of the open kitchen and chicken rotisserie, greet guests at this modern, dark and clubby Columbia grill with live jazz every night; American comfort food is the name of the game – mac 'n' cheese, prime rib, grilled fish – but it's less expensive and in larger portions than you'd expect; tip: it's visible from Route 175, but a GPS comes in handy.

Stone Mill Bakery & Cafe 🖼️ *Bakery*   22 | 12 | 18 | $20

Brooklandville | Greenspring Station | 10751 Falls Rd. (Greenspring Valley Rd.) | 410-821-1358 | www.stonemillbakery.com

"You feel like you're living the high life" at this "wonderful" Brooklandville all-day bakery/cafe offering "delicious" breakfasts, "luxury baked goods" ("don't miss the health bread"), "sinful sandwiches", soups and pizza; true, tabs "may put a dent in your son's college fund", but one philosophical sort notes an "overpriced lunch is an underpriced dinner"; P.S. "outside seating" handles overflow.

Suburban House *Deli*   - | - | - | I

Pikesville | 1700 Reisterstown Rd. (Naylors Ln.) | 410-484-7775 | www.suburbanhousedeli.com

Longtime customers yearning to see pastrami coming through the rye again are having a fressfest since this venerable Pikesville deli reopened in an office complex up the road from the burned-down original; low tabs, on-site bagel baking, snappy service and a long carry-out counter with high throughput keep folks coming back.

	FOOD	DECOR	SERVICE	COST

Sullivan's Steakhouse *Steak*
22 | 21 | 22 | $50

Inner Harbor | 1 E. Pratt St. (entrance on Light St.) | 410-962-5503 |
www.sullivanssteakhouse.com

"A real crowd-pleaser" in the Inner Harbor, this "comfortable", retro
Chicago-style chain outpost is "always lively" with folks chowing
down on "good steaks" amid "deco-themed" digs; "they make a
mean martini" too, though doubters dub it a "wannabe" that "has
some work to do" to catch up with the competition and the cost.

Sushi Hana *Japanese*
23 | 15 | 21 | $30

Mt. Washington | Lake Falls Shopping Ctr. | 6080 Falls Rd. (Lake Ave.) |
410-377-4228

NEW **Timonium** | Yorkridge Shopping Ctr. | 1819 York Rd. (Ridgely Rd.) |
410-560-7090

Towson | 6 E. Pennsylvania Ave. (York Rd.) | 410-823-0372
www.sushihanabaltimore.com

"More sophisticated" than the "student"-friendly Towson original, the
"hard-to-find" Mt. Washington branch tucked behind an "upscale"
shopping center delivers "imaginative" sushi (including "diverse maki
rolls") and other "fresh" Japanese fin fare and cooked options; expect
service that's "friendly" if a bit "slow" at both and tabs that are
"worth your money"; P.S. the Timonium branch opened post-Survey.

Sushi King ☒ *Japanese*
24 | 14 | 21 | $33

Columbia | 6490 Dobbin Rd. (Rte. 175) | 410-997-1269 |
www.sushikingmd.com

Habitués "hooked" on this Columbia Japanese recommend ordering
"one of the specials on the board", a compendium of "outstanding
additions" to a menu already packed with some of the "best sushi in
the area"; perhaps the "decor could be updated" and it's got an "unlikely" business center address "next to the MVA", but modest tabs
and a "friendly, family atmosphere" mean it's "always crowded."

Sushi Sono ☒ *Japanese*
26 | 21 | 24 | $37

Columbia | 10215 Wincopin Circle (Little Patuxent Pkwy.) |
410-997-6131 | www.sushisonomd.com

"Who could ask for anything more?" ponder partisans of this somewhat "pricey" Japanese "Eden" in Columbia, where the "best sushi
around" "takes your palate to new heights" and the sashimi and
"cooked stuff" (shabu-shabu, "fabulous tempura") are "just as
good"; an "attentive" staff and "attractive" quarters with "scenic
views of Lake Kittamaqundi" offer further enticement.

Szechuan House ◑ *Chinese*
23 | 12 | 21 | $21

Lutherville | 1427 York Rd. (Seminary Ave.) | 410-825-8181 |
www.szechuanhouse-md.com

An "unbelievably broad menu" of some of the "best Chinese" around
("sets the bar for Peking duck very high") coupled with "nice touches"
like "sherbet to cleanse your palate" make this Lutherville strip-
maller a real "favorite"; the "decor isn't modern" and the place turns
into a "madhouse" when "crowded", but factor in "fast service",
"low prices" and a delivery option, and "no one seems to mind."

	FOOD	DECOR	SERVICE	COST

Tabrizi's Ⓜ *Mediterranean/Mideastern* — 21 | 23 | 19 | $42

South Baltimore | Harborview | 500 Harborview Dr. (Key Hwy.) | 410-727-3663 | www.tabrizis.com

"Quiet, relaxing and even romantic", this "off-the-beaten-path" eatery in South Baltimore's Harborview development occupies a "wonderful waterside location" and dishes up a "large number" of Med–Middle Eastern dishes from chef-owner Michael Tabrizi; if some nostalgists prefer its long-ago incarnation as a "South Charles hole-in-the-wall" and sniff the "view is better than the food", more say "reasonable prices" and a "welcoming" staff make it "worth the trip."

Talara ◑ *Nuevo Latino* — 23 | 23 | 21 | $35

Harbor East | 615 S. President St. (Fleet St.) | 410-528-9883 | www.talarabaltimore.com

"Key lime mojitos", free salsa lessons (Monday nights) and "outstanding" ceviche power this "fresh and fun" Nuevo Latino that brings "something different" to Harbor East, specifically "glitzy decor and a Miami feel"; "uneven" service kills the buzz for some, but "surprisingly good specialty drinks" and $5 tapas during the "great happy hour" (daily and late-night Saturdays) take care of that.

Tapas Adela *Spanish* — ▽ 25 | 24 | 24 | $35

Fells Point | 814 S. Broadway (bet. Lancaster & Thames Sts.) | 410-534-6262 | www.tapasadela.com

The latest addition to the Kali's Restaurant Group stable (Kali's Court, Meli, Mezze), this "beautiful" Fells Pointer scores points for "delectable" tapas like "lamb meatballs", which can be washed down with "amazing homemade sangria" at a white-marble communal table, in the compact dining room or on sidewalk water-view tables; "excellent" service and modest prices complete the picture.

Tapas Teatro ◑Ⓜ *Eclectic/Mediterranean* — 23 | 19 | 20 | $32

Downtown North | 1711 N. Charles St. (bet. Lafayette Ave. & Lanvale St.) | 410-332-0110 | www.tapasteatro.com

"Dinner and a movie never tasted so good" fawn film buffs who pack this "somewhat cramped" but "always lively" Eclectic-Med "adjacent to the Charles Theatre" in Downtown North; it's the "place that made tapas cool" in these parts, so expect a "creatively prepared" selection of "small plates with big flavor" – just "watch the costs, endure the waits" and "don't miss the sangria"; P.S. "atmosphere out the wazoo" extends to the sidewalk seating.

Tark's Grill *American* — 19 | 18 | 20 | $40

Brooklandville | Greenspring Station | 2360 W. Joppa Rd. (Falls Rd.) | 410-583-8275 | www.tarksgrill.com

"Finally", there's a "trendy" "neighborhood meeting place" that's "showing some staying power" in Brooklandville's Greenspring Station retail complex, albeit one with a "well-prepared" if "uninspiring" surf 'n' turf menu; even so, the "clubby" New American has generated "great buzz", as much for its "dependable" service and "wonderful", "fireplace"-equipped outdoor space as its "hopping bar scene", which can get "turn-up-the-hearing-aid noisy."

☑ Tasting Room ⑧ *American*   27 | 21 | 24 | $48

Frederick | 101 N. Market St. (Church St.) | 240-379-7772 |
www.tastetr.com

The "big windows let everyone see what you're eating" at this "so-phisticated" New American, an "upscale" "gem" whose "fantastic" "seasonal" cuisine, "creative martinis" and vino off one of the "best wine lists for miles around" are "professionally" served "at a Frederick pace"; the decor has a "chic, modern" edge, but seating that's a "lit-tle cramped" means there's little "privacy" and no lack of "noise"; P.S. wallet-watchers can opt for "great lunch deals."

Teavolve *American/Tearoom*   - | - | - | I

Harbor East | 1401 Aliceanna St. (Central Ave.) | 410-522-1907 |
www.teavolve.com

From a weekday study hall for caffeinated laptoppers and nosh-ers to a brunch destination for an after-church crowd replete with big hats, this airy and affordable all-purpose cafe/tearoom in a new East Harbor high-rise appeals to a diverse local crowd; beverages include 50 loose teas served any which way (even in sangria or as iced bubble tea), locally roasted coffee and a full bar; P.S. it's gearing up to add more serious entrees to its menu of salads and sandwiches.

☑ Tersiguel's *French*   26 | 23 | 26 | $57

Ellicott City | 8293 Main St. (Old Columbia Pike) | 410-465-4004 |
www.tersiguels.com

Francophiles "feel pampered" without the "stuffy French attitude" at this "charming" Ellicott City "winner", where chef-owner Michel Tersiguel's "outstanding" creations often include ingredients fresh from his farm; it's a "little pricey", and even a few *amis* consider the "cozy" historic house a bit "cramped", but all in all, it's "still a splen-did experience after all these years."

☑ Thai Arroy Ⓜ *Thai*   27 | 15 | 23 | $21

South Baltimore | 1019 Light St. (bet. Cross & Hamburg Sts.) |
410-385-8587 | www.thaiarroy.com

Lines "often extend outside the door" for tables at this South Baltimore Thai, and for good reason: though portions are "massive", folks just "can't get enough" of its "exceptionally tasty" fare ("some spicy, some not"); a "lovely" staff oversees a dining room "small on space, huge on flavor", while a BYO policy that "makes it acceptable to have a 12-pack at your feet" also makes a "bargain" spot even "cheaper."

Thai Landing *Thai*   27 | 14 | 25 | $27

Mt. Vernon | 1207 N. Charles St. (bet. Biddle & Preston Sts.) |
410-727-1234 | www.thailandingmd.com

"If you like your food spicy", consider this "above-average" Mt. Vernon Thai whose "authentic", "delicious" chow will prompt your taste buds to "send messages you've never heard before"; "service with a smile" outshines the nondescript decor, as do its "reasonable prices" and location "close to the Meyerhoff"; P.S. a post-Survey change in chef and ownership outdates the Food score.

13.5% Wine Bar M *American*

19 | 22 | 20 | $27

Hampden | 1117 W. 36th St. (bet. Falls Rd. & Hickory Ave.) |
410-889-1064 | www.13.5winebar.com

A "trendy spot in a trendy spot", this "vibrant" "oenophile's oasis" in
Hampden helps "hipsters" "feel classy on the cheap", as long as
they "don't mind the strange plastic swivel seats"; there's a limited
menu of "decent" pizzas and New American small plates, but even
fans admit it's "mainly a place for snacks and conversation" – and,
natch, "wine, wine and more wine"; P.S. a fall 2011 opening is
planned for a second branch in Locust Point.

Tidewater Grille *American*

∇ 22 | 22 | 20 | $34

Havre de Grace | 300 Franklin St. (St. John St.) | 410-939-3313 |
www.thetidewatergrille.com

It's a "bit out of the way", but a "beautiful setting" on the
Susquehanna River attracts eaters to this expansive, "casual"
American in "quaint little" Havre de Grace – and the "crab cakes
keep bringing them back"; the food's "fine" and the service
"cheerful", but it becomes "especially nice" if you secure a "table
by the window" or have your "lunch on the patio" and enjoy
the "unbeatable" views.

Timbuktu *Seafood*

21 | 12 | 18 | $29

Hanover | 1726 Dorsey Rd. (Coca-Cola Dr./Rte. 100) | 410-796-0733 |
www.timbukturestaurant.com

Even the "most persnickety of individuals" "rave" about the "humongous, lump-filled" crab cakes at this "informal", "warehouse"-
sized Hanover seafooder patronized by everyone from "church
ladies to suburban yuppies" to Baltimore urbanites; there's "no ambiance", service can be "indifferent" and the other fare is "not inventive", but the droves who make the trek to the "middle of nowhere"
(ok, it's near BWI) ensure it's "busy all the time."

Tio Pepe *Continental/Spanish*

24 | 21 | 23 | $53

Mt. Vernon | 10 E. Franklin St. (bet. Charles & St. Paul Sts.) |
410-539-4675

The "place hasn't changed in forever", but longtime loyalists still
"love everything" about this Mt. Vernon "grande dame", from the
"huge portions" of "consistently delicious" Spanish-Continental cuisine to the "old-world" service; the "unique cellar location" can get
backed up on weekends, but it remains a "major destination for
a special meal."

Trattoria Alberto Ⓢ *Italian*

∇ 25 | 20 | 22 | $68

Glen Burnie | 1660 Crain Hwy. S. (bet. Hospital Dr. & Rte. 100 overpass) |
410-761-0922 | www.trattoriaalberto.com

Although chef-owner Alberto Contestabile recently retired from the
kitchen, they still "put on a show" at this "small" Glen Burnie stalwart, which dishes up an "imaginative menu" of "superb" Northern
Italian fare (e.g. "fresh pasta cooked every day") in a "warm" if "unlikely" strip-mall space; a "friendly" staff enhances the experience,
but "expensive" tabs rattle the thrifty.

NEW Two Boots *Pizza*

- | - | - | I

Downtown North | Fitzgerald Apts. | 1203 W. Mt. Royal Ave. (Oliver St.) | 410-625-2668 | www.twoboots.com

This outpost of an NYC pizzeria chain recently relocated from the Power Plant Live! complex to MICA, where it slings offbeat slices, many with Cajun spice (e.g. its crab, crawfish, andouille and jalapeño version); the spartan space – just a few 1940s-style tables with counter service – is aimed at students, but the Downtown North locale may also yield a quick, inexpensive bite for symphony patrons or light-railers en route to the ball game; P.S. it delivers nearby.

Umi Sake *Asian*

∇ 25 | 18 | 26 | $30

Cockeysville | 9726 York Rd. (Padonia Rd.) | 410-667-6586 | www.umisake.com

"What a find!" exult enthusiasts of this "upscale" Cockeysville "hot spot" churning out "tasty", "artfully presented" sushi and "palate-pleasing" Pan-Asian dishes, plus a "not-to-be-missed" Sunday brunch buffet; "affordable" prices, efficient service and a slick space complete with a sushi bar inspire a lot of "love" from those who've discovered it; P.S. it's expanding, adding a basement lounge.

Victoria Gastro Pub *Eclectic*

21 | 20 | 19 | $32

Columbia | 8201 Snowden River Pkwy. (Waterloo Rd.) | 410-750-1880 | www.victoriagastropub.com

There's a "lively vibe" at this "upscale" Columbia gastropub, no doubt from hopsheads cheering a beer list that "outweighs the food menu" and noshers digging into "fancy-schmancy" Eclectic fare like "fabulous" duck-fat fries ("what I imagine heaven to be like"); it can be "rather costly" and finicky types suggest the fare and service "don't quite make the cut", but given the "pleasant" "old-English feel", overall it's a "neat experience."

Vinny's Cafe Ⓜ *Italian*

- | - | - | M

Dundalk | 6212 Holabird Ave. (Charlotte Ave.) | 410-633-7763 | www.vinnyscafe.com

Convenient to heavy industry and I-95, this robust red-saucer in Dundalk dishes out hefty, midpriced pasta plates and rich Italian standards that lure contractors and salespeople at lunch and families and couples in the evening; the modern, high-ceilinged quarters come equipped with a happy buzz and a weekend piano player, while those seeking a more intimate meal can opt for a smaller dining room; P.S. a serious carry-out operation ensures pizzas get special attention.

Vino Rosina ⬤Ⓢ *American*

- | - | - | M

Harbor East | Bagby Building | 507 S. Exeter St. (Eastern Ave.) | 410-528-8600 | www.vinorosina.com

Blink and you may miss this moderate-priced mid-block wine bar, though that hasn't deterred stylish Harbor East denizens from claiming the slick modern space as a post-work hang for cocktails and vino; there's a big square bar and a few banquettes adjacent to an open kitchen, where the crew turns out nonstandard New American tastes, raw bites (carpaccio, ceviche) and cheese plates.

	FOOD	DECOR	SERVICE	COST

☑ Volt Ⓜ *American* — 28 | 26 | 27 | $73

Frederick | Houck Mansion | 228 N. Market St. (bet. 2nd & 3rd Sts.) | 301-696-8658 | www.voltrestaurant.com

He lost *Top Chef*, but Bryan Voltaggio has a "winner" in this "electrifying" Frederick New American, where the "astonishing", "locally sourced" cuisine packed with "sensational flavors" is eclipsed only by the bounty of 'Table 21', at which the "culinary star" himself presents a "delectable" "21-course tasting menu" (the main dining room is à la carte); set in a "lovely" 1890 mansion awash in "modern" trappings and "over-the-top" service, it's "one of the best dining experiences" around – but "good luck getting a reservation"; P.S. the $20 lunch prix fixe and $15 bar lunch may be the "biggest bargains ever"; closed Mondays and Tuesdays.

Waterstone Ⓜ *Mediterranean* — - | - | - | M

West Baltimore | 311 W. Madison Ave. (Howard St.) | 410-225-7475 | www.waterstonebarandgrille.com

A quick ride from the theaters, an updated old corner bar in an unpopulated area west of Mt. Vernon is the unlikely setting for this hang drawing the post-work drinks crowd and couples sharing mid-priced Mediterranean plates; a waterfall, sidewalk tables and an active bar each soothe in their own way.

Wine Market *American* — 24 | 20 | 21 | $39

Locust Point | 921 E. Fort Ave. (Lawrence St.) | 410-244-6166 | www.the-wine-market.com

"Equally good for romance, girls' night out or just because it's Wednesday", this Locust Pointer features an "awesome concept": "pick your favorite vintage" from the "adjoining wine shop", "pay a $9 corkage fee" ($18 for BYO) then dig into an "ever-changing" "value-priced" New American menu; the "industrial space" can get "noisy", but "enthusiastic" servers and a "fun outside patio" compensate.

☑ Woodberry Kitchen *American* — 26 | 26 | 24 | $47

Hampden | 2010 Clipper Park Rd. (Clipper Mill Rd.) | 410-464-8000 | www.woodberrykitchen.com

It's in a "hard-to-find" "old foundry" west of Hampden, but there's no doubt chef/co-owner Spike Gjerde's "elegant, farm-to-table" New American "has been discovered", inasmuch as it's Baltimore's Most Popular restaurant; expect "crowds" of "beautiful people" poring over an "ever-changing menu" of "stunning" fare made from "local, sustainable" ingredients, all paired with "interesting wines" and "creative cocktails" and served by a "polished" staff; just know that the "rustic-urban" space is "noisy when full" (i.e. almost always) and "reservations are a must"; P.S. a couple of casual spin-offs are planned nearby for late 2011.

Yellow Dog Tavern Ⓜ *American* — 20 | 16 | 20 | $28

Canton | 700 S. Potomac St. (Foster Ave.) | 410-342-0280 | www.yellowdogbaltimore.com

At this "gastronomic haven" set in a "traditional pub", "creative, flavorful" New American cooking (including "great vegetarian items"), "courteous service" and "unique cocktails and tasty microbrews" have tails wagging; the decor is modest, with "local artwork on the walls", but that doesn't stop fans from deeming the place a "top dog" in Canton.

Ze Mean Bean Café *E European*

22 | 17 | 19 | $30

Fells Point | 1739 Fleet St. (Ann St.) | 410-675-5999 | www.zemeanbean.com

"Yes, it has a weird name", but when you're "craving borscht", this "funky" Fells Point "retreat" is the "place to go" for "surprisingly good" Eastern European "comfort food with some oomph" plus an eclectic mix of other choices; service can be "uneven", but that hardly matters to those who say the "romantic, cozy atmosphere" is perfect in "cold weather", and bean-counters contend "ze creative" cuisine is "fairly priced" to boot; P.S. "jazz brunches" add to the "laid-back" vibe.

Zorba's Bar & Grill ☻ *Greek*

21 | 11 | 17 | $22

Greektown | 4710 Eastern Ave. (Oldham St.) | 410-276-4484

For a "true sense of Greektown" and "some of the best lamb chops" in town, make tracks to this "small", "no-frills" taverna turning out "amazing charcoal spit-roasted meats", "grilled fish" and other "traditional dishes" "prepared with love"; it gets "noisy and crowded" (sit upstairs to avoid), but "friendly" service and "reasonable prices" lead many to conclude it's "worth the effort."

Annapolis

	FOOD	DECOR	SERVICE	COST

Austin Grill *Tex-Mex* **15** | **15** | **17** | **$23**

Annapolis | Annapolis Mall | 2002 Annapolis Mall Rd. (Bestgate Rd.) |
410-571-6688 | www.austingrill.com
See review in the Washington, DC, Directory.

Café Normandie *French* **23** | **20** | **20** | **$39**

Annapolis | 185 Main St. (Conduit St.) | 410-263-3382 |
www.cafenormandie.com
Annapolis Francophiles "can count on" this "quaint" fixture for
"magnifique" versions of French bistro "faves" and "courteous" service in a "country inn" setting on Main Street that feels especially
"cozy on a winter night" near the "lovely fireplace"; it "caters to the
locals", but the central location means it's "crowded" "with tourists"
at times – *c'est la vie.*

Cantler's Riverside Inn *Crab House* **23** | **14** | **18** | **$36**

Annapolis | 458 Forest Beach Rd. (Browns Woods Rd.) | 410-757-1311 |
www.cantlers.com
"Feast" on Maryland blue crab at this "cheerful" Annapolis seafood
"shack", which harbors a sprawling "waterfront" deck where multi-
tudes seated at "picnic tables" "covered with sturdy kraft paper"
crack "freshly steamed" crustaceans ("don't bother with anything
else") and guzzle "cold beer"; though "basic" and "a little hard to
find", it "gets crazy crowded" in the summer so "expect to wait."

Carpaccio *Italian* **21** | **23** | **21** | **$41**

Annapolis | Park Pl. | 1 Park Pl. (West St.) | 410-268-6569 |
www.carpacciotuscankitchen.com
"A welcome change" in Annapolis, this "destination" in a shopping/
hotel complex boasts a "broad offering" of "enjoyable" Tuscan fare
(brick-oven pizza, "carpaccio done several ways") paired with a "decent wine list" and "professional service" in a roomy, modern space
with sidewalk seating and a frequently "filled" bar; locals reckon it's
"well above average" for these parts; P.S. the adjacent Carpaccio
2Go dispenses takeout.

Carrol's Creek Cafe *Seafood* **22** | **23** | **21** | **$40**

Eastport | 410 Severn Ave. (4th St.) | 410-263-8102 |
www.carrolscreek.com
The "picturesque waterfront setting" is the lure at this Eastport seafooder, an "inviting" mainstay with a "delightful" deck "overlooking
Spa Creek" and the Annapolis City Dock's "million or so boats"; it
follows through with "delicious" food and a "wonderful" Sunday
brunch, and while penny-pinchers protest it's "expensive for what
you get", it's a "popular" "place to impress" "out-of-town guests."

Cheesecake Factory *American* **19** | **18** | **18** | **$28**

Annapolis | Annapolis Mall | 1872 Annapolis Mall Rd. (Jennifer Rd.) |
410-224-0565 | www.thecheesecakefactory.com
See review in the Washington, DC, Directory.

Chick & Ruth's Delly ◑ *Diner*

19 | 14 | 18 | $15

Annapolis | 165 Main St. (Conduit St.) | 410-269-6737 |
www.chickandruths.com

"Any resemblance to a deli is purely coincidental" at this "bustling" Annapolis "institution", which delivers major "bang for your buck" with "straightforward diner" fare like "thick shakes" and "colossal" sandwiches "named after local politicos"; "it's sure not fancy", but the "cramped" "retro" setting "has character" "you gotta love"; P.S. go in the morning to recite the "Pledge of Allegiance."

Fadó Irish Pub ◑ *Pub Food*

17 | 21 | 17 | $24

Annapolis | Park Pl. | 1 Park Pl. (West St.) | 410-626-0069 |
www.fadoirishpub.com

See review in the Washington, DC, Directory.

☑ Five Guys *Burgers*

22 | 9 | 16 | $11

Annapolis | Annapolis Mall | 1046 Annapolis Mall Rd. (West St.) |
410-573-0581

Annapolis | Village Greens | 509 S. Cherry Grove Ave. (Forest Dr.) |
410-216-7971

NEW Edgewater | 3059 Solomon's Island Rd. (Mayo Rd.) |
410-956-8212

www.fiveguys.com

See review in the Washington, DC, Directory.

Galway Bay *Pub Food*

25 | 23 | 23 | $27

Annapolis | 63 Maryland Ave. (State Circle) | 410-263-8333 |
www.galwaybaymd.com

At this "perfect little pub" set in a "cozy" brick-walled space, "locals" grab a "pint with grown-ups" and dig into "good, hearty" Irish and American food that's "as solid as it can get" – at least in "olde Annapolis"; the "authentic" feel extends down to the "tried-and-true" staff, and even if parking can be "a nightmare", trivia nights, a "Sunday jazz brunch" and "sublime beer" hold critics at bay.

Harry Browne's *American*

24 | 22 | 23 | $46

Annapolis | 66 State Circle (bet. East St. & Maryland Ave.) |
410-263-4332 | www.harrybrownes.com

"Politicians and lobbyists" "meet and mingle" at this Annapolis New American "in the shadow" of the State House, an "old staple" that remains a "sound" purveyor of "well-prepared food" in "charming", clubby surroundings where "the elite" convene to be "pampered"; "though somewhat pricey", it regularly "gets crowded" "when the legislature is in session", so make reservations.

Hell Point Seafood Ⓜ *Seafood*

20 | 19 | 17 | $40

Annapolis | 12 Dock St. (Craig St.) | 410-990-9888 |
www.hp-seafood.com

Anchored at the Annapolis City Dock, this offering from chef-owner Bob Kinkead (of DC's Kinkead's) brings an affordable taste of his seafaring "magic" to a "bright" space with windows overlooking Ego Alley; early critics point to a "rote menu" and service that's "a little spotty", but the pedigree "has real potential."

	FOOD	DECOR	SERVICE	COST

◪ Jalapeños *Mexican/Spanish* 27 | 23 | 25 | $33

Annapolis | Forest Plaza | 85 Forest Dr. (Forest Dr.) | 410-266-7580 | www.jalapenosonline.com

Behind a "dull facade" in an "innocent-looking shopping center" lies one of Annapolis' "best medium-priced restaurants", a "locals' favorite" purveying a "delicious array of Mexican and Spanish dishes" (including "delectable tapas"); it's the "complete package", with "romantic" decor and "wonderful owners" overseeing servers who make you feel like a "guest in their home", albeit one with "out-of-this-world sangria" and a "great tequila selection."

Joss Cafe & Sushi Bar *Japanese* 25 | 16 | 21 | $34

Annapolis | 195 Main St. (Church Circle) | 410-263-4688 | www.josssushi.com

While there's almost "always a line" to get into this Annapolis "favorite" delivering "fabulous sushi, sashimi and other Japanese delights", even impatient types "won't be disappointed" when the food arrives via "efficient" servers; it's "crowded, crazy" and decidedly "not fancy" (the newer Baltimore branch has the edge for decor), but enthusiasts "return frequently" – and "it's clear why once you've eaten" here.

Lebanese Taverna *Lebanese* 21 | 18 | 18 | $30

Annapolis | Annapolis Harbour Ctr. | 2478 Solomons Island Rd. (Aris T. Allen Blvd.) | 410-897-1111 | www.lebanesetaverna.com
See review in the Washington, DC, Directory.

Lemongrass *Thai* 23 | 18 | 21 | $25

Annapolis | 167 West St. (Colonial Ave.) | 410-280-0086
Annapolis | Gateway Village Shopping Ctr. | 2625A Housely Rd. (bet. General Hwy. & Rte. 450) | 410-224-8424
Crofton | 2225A Defense Hwy. (Patuxent River Rd.) | 410-721-1111
www.kapowgroup.com

With a "'heat map' ranging from almost dull to incendiary", this "tasty" trio attracts spice lovers looking for "reasonably priced", "well-served" Thai standards "with a twist"; "deafening noise levels" distract diners at the "tiny" West Street original (though surveyors give it the cooking edge), so regulars suggest checking out the "pleasant" Housely Road strip-maller or the "more spacious" Crofton venue.

◪ Les Folies Brasserie *French* 26 | 23 | 24 | $53

Annapolis | 2552 Riva Rd. (Aris T. Allen Blvd.) | 410-573-0970 | www.lesfoliesbrasserie.com

Amis aver this "lovely" "destination restaurant" is "probably underappreciated" because it's "off the beaten track", but those who venture into the "Annapolis 'burbs" say its "outstanding" French fare is always "worth the drive"; it's predictably pricey, but a "gracious staff" that makes everyone "feel like a regular" and a "comfortable" atmosphere (mirrors, murals, lots of flowers) only add to the "true dining experience"; P.S. valet parking on weekends is essential.

Level ◗ *American*
− | − | − | M

Annapolis | 69 West St. (Calvert St.) | 410-268-0003 |
www.levelsmallplateslounge.com

"Locally produced" flora and fauna go into the "delicious", "innovative" New American small plates at this midpriced Annapolis lounge, outfitted with exposed brick and an open kitchen; "mouthwatering libations" fuel the "fun bar" and there's a DJ on Saturday, further reason for level-headed loyalists to declare it "happening."

☑ Lewnes' Steakhouse *Steak*
25 | 20 | 25 | $56

Eastport | 401 Fourth St. (Severn Ave.) | 410-263-1617 |
www.lewnessteakhouse.com

"Forget the cholesterol count and die happy" at this iconic Eastport meatery that even "works" for carnivores who "like fussy steakhouses (and this one isn't)"; expect "lots and lots" of "wonderful" beef, an "amazing wine list" and "old-school" service in a "great old building", and though it all comes with "expensive" tabs, many agree it "should be tried at least once in your life."

Luna Blu *Italian*
20 | 19 | 23 | $36

Annapolis | 36 West St. (Calvert St.) | 410-267-9950 |
www.lunabluofannapolis.com

For "value and convenience" in Annapolis, everyone from State House pols and office workers to "tourists" flock to this "little" spot with "consistently good" Southern Italian fare and a "hard-working staff"; "huge portions", half-price bottles of wine on Mondays and Wednesdays and a $35 prix fixe seal the deal for bargain-hunters.

Main Ingredient Café *American*
24 | 13 | 21 | $28

Annapolis | 914 Bay Ridge Rd. (Georgetown Rd.) | 410-626-0388 |
www.themainingredient.com

"They really know what they're doing" at this bakery/cafe dishing up a "large" New American menu of "excellent" "b'fast, lunch and dinner" goodies; no wonder enthusiasts exhort the squeamish to "get over the strip-mall" locale in the "wilds of Annapolis" (read: no tourists) and enjoy the "pleasant service" and "great food for the price point"; P.S. "take home a dessert" from its "famous cake case."

McCormick & Schmick's *Seafood*
20 | 20 | 20 | $43

Annapolis | Annapolis Mall | 2100 Annapolis Mall Rd. (West St.) |
410-266-8866 | www.mccormickandschmicks.com

See review in the Washington, DC, Directory.

NEW Nando's Peri-Peri *Chicken*
20 | 16 | 14 | $16

Annapolis | Annapolis Mall | 2002 Annapolis Mall Rd. (Bestgate Rd.) |
410-224-0585 | www.nandosperiperi.com

See review in the Washington, DC, Directory.

O'Learys Seafood *Seafood*
26 | 23 | 25 | $53

Eastport | 310 Third St. (Severn Ave.) | 410-263-0884 |
www.olearysseafood.com

The staff "really cares about getting it right" at this "elegant" Eastport seafooder, from the "exquisite" food and service to the "cozy, intimate" dining room that's "perfect" for "couples, small groups" and "special occasions" of any stripe; it may be a bit pricey, but that doesn't stop "romantic" types and fin fans from vowing to "definitely go back"; P.S. Russell Brown (ex Northwoods) is now cooking.

Osteria 177 *Italian* 25 | 23 | 23 | $48

Annapolis | 177 Main St. (Conduit St.) | 410-267-7700 | www.osteria177.com

Cognoscenti concur it's a "big mistake" if you walk by this "wonderful little place" on Annapolis' main drag, as you'll miss out on its "ever-changing menu" of "first-rate" Northern Italian specialties with a "unique spin"; a "chic, modern" interior where "you can actually talk to your guests" and an "attentive" staff round out the "sophisticated" experience.

Pad Thai *Thai* 20 | 17 | 19 | $29

Annapolis | 38 West St. (Calvert St.) | 410-280-6636

This "solid" Siamese lodged in a narrow storefront near Annapolis' State Circle proffers a "diverse" selection of "flavorful" dishes, including a "delicious" take on the eponymous noodle dish; the unimpressed say it's "nothing to write home about", but showgoers needing a "Thai fix" before Rams Head ("it's right across the street") declare it's the "place to go."

Paul's Homewood Café *American/Greek* 21 | 21 | 24 | $31

Annapolis | 919 West St. (Taylor Ave.) | 410-267-7891 | www.paulscafe-annapolis.com

"Homestyle Greek cooking" and "excellent" New American cuisine share top billing at this "family-run" Annapolis cafe, a "neighborhood gem" that's "off the beaten path" – perfect for a "quiet date"; add in an "everybody-knows-your-name" vibe, and it's "not hard to see why it's lasted" more than 60 years; P.S. "do the impossible and save room for dessert."

P.F. Chang's China Bistro *Chinese* 20 | 20 | 19 | $30

Annapolis | Annapolis Town Ctr. | 307 Sail Pl. (Forest Dr.) | 410-573-2990 | www.pfchangs.com

See review in the Washington, DC, Directory.

Piccola Roma *Italian* ∇ 19 | 16 | 21 | $38

Annapolis | 200 Main St. (Church Circle) | 410-268-7898 | www.piccolaroma.com

A longtime "favorite on Main Street in Annapolis", this "excellent date location" recently reopened "under new ownership" but "kept the same chefs"; the early word is that crowds are rediscovering the "classic Italian dining room", as much for its lower prices as its "delicious" fare and "excellent wine list."

Red Hot & Blue *BBQ* 20 | 14 | 18 | $22

Annapolis | 200 Old Mill Bottom Rd. S. (Rte. 50, exit 28) | 410-626-7427 | www.redhotandblue.com

See review in the Washington, DC, Directory.

	FOOD	DECOR	SERVICE	COST

Rockfish, The *American*

| 18 | 19 | 21 | $38 |

Eastport | 400 Sixth St. (Severn Ave.) | 410-267-1800 |
www.rockfishmd.com

Wayfarers who venture "over the bridge from Downtown Annapolis" discover this "fairly upscale" Eastporter proffering a "varied menu" of "dependable" seafood-slanted New American fare; service that isn't "rushed" and "plenty of parking" are other pluses, but note that the "atmosphere can rock in the evening" thanks to "good happy hours" and live music Tuesday–Saturday.

Ruth's Chris Steak House *Steak*

| 25 | 23 | 25 | $62 |

Eastport | 301 Severn Ave. (3rd St.) | 410-990-0033 | www.ruthschris.com
See review in the Washington, DC, Directory.

☑ Severn Inn *American*

| 20 | 24 | 19 | $42 |

Annapolis | 1993 Baltimore Annapolis Blvd. (Redwood Ave.) |
410-349-4000 | www.severninn.com

"If you want to relax" and "enjoy a cocktail", the "panoramic view of the Naval Academy" from this "easy-access" New American on Annapolis' Severn River "can't be beat"; that vista comes with "adequate" service and fare that divides surveyors ("fresh and tasty" vs. "mediocre and overpriced"), but at least it's in a "beautiful setting"; P.S. closed on Monday from January–March.

Tsunami ● *Asian*

| 20 | 19 | 20 | $32 |

Annapolis | 51 West St. (bet. Calvert St. & Church Circle) |
410-990-9868 | www.tsunamiannapolis.com

Scene-seekers "never know what crowd will be" packing the "rocking" bar at this "hip" Annapolis see-and-be-seenery, but rest assured they'll be having a "fun" time; the chow gets "mixed" grades, with some praising "yummy" sushi and Asian fusion fare, others suggesting the kitchen needs to "figure out what used to work so well."

Wild Orchid Café *American*

| 24 | 21 | 23 | $38 |

Annapolis | 200 Westgate Circle (Taylor Ave.) | 410-268-8009 |
www.thewildorchidcafe.com

Fans of this "absolutely charming restaurant" in Annapolis are hoping for the best now that it's moved (post-Survey) from a "converted older home" into a larger, less "romantic" Annapolis office-building space; happily, much of the "yummy" New American cuisine that "changes seasonally" and a staff that "never disappoints" are reportedly still in place.

Yellowfin *American*

| 20 | 22 | 20 | $38 |

Edgewater | 2840 Solomons Island Rd. (Old S. River Rd.) | 410-573-1371 |
www.yellowfinrestaurant.com

"You can't beat the views" ("especially at sunset") from the "huge deck" of this "happening" Edgewater New American overlooking the South River, though "tasty" seafood and one of the "best extended happy hours" on Friday certainly try; still, a "meat-market atmosphere in the bar" and "unpleasant noise levels" often "overshadow the kitchen's efforts", and even that's deemed "so-so" by a few critics.

Eastern Shore

	FOOD	DECOR	SERVICE	COST

Ava's *Pizza* ▽ 26 | 20 | 23 | $31

St. Michaels | 409 S. Talbot St. (bet. Grace & Thompson Sts.) |
410-745-3081 | www.avaspizzeria.com

Owner Chris Agharabi and chef Chris Fazio "have figured out how to
keep locals and tourists happy year-round" at this "casual", affordable spot in St. Michaels: provide them with "tasty" "gourmet
pizza", "top-notch" wines and a "dedicated staff that works hard to
please"; the "friendly" vibe even extends to Fido, who's welcome on
the "outdoor patio"; P.S. "no reservations, so get there early."

NEW Banning's Tavern *American* - | - | - | M

Easton | Avalon Theatre | 42 E. Dover St. (Harrison St.) | 410-822-1733 |
www.banningstavern.com

Chef Stephen Mangasarian, who pioneered Easton as a dining destination with his erstwhile Restaurant Columbia, fills a local need for a
grown-up collegial corner tavern; the bright windows and burnished
air are nicer than at a typical pub – and the midpriced American fare
works for drop-by quick hits before shows at the adjacent Avalon
Theater or languorous dinners over wine.

Bartlett Pear Inn *American* ▽ 29 | 28 | 27 | $50

Easton | Bartlett Pear Inn | 28 S. Harrison St. (bet. E. Dover &
South Sts.) | 410-770-3300 | www.bartlettpearinn.com

Impressed foodies "love what they've done" to this lovely Easton
venue ensconced in a small boutique inn, a "worth-the-drive" destination with "luscious", locally sourced New American fare that's as
"beautiful" as the setting; a staff that's "helpful without being
stuffy" tends to the "well-behaved crowd of adults", who duck into
the "adorable" bar for a pre-dinner round of drinks and free "popcorn with truffle butter"; P.S. closed Tuesdays.

BBQ Joint *BBQ* - | - | - | I

Easton | 216 E. Dover St. (Aurora St.) | 410-690-3641 | 🛇
www.andrewevansbbqjoint.com

On the east edge of Easton, owner-chef Andrew Evans packs 'em in
for "down and dirty BBQ" (read: sawdust on the floor and plenty of
paper towels) that includes slow-smoked pulled-pork sandwiches,
brisket and ribs, plus a sea of sides like cornbread and greens and
housemade sauces; the tiny space is often jam-packed with happy
eaters, but a few sidewalk tables and carryout provide relief.

Bella Luna *Italian* ▽ 22 | - | 19 | $39

St. Michaels | 1216 S. Talbot St. (Pea Neck Rd.) | 410-745-6100 |
www.bellalunastmichaels.com

A post-Survey move from a "charming" country store to a larger,
more commercial space in St. Michaels gives "engaging" chef-
owner Barbara Helish more breathing space for her midpriced
"homemade" Italian country fare "bursting with flavors"; warm
treatment and soft fabrics in a big windowed dining room (plus

brews and eats at a big bar and patio) may help patrons forget the new external surroundings: the adjacent supermarket and drive-thru espresso hut out front.

NEW Big Pickle FoodBar *American/Deli*   − | − | − | M

St. Michaels | 209 S. Talbot St. (Carpenter St.) | 410-745-8011 | www.bigpicklefoodbar.com

Chef Chad Scott (ex Mason's in Easton) is hoping to jolt staid St. Michaels with this all-purpose den for movers and shakers set to open in June 2011; by day, an affordable family-friendly deli will dispense hearty comfort fare and Illy coffee, but at night, it will morph into a midpriced New American bistro and lounge complete with high-tech sound and video that will allow diners to watch their Wagyu steak's progress on TV.

Bistro Poplar *French*   ∇ 24 | 21 | 20 | $46

Cambridge | 535 Poplar St. (High St.) | 410-228-4884 | www.bistropoplar.com

Set in a classic old mercantile building, this "breath of fresh air" in Cambridge gets "kudos" for everything from its "authentic French food in a crab cake town" to the "bright yet intimate decor"; a few nitpickers knock "spotty service", but most are "thrilled" it's here, even if it is "totally unexpected"; P.S. closed Tuesday–Wednesday.

Bistro St. Michaels *American*   23 | 21 | 22 | $54

St. Michaels | 403 S. Talbot St. (bet. Grace & Thompson Sts.) | 410-745-9111 | www.bistrostmichaels.com

Though "someone famous" may be sitting nearby, the spotlight at this "romantic" St. Michaels stalwart is always on its "wonderful" if "pricey" New American menu, which "changes regularly" and uses only the "freshest ingredients"; service gets mixed marks (some say "engaging", while others cite "a bit of an attitude"), but reservations are still a "must on weekends and holidays"; P.S. closed Tuesday–Wednesday.

NEW Brasserie Brightwell ⓜ *American/French*   − | − | − | E

Easton | 206 N. Harrison St. (Washington St.) | 410-819-3838 | www.brasseriebrightwell.com

Just outside Downtown Easton, a high-ceilinged garage has been converted to a bright, airy brasserie by the operators of 208 Talbot in St. Michaels; beer and wine is paired with traditional French offerings (e.g. escargots, duck confit, frogs' legs) and American items like grilled steaks and fish, plus there's shellfish from the raw bar; P.S. an outdoor patio and bar is an additional perk.

Crab Claw ⏩ *Crab House*   18 | 18 | 17 | $35

St. Michaels | 304 Burns St. (Talbot St.) | 410-745-2900 | www.thecrabclaw.com

"Right on the water" in St. Michaels, this "casual" seasonal seafooder is "an old-time favorite" for steamed "blue crab in particular", with seating both indoors ("don't expect fancy") and "on the pier" with a view of "the harbor action"; although "touristy", it remains "very popular" despite crabbing over "impersonal" service and "cash-only" tabs that can run "pretty high"; P.S. open seasonally, March–November.

Harris Crab House *Crab House*

| 20 | 15 | 18 | $29 |

Grasonville | 433 Kent Narrows Way N. (Rte. 50, exit 42) | 410-827-9500 | www.harriscrabhouse.com

"Roll up your sleeves and dig in" at this "very casual" Grasonville seafood house, where "everyone goes wild for" the "fabulous steamed" crabs, best enjoyed on the "sun-baked" deck "overlooking the bay"; with brown paper–covered tables and views of "watermen unloading" the day's catch, it's "the real thing" when you're ready "to escape the city and relax."

Kentmorr *Crab House*

∇ | 24 | 19 | 23 | $28 |

Stevensville | 910 Kentmorr Rd. (Lane Ave.) | 410-643-2263 | www.kentmorr.com

"Cheap eats, steamed crabs" and "windows open to bay breezes" provide Stevensville seafood seekers with a taste of the "old days" at this waterfront refuge "far from the madding crowd (yet only 10 minutes from Route 50)"; "sit outside" and be entertained "as people try to dock their boats" or in the "calming" dining room, all overseen by a "personal, attentive" staff.

Mason's ⊠ *American*

∇ | 24 | 24 | 26 | $41 |

Easton | 22 S. Harrison St. (South Ln.) | 410-822-3204 | www.masonsgourmet.com

"Whether you're there for lunch or dinner", this "charming" "favorite" in the "quaint town" of Easton is "always a pleasure"; housed in a "historic building" with porch and garden seating, it offers a "wonderful array" of New American fare plus "great pastries and baked goods", all served by an "impeccable" staff; P.S. wallet-watchers can "lower their tabs by asking for the bar menu."

Mitchum's Steakhouse Ⓜ *Steak*

| - | - | - | E |

Trappe | 4021 Main St./Rte. 565 (Maple Ave.) | 410-476-3902 | www.mitchumssteakhouse.com

Beach travelers can't see it, but hiding in tiny Trappe just off Route 50 is this pricey steakhouse surrounded by Eastern Shore farmland; get your sandwich fix from the "cute little" carry-out and lunch outbuildings, or stick around for dinner in the airy dining room brimming with movie memorabilia (including "clips on a big screen") that'll remind you actor Robert Mitchum once lived nearby, so down a Delmonico in honor of the tender tough guy.

Narrows, The *Seafood*

| 23 | 18 | 22 | $43 |

Grasonville | 3023 Kent Narrows Way S. (Rte. 50, exit 41/42) | 410-827-8113 | www.thenarrowsrestaurant.com

There may not be a "better crab cake" around exhort enthusiasts who gladly get in the car and "take the drive" over the Bay Bridge to this "scenic" seafooder on Kent Narrows; "terrific specials" and "well-prepared" standards like "killer cream of crab soup" go hand-in-claw with the "good service" and "wonderful views" – just "go at sunset."

Out of the Fire ⊠Ⓜ *American/Eclectic* | 25 | 19 | 25 | $41 |

Easton | 22 Goldsborough St. (Washington St.) | 410-770-4777 | www.outofthefire.com

Fare that "changes with the season" and an "allegiance to local sustainable farms" keep things "interesting" at this "charming" Easton American-Eclectic with an open kitchen, an "alert" staff and "excellent" stone-hearth pizza; it's "casual" and "cozy", but regulars advise "sitting in the back by the bar" instead of the front space, where "you'll see everyone you don't want to talk to."

Pope's Tavern *American* | - | - | - | M |

Oxford | Oxford Inn | 504 S. Morris St. (Oxford Rd.) | 410-226-5220 | www.oxfordinn.net

You'll have to venture to out-of-the-way Oxford to sample the crab cakes (only served in season) and other moderately priced New American cuisine featured at this "warm", plush place packed with character owing to its setting, a historic Victorian-era inn; try to snag porch seating in warmer weather to admire the water view, or book one of its seven rooms and completely chill out; P.S. closed Tuesday–Wednesday.

Robert Morris Inn *American/Seafood* | - | - | - | E |

Oxford | Robert Morris Inn | 314 N. Morris St. (E. Strand) | 410-226-5111 | www.robertmorrisinn.com

This grand 1710 merchant home–turned-inn near the Oxford-Bellevue ferry is home to pricey American fare from owner-chef Mark Salter (ex Sherwood's Landing); the kitchen's focus is on Chesapeake seafood and Eastern Shore farm output, including fish dishes and crab cakes in warm weather, game by the fire in the atmospheric tavern in cooler times and serious dinners in the more formal dining room; P.S. there's also an outdoor patio.

Rustico *Italian* | ▽ 22 | 19 | 23 | $37 |

Stevensville | 401 Love Point Rd. (Rte. 8) | 410-643-9444 | www.rusticoonline.com

"Huge portions" of "delicious" Southern Italian eats, a "warm and inviting" ambiance and staffers who "work hard at making dining experiences pleasant" add up to a "winning combination" at this "great gem in an old town" (i.e. Stevensville); just count on it being "busy" since those in the know consider it a "blessing to locals" on the Eastern Shore.

☑ Scossa *Italian* | 27 | 27 | 25 | $47 |

Easton | 8 N. Washington St. (Dover St.) | 410-822-2202 | www.scossarestaurant.com

An "unexpected find in a small town", this "elegant" Easton eatery entrances "out-of-town guests" with its "sleek, sophisticated" decor, "big-city" service and "extensive menu" of "outstanding" Northern Italian fare (including "delicious homemade pasta") complemented by a "huge" wine list; naturally, it's "expensive", but insiders insist it's "worth the drive across the Bay Bridge"; P.S. sidewalk dining is "available weather permitting."

208 Talbot Ⓜ *American*

25 | 22 | 24 | $55

St. Michaels | 208 N. Talbot St. (North St.) | 410-745-3838 | www.208talbot.com

"A destination in itself", this "intimate", "relaxed" St. Michaels New American in a "quaint" old house proffers "deceptively creative" fare (a "lot of thought is going into the food") delivered by a "knowledge-able", "courteous" staff; if "expensive" prices leave some grumbling, a new burger menu in the "charming bar" is more "budget-friendly" – plus "it's the best seat in the house"; P.S. also closed Tuesdays.

BALTIMORE, ANNAPOLIS AND THE EASTERN SHORE INDEXES

Cuisines

Includes names, locations and Food ratings.

AFGHAN

Z Helmand | **Mt. Vernon** 26

AMERICAN

Acacia Bistro | **Frederick** 20
NEW Alchemy | **Hampden** -
Annabel Lee | **Canton** 23
Z Antrim 1844 | **Taneytown** 25
b | **D'town N** 25
B&O | **D'town** 22
NEW Banning's | **E Shore** -
Bartlett Pear | **E Shore** 29
Baugher's | **Westminster** 18
NEW Big Pickle FoodBar | **E Shore** -
Birches | **Canton** 24
Bistro Blanc | **Glenelg** -
NEW Bistro Rx | **Hi'town** -
Bistro St. Michaels | **E Shore** 23
Blue Hill Tav. | **Canton** 23
Blue Moon | **Fells Pt** 24
BlueStone | **Timonium** 22
NEW Brass. Brightwell | **E Shore** -
NEW Breakfast Shoppe | **Severna Pk** -
Brewer's Art | **Mt. Vernon** 23
Cafe Hon | **Hampden** 15
Cafe Nola | **Frederick** 21
Chameleon | **NE Balt** 27
Z Charleston | **Harbor E** 28
Cheesecake | **multi.** 19
Christopher Daniel | **Timonium** 23
City Cafe | **Mt. Vernon** 21
Clementine | **NE Balt** 23
Clyde's | **Columbia** 19
Corks | **S Balt** 21
NEW CR Lounge | **Mt. Vernon** -
Crush | **N Balt** 22
Dogwood | **Hampden** 25
Dutch's Daughter | **Frederick** 21
Eggspectations | **Ellicott City** 19
Elkridge Furnace | **Elkridge** 24
Falls | **Mt. Wash** -
Firestone's | **Frederick** 21
Friendly Farm | **Upperco** 22
Galway Bay | **Annap** 25
Garry's Grill | **Severna Pk** 20
Greystone Grill | **Ellicott City** 19
Hard Times | **Frederick** 19
Harry Browne | **Annap** 24
Harryman Hse. | **Reist'town** 22
Henninger's | **Fells Pt** 24

Iron Bridge | **Columbia** 23
Islander Inn | **Dundalk** -
Jennings | **Catonsville** 22
John Steven | **Fells Pt** 18
Kentmorr | **E Shore** 24
Kings Contrivance | **Columbia** 23
Laurrapin | **Havre de Grace** -
Level | **Annap** -
Z Linwoods | **Owings Mills** 27
Louisiana | **Fells Pt** 22
Main Ingredient | **Annap** 24
Mamie's | **Aberdeen** -
M&S Grill | **Inner Harbor** 19
Mason's | **E Shore** 24
McCabe's | **Hampden** -
NEW Meet 27 | **Charles Vill** -
Metropolitan | **S Balt** 18
Mick's | **Frederick** -
Z Milton Inn | **Sparks** 26
Miss Shirley's | **multi.** 24
Monocacy Cross. | **Frederick** 24
Mr. Rain's Fun Hse. | **Fed Hill** -
One-Eyed Mike | **Fells Pt** -
Oregon Grille | **Hunt Valley** 25
Out of the Fire | **E Shore** 25
Pairings Bistro | **Bel Air** -
Pappas | **multi.** 26
Patrick's | **Cockeysville** 22
Paul's Homewood | **Annap** 21
Peerce's | **Phoenix** -
Peppermill | **Lutherville** 18
Z Peter's Inn | **Fells Pt** 27
Pierpoint | **Fells Pt** 24
Pope's Tav. | **E Shore** -
Porter's | **Fed Hill** -
Regi's | **S Balt** 22
Rockfish | **Annap** 18
Z Salt | **E Balt** 27
Sascha's 527 | **Mt. Vernon** 22
Z Severn Inn | **Annap** 20
Soup'r Natural | **Parkton** -
Stanford Grill | **Columbia** -
Tark's Grill | **Brook'ville** 19
Z Tasting Rm. | **Frederick** 27
Teavolve | **Harbor E** -
13.5% Wine Bar | **Hampden** 19
Tidewater | **Havre de Grace** 22
208 Talbot | **E Shore** 25
Vino Rosina | **Harbor E** -
Z Volt | **Frederick** 28
Wild Orchid | **Annap** 24

Wine Mkt. | **Locust Pt**	24
🔁 Woodberry Kit. | **Hampden**	26
Yellow Dog Tav. | **Canton**	20
Yellowfin | **Annap**	20

ASIAN

Jesse Wong's Asean | **Columbia**	23
Jesse Wong's Kit. | **Hunt Valley**	19
Sam's Kid | **Fells Pt**	24
Tsunami | **Annap**	20
Umi Sake | **Cockeysville**	25

BAKERIES

Atwater's | **multi.**	25
Bon Fresco | **Columbia**	-
Goldberg's | **Pikesville**	22
Main Ingredient | **Annap**	24
Stone Mill | **Brook'ville**	22

BARBECUE

Andy Nelson's | **Cockeysville**	25
BBQ Joint | **E Shore**	-
Big Bad Wolf | **NE Balt**	25
Red Hot/Blue | **Annap**	20

BELGIAN

NEW Corner BYOB | **Hampden**	-

BRAZILIAN

Fogo De Chão | **Inner Harbor**	24

BURGERS

BGR | **Columbia**	21
Clyde's | **Columbia**	19
🔁 Five Guys | **multi.**	22
Hamilton Tav. | **NE Balt**	25
Jennings | **Catonsville**	22
🔁 Linwoods | **Owings Mills**	27
McCabe's | **Hampden**	-

CAJUN

Ethel/Ramone | **Mt. Wash**	21

CHESAPEAKE

Gertrude's | **Charles Vill**	23
Narrows | **E Shore**	23
Pierpoint | **Fells Pt**	24
Robert Morris | **E Shore**	-

CHICKEN

Chicken Rico | **Hi'town**	26
Nando's | **Annap**	20

CHINESE

(* dim sum specialist)

Asian Court* | **Ellicott City**	22
Cafe Zen | **N Balt**	20
David Chu's | **Pikesville**	22
Grace Gdn. | **Odenton**	28

Hunan Manor | **Columbia**	21
Hunan Taste | **Catonsville**	-
P.F. Chang's | **multi.**	20
Szechuan Hse. | **Lutherville**	23

COFFEEHOUSES

City Cafe | **Mt. Vernon**	21
Metropolitan | **S Balt**	18
One World Cafe | **Homewood**	19

COFFEE SHOPS/ DINERS

Cafe Hon | **Hampden**	15
Chick/Ruth's | **Annap**	19
Jimmy's | **Fells Pt**	18

CONTINENTAL

Cafe Bretton | **Severna Pk**	24
NEW Corner BYOB | **Hampden**	-
Josef's | **Fallston**	28
Tio Pepe | **Mt. Vernon**	24

CRAB HOUSES

Cantler's Riverside | **Annap**	23
Costas Inn | **Dundalk**	23
Crab Claw | **E Shore**	18
Faidley's | **D'town W**	27
Gunning's Seafood | **Hanover**	-
Harris Crab | **E Shore**	20
Islander Inn | **Dundalk**	-
Kentmorr | **E Shore**	24
Mr. Bill's | **Essex**	26
Obrycki's | **E Balt**	23
Schultz's Crab | **Essex**	-

CREOLE

Ethel/Ramone | **Mt. Wash**	21
Louisiana | **Fells Pt**	22

CUBAN

NEW Havana Rd. | **Towson**	-

DELIS

Attman's Deli | **E Balt**	25
NEW Big Pickle FoodBar | **E Shore**	-
Suburban Hse. | **Pikesville**	-

DESSERT

Broom's Bloom | **Bel Air**	27
Cheesecake | **multi.**	19
Paul's Homewood | **Annap**	21
Stone Mill | **Brook'ville**	22

EASTERN EUROPEAN

Ze Mean Bean | **Fells Pt**	22

ECLECTIC

Jack's Bistro | **Canton**	26
Meli | **Fells Pt**	22
Orchard | **Frederick**	19
Out of the Fire | **E Shore**	25
Regions | **Catonsville**	-
Rocket/Venus | **Hampden**	19
Sabor | **Lutherville**	24
Tapas Teatro | **D'town N**	23
Victoria Gastro | **Columbia**	21

ETHIOPIAN

Dukem | **Mt. Vernon**	24

FRENCH

☑ Antrim 1844 | **Taneytown**	25
Cafe Bretton | **Severna Pk**	24
☑ Les Folies | **Annap**	26
Marie Louise | **Mt. Vernon**	20
☑ Tersiguel's | **Ellicott City**	26

FRENCH (BISTRO)

Bistro Poplar | **E Shore**	24
NEW Brass. Brightwell | **E Shore**	-
Café de Paris | **Columbia**	21
Café Normandie | **Annap**	23
Crêpe du Jour | **Mt. Wash**	21
☑ Petit Louis | **Roland Pk**	25

GREEK

☑ Black Olive | **Fells Pt**	26
Ikaros | **Gr'town**	24
Paul's Homewood | **Annap**	21
☑ Samos | **Gr'town**	27
Zorba's B&G | **Gr'town**	21

HAWAIIAN

Roy's | **Harbor E**	25

ICE CREAM PARLORS

Broom's Bloom | **Bel Air**	27

INDIAN

Akbar | **multi.**	24
Ambassador | **Homewood**	24
Carlyle Club | **Homewood**	22
Flavors/Hse. of India | **Columbia**	24

IRISH

Fadó | **Annap**	17
Galway Bay | **Annap**	25

ITALIAN

(N=Northern; S=Southern)

Aida | **Columbia**	23
Aldo's | S | **Little Italy**	25
Amicci's | **Little Italy**	21
Ava's | **E Shore**	26
Bella Luna | **E Shore**	22
Caesar's Den | S | **Little Italy**	21
Café Gia | S | **Little Italy**	20
Café Troia | **Towson**	21
Café Tuscany | **Westminster**	22
Carpaccio | N | **Annap**	21
NEW Chazz | S | **Harbor E**	-
Chiapparelli's | **multi.**	20
Ciao Bella | **Little Italy**	22
☑ Cinghiale | **Harbor E**	24
Da Mimmo | **Little Italy**	22
Della Notte | **Little Italy**	22
☑ Di Pasquale's | **E Balt**	27
Grano | **Hampden**	25
Germano's | N | **Little Italy**	23
La Famiglia | N | **Homewood**	21
La Scala | **Little Italy**	26
La Tavola | **Little Italy**	24
Liberatore's | S | **multi.**	21
Luna Blu | S | **Annap**	20
Mamma Lucia | **multi.**	18
Osteria 177 | **Annap**	25
Piccola Roma | **Annap**	19
Portalli's | **Ellicott City**	-
Rocco's Capriccio | **Little Italy**	23
Rustico | S | **E Shore**	22
Sabatino's | **Little Italy**	20
Sammy's Tratt. | S | **Mt. Vernon**	21
☑ Scossa | N | **E Shore**	27
Sotto Sopra | N | **Mt. Vernon**	24
Tratt. Alberto | N | **Glen Burnie**	25
Vinny's Cafe | **Dundalk**	-

JAPANESE

(* sushi specialist)

Chiu's Sushi* | **Harbor E**	23
Edo Sushi* | **multi.**	24
Hinode* | **Frederick**	19
Joss Cafe/Sushi* | **multi.**	25
Matsuri* | **S Balt**	22
Minato* | **D'town N**	22
San Sushi/Thai* | **multi.**	23
Sushi Hana* | **multi.**	23
Sushi King* | **Columbia**	24
Sushi Sono* | **Columbia**	26

KOREAN

(* barbecue specialist)

Honey Pig* | **Ellicott City**	26
Shin Chon* | **Ellicott City**	-

KOSHER-STYLE

David Chu's | **Pikesville**	22
Goldberg's | **Pikesville**	22

LEBANESE

Lebanese Tav. | **multi.**   21

MEDITERRANEAN

Kali's Ct. | **Fells Pt**   24
Marie Louise | **Mt. Vernon**   20
Mezze | **Fells Pt**   25
Orchard Mkt. | **Towson**   25
🆕 Pazo | **Harbor E**   24
Tabrizi's | **S Balt**   21
Tapas Teatro | **D'town N**   23
Waterstone | **W Balt**   ⌐

MEXICAN

Blue Agave | **S Balt**   20
Cacique | **Frederick**   21
El Trovador | **Fells Pt**   23
🆕 Jalapeños | **Annap**   27
Mari Luna | **multi.**   26
Miguel's Cocina | **Locust Pt**   ⌐

MIDDLE EASTERN

Tabrizi's | **S Balt**   21

NEW MEXICAN

Golden West | **Hampden**   20

NUEVO LATINO

Talara | **Harbor E**   23

PAN-LATIN

Mari Luna | **multi.**   26

PERUVIAN

Salsa Grill | **Woodlawn**   ⌐

PIZZA

Ava's | **E Shore**   26
🆕 Chazz | **Harbor E**   ⌐
Coal Fire | **Ellicott City**   20
Iggies | **Mt. Vernon**   25
Matthew's Pizza | **Hi'town**   25
Out of the Fire | **E Shore**   25
🆕 Two Boots | **D'town N**   ⌐

PUB FOOD

Clyde's | **Columbia**   19
Fadó | **Annap**   17
Galway Bay | **Annap**   25
Hamilton Tav. | **NE Balt**   25
Jennings | **Catonsville**   22
Koco's | **NE Balt**   26
McCabe's | **Hampden**   ⌐
Mick's | **Frederick**   ⌐

SALVADORAN

El Trovador | **Fells Pt**   23

SANDWICHES

Attman's Deli | **E Balt**   25
Atwater's | **multi.**   25
Bon Fresco | **Columbia**   ⌐
Broom's Bloom | **Bel Air**   27
Chick/Ruth's | **Annap**   19
Grilled Cheese | **multi.**   ⌐
Stone Mill | **Brook'ville**   22

SEAFOOD

Bertha's | **Fells Pt**   18
🆕 Black Olive | **Fells Pt**   26
BlueStone | **Timonium**   22
Cantler's Riverside | **Annap**   23
Carrol's Creek | **Annap**   22
Catonsville Gourmet | **Catonsville**   24
Crab Claw | **E Shore**   18
Dutch's Daughter | **Frederick**   21
Faidley's | **D'town W**   27
G&M | **Linthicum**   24
Gertrude's | **Charles Vill**   23
Harris Crab | **E Shore**   20
Hell Pt. Seafood | **Annap**   20
Islander Inn | **Dundalk**   ⌐
Jerry's Seafood | **Bowie**   24
John Steven | **Fells Pt**   18
Kali's Ct. | **Fells Pt**   24
L.P. Steamers | **Locust Pt**   23
Mama's/Half Shell | **Canton**   23
M&S Grill | **Inner Harbor**   19
McCormick/Schmick | **multi.**   20
Mr. Bill's | **Essex**   26
Narrows | **E Shore**   23
Obrycki's | **E Balt**   23
Oceanaire | **Harbor E**   24
O'Learys | **Annap**   26
Pappas | **multi.**   26
Robert Morris | **E Shore**   ⌐
Rockfish | **Annap**   18
Schultz's Crab | **Essex**   ⌐
🆕 Severn Inn | **Annap**   20
Timbuktu | **Hanover**   21
Zorba's B&G | **Gr'town**   21

SMALL PLATES

(See also Spanish tapas specialist)
Aida | Italian | **Columbia**   23
Café Tuscany | Italian | **Westminster**   22
Iron Bridge | Amer. | **Columbia**   23
Level | Amer. | **Annap**   ⌐
Mezze | Med. | **Fells Pt**   25
🆕 Pazo | Med. | **Harbor E**   24
Talara | Nuevo Latino | **Harbor E**   23
Tapas Teatro | Eclectic | **D'town N**   23

SOUP

Atwater's | **multi.** 25
Stone Mill | **Brook'ville** 22

SOUTH AMERICAN

Chicken Rico | **Hi'town** 26

SOUTHERN

Langermann's | **Canton** –

SPANISH

(* tapas specialist)
Cacique | **Frederick** 21
Centro* | **S Balt** –
Isabella's* | **Frederick** 25
Ⓩ Jalapeños* | **Annap** 27
Tapas Adela* | **Fells Pt** 25
Tio Pepe | **Mt. Vernon** 24

STEAKHOUSES

Ⓩ Capital Grille | **Inner Harbor** 25
Fleming's Steak | **Harbor E** 24
Fogo De Chão | **Inner Harbor** 24
Greystone Grill | **Ellicott City** 19
Ⓩ Lewnes' Steak | **Annap** 25
M&S Grill | **Inner Harbor** 19
Mitchum's Steak | **E Shore** –
Morton's | **Inner Harbor** 25
Oregon Grille | **Hunt Valley** 25
Ⓩ Prime Rib | **D'town N** 27

Ruth's Chris | **multi.** 25
Sullivan's Steak | **Inner Harbor** 22

TEAROOMS

Teavolve | **Harbor E** –

TEX-MEX

Austin Grill | **Annap** 15

THAI

Bân Thai | **D'town** 19
Lemongrass | **Annap** 23
Little Spice | **Hanover** 25
Pad Thai | **Annap** 20
San Sushi/Thai | **Towson** 23
Ⓩ Thai Arroy | **S Balt** 27
Thai Landing | **Mt. Vernon** 27

TURKISH

Cazbar | **D'town** 22

VEGETARIAN

(* vegan)
Great Sage* | **Clarksville** 22
One World Cafe | **Homewood** 19

VIETNAMESE

An Loi | **Columbia** 24
Mekong Delta | **D'town W** 25
Pho Dat Thanh | **multi.** 25
Pho Nam | **Catonsville** 23

Locations

Includes names, cuisines and Food ratings.

Baltimore

BUSINESS DISTRICT/ CAMDEN YARDS/ CONVENTION CTR./ DOWNTOWN/ INNER HARBOR

B&O	*Amer.*	22
Bân Thai	*Thai*	19
☑ Capital Grille	*Steak*	25
Cazbar	*Turkish*	22
Cheesecake	*Amer.*	19
Edo Sushi	*Japanese*	24
☑ Five Guys	*Burgers*	22
Fogo De Chão	*Brazilian/Steak*	24
M&S Grill	*Seafood/Steak*	19
McCormick/Schmick	*Seafood*	20
Miss Shirley	*Amer.*	24
Morton's	*Steak*	25
P.F. Chang's	*Chinese*	20
Ruth's Chris	*Steak*	25
Sullivan's Steak	*Steak*	22

CANTON

Annabel Lee	*Amer.*	23
Birches	*Amer.*	24
Blue Hill Tav.	*Amer.*	23
☑ Five Guys	*Burgers*	22
Jack's Bistro	*Eclectic*	26
Langermann's	*Southern*	-
Mama's/Half Shell	*Seafood*	23
Yellow Dog Tav.	*Amer.*	20

CHARLES VILLAGE

Gertrude's	*Chesapeake*	23
NEW Meet 27	*Amer.*	-

DOWNTOWN NORTH/ CHARLES ST./ MT. VERNON

Akbar	*Indian*	24
b	*Amer.*	25
Brewer's Art	*Amer.*	23
City Cafe	*Amer.*	21
NEW CR Lounge	*Amer.*	-
Dukem	*Ethiopian*	24
☑ Helmand	*Afghan*	26
Iggies	*Pizza*	25
Joss Cafe/Sushi	*Japanese*	25
Marie Louise	*French/Med.*	20
Mari Luna	*Mex./Pan-Latin*	26
Minato	*Japanese*	22
☑ Prime Rib	*Seafood/Steak*	27
Sammy's Tratt.	*Italian*	21
Sascha's 527	*Amer.*	22
Sotto Sopra	*Italian*	24
Tapas Teatro	*Eclectic/Med.*	23
Thai Landing	*Thai*	27
Tio Pepe	*Continental/Spanish*	24
NEW Two Boots	*Pizza*	-

EAST BALTIMORE

Attman's Deli	*Deli*	25
☑ Di Pasquale's	*Italian*	27
Obrycki's	*Seafood*	23
☑ Salt	*Amer.*	27

FELLS POINT

Bertha's	*Seafood*	18
☑ Black Olive	*Greek/Seafood*	26
Blue Moon	*Amer.*	24
El Trovador	*Mex./Salvadoran*	23
Henninger's	*Amer.*	24
Jimmy's	*Diner*	18
John Steven	*Seafood*	18
Kali's Ct.	*Med./Seafood*	24
Louisiana	*Amer./Creole*	22
Meli	*Eclectic*	22
Mezze	*Med.*	25
One-Eyed Mike	*Amer.*	-
☑ Peter's Inn	*Amer.*	27
Pierpoint	*Amer.*	24
Sam's Kid	*Asian*	24
Tapas Adela	*Spanish*	25
Ze Mean Bean	*E Euro.*	22

HAMPDEN/ ROLAND PARK

NEW Alchemy	*Amer.*	-
Cafe Hon	*Amer.*	15
NEW Corner BYOB	*Continental*	-
Dogwood	*Amer.*	25
Grano	*Italian*	25
Golden West	*New Mex.*	20
McCabe's	*Pub*	-
Miss Shirley	*Amer.*	24
☑ Petit Louis	*French*	25
Rocket/Venus	*Eclectic*	19
13.5% Wine Bar	*Amer.*	19
☑ Woodberry Kit.	*Amer.*	26

HARBOR EAST/ LITTLE ITALY

Aldo's | *Italian*	25
Amicci's | *Italian*	21
Caesar's Den | *Italian*	21
Café Gia | *Italian*	20
⚡ Charleston | *Amer.*	28
NEW Chazz | *Italian/Pizza*	-
Chiapparelli's | *Italian*	20
Chiu's Sushi | *Japanese*	23
Ciao Bella | *Italian*	22
⚡ Cinghiale | *Italian*	24
Da Mimmo | *Italian*	22
Della Notte | *Italian*	22
Fleming's Steak | *Steak*	24
Germano's | *Italian*	23
La Scala | *Italian*	26
La Tavola | *Italian*	24
Lebanese Tav. | *Lebanese*	21
Oceanaire | *Seafood*	24
⚡ Pazo | *Med.*	24
Rocco's Capriccio | *Italian*	23
Roy's | *Hawaiian*	25
Sabatino's | *Italian*	20
Talara | *Nuevo Latino*	23
Teavolve | *Amer./Tea*	-
Vino Rosina | *Amer.*	-

HIGHLANDTOWN/ GREEKTOWN

NEW Bistro Rx | *Amer.*	-
Chicken Rico | *Chicken*	26
Ikaros | *Greek*	24
Matthew's Pizza | *Pizza*	25
⚡ Samos | *Greek*	27
Zorba's B&G | *Greek*	21

HOMEWOOD

Ambassador | *Indian*	24
Carlyle Club | *Indian*	22
La Famiglia | *Italian*	21
One World Cafe | *Veg.*	19

LOCUST POINT

L.P. Steamers | *Seafood*	23
Miguel's Cocina | *Mex.*	-
Wine Mkt. | *Amer.*	24

MT. WASHINGTON

Crêpe du Jour | *French*	21
Ethel/Ramone | *Cajun/Creole*	21
Falls | *Amer.*	-
Sushi Hana | *Japanese*	23

NORTH BALTIMORE/ YORK ROAD CORRIDOR

Atwater's | *Bakery*	25
Cafe Zen | *Chinese*	20
Crush | *Amer.*	22

SOUTH BALTIMORE

(Including Federal Hill)

Blue Agave | *Mex.*	20
Bluegrass | *Amer.*	-
Centro | *Spanish*	-
Corks | *Amer.*	21
Matsuri | *Japanese*	22
Metropolitan | *Amer.*	18
Mr. Rain's Fun Hse. | *Amer.*	-
Porter's | *Amer.*	-
Regi's | *Amer.*	22
Tabrizi's | *Med./Mideast.*	21
⚡ Thai Arroy | *Thai*	27

WEST BALTIMORE

Faidley's | *Seafood*	27
Mekong Delta | *Viet.*	25
Waterstone | *Med.*	-

Outer Baltimore

ABERDEEN/ HARFORD COUNTY/ HAVRE DE GRACE

(Including White Marsh)

Broom's Bloom | *Ice Cream*	27
Chiapparelli's | *Italian*	20
⚡ Five Guys | *Burgers*	22
Josef's | *Continental*	28
Laurrapin | *Amer.*	-
Liberatore's | *Italian*	21
Mamie's | *Amer.*	-
Pairings Bistro | *Amer.*	-
P.F. Chang's | *Chinese*	20
Tidewater | *Amer.*	22

BOWIE

⚡ Five Guys | *Burgers*	22
Jerry's Seafood | *Seafood*	24

BROOKLANDVILLE

Stone Mill | *Bakery*	22
Tark's Grill | *Amer.*	19

BWI/ELKRIDGE/ HANOVER/ LINTHICUM

Elkridge Furnace | *Amer.*	24
⚡ Five Guys | *Burgers*	22
G&M | *Seafood*	24

Gunning's Seafood | *Seafood* — |
Little Spice | *Thai* 25 |
Mamma Lucia | *Italian* 18 |
Timbuktu | *Seafood* 21 |

CATONSVILLE/ WOODLAWN

Atwater's | *Bakery* 25 |
Catonsville Gourmet | *Seafood* 24 |
Grilled Cheese | *Sandwiches* — |
Hunan Taste | *Chinese* — |
Jennings | *Pub* 22 |
Pho Nam | *Viet.* 23 |
Regions | *Eclectic* — |
Salsa Grill | *Pan-Latin/Peruvian* — |

CLARKSVILLE/ GLENELG

Bistro Blanc | *Amer.* — |
Great Sage | *Vegan* 22 |

COLUMBIA/ ELLICOTT CITY

Aida | *Italian* 23 |
Akbar | *Indian* 24 |
An Loi | *Viet.* 24 |
Asian Court | *Chinese* 22 |
BGR | *Burgers* 21 |
Bon Fresco | *Sandwiches* — |
Café de Paris | *French* 21 |
Cheesecake | *Amer.* 19 |
Clyde's | *Amer.* 19 |
Coal Fire | *Pizza* 20 |
Eggspectations | *Amer.* 19 |
Flavors/Hse. of India | *Indian* 24 |
Greystone Grill | *Amer.* 19 |
Honey Pig | *Korean* 26 |
Hunan Manor | *Chinese* 21 |
Iron Bridge | *Amer.* 23 |
Jesse Wong's Asean | *Asian* 23 |
Kings Contrivance | *Amer.* 23 |
P.F. Chang's | *Chinese* 20 |
Pho Dat Thanh | *Viet.* 25 |
Portalli's | *Italian* — |
Shin Chon | *Korean* — |
Stanford Grill | *Amer.* — |
Sushi King | *Japanese* 24 |
Sushi Sono | *Japanese* 26 |
Z Tersiguel's | *French* 26 |
Victoria Gastro | *Eclectic* 21 |

ESSEX/DUNDALK

Costas Inn | *Crab* 23 |
Islander Inn | *Crab* — |
Mr. Bill's | *Crab* 26 |
Schultz's Crab | *Crab* — |
Vinny's Cafe | *Italian* — |

GLEN BURNIE/ ODENTON/ SEVERNA PARK

NEW Breakfast Shoppe | *Amer.* — |
Cafe Bretton | *French* 24 |
Z Five Guys | *Burgers* 22 |
Garry's Grill | *Amer.* 20 |
Grace Gdn. | *Chinese* 28 |
Pappas | *Amer./Seafood* 26 |
Tratt. Alberto | *Italian* 25 |

HUNT VALLEY/ NORTH BALTIMORE COUNTY

Friendly Farm | *Amer.* 22 |
Jesse Wong's Kit. | *Asian* 19 |
Z Milton Inn | *Amer.* 26 |
Oregon Grille | *Seafood/Steak* 25 |
Peerce's | *Amer.* — |
Soup'r Natural | *Amer.* — |

LUTHERVILLE/ COCKEYSVILLE/ TIMONIUM

Andy Nelson's | *BBQ* 25 |
BlueStone | *Seafood* 22 |
Christopher Daniel | *Amer.* 23 |
Edo Sushi | *Japanese* 24 |
Z Five Guys | *Burgers* 22 |
Liberatore's | *Italian* 21 |
Patrick's | *Amer.* 22 |
Peppermill | *Amer.* 18 |
Sabor | *Eclectic* 24 |
San Sushi/Thai | *Japanese* 23 |
Sushi Hana | *Japanese* 23 |
Szechuan Hse. | *Chinese* 23 |
Umi Sake | *Asian* 25 |

NORTHEAST BALTIMORE/ PERRY HALL

Big Bad Wolf | *BBQ* 25 |
Chameleon | *Amer.* 27 |
Clementine | *Amer.* 23 |
Hamilton Tav. | *Pub* 25 |
Koco's | *Pub* 26 |
Liberatore's | *Italian* 21 |
Pappas | *Amer./Seafood* 26 |

OWINGS MILLS/ REISTERSTOWN/ FINKSBURG

Edo Sushi | *Japanese* 24 |
Harryman Hse. | *Amer.* 22 |
Z Linwoods | *Amer.* 27 |

PIKESVILLE

David Chu's | *Chinese/Kosher* — 22
Goldberg's | *Bagels/Kosher* — 22
Mari Luna | *Mex./Pan-Latin* — 26
Ruth's Chris | *Steak* — 25
Suburban Hse. | *Deli* — −

TOWSON

Atwater's | *Bakery* — 25
Café Troia | *Italian* — 21
Cheesecake | *Amer.* — 19
☒ Five Guys | *Burgers* — 22
🆕 Havana Rd. | *Cuban* — −
Orchard Mkt. | *Persian* — 25
P.F. Chang's | *Chinese* — 20
Pho Dat Thanh | *Viet.* — 25
San Sushi/Thai | *Japanese/Thai* — 23
Sushi Hana | *Japanese* — 23

WESTMINSTER/ ELDERSBURG/ SYKESVILLE

Baugher's | *Amer.* — 18
Café Tuscany | *Italian* — 22
☒ Five Guys | *Burgers* — 22
Grilled Cheese | *Sandwiches* — −
Liberatore's | *Italian* — 21

Frederick/ Central Maryland

Acacia Bistro | *Amer.* — 20
☒ Antrim 1844 | *Amer./French* — 25
Cacique | *Mex./Spanish* — 21
Cafe Nola | *Amer.* — 21
Dutch's Daughter | *Amer.* — 21
Firestone's | *Amer.* — 21
☒ Five Guys | *Burgers* — 22
Hard Times | *Amer.* — 19
Hinode | *Japanese* — 19
Isabella's | *Spanish* — 25
Mamma Lucia | *Italian* — 18
Mick's | *Amer.* — −
Monocacy Cross. | *Amer.* — 24
Orchard | *Eclectic* — 19
☒ Tasting Rm. | *Amer.* — 27
☒ Volt | *Amer.* — 28

Annapolis/ Anne Arundel

Austin Grill | *Tex-Mex* — 15
Café Normandie | *French* — 23
Cantler's Riverside | *Crab* — 23
Carpaccio | *Italian* — 21
Carrol's Creek | *Seafood* — 22
Cheesecake | *Amer.* — 19

Chick/Ruth's | *Diner* — 19
Fadó | *Pub* — 17
☒ Five Guys | *Burgers* — 22
Galway Bay | *Pub* — 25
Harry Browne | *Amer.* — 24
Hell Pt. Seafood | *Seafood* — 20
☒ Jalapeños | *Mex./Spanish* — 27
Joss Cafe/Sushi | *Japanese* — 25
Lebanese Tav. | *Lebanese* — 21
Lemongrass | *Thai* — 23
☒ Les Folies | *French* — 26
Level | *Amer.* — −
☒ Lewnes' Steak | *Steak* — 25
Luna Blu | *Italian* — 20
Main Ingredient | *Amer.* — 24
McCormick/Schmick | *Seafood* — 20
Nando's | *Chicken* — 20
O'Learys | *Seafood* — 26
Osteria 177 | *Italian* — 25
Pad Thai | *Thai* — 20
Paul's Homewood | *Amer./Greek* — 21
P.F. Chang's | *Chinese* — 20
Piccola Roma | *Italian* — 19
Red Hot/Blue | *BBQ* — 20
Rockfish | *Amer.* — 18
Ruth's Chris | *Steak* — 25
☒ Severn Inn | *Amer.* — 20
Tsunami | *Asian* — 20
Wild Orchid | *Amer.* — 24
Yellowfin | *Amer.* — 20

Eastern Shore

Ava's | *Pizza* — 26
🆕 Banning's | *Amer.* — −
Bartlett Pear | *Amer.* — 29
BBQ Joint | *BBQ* — −
Bella Luna | *Italian* — 22
🆕 Big Pickle FoodBar | *Amer./Deli* — −
Bistro Poplar | *French* — 24
Bistro St. Michaels | *Amer.* — 23
🆕 Brass. Brightwell | *Amer./French* — −
Crab Claw | *Crab* — 18
Harris Crab | *Crab* — 20
Kentmorr | *Crab* — 24
Mason's | *Amer.* — 24
Mitchum's Steak | *Steak* — −
Narrows | *Seafood* — 23
Out of the Fire | *Amer./Eclectic* — 25
Pope's Tav. | *Amer.* — −
Robert Morris | *Amer./Seafood* — −
Rustico | *Italian* — 22
☒ Scossa | *Italian* — 27
208 Talbot | *Amer.* — 25

Special Features

Listings cover the best in each category and include names, locations and Food ratings. Multi-location restaurants' features may vary by branch.

ADDITIONS

(Properties added since the last edition of the book)

Alchemy	**Hampden**	-
Banning's	**E Shore**	-
Big Pickle FoodBar	**E Shore**	-
Bistro Rx	**Hi'town**	-
Brass. Brightwell	**E Shore**	-
Breakfast Shoppe	**Severna Pk**	-
Chazz	**Harbor E**	-
Corner BYOB	**Hampden**	-
CR Lounge	**Mt. Vernon**	-
Falls	**Mt. Wash**	-
Havana Rd.	**Towson**	-
Islander Inn	**Dundalk**	-
Meet 27	**Charles Vill**	-
Mick's	**Frederick**	-
Miguel's Cocina	**Locust Pt**	-
Peerce's	**Phoenix**	-
Suburban Hse.	**Pikesville**	-
Teavolve	**Harbor E**	-
Two Boots	**D'town N**	-
Waterstone	**W Balt**	-

BOAT DOCKING FACILITIES

Cantler's Riverside	**Annap**	23
Crab Claw	**E Shore**	18
Harris Crab	**E Shore**	20
Kentmorr	**E Shore**	24
Narrows	**E Shore**	23
☑ Severn Inn	**Annap**	20
Tabrizi's	**S Balt**	21
Tidewater	**Havre de Grace**	22
Yellowfin	**Annap**	20

BREAKFAST

(See also Hotel Dining)

Baugher's	**Westminster**	18
Blue Moon	**Fells Pt**	24
NEW Breakfast Shoppe	**Severna Pk**	-
Cafe Hon	**Hampden**	15
Chick/Ruth's	**Annap**	19
City Cafe	**Mt. Vernon**	21
Goldberg's	**Pikesville**	22
Jimmy's	**Fells Pt**	18
Main Ingredient	**Annap**	24
Miss Shirley	**Roland Pk**	24
Stone Mill	**Brook'ville**	22

BRUNCH

Acacia Bistro	**Frederick**	20
Ambassador	**Homewood**	24
b	**D'town N**	25
Bertha's	**Fells Pt**	18
Cafe Nola	**Frederick**	21
Carrol's Creek	**Annap**	22
City Cafe	**Mt. Vernon**	21
Clyde's	**Columbia**	19
Dutch's Daughter	**Frederick**	21
Firestone's	**Frederick**	21
Gertrude's	**Charles Vill**	23
Harryman Hse.	**Reist'town**	22
Jesse Wong's Asean	**Columbia**	23
Jesse Wong's Kit.	**Hunt Valley**	19
Main Ingredient	**Annap**	24
Orchard Mkt.	**Towson**	25
Regi's	**S Balt**	22
Ze Mean Bean	**Fells Pt**	22

BUSINESS DINING

☑ Capital Grille	**Inner Harbor**	25
Carpaccio	**Annap**	21
☑ Charleston	**Harbor E**	28
☑ Cinghiale	**Harbor E**	24
Fleming's Steak	**Harbor E**	24
Greystone Grill	**Ellicott City**	19
Harry Browne	**Annap**	24
La Famiglia	**Homewood**	21
☑ Lewnes' Steak	**Annap**	25
☑ Linwoods	**Owings Mills**	27
Morton's	**Inner Harbor**	25
Oceanaire	**Harbor E**	24
Roy's	**Harbor E**	25
Ruth's Chris	**Inner Harbor**	25
Sullivan's Steak	**Inner Harbor**	22
Vinny's Cafe	**Dundalk**	-

BYO

Andy Nelson's	**Cockeysville**	25
Atwater's	**N Balt**	25
Catonsville Gourmet	**Catonsville**	24
Clementine	**NE Balt**	23
NEW Corner BYOB	**Hampden**	-
Edo Sushi	**multi.**	24
Grano (Little)	**Hampden**	25
NEW Havana Rd.	**Towson**	-
Hunan Taste	**Catonsville**	-
Iggies	**Mt. Vernon**	25
Mekong Delta	**D'town W**	25

Orchard Mkt. | **Towson**	25
Regions | **Catonsville**	-
Sabor | **Lutherville**	24
Salsa Grill | **Woodlawn**	-
☑ Samos | **Gr'town**	27
Soup'r Natural | **Parkton**	-
Sushi Hana | **Timonium**	23
☑ Thai Arroy | **S Balt**	27
Wild Orchid | **Annap**	24

CATERING

Andy Nelson's | **Cockeysville**	25
Attman's Deli | **E Balt**	25
Big Bad Wolf | **NE Balt**	25
Main Ingredient | **Annap**	24
Paul's Homewood | **Annap**	21
Peerce's | **Phoenix**	-
☑ Samos | **Gr'town**	27
Sascha's 527 | **Mt. Vernon**	22
Wild Orchid | **Annap**	24

CHILD-FRIENDLY

(Alternatives to the usual fast-food places; * children's menu available)

b* | **D'town N**	25
Baugher's* | **Westminster**	18
Broom's Bloom | **Bel Air**	27
Cafe Hon* | **Hampden**	15
Chick/Ruth's* | **Annap**	19
Clementine | **NE Balt**	23
Friendly Farm* | **Upperco**	22
Hunan Manor | **Columbia**	21
P.F. Chang's | **Columbia**	20

DESSERT SPECIALISTS

Baugher's | **Westminster**	18
Broom's Bloom | **Bel Air**	27
Cafe Hon | **Hampden**	15
Cheesecake | **Inner Harbor**	19
Chick/Ruth's | **Annap**	19
City Cafe | **Mt. Vernon**	21
Crêpe du Jour | **Mt. Wash**	21
Paul's Homewood | **Annap**	21
Stone Mill | **Brook'ville**	22
Teavolve | **Harbor E**	-

ENTERTAINMENT

(Call for days and times of performances)

Aida | jazz | **Columbia**	23
Bertha's | blues/jazz | **Fells Pt**	18
Germano's | cabaret | **Little Italy**	23
Gertrude's | jazz | **Charles Vill**	23
Jesse Wong's Asean | jazz/piano | **Columbia**	23
☑ Prime Rib | jazz | **D'town N**	27
Sotto Sopra | opera | **Mt. Vernon**	24
Tabrizi's | varies | **S Balt**	21
Ze Mean Bean | jazz | **Fells Pt**	22

FIREPLACES

☑ Antrim 1844 | **Taneytown**	25
Bartlett Pear | **E Shore**	29
Brewer's Art | **Mt. Vernon**	23
Cafe Bretton | **Severna Pk**	24
Café Normandie | **Annap**	23
Ciao Bella | **Little Italy**	22
Da Mimmo | **Little Italy**	22
Dutch's Daughter | **Frederick**	21
Elkridge Furnace | **Elkridge**	24
Harry Browne | **Annap**	24
Harryman Hse. | **Reist'town**	22
Isabella's | **Frederick**	25
☑ Jalapeños | **Annap**	27
Kentmorr | **E Shore**	24
La Famiglia | **Homewood**	21
Langermann's | **Canton**	-
Liberatore's | **Eldersburg**	21
Louisiana | **Fells Pt**	22
Mason's | **E Shore**	24
☑ Milton Inn | **Sparks**	26
Oregon Grille | **Hunt Valley**	25
Pappas | **NE Balt**	26
Patrick's | **Cockeysville**	22
Peerce's | **Phoenix**	-
☑ Petit Louis | **Roland Pk**	25
Regi's | **S Balt**	22
Robert Morris | **E Shore**	-
Tidewater | **Havre de Grace**	22
Ze Mean Bean | **Fells Pt**	22

HISTORIC PLACES

(Year opened; * building)

1710 | Robert Morris* | **E Shore**	-
1740 | Milton Inn* | **Sparks**	26
1744 | Elkridge Furnace* | **Elkridge**	24
1799 | Peter's Inn* | **Fells Pt**	27
1820 | Bertha's* | **Fells Pt**	18
1844 | Antrim 1844* | **Taneytown**	25
1864 | Louisiana* | **Fells Pt**	22
1880 | Pope's Tav.* | **E Shore**	-
1886 | Mason's* | **E Shore**	24
1890 | Lewnes' Steak* | **Annap**	25
1890 | Petit Louis* | **Roland Pk**	25
1890 | Volt* | **Frederick**	28
1896 | Chiapparelli's* | **Havre de Grace**	20
1900 | Kings Contrivance* | **Columbia**	23
1905 | Annabel Lee* | **Canton**	23
1906 | Brewer's Art* | **Mt. Vernon**	23

1920 | Hamilton Tav.* | **NE Balt**	25
1920 | Josef's* | **Fallston**	28
1943 | Matthew's Pizza | **Hi'town**	25
1944 | Obrycki's | **E Balt**	23

HOTEL DINING

Antrim 1844	
🅩 Antrim 1844 | **Taneytown**	25
Bartlett Pear Inn	
Bartlett Pear | **E Shore**	29
Monaco Baltimore	
B&O | **D'town**	22
Oxford Inn	
Pope's Tav. | **E Shore**	–
Pier 5	
Ruth's Chris | **Inner Harbor**	25
McCormick/Schmick | **Inner Harbor**	20
Robert Morris Inn	
Robert Morris | **E Shore**	–
Sheraton Inner Harbor	
Morton's | **Inner Harbor**	25

LATE DINING

(Weekday closing hour)

Clyde's | 12 AM | **Columbia**	19
Costas Inn | 1 AM | **Dundalk**	23
Fadó | 1 AM | **Annap**	17
Honey Pig | 24 hrs. | **Ellicott City**	26
Hunan Taste | 12 AM | **Catonsville**	–
Jennings | 12:30 AM | **Catonsville**	22
Level | 1 AM | **Annap**	–
Mezze | 12 AM | **Fells Pt**	25
Sabatino's | varies | **Little Italy**	20
Szechuan Hse. | 12 AM | **Lutherville**	23
Talara | 12 AM | **Harbor E**	23
Tapas Teatro | 12 AM | **D'town N**	23
Tsunami | 1 AM | **Annap**	20
Zorba's B&G | 2 AM | **Gr'town**	21

LOCAL FAVORITES

🆕 Breakfast Shoppe | **Severna Pk**	–
Chameleon | **NE Balt**	27
City Cafe | **Mt. Vernon**	21
Costas Inn | **Dundalk**	23
Faidley's | **D'town W**	27
🅩 Helmand | **Mt. Vernon**	26
Islander Inn | **Dundalk**	–
Jennings | **Catonsville**	22
Mari Luna | **multi.**	26
Miss Shirley | **Roland Pk**	24
Mr. Bill's | **Essex**	26
Narrows | **E Shore**	23
Paul's Homewood | **Annap**	21
Peppermill | **Lutherville**	18

🅩 Samos | **Gr'town**	27
Suburban Hse. | **Pikesville**	–
Szechuan Hse. | **Lutherville**	23
Teavolve | **Harbor E**	–
Wine Mkt. | **Locust Pt**	24
Zorba's B&G | **Gr'town**	21

MEET FOR A DRINK

Acacia Bistro | **Frederick**	20
Aida | **Columbia**	23
🆕 Banning's | **E Shore**	–
Bella Luna | **E Shore**	22
🆕 Bistro Rx | **Hi'town**	–
🆕 Brass. Brightwell | **E Shore**	–
Brewer's Art | **Mt. Vernon**	23
Café de Paris | **Columbia**	21
Carpaccio | **Annap**	21
🆕 Chazz | **Harbor E**	–
🅩 Cinghiale | **Harbor E**	24
City Cafe | **Mt. Vernon**	21
🆕 CR Lounge | **Mt. Vernon**	–
Crush | **N Balt**	22
Dogwood | **Hampden**	25
Falls | **Mt. Wash**	–
Firestone's | **Frederick**	21
Galway Bay | **Annap**	25
Henninger's | **Fells Pt**	24
Iron Bridge | **Columbia**	23
John Steven | **Fells Pt**	18
La Famiglia | **Homewood**	21
🅩 Lewnes' Steak | **Annap**	25
Mick's | **Frederick**	–
One-Eyed Mike | **Fells Pt**	–
One World Cafe | **Homewood**	19
Out of the Fire | **E Shore**	25
🅩 Pazo | **Harbor E**	24
Porter's | **Fed Hill**	–
Rocket/Venus | **Hampden**	19
Sullivan's Steak | **Inner Harbor**	22
Tark's Grill | **Brook'ville**	19
🅩 Tasting Rm. | **Frederick**	27
Teavolve | **Harbor E**	–
13.5% Wine Bar | **Hampden**	19
Victoria Gastro | **Columbia**	21
Vino Rosina | **Harbor E**	–
Waterstone | **W Balt**	–
Wine Mkt. | **Locust Pt**	24
Yellow Dog Tav. | **Canton**	20

OFFBEAT

Bertha's | **Fells Pt**	18
Blue Moon | **Fells Pt**	24
Brewer's Art | **Mt. Vernon**	23
Cafe Hon | **Hampden**	15
Chick/Ruth's | **Annap**	19

City Cafe	Mt. Vernon	21
Ethel/Ramone	Mt. Wash	21
Golden West	Hampden	20
Islander Inn	Dundalk	-
☑ Peter's Inn	Fells Pt	27
Teavolve	Harbor E	-

OUTDOOR DINING

(G=garden; P=patio; S=sidewalk; T=terrace)

Ambassador	G	Homewood	24
b	S	D'town N	25
Birches	S	Canton	24
BlueStone	T	Timonium	22
Cantler's Riverside	T	Annap	23
Carlyle Club	P	Homewood	22
Carrol's Creek	P	Annap	22
☑ Charleston	S	Harbor E	28
☑ Cinghiale	S	Harbor E	24
City Cafe	S	Mt. Vernon	21
Crab Claw	P	E Shore	18
Crêpe du Jour	P	Mt. Wash	21
Gertrude's	G	Charles Vill	23
Harris Crab	T	E Shore	20
John Steven	P, S	Fells Pt	18
Kentmorr	T	E Shore	24
Mason's	G	E Shore	24
☑ Milton Inn	P	Sparks	26
Monocacy Cross.	P	Frederick	24
Oregon Grille	P	Hunt Valley	25
☑ Peter's Inn	S	Fells Pt	27
Stone Mill	P	Brook'ville	22
Tapas Teatro	S	D'town N	23
Tark's Grill	P	Brook'ville	19
Wild Orchid	P	Annap	24
Wine Mkt.	P	Locust Pt	24

PEOPLE-WATCHING

Chick/Ruth's	Annap	19
Faidley's	D'town W	27
Harry Browne	Annap	24
Jimmy's	Fells Pt	18
☑ Pazo	Harbor E	24

POWER SCENES

NEW Banning's	E Shore	-
☑ Capital Grille	Inner Harbor	25
☑ Charleston	Harbor E	28
Harry Browne	Annap	24
☑ Lewnes' Steak	Annap	25
☑ Linwoods	Owings Mills	27
☑ Prime Rib	D'town N	27
☑ Volt	Frederick	28
☑ Woodberry Kit.	Hampden	26

PRIVATE ROOMS

(Restaurants charge less at off times; call for capacity)

☑ Antrim 1844	Taneytown	25
Broom's Bloom	Bel Air	27
Cafe Hon	Hampden	15
☑ Capital Grille	Inner Harbor	25
☑ Charleston	Harbor E	28
☑ Cinghiale	Harbor E	24
Clyde's	Columbia	19
Dutch's Daughter	Frederick	21
Elkridge Furnace	Elkridge	24
Fleming's Steak	Harbor E	24
Harry Browne	Annap	24
Ikaros	Gr'town	24
Kings Contrivance	Columbia	23
La Famiglia	Homewood	21
☑ Lewnes' Steak	Annap	25
Mezze	Fells Pt	25
☑ Milton Inn	Sparks	26
Morton's	Inner Harbor	25
O'Learys	Annap	26
Oregon Grille	Hunt Valley	25
☑ Pazo	Harbor E	24
Portalli's	Ellicott City	-
Sabatino's	Little Italy	20
Sushi Hana	Timonium	23
☑ Tersiguel's	Ellicott City	26
Vinny's Cafe	Dundalk	-

PRIX FIXE MENUS

(Call for prices and times)

☑ Antrim 1844	Taneytown	25
Café de Paris	Columbia	21
Café Troia	Towson	21
Jesse Wong's Kit.	Hunt Valley	19
Luna Blu	Annap	20
☑ Milton Inn	Sparks	26
☑ Petit Louis	Roland Pk	25
Tabrizi's	S Balt	21
☑ Tersiguel's	Ellicott City	26
Wild Orchid	Annap	24

QUIET CONVERSATION

Acacia Bistro	Frederick	20
Ambassador	Homewood	24
Bân Thai	D'town	19
Bella Luna	E Shore	22
NEW CR Lounge	Mt. Vernon	-
Dogwood	Hampden	25
Falls	Mt. Wash	-
Great Sage	Clarksville	22
NEW Havana Rd.	Towson	-
Little Spice	Hanover	25

Mari Luna	Mt. Vernon	26
NEW Meet 27	Charles Vill	-
Mick's	Frederick	-
Orchard	Frederick	19
Pairings Bistro	Bel Air	-
Paul's Homewood	Annap	21
Teavolve	Harbor E	-
Waterstone	W Balt	-

ROMANTIC PLACES

Ambassador	Homewood	24
Z Antrim 1844	Taneytown	25
Chameleon	NE Balt	27
Z Charleston	Harbor E	28
Corks	S Balt	21
Dogwood	Hampden	25
El Trovador	Fells Pt	23
Z Linwoods	Owings Mills	27
Z Milton Inn	Sparks	26
Narrows	E Shore	23
Pairings Bistro	Bel Air	-
Paul's Homewood	Annap	21
Z Petit Louis	Roland Pk	25
Pope's Tav.	E Shore	-
Sotto Sopra	Mt. Vernon	24
Z Tersiguel's	Ellicott City	26

SENIOR APPEAL

Z Capital Grille	Inner Harbor	25
Josef's	Fallston	28
Liberatore's	multi.	21
Patrick's	Cockeysville	22
Peppermill	Lutherville	18
Z Prime Rib	D'town N	27
Suburban Hse.	Pikesville	-
Tio Pepe	Mt. Vernon	24

SINGLES SCENES

Brewer's Art	Mt. Vernon	23
Liberatore's	multi.	21
Mama's/Half Shell	Canton	23
Z Pazo	Harbor E	24
Sullivan's Steak	Inner Harbor	22
Z Tasting Rm.	Frederick	27
Tsunami	Annap	20

SLEEPERS

(Good to excellent food,
but little known)

An Loi	Columbia	24
Asian Court	Ellicott City	22
Bella Luna	E Shore	22
Big Bad Wolf	NE Balt	25
Birches	Canton	24
Bistro Poplar	E Shore	24

Broom's Bloom	Bel Air	27
Cafe Bretton	Severna Pk	24
Café Tuscany	Westminster	22
Carlyle Club	Homewood	22
Cazbar	D'town	22
Chicken Rico	Hi'town	26
Costas Inn	Dundalk	23
David Chu's	Pikesville	22
El Trovador	Fells Pt	23
Flavors/Hse. of India	Columbia	24
Germano's	Little Italy	23
Grace Gdn.	Odenton	28
Great Sage	Clarksville	22
Hamilton Tav.	NE Balt	25
Harry Browne	Annap	24
Henninger's	Fells Pt	24
Honey Pig	Ellicott City	26
Jennings	Catonsville	22
Josef's	Fallston	28
Kentmorr	E Shore	24
Z Les Folies	Annap	26
Little Spice	Hanover	25
Louisiana	Fells Pt	22
L.P. Steamers	Locust Pt	23
Main Ingredient	Annap	24
Mekong Delta	D'town W	25
Minato	D'town N	22
Monocacy Cross.	Frederick	24
Mr. Bill's	Essex	26
Out of the Fire	E Shore	25
Pappas	multi.	26
Patrick's	Cockeysville	22
Pho Nam	Catonsville	23
Pierpoint	Fells Pt	24
Sam's Kid	Fells Pt	24
Szechuan Hse.	Lutherville	23
Thai Landing	Mt. Vernon	27
Tratt. Alberto	Glen Burnie	25
Umi Sake	Cockeysville	25
Wild Orchid	Annap	24

TRENDY

NEW Alchemy	Hampden	-
NEW Banning's	E Shore	-
Brewer's Art	Mt. Vernon	23
NEW Chazz	Harbor E	-
Clementine	NE Balt	23
NEW Corner BYOB	Hampden	-
Crush	N Balt	22
Hamilton Tav.	NE Balt	25
Z Pazo	Harbor E	24
Rocket/Venus	Hampden	19
13.5% Wine Bar	Hampden	19
Z Volt	Frederick	28
Z Woodberry Kit.	Hampden	26

VALET PARKING

Aldo's | **Little Italy**	25
Ambassador | **Homewood**	24
Z Black Olive | **Fells Pt**	26
Bluegrass | **S Balt**	-
Blue Hill Tav. | **Canton**	23
Caesar's Den | **Little Italy**	21
Café Troia | **Towson**	21
Z Capital Grille | **Inner Harbor**	25
Carlyle Club | **Homewood**	22
Centro | **S Balt**	-
Z Charleston | **Harbor E**	28
NEW Chazz | **Harbor E**	-
Cheesecake | **Inner Harbor**	19
Chiapparelli's | **Little Italy**	20
Ciao Bella | **Little Italy**	22
Z Cinghiale | **Harbor E**	24
City Cafe | **Mt. Vernon**	21
Crêpe du Jour | **Mt. Wash**	21
Fleming's Steak | **Harbor E**	24
Germano's | **Little Italy**	23
Harry Browne | **Annap**	24
Kali's Ct. | **Fells Pt**	24
La Famiglia | **Homewood**	21
La Scala | **Little Italy**	26
La Tavola | **Little Italy**	24
Lebanese Tav. | **Harbor E**	21
Louisiana | **Fells Pt**	22
Mari Luna | **Pikesville**	26
McCormick/Schmick | **Inner Harbor**	20
Meli | **Fells Pt**	22
Mezze | **Fells Pt**	25
Morton's | **Inner Harbor**	25
Oceanaire | **Harbor E**	24
Z Pazo | **Harbor E**	24
P.F. Chang's | **Annap**	20
Piccola Roma | **Annap**	19
Portalli's | **Ellicott City**	-
Z Prime Rib | **D'town N**	27
Rocco's Capriccio | **Little Italy**	23
Roy's | **Harbor E**	25
Ruth's Chris | **multi.**	25
Sabatino's | **Little Italy**	20
Sotto Sopra | **Mt. Vernon**	24
Sullivan's Steak | **Inner Harbor**	22
Talara | **Harbor E**	23
Tapas Adela | **Fells Pt**	25
Z Woodberry Kit. | **Hampden**	26
Yellowfin | **Annap**	20

VIEWS

Z Antrim 1844 | **Taneytown**	25
Blue Hill Tav. | **Canton**	23
Broom's Bloom | **Bel Air**	27

Cantler's Riverside | **Annap**	23
Carrol's Creek | **Annap**	22
Z Charleston | **Harbor E**	28
Cheesecake | **Inner Harbor**	19
Z Cinghiale | **Harbor E**	24
Crab Claw | **E Shore**	18
Edo Sushi | **Inner Harbor**	24
Friendly Farm | **Upperco**	22
Gertrude's | **Charles Vill**	23
Harris Crab | **E Shore**	20
Kentmorr | **E Shore**	24
L.P. Steamers | **Locust Pt**	23
McCormick/Schmick | **Inner Harbor**	20
Narrows | **E Shore**	23
Pope's Tav. | **E Shore**	-
Robert Morris | **E Shore**	-
Z Severn Inn | **Annap**	20
Stone Mill | **Brook'ville**	22
Sushi Sono | **Columbia**	26
Tabrizi's | **S Balt**	21
Tidewater | **Havre de Grace**	22
Yellowfin | **Annap**	20

VISITORS ON EXPENSE ACCOUNT

Z Black Olive | **Fells Pt**	26
Z Capital Grille | **Inner Harbor**	25
Z Charleston | **Harbor E**	28
Z Cinghiale | **Harbor E**	24
NEW Corner BYOB | **Hampden**	-
Da Mimmo | **Little Italy**	22
Fleming's Steak | **Harbor E**	24
Greystone Grill | **Ellicott City**	19
Harry Browne | **Annap**	24
La Famiglia | **Homewood**	21
Z Les Folies | **Annap**	26
Z Lewnes' Steak | **Annap**	25
Z Linwoods | **Owings Mills**	27
Z Milton Inn | **Sparks**	26
Morton's | **Inner Harbor**	25
Oceanaire | **Harbor E**	24
O'Learys | **Annap**	26
Oregon Grille | **Hunt Valley**	25
Z Petit Louis | **Roland Pk**	25
Z Prime Rib | **D'town N**	27
Roy's | **Harbor E**	25
Ruth's Chris | **Inner Harbor**	25
Z Tersiguel's | **Ellicott City**	26
Z Volt | **Frederick**	28

WATERSIDE

Cantler's Riverside | **Annap**	23
Carrol's Creek | **Annap**	22
Z Charleston | **Harbor E**	28

Cheesecake | **Inner Harbor**	19
Z Cinghiale | **Harbor E**	24
Clyde's | **Columbia**	19
Crab Claw | **E Shore**	18
Harris Crab | **E Shore**	20
John Steven | **Fells Pt**	18
Kentmorr | **E Shore**	24
M&S Grill | **Inner Harbor**	19
McCormick/Schmick | **Inner Harbor**	20
Narrows | **E Shore**	23
Robert Morris | **E Shore**	-
Z Severn Inn | **Annap**	20
Tabrizi's | **S Balt**	21
Tidewater | **Havre de Grace**	22
Yellowfin | **Annap**	20

WINNING WINE LISTS

Z Antrim 1844 | **Taneytown**	25
Café de Paris | **Columbia**	21
Z Capital Grille | **Inner Harbor**	25
Z Charleston | **Harbor E**	28
Z Cinghiale | **Harbor E**	24
Corks | **S Balt**	21
Della Notte | **Little Italy**	22
Fleming's Steak | **Harbor E**	24
Iron Bridge | **Columbia**	23
Oregon Grille | **Hunt Valley**	25
Out of the Fire | **E Shore**	25
Z Pazo | **Harbor E**	24
Z Petit Louis | **Roland Pk**	25

Z Tasting Rm. | **Frederick**	27
Z Tersiguel's | **Ellicott City**	26
208 Talbot | **E Shore**	25
Vino Rosina | **Harbor E**	-
Z Volt | **Frederick**	28
Wine Mkt. | **Locust Pt**	24

WORTH A TRIP

Annapolis	
Cantler's Riverside	23
Paul's Homewood	21
Bel Air	
Broom's Bloom	27
Eastport	
Z Lewnes' Steak	25
O'Learys	26
Essex	
Mr. Bill's	26
Schultz's Crab	-
Frederick	
Z Volt	28
Grasonville	
Harris Crab	20
Narrows	23
Oxford	
Pope's Tav.	-
Robert Morris	-
Taneytown	
Z Antrim 1844	25
Westminster	
Baugher's	18
Café Tuscany	22

Wine Vintage Chart

This chart is based on our 0 to 30 scale. The ratings (by U. of South Carolina law professor **Howard Stravitz**) reflect vintage quality and the wine's readiness to drink. A dash means the wine is past its peak or too young to rate. Loire ratings are for dry whites.

Whites	95	96	97	98	99	00	01	02	03	04	05	06	07	08	09
France:															
Alsace	24	23	23	25	23	25	26	23	21	24	25	24	26	25	25
Burgundy	27	26	22	21	24	24	24	27	23	26	27	25	26	25	25
Loire Valley	-	-	-	-	-	-	-	26	21	23	27	23	24	24	26
Champagne	26	27	24	23	25	24	21	26	21	-	-	-	-	-	-
Sauternes	21	23	25	23	24	24	29	24	26	21	26	24	27	25	27
California:															
Chardonnay	-	-	-	-	22	21	25	26	22	26	29	24	27	25	-
Sauvignon Blanc	-	-	-	-	-	-	-	-	-	26	25	27	25	24	25
Austria:															
Grüner V./Riesl.	22	-	25	22	25	21	22	25	26	25	24	26	25	23	27
Germany:	21	26	21	22	24	20	29	25	26	27	28	25	27	25	25

Reds	95	96	97	98	99	00	01	02	03	04	05	06	07	08	09
France:															
Bordeaux	26	25	23	25	24	29	26	24	26	25	28	24	23	25	27
Burgundy	26	27	25	24	27	22	24	27	25	23	28	25	25	24	26
Rhône	26	22	23	27	26	27	26	-	26	25	27	25	26	23	26
Beaujolais	-	-	-	-	-	-	-	-	-	-	27	24	25	23	27
California:															
Cab./Merlot	27	25	28	23	25	-	27	26	25	24	26	23	26	23	25
Pinot Noir	-	-	-	-	-	-	25	26	25	26	24	23	27	25	24
Zinfandel	-	-	-	-	-	-	25	23	27	22	24	21	21	25	23
Oregon:															
Pinot Noir	-	-	-	-	-	-	-	26	24	26	25	24	23	27	25
Italy:															
Tuscany	25	24	29	24	27	24	27	-	25	27	26	26	25	24	-
Piedmont	21	27	26	25	26	28	27	-	24	27	26	25	26	26	-
Spain:															
Rioja	26	24	25	-	25	24	28	-	23	27	26	24	24	-	26
Ribera del Duero/ Priorat	26	27	25	24	25	24	27	-	24	27	26	24	26	-	-
Australia:															
Shiraz/Cab.	24	26	25	28	24	24	27	27	25	26	27	25	23	-	-
Chile:	-	-	-	-	25	23	26	24	25	24	27	25	24	26	-
Argentina:															
Malbec	-	-	-	-	-	-	-	-	25	26	27	25	24	-	-

Vote at ZAGAT.com